Richard the Third

up to Shakespeare.

By

George B. Churchill, Ph. D. (Berlin)
Associate Professor in Amherst College.

ALAN SUTTON
ROWMAN & LITTLEFIELD
1976

First published in Berlin 1900

This edition published 1976 by
Alan Sutton
Dursley
Gloucestershire, England

and in the United States of America by
Rowman & Littlefield
Totowa, New Jersey

ISBN 0 904387 05 4
(Alan Sutton)

ISBN 0 87471 773 6
(Rowman & Littlefield)

Printed in Great Britain by
REDWOOD BURN LIMITED
Trowbridge & Esher

Preface.

The following pages, especially those of Part I, may seem to require some word of explanation, if not of apology. The book has grown out of a study which had for its object to determine exactly what was the nature of the raw material ready to Shakespeare's hand when he began to write his Richard III. That the Richard whose character and career were the subject of Shakespeare's work was not the Richard of history has long been well known. His story had been moulded and remoulded by successive chroniclers down to the Hall and Holinshed from whom the great dramatist drew most of his material. But Richard had also been the subject of literary treatment before Shakespeare's, in the Mirror for Magistrates, for example, and in two other still extant plays; and it was thought that a careful analysis of these, with a study of their relations to each other and to Shakespeare's play, would be an assistance of some value in the appreciation of the latter. It had not been intended to consider in detail the work of the chroniclers, but the attempt to determine the historical sources of the material presented by the plays soon led to the discovery that none of Shakespeare's commentators has presented this material completely or even without considerable error so far as he has gone. It was necessary, therefore, first to analyze the growth of the Richard saga in the chronicles. The results of this study appear in Part I. Where others of such note have failed, I cannot hope that my own work will be found wholly free from mistakes; but I venture to hope that the reader will here be able to trace without essential error the development of Richard's story in the various chronicles and histories, and to perceive clearly the contributions of each. The product in the complete form that lay before Shakespeare may be seen in Boswell-Stone's Shakspere's Holinshed, if to the citations there given are added certain omitted passages which I have noted elswhere (Herrig's Archiv, Bd. XCVIII, p. 159) and the special contributions of Hall (cf. p. 206).

The exigencies of the press and the author's distance from the place of publication, which have prevented him from reading his own proof-sheets, will, I trust, be considered sufficient excuse for the rather large number of misprints, the most important of which are recorded in the Corrigenda, and for certain uncorrected inconsistencies in the spelling of proper names, such as Fabyan and Hardyng.

I wish here to record my hearty appreciation of obligation to Prof. Brandl, to whom the book owes its origin and from whom I have received constant help and encouragement; to Dr. Wolgang Keller, from whom came the information of the date assigned by the Caius College Ms. to Legge's Richardus Tertius, and many other friendly suggestions; to Prof. A. Keller of the German University of Prague, who furnished me the source of Rous's quotation from Claudian (cf. p. 46) and the note on André's quotation from Seneca (cf. p. 60); and to Mr. Wilfrid Perrett, who has with unfailing kindness performed the difficult and tedious task of correcting the proof-sheets.

Amherst College, Mass., October 20, 1899.

Contents.

Part I. Richard in the Chronicles.

	Page
Introduction	1

    The Lancastrian chroniclers, 1 . . . the Richard saga, 2 . . . historical table, 3.

I. Historie of the Arrival of Edward IV   6
    Authorship, date, use by later chroniclers, 6 . . . contents, 7—11 . . . summary, 11—13 . . . Yorkist character, 11 . . . contribution to the saga, 12.

II. Warkworth's Chronicle   13
    Date, authorship, 13 . . . use by Stow and Holinshed, 14 . . . contents, 14—19 . . . summary, 19, 20.

III. Ms. References to the death of Henry VI . . .   20

IV. A Chronicle of London from 1089 to 1483 . . .   21

V. The First Continuation of the History of Croyland Monastery   22
    Authorship, date, 22 . . . contents, 22,23 . . . summary, 24.

VI. The Second Continuation of the History of Croyland Monastery   24
    Authorship, date, 24 . . . contents, 24—41 . . . summary, 41—46 . . . characterization of Richard, 42 . . . Richard's crimes, 42 . . . contributions to the saga, 45.

VII. Rous's Historia Regum Angliae   46
    Date, 46 . . . contents, 46—49 . . . summary, 49—52 . . . Tudor flattery, characterization of Richard and Richmond, 49 . . . Richard's deformity, his crimes, 50 . . . classical influence in Rous, 51.

VIII. The Memoirs of Philippe de Comines   52
    Date, use by Hall, 52 . . . contents, 52—57 . . . summary, 57—59 . . . Clarence's death in the butt of malmsey, 58 . . . divine justice in the York-Lancaster struggle, 59.

	Page
IX. Bernard André's History of Henry VII	59

Date, 59 ... contents, 59—63 ... summary, 64—66 ... contributions to the saga, 64 ... characterization of Richmond, the messenger of God, and of Richard, the "blood-sucker", 64 ... Richard's crimes, 65 ... classical influence, 65 ... speeches, divine justice, 66.

X. Fabyan's Chronicle	66

Date, 66 ... contents, 67—73 ... summary, 74, 75 ... contributions to the saga, 74.

XI. More's History of King Richard III	75

A. The English version — author, publication, 75 ... relation to the Latin version, 76 ... date, 77 ... contents 78—116.

B. The Latin version — contents, 116—118 ... summary, 118—127 ... use by later chroniclers, 119 ... contributions to the saga, 119 ... Richard's person 119 ... his character, 120 ... his protectorship, 123 ... his conscience, 124 ... little reference to divine justice, lack of classical influence, 126.

XII. Polydore Vergil's Historia Angliae	127

Date, 127 ... English translation, 128 ... use by Hall and the Hardyng continuator, 128 ... contents, 128—155 ... summary, 155—161 ... importance of Vergil's work in the development of the saga, 155 ... use by later chroniclers and Shakespeare, 156 ... account of Richard's early life, 156 ... varying accounts of the character and death of Warwick, 157 ... comparison of Vergil with More, 157 ... Richard's later life, person and character in Vergil, 158 ... his conscience, 159 ... the motives of divine vengeance and of destiny, and their use by Shakespeare, 160.

XIII. Rastell's Pastime of People	161

Author, use of Fabyan, 161 ... the death and burial of the two princes, 161.

XIV. The Continuation of Hardyng's Chronicle	162

Authorship, 163 ... translation and adaptation of Vergil, 164 ... contents, 164—172 ... summary, 172, 173 ... contributions to the saga, 172 ... use by Hall, 172.

XV. Hall's Chronicle	173

Author, editions, date, 173 ... use of Vergil, Fabyan, de Comines, More, 174 ... contents, 174—201 ... summary, 201—207 ... purpose of Hall's work, 201 ...

additional information of Richard's early career, 202 ... his character and crimes, 202 ... description of Richmond, 204 ... speeches, 205 ... additions to the saga, 205 ... use by later chroniclers, especially Holinshed, 206 ... use by Shakespeare, 206.

XVI. Grafton's Chronicle 207
Author, 207 ... date, 208 ... use of Hall. Vergil, Fabyan, More, 208 ... contents, 208—211.

XVII. Holinshed's Chronicle 211
Author, editions, 211 ... use of Hall, Stow, other sources, 212 ... contents, 212—222 ... use of Hall by Shakespeare in 3 Henry VI, 213 ... summary, 222, 223 ... but one addition to the saga, 222 ... Shakespeare's use of Holinshed, 223.

XVIII. Stow's Annals 223
Author, editions, sources, 223 ... contents, 224—227 ... the case of Burdet, 225 ... the indictment of Clarence, 225 ... faithful use of More, 227.

Part II. Richard in Poetry and the Drama.

I. The Song of Lady Bessy 231
Authorship, date, 231 ... contents, 231—234 ... summary, 234—235 ... popular feeling toward Richard and Richmond, 234.

II. A Mirror for Magistrates 235
Purpose of the work, 235 ... editions, legends of the time of Richard, 237.
1. King Henry VI, murders of Edward and Henry, 238 ... use of Hall, 238.
2. George Plantagenet [Clarence], contents, 239—241 ... addition to the saga, 241 ... Clarence murdered by Richard in person, 242 ... other evidences that popular tradition regarded Richard as Clarence's murderer, 242, 243 ... possible use of the legend by Shakespeare, 245.
3. King Edward IV, contents, 246.
4. Syr Anthony Wodvile, contents, 246—248 ... summary, 248.
5. Lord Hastings, contents, 250, 251 .. summary, 252.
6. Henry Duke of Buckingham, contents, 252—256 ... summary, 256 ... Buckingham's motive for rebellion, 256 ... comparison with Shakespeare's play, 257.

		Page

7. Collingbourne, contents, ground of his execution, 258.
8. Richarde Plantagenet Duke of Glocester, contents, 259 ... summary, 260 ... omission of Richard's deformity and of his dream, 260.
9. Shore's Wife, contents, 260—263 ... summary, 263—264 ... her beggary, 263 ... use by The True Tragedy, 264.

III. Legge's Richardus Tertius 265

Allusions to the play, 265 ... life of Legge, 265 ... place, time and circumstances of production, 266 [see also Addendum]... manuscripts, 269 ... printed editions, 269 ... historical position of the play, 269 ... influence upon popular dramatists, 271 ... historical sources, 273 ... analysis of the play, with sources of the scenes, imitations of Seneca, and comparison with Shakespeare's play, 280—371 ... other imitations of Seneca, 371 ... the character of Richard in Richard Tertius, 375 ... formal imitation of Seneca in material, theme, and "fable", 381 ... epic scenes, 385 ... lyric scenes, 387 ... dramatic scenes, 388 ... the chorus, 390 ... construction, organization of the material, 390 ... the relation of Legge's play to Shakespeare's, 393.

IV. Lacey's Richardus Tertius, a transcript of Legge's play 395

V. A Tragical Report of King Richard the Third · 395
Entry in the Stationers' Register, 395.

VI. The True Tragedy of Richard the Third . . . 396

Entry in the Stationers' Register, 396 ... previous notices and comments, 396 ... historical position of the play, its nature and style, 398 ... influence of the chronicles and of Marlowe, 399 ... of the revenge-plays, 400 ... verse and prose in the play, 403 ... corruption, 404 ... historical sources, 404 ... use of the Mirror for Magistrates, 409 ... analysis of the play, with sources of the scenes and relation to other early plays, 413—469 ... supposition of reference to Drayton's Heroical Epistles unfounded, 439 ... William Slaughter not an actor in the Queen's company, 444 ... Denis in the True Tragedy and in Alleyn's play, 456 ... the character of Richard in the True Tragedy, 469 ... influence of Legge's play upon the True Tragedy

	Page
— of Marlowe's plays, 480 ... Henry VI and the True Tragedy, 484 ... the True Tragedy and Shakespeare's Richard III, 497 ... the date of the True Tragedy, 524 ... the authorship of the True Tragedy, 528.	
VII. Chute's Shore's Wife	528
Entry in the Stationers' Register, date, extant copies, composition, 528.	
VIII. Fletcher's The Rising to the Crowne of Richard the Thirde	529
Authorship, date, contents, 529 ... sources More and Holinshed, 530 ... influence of popular tradition, 530.	
IX. Henslowe's Play on Richard III	531
X. A Possible Original of Shakespeare's Play	531
Opinions of Lloyd, Fleay and Lowell, 532 ... opinion of Halliwell and quotation from supposed previous play, 533.	
XI. Drayton's Heroical Epistles	534
The argument for reference to Drayton in the True Tragedy, 534 ... date of the Epistles, 535.	
1. Queene Margaret to William de-la-Poole, contents, 536.	
2. Edward the fourth to Shore's wife, contents, 537.	
3. Shore's wife to Edward the fourth, contents, 538 ... note on portrait of Shore's wife, 539.	
XII. Index Table of some of the Sources of Shakespeare's Richard III	539

Richard the Third

up to Shakespeare.

Part I:

Richard in the Chronicles.

Introduction.

The success of Henry of Richmond at the battle of Bosworth, August 22, 1485, and his subsequent marriage to Elizabeth of York, daughter of Edward IV, ended the contest of nearly ninety years between the houses of Lancaster and York for the throne of England. The history of that contest, as it culminated in the claims of Richard of York, in his wars and those of his sons Edward and Richard, was written by Lancastrian chroniclers. Two of them were foreigners, to whom the task was assigned by Henry himself. Another doubtless derived his information largely if not wholly from a patron who had been a leading opponent of the last Yorkist king and an important aider to Henry's success. All had the strongest material inducements to favor the reigning house, and none at all to excite royal disfavor by even describing impartially such acts of the House of York as really deserved approbation. These inducements diminished little if any in power during the reigns of Henry VIII, of Edward VI and of Mary, and they were greatly increased in the reign of Elizabeth, whose nature imperiously demanded homage and rebuked favor shown to her historical as well as actual foes.

There was besides an inducement other than material or political to describe the last stage in that contest, the reign of Richard III, in terms most disparaging to the house of York. Richard had not only been the reigning head of a family that had usurped the throne; he had become that reigning head by murder and usurpation within the usurping family itself. His short rule had been that of a tyrant, and no tyrant could win approbation in genuine English feeling. It is highly natural, therefore, that the Lancastrian historians should have painted Richard in dark colors, and that those colors should have grown darker with time. Crimes known to be his were treated with ever-increasing emphasis: other crimes were with plausibility suggested or insinuated as his, and in the course of years accepted as certain. His person, too, was subjected to the same treatment. From the Richard, one of whose shoulders, it was asserted, was higher than the other, was developed "crookbacked Richard", repulsive in figure as in life. Legend and prophecy were made to contribute their part to the picture. Thus but a few years after the historical Richard's death there existed what has not inaptly been called a Richard saga, the historical elements of which modern scholars have attempted to discover only with most unsatisfactory results.

This saga was not shaped by the chroniclers alone. The life of Richard was made the subject of literary treatment in the poems of the Mirror for Magistrates and in various ballads, and of dramatic treatment in a Latin university play, in an English play for a popular audience, and in other plays that have not come down to us. All these, according to their purpose and point of view, had a share in giving form to the conception of the chroniclers.

Thus at the beginning of the last decade of the sixteenth century, when the so-called chronicle history, or history-play, was for the first time attempted by the master who brought it to fullest perfection, a historical Richard III did not exist. It was the Richard of a hundred year old saga whom alone Shakespeare knew and made the subject of his play.

It is the purpose of this dissertation to trace the development of that saga through the sixteenth century, in chronicle, poem, and drama, and to show what that Richard was whose character and deeds Shakespeare found ready to his hand as raw material for his dramatic picture. The historical Richard will need to be considered only so far as the mythical Richard may thus he better understood.

To trace the development of the Richard saga it is necessary to consider the writers in chronological order. That their references may be more clearly understood, I subjoin a brief table of the important historical events in the struggle between York and Lancaster.

1399. Richard II is deposed by Henry Bolingbroke, son of Richard's uncle, the Duke of Lancaster: he is crowned as Henry IV. The lineal heir was Edmund, Earl of March, great-grandson of Lionel, Duke of Clarence, third son of Edward III. Bolingbroke was son of the fourth son, John of Gaunt, Duke of Lancaster.
1413. Death of Henry IV. His son crowned as Henry V.
1415. A conspiracy in favor of Edmund Earl of March defeated.
1422. Death of Henry V. The Duke of Gloucester made Protector of the infant Henry VI.
1452. Contest between the Duke of York, great-great-grandson of Lionel, Duke of Clarence, and the Duke of Somerset, grandson of John of Gaunt, Duke of Lancaster (by his mistress, Katherine Swynford). York claims the crown. The wars of the Roses begin. Birth of Richard, Oct. 2, 1452.
1454. York made Protector, on account of Henry's illness.
1455. First battle of St. Albans, between the parties of York and Somerset. York victorious.
1460. York declared by Parliament heir to the crown, after the death of Henry VI. Battle of Wakefield, Dec. 30; defeat and death of York and his son Rutland. George (Clarence) and Richard sent by their mother to Utrecht for safety.
1461. Battle of Mortimer's Cross: Yorkists under Edward victorious. Second battle of St. Albans: Yorkists

defeated. Edward succeeds however in reaching London and assumes crown as Edward IV.

Battle of Towton: great victory for Edward. Henry VI driven to Scotland. George and Richard return to England.

1464. Alliance between Queen Margaret and France. Battle of Hexham: Lancastrians defeated.

Henry imprisoned in the Tower.

Marriage of Ed. IV with Elizabeth Gray. Warwick estranged thereby from the king.

1469. George, Duke of Clarence, joins Warwick and marries his daughter Isabel.

1470. Warwick and Clarence join Margaret. Edward, deserted by Lord Montague, Warwick's brother, is driven over seas, and Henry VI is restored. Clarence declared his heir, in case direct heirs (Prince Edward) fail.

1471. Battle of Barnet, Apr. 14. Clarence rejoins his brother Edward. Richard leads the van. Warwick defeated and killed.

Battle of Tewkesbury, May 3. Richard again leads the van. Margaret's troops defeated; Prince Edward killed. Unsuccessful attack on London by Faulconbridge. Edward and Richard arrive together in London, May 21.

Death of Henry VI, May 21.

1473. Richard marries Anne, daughter of Warwick and formerly betrothed (not wife) of Edward, son of Henry VI.

1478. Execution of Clarence for treason.

1483. Death of Ed. IV. Prince Ed. returns from Wales to London. Capture and subsequent execution of Rivers and Gray. Gloucester confirmed as Protector by the Council. Duke of York taken to his brother in the Tower. The princes declared by Buckingham and Dr. Shaw to be bastards. Richard mounts the throne with the consent of the peers, June 26. R's coronation July 6. The Princes murdered in the Tower. Revolt of Buckingham. First and unsuccessful attempt of Richmond to land in England.

1485. Death of Anne. Richard woos his niece, the Princess Elizabeth. Second and successful attempt of Richmond. The Battle of Bosworth, Aug. 22. Richard killed, Richmond becomes Henry VII.

---

cf. Pauli, *Geschichte Englands*; Gairdner, *Life of Richard III*; Warner, *Engl. Hist. in Shakespeare's Plays*, of the tables of which I have freely availed myself.

I. Historie of the Arrival of Edward IV in England and the finall recouerye of his Kingdomes from Henry VI, A. D. MCCCCLXXI.

From the end of the 16th Century this work was unknown until used by Sharon Turner in his History of England during the Middle Ages. It was edited by John Bruce for the Camden Society, 1838, from a Ms. copy made by the chronicler Stowe. My citations are from Bruce's edition.

This narrative was written immediately after the events it relates, in 1471, by one who represents himself as "a servaunt of the Kyngs, that presently saw in effect a great parte of his exploytes, and the resydewe knewe by true relation of them that were present at every tyme" (p. 1). In it we have, as its editor says, "an authorised relation put forth by the Yorkists themselves, and giving their own account of the events upon which many of the heavy charges brought against their 'house' have been founded" (Introd. p. VI). Unknown, or ignored by Lancastrian writers, part of it made its way eventually into Stowe's and Holinshed's Chronicles. I cannot do better than to give Mr. Bruce's account of its fate. "A Ms. of it is ascertained to have been extant in the library of Fleetwood, the well-known recorder of London in the time of Elizabeth; and from that Ms., Fleetwood, without acknowledging his authority, compiled a narrative of Edward's restoration, which was inserted in Holinshed's Chronicle, and is referred to its author by the name 'W. Fleetwood' in the margin. In passing under Fleetwood's hand . . . . many passages were omitted, many softened, and in some of the most important places the narrative of Hall, translated from Polydore Vergil, was adopted as 'more pleasing to Lancastrian ear'. After it had been thus diluted by Fleetwood, it received an infusion of Lancastrian spirit by Abraham Fleming, the editor of that part of Holinshed, who interpolated a number of passages from Stowe, derived from the Chronicler [Warkworth, see III] with whom we are made acquainted by the extracts in Leland's Collectanea. In these various ways the red rose was blanched [sic!], the colour of the narrative was changed in all its more important passages, and the servant of Edward IV was transformed into a Lancastrian chronicler" (Introd. p. XIII).

The history begins with the landing of Edward in England. After suffering adverse winds in the harbor of Flushing for nine days, he came to Crowmere in Norfolk. Men sent on shore reported the presence of strong opposing forces, and Edward sailed toward the north, where after a great storm and separation from his companion ships the King landed with Hastings "within Humber, on Holdernes syde, at a place callyd Ravenersporne, even in the same place where somtime the Usurpowr Henry of Derby, aftar called Kynge Henry the IV, landed, aftar his exile, contrary and to the dissobeysance of his sovereigne lord, Kynge Richard the II, whome, aftar that, he wrongfully distressed, and put from his reigne and regalie, and usurped it falsely to hymselfe and to his isswe, from whome was linially descended Kynge Henry, at this tyme using and usurpinge the corone, as sonne to his eldest sonne, somtyme callyd Kynge Henry the V" (p. 2). Gloucester landed four miles away, Earl Rivers at Pole, fourteen miles away, and the others where they best could.

The people were not ready to join Edward's standard in an attempt to regain the kingdom, but for love of "that prince of ful noble memorye", his father, were ready to allow him to proceed unmolested in prosecution of his claim to the dukedom of York; and this Edward gave out as his sole purpose. Approaching York, he was met by the Recorder and warned to return, because he would not be allowed to enter. Continuing, he was met by others, who declared that he would be admitted if his claim were merely to the dukedom. Afterward he "came to the worshipfull folks whiche were assembled a little within the gates" (p. 5), and satisfying them in a parley, was admitted. At Nottingham "came unto hym two good Knyghts, Syr William Parre, and sir James Harington, with two good bands of men . . . the nombar of VI^c men" (p. 7). Edward then besieged Warwick in Coventry, where Warwick offered to come over to the King if he might have "some gode and expedient appoyntment", which the King refused, as not standing with his honor and surety. Clarence now joined Edward, having previously become reconciled to him, because all his family, he saw, would be deprived of the realm, because mortal war was likely to fall between him and his brothers, and the winner would probably be in as great danger as before, and especially because he was in great suspicion and hatred with all the followers of Henry, who were likely to procure the destruction of him and all his blood, and because it was unnatural and against God to suffer a war between himself and his brother to continue. There had been many mediators between them, the most active being the duchess of Burgundy, Edward's and Clarence's sister. When the brothers met, "there was right kynde and lovynge langwage betwixt them twoo, with parfite accord knyt togethars for ever here aftar" (p. 11). "And than, in lyke wyse, spake togethar the two Dukes of Clarence and Glocestar" (p. 11).

Clarence tried to reconcile Warwick to his brother, but failed. Leaving his host before Coventry, Edward proceeded to London, stopping by the way at Daventry, where on Palm Sunday he heard divine service and worshipped God and St. Anne, who shewed him "a fayre miracle; a goode pronostique of good aventure that aftar shuld befall unto the Kynge by the hand of God, and mediation of that holy matron Seynt Anne" (p. 11). Admitted into London, Edward took possession of King Henry, and then went to Westminster, where he "honoryd, made his devout prayers, and gave thankyngs to God" (p. 17). Thence Edward went to his queen, who had borne him a son in sanctuary.

Warwick now left Coventry and drew toward London as far as Barnet, ten miles from the city, where Edward met him, "committing his cawse and quarell to Allmyghty God" (p. 19). The battle of Barnet is described in detail. It began between four and five in the morning, in a great mist, because of which the two fronts did not meet evenly, but Warwick's overlapped Edward's at the west end, where Edward's men were outnumbered and broke. Hence ran the news to London that the King had been defeated. But it was not so, "for the Kynge, trusting verely in God's helpe, owr blessyd ladyes, and Seynt George, toke to hym great hardies and corage for to supprese the falcehode of all them that so falcely and so traytorowsly had conspired agaynst hym, where thrwghe . . . he, with great violence, bett and bare down afore hym all that stode in hys way, and, than, turned to the range, first on that one hand and than on that othar hand, in lengthe, and so bet and bare them downe, so that nothing myght stande in the syght of hym and the welle assured felowshipe that attendyd trewly upon hym; so that, blessed be God! he wan the filde there" (pp. 19—20). In the battle was slain, by whom is not mentioned, the Earl of Warwick, "somewhat fleinge". Then again is great glory given to God, who gave Edward the victory.

Margaret now entered England and fought the battle of Tewkesbury. Here Edward "ordeined three wards; displayed his bannars; dyd blowe up the trompets; commytted his caws and quarrel to Almyghty God, to owr most blessyd lady his mothar, Virgyn Mary, the glorious martyr Seint George, and all the saynts; and avaunced, directly upon his enemyes" (p. 29). The king's van attacked with "right-a-sharpe shwre" of arrows. In front of the enemy's field were many lanes and deep dikes, hedges and trees, so that it was hard to approach them near; but the duke of Somerset, leading Margaret's van, came out into the open and attacked the king. "The Kynge, full manly, set forthe even upon them, enteryd and wann the dyke, and hedge, upon them into the cloose, and, with great vyolence, put them upe towards the hyll, and, so also, the Kyng's vaward, being in the rule of the Duke of Gloucestar". Then a reserve force of Edward's burst upon Somerset's men from the side, and dismayed by the double attack they broke and fled. "At this point of theyr flyght, the Kynge coragiously set upon that othar felde, where was chefe Edward, called Prince, and in short while put hym to discomfiture and flyght". "In the wynnyge of the fielde such as abode hand-stroke were slayne incontinent; Edward, called Prince, was taken, fleinge to the towne wards, and slayne, in the fielde" (p. 30).

After the battle, Gloucester, as Constable of England, and the Duke of Norfolk, as Marshal, tried and condemned to death the Duke of Somerset and others of the prisoners. Nothing is said of their having been among the number of certain fugitives who, it is stated, were found by Edward in the Abbey church and there pardoned by him, although the place had no franchise as a sanctuary.

News of the death of the Prince, the capture of the Queen, the downfall of Henry's party everywhere, was brought to "Henry, late called Kyng, being in the Tower of London; not havynge, afore that, knowledge of the saide matars, he toke it to so great dispite, ire, and indingnation, that of pure displeasure, and melencoly, he dyed the XXIII day of the monithe of may. Whom the Kynge dyd to be browght to the friers prechars at London, and there, his funerall service donne, to be carried, by watar, to an Abbey upon Thamys syd, XVj myles from London, called Chartsey, and there honorably enteryd" (p. 30).

Margaret was taken prisoner three days after the battle in a poor religious place, "where she had hyd hir selfe, for the surty of hir parson, the Saturdaye, erlye in the mornynge, after his [read: hir] sonne Edward, callyd Prince, was gon to the filde for to withdraw hirselfe from the adventure of the battayle" (p. 31).

The narrative concludes with an account of the bastard Fauconbridge's rebellion in Kent, his assault upon London, his repulse and final submission at Sandwich, where he and his ships were received on the King's behalf by the Duke of Gloucester.

Such is the only purely Yorkist account that we have of this period. Its character naturally corresponds to its official authorship. Edward forms throughout the central figure, is in all the leader, and the winner of his own battles against the forces of a usurper, calling himself king. Gloucester is rarely mentioned, as landing with Edward, as speaking with Clarence at the reconciliation, as commanding the kings van at Tewkesbury, and following or accompanyng him in a charge, as judging the captured Somerset, and as receiving for the king the surrender of Fauconbridge. All Edward's acts are handled favorably; Clarence is praised for his return to his brother; there is no suggestion of Gloucester's part in any crime. Henry dies of pure melancholy, Prince Edward is slain in the field. In the account of his death the position of the words "in the fielde" awakens a little suspicion, and whether we are to suppose that Edward "abode hand-stroke" and fought for his life is not clear. At all events, the writer gives one to understand — as Edward's historian would have to do — that the prince was slain in fair battle. The death of Warwick, as here related, is not that of the Warwick who in 3 Hen. VI,5 : 2, cries, "Why, then, I would not fly". The editor of Chronicles of the White Rose (p. 65) condemns this as an unwarranted "aspersion upon the personal bravery of the bravest man of a brave age", and accounts for it by the fact that the writer is biassed by his Yorkist predilections. Warkworth, however, whose bias is wholly Lancastrian, has a more extended account of Warwick's flight (cf. p. II), and his account was copied by Stowe and Holinshed. The Queen is with historical truth represented as not present at the battle of Tewkesbury.

However much is concealed or mis-related, the chief value of the work for the present purpose lies in its very partisanship. The account presents the picture to which all the later Lancastrian pictures are opposed; and by comparing it with these we are better able to estimate how much of them also may be due to partisanship. The most important result of such a comparison is the perception that the religious devotion of Richmond, his faith in himself as the minister of God's vengeance upon a usurper, was not the characteristic of Richmond alone. The Richmond who in Richard III, 5, 3 prays on the night before the battle of Bosworth,

> "O Thou whose captain I account myself,
> Look on my forces with a gracious eye:
> Put in their hands thy bruising irons of wrath,
> That they may crush down with a heavy fall
> Th' usurping helmets of our adversaries!"

was successful, and this picture of him lives: the Edward who on Palm Sunday before the battle of Barnet prayed to God, our Lady, Saint George, and Saint Anne, and to whom was vouchsafed a miracle as "a good sign and token of good and prosperous aventure that God wold send hym in that he had to do", namely, to overthrow "the usurpoure Henry and his complices", is to be found in this single Yorkist account alone. Throughout the relation Edward's devotion and belief in God's help are emphasized, and at the close, in an extended paragraph, is a paean of praise for "the helpe and grace of Almyghty God", to whom the success was due. His religious feeling did not prevent Edward from putting King Henry to death;

and no more did it prevent Richmond from putting to death the son of Clarence, an act in some respects even more damnable than Richard's murder of his nephews. Such religious devotion did not, then, belong to character; it belonged to the times. Partisan writers, however, many of them priests, emphasized it as a characteristic of their masters; throughout the sixteenth century there was but one party; in Shakespeare, therefore, Richmond is truly the captain of the Lord. That attitude of the chroniclers which gave Shakespeare a saga Richmond whom he could reasonably present as the Lord's captain, makes its appearance in the first chronicle we have had to consider.

II. Warkworth's Chronicle of the first thirteen years of the reign of King Edward.

This work was written by John Warkworth, master of St. Peter's College, Cambridge, from 1473 to 1498. The greater portion of the manuscript volume in which it is contained is a mere transcription of "Caxton's" Chronicle of Brute. To this is added an account by Warkworth himself of the earlier part of Edward's reign, ending with the year 1473, and apparently written not long after that date. Halliwell calls attention to the fact that a passage upon certain prophetic wells must have been penned in the same year, 1473, as the prodigies recounted, as is indicated by the use of the present tense. The same is shown by the spirit of the passage itself. The prodigies are recent enough to be a very vivid warning of events not yet come to pass. As a matter of fact, they never did come to pass. That there were later additions, however, Halliwell does not appear to have noticed. Two such are apparent. In the passage above mentioned, Warkworth says of the well called Wemere that it not only ran hugely this year (the thirteenth), but "ranne stylle to the XIIj day of June next yere followynge" (p. 24). A passage on the consequences of Clarence's perjury cannot have been written before his death in 1478.

The book was presented by Warkworth to the library of his college and remained, as a whole, unpublished till 1839, when it was edited for the Camden Society by James O. Halliwell (Halliwell-Phillips), the well-known Shakespearian scholar. But it was not unknown earlier, for Leland, in his Collectanea, gathered 1534—1543, made copious selections from it; and Stowe, who mentions it among his authorities, apparently twice, as Chronica Petri Colleg. and again as Liber Collegij S. Petri, adopted large portions of it in his Annals, from which they passed into the second edition of Holinshed. That it was known in the time of Henry VII does not admit of assertion. It shows, at all events, what reports were circulated concerning some of Richard's deeds even during his lifetime. That these are highly important will be clear enough when it is seen how many of the reports of the later chronicles depend on oral tradition. The crimes with which Richard was charged were of course nearly all committed in secret, and did not admit of written proof. His connection with them was first suggested by one man to another, and found its authority always in what "men said" or "wise men weened". That rumors of Richard's crimes were early wide spread is proved by such a book as Warkworth's; and these rumors, which as current on men's lips were known to the writers of Henry VII, form the beginning of the saga. The following citations are from Halliwell's edition.

Warkworth's story begins with the coronation of Edward, where his brother George is made Duke of Clarence, and Richard Duke of Gloucester. "The III j^e yere of Kynge Edwarde, the Erle of Warwyke was sent into France for a maryage for the Kynge, for one fayre ladye, suster-doughtere to the Kynge of Fraunce. And whiles the seyde Erle of Warwyke was in Fraunce, the Kynge was wedded to Elisabethe Gray, wedow; .... and the weddynge was prevely in a secrete place. And when the Erle of Warwyke come home and herde hereof, thenne was he gretely displesyd withe the Kyng; and after that rose grete discencyone ever more and more betwene the Kyng and hym". They were accorded diverse times: "but thei nevere loffyd togedere aftere" (p. 3).

The capture of King Henry is thus described: "Kynge Herry was takene bysyde a howse of religione in Lancaschyre, by the mene of a blacke monke of Abyngtone, in a wode called Cletherwode, besyde Bungerly Hyppyngstones, by Thomas Talbott, sonne and heyre to Sere Edmunde Talbot of Basshalle, and Jhon Talbott his cosyne of Colebry, withe other moo; which disseyvide, beynge at his dynere at Waddyngtone Halle, and caryed to Londone on horse bake, and his legs bownde to the styrope, and so brought thrugh Londone to the Toure" (p. 5).

In the ninth year Clarence married Warwick's daughter [Isabel] in Calais, and with him, though absent from England, stirred up the rebellion of Robin of Redesdale. Returned to England, they took advantage of the defeat of Edward's forces at Banbury by Robin [said by Warksworth to be Sir William Conyars]. Lord Rivers [Edward's father-in-law] and his son were captured in the forest of Dene, and beheaded at Northampton by Clarence's and Warwick's order. Edward, deserted by his troops, was captured by the Archbishop of York, and carried "to Yorke cite; and ther, by fayre speche and promyse, the Kynge scaped oute of the Bisshoppys handes, and came unto Londone, and dyd what hym lykede" (p. 7). Later, forces of the son of Lord Welles and Sir Thomas Dimmock, stirred up by Clarence and Warwick, were defeated by Edward in Lincolnshire; whereupon the two conspirators fled the kingdom.

They joined Margaret in France, and decided to make a marriage between another of Warwick's daughters [Anne] and Prince Edward, "which was concluded, and in Fraunce worschippfully wedded". On the return of Clarence and Warwick to England, Edward purposed to oppose them with a force under the command of Marquis Montague. "Nevere the lattere, the seide Markes Montagu hatyde the Kynge, and purposede to have taken hym" (p. 10). Warned of this and of the insufficiency of the forces on which he could rely, Edward fled from England, "overe the see into Flaunders, to his brother-in-lawe, the Duke of Burgeyne, for socoure and help" (p. 11).

"The more parte of peple" were glad of Henry's restoration. Before, they had hated him. The cause of this was the putting to death of "the good Duke of Glouceter" [Humphrey, the Protector], and others, the covetousness and selfishness of those about the king, and the loss of the French provinces. But this was "alle by cause of his fals lordes, and nevere of hym". Men had expected peace and amendment from another king, but they had not come.

Edward now returned to his kingdom. Troubled on the sea by storms, and opposed by strong forces in Norfolk, where he had intended to land, Edward was obliged to land "in Yorkeschyre at Ravenys-spore". Here he was opposed by forces of the men of Holderness under a priest, and Sir John Westerdale; but he declared to them "that he came thedere by the Erle of Northumberlondes avyse, and schewede the Erles lettere y-send to hym &c. undere his seale; and also he came for to clayme the Duchery of Yorke, the whiche was his inherytaunce of ryght, and so passed forth to the cite of Yorke, where Thomas Clyfford lete hym inne, and ther he was examynede ayenne; and he seyde to the mayre and aldermenne and to alle the comons of the cite, in likewyse as he was afore in Holdernes at his landyng: that was to sey, that [he] nevere wulde clayme no title, ne take uppone honde to be Kynge of Englond, ... and therto afore alle peple, he cryed "A! Kynge Herry! A! Kynge and Prynce Edwarde!" and wered ane estryche feder, Prynce Edwardes lyvery. And after this he was sufferd to passe the cite, and so helde his wey southwarde, and no man lettyd hym ne hurtyde him."

Arrived at Nottingham he was met by Sir William a Stanley, Sir William Norys, and others, with many soldiers, "an anone aftere he made his proclamacyone, and called hym self Kynge of Englonde and of Fraunce" (p. 14). "The Erle of Warwyke had a letter from the Duke of Clarence, that he schulde not feght withe hym tylle he came hym self; and alle was to the distruccion of the Erle of Warwyke, as it happenede aftyrwarde". "A litelle oute of Warwyke mett the Duke of Clarence with Kynge Edward ... and ther thei were made acorde, and made a proclamacion forthewithe in Kynge Edwardes name; and so alle covandes of fydelitie, made betwyx the Duke of Clarence, and the Erle of Warwyke, Quene Margarete, Prince Edwarde hir sonne, bothe in Englonde and in France, were clerly brokene and forsakene of the seide Duke of Clarence; whiche, in conclusione, was distruccion bothe to hym and them: for perjury schall nevere have bettere ende, witheoute grete grace of God. Vide finem &c."

The battle of Barnet is thus briefly described:

"On Ester day in the mornynge, the xiiij. day of Apryl, ryght erly, eche of them came uppone othere; and ther was suche a grete myste, that nether of them myght see othere perfitely; ther thei faughte, from iiij. of clokke in the mornynge unto x of clokke the fore-none. And dyverse tymes the Erle of Warwyke party hade the victory, and supposede that thei hade wonne the felde. But it hapenede so, that the Erle of Oxenfordes men hade uppon them ther lordes lyvery, bothe before and behynde, which was a sterre withe stremys, wiche [was] myche lyke Kynge Edwardes lyvery, the sunne with stremys; and the myste was so thycke, that a manne myghte not profytely juge one thynge from anothere; so the Erle of Warwikes menne schott and faught ayens the Erle of Oxenfordes menne, wetynge and supposynge that thei hade bene Kynge Edwardes menne; and anone the Erle of Oxenforde and his menne cryed "treasoune! treasoune!" and fledde awaye from the felde withe vIIj. c. menne. The Lorde Markes Montagu was agreyde and apoyntede with Kynge Edwarde, and put uppone hym Kynge Edwardes lyvery; and a manne of the Erles of Warwyke sawe that, and felle uppone hyme, and kyllede hym. And whenne the Erle of Warwyke saw his brother dede and the Erle of Oxenforde fledde, he lepte one horse-backe, and flede to a wode by the felde of Barnett, where was no waye forthe; and one of Kynge Edwardes menne hade espyde hyme, and one came uppone hym and kylled hym, and dispolede hyme nakede" (p. 16).

Now Margaret entered England and there was fought and lost the battle of Tewkesbury. "And ther was slayne in the felde, Prynce Edward, whiche cryede for socoure to his brother-in-lawe the Duke of Clarence." Margaret's followers, including Somerset, took refuge in Tewkesbury Abbey Church, whither Edward pursued them, sword in hand. But a priest who was saying mass conjured him upon the Sacrament he bore to pardon them, and the King did so. But two days later they were beheaded nevertheless.

The bastard Falconbridge now attacked London and was repulsed. At Sandwich the King received him and his ships in submission. "After, by the Duke of Gloucetre in Yorkeschyre, the seide Bastarde was behedede, noght with stondynge he hade a chartere of pardone."

"And the same nyghte that Kynge Edwarde came to Londone, Kynge Herry, beynge inwarde in presone in the Toure of Londone, was putt to dethe, the xxj. day of Maij, on a tywesday nyght, betwyx xj. and xIj. of the cloke, beynge thenne at the Toure the Duke of Gloucetre, brothere to Kynge Edwarde, and many other; and one the morwe he was chestyde and brought to Paulys, and his face was opyne that every manne myghte see hyme;

and in hys lyinge he bledde one the pament ther; and afterward at the Blake Fryres was broughte, and ther he blede new and fresche; and from thens he was caryed to Chyrchesey Abbey in a bote, and buryed there in oure Lady Chapelle."

The brief chronicle concludes with an account of the taking of the Archbishop of York and of the Earl of Oxford.

With this chronicle begins the long Lancastrian series. Occupying an important position and writing while Edward was king, Warkworth possibly did not dare to be very strongly Lancastrian in what he wrote, even though he may have preserved it from public view till a later time. But his feeling is plain enough. In his description of King Henry, while stating faithfully the reasons why men hated him, he takes pains to say that Henry himself was never to blame. His picture of Edward is far different from that of "The Arrival". We hear in detail of the deception by which Edward recovered the crown, of his broken promises to the citizens of York, of his beheading the nobles at Tewkesbury contrary to his plighted faith, of the execution of Falconbridge despite the King's pardon. Thus early is sounded the Lancastrian note of condemnation of Clarence's perjury, with the assertion that his end was fitting retribution. Here first in the long row of works that chronicle the struggle of York and Lancaster does Fate appear as the agent of God's vengeance for crime. There is no condemnation of Clarence's unnatural conduct in forsaking his brother.

As for Gloucester, his acts are hinted at, rather than stated. In the account of Prince Edward's death there is no indication that he was murdered, and much less any mention that Richard was connected with such a murder. In fact Richard is not mentioned at all as present at Tewkesbury or Barnet, thought in both battles he was his brother's stoutest champion. In the circumstantial account of King Henry's death, Gloucester is not

2*

mentioned as the murderer; but the implication is pretty plain Warkworth evidently regarded Richard as the executor of a deed considered by Edward and his friends to be a political necessity. It was an act the responsibility for which, by whomsoever executed, no one member of the house of York can be made to bear. That this view was common there is, as will be seen, abundant evidence. But already, shortly after the deed, Richard is suggested as its executor. Otherwise he is mentioned only as created Duke of Gloucester, and as the executor of the previously pardoned Falconbridge.

Considering its Lancastrian feeling Warkworth's account is noteworthy for what it omits to say of the death of Prince Edward. How much is meant by the statement that the prince called to Clarence for succor it would be difficult to say. At all events he is said to have been killed "in the field" with others who are admitted to have been fairly slain, and there is nothing in Warkworth's statement inconsistent with a belief that Warkworth knew nothing of any unfair treatment of Edward. Noteworthy, too, from the came consideration, is the account of Warwick's death, a much more open aspersion on his character as a brave man than the account in the Yorkist "Arrival".

III. Ms. References to the death of Henry VI.

I take the occasion here to cite from Halliwell's preface to Warkworth other references to Henry's death, dating from nearly the same time as Warkworth's statement. They show more fully the nature of the rumors then current.
    a. Ms. Cotton Otho, B. XIV. fol. 221, v°. "Rex Henricus Sextus in arce London ferro transfigitur et occiditur."
    b. Ms. Arundel, (College of Arms) No. 5, fol. 171, v°. "Et Henricus, nuper Rex, reponitur in Turrim London,

et, in vigilia Ascensionis dormiente, ibidem feliciter moriens, per Tamisiam navicula usque ad Abbathiam de Cheltosye deductus, ibi sepultus est."

c. Ms. London Chronicle, Bibl. Cotton. Vitell. A. XVI fol. 133, r⁰. "Also upon ascencion evyn, Kyng Henry was brought from the tower thrugh Chepe unto Powlys upon a bere, and abowte the beere more glevys and stavys than torches; who was slayne, as it was said, by the Duke of Glowcetir; but howe he was deed thedir he was brought deed; and in the chirch the corps stode all nyght, and on the morne he was conveyed to Chertsey, where he was buryed."

Between the words "deed" and "thedir" Halliwell inserts, as lacking to the sense, [nobody knewe, but]. Rather, the words "how he was dead" — however he died.

d. Three other Ms. references of early date do not mention the manner of Henry's death. Herd's metrical history, also quoted by Halliwell, dates from the middle of the 16th century. Cf. for the whole collection, Halliwell's preface to Warkworth, XI—XVIII.

These citations show that the rumors current at the end of the 15th century by no means unanimously assign Gloucester a share, and much less a principal role, in the death of Henry. Two mention the rumor, one says that he died happily, three mention simply that he died.

IV. A Chronicle of London, from 1089 to 1483; written in the Fifteenth Century.

Printed from Mss. in the British Museum in 1827.

This account from the twenty-second year of Henry VI, when a new hand begins, is a very meagre statement of a few facts. Of Prince Edward's death the statement is only "Than was quene Margret and prynce Edward hir sone with theare compeigny, landid in the west; and kyng Edward met them at Tewkesbury; and there was the prynce slayne with many others" (p. 144). Of Clarence it is said: "The duke of Clarence was atteyntid of high treason, and afterward put to deth in the Tour of London" (p. 146).

Henry's death is not mentioned at all. The account closes with a statement of the death of King Edward.

This chronicle, though said by Pauli to have been one of Fabyan's sources, clearly furnished him nothing about this period. It is confined to the meagrest statement of facts, and furnishes no rumors concerning the deeds of Gloucester or Edward.

V. The First Continuation of the History of Croyland Monastery.

This was written by the Prior of the monastery, who brought the account from the beginning of the reign of King Stephen, to which point the history had been written by Petrus Blesensis, down to the year 1470, in which year the conclusion was written. It is admitted here, somewhat out of its chronological position, because, noting as it does but a few events of the first years of Edward's reign, it rather serves as an introduction to the second continuation than is an independent story of importance in itself.

Under date of 1465, and written in that year, is a notice of Henry's capture in the North, and of his being brought to the Tower "cum manu forte". Here "sub salva custodia omnem ei humanitatem Rex Edwardus uberrime jussit impendi, & quaeque sibi necessaria congrua cum reverentia exhiberi" (p. 539). Mention follows of the execution and fining of many nobles, bishops, and abbots, for sending money to Margaret and her son and urging them to return to England.

Edward's marriage follows. "Rex Edwardus cum jam fervore juventutis urgeretur, propria fretus electione, cujusdam militis relictam viduam, Elizabeth nomine, ex patre quidam milite, matre vero Ducissa progenitam; inconsultis Regni proceribus, clandestius desponsavit matrimonio; atque post haec ipsam solemniter in Reginam coronari fecit. Quod quidem Regni Optimates aegre tulerunt & idigne; quia de tam mediocri stirpe procreatam, ad Regni consortium secum praepropere sublimaret" (p. 539).

In 1469, "inter ipsum Regem & illustrissimum Comitem Warwici Richardum, ejus cognatum, magna, & non sine multorum sanguine sopienda, accidit discordia; eo quod Rex affectuosis allectus nimium Reginae suggestionibus, singulos ejusdem Reginae propinquos, & qui eam aliquo sanguinis titulo contingebant, in specialem sibi admittens familiaritatem, immensis ditabat numeribus, & ad digniora semper circa personam suam officia promovebat; fratres quoque suos & cognatos Regio de sanguine progenitos, & ipsum Comitem Warwici Richardum, cum ceteris sibi fidelibus Regni Proceribus, a sua praesentia profligavit" (p. 542).

Thereupon seizing the opportunity, they stirred up an insurrection among the commons of the north, who, complaining that they were "taxis & tributis animis per eosdem Regis & Reginae familiares graviter oppressos", elected a certain Robert of Redesdale their captain and hastened toward Warwick, who was in London. Meeting at Hedgecote near Banbury the forces of Pembroke, who was hastening to Edward's relief, Robin's men were victorious, and Pembroke and other nobles of Wales, "generosi captivi" were beheaded at Northampton, "ad arbitrium praefati Comitis Warwici, nulla interveniente redemptione" (p. 543). Edward, much disturbed, admitted to conference with him Warwick, Clarence and others, "quibus ille in primo adventu ex indignantis animi rigore turbidum praetendebat vultum;" but after they had promised to be faithful to him and to abandon their adherents,

„complacitior jam effectus, eos in favorem & benevolentiam admisit uberiorem".

There is little in the above account to require comment. It is noticeable, however, that Warwick's dissension was caused, according to the scribe, because the King's favor had been turned from him to the relations of the queen. Nothing is said of his mission to France or anger at Edward's marriage. The account of Warwick's and Clarence's reconciliation to Edward will be found to differ from later accounts.

VI. The second Continuation of the History of Croyland Monastery.

The second continuation of the Croyland Chronicle covers the period from 1470 to a date shortly after the battle of Bosworth, 1485. Its author was Prior of the monastery, a doctor of canonical law, a member of Edward IV's Council, and had been employed by him in diplomatic service (cf. p. 557). The continuation, as various statements in the work seem to show, appears to have been wholly written after the battle of Bosworth. Cf. Pauli 5: 695.

Finding the account of the preceding writer, either because of lack of interest in worldly affairs, or from a desire to be brief, an insufficient preface to his own work, the second continuator first briefly reviews the events leading up to those of the year 1470. In this review he mentions the battle of Rudlow; the exile of Richard of York to Ireland and of his son Edward with Warwick to Calais; the return of Warwick and the battle of Northampton; York's return from Ireland and his claim to the throne; the decree of Parliament; the oath sworn by York, Edward, and Rutland to be faithful to Henry. The battle of Wakefield was caused, according to the scribe, by partisans of the Queen who opposed the decree and wished to reverse it. York came to battle against them "pro reprimendis eorum conatibus" (p. 550).

The battle of St. Albans followed. Meanwhile Edward had been waging successful battle at Mortimer's Cross against like supporters of the Queen. Hearing of his father's death, and holding himself released from his oath to Henry because the latter had associated himself with the slayers of York, he marched to London and was proclaimed king. The birth of Edward's daughter Elizabeth, and the marriage of his sister Margaret to the duke of Burgundy follow. "Super quo Richardus Nevyl, Comes Warwici, qui partibus Francorum contra Burgurdiones jam aliquot annis favere visus est, magnam animi indignationem cepit". For he hated the duke of Burgundy with a deadly hatred. "Hanc ego reputo veriorem causam discidii inter Regem & Comitem, quam ipsum matrimonium Regis cum Elizabeth Regina (p. 551). This marriage, though he had at first murmured at it, because he had before labored to have Edward take to wife the widowed queen of Scotland, Warwick had subsequently with all the prelates and greater lords solemnly praised and approved at Radingham. His favor towards the queen's kin continued until they assisted in bringing about Margaret's marriage to the duke of Burgundy. The battle of Hedgecote followed and there not only Herbert, Earl of Pembroke perished, as stated by the preceding scribe, but also Rivers and John Woodville, the father and brother of the queen.

In 1469 Edward was captured by Clarence, Warwick, and the Archbishop of York, and conveyed first to Warwick and then to Middleham, "a quo tamen praeter omnem spem paene miraculos, non tam evasit, quam de expresso ipsius Comitis Warwici consensu dismissus est" (p. 552). For an insurrection arose in the north which Warwick could not suppress without forces which could be called together only by proclamation in the name of the king, and no such proclamation would the people obey till they saw the king in full liberty at York. Edward, seizing his opportunity, hastened to London. There Clarence and Warwick came to him, and "pax & omnium impacabilium abolitio foris conceditur. Manet tamen fortassis alta mente reposita, illic despectae Majestatis injuria; hic nimis elati rea mens sibi conscia facti" (p. 552).

There followed the insurrection under the son of Lord Wells. When this was successfully put down by Edward, Clarence and Warwick, as if conscious of participation in rebellion, fled the kingdom. Arrived in France and kindly received by King Louis, they were taken into favor by Margaret and Prince Edward, and "eorum ac Regis Henrici partes se de cetero fideliter observaturos promittunt. Et ut tam dilectis quam fides ita renovata indubitatior futuris saeculis appareret, contrahunt sponsalia inter dictum Principem & dominam Annam praefati Comitis Warwici filiam juniorem. Nam seniorem, Isabellam nomine, Dux ipse Clarentiae ante sibi uxorem devinxerat".

Returning to England after an exile of six months, Clarence and Warwick soon gathered so large a force that the soldiers of Edward, assembled at Doncaster, abandoned him. The Marquis of Montague, on hearing of the arrival of his brother Warwick, determined to abandon the cause of Edward, and to capture the king with the very forces he had raised to defend him. This purpose was reported to Edward, and he thereupon fled over sea to his brother-in-law in Burgundy. His wife took refuge in sanctuary at Westminster, where she bore a son, a happy event that somewhat revived the hopes of Edward's well-wishers.

Henry was restored to his throne. "Vidisses populum innumerum hanc piissimi Regis Henrici restitutionem miraculo, mutationemque ipsam dextrae excelsi operibus ascripsisse" (p. 554); and yet how past finding out are the ways of God was within six months sufficiently evident. For Edward, aided by ships and forces from the duke of Burgundy, landed in England, at Holderness, "eodem quidem in loco quo quondam Henricus quartus Regem Richardum depositurus applicuit. Passing through the city of York, "non aliter se intitulans nisi Ducem, tanquam haeredem patris sui, ita enim propter illic adversantes dissimulare oportuit" (p. 554), he came without resistance to Coventry, in which Warwick and Oxford had shut themselves up.

Meanwhile Clarence, "Regi dulciter conciliatus", through the mediation of his sisters Margaret of Burgundy and the Duchess of Exeter, came to him with a large army from the west. Hastening to London, Edward once more imprisoned King Henry, and two days after set out again toward the enemy, who had followed him, thinking that the king would be more intent upon devotions than upon arms at this Easter time. On Easter day he met the enemy at Barnet. "Mane fit conflictus terribilis". On Henry's side fell "duo clarissimi domini fratres germani", Warwick and Montague. To Edward, despite considerable losses "cessit mirabilis, insperata, & gloriosa victoria".

Edward returned with Gloucester and Clarence to London; but he had no long time of rest, for Margaret and her son now entered England. Many nobles joined her. They marched from Cornwall and Devonshire toward Gloucestershire and Chester, where were bowmen whom they expected to find favorable to the house of Lancaster. Edward was too quick for them, and intercepted them at Tewkesbury in Gloucestershire. "Tandem potitus est Rex Edwardus praeclara victoria, interfectis de parte Reginae, tum in campo tum postea ultricibus quorundam manibus, ipso Principe Edwardo unigenito Regis Henrici, victo Duce Somersetiae, Comiteque Devoniae, ac aliis dominis omnibus ac singulis memoratis" (p. 555). Margaret was captured and brought to London. But even yet Edward was not free from trouble, for there followed the uprising of the bastard Falconbridge in Kent, and his unsuccessful attack on London. Edward, on his triumphant entrance into London, seemed to have won the hearts of all, but knowing the mutability of the people of Kent, he hastened thither to punish Falconbridge.

"Taceo, hoc temporum interstitio, inventum esse corpus Regis Henrici in turri Londoniarum exanime: parcat Deus, & spatium poenitentiae ei donet, quicunque tam sacrilegas manus in Christum Domini ausus est immittere. Unde & agens, tyranni; patiensque, gloriosi martyris titulum mereatur. Ostensum est corpus per dies aliquot in Ecclesia sancti Pauli Londoniis, atque abhinc per fluvium Thamasis ad Ecclesiam conventualem monachorum de Chertesey . . . in quadam ad hoc cum luminaribus solemniter praeparata barga, defertur humandum. Qui quidem quanti apud eum meriti pro vitae innocentia, dilectione Dei & Ecclesiae, patientia in adversis, ac aliis egregiis virtutibus inventus sit; testantur mirabilia quae operatus est Deus ad preces eorum, qui ipsius implorant suffragia devoto corde".

After this is mentioned an embassy on the part of the writer himself from Edward to the Duke of Burgundy, to confer with him concerning a proposed war to be undertaken by both against King Louis.

Then appears an account of a quarrel between Gloucester and Clarence, which seemed most difficult of settlement. After the death of Prince Edward in the battle of Tewkesbury, "cui domina Anna minor filia Comitis Warwici desponsata fuit", Richard himself sought her to wife. This did not suit Clarence, who had married Warwick's eldest daughter, so he hid Anna away, "metuens divisionem haereditatis, quam sibi soli ratione conjugis suae applicari malluit, potius quam partitionem cum alio quovis inire" (p. 555). But the shrewdness of Gloucester prevailed. He found Anna in London disguised in the garb of a kitchen-maid, and carried her to the sanctuary of St. Martin. This caused great discord between the dukes, who argued their respective cases before the king in the council chamber, with such extended and acute reasoning that even the lawyers who were present were astonished at the wealth of arguments they produced. "Porro tres hi germani, Rex atque Duces, tam excellenti valebant ingenio, ut si discordare non potuissent, funiculus ille triplex difficillime rumperetur" (p. 557). The king, who loved each equally, and desired that their dissension should be no impediment to his proposed expedition into France, at length intervened, and the matter was settled. Gloucester was allowed to marry Anna, and should have so many and such lands as should be agreed upon between the brothers by means of arbitrators. All the rest should remain in the possession of Clarence. Thus little or nothing was left to Warwick's widow, who was his real heir. "Transeo faciliter", continues the scribe, "rem incurabilem sine cura, & dimittens hominos voluntarios voluntati; residuum historiae quoad menti occurit, libera voce, nullo scienter admixto mendacio, prosequi dignum duxi" (p. 557).

Edward now prepared for his expedition into France. A tenth and a fifteenth were levied in taxes upon the people by Parliament and in addition was imposed a new and unheard of kind of burden, "ut per benevolentiam quilibet daret id quod vellet, imo verius quod nollet" (p. 558). The sums resulting from these concessions reached such an amount as had never been before seen together, and in the scribe's opinion, were not likely ever to be seen again. Sending embassies to the Hanseatic League and to Scotland, that he might have no enemies behind his back, Edward set out for France. Here, for many reasons, including want of money, he made peace with Louis, on condition that he should receive £1000 yearly, and that the Dauphin should marry Elizabeth his daughter, conditions which to the writer seem entirely honorable, but which many condemned. The next few years were spent by Edward in filling by various means the royal coffers; among them, the resumption of all property formerly bestowed on others by royal concessions.

Now the glory of this most provident king was disturbed by a new disaffection between him and Clarence.

He appeared to withdraw more and more from the king's presence, had scarcely a word to say in the council, and seemed unwilling to eat or drink in the king's house. This alienation was caused, as many thought, by the fact that on the general resumption of the royal concessions Clarence had lost the lordship of Tutbury, and many other lands. Moreover, Margaret, widow of the duke of Burgundy, who had fallen in battle in Lorraine in 1477, proposed to marry the duke's daughter and sole heir, Maria, to Clarence, whom she had always loved more than any other of her kin. Such an elevation of his ungrateful brother was displeasing to Edward, and he threw all possible impediments in its way. At this the indignation of the duke was greatly increased. "Jamque alter alterum non satis fraternis oculis respicere coepit". Then might have been seen such flatterers as are always to be found in kings' courts running back and forth from the one brother to the other, reporting their words, in however secret conclave uttered. The duke's fall was brought about thus: a certain necromancer named John Stacy was accused of having endeavored to procure by means of leaden images and other things the death of Lord Beauchamp, at the request of Beauchamp's adulterous wife. At his examination he not only confessed this, but implicated one Thomas Burdet, a servant of Clarence. Burdet was arrested and condemned, and perished with Stacy on the gallows at Tyburn, strongly maintaining his innocence. On the next day Clarence came to the council chamber at Westminster, bringing with him the famous preacher Dr. Godard, who reported to the council Burdet's confession and declaration of innocence.

At this time the king was at Windsor. When he heard of what had happened in the council, he was greatly displeased; and meditating on the informations against Clarence which had been brought to him, he summoned his brother to appear at the royal palace in Westminster. There in the presence of the mayor and aldermen of London he upbraided Clarence vehemently for his act, as imputing injustice to the government, and as perilous to judges and juries. The duke was placed in custody and remained there till his death. "Quae autem in Parliamento proximo secuta sunt", says the writer, "mens refugit enarrare: tam tristis visa est disceptatio ea habita inter duos tantae humanitatis germanos". For no one argued against the duke save the king; no one replied to the king save the duke. Men were brought who seemed to many to fulfil the functions of accusers rather than of witnesses. Clarence offered to defend his cause by personal combat. Parliament decided that the testimony was sufficient, and sentenced him, by the mouth of Buckingham, created Lord High Steward for the purpose, to death. The execution of the sentence was long delayed, till the Speaker of the House of Commons appeared with his associates in the Upper House, and asked that the sentence might be carried out. "Consequenter infra paucos dies factum est id qualecunque erat genus supplicii secrete infra Turrim Londiniarum (utinam finis mali)" (p. 562).

In consequence of this act many persuaded the king that he might rule at will over the whole kingdom, for all the idols of the people had been put away. And the king, "licet intra se (ut abitror) saepissime poenitens facti", ruled so magnificently that he seemed to be feared by all while he himself feared no one.

At this time began renewed troubles for Edward, on the side of France, from which his yearly tribute failed to come, and from Scotland. To Scotland was sent a large army under the command of Gloucester. What he accomplished in that expedition, and how much money he foolishly spent, is evident enough from the results. For he reached Edingburgh with his whole army unresisted, but left that richest of cities untouched, and returned by way of Berwick. That town, lying at the very entrance of the country, was captured, and the castle, which held out longer, at length fell into the hands of the English at the cost of some slaughter and blood. This little acquisition, or perhaps better perdition, says the writer, for it cost 2000 marks per year to maintain, cost the realm more than 100,000 pounds. "Haec sunt quae in Scotia Dux ille confecerat" (p. 563).

As for France, Edward, enraged at the loss of his tribute and still more by the failure to marry his daughter to the Dauphin, determined to undertake another expedition. Preparations for this were making, "cum Rex ille neque senio, neque quovis intellecto certo genere morbi, cujus cura in minori persona facilis non videretur, affectus esset; decidit in lectum" April 9, 1483 (pp. 563—4). "Is Princeps licet diebus suis cupiditatibus & luxui nimis intemperanter indulsisse credatur, in fide tamen Catholicus summe, haereticorum severissimus hostis, sapientium & Doctorum hominum Clericorumque promotor amantissimus; sacramentorum Ecclesiae devotissimus reverator; peccatorumque suorum omnium poenitentissimus fuit" (p. 564). Those present at his death, and especially the executors of his will, testified that he wished all men to whom he owed anything, by contract, fraud, or extortion, to be fully satisfied of their claims. Long before his death he had made his will, and at the time of his death he added some codicils. What a wretched and unhappy sequel this wise disposition of everything had, the following tragedy will show.

The Privy Council met to determine the day on which the young Prince, who was at that time in Wales, should be crowned, and with how large a retinue he should come up to London. On this point there was a great divergence of opinion, the occasion of which was this: all desired to see the prince succeed his father; but the wiser desired to withdraw him from the guardianship of his uncles and his brothers of the queen's blood. Which was not an easy thing to accomplish if these same men through their influence with the prince were allowed to set the number as high as they would. Hastings declared that he would flee to Calais, of which he was captain, if the king did not come up with a moderate number; for he feared if the power fell into the hands of the the queen's kindred they would avenge the injuries they pretended he had done them. "Duravit enim jam diu malevolentia grandis inter ipsum Dominum de Hastyngs atque eos". "Benignissima autem Regina", wishing to prevent any trouble, wrote to the prince to bring not more than 2000 men. With this number Hastings was satisfied, for he was sure that Gloucester and Buckingham, "in quibus maxime confidebat", would bring up no less a number.

All now awaited the coronation upon the 4th of May. "Interea scribit Dux Glocestriae ad consolationem Reginae dulcissimas litteras; promittit adventum, obsequium, fidelitatem, & omne debitum suum Regi & domino suo Edwardo quinto, fratris sui defuncti Regis atque ipsius Reginae primogenito. Veniens itaque Eboracum cum decenti familia, singulis veste lugubri indutis, solennes atque lachrymis plenas Regis exequias facit. Omnem Nobilitatem illarum partium ad fidelitatem filii Regis sacramentis constringens: ipse prior omnium jurat" (p. 565).

When Richard had reached Northampton, he was met by Buckingham, and there came to him there Lord Rivers, and Richard Grey, and others sent by the king, "ut omnia agenda arbitrio patrui sui Ducis Gloucestriae submitterent" (p. 565). They were received "jocundo nimis atque hilari vultu", dined with the Duke and Buckingham, with courteous conversation, and parted for the night to their several inns. Early the next morning, "pessimo, ut postea visum est, hac nocte capto consilio", all the lords went out together to present themselves to the young king, who was at Stony Stratford, a few miles away. Scarcely were they arrived at the entrance to this village, when Rivers and Grey were arrested and ordered to be sent north. And straightway, before this was known in the village, Gloucester and Buckingham hastened in and arrested others of the king's train, among them Sir Thomas Vaughan. "Dux tamen ille Glocestriae, qui hujus factionis Princeps erat, nihil reverentiae quod capitis nudatio, genuflectio, aliusve quilibet corporis habitus in subdito exegit, dicto nepoti suo Regi facere distulit aut recusavit. — Tantum dicebat se prospicere tutelae corporis sui, cum certo sciebat hujuscemodi homines assistere lateri Regis, qui in honoris vitaeque suae exterminium conjurarunt" (p. 565). Thereupon all the king's followers were bidden to withdraw.

On the following night rumors of what had happened were brought to London, and the queen fled to sanctuary in Westminster with all her children. The next morning many of the citizens took sides, some appearing at Westminster to support the queen; others in London, under the shadow of Hastings.

After a few days had elapsed, Buckingham aud Gloucester appeared in London with the young king, whom they lodged in the palace of the bishop of St. Paul's. They compelled all the lords, the mayor and aldermen, to swear an oath of fidelity to the king. At a meeting of the council various places were proposed for the king's residence — "aliquem alium laxiorem locum" — till he should be crowned; Buckingham's suggestion of the Tower was accepted. "Acceiptque dictus Richardus . . . illum solennem magistratum, qui Duci Humfrido Glocestriae, stante minore aetate Regis Henrici, ut Regni Protector appellaretur, olim contingebat". This authority he used with the consent and good will of all the lords. The king's coronation was set down for June 22, and "sperabant & expectabant universi pacem & prosperitatem Regni" (p. 566).

Hastings, who seemed to assist the two dukes in every way and to have deserved their especial favor, declared his joy that the rule had been transferred from two of the queen's blood to two nobler men of the king's blood; and that without so much bloodshed as would happen from a cut finger. But a little while after his great joy was turned to mourning. For by the Protector's wonderful shrewdness divided Council-meetings were held, one at

Westminster, one in the Tower, where the king was. On the thirteenth of June, Hastings, coming to the Council-meeting at the Tower, by the Protector's order was beheaded. The Archbishop of York and the Bishop of Ely, saved by their cloth from death, were imprisoned in different castles in Wales. "Ita sublatis sine justitia aut judicio tribus fortioribus funibus novelli Regis, caeterisque omnibus fidelibus ejus similia formidantibus, fecerunt amodo hi duo Duces quicquid cupiebant" (p. 566).

On the following Monday they came "cum multitudine maxima . . . cum gladiis & fustibus" to Westminster, where they compelled the Lord Cardinal of Canterbury to appeal to the queen to give up the young duke of York for the solace of the king his brother. "Illa verbis gratanter annuens, dimisit puerum", and the Cardinal took him to the Tower.

From that day the two dukes showed their plans openly. "Nam evocatis ab Aquilone, Wallia, & ceteris quibusvis partibus sub eorum ditione & potestate constitutis, hominibus armatis in numero terribili & inaudito, dictus Richardus Protector vicesimo sexto die praefati mensis Junii Regimine Regni sub titulo Regii nominis sibi vendicavit; seque eodem die apud magnam aulam Westmonasterii in cathedram marmoream ibi intrusit" (p. 566).

The means by which this was brought about is as follows. A petition was brought forward, in which it was declared that Edward's children were bastards, as before he had married Elizabeth he had entered into a contract "cum quadam Domina Alienora Boteler", and as the descendants of Clarence had been attainted, Gloucester was left as the only undoubted heir of Richard, Duke of York. Wherefore Gloucester was besought, at the end of the petition, on the part of the Lords and Commons. that he would assume what was his right. It was given out that this petition was composed in the North, but all knew who in London was the sole author of so great and infamous a sedition (p. 567).

3*

From the North came a large number of troops, commanded by Richard Ratcliff, who stopped on his way at Pomfret, to put to death, "absque ulla .... forma judicii observata", Rivers, Grey and Vaughan. "Et is est secundus sanguis qui in hac subitanea mutatione innocenter effusus est" (p. 567).

On July 6 Richard and Anne were crowned. "Ab eo die dum viveret, homo iste appelatus est Rex Richardus a conquaestu tertius" (p. 567). Richard now made a progress into the North, passing through Windsor, Oxford, and Coventry to York. Here a second coronation was celebrated for the sake of impressing the people, with all possible pomp. For this he had money enough, having taken to himself all the treasures which King Edward had accumulated and placed at the disposal of the executors of his will. Richard's only son, Edward, was here made Prince of Wales.

While all this was going on, the two princes remained under guard in the Tower. Many, especially in the South and West, urged the queen to send her daughters secretly into France, that, if anything befel the princes, the true royal blood might yet exist. Hearing of this, Richard set strict guard about the sanctuary. Throughout the South and West men began to rise in rebellion, and "factis proclamationibus publicis quod Dux Bukynghamiae Henricus, qui per id temporis habitabat apud Brekenok in Wallia, facti poenitens, Capitaneus in hac re principalis existeret, vulgatum est, dictos Regis Edwardi pueros, quo genere violenti interitus ignoratur, decessisse in fata" (p. 568).

On hearing of this the conspirators called to mind Henry of Richmond, who was living in Britanny in exile, and, on the advice of the Bishop of Ely, Buckingham sent to Richmond, urging him to come to England as quickly as possible, marry the Princess Elizabeth, and with her take possession of the whole realm. Richard was not unaware of the conspirators' plans, but had followed them with the greatest vigilance. Buckingham's whole country was surrounded by men to whom Richard had promised the duke's possessions, who should intercept him the moment he left his home; every way into England was beset. Buckingham was at this time with the Bishop of Ely and other conspirators in the house of Walter Devereux, Lord Ferrers. Seeing that he was so hemmed in that it was impossible to find a safe egress, he fled by night in disguise; "qui tandem in cujusdam pauperis tugurio per uberiorem solito provisionem victualium illic allatorum, discoopertus capitur, & usque ad civitatem Sarisburiensem, quo Rex se cum maximo exercitu contulerat, perductus in die commemorationis Animarum ... in publico mercato ... capitalem subiit sententiam" (p. 568).

Of the other conspirators, some, including Dorset, fled to Britanny, some to sanctuary; one, Thomas Saintleger, was captured and beheaded.

Meanwhile Richmond came with certain ships to the harbor of Plymouth; but learning what had happened sailed away again. Richard returned from the West to London in triumph. At the next Parliament he made such proscriptions of his foes as were unheard of even from Octavian, Antony, and Lepidus. The property of the exiles was given to men of the North, whom he placed all about himself, "in opprobrium & murmur perpetuum omnium Australium populorum, qui magis quotidie ad veterum dominorum suorum speratum reditum, quam istorum praesentaneam tyrannidem respexerunt" (p. 570). Now the queen,"frequentibus intercessionibus terribilibusque minis adhibitis, ad id sollicitata", sent out all her daughters from sanctuary to King Richard. Shortly after, almost all the temporal and spiritual lords of the realm, headed by the Duke of Norfolk, took an oath to be faithful to Richard's son Edward, as their supreme lord, should anything befal the king.

"Sed quam vana est cogitatio hominis cupientis res suas stabilire sine Deo, brevi postea compertum est. Nam sequenti mense Aprilis, die non multum vario ab anniversario Regis Edwardi, puer ille unicus, in quo tantis sacramentis tota Regalis successionis spes reponebatur . . occubuit. . . . Vidisses tantisper patrem & matrem . . prae subitis doloribus pene insanire" (p. 571).

It was now reported that the conspirators would shortly appear in England, and Richard took such excellent precautions, by means of concessions and distributions throughout the whole realm, that he was better prepared in that year than any time afterward. A truce was concluded with the Scotch king at Nottingham.

Christmas (1482) was celebrated in the palace at Westminster with especial splendor. On Twelfth Night the King appeared crowned in the great hall as on the day of his coronation. Here, in the midst of the festivities, he was informed by his spies, that without any doubt his foes would enter or try to enter England the next summer. Nothing could be more pleasing to him than this, for it would put an end to all his anxieties and evils; but thinking shrewdly that money, the sinews of war, was beginning to fail him, he had recourse to the exactions he had so condemned in his brother Edward. Chosen men were sent out to collect money "precibus atque minis, per fas & nefas" from men of almost every rank. Much else the scribe omits from very shame; this nevertheless ought not to be passed over in silence, that at the Christmas festivities attention was attracted to the fact that changes of garment of the same color and form were presented to the queen and to the Lady Elizabeth. At this people began to talk and wonder greatly, and many said that the king, either expecting the death of the queen or intending to obtain a divorce, for which he thought he had sufficient grounds, was turning his mind to bringing about by any means a marriage with the Lady Elizabeth. Only so, it seemed, could he be sure of his kingdom, and the hopes of his rival be blighted.

A few days after this the queen began to become

exceedingly ill, "cujus languor ideo magis atque magis excrevisse censebatur, quod Rex ipse thori sui consortium omnino aspernabatur. Itaque a medicis sibi consultum, ut faceret, judicavit". About the middle of March [March 16], on the day of a great eclipse of the sun, Anna died.

But the purpose of the king to marry his niece being brought to the ears of some who did not wish it to take place, he was compelled at a meeting of the Council to declare that such an idea had never entered his head; though there were men present who knew the contrary to be true. Those who were especially opposed to this marriage, and whose opinions Richard himself scarcely dared to oppose, were Ratcliffe and Catesby. These declared to the king that if he did not in person repudiate this design in the presence of the mayor and citizens of London, the men of the North, in whom he especially trusted, would rise against him, imputing to him the death of the queen, Warwick's daughter and heir, through whom he had first obtained his honors. They also brought in more than twelve doctors of theology, who declared that even the Pope could not give a dispensation for marriage within so close a degree of consanguinity. It was thought by many that the real reason of Catesby's and Ratcliffe's opposition was a fear that if Elizabeth became queen she would have it in her power to be revenged on them for the death of Rivers and Gray. So a little before Easter, in presence of the mayor and citizens convoked for the purpose, Richard repudiated any design to marry his niece.

And now came news that Richmond would soon be on his way. From a certain prophecy Richard expected his foe to land at Milford near Southampton, and arranged special defences there; but he was deceived. On the first day of August Richmond landed without opposition at Milford in Wales.

On hearing the news, the king, who was at Nottingham, rejoiced greatly, or at least seemed to rejoice, writing everywhere that the longed-for day was come, when he could once more give peace to the state. Meanwhile he sent out terrible mandates that all men who were born to any inheritance in the realm should prepare to fight on the king's side, on penalty of all their goods, possessions and lives.

A little before Richmond landed, Thomas Stanley, husband of Richmond's mother, had been allowed to depart to his home in Lancaster, on condition of sending his son George, Lord Strange, as a pledge to Richard at Nottingham. This he did. When Richmond landed, the king fearing Stanley's defection wrote bidding him present himself at once before the king. Stanley made answer that he was suffering from the sweating-sickness and could not come. His son, who was preparing to escape from Richard, was captured, and a plot on the part of his father, his uncle William Stanley, and Sir John Savage, to go over to Richmond was revealed. He begged for mercy and promised that his father should come at once with all his power to aid the king. In addition he wrote his father of the peril in which he was, and begged for the aid he had promised Richard.

William Stanley and Savage were proclaimed traitors, and the army, though not wholly gathered, advanced to Leicester. There was found a number of men fighting for the king greater than was ever before seen in England fighting on one side. Thence Richard, wearing his crown and accompanied by Norfolk and Northumberland, proceeded with great pomp to a spot about 8 miles from Leicester, where he pitched his camp.

The next morning Richard rose as the dawn was beginning to glimmer. His chaplains were not ready to say mass, no breakfast was ready to re-enkindle the king's fainting (tabescentem) spirit, and he, it is said, reported that he had had terrible visions, as if he had been surrounded by a multitude of demons. "Faciem uti semper attenuatam, tunc magis discoloratam & mortiferam prae se tulit"; and he declared that the result of the battle would be the destruction of the realm, for the victor, which ever he should be, would destroy those who had opposed him. Finally, as he saw the enemy approaching, he gave orders to behead Lord Strange. "Illi autem quibus hoc officium datum est, videntes ancipitem rem nimis majorisque ponderis quam unius hominis exterminium in manibus esse, differentes crudele Regis mandatum exequi dimiserunt hominem suo arbitrio, & ad interiora belli reversi sunt" (p. 574).

When battle was joined, Richmond proceeded straight toward King Richard; Oxford attacked the wing commanded by Norfolk. Where Northumberland stood, no strokes were seen either given or taken. Finally Richmond won a glorious victory, together with that most precious crown which Richard had formerly worn on his head. "Nam inter pugnandum, & non in fuga, dictus Rex Richardus multis letalibus vulneribus ictus, quasi Princeps animosus & audentissimus, in campo occubuit" (p. 574).

"Invento inter alios mortuos corpore dicto Richardi Regis, ... multasque alias contumelias illatas, ipsoque non satis humaniter propter funem in collum adjectum usque at Leicestriam deportato; novus Rex corona tam insigniter conquaesita decoratus Leicestriam vadit" (pp. 573-4). Northumberland and Surrey gave themselves up. Catesby was captured and beheaded at Leicester, a father and son named Brecher were hanged. And since no other executions were heard of, "sed Principem hunc novum in omnes suam clementiam impartisse, coepit laudari ab omnibus, tanquam Angelus de coelo missus, per quem Deus dignaretur visitare plebem suam, & liberare eam de malis quibus hactenus afflicta est supra modum" (p. 575).

Et ita finit historia, quam usque ad exitum dicti Regis Richardi, quoad veritas gestorum se menti offerebat, sine ulla scita intermixtione mendacii, odii, aut favoris, declarare promisimus" (p. 575).

That the statement with which the continuation closes is a true characterization of the work has been universally admitted. Faulty in a few points, it nevertheless remains the most important and authoritative source of knowledge of the period it covers. Conscientiously devoted to the service of King Edward, the writer is not by any means in his history a bigoted partisan of the House of York. His statement of the murder of that "glorious martyr" King Henry, committed by a "tyrant", is sufficient to prove that. Whoever actually committed the crime, the burden of it had to be borne by the whole royal house. The writer knows how also to recognize all Henry's "remarkable virtues", and the miracles worked at his tomb. Edward, too, is not free from his criticism, although the eulogy which follows the account of his death is sufficiently strong. In considering the account of these two kings, it is important to remember that it was written after the beginning of a Lancaster-Tudor dynasty. Whatever influence that fact may have had in opening the eyes of the writer to Henry's virtues, it certainly did not tend to weaken his faith in Edward's.

The treatment of Richard, however, rests upon a wholly different basis. There is nowhere evident any favorable disposition on the part of the scribe toward him. One may be certain that, if spared at all, he is spared through the writer's desire to write the truth, free from all admixture of hatred. Unsparing as the treatment of Richard is, it bears every mark that it is written from a conscientious historian's point of view, and not that of a personal foe. The only trace of what might be called personal feeling is an occasional expression like "homo iste". It is in no sense artful, there is no dependence upon prophecy, legend or hearsay in an attempt to add color to the picture of a tyrant.

Such considerations make exceedingly noteworthy the writer's treatment of those early crimes with which Richard was charged. Neither he nor anyone else is mentioned as connected with a murder of Prince Edward, who is said to have been slain in the field. Of this account Gairdner says: "These words, I think, naturally imply that the first-named person, at least, was slain in the field, and some others after the battle 'by the vindictive hands of certain persons'. It seems probable, however, that the writer, who was one of Edward IV's council, expressed himself ambiguously on purpose to shield the guilty. This he evidently did in his allusion to the death of Henry VI" (Life of Richard III, p. 12). In reply to this, it must be said that there can be little doubt that this passage, like the rest of the history, was written after the death of Richard, when the writer could have had no reason, as he clearly had no disposition, to shield him. A strong proof that these passages were written after Edward's and Richard's deaths is found in the reason offered by the scribe for not continuing his history into the reign of Henry VII: "Cum mos scribentium historias viventium gesta reticere solet, ne vitiorum descriptio odium pariat virtutum recitatio adulatoris crimini detur: statuit praefatus scriptor una cum morte Richardi Regis suo labori finem imponere" (p. 577).

At all events, if, as is possible, the passage was written before Richard's death, it must have been written at about the same time as that on the death of Henry, where the statement is not only "remarkably strong", as Gairdner calls it, but simply unthinkable as written while the author was a member of Edward's council. If the deed was, as Gairdner says, and as there can be no doubt, "so clearly abetted by authority that it was not expedient then to speak the whole truth about it" (Life of Richard III, p. 20), there can be no reasonable doubt that it could not have been expedient for a member of Edward's council to have called the doer of the deed a tyrant or its victim a martyr. If the writer could venture to write this passage, he could certainly have ventured to write what he knew about the death of Henry. Further, the passage, rightly considered, seems clear enough. Somerset, who is therein mentioned, was beheaded with others two days after the battle. That fact must have been known to the writer, and by "certain avenging hands" he clearly means those of the executioners of Somerset and his companions. Courtney was slain on the field; and it is clear enough that the writer simply meant to mention the important deaths, without distinguishing as to whether they took place on the battle-field, or at the execution later.

If the passage on Henry's death was, as seems nearly certain, written after the death of Richard, the pious wish that the murderer may be spared to repent, shows that the writer intends no reference to Richard. If, on the other hand, it was written before Richard's death, the most reasonable conclusion seems to be that the writer here as elsewhere, refrains from stating rumors where he is not certain of the truth. Noteworthy in this connection is the writer's treatment of the death of Anna. We are told that Ratcliffe and Catesby asserted to Richard that he would be accused of the death of his wife, if he married Elizabeth, but the scribe carefully refrains from stating or suggesting that Richard poisoned Anna.

No hint is given that Richard had a hand in Clarence's death.

Thus with four great crimes imputed to Richard by later writers he remains in the Croyland history unconnected; and with only one of them is his connection even suggested.

With the deaths of Hastings, of Rivers and his companions, and of the princes, he is of course charged; but the facts are scarcely more than mentioned. There is no lamentation, no rhetorical pathos, least of all in connection with the deaths of the princes. The most that is said in such sort is that the death of Rivers was the second shedding of innocent blood in this sedition.

But if there is evident a determination to keep within the bounds of known fact in the writer's treatment of Richard, there is on the other hand, as said before, no sign of any disposition to shield him. The facts spoke for themselves without any rhetorical ornamentation. Richard is the tyrant and murderer. His dissimulation and perjury are brought out by the statement of his oath of fidelity to the young King, taken by his command and by him first of all, at York, by his letters to the Queen, his devotion to the Prince on meeting him at Stony Stratford, his compelling the lords and the authorities of London to take the oath of fidelity to Edward at the Bishop's palace. Another dark side of his character is shown by insisting on Richard's eagerness to enter on an incestuous marriage with his niece. With how little favor the Croyland continuator looked on Richard, and how little disposed he was to find good in his acts is seen in his treatment of Richard's Scotch campaign. His success in this was of very great value to England, and his services were gratefully recognized by the King, by Parliament, and by the whole nation. According to the writer, however, Richard not only refused to obtain important success that was within his grasp, but saddled the nation with a monstrous expense by the capture of Berwick, which he calls "perditio" rather than "acquisitio". All that the continuator finds of good to say of Richard is a mention of his "ingenium excellens", and of his brave death in battle.

Throughout the account there are very few traces of reflexion, pious, philosophical, or rhetorical, upon the events narrated. There is almost no insistence upon God's punishment for crimes committed by Richard. How vain are the purposes of a man who endeavors to establish his plans without God, was shown by the loss of Richard's one son, on whom lay all his hope of founding a dynasty. How past finding out are God's ways, was shown by Edward's final overthrow of Henry, who had been, in the people's belief, restored by the hand of the Most High. Richmond — and this is the most important touch — seemed an angel sent from heaven by whom God deigned to visit his people and free them from their unheard-of ills. These are practically all the reflections to which the author turns aside from the plain current of his story. In the words about Richmond, however, is seen the beginning of a spirit destined in the succeeding years to an enormous extension.

VII. Joannis Rossi Historia Regum Angliae.

This book was written by John Rous, an antiquary, who was chaplain at Guy's Cliffe, near Warwick, and died in 1491. The last fact mentioned in his work is that God blessed King Henry [VII] with offspring of both sexes. Prince Arthur was born September 19, 1486, Princess Margaret Nov. 29, 1489. The birth of Henry, June 28, 1491, is not mentioned, and between these last two dates the composition of this part of Rous's narrative must lie. His work was dedicated to Henry VII. It was published from a manuscript in the Bodleian Library by Thomas Hearne in 1716, and again in 1745. The following citations are from the second edition.

Of the character of Henry VI Rous says, "Rex iste Henricus sextus, ut crevit aetate, crevit similiter & virtutibus, omni aetate discretionis capax, Deo & beatae virgini Mariae devotissimus, sed mundo & mundanis operibus minime deditus, ea semper committens Concilio". "Iste etiam sanctissimus vir a regno turpiter fugatus .... tandem captus & incarceratus est, plurimis annis pacifice omnia sufferens" (p. 210). Of his death — "Iterum thronum regium ascendens, non diu ita residens, sed iterum incarceratus demum martirio coronatus migravit ad Electorum Dei sempiternum consortium, miraculis mirabiliter choruscans, patientia vincens, & per hoc patientiam cunctis edocens" (p. 210). Later, Rous says in speaking of Richard's crimes, "ipsum sanctissimum virum regem Henricum sextum per alios, vel multis credentibus manu pocius propria interfecit" (p. 215).

Edward, who succeeded, had as guide in all his acts "fortuna vultu hilari arridens & in adversis scuto suae". He was always favored by the people, "juxta illud poeticum: mobile versatur semper cum principe vulgus".[1]

---

[1] From Claudian IV cons. of Honorius, vs. 302.

To Edward succeeded his son, a child of about thirteen years and a half [really twelve and a half]. At that time he was at Ludlow, whither the friends of his father hastened to him, and whence "militum Gartorii solito servicio cum splendido convivio dictus juvenis rex removit se . . versus Londinias" (p. 212). Coming upon them at StonyStratford Richard, "dux Gloucestriae & sua ordinatione protector Angliae" (p. 212), with a strong hand took the young Prince under his own rule as Protector, arrested Rivers, Richard Grey and Vaughan, and sent them to Pomfret, where a short time after they were unjustly put to death. Later, the Earl of Northumberland is stated to have been their principal judge. Thus the young king, torn from those most faithful to him and received [by Richard] with kisses and embraces, fell "ut innocens agnus in manus luporum" (p. 212). He was brought to London and lodged in the palace of the Bishop. Everything pertaining to the royal dignity was done after the wonted fashion, in his name, and coins were struck off bearing his name.

On hearing of the fate of her kinsmen the queen mother fled with the young Duke of York and her daughters to sanctuary in Westminster Abbey. Her son Dorset and her brother-in-law Edward Grey fled elsewhither, being accused of plotting the death of the Protector. Upon the arrival of the Earl of Northumberland in London, "statim dux Gloucestriae regni Protectoris titulum ad exheredationem domini sui regis Edwardi quinti invenit, pro sua propria promotione non invenit sed proprius finxit" (p. 214). Then Edward the fifth, king in fact though not crowned, with his brother Richard, obtained from Westminster under a promise that he should be safe, were put into prison, "ita quod ex post paucissimis notum fuit qua morte martirizati sunt" (p. 214).

Then mounted the throne "tyrannus rex Ricardus, qui natus est . . . biennio matris utero tentus, exiens cum dentibus et capillis ad humeros" (p. 215). At his nativity

Scorpio, the sign of the house of Mars, was ascendant, and like the scorpion, "vultu blandiens, cauda pungens", he showed himself to all. For he received Edward the fifth smilingly with embraces and kisses and then killed him; and his wife Anna the Queen he poisoned. And because there was a certain prophecy that after E. should reign G., George, Duke of Clarence, "peremptus est" (p. 215); and the other G., Gloucester, was preserved to fulfil the prophecy. "Simili prophetia Humfridus, dux Gloucestriae, funditus peremptus dicebatur, nempe quod dux Gloucestriae ipsum interficeret, et totum completum est in isto misero rege Ricardo tercio prius Gloucestriae duce" (p. 215). The Lord Hastings he beheaded without trial, the Archbishop of York and the Bishop of Ely he imprisoned, "ad haec maxime desudante Henrico duce Bukkynghamiae" (p. 316). The Lord Stanley was wounded, arrested, and put in prison, but restored to liberty. He had been made by Richard Lord Chamberlain and High Constable of England. "Rege Edwardo quinto incarcerato rex Ricardus tercius omnes gazas suas contulit Henrico duci Bukkynghamiae, qui tunc liberaturam dans de nodis Staffordensium gloriabatur, se tot de illis habere sicut prius habuit Ricardus Nevel comes Warwici de baculis ramosis, id est, raggid staves. Multum tamen numero erant impares, & non diu quin crevit latens odium inter regem & ducem" (p. 216). Buckingham's rebellion, his capture, and execution at Salisbury, follow.

Richard's progresses to Gloucester and to York are mentioned. At the latter place Richard's son, "parvulus septem annorum" was proclaimed Prince of Wales, but died shortly after. Then Edward, son of the dead Clarence, was proclaimed heir apparent, but subsequently John, Earl of Lincoln, was preferred to him.

And now, the life of King Richard hastening toward its setting, many secretly withdrew from him to join Richmond, who appeared at Milford Haven in Wales. He had comparatively few against many, yet he slew Richard in battle. This Richard, cruel beyond compare, had reigned "ad instar Antechristi regnaturi"; and as Antechrist shall fall hereafter in the midst of his greatest glory, so Richard perished wretchedly, having with him on the field his crown and many of his treasures and in the midst of a great throng. Yet, desiring to tell the truth in Richard's honor, Rous says that he, though small of body and weak of strength, fought like a noble soldier to his last breath, defending himself with the greatest skill (clarissime), often crying out that he was betrayed, and shouting, Treason, treason, treason, and thus, tasting the cup which he had often given others to drink ("gustans quod aliis saepius propinaverat"), ended his life most wretchedly (p. 218).

Rous is the first of the chroniclers to describe Richard's person. "Parvae staturae erat, curtam habens faciem, inaequales humeros, dexter superior sinisterque inferior" (p. 216). Richmond, on the other hand, had an angelic face, ever inciting love in all who gazed upon it. Rous ends his book with a direct address to Henry, full of extravagant praise, "quia in amoris ardore te intuens, o nobili rex, si tantam gratiam permissivam in oculis munificentiae tuae inveni, sub tua speciali licentia et favore alloquor" (p. 219). Ancient prophecies, the favor of God shown in his success, and gifts from the pope, are signs of glory to come. And a further sign is that God has blessed him with offspring of both sexes. "Tuo nempe ex femore prodiit modernus princeps Walliae inclitus Arthurus filius tuus primogenitus & heres Angliae Deo ordinante futurus, alterius Arthuri magni in futuro divina providentia probitatem suscepturus" (p. 219).

The foregoing account is not merely Lancastrian. It was written directly for the perusal of Henry VII, and its whole spirit is accommodated to that end. The descriptions of Henry VI, of Henry VII, most of all of Richard himself, Rous painted in the colors likeliest to be pleasing to his royal patron. Henry VI is the "holiest of men" patient of all misfortune, "refulgent with miracles" after his death;

and Henry VII has an angelic countenance that wins the love of all who behold it. To this flattering portrait that of Richard is naturally a contrast. In Rous's work first do we find details of Richard's person, weak of body, short of stature and of face, with the right shoulder higher than the left — curiously different from the later picture, in which Richard's left shoulder is represented as higher than the right. Here first we begin to hear tales of Richard's monstrous birth, haired and toothed, having been in his mother's womb two years — again an interesting contrast to Shakespeare's representation that Richard's physical peculiarities were due to the fact that he was sent before his time into this breathing world, unfinished, scarce half made up. Astrology is drawn into the picture. Scorpio was ascendant at Richard's birth and like the scorpion "vultu blandiens cauda pungens" he showed himself. Shakespeare would certainly have made use of the simile, had he known it, in his picture of the Richard who could smile and murder while he smiled. Toad, spider, hog, a cockatrice with murderous eye, all these is Richard in Shakespeare's picture, but the scorpion fails. The bit of astrology, too, might well have been included in the treatment of the Richard who accounts to the queen for the death of her murdered sons with the words "Lo, at their births good stars were opposite". Prophecy, too, plays its part in Rous's picture of Richard. He is the fulfiller of the prophecy that after E., G. should reign — a prophecy which here makes its first appearance in the chronicles; he fulfils likewise a prophecy which according to the author had caused the death of Humphrey the good duke of Gloucester.

Deformed as Richard is in person, and monstrous in his birth, even so deformed and monstrous is he in his character — a very Antechrist. He receives the young king with kisses and embraces, and within three months murders him and his brother. He is the murderer of Henry VI; he beheads Rivers and his companions against justice, Hastings without a trial; he poisons his own wife Anne. It is instructive to note, that at this early date is told bluntly, as a fact, what later Lancastrian-Tudor historians, like More, told with reservations. This could never have been more than a rumor, and its statement here as fact shows that Rous was eager to charge Richard with all the crimes which he had any reasonable pretext for charging him with. Interesting, therefore, is what Rous omits to say. That Richard with his own hands murdered King Henry is told only on the authority of "multis credentibus". Richard's agency in bringing about Clarence's death is not even suggested. Had any rumor of it been known to Rous he would surely have mentioned it in his catalogue of Richard's crimes.

Noteworthy, further, is the fact that Rous, like Shakespeare, represents the prophecy about G. as the sole cause of Clarence's death. In the days of Henry VII, it appears, such a prophecy was considered cause enough.

In Rous begins very slightly to appear in Richard's story the classical influence. Fortune smiles on Edward with cheerful look, and protects him beneath her shield; and another bit of Seneca-like reflection on the fickle populace appears in the line quoted from Claudian, 'mobile versatur semper cum principe vulgus".

In conclusion it must once more be emphasized that this tolerably complete picture of Richard the monster and tyrant, born under a hostile star and perishing like Antechrist, is the product not of a historical feeling, but of a courtier's. There is no need to assert that it is a dishonest picture; but it is a work of art, the work of an artist, whose sight is of the kind that finds the face of a king angelic. It must be said, moreover, that Rous could on occasion draw a very different portrait of Richard, as Mr. Gairdner has shown. "In the Warwick Roll composed by him he pays him [Richard] the following tribute: 'The most mighty prince Richard by the grace of of God king of England and of France, and Lord of

Ireland, by very matrimony, without discontinuance or any defiling in the law, by heir male lineally descending from King Harry the Second, all avarice set aside, ruled his subjects in his realm full commendably, punishing offenders of his laws, specially extortioners and oppressors of his commons, and cherishing those that were virtuous; by the which discreet guiding he got great thanks of God and love of all his subjects, rich and poor, and great land of the people of all other lands about him'. Though written in the past tense there can be little doubt this eulogium was composed during Richard's life, and for the king's own gratification". (Gairdner, Life of Richard III, p. 323, fn.) Which only makes one wonder the more what Rous's portrait of Richmond would have been had Richard been victorious.

There are two original drawings of Richard in existence made by Rous himself: in neither of these appears any trace of Richard's alleged deformity.

VIII. The memoirs of Philippe de Comines.

Philippe de Comines, counsellor, chamberlain and diplomatic agent of Charles the Bold, later of Louis XI, was born in 1447, died 1511. The first six books of his memoirs were written between 1488 and 1504, and the passages quoted below were, like Rous's book, written between the birth of Arthur, 1486, and that of Margaret, 1489, as is shown by de Comines' reference to Henry VII as having two beautiful children (Ed. Mlle. Dupont, 2 : 245). The memoirs were first printed in 1524, and went through many editions before 1548, when Hall used the book in compiling his chronicle.

I quote from the three volume edition of the Société de l'histoire de France, edited by Mlle. Dupont, 1840.

In chapters 4, 5, 6 and 7 of Book III, de Comines relates the preparations of Warwick and Clarence in France for their invasion of England, and subsequent events down to Edward's definitive success at Tewkesbury. He speaks of the marriage, not betrothal, of Prince Edward and the second daughter of the Earl of Warwick. While Warwick and Clarence were preparing for the invasion there came to Calais from King Edward a young lady who deceived the intendant of Calais, Waneloc[1]), who was friendly to Warwick, into believing that she bore overtures of peace from King Edward. As a matter of fact, she bore a message from the king to Clarence, urging him not to be a cause of the destruction of his own house to the benefit of that of Lancaster, and that from the marriage of Warwick's daughter to Henry's son Edward there could be no doubt that he intended to make the latter king of England. So well did this woman fulfil her mission that she won over Clarence, who promised to join his brother as soon as he arrived in England.

Warwick descended upon England and drove out Edward, "qui n'estoit point homme de grant ordre, mais fort beau prince, plus que nul que j'aye jamais veu en ce temps là, et tres vaillant" (1 : 239). He fled hurriedly with Gloucester, and after being in great danger from certain ships of the Easterlings (merchants of the Hanseatic League) reached Holland. On coming to power in England Warwick restored Henry to the throne, "en la presence du duc de Clarence, à qui ce cas ne plaisoit pas" (1 : 250). Edward came to the Duke of Burgundy, de Comines' master, and received from him secret aid, in ships and money, while the duke openly supported Henry, and thought he had made friends on both sides, however Edward's expedition should turn out. Edward landed in England, reached London before Warwick could (get) there, then went to meet Warwick. When the armies were opposite

---

[1]) Instead of the above-mentioned Waneloc, that is, Lord Wenlock, all the printed editions before Mlle. Dupont's, and one of the Mss. used by her have the name Vaucler. Hence this is the name found in Hall's (and Holinshed's) account, taken from de Comines.

each other, Clarence came over to Edward. "Vous avez bien entendu, par cy devant, comme ceste marchandise dudict duc de Clarence avoit esté mence" says de Comines (1 : 259), referring to the mission of the young lady mentioned before.

Of the battle of Barnet, de Comines says that it was "tres aspre et tres forte". It was fought entirely on foot, and so closely did the two armies join "que le roy d'Angleterre combatit en sa personne autant ou plus que nul homme qui fut des deux costez" (1 : 259). In battle, says de Comines, it was Warwick's custom never to fight on foot, but to set his followers to fighting and then mount on horseback. If all was going well he would join in the mêlée, "et si elle alloit mal il se deslogeoit de bonne heure". But this time his brother, Marquis Montague, who was a very brave knight, made him send away his horses and fight on foot. And in this battle he was killed, under what circumstances we are not told. The loss in the battle was great, for Edward, who had conceived a great hatred toward the people of England on account of the favor they showed Warwick, did not make use of his customary battle-cry, "Save the people and slay the nobles" (1 : 260).

Of Henry and his death, de Comines says "Le dict roy Henry estoit homme fort ignorant, et presque insensé: et, si je n'en ay ouy mentir, incontinent apres ceste bataille, le duc de Clocestre, frere dudict roy Edouard, lequel depuis a esté roy nommé Richard, tua de sa main, ou feit tuer en sa presence, en quelque lieu a part, ce bon homme roy Henry" (1 : 261). In the battle of Tewkesbury, "le dict roy Edouard en eut la victoire, et fut le prince de Galles tué sur le champ, et plusieurs autres grans seigneurs, et tres grant nombre de peuple" (1 : 262). After that day Edward had peace until his death; "mais non pas sans grant travail d'esperit et grans pensees" (1 : 263).

Of the death of Clarence de Comines says, "Le roy Edouard feit mourir son frere le duc de Clarence en une pippe de malvoysie, pour ce qu'il se vouloit faire Roy comme on disoit" (1 : 69).

There is an extended account of Edward's expedition to France and the treaty at Picquigny, with mention of various prophecies of the English connected with these events, apropos of which the author remarks that the English are never unprovided with prophecies. The death of Edward was, according to de Comines, caused by the marriage of Marguerite of Flanders with the dauphin, whom Edward had desired for his own daughter, Elizabeth.

Thereupon the Duke of Gloucester took upon himself the government of his nephew, some ten years of age; did him homage as king; led him to London, pretending that he intended to crown him, and for the purpose of getting the other son out of sanctuary (2 : 156). He then declared his nephews bastards, on the authority of the Bishop of Bath, who told Richard that he had married Edward to a certain lady of England, of whom he desired to obtain possession; and that none were present at the marriage but himself, Edward and the lady. Thus he aided Richard to execute his evil desire. Richard then "feit mourir ses deux neveux, et se feit appeller roy Richard" (2 : 158). The two children he had caused to be declared bastards in full Parliament.

The news of this murder was soon received in France; and when Richard wrote signing himself king, asking the friendship of King Louis and doubtless hoping to receive the "pension" which Louis had paid Edward, "le Roy ne voulut respondre à ses lettres ne ouyr le messagier, et l'estima tres cruel et mauvais: car apres le trespas du dict roy Edouard, le dict duc de Clocestre avoit faict hommaige à son neveu, comme à son roy et souverain seigneur, et incontinent apres commit ce cas" (2 : 244).

But this cruelty did not last long, for being in greater pride than any King of England for a hundred years, and having put to death the Duke of Buckingham, God raised up against him in the Earl of Richmond an enemy without any force, "ne nul droict a la couronne d'Angleterre" (2:245). Richmond had been from the age of fifteen or thereabouts (2 : 158; eighteen, 2 : 246) a prisoner in Brittany.

On the occasion of Buckingham's rebellion he made an unsuccessful attempt to land in England. A second attempt was successful, a battle ensued in which Richmond had the help of his stepfather Stanley with 26,000 men, Richard was slain and Richmond crowned on the field with Richard's crown. "Est-ce cecy fortune? C'est vray jugement de Dieu". That this may be more apparent, de Comines adds, "des que le roy Richard eut faict ce cruel meurtre, il perdit sa femme: aucuns veullent dire qu'il la feit mourir. Il n'avoit que ung fils, lequel incontinent mourut" (2 : 160).

I have here united the two accounts which are given in Book V Chap. 20 and Book VI Chap. 8. The first account is found in a chapter headed: "Exemples des malheurs des princes et revolutions des estats arrivez par jugement de Dieu" (2 : 153). Of these the best example was the fate of Richard, but there had been many other examples before his time in England. The line of Lancaster had fallen at Edward's hands, Warwick had perished and his brothers with him. Many English lords had slain their enemies, only to suffer the revenge of their dead enemies' sons. "Or est il bien à penser que telles playes ne viengnent que par la divine justice" (2 : 154). The second account closes with the words "ailleurs ay parlé de ceste matiêre, mais il servoit encores d'en parler icy, et par especial pour monstrer comme Dieu a payé contant, en nostre temps, telle cruaultez, sans attendre". Elsewhere (1 : 66) de Comines has another chapter: "Digression sur les estatz, offices et ambitions, par l'exemple des Anglois". Here again is recited the long series of English calamities: Henry sixth, crowned king, is deposed, imprisoned, and killed; Richard of York names himself king and perishes a few days after; Warwick supports the House of York, Somerset that of Lancaster: in the end, all of Warwick's and Somerset's houses are beheaded or fall in battle; Edward puts to death his brother Clarence for aspiring to the crown, he dies, and Gloucester puts to death Edward's children, and makes himself ruler in their place; incontinent thereafter Richmond enters England, and puts to death this cruel murderer. Thus in these quarrels of England about eighty men of the royal line of England perish. Wherefore de Comines warns princes against allowing divisions to spring up in their realms. "Mais mon advis est que il ne se faict pas que par disposition divine: car quant les princes ou royaulmes ont esté en grant prosperité ou richesses, et ilz ont mescongnoissance dont procede telle grace, Dieu leur dresse ung ennemy ou ennemye, dont nul ne se doubteroit, comme vous porez veoir par les roys nommez en la Bible, et par ce que puis peu d'annees en avez veu en ceste Angleterre" (1 : 70).

De Comines had a certain personal connection with the English affairs of which he writes. He was the diplomatic agent of Charles of Burgundy, when Warwick and Clarence took refuge in France; was the duke's agent when, later, Edward took refuge with him, and obtained help, while the partisans of Henry were being assured no help would be given. He was, again, the counsellor of Louis XI when Edward made his treaty in peace with him in 1475. On this occasion and on others he had spoken with Edward, and learned from the king's own lips that his warcry was, "Slay the nobles and spare the people". With Richmond, too, he had talked, and learned from him the story of his imprisonment in Brittany. But of what went on on English soil, de Comines had only hearsay evidence. His account of the battle of Tewkesbury and prince Edward's death was evidently derived from English refugees in Burgundy, for it contains the words, "comme m'ont dict, ceulx qui y estoient"; and his story of Henry's death is conditioned by "si je n'en ay ouy mentir", "if what I have heard be correct". But de Comines' story is of great value as bearing testimony to the rumors afloat among Englishmen of high rank, especially among Lancastrian partisans.

He has the rumors that Richard murdered with his own hand, or caused to be murdered in his presence, King Henry; the statement of some that he put his wife to death; the fact that he slew his nephews. It is upon this alone that all de Comines' hatred of Richard is based. Prince Edward, he states, was slain on the field, and the statement is especially noteworthy, since de Comines almost certainly, as before said, got his information from Lancastrian refugees in Burgundy. These, if unaware from personal experience of what happened on the field of battle, must, it seems, have been in possession of all Lancastrian reports concerning it. There is no statement, either, of Richard's complicity in the death of Clarence.

Henry VI appears in de Comines' account as a man very ignorant and almost without sense. Edward is praised for his good looks, and his courage; his inordinate love of women is mentioned, and he is called a man of no high order.

De Comines' account of Warwick is especially noteworthy. He may have shared the hatred of his former master, Charles of Burgundy, for Warwick; but when he wrote he was in the service of Louis, who was Warwick's friend and helper. It is remarkable, therefore, that while we have no account of the manner of Warwick's death, his portrait, — quite consistent with the account is his death in Warkworth, and "The Arrival", — is that of a coward. Such appears to have been the common opinion of French historians. Chastellain, for example, (quoted by Mlle. Dupont in her ed. of de Comines, 1 : 250) says of him: "Warwyc .. estoit laiche et couard, ne oncques ne se trouva en lieu, fort fuitif."

In de Comines' account appears for the first time the famous butt of malmsey in which Clarence is said to have been drowned.

Not the least noteworthy part of de Comines' treatment is his insistence that the hand of divine justice is clearly to be seen throughout the struggle of Lancaster and York. His view is in most points a somewhat general one; the disasters he recounts are God's vengeance upon princes because they do not recognize Him as the source of their prosperity; or they are sent by God as punishment for partisan quarrels and divisions. But with regard to Edward and Richard his statement is more direct. Edward is punished for the murder of Clarence by Richard's murder of his children; and for that murder in turn Richard is punished by the loss of his wife, of his son, and finally of his own life, at the hands of Richmond, his enemy raised up by God.

IX. Bernard André's History of Henry VII.

André was an Augustinian friar, a native of Toulouse, who accompanied Henry in his descent upon England. He was made poet laureate, tutor to Prince Arthur, and royal historiographer. His work was begun in 1500, and most of it composed two years later (cf. Dic. Nat. Biog. sub nom.). In the account following the battle of Bosworth, Fox is mentioned as bishop of Winchester, to which see he was elevated Oct. 17, 1501. Gairdner's reprint, from which I quote, is from the unique Ms. of the Cottonian library (Dom. XVIII, ff. 126—228), which is thought to be the identical copy presented to the king.

The work is, as André says, (p. 19) "not so much a history as a biography", and even as such it is singularly short and incomplete. He complains of lack of material, that he is, as it were, wandering blindly in darkness without a guide, that he has nothing save what he has heard. But the work was written for Henry himself, and undoubtedly represents the view he wished to be taken of the events that preceded his enthronement.

After speaking at length of Henry's descent and birth, and of his wonderful ability in learning, André mentions a "divine prophecy" of Richmond's future kingship, made by Henry VI: "Henrico Sexto quadam die cum proceribus et optimatibus regni convivium amplissimum agente, idem rex inter lavandum manus, comite Richemundiae accito, praedixerat illum aliquando regni gubernacula suscepturum, omniaque manu sua (ut nunc videmus feliciter possidet) habiturum" (p. 14). Because of this prophecy, and by Henry's advice, young Richmond was sent by his mother across the channel for safety. Here he was welcomed by Francis of Britanny, because he knew, for so he had learned from others, that Richmond would one day reign in England.

Meanwhile Edward, "nescio qua stimulatus accensusque Furia", aspired to the throne. "Pallida Tisiphone faces accendit mortiferas, quibus illos ad violandum fidem ac jusjurandum excitat" (p. 18). War ensues. Of Prince Edward's death André says only, "is . . . in Theoxberye praelio ceciderat" (p. 22).

Coming to speak of the death of the "holy king", André observes "mirum dictu est quid sit occulti potentia fati; quo alii ad bona, alii ad mala feruntur praecipites. Unde non injuria tragicus [in margin, Seneca][1] exclamat. 'Fata nolentem trahunt, volentem ducunt'. Hoc ideo dixerim quia Richardus, comitis praefati marchiorum frater (Edward IV, at first Earl of March), Gloucestriae dux, si vera est fama, ad regem innocentissimum trucidandum decernitur; huic namque ab unguiculis sanguinolenta placuere facinora" (p. 17). In a later passage, André expressly mentions that Henry's death was resolved upon by Edward. Whereupon he says: "Non possum hoc in loco me lacrymis abstinere, dum mecum in sanctum virum truculentiam, imma-

---

[1] This quotation is not from any of Seneca's plays. His dialogue De Providentia Cap. 5 has "et volentes quidem non trahuntur a fortunia", and later on "Fata nos ducunt". It may be that a mediaeval writer formed these into one sentence.

nitatem, crudelitatem, secreta mente revolvo" (p. 20). And then follows, in the most approved style of lamentation, a passage entitled "Auctoris lacrymosa exclamatio". "His itaque gestis, ecce humani sanguinis sititor ille Richardus Gloucestriae dux a fratre suo Eduardo Quarto missus ad ipsum Henricum trucidandum accessit, illumque . . . [Blank in Ms.]

To the evils that followed this cruel murder, almost the whole world bears witness. "Calamitates siquidem ad cumulum innumerabiles post illa consecutae sunt" (p. 23). For Edward, though during his life (alioquin) a most potent and glorious king, after his death was punished in the persons of his children, whom he had committed to the protection of his brother Richard. While he lived, too, he was often in terror lest Richmond should succeed him. "Propheticis quorumdam testimoniis exterritus" he sought by money, entreaties, and great promises, to induce the Duke of Brittany to yield up Richard to him, then by stealth to obtain possession of him, but in vain. "Verum nec praevaluit unquam in Deum mortalis astutia; quare post haec adversa valetudine correptus obiit" (p. 23).

Then Richard, "protector a rege vocatus et declaratus", named protector by the king and publicly proclaimed as such, first bade summon from Wales his brother's sons (filios. André thought that the Duke of York was with his brother), concealing the tyrannical purpose he had already conceived. The queen fled to sanctuary. Then the tyrant, after putting to death the lords whom he knew to be faithful to his brother, "nepotes quoque clam ferro incautos feriri jussit; sicque mors morte, exitium exitio pensatum est" (p. 24). Thus, while the nobles were faithful in words but far estranged from him in their hearts, Richard was raised to the throne.

Meanwhile Richmond was informed of what went on in England. On Buckingham's rebellion he determined to land in England, but was dissuaded by Dorset. Afterwards, Dorset, "Richardo sollicitatus", started to return home, but was pursued by men whom Richmond sent, and brought back. Now Francis proved treacherous, intending to win Richard's favor by delivering up Richmond; but the latter, getting wind of this, fled to Charles of France, who, "divino velut oraculo admonitus" gave him aid, and Richmond set out, after prayer to God and a speech by Oxford, largely composed of quotations from Lucan. In his prayer Richmond declares that he is embarking in accordance with God's order, not, as God is his witness, drawn thereto by avarice, ambition, or thirst for blood; "sed Angliae regnique populorum longam miseratus calamitosam captivitatem illuc accedo" (p. 25). In his task he prays for God's guidance. Addressing his forces, he declares that the tyrant has slain all his kin save his mother, has filled the whole land with blood, has put to death Buckingham, who was formerly most dear to him, many innocent nobles of the realm, and finally his own nephews. "Nos autem, qui Dei nutu relinquimur, sitibundus sanguinis pari modo discupit. Nunc vero tempus nostrum advenit, quo Deus Judex justus illius scelera manibus nostris puniet." Contrary to his nature, he asserts, does he undertake this cruel war, but it is better to obey God's commands than spend his life amid a foreign people. His forces are small, but God will grant him the victory, as he did to Moses, as victory came to small armies over Xerxes, Darius, Croesus and many others. His adress ends with a request to the priests to pray without ceasing till victory come.

When Richard heard the news of Richmond's arrival in Wales, "ut coluber mala gramina pastus in furorem ac rabiem inflammatur atque accenditur, non secus ac Hyrcana tigris aut Marsus aper ubi vulnera sentit. Itaque repentinum in clamorem erumpens, furibundus ita suos alloquitur" (p. 31). Then follows the "Tyranni in suos furibunda oratio", composed in accordance with the character ascribed to Richard. One passage will suffice to show its nature. "Edico autem vobis, jubeo atque impero ut sine misericordia, sine pietate, sine gratia, omnes igne ferroque perdatis; Gallos autem et exteros quosque ad unum jugulate, enecate, ac cruci affigite. Ipsum vero Richemundiae comitem sine ullo vel sanguinis vel nobilitatis respectu trucidare, aut vivum si potestis adducite, ut illum prae sententia mea excogitatis novis atque inauditis suppliciis, vel mea manu trucidem, jugulem, interimam" (p. 31). We are presented with the opposite picture in Richmond's "Ad Angliam salutatio ad suosque secunda justaque oratio." He greets his native land in much the style of an Agamemnon or Thyestes, „Salve, belli potens, pacisque magistra, ingeniis ornata sacris, dotataque cunctis fortunae donis: excellis omnes quas maximus ambit Oceanus", etc. (p. 30). He comes not to lay the land waste by fire and sword, but to free it from a tyrant and with the help of God to receive back the ancient right of his family, the throne. His men are directed in the strongest terms to beware of committing any injury against the inhabitants for the sake of money or food, and not to receive such without paying for it, "vos autem itidem in alios faciatis, nihil aut verbo aut facto quod quod vobis metipsis facere minime voletis perpetrantes. Si ita feceritis Deus erit nobis propitius, quippe alienis diu non gaudet illicitus usurpator" (p. 31.)

All account of the battle of Bosworth is omitted, for lack of knowledge. After the battle "parta Dei optimi maximique divina dispositione a Richemundiae comite feliciter victoria, tyrannoque pro meritis trucidato" (p. 33), Henry indulges in a speech of thanksgiving, to Jesus and the Virgin, beginning with the hexameter "gratia nulla potest a me nunc digna referri" and ending with a sapphic strophe. He expresses his sorrow for the fallen and bids bury them honorably. "Imprimis ipsius Richardi Regis in . . . . [Blank in Ms.] cum omni moda reverentia sepeliendum sentio" (p. 33), an order which leaves out of account the real way in which Richard's body was brought, lying stark naked across a horse's back, "like a hog or a calf", into Leicester, and there buried "without any solemnity" (Hardying con. ed. Lumby, p. 127).

With the account of André, the Richard-saga has taken a long step forward. The account is not a history; it is a portrait of two figures, the one of darkness, the other of light, black Richard and the angelic Richmond. Richard is not merely a tyrant, usurper and murderer, he is the monster who from his cradle finds his joy in deeds of blood, the butcher selected because of his nature for the execution of murder. He is the Shakesperian Richard to whom Anna says:

> "Thou wast provoked by thy bloody mind,
> That never dreamt on aught but butcheries" R. III, 1 : 2,

and of whom Margaret says:

> murder is thy alms-deed;
> Petitioners for blood thou ne'er putt'st back. 3 H. VI, 5 : 5.

The "sanguinis sititor" of André is the "blood-supper" and "blood-sucker" of the later chronicles and Shakespeare. The tyrant who, swollen with rage like a serpent that has fed on noxious herbs, like a Hyrcanian tiger or a Marsian boar that feel a wound, bursts out in a wild command to his soldiers that with his own hand he may slay Richmond with new and unheard-of tortures, is the Richard whom Shakespeare makes Richmond call

> "The wretched, bloody, and usurping boar,
> That . . . . . .
> Swills your warm blood like wash, and makes his trough
> In your embowelled bosoms". —

There is in the revenge tragedies little more savage than this speech of Richard to his troops. It is scarcely surpassed by the speech of Richard in the True Tragedy: "This, ay this verie day, I hope with this lame hand of mine, to rake out that hatefull heart of Richmond, and when I haue it, to eat it panting hote with salt, and drinke his blood luke warme, tho I be sure twil poyson me" (Sh. Lib. 5 : 120). There is no offset to this black picture, nothing that counts in Richard's favor. His tyrannical purpose he is said to have conceived before the prince came from

Wales, and to have sent for him that the purpose might be executed. The princes were, according to André, slain by the sword.

But if not one thing is said in favor of Richard, some things that are not said do so count. André does not mention that Prince Edward was murdered at all, but says that he fell fighting in the battle of Tewkesbury. Nothing is said of Clarence's death or of Anna's. That he would have mentioned any reputed crimes of Richard in this connection, if he had heard of them, his whole characterization leaves no doubt; yet how should he, living in Henry's court and surrounded by Henry's friends, have failed to hear of them? There is no satisfactory answer, save that no such charges were current at this time.

One more fact concerning Richard remains to be noted. André says that he had been named and declared Protector by King Edward, a statement here met with for the first time.

The picture of Richmond is naturally the greatest contrast to that of Richard. Long exiled, his future kingship is prophesied by the holiest of men — a prophecy here mentioned for the first time. He returns to his native land as God's messenger, sent by Him to punish Richard's crimes. He enters England not because of avarice, ambition, or thirst of blood, but out of pity for the oppressed. The war which he is compelled to enter upon, contrary to his nature, is God's war, and He will grant the victory. Richmond is a princely advocate of the Golden Rule, loves and shows mercy. In most effective contrast to Richard's blood-thirsty desire to slay Richmond with his own hand, he bids bury his conquered foe with every kind of honor. The Richmond of André is the Richmond of Shakespeare.

To make these two figures effective, new literary means are employed. The story is infused throughout with André's classical learning, embellished with Latin poetry from Lucan, Vergil, and others. Now for the first time is Senecan philosophy applied to Richard. He has become the willing follower whom the fates hurry on to evil. Edward, too, is impelled to his measures against Henry by some Fury, while pale Tisiphone, avenger of murder, kindles her fatal torches.

André is also the first writer to frame long speeches, somewhat after the style of Livy, for the characters of his story. Out of about 22 pages actually devoted to an account of the events preceding the beginning of Henry's reign, nine are taken up in speeches. More, Vergil, and Hall followed André in carrying this trick to excess, but nowhere are there such absurd and preposterous examples. We do not wonder that after closing his speech of thanksgiving with a stanza of Latin sapphics, Richmond exclaims, "I know not what I shall say more". For what these speeches became as revealers of character it is only necessary to refer to Shakespeare's play: yet the Richmond and Richard of Shakespeare's speeches — modelled on those of Vergil and Hall — are in all essentials the Richard and Richmond of André.

In André, too, is far more strongly emphasized than ever before, the part played in the gruesome story by divine justice. Not only Richard pays the penalty of his crimes, but Edward also is punished for the murder of Henry by his fear of Richmond while he lives, by his own death, and most of all by the death of his children after him — "mors morte exitium exitio pensatum".

X. Fabyan's Chronicle.

Robert Fabyan was a merchant and alderman of London in the reign of Henry VII. He resigned the office of alderman in 1502, to avoid the expense of the mayoralty. His death occurred in 1512. According to his own statement (p. 681) his chronicle, which ends with the beginning of Henry VII's reign, was finished Nov. 7, 1504. The first edition of his work appeared in 1516, edited by

Richard Pynson, and ended with the battle cf Bosworth. A second edition by William Rastell, including the reign of Henry VII, appeared in 1533, a third in 1542. An edition in 1559 brought the account down to Elizabeth. The following citations are from Ellis's reprint, 1811.

Fabyan's account is that of a city, and not a royal, chronicler. According to the list of authorities mentioned by him he had no extended Ms. or printed work upon which to base his story of the reigns of Edward and Richard, and his sources must have been only such oral and written testimony as was possible to a member of the London city government. His report, therefore, is of great importance as showing the view of Richard held in the city — tradition and saga shaped by a different circle from any that had a hand in the accounts hitherto examined.

Our summary begins after the battle of St. Albans, in which was killed Richard's father, Duke of York. Hearing of the loss of this field, the Duchess of York sent her two younger sons, George and Richard, to Utrecht, where they remained a while. Edward was made king, by help of Warwick, and Henry fled to Scotland, while "that noble and most bounteuous pryncesse quene Margarete, of whom many and vntrewe surmyse was imagened and tolde, was fayne to flye comfortlesse" (p. 640). Toward the end of Edward's first year Richard was created duke of Gloucester.

The marriage of Edward to Elizabeth Grey and the measures adopted to ensure secrecy are detailed at length. "And so this maryage was kept secret after, tyll nedely it muste be discoueryd & disclosed, by meane of other whiche were offeryd vnto the kynge, as the quene of Scottes and other. What obloquy ran after of this maryage, howe the kynge was enchaunted by the duchesse of Bedforde [mother of Elizabeth Grey] and howe after he wolde haue refusyd her, with many other thynges concernyng this matier, I here passe it ouer" (p. 654). This year Henry was taken prisoner in a wood in the

North country by one named Cantlowe, and after presented to the king, who sent him to the Tower.

In the ninth year of Edward "the dissymuled fauore, which atwene the king and the erle of Warwyke hadde this (read: styll, as in later ed.) contynued syne the maryage of the quene, beganne to appere; in somoch that the erle with drewe hym from the kinge, and confederyd vnto hym the duke of Clarence, that before hadde maryed his doughter" (p. 657). Whereupon ensued the rebellion of Robin of Redesdale. Clarence and Warwick fled to France, returned with help, and drove out Edward. He fled to Charles, duke of Burgundy, who had married his sister, while his queen took sanctuary at Westminster. King Henry was restored to his throne. During the parliament that ensued, Edward was proclaimed usurper, and Richard traitor.

Then Edward returned to England, landed at Ravenspore, and drew toward York, "makyng his proclamations in the name of Kyng Henry, and shewyd to the people, that he came for none entent, but oonly to clayme his enherytaunce, ẙ dukedome of Yorke; and soo passyd the countres tyll he came to ẙ cytie of Yorke, where the cytezyns helde hym oute tyll they knewe his entent. And when he had shewyd vnto theym, as he before had done vnto other, & confermed it by an othe, he was there receyued" (p. 660). Coming to London, Edward took possession of the city and imprisoned Henry in the tower. Then followed the battle of Barnet. "In whiche season the duke of Clarence, contrary to his othe and promyse made vnto the Frenshe kynge, refusyd the title of kyng Henry, & sodaynly with ẙ strength as he hadde, rode streight vnto his broder kynge Edwarde, wherwith the other lordes were somdeale abasshed" (p. 661). After a long and cruel fight Edward obtained the upper hand, and Warwick was slain — how, we are nor told.

"Of the mystes and other impedymentes whiche fyll upon the lordes partye, by reason of the incantacyons wrought by fryer Bungey, as the fame went, me lyst nat to wryte" (p. 661).

Margaret and her son now landed in England and advanced to Tewkesbury, "where the kinge mette with her and her distressyd, and chasyd her company and slewe many of theym. In the whiche batayll she was taken, and Sir Edward her sone, and so brought vnto the kynge. But after the kynge hadde questyoned with the sayd Sir Edwarde, and he had answeryd vnto hym contrarye his pleasure, he thenne strake hym with his gauntelet vpon the face: after whiche stroke so by hym recyued, he was by the kynges seruaunts incontynently slayne vpon the .IIII. day of the moneth of May. Whan Kynge Edwarde hadde thus subduyd his enemyes, anone he sent quene Margarete vnto London, where she restyd a season, and fynally she was sent home into her countre" (p. 662).

"Thanne vpon Assencion Euyn next ensuynge, $\tilde{y}^e$ corps of Henry the .VI. late kynge was brought unreuerently from $\tilde{y}^e$ Tower thorugh $\tilde{y}^e$ hygh stretes of $\tilde{y}^e$ cytie vnto Paulis Church, and there lefte for that nyght, and vpon $\tilde{y}^e$ morowe conueyed with gleyuys & other wepyns, as he before thyther was broughte vnto Chertyssey, where he was buryed. Of $\tilde{y}^e$ deth of this prynce dyuerse tales were tolde: but the most common fame wente, that he was stykked with a dagger, by the handes of the duke of Glouceter" (p. 662). (cf. with the passage from a Ms. London chron., c under III. One account was evidently influenced by the other, or the two had a common source).

In the 17th year "that is to meane $\tilde{y}^e$ .XVIII. daye of February, the duke of Clarence and . . . brother to the kynge, thanne beyng prysoner in $\tilde{y}^e$ Tower, was secretly put to deth & drowned in a barell of maluesye within the sayd Tower" (p. 666).

As soon as King Edward was dead, "grudge and vnkyndnesse beganne to take place atwene the kynges and the quenes allye, for the lorde marquys of Dorset broder [Rivers. Dorset was the queen's son. Fabyan has

the same mistake in the name below] vnto the quene &
other of his affynytie, had then the rule and kepynge of
this yonge kynge, whiche at the tyme of his faders dethe
was of the age of . XI . yere or there about, and so beynge
in this gydynge in the Marche of Walys, conueyd hym
towarde London" (p. 668). The duke of Gloucester now
intervened. With a number of men from the North he
met the king at Stony Stratford, and "after dissymuled
countenaunce made atwene hym and the foresayd marquys",
took the king under his own charge, and accompanied by
Buckingham brought him "with all honour" to London.
Upon receipt of the news, the queen took sanctuary in
Westminster with the young duke of York. The king was
met by mayor and citizens at Harnesay Park and conveyed to the bishop's palace. Then Gloucester "inuegelyd
so the arbysshop of Caunterbury namyd Bowchier, that he
went with hym to the quene" (p. 668), and by promises
obtained from her the duke of York.

While provision was making for the king's coronation,
Gloucester was "admitted for lord protector", and caused
to be beheaded at Pomfret, Sir Antony Wydyuyle [Earl
Rivers], the lord Richard Gray, Sir Richard Hawte, and
Sir Thomas Vaghan. Gloucester now sent "for the more
partie" of the nobles and counselled with them, feeling
their minds without letting them perceive his wicked purpose.
"Sodaynly vpon the . XIII . day of Iuny, beyng within the
Tower in the counsayll chambre, with dyuerse lordes with
hym, as the duke of Bukkyngham, erle of Derby, the lorde
Hastynges, than lorde chamberlayne, with dynerse other,
an owte crye by his assent of treason was made in the
vtter chambre, wherwith the sayd lorde protectour beynge
warnyd, roose vp & yode hymselfe to the chamber dore,
and there receyued in suche persones as he before had
appoynted to execute his malycious purpose, the whiche
incontynently set hande vpon the forenamyd lord chamberlayne and other: in the whiche styrrynge the erle of Derby
was hurte in the face, and kepte a whyle vnderholde.

Thanne by commaundement of the sayd lorde protectour, the sayd lorde chamberlayne in all hast was ladde in the court or playne where the chapell of the Tower standeth, and there without iugement, or longe tyme of confession or repentaunce, vpon an ende of a longe and great tymber logge, whiche there laye with other for the repayrynge of the sayd Tower, caused his hedde to be smytten of, and all for he knewe well that he wolde nat assent vnto his wycked entent" (p. 668). Then the bishops of York and Ely were set in sure keeping, while the earl of Derby, for fear of his son the lord Strange, lest he should array Cheshire and Lancashire against Richard, was set at large.

"Thanne beganne the longe couert dissymulacion, whiche of the lorde protectour had been so craftly shadowyd, to breke out at large" (p. 669). Upon the Sunday following, Doctor Rafe Shaa, in a sermon at Paul's cross, before Richard, Buckingham, and others, declared that the children of Edward were illegitimate. Few of the audience favored the matter. "Of the whiche declaracion, as the fame went after, the sayd doctour Shaa toke such repentaunce, that he lyued in lytell prosperite after". On the Tuesday following, in a speech at Guildhall before the mayor and citizens, Buckingham, in an eloquent oration, set forth Richard's right to the crown. On the next Thursday "the sayd lorde protectour takyng then vpon hym as kyng and gouernour of the realme" went to Westminster, took possession, made the royal oath, and exhorted the judges of the law to execute justice (p. 669). "Which passetyme the two princes were put under suer kepynge within the Tower". On Friday the protector was proclaimed king. Then "for fere of the quenes blode and other" (p. 669) he sent for men from the North; they came to the number of 4000 men and remained till after they coronation. "In which foresayd passe tyme, the marquys of Dorset, broder [sic! cf. above] vnto quene Elizabeth, that before was fled, escapyd many wonderfull daungers, both aboute London, Ely, and other places" (p. 670).

Here Fabyan declares: "Tedyous it is to me to wryte the tragedyous hystory" of Richard, "except that I remembre that good it is to wryte and put in remembraunce the punysshment of synners, to the ende that other may exchewe to fall in lyke daunger" (p. 670). From now on few or none favored Richard except for dread or for the great gifts they received of him. For Richard spared not to use in this way the treasure accumulated by Edward, and borrowed more from the citizens of London. Those so won deceived him afterwards. Richard was crowned and then went North to pacify a rebellion. He created his legitimate son Prince of Wales, and his illegitimate son Captain of Calais, "whiche encreasyd more grudge to hymwarde" (p. 670).

In the next year, "the foresayd grudge encreasinge, and the more for asmoche as the common fame went that kynge Richarde hadde within the Tower put vnto secrete deth the .II. sonnes of his broder Edwarde the .IIII. for the whiche, and other causes hadde within the brest of the duke of Bukkyngham, the sayd duke, in secrete manner, conspyred agayne hym, and allyed hym with dyuerse gentylmen, to the ende to bryng his purpose aboute" (p. 670). Learning of this, Richard sent to arrest him, and Buckingham, who was at his manor of Brecknock "smally accompanyed", fled to the house of a servant of his, named Banaster. For the sake of the reward offered by Richard, £ 1000 and land £ 100 in value, or else for fear of his life, Banaster delivered up Buckingham to the sheriff of the shire [not named], and the prisoner was brought to Richard at Salisbury. Here he was beheaded after vainly requesting to be allowed to see the king.

Now, while Richard was "ledynge his lyfe in great agony and doubte, trustynge fewe of such as were about hym" (p. 671), many passed over to France and there allied them to "that vertuous prynce Henry, sone vnto the erle of Richmonde, discendyd lyneally from Henry the .IIII. lately kyng of this realme", and agreed to help him to become King of England if he would marry Princess Elizabeth. Among these were Sir James Blount, keeper of the castle of Guynys (Guines: otherwise Ham Castle), and the Earl of Oxford, who had been his prisoner since the eleventh year of Edward IV.

"Whyle thyse..escapyd..was one named Wyllyam Colyngbourne taken, and after he.. was caste for sondry treasons: & for a ryme which was layde to his charge,.. as folowith.

>   The catte, the ratte, and Louell our dogge,
>   Rulyth all Englande vnder a hogge.

The whiche was ment, that Catisby, Ratcliffe, and the lorde Louell, ruled the lande under the kynge, which bare the whyte bore for his conysaunce. For the whiche and other .. he was put to the moost cruell deth" (p. 672). Then follows a gruesome account of his execution.

Richmond landed at Mylbourne (there is no mention of his first unsuccessful attempt), "for whose defence of landynge, kynge Richarde, for somoche as he feryd hym lytell, made but small prouycion" (p. 672). When Henry landed "he incontyently [sic!] knelyd downe upon the erth, and with meke countenaunce and pure deuocion began this psalme: 'Judica me Deus, et decerne causam meam' &c. The whiche whenne he hadde fynysshid to the ende, and kyssed the grounde mekely and reuerently, made the signe of the crosse vpon hym, he commaundyd suche as were aboute hym boldly in the name of God and seint George to sette forewarde" (p. 672). At Bosworth ensued a sharp battle, which would have been sharper if Richard's men had remained true to him; but many left him and went over to Richmond, "and some stode houynge a ferre of, tyll they sawe to whiche partye the victory fyll." Richard was slain, with Norfolk and Brackenbury, and his corpse, "spoyled, &, naked, as he was borne, cast behynde a man, and so caryed unreuerently overthwarte the horse backe vnto the fryers at Leyceter; where after a season that he had lyen, that all men myght beholde hym, he was there with lytel reuerence buryed" (p. 673).

Of the greatest interest in Fabyan's narrative is the detailed account of Prince Edward's death. Here for the first time, thirty years after the event, do we meet with the statement that the prince was captured in the battle and brought to the king. For a displeasing answer — not given — King Edward strikes him — but only with his gauntlet: whereupon the prince is murdered by the king's servants — no names given.

The account of Henry's death agrees so nearly with that of the Ms. chronicle cited in III c., that the one account was evidently taken from the other, or else they had a common source.

For the second time occurs the statement that Clarence was put to death in a butt of wine. De Comines' work, if seen by Fabyan, must have been seen in Ms. It is not mentioned by Fabyan as one of his sources, and there is no indication elsewhere that he ever used it. It is more probable therefore that both authors derived their account from popular report (cf. Chronicles of the White Rose, p. 251 to the contrary).

Among the facts mentioned for the first time by Fabyan are the capture of Margaret in the battlefield of Tewkesbury (historically incorrect); the betrayal of Buckingham by Banister; Collingbourne's rime; and the manner of Richard's bringing to Leicester, and his burial there.

As for the chronicler's attitude toward Richard, it is plainly enough one of intense opposition, but he confines himself mostly to a statement of his deeds, with no attempt at embellishment, and with few reflections save the statement that he writes the "tragedious history" of Richard as a warning to sinners. Richmond is treated in much the same way from the opposite point of view. He is a virtuous prince and the lineal descendant of Henry IV; meekly and reverently, with pure devotion he calls on God to judge him and decide his cause. But there is no flattery aside from that conveyed by the speeches, and no rhetorical attempts to enhance the picture of him that is presented by the facts of his story.

In addition it should be noted that Fabyan makes no mention of Richard's appointment as Protector by the king, and that nothing is said of the visit by the mayor and aldermen of London to Baynard Castle to urge Richard to take upon himself the crown. Considering Fabyan's knowledge of city affairs this would seem surprising, were it not for the consideration that the writer doubtless wished to shield his fellow-citizens.

The cardinal who goes to the queen in sanctuary to beg for the young Duke of York is called by Fabyan the Archbishop of Canterbury.

XI. More's History of King Richard III.

A. The English Version.

Sir Thomas More was born 1477, and died 1535. At the age of thirteen he was placed in the household of Doctor Morton, then Archbishop of Canterbury; and he, it is generally, and doubtless rightly, assumed, was the authority for most of the facts which appear in this history. As bishop of Ely, Morton had opposed Richard, been confined by him, had escaped, had rendered important assistance in bringing Henry to the throne, and had been raised by him to the primacy of England.

The work first appeared in somewhat mangled form in Grafton's continuation of Hardyng's Chronicle, 1543, and again in Hall's "The Unyon of the two noble and illustre famelies of Lancastre and Yorke", as published in 1548. It was printed from an authentic copy by More's nephew William Rastell, in his edition of More's works, 1557. As there printed it contains certain passages said by the editor not to be contained in More's English work, but to be translated out of that which he wrote in Latin. This Latin history was first printed in the 1566 edition of More's works. The relation of the two versions is in doubt. Harington, Metamorphosis of Ajax, had "heard" that the Latin version was by Archbishop Morton, and Buck, History of Richard III, 1646, says that Morton wrote "a booke in Latine against king Richard, which came afterward to the hands of Mr. Moore, sometime his servant". This book had been seen by a friend of Buck's, who told him of it. The theory of Morton's authorship has been held by many of the best historians since, among them Pauli (5 : 647). The Latin is considered to be much inferior to More's, and "the tone often implies that the writer was a contemporary witness of some of the events described" (Dic. Nat. Biog. sub More).

An opposite theory, however, was proposed by Sir Henry Ellis in the preface to his edition of Grafton's Hardyng. He was "inclined to think that the English copy was the work of Morton", on account of a sentence occurring in Grafton's copy of More. Speaking of Edward's last sickness, the writer says that it "continued longer then false and fantasticall tales have untruly and falsely surmised, as I myself that write this pamphlet truly knew". This, Ellis thinks, bears evidence to an earlier pen than More's; and the editor of Chronicles of the White Rose agrees with him that there is "much greater probability" that Morton wrote the English rather than the Latin. Ellis also finds "the colour of eloquence . . so richly spread over the whole tract that it has no appearance of having been translated from another language"; and thinks it "singular that the passage quoted should be omitted in the editions of the reign printed in Hall, Holinshed, Stow and Speed" (p. xx). As a matter of fact, the passage does occur in Hall (p. 343, ll. 41—43), who copied More's work as it appeared in the continuation of Hardyng. Holinshed, Stow, and Speed copied Rastell's edition from the copy in More's own hand, where the passage is not to be found.

The question of date has its importance in determining

the authorship. Pauli says of the English version: "Es ist unstreitig, wie sich nachweisen lässt, um das Jahr 1509, aus More's Feder geflossen." Upon what evidence he relies for this early date I do not know. The date generally accepted is that assigned by Rastell on the title page of the first published edition — "about the yeare of our Lorde. 1513"; and this was copied by Holinshed (vol. 3, p. 360). At the beginning of the work, however, occurs the statement that Anne, daughter of Edward IV, was married to "Thomas, than Lorde Hawarde, and after Earle of Surrey". This passage, at least, must have been written after Feb. 1, 1514, when Howard was made Earl of Surrey upon his father's elevation to the dukedom of Norfolk. But as the passage is found in the Latin version also, it proves that if the Latin version was originally Morton's, one addition at least was made after his death. Beside this, the portion of the English version that follows Richard's coronation — with which the Latin version ends — cannot have been written by Morton, who died in 1500, since it mentions (ed. Lumby, p. 81) "the late . . king Henry", who died Apr. 21, 1509.

While it appears impossible to decide with absolute satisfaction the question of authorship, it is beyond doubt that the Latin version is the basis of the English, which follows the other with much greater faithfulness than has often been asserted, though it is somewhat fuller, and in a few places a paraphrase rather than a translation. But that, contrary to Ellis's opinion, it is a translation from the Latin, the constant recurrence of Latin constructions and idioms, which appears on comparison, is fully sufficient to prove.

The English book begins with the death of Edward IV and ends abruptly, in the midst of a conversation between Buckingham and Bishop Morton which is said by More to have led to Buckingham's rebellion.

The following citations are taken from the edition of Dr. Lumby, printed by the Pitt Press, 1883.

The person of King Edward is first described, his virtues recounted, and the quiet state of the realm and general affection of the people brought forward as an indication that his children would have been securely protected, had they not been removed by the Duke of Gloucester.

Before writing the deeds of this man it is necessary to show what manner of man he was, and, to that end, to go back a little, Richard was the son of Richard, Duke of York, "a noble man and a mighty", who "beganne not by warre, but by lawe, to challenge the crown, putting his claime into the parliamente". Here it was decided that the crown should fall to York and his issue, after the death of Henry. For this he could not bear to wait, battled for the crown at Wakefield, and lost it. He left three sons, Edward, George and Richard. "Al three as they wer great states of birthe, soo were they greate and statelye of stomacke, gredye and ambicious of authoritie, and impacient of parteners. Edward, reuenging his fathers death, deprived King Henrie, and attained the crown. George Duke of Clarence was a goodly noble prince, and at all pointes fortunate, if either his owne ambicion had not set him against his brother, or the enuie of his enemies his brother agaynste him". For either through the malignity of the queen and her kindred, or the duke's own intention to become king, faulty or faultless, he was attainted of treason by parliament, condemned to death, "and therupon hastely drouned in a Butte of Malmesey, whose death kyng Edwarde (albeit he commaunded it) when he wist it was done, pitiously bewailed and sorowfully repented".

Then follows the famous description of Richard's person. "Richarde the third sonne, of whom we nowe entreate, was in witte and courage egall with either of them, in bodye and prowesse farre vnder them bothe, little of stature, ill fetured of limmes, croke backed, his left shoulder much higher then his right, hard fauoured of visage, and suche as is in states called warlye, in other menne otherwise, he was malicious, wrathfull, enuious and, from afore his birth, euer frowarde. It is for trouth reported, that the Duches his mother had muche adoe in her trauaile [that she could not be deliuered of hym vncut]¹), and that hee came into the worlde with the feete fowarde, as menne bee borne outwarde, and (as the fame runneth) also not vntothed, whither menne of hatred reporte aboue the trouthe, or elles that nature chaunged her course in hys beginninge, whiche in the course of his lyfe many thinges vnnaturallye committed. None euill captaine was hee in the warre, as to whiche his disposicion was more metely then for peace. Sundrye victories hadde hee, and sommetime ouerthrowes, but neuer in defaulte, as for his owne parsone, either of hardinesse or polytike order; free was hee called of dyspence, and sommewhat aboue hys power liberall, with large giftes hee get him vnstedfaste frendeshippe, for whiche hee was fain to pil and spoyle in other places, and get him stedfast hatred. He was close and secrete, a deepe dissimuler, lowlye of counteynaunce, arrogant of heart, outwardly coumpinable where he inwardely hated, not letting to kisse whome hee thoughte to kyll; dispitious and cruell, not for euill will alway, but ofter for ambicion, and either for the suretie or encrease of his estate. Frende and foo was muche what indifferent, where his aduauntage grew, he spared no mans deathe, whose life withstoode his purpose. He slewe with his owne handes king Henry the sixt, being prisoner in the Tower, as menne constantly saye, and that without commaundemente or knoweledge of the king, whiche woulde vndoubtedly, yf he had entended that thinge, haue appointed that boocherly office, to some other then his owne borne brother. Somme wise menne also weene, that his drifte couertly conuayde, lacked not in helping furth his brother Clarence to his death: whiche hee resisted

---

¹) Hall. p. 343. Omitted by Lumby, who "expurgates" without so much as the hint of an asterisk!

openly, howbeit somwhat (as menne demed) more faintly then he that wer hartely minded to his welth. And they that thus deme, think that he long time in king Edwardes life forethought to be king in case that the king his brother (whose life hee looked that euil dyete shoulde shorten) shoulde happen to decease (as in dede he did) while his children wer yonge. And thei deme, that for thys intente he was gladde of his brothers death the Duke of Clarence, whose life must nedes haue hindered hym so entendynge, whither the same Duke of Clarence hadde kepte him true to his nephew the yonge king, or enterprised to be kyng himselfe. But of al this pointe is there no certaintie, and whoso diuineth vppon conjectures maye as wel shote to farre as to short" (pp. 5—7).

Since Richard "well wiste and holpe to mayntayn a long continued grudge and hearte brennynge betwene the Quenes kinred and the kinges blood, eyther partie enuying others authoritye," he thought to find a good start for his plan in this dissension. Edward during his life had suffered this because he felt himself able to rule both parties, but coming to die he perceived in it disastrous consequences for his children. He summoned to him, therefore, some of those who were at variance, and especially Dorset and Hastings, "agayne whome the Quene specially grudged, for the great fauoure the kyng bare hym, and also for that shee thoughte hym secretelye familyer with the kynge in wanton coumpanye" (p. 9). The king called the attention of his nobles to the fact that the only surety for his children lay in their concord. It was not sufficient that all loved his sons; if the nobles hated each other no good conclusion could be arrived at, and by their authority alone could the children be supported. Whereas there was every reason that they should love each other, hatred did exist among them, "suche a pestilente serpente is ambicion and desyre of vaine glorye and soueraintye" what trouble that had caused of late in England they all knew, but now everything was peaceful. "But yf you among youre selfe in a childes reygne fall at debate, many a good man shal perish and happely he to, and ye to, ere thys land finde peace again". Wherefore he exhorted them by their love for him, by his for them, and by the love of the Lord for them all, to love each other. Then the King ended, being no longer able to sit up.

To his speech the lords made answer as he wished, and "there in his presence (as by their wordes appered) ech forgaue other, and joyned their hands together, when (as it after appeared by their dedes) their herts wer far asonder" (p. 12).

At the death of his father the young Prince Edward was at Ludlow in Wales, whither he had been sent that his presence might help to keep the lawless population in order. As his governor had been appointed Lord Rivers, brother of the Queen, and the others of the Prince's household all belonged to the Queen's party. This fact Richard turned to their destruction. For he sent secret messengers and letters to all whom he knew to be opposed to the Queen's party, declaring it insufferable that the Prince should be in the hands of his mother's low-born kin, while those of the royal blood were removed from him. Such power in the hands of these men was sure to lead to the undoing of those whom they opposed. Of this there was no less fear to be felt because of the late atonement, made for the king's pleasure and not of their own wills. No one would be so unwise as to trust a new friend made of an old foe, or to think that an hourly kindness would be deeper seated than a malice many years rooted.

Thus Richard "set afire" those who were of themselves easy to kindle, and especially Buckingham and Hastings, who did not bear "eche to other so muche loue, as hatred bothe vnto the Quenes parte". So they agreed with Richard to remove from the king's company all his mother's friends. Learning that these intended to bring the king up to London with a strong train, Richard "secretely by divers meanes, caused the Quene to be perswaded . . .

that it neither wer nede, and also shold be jeopardous, the King to come vp strong" (p. 14). For the lords of her kindred would by a large train give the others with whom they had been at variance cause to suspect that it was meant not so much for the King's safeguard as for their destruction. These would assemble a power for their defence,. and the kingdom would be in uproar. For which her kindred would surely be blamed, as having "broken the amitie and peace that the king her husband so prudentelye made betwene hys kinne and hers in his deathbed, and which the other party faithfully obserued".

The Queen was persuaded, and wrote to her son and to Lord Rivers that they should come with few, and Gloucester and his friends wrote so reverently to the King and so lovingly to the Queen's friends, that they suspected nothing and complied.

The King had reached Stony Stratford, ten miles from Northampton, and Rivers was at the latter city intending to overtake the King next day, when Buckingham and Gloucester arrived. In the evening there was "much friendely chere" between them and Rivers. But during the night they possessed themselves of the keys of Rivers' inn, and set guards in the roads that none of Rivers' men should reach Stony Stratford. When Rivers in the morning found himself locked in, "in so few houres so gret a chaunge marueylouslye misliked". Lest he should seem to be afraid of some fault on his own part, "he determined vppon the suretie of his own conscience, to goe boldelye to them, and inquire what thys matter myghte meane" (p. 16). Richard and Buckingham immediately accused him of intending to set distance between the King and them and to bring them to confusion; and when he attempted to excuse himself they interrupted him, and put him in ward. Then they made haste to Stratford, where they came to the King. "And as sone as they came in his presence, they lighte adowne with all their companie aboute them. To whome the Duke of Buckingham saide, goe afore. Gentlemenne and yomen, kepe youre rowmes. And thus in a goodly arraye thei came to the kinge, and on theire knees in very humble wise salued his grace; whiche receyued them in very joyous and amiable maner, nothinge earthlye knowing nor mistrustinge as yet. But euen by and by in his presence they piked a quarrell to the Lorde Richard Graye, the kinges other brother by his mother, sayinge that hee, with the lorde Marques his brother and the Lorde Rivers his vncle, hadde coumpassed to rule the kinge and the realme, and to sette variaunce among the states, and to subdewe and destroye the noble blood of the realm. Toward the accoumplishinge whereof, they sayde that the Lorde Marques hadde entered into the Tower of London, and thence taken out the kinges Treasor, and sent menne to the sea. All whiche thinge these Dukes wiste well were done for good purposes and necessari by the whole counsaile at London, sauing that sommewhat thei must sai. Unto whiche woordes the king aunswered, what my brother Marques hath done I cannot saie. But in good faith I dare well aunswere for myne oncle Riuers and my brother here, that thei be innocent of any such matters. Ye, my liege, quod the Duke of Buckingham, thei haue kepte theire dealing in these matters farre fro the knowledge of your good grace" (pp. 17—18).

Hereupon they arrested Gray and Vaughan and brought the King back to Northampton. Here the King's former servants were removed and new ones set about him, at which the King "wepte and was nothing contente, but it booted not". At dinner Richard sent Rivers a dish from his own table, "Prayinge him to bee of good cheere, all should be well inough". Rivers sent it to his nephew Richard Gray, with the same message for his comfort, as one to whom adversity was less well known. Yet "for al this coumfortable courtesye" Rivers, Grey and Vaughan were sent north to divers prisons, and afterwards beheaded at Pomfret.

Thus Richard "tooke upon himself the order and

gouernance of the young king, whom with much honor and humble reuerence he conuayed vppewarde towarde the citye" (p. 18). On receiving the news of the disaster a little before the midnight following, the Queen "in gret fright and heuines, bewailing her childes rain, her frendes mischance, and her own infortune, damning the time that euer shee diswaded the gatheryng of power aboute the kinge, gate her selfe in all the haste possible with her yonger sonne and her doughters . . . into the Sainctuarye" at Westminster (p. 19).

Not long after midnight came a message from Hastings to the Archbishop of York, then Chancellor of England, conveying to him the news of what had been done at Stratford. The frightened Archbishop called up his servants, armed them, took the great seal, and before daylight came to the Queen. Her he found in the midst of great confusion, owing to the conveyance of her stuff — "chestes, coffers, packes, fardelles, trusses" — into sanctuary. He comforted her as best he might, and gave up to her the great seal. Returned home, he saw the Thames covered with boats containing the Duke of Gloucester's men, watching that nobody should go to sanctuary. "Then was there greate commocion and murmure as well in other places about, as specially in the city, the people diuersclye diuininge vppon this dealinge" (p. 20). Many of the lords armed themselves out of fear for themselves or favor of the Queen. At a meeting of the lords to counsel about the matter the Archbishop of York and Hastings were present. The former had sent for the great seal again "fearing that it wold be ascribed (as it was in dede) to his ouermuch lightnesse, that he so sodainly had yelded" it up to the Queen. Hastings, "whose trouth towarde the King no manne doubted nor neded to doubte", persuaded the lords that Richard was faithful to the King, that Rivers and the others had been arrested for attempts against Richard and Buckingham, and that they would later be judged by the Council. He advised them not to stir up trouble by judging the matter too hastily". With these parswaseons of the Lorde Hastynges, whereof parte hymselfe belieued, of parte he wist the contrarye, these commocions were sommewhat appeased" (p. 21).

When the king approached the city he was met at Harnesay by the mayor and many citizens, and conducted into London. "The Duke of Gloucester bare him in open sighte so reurentlye to the Prince, with all semblaunce of lowlinesse, that from the great obloquy in which hee was soo late before, hee was sodainelye fallen in soo greate truste, that at the counsayle next assembled, hee was made the onely manne chose and thoughte most mete, to bee protectoure of the king and hys realme, so that (were it destenye or were it foly) the lamb was betaken to the wolfe to kepe" (p. 23).

At this meeting the bishop of Lincoln was made Chancellor in place of York, and other appointments were made. Now Richard, thirsting sore to finish what he had begun, and knowing that if he deposed the king the realm would fall to his brother, who was in sanctuary, determined to have him out. At the next meeting of the council, the declared it a heinous deed of the Queen to keep the Duke of York from his brother "whose specyall pleasure and coumforte were to haue his brother with hym"; that her purpose was to bring the lords into obloquy. "As thoughe they were not to bee trusted with the Kynges brother, that by the assente of the nobles of the lande wer appoynted, as the Kynges nereste friendes, to the tuicyon of his owne royall parsone". The King needed a companion, and who more fit than his brother? If the Duke were kept in sanctuary people would suspect that there was some grave cause for it, and harm would grow. Therefore Richard proposed that some should go to persuade the Queen to give the Duke up. "For al which consideracions, none seemeth mee more metelye than oure reuerente father here presente, my Lorde Cardynall" (p. 14). If the Queen would not give up the child, Richard urged that the Cardinal should take him by force, under the King's authority. Such was his opinion, unless the council willed otherwise, for he was always ready to change his own will upon their better advices.

The council agreed, and the Archbishop of York undertook the task, declaring however, that if the Queen would not give up the boy, the sanctuary, hallowed as it was by being dedicated at night by Saint Peter and multitudes of angels (for proof of which they had Saint Peter's cope in the Abbey to show) and kept sacred ever before, should not be violated. If the Queen would not deliver up the Duke the hindrance would he only a mother's dread and womanish fear. "Womannishe feare, naye womannishe frowardenesse (quod the Duke of Buckyngham)". In his opinion the Queen had nought to fear. She might come out herself and abide with her sons. If men were really bent upon doing her children a mischief the sanctuary would not hinder them. He did not wish to break sanctuary: debtors and partisans in civil wars should have a place of refuge; yet everybody knew "what a rabble of theves, murtherers, and malicious heyghnous traitours" took advantage of it. As for the prince, he had no need of sanctuary for no one threatened him with harm. Jurther, he had no claim to it, for each person needing sanctuary must ask it for himself, which this "babe" had not done. Indeed, of those who were rightfully sanctuary men, he would treat debtors "somewhat more homely" than had been done. Their bodies might be allowed liberty, but their goods, even within the sanctuary, should be taken to pay their debts. To this "diuers of the clergy that wer present" agreed that by the law of God and of the church the goods of a sanctuary man should be delivered to pay his debts, and stolen goods to their owner, and he have liberty only to get his living with his hands. The duke agreed, and continued, that to his mind a man might recover his wife from sanctuary, if she had no cause save that she desired to run from her husband. If nobody might be taken from sanctuary a child might run thither because he feared to go to school and his master must let him alone. In this case there was even less reason, for this child had no fear at all. "And verelye", said he, "I haue often heard of saintuarye menne. But I neuer heard erste of saintuarye chyldren".

Thereupon the temporal men, and most of the spiritual, agreed that if the boy were not delivered he should be fetched. The Protector and council went to the star chamber, and the Cardinal with others went into the sanctuary to the Queen. There the Cardinal asked for the child, offering the same reasons that Richard had given, and insisting especially on the necessity of both King and Duke to have youthful recreation, and together.

The Queen agreed that they ought to be together, but under her own care, being so young, and the younger not yet wholly recovered from a sickness; "he might relapse, and there was "double the perill in the recidiuacion that was in the first sickness" (p. 34). The Cardinal replied that no one doubted that the mother should be with her children, but it should be in some place consistent with their honor, not in a place which meant dishonor and obloquy. Occasions, too, sometimes appeared when it was best for the child to be away from his mother: she herself had been well content to let her son Edward be away from her in Wales. Not very well content, answered the Queen. But then Edward was in health, while the Duke was now sick. She wondered that the Protector desired the child to strongly when if he miscarried from his sickness it would bring the Protector into suspicion. As for her child's honor, it was to the honor of all that he should stay where he was best kept. That was with her, and she did not intend to come out and run into dauger, as her friends had done. "Whye madame (quod another Lorde) know you any thing why thei should be in jubardye? Nay verely sur, quod shee, nor why they should be in prison neither, as they now be" (p. 35). She feared that those who had put them in prison without color would not fail to procure their destruction without cause.

"The Cardinall made a countinance to the tother Lord, that he should harp no more vpon that string". Then he said to the Queen that her kindred would on examination doubtless do well enough. For herself there could be no danger. This the Queen could not believe. Any cause for hating her kindred was doubly valid of herself. The more eager men were without cause to have the Duke, the less ready was she to deliver him. "And the farder that you be to delyuer him the farder bene other men to suffer you to kepe hym", was the Cardinal's reply. He was certain that if the Duke were not delivered he would be removed by force. "So much drede hath my Lorde his vncle, for the tender loue he bereth him, lest your grace shold hap to send him awaye" (p. 36). "A syr, quod the Quene, hath the protectour so tender zele to him, that he fereth nothing but lest he should escape hym?" To what safer place could she send the prince? It was a "goodly glose" that a place which could defend a thief might not save an innocent. She prayed that the Duke, as they said, had no need of sanctuary. As for the King's need of a playfellow, there were plenty of others, who were not sick, and playfellows need not be kindred, who indeed rarely agreed as well as strangers. The Protector asserted that the Duke could not ask the privilege of sanctuary: he should hear him ask for it. But even if he could not ask for it, she was his legal guardian, and entitled to have her ward with her, as well as her goods. If example were wanted, it was present in her son the King, who was born in this same sanctuary, to which she had fled when her husband was driven out, and where she met him on his return.

The Cardinal, perceiving that the Queen "waxed euer the lenger the farder of", and that she was beginning to attack the Protector, desired to bring the matter to a conclusion. He said that if she would deliver the Duke he would lay his own body and soul as pledge of the child's surety: if she would not, he would go and leave others to attend to the matter. Thereat the Queen stood a good while in a great study. Some of the others did not seem as ready as the Cardinal to depart, and she knew that the Protector was close by. She feared that the child would be taken from her, and she did not doubt the faith of the Cardinal, though she thought he might be deceived. She deemed it wisest therefore to give up the child of her own accord. So turning to the lords she declared that she neither mistrusted their wits, nor their truth; which she purposed to put to the proof in a way sure to bring great harm if she were deceived. She knew that the child had enemies. "The desire of a kingdome knoweth no kindred. The brother hath bene the brothers bane. And may the nephews be sure of their vncle?" As long as the two children were apart each was the other's protection. "All this not withstanding, here I deliuer him, and hys brother in him, to kepe, into your handes, of whome I shall ask them both afore God and the world". "And there with all she said vnto the child: Farewel, my own swete sonne, God send you good keping, let me kis you ones yet ere you goe, for God knoweth when we shal kis togither agayne. And there with she kissed him, and blessed him, turned her back and wept and went her way, leauing the child weping as fast" (pp. 40—1).

The young Duke was brought to Richard, who "toke him in his armes and kissed him with these wordes: Now welcome, my lord, euer with al my very hart. And he sayd in that of likelihood as he thought". The child was then taken to his brother in the Bishop of London's palace, and then both went to the Tower, whence they never again came abroad.

Now Richard opened himself more boldly to his friends, especially to Buckingham. Many thought, indeed, that Buckingham knew all Richard's plans from the first, and some said that Buckingham was the first mover of the Protector in the matter, sending him a secret message at once after King Edward's death. But others knew that the Duke was not made privy to Richard's plans till the two children were in the Tower. "The matter was broken vnto the duke by suttell folks" who told him that the King was bound to revenge on him the misfortune of his kinsfolk. If they escaped they would urge the King on; if put to death the King would surely avenge them. There was no opportunity to repent, for Richard had set spies for the Duke, and would catch him if he turned back. These things brought the Duke to the point "that where he had repented the way that he had entred, yet wold he go forth in the same .... and determined, that since the comon mischief could not be amended, he wold tourne it as much as he might to hys owne commodite" (p. 42).

So Buckingham agreed to help Richard become king, for which Richard's son was to marry the duke's daughter, and he was to be grantes the earldom of Hertford, which he claimed as his inheritance and could not obtain from King Edward. Beside this, there was promised him "a great quantite of the kinges tresure and of his howsehold stuffe" (p. 43). Then the two pretended to prepare for the king's coronation. They set York, Ely, Stanley, Hastings and others "to commune and deuise about the coronacion in one place", while they and their friends were busy elsewhere planning to make Richard king. There began then, "here and there about, some maner of muttering amonge the people, as though al should not long be wel, though they neither wist what thei feared nor wherfore; were it that before such great thinges mens hartes of a secret instinct of nature misgiueth them, as the sea without wind swelleth of himself somtime before a tempest: or were it that some one man, happely somwhat perceiuing, filled mani men with suspicion, though he shewed few men what he knew" (p. 43). The court of the Protector began now to be thronged, while the King was left with few.

Stanley mistrusted the holding of two separate councils, and told Hastings so. "For while we (quod he) talke of one matter in the tone place, litte wote we wherof they talk in the tother place" (p. 44). Hastings replied that there was no cause for doubt; his friend Catesby, who was much beholden to him and by his favor had large authority in Leicestershire, where Hastings' power chiefly lay, was always present at the other council, and on him he could always depend for news, and that no harm would be intended him in a council where Catesby was. Buckingham and Richard always treated Hastings favorably, and there is little doubt that Richard loved him and was loath to lose him. So through Catesby he sought to move him to enter the conspiracy. "But Catesby, whither he assayed him or assaied him not, reported . . . that he founde him so fast, and hard him speke so terrible woordes, that he durst no further breke". In fact Hastings showed Catesby that others were beginning to mistrust the matter, and Catesby "fering lest their mocions might with the lord Hastinges minishe his credence, whereunto onely al the matter lenid, procured the protectour hastely to ridde him. And much the rather, for that he trusted by his deth to obtaine much of the rule that the lorde Hastinges bare in his countrey; the only desire whereof, was the allectiue that induced him to be partener and one specyall contriuer of al this horrible treson.

Whereupon sone after, that is to wit, on the Friday the — day of — many Lordes assembled in the Tower, and there sat in counsaile, deuising the honorable solempnite of the kinges coronacion, of which the time appointed then so nere approched, that the pageauntes and sutteties were in making day and night at Westminster, and much vitaile killed therfore, that afterward was cast away. These lordes so sytting togyther comoning of thys matter, the protectour came in among them, fyrst aboute .IX. of the clock, saluting them curtesly, and excusyng hymself that he had ben from them so long, saieng merely [merrily] that he had bene a slepe that day. And after a little talking with them, he sayd vnto the Bishop of Elye: My lord you haue very good strawberies at your gardayne in

Holberne, I require you let vs haue a messe of them.
Gladly my lord, quod he, woulde God I had some better
thing as redy to your pleasure as that. And ther with
in al the hast he sent hys seruant for a messe of strauberies.
The protectour sette the lordes fast in comoning, and
therupon prayeng them to spare hym for a little while
departed thence. And sone, after one hower, betwene
.X. and .XI. he returned into the chamber among them,
al changed, with a wonderful soure angrye countenaunce,
knitting the browes, frowning and froting and knawing
on hys lippes, and so sat him downe in hys place; al the
lordes much dismaied and sore merueiling of this maner
of sodain chaunge, and what thing should him aile. Then
when had sitten still a while, thus he began: What were
they worthy to haue, that compasse and ymagine the
distruccion of me, being so nere of blood vnto the king
and protectour of his riall person and his realme? At
this question, al the lordes sat sore astonied, musyng much
by whome thys question should be ment, of which euery
man wyst himselfe clere. Then the lord chamberlen, as
he that for the loue betwene them thoughte he might be
boldest with him, aunswered and sayd, that thei wer
worthye to bee punished as heighnous traitors, what soeuer
they were. And al the other affirmed the same. That is
(quod he) yonder sorceres my brothers wife and other
with her, meaning the quene. At these wordes many of
the other Lordes were gretly abashed that fauoured her.
But the lord Hastinges was in his minde better content,
that it was moued by her, then by any other whom he
loued better. Albeit hys harte somewhat grudged, that
he was not afore made of counsell in this mater, as he
was of the taking of her kynred, and of their putting to
death, which were by his assent before deuised to bee
byhedded at Pountfreit, this selfe same day, in which he
was not ware that it was by other deuised, that himself
should the same day be behedded at London. Then said
the protectour; ye shal al se in what wise that sorceres

and that other witch of her counsel, Shoris wife, with
their affynite, haue by their sorcery and witchcraft wasted
my body. And ther with he plucked vp hys doublet sleue
to his elbow vpon his left arme, where he stewed a werish
withered arme and small, as it was neuer other. And
thereupon enery mannes mind sore misgaue them, well
perceiuing that this matter was but a quarel. For wel
thei wist, that the quene was to wise to go aboute any
such folye. And also if she would, yet wold she of all
folke leste make Shoris wife of counsaile, whom of al
women she most hated, as that concubine whom the king
her husband had most loued. And also no man was there
present, but wel knew that his harme [arm] was euer such
since his birth. Natheles the lorde Chamberlen aunswered
and sayd: certainly my lorde if they haue so heinously
done, thei be worthy heinouse punishement. What, quod
the protectour, thou seruest me, I wene, with iffes and
with andes, I tel the thei haue so done, and that I will
make good on thy body, traitour. And therwith as in a
great anger, he clapped his fist vpon the borde a great
rappe. At which token giuen, one cried treason without
the c[h]ambre. Therewith a dore clapped, and in come
there rushing men in harneys as many as the chambre
might hold. And anon the protectour sayd to the lorde
Hastinges: I arest the, traitour. What, me, my Lorde?
quod he. Yea the, traitour, quod the protectour. And
another let flee at the Lorde Standley which shronke at
the stroke and fel vnder the table, or els his hed had ben
clefte to the tethe: for as shortely as he shranke, yet
ranne the blood aboute hys eares. Then were they al
quickly bestowed in diuerse chambres, except the lorde
Chamberlen, whom the protectour bade spede and shryue
hym apace, for by saynt Poule (quod he) I wil not to
dinner til I se thy hed of. It boted him not to aske why,
but heuely he toke a priest at aduenture, and made a
short shrift, for a longer would not be suffered, the protectour made so much hast to dyner; which he might not

go to til this wer done for sauing of his othe. So was he brought forth into the grene beside the chappel within the Tower, and his head laid down vpon a long log of timbre, and there striken of, and afterward his body with the hed entred at Windsore beside the body of kinge Edward" (pp. 45—48).

Then follows an account of certain marvelous warnings which Hastings had but did not heed. The night before his death, at midnight, Stanley sent him a messenger, "requiring hym to rise and ryde away with hym, for he was disposed vtterly no lenger to bide; he had so fereful a dreme, in which him thoughte that a bore with his tuskes so raced them both bi the heddes, that the blood ranne aboute both their shoulders" (p. 48). Now the boar was Richard's cognisance; and Stanley begged Hastings to ride with him that same night so far that they should be out of danger before day. "Ey, good lord, quod the lord Hastinges to this messenger, leneth mi lord thi master so much to such trifles, and hath such faith in dremes, which either his own fere fantasieth or do rise in the nightes rest by reson of his daye thoughtes? Tel him it is plaine witchcraft to beleue in suche dremes" (pp. 48—49). If they fled they were likely to be pursued and brought back, whereby they should seem to have been guilty of some fault. Stanley should have no fear, said Hastings, "for I ensure hym I am as sure of the man that he woteth of, as I am of my hand" (p. 49). As Hastings was riding toward the Tower where death awaited him, his horse stumbled two or three times, which "hath .. ben, of an olde rite and custome, obserued as a token often times notably foregoing some great misfortune" (p. 49). Another thing that happened "was no warning, but an enemiouse scorne". On that morning, before Hastings was up, came a knight to him, as if of courtesy to escort him to the Council, but really sent by Richard to hurry him thither. On their way they met a priest, with whom Hastings stopped to "comen a while". The knight interrupted, "and said merely [merrily] to him: What, my lord, I pray you come on, whereto talke you so long with that priest, you haue no nede of a pri[e]st yet; and therewith he langhed vpon him, as though he would say, ye shal haue sone. But so little wist that tother what he ment, and so little mistrusted, that he was neuer merier nor neuer so full of good hope in his life; which self thing is often sene a signe of chaunge" (p. 50).

On the Tower wharf Hastings met "one Hastinges, a purseuant of his own name". Once before he had met him in the same place, at a time when Rivers had accused him to the king, and "he was for the while (but it lasted not long) farre fallen into the kinges indignacion, and stode in gret fere of himselfe". "And therfore he said: Ah Hastinges art thou remembred when I met thee here ones with an heuy hart? Yea, my lord (quod he), that remembre I wel: and thanked be God they gate no good nor ye none harme thereby. Thou wouldest say so, quod he, if thou knewest as much as I know, which few know els as yet and moe shall shortly. That ment he by the lordes of the quenes kindred that were taken before, and should that day be behedded at Pounfreit... In faith, man, quod he, I was neuer so sory, nor neuer stode in so great dread in my life, as I did when thcu and I met here. And lo, now the world is turned, now stand mine enemies in the daunger .. and I neuer in my life so mery nor neuer in so great surety".

The news of Hastings' death was at once spread in the city. "Entending to set some colour vpon the matter", Richard sent in haste for "many sembstauncial men out of the city into the Tower. And at their comming, himself with the Duke of Bukingham, stode harnesed in old il-faring briginders, such as no man shold wene that thei wold vouchsafe to haue put vpon their backes, except that some sodaine necessitie had constrained them" (p. 51). Then Richard declared that Hastings and others had intended to destroy him and Buckingham at the council, a fact of which he had not known till ten o'clock. "Whiche sodain fere draue them to put on for ther defence such harneis as came next to hande. And so had God holpen them, that the mischief turned vpon them that wold haue done it. And this he required them to report. Eueri man answered him fair, as though no man mistrusted the mater which of trouth no man belued" (p. 51).

Beside this, Richard sent a herald through the city, with a proclamation declaring that Hastings and others had conspired against his life and Buckingham's, "and after to haue taken vpon them to rule the king and the realm at their pleasure, and therbi to pil and spoil whom thei list vncontroled" (p. 52). Other charges were included, that Hastings had given King Edward IV evil counsel, and furthered him in vicious living; that he had himself lived viciously, especially with Shore's wife, who had urged him on to the treason. It was declared that Hastings had been beheaded in haste only to prevent his deliverance and further conspiracy. "Now was this proclamacion made within .II. houres after that he was beheded, and it was so curiously indited, and so fair writen in parchment in so wel a set hande, and therwith of it self so long a processe, that eueri child might wel perceiue that it was prepared before. For al the time betwene his death and the proclaming could scant haue suffised vnto the bare wryting alone, all had it bene but in paper and scribled forth in hast at aduenture. So that vpon the proclaming therof, one that was scole master of Poules of chaunce standing by and comparing the shortnes of the time with the length of the matter, said vnto them that stode about him, here is a gay goodly cast foule cast awai for hast. And a merchant answered hym, that it was writen by profecy" (pp. 52, 53).

After this, "as it wer for anger, not for couetise, the protector sent into the house of Shores wife . . . . and spoiled her of al that euer she had, aboue the value of II. or III. M. marke, and sent her body to prison". Her charged her with bewitching him and with aiding Hastings in his treason, and "when that no colour could fasten vpon these matters", he charged her with being "nought of her body". "And for thys cause (as a goodly continent prince, clene and faultles of himself, sente oute of heauen into this vicious world for the amendement of mens maners) he caused the bishop of London to put her to open penance, going before the crosse in procession upon a Sonday with a taper in her hand. In which she went in countenance and pace demure so womanly, and albeit she were out of al array saue her kyrtle only: yet went she so fair and louely, namelye while the wondering of the people caste a comely rud in her chekes (of which she before had most misse) that her great shame wan her much praise. And many good folke also, that hated her liuing, and glad wer to se sin corrected, yet pitied thei more her penance, then rejoyced therein, when thei considred that the protector procured it, more of a corrup; intent then ani vertuous affecion".

"This woman was born in London, worshipfully frended, honestly brought vp, and very wel maryed, sauing somewhat to sone, her husbande an honest citezen, yonge and goodly and of good substance ... but forasmuche as they were coupled or ere she were well rype, she not very feruently loued for whom she neuer longed", so that she easily yielded to the king. "When the kyng had abused her, anone her husband beyng an honest manne and one that could his good, not presumyng to tcuche a kynges concubyne left her vp to hym altogether. When the kyng dyed, the lorde Hastynges toke her. Proper she was and faire ... yet delited not men so much in her bewty, as in her plesant behauiour. For a proper wit had she, and could both rede wel and write, mery in company, redy and quick of aunswer, neither mute nor ful of bable, sometime taunting without displesure and not without disport. In whom the king therfore toke speciall pleasure". But his favor "she neuer abused to any mans hurt, but to

Palaestra. X.   7

many a mans comfort and relief: where the king toke
displeasure she would mitigate and appease his mind;
where men were out of fauour, she wold bring them in
his grace. For many that had highly offended, shee obtained
pardon. Of great forfetures she gate men remission. And
finally in many weighty sutes, she stode many men in
gret stede". But now [in More's time] she is in a "beggerly
condicion, vnfrended and worne out of acquaintance . . . .
at this daye she beggeth of many at this daye liuing, that
at this day had begged if she had not bene" (pp. 54, 55.)

[In this description of Shore's wife Lumby has again
"expurgated" without indicating the fact. I add most of
the omitted lines from Hall.]

Now it had been arranged that on the same day that
Hastings was beheaded the lords taken at Northampton
and Stony Stratford should be beheaded at Pomfret; which
was done, under the direction of Sir Richard Ratclif, whom
Richard made special use of "as a man that had ben long
secret with him, hauing experience of the world and a
shrewde wit, short and rude in speche, rough and boustiouse
of behauiour, bold in mischief, as far from pitie as from
al fere of God. This knight bringing them out of the prison
to the scafold, and shewing to the people about that thei
were traitors, not suffring them to speke and declare their
innocence, lest their wordes might haue inclined men to
pity them, and to hate the protectour and his part, caused
them hastly without jugement, processe, or maner of order
to be behedded".

Now that Hastings and the others were out of the
way, Richard thought "it were best hastly to pursue his
purpose and put himself in possession of the crowne, ere
men could haue time to deuise ani wais to resist". The
first necessity was to break the matter skilfully to the
people, and among those chosen to counsel about this was
"Edmond Shaa knight, then maier of London, which, vpon
trust of his owne aduauncement, whereof he was of a
proud hart highly desirouse, shold frame the cite to their

appetite. Of spiritual men thei toke such as had wit, and were in aucthoritie among the peple for oppinion of ther lerning, and had no scrupilouse conscience. Among these had thei John Shaa clerke, brother to the maier, and freer Peuker, prouincial of the Augustine freers, both doctor of diunitie, both gret prechars ... Of these two the tone had a sermon in praise of the protectour before the coronacion, the tother after, both so ful of tediouse flatery, that no mans eares could abide them. Peuker in his sermon so lost his voice that he was faine to leaue of and come downe in the middes. Doctor Shaa by his sermon lost his honestie, and sone after his life, for very shame of the worlde, into which he durst neuer after come abrode" (p. 57).

Shaw's sermon was delivered at Paul's Cross, for the purpose of offering the people a pretext for deposing the prince and making Richard king. He was instructed to allege bastardy "either in king Edward himself, or in his children, or both. To lay bastardy in kynge Edward sowned openly to the rebuke of the protectours owne mother, whiche was mother to them both; for in that point could be none other colour, but to pretend that his own mother was one aduouteresse which notwithstanding, to farther this purpose, he letted not; but natheles he would that point should be lesse, and more fauorably, handled, not euen fully plain and directly, but that the matter should be touched aslope craftely, as though men spared in that point to speke al the trouth for fere of his cispleasure. But the other point concerning the bastardy that they deuised to surmise in king Edwards children, that wold he should be openly declared and inforsed to the uttermost. The coloure and pretext wherof cannot be wel perceiued, but if we first repete you some thinges longe before done about king Edwardes mariage". Edward, wishing to marry, sent Warwick "vnto Spaine, to intreate and conclude a mariage betwene king Edward and the kinges doughter of Spaine". He succeeded easily, but meanwhile there

7*

came to Edward the Lady Elisabeth Gray, suing for restoration of the lands of her husband, who fell at Barnet, fighting for King Henry. "Whom when the kyng beheld, and hard her speke, as she was both faire, of a good fauor, moderate of stature, wel made and very wise: he not alonely pitied her, but also waxed enamored on her, [and takyng her secretly a sydd began to enter into talkyng more familierly, whose appetite when she perceyued, she verteously denied hym, but that she dyd so wysely and that with so good maner and woorde so wel set, that she rather kyndeled his desyre then quenched it. And finally, after many a metyng and much wowyng and many great promises she well espied the kyng his affeccion towarde her so greatly encreased that she durste somewhat the more boldely saye her mynde as to him whose hert she perceyued more feruently set then to fall of for a worde. And in conclusion she shewed him plain, that as she wist her self to simple to be his wife, so thought she her self to good to be his concubine. The kyng muche marueilyng of her constancy, as he that had not been wonte els where so stiefly sayed nay, so muche estemed her continency and chastitee, that he sette her vertue in steade of possession and richesse: And this takyng counsaill of his owne desyre determined in haste to mary her". Hall, p. 366; "expurgated" by Lumby.]

His mother tried to dissuade him, urging that Elizabeth was not sufficiently noble, that the king for policy's sake should not marry his own subject, that as she was a widow Edward would be committing bigamy [as regarded by the canon law of that time], and that Warwick would be angry. Edward answered that love was the first requisite in marriage, that marrying his subject would bring him favor in his own land, which was more important to him than that of a foreign land, that he could obtain the latter by the marriages of his kin, that Warwick loved him too well to be angry, and that as for bigamy he understood it to be forbidden to a priest, but not to a prince.

Then the duchess determined to disturb the marriage by alleging a pre-contract on Edward's part with "one dame Elizabeth Lucy, whom the king had also not long before gotten with child". But this woman, though urged thereto, would not declare that they had been "insured", though she had hoped from the king's loving words that he would marry her. Thus Edward was married to the lady Grey, to the intense displeasure and subsequent enmity of Warwick, "a wise man and a couragiouse warrior, and of such strength .... that he made kinges and put down kinges almost at his pleasure, and not impossible to haue attained it himselfe, if he had not rekened it a greater thing to make a king then to be a king".

Thus Shaw, beside asserting the bastardy of Edward himself and of Clarence, was to show that Edward's children were bastards because he had been contracted to Elizabeth Lucy before his marriage.

Shaw took for his text "spuria vitulamnia non agent radices altas. That is to say, bastard slippes shall neuer take depe roote". After showing the great grace attending generation in lawful matrimony, he declared that bastards, though they may for a season inherit other men's lands, are sure to be found out, and "the bastard slip pulled up, ere it can be roted depe". Of this he cited examples from the Old Testament "and other auncient histories". Then he began to praise the dead Richard duke of York and showed the title of his heirs to the crown. Then he tried to prove that Richard was the duke's only lawful heir, on account of Edward's marriage with Elizabeth Lucy, and because Edward and Clarence themselves were not reckoned surety as the duke's sons, "as those that by their fauors more resembled other knowen men then him". "But the lord protectour he said, that very noble prince, the special paterne of knightly prowes, as well in all princely behaueor as in the liniamentes and fauor of his visage, represented the verye face of the noble duke his father. This is, quod he, the fathers owne figure, this is his own countenance, the very prent of his visage, the sure vndoubted image, the playne expresse likenes of that noble Duke" (pp. 64, 65).

Now it had been arranged that just at this point Richard should appear, that these words "might haue been taken among the hearers, as thoughe the Holye Ghost had put them in the preachers mouth, and should haue moued the people euen ther to crie, king Richard, king Richard, that it might haue bene after said, that he was specially chosen by God and in maner by miracle" (p. 65). But Shaw, fearing to reach the passage too late, hurried, and Richard fearing to come too early delayed; so that when he did arrive the preacher was far on in his sermon. When he saw Richard coming, he "out of al order, and oute of al frame began to repete those wordes again" (p. 65). "But the people wer so farre fro crying king Richard, that thei stode as thei had bene turned into stones, for wonder of this shamefull sermon".

After this the preacher kept himself at home "out of sight lyke an owle. And when he once asked one that had bene his old frend, what the people talked of him, al wer it that his own conscience wel shewed him that thei talked no good, yet when the tother answered him that there was in euery mans mouth spoken of him much shame, it so strake him to the heart, that within fewe daies after he withered and consumed away" (p. 65). On the Tuesday following, in the Guildhall, the duke of Buckingham, "as he was neither vnlearned, and of nature marueilouslye wel spoken" addressed "all the commons of the citie" (p. 65).

Buckingham declared that he had come to bring them what they had sore longed for — the surety of their own bodies, the quiet of their wives and daughters, and the safeguard of their goods. This they had long lacked. Edward had taken from them great sums, whatever he wished, under the easy name of benevolence. Every offence had been regarded by him as greater than it was, as for example the offence of Burdet, who "for a word spoken in hast" was "cruelly behedded, by the misconstruing of the lawes of thys realme for the princes plesure", though Markam, the chief justice, left his office sooner than give consent. There was the destruction of Cooke, formerly their own mayor. Never had there been such long dissension or so many battles as under Edward's reign; at the cost of more English blood than would have won France twice. No time was free from fear of the king, for whom spared he that killed his own brother? Those whom he favored were scarce fit to speak of, for "whoso was beste, bare away lest rule, and more sute was in his dayes vnto Shores wife, then to al the lordes in England, except vnto those that made her their proctoure". Shore's wife had been honest till the king corrupted her. But she was not his only victim. There was, as they well knew, no woman, young or old, rich or poor, whom he had desired, that he had not corrupted. The citizens of London had been specially annoyed, though the king should have shown them special favor.

But there lived a member of the house of York who would requite them for this. They had on Sunday heard from a preacher of the word of God the title of Richard of Gloucester to the throne. He had shown that the princes were bastards, as the king, since his true wife, dame Elizabeth Lucy, lived, was never lawfully married to their mother. "For lack of which lawfull accoupling, and also of other thinges, which the said worshipful doctor rather signified than fully explained, and which thynges shal not be spoken for me, as the thing wherin euery man forbereth to say that he knoweth, in auoidinge dyspleasure of my noble lord protector, bearing as nature requireth a filial reuerence to the duches his mother" (p. 70) — for these causes the title to the throne belonged to Richard. On consideration of these things, and of "the greate knightly prowes and manyfolde vertues which in his noble parson singularly" abounded, the nobles and commons, especially of the north, had determined to petition Richard to take the kingly office. Without doubt he would be loth to take up such a burden. It was no child's office. "And that the greate wise manne well perceiued, when hee sayde: veh regno cuius rex puer est. Woe is that Realme, that hathe a chylde to theyre kynge". They should be glad that a man of such wisdom and experience existed for the office, and though loth, he would take it if the citizens of London joined in the request. Which he doubted not they would do. "Wherin", concluded he, "dere frendes, what mind you haue, wee require you plainely to shew vs".

Here Buckingham had expected that the people, "whome he hoped that the mayer had framed before", would cry "King Richard"; but all was still. "Wherewith the duke was meruailously abashed", and taking the mayor aside he asked him what was the matter. "Sir, quod the mayer, parcase they perceyue you not well". Whereon he repeated his speech in other words, most eloquently. "But al was as styl as the midnight, no so much as rowning [whispering] among them, by whych the myght seme to comen what was best to doe". Then the mayor said that the people were not wont to be spoken to but by the recorder, to whom they might answer. So the recorder, FitzWilliam, rehearsed the matter, but "he shewed euery thing as the dukes wordes and no part his owne". Yet the people still "stode as they had ben men amased". Then Buckingham addressed them again. He said that they had come to the citizens not out of need, but of love. "Wherefore we requere you giue vs aunswer one or other, whither you be mynded as all the nobles of the realme be, to haue this noble prynce now protectour to be your kyng or not". Then the people began to whisper, "tyl at the last in the nether ende of the hal, a bushement of the dukes seruantes, and Nashefeldes and other longing [belonging] to the protectour, with some prentises and laddes that thrust into the hal amonge the prese, began sodainelye at mennes backes to crye owte as lowde as their throtes would gyue, king Richarde, kinge Rycharde, and threwe vp their cappes in token of joye. And when the duke and the maier saw thys maner, they wysely turned it to theyr purpose. And said it was a goodly cry and a joyfull to here, euery man with one voice, no manne sayeng nay. Wherfore frendes, quod the duke, sine that we parceiue it is all your hole mindes to haue this noble man for your king . . . . we require ye that ye to morow go with vs and wee with you vnto his noble grace, to make our humble request vnto him in maner before remembered" (p. 74).

Then the assembly dissolved, "the more part al sad . . . and some of those that came thyther with the duke, not able to dissemble theyr sorow, were faine at his backe to turne their face to the wall, while the doloure of their heart braste oute at theyr eyen" (p. 74).

"Then on the morowe after, the mayre with all the aldermen and chiefe comeners of the citie in their beste maner apparailed, assembling themself together resorted vnto Baynardes castell where the protector lay. To which place repaired also according to their appointmente the duke of Buckingham, with dyuers noble menne with him, beside manye knightes and other gentlemen. And thereupon the duke sent worde vnto the lord protectour, of the being there of a great and honourable coumpanye, to moue a great matter vnto his grace. Whereupon the protectour made difficultie to come oute vnto them, but if he first knewe some part of theyr errande, as though he doubted and partelye dystrusted the commyng of suche noumber vnto him so sodainlye, withoute any warnyng or knowledge, whyther they came for good or harme. Then the Duke when he had shewed this vnto the maier and other, that they mighte thereby see howe lytle the protectour loked for this matter, thei sent vnto him by the messenger suche louyng message againe, and therewith so humblye besought hym to vouchesafe that thei might resort to hys presence, to purpose their intent, of which they would vnto none other parson any part disclose, that at the laste hee came foorth of his chamber, and get not down vnto them, but stode aboue in a galarye ouer them, where they mighte see hym and speake to him, as though he woulde not yet come to nere them tyll he wist what they mente. And thereuppon the Duke of Buckingham fyrste made humble peticion vnto him, on the behalfe of them all, that his grace woulde pardon them and lycence them to purpose vnto hys grace the intent of their commyng withoute his displeasure, whithoute whiche pardon obtayned, they durst not be bold to moue him of that matter. In whiche albeit thei ment as muche honor to hys grace as wealth to al the realm beside, yet were they not sure howe hys grace woulde take it, whom they would in no wyse offende. Then the protector as hee was very gentle of hymselfe, and also longed sore to wit what they mente, gaue hym leaue to purpose what hym lyked, verely trusting for the good minde that he bare them al, none of them ani thing would intende vnto hym warde, where with he ought to be greued. When the duke had this leaue and pardon to speake, then waxed he bolde to shewe hym theyr intent and purpose, with all the causes mouing them thereunto as ye before haue harde, and finally to beseche hys grace, that it wold lyke him of his accustomed goodness and zeale vnto the realm, now with his eye of pitie, to beholde the long continued distres and decay of the same and to sette his gracious handes to the redresse and amendement therof, by taking vppon him the crowne and gouernaunce of this realme, according to his right and tytle lawfully descended vnto hym, and to the laude of God, profyte of the land, and vnto his grace so muche the more honour and lesse paine, in that neuer prince raigned vpon any people, that were so glad to liue vnder hys obeysaunce as the people of this realme vnder his.

When the protector had hard the proposicion, he loked very strangely therat, and answered: That all were it that he partli knew the thinges by them alledged to be true; yet such entier loue he bare vnto king Edward and his children, that so muche more regarded hys honour in other realmes about, then the crowne of any one, of which he was neuer desyrous, that he could not fynde in his hearte in this poynte to enclyne to theyr desyre. For in all other nacyons where the trueth wer not wel knowen, it shold paraduenture be thought, that it were his owne ambicious minde and deuise, to depose the prince and take himself the crown. With which infami he wold not haue his honoure stayned for anye crowne. In which he had euer parceyued muche more labour and payn, then pleasure to hym that so woulde so vse it, as that he that woulde not were not worthy to haue it. Notwithstanding he not only pardoned them the mocion that they made him, but also thanked them for the loue and hearty fauoure they bare him, prayinge them for his sake to geue and beare the same to the prynce, vnder whom he was and would be content to lyue, and with his labour and counsel as farre as should like the kyng to vse him, he woold doe his vttermost deuor to set the realm in good state. Whiche was alreadye in this litle while of his protectorship (the prayse geuen to God) wel begon, in that the malice of such as wer before occasion of the contrary, and of new intended to bee, were nowe partelye by good policye, partly more by Goddes special prouidence then mans prouision repressed. Vpon this answer geuen, the Duke by the protectours lycence, a lytle rouned, as well with other noble men about him as with the mayre and recorder of London. And after that vpon lyke pardone desyred and obtayned, he shewed aloude vnto the protectour that for a fynal conclusion, that the realm was appointed king Edwardes lyne shoulde not any longer reigne vpon them, both for that thei had so farre gone, that it was now no surety to retreate, as for that they thought it for the weale vniuersal to take that wai although they had not yet begonne it. Wherfore yf it would lyke hys grace to take the crowne vpon him, they would humblye beseche hym thereunto. If he woulde geue them a resolute aunswere to the contrarye, whyche they

woulde bee lothe to heare, than muste they needes seke and
shold not faile to fynd some other noble manne that woulde.
These wordes much moued the protectoure, whiche els, as euery
manne may witte, would neuer of likelyhoode haue inclyned
therunto. But when he saw ther was none other way, but
that eyther he must take it or els he and his bothe goe
fro it, he saide vnto the lordes and commons: Sith we
parceiue wel that al the realm is so set, whereof we be
very sorye that they wil not suffer in any wise king
Edwardes line to gouerne them, whom no manne earthly
can gouerne again their willes, and we wel also perceue,
that no manne is there, to whom the crowne can by so
just tytle appertayn as to our self, as verye ryghte heyre
lawfullye begotten of the bodye of oure moste deere father
Rycharde late Duke of Yorke, to whiche tytle is nowe
joyned your elleccion, the nobles and comons of this realm,
whiche wee of all titles possible take for most effectual:
we be content and agre fauourably to incline to your
peticion and request, and accordyng to the same, here we
take vppon vs the royall estate, preeminence and kyngdome of the twoo noble realmes, England and Fraunce, the
tone fro this day forward by vs and our heires to rule,
gouerne and defend, the tother by Goddes grace and
youre good helpe to geat again and subdewe, and establish
for euer in due obedyence vnto this realme of Englande,
thaduancement wherof we neuer aske of God longer to
lyue then we entende to procure. With this there was a
great shout, crying, kyng Richard, king Rychard. And
then the lordes went vp to the kyng (for so was he from
that time called) and the people departed, talkyng diuersly
of the matter euery man as his fantasye gaue hym. But
muche they talked and marueiled of the maner of this
dealing, that the matter was on bothe partes made so
straunge, as though neither had euer communed with other
therof before, when that themself wel wist there was no
man so dul that heard them, but he perceiued well inough,
that all the matter was made betwene them. Howbeit

somme excused that agayne, and sayde all must be done
in good order though. And menne must sommetime for
the manner sake not bee a-knowen what they knowe. For
at the consecracion of a bishop, euery man woteth well
by the paying for his bulles, that he purposeth to be one,
and thoughe he paye for nothing elles. And yet must he
be twise asked whyther he wil be bishop or no, and he
muste twyse say naye, and at the third tyme take it as
compelled ther vnto by his owne wyll. And in a stage
play all the people know right wel, that he that playeth
the sowdayne is percase a sowter. Yet if one should can
so lyttle good, to shewe out of seasonne what acquaintance
he hath with him, and calle him by his owne name whyle
he standeth in his magestie, one of his tormentors might
hap to breake his head, and worthy for marring of the
play. And so they said that these matters bee Kynges
games, as it were stage playes, and for the more part
plaied vpon scafoldes. In which pore men be but the
lokers on. And thei that wise be, wil medle no farther.
For they that sometyme step vp and playe with them,
when they cannot play their partes, they disorder the play
and do themself no good" (pp. 74—79).

The next day Richard went to Westminster Hall "and
there when he had placed himself in the court of the
kinges bench declared . . . that he woulde take vpon
him the crowne in that place there, wher the king himself
sitteth and ministreth the law". He then made an oration,
seeking to win to himself the nobles, merchants, artificers
and especially the lawyers. Then that by clemency he
might win good will, he declared himself ready to forgive
all offences against him, and summoned from sanctuary
one Fogge, "whom he had long deadly hated", took him
by the hand and pardoned him. As Richard returned
home he saluted all he met. For a minde that knoweth
it self giltye, is in a maner dejected to a seruile flattery"
(p. 80). Having thus begun his reign, Richard was crowned
soon after. [The date is lacking in More.]

"Now fell ther mischieues thick". As Richard ended his reign with the best and most righteous death, his own, so he began it with the most piteous and wicked, that of his nephews. There were [in More's time] some who doubted that they were in Richard's days destroyed, not only because of the pretence of Perkin Warbeck, but because nothing could be plainly and openly proved. Wherefore, says More, "I shall rehearse you the dolorous end of those babes, not after euery way that I haue heard, but after that way that I haue so hard by suche men and by such meanes, as me thinket it wer hard but it should be true". King Richard after his coronation visited Gloucester, and as he rode thither determined for his security to kill his nephews. He therefore sent one John Green to Brakenbury, constable of the Tower, bidding him in any wise put the two children to death. "This John Grene did his errande vnto Brakenbery kneling before our Lady in the Tower, who plainely answered that he would neuer putte them to death to dye therfore" (p. 81). This answer Green reported to Richard at Warwick. "Wherwith he toke such displeasure and thought, that the same night, he said vnto a secrete page of his. Ah whome shall a man trust? those that I haue broughte vp my selfe, those that I had went would most surely serue me, euen those fayle me, and at my commaundemente wyll do nothyng for me. Syr, quod his page, there lyeth one on your paylet without, that I dare well say, to do your grace pleasure, the thyng were right harde that he wold refuse meaning this by sir James Tyrell, which was a man of right goodlye parsonage, and for natures gyftes, worthy to haue serued a muche better prince, if he had well serued God, and by grace obtayned as muche trouthe and good wil as he had strength and witte. The man had an high heart, and sore longed vpwarde, not rising yet so fast as he had hoped, being hindered and kept vnder by the meanes of sir Richarde Ratclife and sir William Catesby" (p. 82), who wanted no partners in Richard's favor.

Richard thereupon came out into the pallet chamber where were sleping Tyrell and his brother Sir Thomas. "Then said the king merely [merrily] to them: What sirs, be ye in bed so soone? And calling vp syr James, brake to him secretely his mind in this mischieuous matter. In whiche he founde him nothing strange". He was sent to Brakenbury with a letter bidding Brakenbury deliver to him all the keys of the Tower for one night. Which being fulfilled, Tyrell appointed the next night for the deed. "The prince, as soone as the protector lefte that name and toke himself as king, had it shewed vnto him, that he should not reigne, but his vncle should haue the crowne. At which worde the prince sore abashed, began to sigh and said: Alas I woulde my vncle woulde lette me haue my lyfe yet, though I lese my kingdome. Then he that tolde him the tale, vsed him with good wordes, and put him in the best comfort he could. But forthwith was the prince and his brother bothe shet vp, and all other remoued from them, onely one called black Wil or William Slaughter except, set to serue them and see them sure. After whiche time the prince neuer tyed his pointes, nor ought rought of hymselfe, but with that young babe hys brother, lingered in thought and heauines til this tratorous death deliuered them of that wretchednes. For sir James Tirel deuised that thei shold be murthered in their beddes. To the execucion wherof, he appointed Miles Forest, one of the foure that kept them, a felowe fleshed in murther before time. To him he joyned one John Dighton, his own horsekeper, a big brode square strong knaue. Then al the other beeing remoued from them, thys Miles Forest and John Dighton, about midnight (the sely children lying in their beddes) came into the chamber, and sodainly lapped them vp among the clothes, so bewrapped them and entangled them, keping down by force the fether bed and pillowes hard vnto their mouthes, that within a while smored and stifled, theyr breath failing, thei gaue vp to God their innocent soules into the joyes of heauen, leauing to the tormentors their bodyes dead in the bed. Whiche after that the wretches parceiued, first by the strugling with the paines of death, and after long lying styll, to be throughly dead; they laide their bodies naked out vppon the bed, and fetched sir James to see them. Which vpon the sight of them, caused those murtherers to burye them at the stayre foote, metely depe in the grounde vnder a great heape of stones. Than rode sir James in great hast to king Richarde, and shewed him al the maner of the murther, who gaue hym gret thanks and, as som say, there made him knight. But he allowed not, as I haue heard, the burying in so vile a corner, saying that he woulde haue them buried in a better place, because thei wer a kinges sonnes. Loe the honourable corage of a kynge! Wherupon thei say that a prieste of syr Robert Brakenbury toke vp the bodyes again, and secretelye entered them in such place, as by the occasion of his deathe, whiche onely knew it, could neuer synce come to light.

In the time of Henry VII, Tyrell was committed to prison for treason, and while there he and Dighton "confessed the murther in maner aboue writen". "What wretched end ensueth such dispiteous crueltie" may be seen from the fate of those who committed this deed. Forest "pecemele rotted away"; Dighton was in More's day still alive but likely to be hanged. Tyrell was beheaded for treason, and Richard was "slain . . hacked and hewed of his enemies handes, haryed on horsebacke dead, his here in despite torn and togged lyke a cur dogge". Until that happened he was torn by anguish. "For I haue heard by credible report of such as wer secrete with his chamberers, that after this abhominable deede done, he neuer hadde quiet in his minde, hee neuer thought himself sure. Where he went abrode, his eyen whirled about, his body priuily fenced, his hand euer on his dager, his countenance and maner like one alway ready to strike againe, he toke ill rest a nightes, lay long wakyng and musing, sore weried with care and watch, rather slumbred then slept, troubled wyth feareful dreames, sodainly sommetyme sterte up, leape out of his bed and runne about the chamber, so was his restles herte continually tossed and tumbled with the tedious impression and stormy remembrance of his abominable dede" (p. 85).

Outwardly, too, he had no long time of rest, for soon after began Buckingham's conspiracy against him, the occasion of which "is of diuers folke diuerse wyse pretended". The duke had, as More was informed, immediately on Edward's death sent to Richard at York a messenger named Persal, who was admitted by Richard "in the dead of the night after al other folk auoyded". The message borne by Persal was that "in this new worlde" Buckingham would take the same part as Richard and wait on him at need with 1000 men. Persal, "sent back with thanks, and some secret instruccion of the protector's mind", met Richard again with a further message from Buckingham at Nottingham, whither the protector from York with 600 men was come on his way to London. Buckingham met him at Northampton with 300 horse, and from then on continued to be a partner of his devices till after the coronation, when they separated, "as it semed very great frendes" at Gloucester. Once home, Buckingham began his conspiracy. Some said the cause was that Buckingham had required of the protector the duke of Hereford's lands, and since the title to these lands "was somewhat enterlaced with the title to the crowne by the line of king Henry before deprived; the protector conceiued such indignacion, that he rejected the dukes request with many spitefull and minatory wordes". Whereat Buckingham was so wounded with hatred and mistrust that he could never afterward bear to look on king Richard, and feigned himself sick that he might not have to ride with Richard to his coronation.

"And the tother taking it in euil part, sent hym worde to ryse, and come ride or he wold make him be caried. Wherupon he rode on with euil wil, and that notwithstanding on the morow rose from the feast faining himself sicke, and kyng Richard said it was done in hatred and dispite of him. And they say that euer after continually ech of them liued in suche hatred and distrust of other, that the duke verilye looked to haue bene murthered at Gloucester. From which nathles he in fair maner departed" (p. 87).

But many "right secret at the daies deny this" and think it unlikely, considering the "depe dissimuling nature" of both, and the need each had of the other, "that either the protector wold geue the duke occasion of displeasure, or the duke the protector occasion of mistrust. And vtterly men think, that yf kyng Richard had any such oppinion conceiued: he would neuer haue suffred him to escape his handes". It is true, says More, that Buckingham was a "high minded man, and euyll could beare the glory of an other, so that I haue heard of som that said thei saw it, that the duke at such time as the crown was first set vpon the protectors hed, his eye could not abide the sight thereof, but wried hys hed an other way" (p. 88). Some said that Buckingham was really "not wel at ease" [i. e. was sick], and was therefore allowed by Richard to depart, with great gifts, "in most louing and trusty maner".

But when Buckingham came home to Brecknock he began to talk familiarly with Doctor Morton, bishop of Ely, who had been in Buckingham's custody since the meeting of the council where Hastings came to his end. Morton had been fast upon the side of Henry VI, had fled with Margaret and her son, and returned with them to the fatal field at Barnet. After that Edward "woed him to come and had him from thence forth in secret trust and very speciall fauor". For his truth to the young king Edward he was taken prisoner and given into Buckingham's charge, from which he escaped, as we learn later. He it was that devised the marriage between Henry and Elizabeth. He was summoned home from Rome, whither he had gone after Henry entered England, and was made archbishop of Canterbury and chancellor of England, receiving the title of Cardinal from the Pope.

Now the bishop "had gotten by great experience, the verye mother and maistres of wisdom, a depe insighte in politike worldli driftes". Seeing that Buckingham was glad to talk with him, and would "now and then balke oute a lytle breide of enuy. toward the glory of the king . . . he craftelye sought the waies to pricke him forwarde". "For when the duke first began to praise and bost the king, and shewe how much profit the realm should take by his reign", Morton replied that Buckingham well knew that if he could have had his way, Henry's son would have had the crown, and not Edward. But as God ordered otherwise, he was not so mad as to strive with a dead man against a living. So he had been Edward's faithful chaplain, and would have been glad to see his son succeed him. But again he did not intend to labor to set up what God pulled down. "And as for the late protector and now kyng. And euen there he left, saying that he had alredy medled to muche with the world, and would fro that day medle with his boke and his beedes and no farther".

"Then longed the duke sore to here what he would haue sayd, because he ended with the king and there so sodeinly stopped", and urged him to speak openly. He had procured of the king the custody of the bishop precisely for the purpose of making use of his advice and counsel.

"The bishop right humbly thanked him and said; In good faith, my lord, I loue not much to talke muche of princes, as thing not all out of peril, thoughe the word be without fault, forasmuch as it shal not be taken as the party ment it, but as it pleaseth the prince to conster it. And euer I think on Esop's tale, that when the lion had proclamed that on pain of deth there should none horned beast abide in that wood, one that had in his forehed a bunch of flesh, fled awaye a great pace. The fox that saw him run so faste, asked him whither he made al that hast. And he answered, in faith I neither wote nor reck, so I wer once hence because of this proclamacion made of horned beastes. What, fole, quod the fox, thou maist abide wel inough, the lyon ment not by thee, for it is none horne that is in thine head. No mary, quod he, that wote I wel ynough. But what and he cal it an horn, wher am I then? The duke laughed merely at the tale, and said; My lord I warant you, neither the lyon nor the bore shal pyke anye matter at any thyng here spoken, for it shall neuer come nere their eare. In good fayth, sir, said the bishop, if it did, the thing that I was about to say, taken as wel as afore God I ment it, could deserue but thank. And yet taken as I wene it wold, might happen to turn me to litle good and you to lesse. Then longed the duke yet moch more to wit what it was" (pp. 90, 91).

Then the bishop declared that as Richard was king in possession he did not purpose to dispute his title. He only wished that in addition to Richard's many abilities God had given him some of such other excellent virtues meet for the rule of a realm as the Lord had planted in the person of Buckingham himself.

And here More's work breaks abruptly off.

B. The Latin Version of More's Richard III.

I note here the only important differences of the Latin from the English version. The citations are taken from the Frankfort edition of More's works, 1689.

Of Clarence's death it is stated that Parliament had condemned him "acerbissimo supplicio; sed Rex atrocitatem poenae sustulit, mortem tulit, qua ut levissima defungeretur, in vini Cretensis dolium immerso capite, respirare prohibitus, expiravit.

In the description of Richard's person, for the "prowesse" of the English is found "probitate"; "ill fetured of limmes" is the equivalent of "inaequalibus atque informibus membris", and for the "his left shoulder much higher than his right" we have the milder and less definite "alteroque humero erectior".

For the "close and secret" of the English version we have the more definite and interesting statement that he would intrust his plans to nobody save those that had to carry them out, and not even to these before the moment for action, or further than was absolutely necessary.

For "He slew King Henry" stands the more definite "Henricum ... ab isto crudeliter adacto sub costas pugione confossum ac trucidatum".

In the story of Rivers's capture no statement is found to the effect that Richard and Buckingham had taken possession of the keys of the inn; instead stands only "omnibus itineribus oppidi obsessis".

In Richard's charge that Dorset had taken money from the tower is found "stipendium in milites elargitum, quos in classem ad confirmandas illius factionis opes coegisset".

Gray, on his capture, is said to have put his hand to his sword, intending to defend himself, but gave it up, being admonished that it was too late.

The queen is said to have had "filias quatuor" with her in sanctuary.

In Richard's speech urging that the duke of York be brought out of sanctuary for "they that by the assent of the nobles of the land wer appoynted .. to the tuicyon of his owne royall parsone", we have "cujus ipsum corpus mihi vos alendum tuendumque credidistis" (p. 9).

The cardinal sent to the queen is not named as either York or Canterbury.

The description of the council where Hastings met his death has a few further details and slight differences. The beginning reads: "Igitur consultantibus paulo post in arce proceribus, quos eos protector conculcaverat, ipse serius veniens in consilium excusat tarditatem: Tum hilaris, ac prope jocanti similis accubuit protinusque in Eliensem versus Episcopum: Pater, inquit, fraga tibi in hortis audio insignia nasci, non gravatim scio ferculum unum tot nobilibus in prandium, velut symbolum tuum conferes". Ely sends for the strawberries. Then "protector velut nescio quid necessariae rei in proximo facturus cubiculo, statimque in consilium redditurus egreditur, proceribus interim tanta ejus festivitate oblectatis, quantam haud temere ante in illo viderant, simulque humanitatem benignitatemque animi laudantibus, ille non diu moratus revertitur". Hence the narrative proceeds as in the English. Richard's answer to Hastings reads: "Quid tu mihi inquit, si ego tibi fecisse ajo: idque si defendas, duello tecum proditor approbavero".

Of Stanley's wound we have additional information. "Mideltonus quidem in Darbiae Comitem securim libravit, sic ut nisi propere sub mensam dilapsus evitasset ictum, ad dentes usque caput fuerit divisurus, quippe quem sic quoque celeri lapsu ictum declinantem, extrema tamen acies consecuta vertici impacto vulnere totum cruore perfuderit. Inter Comitem & percussorem hunc lis de praediis olim, atque hinc inimicitia vetus intercesserat. Nam Comes eum de possessione, vine an jure incertum, invitum certe dejecerat, unde ille plus ausus, quam imperatum est in aliena causa, suo dolori serviebat". Of Hasting's death we have, "urgente Bukyngamiae Duce (quem ille [Hastings] suppliciter intuens ut sui misereretur obsecrabat) vix temere facta confessione, producitur . . . finem recepit" (p. 17).

Stanley's dream is thus related. "Visum enim aprum prostratos ambos appetere dentibus: Hastyngum repente confectum, ipsi vero sic lancinatum caput, ut sanguis ubertim sic sinus efflueret" (p. 17).

Hastings' former imprisonment is said to have been the result of a charge by Rivers, that Hastings, who was captain of Calais, intended to betray the place to the French (p. 17).

The Latin version ends with the statement of Richard's coronation.

In More's history the Richard saga made its greatest advance. The work not only gives in minute detail an account of all the important events from the death of

Edward to the outbreak of Buckingham's rebellion, but it presents the most finished portrait of Richard's person and character. Added to this is a style which has caused it to be considered the first piece of historical writing that has just claim to be called literature. It is not strange, therefore, that it fixed in practically definitive form the character and person of Richard, as they were to appear in later history and literature, and with these the history of the events in Richard's life, so far as More spoke of them. The work was adopted with but slight changes of phraseology and meagre additions of fact into all the succeeding chronicles — the Hardyng continuation, Hall, Grafton, Holinshed and Stow. Thus it formed also the, basis of Shakespeare's picture.

That More's account contains not only many inaccuracies, but also seemingly wilful misstatements of fact, has been abundantly proved by Buck, Walpole, Gairdner and others. What is still more apparent is the feeling of actual hatred of Richard that informs the whole work. It goes beyond the righteous detestation of a tyrant and murderer, goes beyond even the exaggerated feeling of a court chronicler like André. This, too, it is most probable, as well as his facts, was due to his contact with Bishop Morton, who had been Richard's personal foe.

Nowhere is this feeling more clearly shown than in the description of Richard's person, and nowhere does the saga make a more distinct advance. Up to this point we have heard only that Richard was short of stature and had the right shoulder higher than the left. In More, for the first time does he become "croke backed Richard", the name by which he was known to the succeeding generations. His left shoulder now becomes not only higher but much higher than his right. His very face is hard-favored", his limbs "ill-featured", his arm "werish, withered and small". Of his birth Rous had reported the legends that he was born haired and toothed. More adds that he was brought into the world by the physician's knife, and that he appeared with the feet forward, as men "bee borne outward" to burial. That nature changed her course in Richard's very beginning is More's plain belief.

The analysis of Richard's character is far more extended than any before written. Rous had suggested that Richard's monstrous nature was foretold by his birth. André had charged him with loving deeds of blood from the very cradle. More likewise dates his disposition from even before his birth as ever froward. The dissimulation and hypocrisy which other writers had mentioned is emphasized by More in detail. New qualities are insisted upon, malice, wrath, envy. On the other side, More, as others had done before him, praises Richard's courage and policy in war. In More's treatment of Richard's crimes the saga again takes an important step forward. Prince Edward's death, it is noticeable, is not mentioned by More, but the murder of Henry VI is ascribed to Richard. It is, moreover, for the first time ascribed to his own impulse, as done without the commandment or knowledge of Edward, who, More thinks, if he had wished the deed done, would have had it executed by some other than his own brother. This reasoning, with its entire lack of consideration of the political situation, reveals clearly enough More's inclination to picture Richard in the worst possible light. A further step is the veiled suggestion that Richard was glad of Clarence's death and by secret expressions helped it on. But More is careful to indicate that this is based on rumor only, and that conjecture may as well shoot too far as too short. That Richard played any active part in inducing the condemnation of Clarence or in procuring the carrying out of the sentence is not suggested.

In the reason assigned for the statement that Richard was glad of Clarence's death, the saga again advances and Richard's character grows blacker. Till now there had been but slight discussion concerning the time when Richard first conceived his purpose to reign. In More we find the report that "he long time in king Edwardes life forethought to be king". It is true that More declares that there is no certainty on this point, and that Richard may first have been put in hope by the tender age of his nephews; but, as in other places, it is the worse report that is emphasized, supported, and apparently believed. It is of course impossible here to indicate all that is new in More's account; so much of it is new. I content myself with calling attention to some of the salient points in the story.

More's account is not a chronicle, but a biography of Richard. In all the history of the events that followed Edward's death, Gloucester is therefore not only made the chief and central figure, but the moving impulse. All that happens proceeds originally from him. And since the biography is written by a foe, Richard's motives for the impulses he gives to events are invariably represented as infamous and springing from his desire to become king. Thus, on the other side, the motives of Richard's opponents are placed in the most favorable light: a fact which at once appears by a comparison with the account of the Croyland continuation. The position of the queen's kindred about the young prince, their desires and aims, are represented by More as wise and just. The renewal of the old malice against them after the reconciliation at Edward's bedside, was, according to More, wholly the work of Richard, though he set on fire those who were themselves easy to kindle. Buckingham and Hastings both follow Richard's urging. In More it is Richard who, perceiving that a large train attending upon the young prince will prevent the attaining of his purpose, persuades the queen to send word to her son to come with only a small attendance. But the Croyland continuation makes it plain enough that Hastings and a majority of the council were of themselves opposed to the queen's kin, and to the train with which they proposed to bring the king up to London. Nothing is clearer than that the queen's kin were perfectly aware of the strong opposition to them, and that they intended to bring up a large army for the sake of maintaining themselves in power. Richard was at the time of Edward's death in Yorkshire, a fact which More does not mention or suggest in this place, though he does later, and it is unlikely that Richard knew much of the proceedings of the councils in London or of what was to be feared from the queen's kin, till he met Buckingham in Northampton (cf. Gairdner, p. 61). The charge brought by Buckingham and Richard against Dorset that he had taken treasure from the Tower and sent men to sea, is asserted by More to have been a mere pretext because they had to say something, and the act itself is declared to have been done for good and necessary purposes at the bidding of the whole council. It is not without great interest that the English version softens very much the charge as it appears in the Latin version, where the dukes assert that Dorset's purpose in his act was to strengthen his own faction. Here again the partisanship of More is plain, for it is perfectly clear that Richard's charge was true. Dorset, as constable of the Tower, had no authority to expend this money and no authority to fit out ships, a function which belonged to Richard in his office of Admiral of England. The situation was clearly this. Both parties, the queen's kin and their foes, were bent on a struggle for the supremacy. The latter party naturally intended to make all the use possible of the powerful Duke of Gloucester, and sooner or later he made up his mind to use them.

A further analysis of the relation of More's statements to history does not belong to my purpose. The above is sufficient to make clear that it was More's partisanship that brought about three important characteristics of the saga as shaped by him and accepted by those who followed him; viz., Richard the guiding spirit of all the events that followed Edward's death; his purpose therein the attainment of the crown; Rivers and his companions animated merely by the spirit of innocent and faithful defenders of the young king's rights.

In this connection it is important to note that More has not the slightest suggestion that Richard had any claim to a position of authority near the king. Mention of his protectorship occurs first at his appointment by the council. His actions as he "tooke upon himself the order and gouernance of the young king" bear at least the tacit charge of usurpation. It is an interesting question whether it was to heighten this appearance that More simply mentions that Lord Rivers "remained behynd" at Northampton. The Croyland continuator tells us that his purpose in so doing was to submit his proceedings to the approval of the king's uncle.

Richard's appointment to the protectorship by the council is represented by More as brought about by his humble and reverent bearing toward the king. So that from the great obloquy which his arrest of the queen's kin had brought upon him he was suddenly fallen into great trust. Here again it is Richard's hypocrisy, according to More, that brings him success. In fact, however, his appointment was but the consistent outcome of the purpose of those opposed to the queen; and this appointment was in reality but the ratification by the council of an appointment made by Edward IV in his will.

From this point on, among the numerous details here for the first time given, Richard's hypocrisy and crafty policy are most strongly emphasized. The winning of the young duke of York away from his mother's protection, the subtle messages by which Buckingham is induced to follow Richard in all his plans, the double councils, the dramatic plot which brings Hastings to his death, the statement to the citizens of Hastings' treason, with the device of the rusty armor, the previously prepared proclamation of a subsequently discovered crime, the sermon of Shaw and the intended coup of Richard's opportune appearance, Buckingham's speech at Guildhall, the scene at Baynard's castle where the crown is pressed upon the reluctant Richard, the reconciliation with Fogge — in all these, next to their cruel purpose, it is Richard's devilish craft that is made most prominent. That he was "a deepe dissimuler" others had stated before; but More's account seems one continued attempt to prove that thesis.

The next most important contribution of More to the saga, aside from the events, is his picture of the power of Richard's conscience. The Croyland continuator had mentioned Richard's dream at Bosworth, and the gloomy spirit that oppressed him before the battle; but these rather as prophecies of disaster than as stings of conscience. Nearly all preceding writers had in one way or another called attention to the fact that God's justice overtook the tyrant before he had long enjoyed his ill-gotten spoil. But it is in More that we find for the first time a Richard punished by his own heart. Even Shakespeare's picture of the torment in Richard's soul is not greatly superior in vivid power to that description of More which forms its basis. That precisely in this torment of soul and not in his death lay Richard's real punishment was seen by two of the dramatists that treated the story, the author of The True Tragedy, and Shakespeare. Among the events first reported by More the most important is the detailed account of the manner of the young princes' death. The account was, according to the author, obtained from the confession of Tyrell, when confined in the Tower for treason in 1502. It contains certain inaccuracies, as in the account of Tyrell himself and his introduction to Richard by a page (cf. Gairdner, p. 155, 156); and doubts have been cast on the truth, and on the genuineness of the whole confession. Such however was the account given out by Henry VII, and as related by More it supplanted in all subsequent histories the uncertain rumors that had before been current.

More's statement of the cause of Buckingham's rebellion is much confused. Several rumors of the reason that led Buckingham to fall away from the king, including Richard's refusal to give him the earldom of Hereford, are mentioned only to be rejected. The ground which seems to have been accepted by More is Buckingham's pride and envy of Richard's glory. This pride, says More, the bishop of Ely abused to Buckingham's destruction and his own deliverance. Unfortunately, More's account breaks off in the midst of the conversation between Buckingham and Ely, before Buckingham states his own feelings toward Richard. The lack of definiteness was afterwards somewhat supplied by those who continued More's story.

To More, perhaps originally to Archbishop Morton, is due the famous account of the council meeting where Hastings was arrested and beheaded. The slight differences between the English and the Latin accounts are of much interest. In the Latin far more is made of Richard's cheerful and almost jocular manner at his first appearance. During his absence the members of the council comment upon and praise it, as they do in Shakespeare's play, but not in the English version of More.

Ely's strawberries, it appears from the Latin version, were intended for the breakfast of the council — a further indication of Richard's pacific feeling and intention at the time of his first entrance.

In the Latin Richard returns shortly, while in the English version the time of his first appearance is exactly fixed at about nine, and his return an hour later, between ten and eleven. This is evidently made to fit the later statement by Richard to the mayor, that he had not known of Hastings' treason till ten o' clock. The statement in the Latin is "paulo ante prandium". In both accounts the evident intention is to represent Richard as giving out that he first heard of Hastings' treason during his absence from the council chamber. In the Latin account Hastings' arrest for the treason is made a little more plausible, for here Richard asserts that Hastings' reply is an attempt to defend the queen and Shore, and that this defence shows him to be a fellow conspirator.

Certain points in More's handling of his story remain to be noticed. Like André before him, he is very fond of long speeches. There is a deathbed speech of Edward, which is in its way effective, the long interchange of speeches between the Cardinal and the Queen, most unnecessarily prolix, the interchange of speeches between King Edward IV and his mother, Shaw's sermon, Buckingham's speech in Guildhall, the conversation between Buckingham and Ely, and many others. In all, considerably more than a third of More's work is taken up by speeches. Their importance in the drama, and especially in Shakespeare has already been spoken of (cf. p. 66).

The prophecies and warnings of which other historians were so fond appear in More also. But one, however, has reference to Richard himself: namely, his monstrous birth. The others have reference to the fate of Hastings — Stanley's dream, the repeated stumbling of Hastings' horse, his meeting with the priest and with the pursuivant. All have much dramatic value and are found in Shakespeare's play.

Of divine justice More has little to say. It is insisted upon in a single passage only, that where the fate of those who murdered the princes, including Richard himself, is pointed to as a most notable example given by God of the uncertainty of worldly wealth and the wretched end of dispiteous cruelty.

Of classical influence there is almost no trace, except in the Latinising style of the translation. There is absolutely no classical allusion in the English, a few which occurred in the Latin version, having been omitted. A passage in Shakespeare's Richard III, 2:3:41 et seq., referred to by Cunliffe, Infl. of Seneca on Eliz. Tragedy, as going to prove Shakspeare's acquaintance with Seneca, is taken almost verbally from More. The lines in Richard III read:

> "By a divine instinct men's minds mistrust
> Ensuing dangers; as, by proof, we see
> The waters swell before a boisterous storm".

More's words are, "before such great thinges mens hartes of a secret instinct of nature misgiueth them, as the sea

without wind swelleth of himself somtime before a tempest".
Cunliffe compares Thyestes 961—4

> mittit luctus signa futuri
> mens ante sui presaga mali,
> instat nautis fera tempestas,
> cum sine uento tranquilla tument.

If there is Senecan influence, it is, as shown, upon More, not Shakespeare; but the fact itself is open to some doubt. The passsage in the Latin version bears little resemblance to Seneca. It reads "animis ingentia mala secretiore naturae vi praesagientibus, pelagi in morem, sponte sua exaestuantis adversus instantem procellam" (p. 15). At all events this is the only passage where the influence of Latin literature can with plausibility be asserted of More's story. The habit of putting long speeches in the mouths of the persons in the history is without doubt ultimately derived from the classic historians; but it would be difficult to maintain that these had a direct influence on the present work.

XII. Polydore Vergil's Historia Angliae.

Polydore Vergil, a native of Urbino, was sent by Pope Alexander VI about 1501 to England as sub-collector of Peter's pence. He had written two works of great repute in Europe, was recommended to the king, received from him various ecclesiastical appointments and was requested by him to undertake a history of England. In a letter to his brother dated 1517, published in the 1521 Basel edition of his "De Inventoribus", he declares that he has been busy on this history already twelve years, and that it is not yet finished. Of some assistance toward determining the date at which the account of the reigns of Edward IV and of Richard III was written is the fact to which Pauli (5:701) calls attention, that in some places Vergil indicates the year in which he writes. Speaking of the war waged by Charles VIII in Italy, 1493 (p. 581, 1st ed.) Vergil says, "coepit haec malorum lues . . . duratque etiam nunc, qui est annus salutis humanae M D XII", and later, in writing of events in 1497, he says that Charles VIII when in Italy "in varios Italici belli laqueos sese & suam gentem induerat, ex quorum nullo illa ad hunc diem, qui est annus salutis M D XXIIII, se expedire potuit" (p. 593). This proves simply that Vergil was busy working on the reign of Henry VII as early as 1512 and as late as 1524. We cannot conclude that what precedes Henry's reign was written before 1512. In the reign of Edward IV he mentions that Henry I "began a few years past" to seek the canonization of Henry VI but was "prevented by hasty death". Henry died in 1509.

The first edition of Vergil's history appeared in Basel in 1534, a second in 1546, with the work brought down to 1509. Vergil died in 1555. A third edition appeared in that year, bringing the history down to 1538. Four other editions followed, Basel 1555, Ghent 1556—7, Basel 1570, Leyden 1651.

The quotations following are made from the translation published by Sir Henry Ellis in 1844 for the Camden Society. This translation is one of the Mss. of the old Royal Library in the British Museum. It was written, according to Ellis, in the latter part of the reign of Henry VIII, but this is incorrect. The translation used by Hall and the continuation of the Hardyng chronicle was made from the first edition, 1534, but Ellis's translation was made from the second edition of 1546, which differs in several passages from the earlier edition. Henry died in January 1547. The translation is literal and, with slight and unimportant exceptions, accurate. Quotations are made from it for convenience' sake, but in any case of necessity, owing to lack of clearness, mistranslation or omission, reference is made to the original in the first edition, 1533.

After the death of the Duke of York at the battle of St. Albans, 1461, Edward, his son, then earl of March, hastened to Wales and prepared a new army, joined with the earl of Warwick, and hastened to London, where he was proclaimed king. Henry fled to York. At Towton, near York, he was met by Edward, was defeated, and fled to Scotland. Queen Margaret and her son hastened to France to raise up a new army. Edward, now reigning in triumph, created his brother George duke of Clarence and Richard duke of Gloucester. Meanwhile Henry gathered an army in Scotland, re-entered England, was defeated at the battle of Hexam, and fled again to Scotland. Later, "whether he wer past all feare, or dryven depely to soome kynd of madnes", he "was not long in secret, who enterprysing to enter England disguysed in apparell had scarce set foote therein when he was taken by the watche, and browght to king Edward at London, was commyttyd to warde" (p. 115). Edward now sent Warwick into France "to demand in marriage a young lady cawlyd Bone, syster to Carlot queene of France, and dowghter of Lewys duke of Savoy. But whyle the earle travalyed into France and delt with king Lewys touching this new affynytie, with whom this yowng lady Bone was attending uppon the queene, king Edwardes mynde alteryd uppon the soddayn. and he tooke to wyfe Elyzabeth, dowghter to Richard earle Ryvers, wyfe soomtyme to John Gray knight, by whom she had two soones, Thomas and Richerd; which mariage because the woman was of meane caulyng he kept secret" (p. 116). The nobility "found muche fault with him in that mariage, and imputyd the same to his dishonor, as the thing wherunto he was led by blynde affection, and not by reule of reason" (p. 117). And this was the reason of the strife that sprang up between Warwick and the king; or else it was made an occasion, as some thought, to utter a malice before conceived, for Edward had begun to be jealous of Warwick's power. Warwick did not reveal his feeling, however, reserving it for a time when the king should be in distress. There was besides a report, which "caryeth scome colour of truthe" (p. 117) ("nec abhorret a ueritate", p. 506), that

Edward had made an attempt against the honor of some woman in Warwick's house. Another rumor, that Warwick was angry because, contrary to his advice, Edward had married his sister to the Duke of Burgundy, whom the earl hated, Vergil puts aside as "a mere fabell of the common people". Whatever the cause, on receiving the news, Warwick "excusyd king Edward unto king Lewys as well as wold be", and returned to Edward. To him he made his report "without any shew of greife conceavyd" (p. 118). A few days later he left the court and united his brothers with him in his intended enterprise against the king. Montacute was not easily persuaded, "for he cowld never be movyd from the begyning to alow uppon any practyce agaynst king Edward; but in thende, whan therle of Warweke was promysed the ayd . . . of many noble men", he was induced to join the others (p. 120).

Warwick then approached Clarence, who "was for soome secrete, I cannot tell what cause, alyenated in mynde from his broother", and won him finally by promising him his daughter in marriage. They hastened together to Calais, and there "after the duke [Clarence] had sworne never to breake the promyse which he had made", he was married to the earl's eldest daughter Isabel. Meanwhile a rebellion was stirred up by Warwick's brothers in Yorkshire, in pursuance of the earl's wishes. On hearing of this, Warwick and Clarence returned to England, and fought a battle at Banbury with Edward's leader, the earl of Pembroke, who was defeated and beheaded, while Earl Rivers, father of the queen, and his son, John Woodville, were slain. Edward was captured in camp by Warwick, who "approchyd the kinges camp as secretly as he could in the night, and having kyllyd the watche and ward tooke the king unawares" (p. 124). Edward was sent to Middleham, under the care of the Archbishop of York, Warwick's brother, whence he escaped by bribing his jailers and through the aid of his friend Hastings made his way to London. Here Warwick and Clarence had a conference with him, but without result, both parties were so "replenyshyd with ire" (p. 126).

The battle of Edgecote followed, and Warwick and Clarence were forced to fly to France, and sought aid at the court of Louis. Here Margaret and her son joined them. A league was concluded, under the impulse of King Louis. Anne, daughter of Warwick, was affianced ["Eduardo despondetur"; the word should be noted] to prince Edward; the earl and duke promised by oath not to cease warring till the kingdom should be restored to Henry or his son; and Margaret and Edward on their part swore to make Clarence and Warwick protectors of the state till the prince should be old enough to take that charge upon himself. Warwick now descended upon England, where so many joined him that he was irresistible. Edward and Richard his brother fled to Flanders, while Queen Elizabeth went into sanctuary, where she brought forth a son, prince Edward. Henry was restored to the throne and Warwick was made protector of the realm, "with whom was joyned in commission the duke of Clarence" (p. 134).

"John marquyse Montacute came to that parlyament, who purgying his fault by long discours that his late inclyning to king Edwardes syde was for feare of lyfe onely, obtayned pardon that as he dyd the same unwillingly, so he should neuer afterward do his frinds good, for yf he had stand fast with king Edward lesse harme undoutydly showld he have doone being an open enemy than a faynyd frynd" (p. 134).

"During the same season Jaspar earle of Pembrowghe returnyd into Wales to his earledome, wher he fownd Henry, soone to his brother Edmund earle of Richemond, not fully x. yeres owld, kept as prysoner. but honorably browght up with the wyfe of William Herbert" [created Earl of Pembroke by Edward and beheaded after the battle of Banbury]. "This chylde dyd his mother Margaret . . . bring foorth whan she was scarse xIIIj^{ten} yeres

9*

owld, who thowghe afterward she maryed to Henry soone to Humfrey duke of Buckingham, and thirdly to Thomas earle of Darby, yeat never had any mo chyldren, as one thinking yt sufficient for hir to have browght into this world one onely, and suche a soone. And so Jaspar took the boy Henry ... and browght him with himself a lyttle after whan he cam to London unto King Henry. Whan the king saw the chylde, beholding within himself without speache a prety space the haultie disposition therof, he ys reportyd to have sayd to the noble men ther present, 'This trewly, this is he unto whom both we and our adversaryes must yeald and geave over the doymynion'. Thus the holy man shewyd yt woold coome to passe that Henry showld in time enjoy the kingdom".

In this account the translation omits a passage of the first edition: "Is est Henricus, qui deuicto Ricardo tertio Edouardi fratre, regnum, ut deinde dicetur, assecutus est, de quo illud credendum est, ut diuinitus ad regnum peruenerit, ad extinguendas tam Henrici quam Edouardi factiones Anglicae in primis nobilitati exitiosas, quando nihil fuit, quod potius fecerit" (p. 515).

Edward now landed in England with a force of scarce 2000 men. It is not likely, says Vergil, that he would have dared enter England with so small a force unless he had expected to receive great help; "by which reason, yt ys not to he dowtyd but the duke of Clarence was even than secretly reconcylyd unto him and that the marquyse also Montacute was becoome his partaker, wherof afterward the show was evydent" (p. 136). Yet as the countrymen failed to come over to him "he causyd yt to be blowen abrode that he sowght onely for his dukedom of Yorke", whereby the people were moved to favor him. As he approached York the gates were shut against him, and two chief men of the city informed him that he could not be admitted; but he sent them back bidding them tell the citizens that he came not to claim the crown, but only his dukedom. "The cytecynes wer soomwhat softenyd with king Edwardes aunswer, for that he semyd, as he sayd, to purpose no practyse agayst king Henry" (p. 138). "They commounyd with him from the waule" telling him that he might depart in safety, but if he remained his life would be in danger. Edward in return "gave curtesse speaches to every of tholder men and rewlers by name, cawling them worshippfull and grave magistrates" (p. 138) and making many fair promises. After nearly a whole day's parley the citizens agreed to admit him, if Edward would give his oath to treat the citizens courteously and from thenceforth to be obedient and faithful to King Henry. Next morning, while a priest said mass, "he emong the holy mysteryes promysyd by othe, devoutly and reverently, to observe both two", and was admitted.

"Thus oftentimes as well men of highe as of low cawling blyndyd with covetousnes, and forgetting all religyon and honesty, ar woont to make promyse in swearing by thimmortal God, which promyse neverthelesse they are already determynyd to breake before they make yt. Of this matter yt shall not yrk me to make mentyon in the lyfe of king Richerd the third ... wher perchaunce yt may be well conceavyd that thissew of king Edward did partycypate also the fault of this perjury" (p. 139).

Once within the walls of York, Edward put aside all memory of his oath — a heinous fact. Thence he set out for London, passing the army of Montacute, who had been ordered by Warwick to oppose Edward, but who made no resistance. Warwick now sent in haste for Clarence, "eaven than suspectyng that he was corruptyd by his broothers" (p. 141), and shut himself up in Coventry. When Clarence came within view of his brother's army, "Richerd duke of Glocestre, as thowghe he had bene apoyntyd arbyter of all controversy, first conferryd secretly with the duke; than he returnyd to king Edward, and dyd the very same with him" (p. 141). Here the translation again omits to render a passage in the first edition: "veruntamen Deus uisus est non remisisse duci meritas ob uiolatum iusiurandum poenas, quas postea miser crudeli morte pependit". Finally the brothers gladly embraced one another. Clarence sent messengers to Warwick, urging him to make some composition with the king, but when the duke's message was brought him, "first he accursyd and cryed owt uppon him, that contrary to his faith and promise geaven, he had in suche shamefull maner fled unto King Edward. . . . He gave none other awnswer but that he had rather be lyke himself than a false duke, and that therfor he wold not surcease the warre tylle ether he had lost his lyfe or wer revengyd uppon his ennemyes" (p. 142).

Edward now hastened to London, where he again took Henry prisoner. Warwick followed as far as Barnet. With him were the duke of Exeter, the earl of Oxford, the duke of Somerset and the marquis Montacute, "brother to therle [Warwick], whom therle himself perceavyd well now to serve in this warre agaynst his owne mynde, and therfor knew not how muche he might trust unto him, but the brootherlie loove tooke away almost all suspycion" (p. 144). After short speeches by Warwick and Edward to their respective armies, battle was joined, in which Edward, trusting to numbers, pressed on earnestly, while Warwick, "remembryng his renowmyd vertew and prowesse, resystyd valyantly" (p. 145). "He, with invincible corage, made way emongest the myddest of his enemyes, wher, whyle he entryd unadvysydly, beating down and killing thennemy, farre from his owne forces, him also was thrust throughe and slane, manfully fyghting, together with the marquise his broother, who folowyd him, having almost the victory in his hand . . This end happenyd unto him throwgh haultines of corage long before his tyme by course of yeres" (p. 146). This is a very different picture of Warwick and his death from that we have had before. In V.'s account of the battle, Gloucester is not once mentioned.

When Prince Edward and Margaret arrived in England and heard the news of Warwick's defeat, "the myserable woman swownyd for feare; she was distraught, dismayd, and tormentyd with sorow; she lamentyd the calamyty of the time, the adversity of fortune (p. 147), hir owne toyle and mysery; she bewaylyd the unhappy end of King Henry, which now she accowntyd assurydly to be at hand; and to be short, she so afflictyd hir self as one more desyrus to dy than lyve. . . . Than might quene Margaret have caulyd to mynde that these maner myschiefes had chancyd princypally for the death of Humfrey duke of Glocester, of which practise, thowgh percase she wer no partaker, yeat not giltles, because she myght have preservyd that good nobleman" (p. 148). In despair she took sanctuary, in the abbey of Beaulieu. Here she was found by Somserset and others, who sought a long while in vain to comfort her and give her courage. The queen refused to be persuaded and wished to send her son back to France; she was brought to consent to go on only by the firm determination of all the leaders to give battle. The battle was fought at Tewkesbury. The account of the battle is short, and there is no mention of the part Gloucester played in it. "Ther wer taken, Margaret the quene, Edward the prince, Edmund duke of Soomerset" and others. "Edward the prince and excellent yowth, being browght a lyttle after to the speache of king Edward, and demaundyd how he durst be so bowld as to enter and make warre in his realme, made awnswer, with bold mynde, that he came to recover his awncyent inherytance; hereunto king Edward gave no awnswer, onely thrusting the young man from him with his hand, whom furthwith, those that wer present wer George duke of Clarence, Richerd duke of Glocester, and William lord Hastings, crewelly murderyd" (p. 152).

Margaret was taken to London, and not long after, being ransomed, was sent back to France, where she lived in perpetual mourning.

Speaking of Edward's success, Polydore says: "Thus may we se that . . . . the good fortune of a man ys all" [cf. Rous on fortune's smiling upon Edward]. "Yeat yt may be peradventure that this came to passe by reason of thinfortunacy of the howse of Lancaster, which wyse men thowght eaven than was to be adscrybyd to the rightewousness of God; because the soveraignty extortyd forceably by Henry the Fourth, grandfather to king Henry the sixt, cowld not therby be long enjoyed of that famyly, and so the grandfathers offence redowndyd unto the nephews" (p. 154; not in the first edition of Vergil's work).

Then "to thintent every man might conceave a perfyte peace to be attainyd, and that all feare of enemyes might be abolisshed, Henry the Sixt . . was put to death in the tour of London. The contynuall report is, that Richard duke of Glocester killyd him with a sword [gladio], whereby his brother might be delyveryd from all fear of hostylytie. But who so ever wer the killer of that holy man, yt is apparant ynoughe, that as well the murtherer as the procurers thereof sufferyd punysshement for ther offences, who, whan as afterward they had none enemyes uppon whom to satisfy and satyate ther crueltie, exercysyd the same uppon themselves, as hereafter in place convenyent shalbe declaryd, and embrewyd ther handes in ther own bloode. Afterward the corse of king Henry was without any honor browght from the towre to Saint Paules churche, wher yt lay uppon the beere all one day, and the day folowing was caryed unto an abbay . . in Chertsey . . . and ther was buryed; but not long after yt was transferryd . . to . . Wyndsore" (p. 156).

There follows a description of Henry VI, not differing in character from that of other Lancastrian and Tudor writers, but more extended. "He dyd of his owne naturall inclynation abhorre all vices both of body and mynde, by reason wherof he was of honest conversation eaven from a chylde, pure and clene, partaken of none evell, ready to conceave all that was good, a contemner of all those thinges whiche commonly corrupt the myndes of men, so patient also in suffering of injuryes, receavyd now and then, as that he covetyd in his hart no revenge, but for the very same gave God Almighty most humble thankes, because therby he thought his sinnes to be wasshyd away; yea, what shalle we say, that this good, gratious, holy, sober, and wyse man, wold affirme all these myseryes to have happenyd unto him both for his owne and his ancestors manyfold offences" (p. 157).

Edward now started to make war with the duke of Burgundy against Lewis of France, but concluded a peace. He then induced the duke of Brittany to deliver up Richmond to his ambassadors, pretending that he meant to marry him to his daughter Elizabeth. Thus the duke had unwittingly "commyttyd the sheepe to the woolffe" thinking he had only given the son to the father. But being informed of his mistake, that he had delivered Henry "to be torn in peces by bloody butchers", he sent Peter Landoise, his treasurer, who overtook the ambassadors at St. Malo, and by a clever trick got Richmond into sanctuary, whence he afterward returned into Brittany.

Edward was busying himself with filling his coffers, and afterwards was showing himself a bountiful prince to the state, when "loe sudaynly he fell into a fact most horryble, commandyng rashly and uppon the suddane his brother George duke of Clarence to be apprehendyd and put to death, who was drowned (as they say) in a butte of malmesey" (p. 167). The cause of this act Vergil declares his inability to give, although he had inquired of many who were of authority in the king's counsel at the time. The report among the common people was that the king was afraid because of a soothsayer's prophecy that after Edward should reign someone the first letter of whose name should be G. "And because the devels ar wont in that sort to envegle the mynds of them who conceave pleasures in suche illusions" (p. 167), men said afterwards that the prophecy was fulfilled when Gloucester usurped the kingdom. Others declared the cause of hatred to be that Clarence desired to marry the daughter of the duke of Burgundy, and Edward hindered it out of jealousy. At the same time a servant of Clarence was executed for sorcery, "against which dede whan the duke could not hold him content, but vehemently speake and cry owt, the king muche movyd with this exclamation commyttyd the duke to warde, and not long after, being condemnyd, by right or wrong, put him to death. But yt ys very lykly that king Edward right soone repentyd that dede; for (as men say) whan so ever any sewyd [sued] for saving a mans lyfe, he was woont to cry owt in a rage, 'O infortunate broother, for whose lyfe no man in this world wold once make request'; affirming in that manyfestly, that he was cast away by envy of the nobylytie" (p. 168).

Gloucester and others were now sent against the Scots, and fought a successful campaign, which is very briefly described. Gloucester's share in it is confined to wasting the country and striking a truce with King James. Edward then intended to wage war on France, "but behold, while king Edward taketh care and thowght for these matters, he fell sicke of an unknowen disease", whereupon he reconciled himself to God and made his will, "wherin he constitutyd his soones his heyres, whom he commyttyd to the tuytion of Richerd his brother, duke of Glocester". And so he departed this life "being abowt fifty yeres old" (p. 175). Then follows a description of Edward, corresponding in all essentials to More's.

When Edward died, Richard was in Yorkshire, where he received letters from Hastings informing him of the event, and that the king had committed to him wife, children, goods, and all that he had; and urging Gloucester to repair to Wales and bring the young prince up to London. "Whan Richard had intelligence hereof he began to be kindled with an ardent desyre of soveraigntie" (p. 173). He wrote most loving letters to the queen, and at York "comandyd all men to sweare obedience unto prince Edward; hymself was the fyrst that tooke the othe, which soone after hee was the fyrst to vyolate" (p. 174).

Richard met Buckingham at Northampton and "as is commonly beleeved he eaven then discoveryd to Henry [Buckingham] his intent of usurpyng the kingdom" (p. 174). He did not realize that purpose meant extreme detriment to the state, and the utter subvertion of his house. "Surely so yt happeneth to graceles people, that who seketh to overthrow an other, his owne frawd, wicked and mischevous intent, his owne desperate boldenes, maketh him frantyke and mad" (p. 174). Nothing is said of Richard's agency, or Buckingham's, in lessening the train of the young prince. Anthony Woodville and Thomas Vaughan are the only two mentioned by name as arrested. The queen is said to have taken Dorset with her into sanctuary at Westminster; nothing is said of the Archbishop of York coming to her. Hastings, who had out of hatred to the marquis and others of the queen's side urged Richard to take upon him the government of the prince, repented of his action when he saw how matters turned out, and called a council of Prince Edward's friends in Paul's church. Here some urged that the prince should be rescued from Richard's hands, but it was determined to wait till Richard should arrive and give some reason for his act. Richard's speech to the nobles urging that the duke of York should be brought out of sanctuary differs wholly from More as regards the words, and largely in matter. Here Richard declares that he knows any harm to his nephews would redound to the harm of the state and of himself. "Therfor, seing that my [his] broother Edward our [their] king dyd uppon his death-bed constytute and appoint me [him] Protector of the Realme" (p. 176), he had brought his nephew where all might be associated in deciding what should be done. Rivers had attempted to hinder him in this, and had therefore been committed to prison. But worse had been done by those who had counselled the queen to fly with her children to sanctuary, a refuge meant for the poor, for debtors and those of lewd behavior, as if the protector intended them violence. This "womanish disease" creeping into the state needed remedy. What a sight if, when the king were crowned, his mother, brothers and sisters should be in sanctuary! Such a fact were really a violation of the majesty of the law. So Richard proposed that some should go to give her assurance, and induce her to yield up the duke of York that he might be present at his brother's coronation. So it was agreed that "Thomas archebisshop of Canterbury, Henry duke of Buchyngame, John lord Howard (p. 178)" should go. They succeeded in obtaining the duke.

Richard now conveyed his nephews to the Tower, which "causyd no suspytion, for that thusage ys at the kings coronation for the whole assembly to coom out from thence solemly and so procede to Westmynster. This doone, Richerd, whose mynde partly was enflamyd with desire of usurping the kyngdom, partly was trubblyd by guyltynes of intent to commyt so haynous wickednes (for a guiltie conscience causeth thoffendor to have dew punishment alway in imagination before his eyes)" (pp. 178—9) began to give large gifts to those he wished to win. Hastings, through fear of his power or through despair of winning him, he determined to rid out of the way.

Vergil's account of the council meeting varies somewhat from More's. There is no mention of Richard's first pleasant appearance. When the council was gathered and Richard's men posted outside, he said, "My lords, I have procuryd you all to be caulyd hyther this day for that onely cause that I might shew unto you in what great danger of death I stand; for by the space of a few days by past nether nyght nor day can I rest, drynk, nor eat, wherfor my blood by lyttle and lyttle decreaseth, my force fayleth, my breath shorteneth, and all the partes of my body do above measure, as you se (and with that he shewyd them his arme), faule away; which mischief veryly procedeth in me from that sorceres Elyzabeth the quene, who with hir witchcraft hath so enchantyd me that by thanoyance thereof I am dissolvyd" (p. 180). Thereupon

Hastings "who hatyd not duke Richard and was woont to speke all thinges with him very frely" answered that the queen ought to be punished, "yf yt might appeare that by use of witchcraft she had doone him any harme". Richard made the same assertion as before and Hastings the same answer. "Than Rycherd, to geve a sygne for them who wer withowt layd pryvyly for the nonce, spak with more shirle voyce: 'What than, William, yf by thine owne practises I be brought to destruction?' " (Quid igitur Gulielme, sic tuis rationibus ducar ad interitum? p. 536 1st ed. Translator evidently read si.) Whereupon the men without entered, and Hastings, the bishops of York and Ely, and Stanley were apprehended, and Hastings was at once beheaded.

"So the lord Hastinges learnyd, by his owne losse at the last, that the law of nature wherof the gospell speaketh (what soever you will that men do unto yow, do you so also unto them) can not be broken without punishment. He was one of the smyters of prince Edward, king Henry the vj$^{ths.}$ soon, who was fynally quyt with like maner of deth. Would God suche kind of examples might once be a learning for them who think yt lawfull to do whatsoever lyketh them" (p. 181). Vergil mentions rightly that Rivers and the rest were beheaded "soon after", not on the same day. So too there is no mention of the wonderful warnings Hastings had.

According to Vergil's account of Shaw's sermon, the preacher mentioned only the bastardy of King Edward himself; he expressly denies the common report that Shaw called Edward's children bastards. Richard was present at the sermon, but there is no mention of a trick whereby he was to appear at an opportune moment. As in More, Shaw died "shortly for very sorow". No mention is made of Penker. In Buckingham's speech in the Guildhall, he "delyveryd... duke Rychard's mynd", declared that Richard with right and justice "demaundyd the kingdom from the which he had bene defraudyd before by his broother Edward", and "therfor prayed that by ther authorytie they wold deale and determyn of so weyghtie a matter, wherbie he might, with good will of the commonaltie . . . enjoy once at the last his royall right" (p. 186). No man durst gainsay Richard's demand and determination, and on the next day he appeared as king. For his protection he sent for 5000 soldiers out of Yorkshire, commanded by Ratcliff, who turned aside at Pomfret to execute Rivers and his companions.

After Richard's coronation he went to Gloucester "where the whyle he taryed the haynous guylt of wicked conscyence dyd so freat him every moment as that he lyvyd in contynuall feare, for thexpecting wherof by any kind of meane he determynyd by death to dispatche his nephewys" (p. 187). When Brakenbury refused to fulfil his wishes he sent James Tyrell, who, being forced to do the king's commandment, rode sorrowfully to London, and "to the woorst example that hath been almost ever hard of, murderyd those babes of thyssew royall. Thys end had Prince Edward and Richarde his brother; but with what kinde of death these sely chyldren wer executyd yt is not certanely known" (p. 189). Vergil has a moving description (copied afterwards by Hall and Grafton and so passing into Shakespeare) of the queen's lamentation on hearing the news. She swooned and lay long lifeless; on recovering she made the house ring with her shrieks, striking her breast and cutting and tearing her hair, condemning herself for a mad woman in having given up her son. "But after long lamentation, whan otherwise she cowld not be revengyd, she besowght help of God (the revenger of falshed and treason) as assuryd that he wold once revenge the same" (p. 189). Who "wyll not tremble and quake, seing that suche matters often happen for thoffences of our ancestors, whose faults doo redownd to the posterytie? That fortunyd peradventure to these two innocent impes because Edward ther fathyr commytted thoffence of perjury, by reason of that most solemne othe . . . which he tooke at the gates of the cytie of

York ... and for that afterwardes, by reason of his brother the duke of Clarence death, he had chargyd himself and his posterytie before God with dew desert of grevous punysshement" (p. 190).

After his second coronation, in York, Richard called a parliament there. His only son Edward "abowt IX^{ne} yeres owld", was made prince of Wales, and "because ther was no myschyef, none adversytie, which the kinges head, guiltie of so many crymes, dyd not mystrust", Thomas Hutton was sent to induce the duke of Brittany to detain Richmond in prison. "Thus had kinge Richerd by a strange kinde of owtrageous creweltie attayned the type of glory and promotion, aud in the eye of the people was accountyd a happy man, whan as soon after he perceavyd himself to declyne from his state by lyttle and lyttle, that he could not kepe fast therein by any pollycy" (p. 191). For after the death of the princes, the people accused and detested him, and besought God to take extreme vengeance upon him. So Richard determined to turn over a new leaf and by good government make the people forget his past sins. But his purpose waxed cold again: for first he lost Edward his only son three months after he was made Prince of Wales, and then there arose the conspiracy of Buckingham. The cause assigned by Vergil for the dissension between Buckingham and Richard is the matter of the Hereford lands. Vergil does not mention that Richard promised the crown's half of these lands to Buckingham; so when Buckingham makes request for it, "king Richerd, who supposyd that matter to have bene now forgotten [i. e. that the crown half really belonged to Buckingham, after the death of Henry VI] ys reportyd to have awnsered furthwith in great rage: 'What now, duke Henry, will yow chalenge unto you that right of Henry the Fourth wherby he wickedly usurpid the crowne, and so make open fov yourself the way therunto?" (p. 193). Whereat, in indignation, Buckingham repaired to Brecknock and discovered to the bishop of Ely his purpose to overthrow Richard.

Here we reach the point where More's story ends.

Such was the real cause of dissension between the king and the duke, but among the people the rumor was current that Buckingham had not tried to dissuade Richard from his wicked deeds, to the end that he might eventually be driven out and Buckingham himself called to the throne.

Ely, continues Vergil, approved of Buckingham's plan and procured Renold Bray, a servant to Margaret, Richmond's mother, as a go-between, between the duke and Margaret. Now before the duke had began to be alienated from Richard, Margaret and Queen Elizabeth, communicating by a certain Lewis, physician to both ladies, had already entered upon a plan to bring Richmond to the throne, provided he married the princess Elizabeth, or in event of her death, Cecile, her sister. Margaret had evolved the plan, had had Lewis communicate it to Elizabeth as coming from himself, and the queen in joy had sent him back to Margaret to propose his plan to her. Now that Buckingham had devised the same plan, the way seemed clear. Bray rapidly brought others into the conspiracy. Margaret had intended to send to Henry with the news Christopher Urswicke, a priest introduced to her by Lewis. Now that Buckingham had joined the conspiracy, she sent a more important man, Hugh Conway. By another conspirator, Guilford, Thomas Ramney was sent, and the two messengers came to Henry at almost the same moment. Whereat Henry was wonderfully rejoiced, and communicated his hopes to the duke of Brittany, who promised aid, though Richard had tried hard to bribe him to give up Richmond, and messages were sent in return, urging on the conspirators.

Richard now became aware of the conspiracy, but wisely concealed his knowledge, that he might the more easily entrap his foes. Buckingham, whom he knew to be the chief conspirator, he determined to cut off at once, and summoned him to the court by "exceding curteous letters" and "many fayre promyses". Buckingham replied excusing himself on account of "infyrmytie of stomake". Richard would not admit the excuse, but sent again with threats, and now Buckingham was forced to declare himself. Thereupon other conspirators, including Dorset, began to stir. Richard with a large army marched toward Salisbury, and was within two days of the town, near which he expected to find Buckingham, when the latter's soldiers, a body of Welshmen, whom Buckingham had compelled to follow him "rather by rigorus commandment than for money", deserted their leader. Buckingham was compelled to fly, and took refuge in the house "of a certane servant [familiaris] of his namyd Humfrey Banyster, whom because he had found an honest man eaven from his chyldehoode [a puero bonum virum habuerat], therfor he trusted to fynde him most faythfull" (p. 199). Deprived of their leader the conspirators fled in different directions, most of them, including Dorset, to Henry in Brittany, others, including Ely, to Flanders.

Richard, to prevent the conspirators from getting away, and to intercept Henry, who, he now knew, was fitting out an expedition with the help of the duke of Brittany, sent soldiers to all the ports and fitted out ships to cruise in the channel. Banister, "whether for feare or money [Richard had offered a large reward — freedom to a bondman, to a freeman immunity and £ 1000] yt is scom dowt", betrayed his guests to Richard's searchers, who brought him to the king at Salisbury; and there having confessed, and vainly asked for the privilege of speaking with Richard, he was beheaded. "Hereof surely may we marke that he loseth his labor, and chargeth his owne lyfe with haynous offence, who helpeth an evell and wicked man, seing that he both receaveth of him for the most parte an evell dede for a good, and of God alway in the ende condigne punishment" (p. 201).

Meanwhile Richmond made an attempt to land in England. A sudden tempest arose and all his ships were driven back, except his own and one other, which came to Pole, on the south coast of England. There soldiers were seen on shore, and Richmond sent out a boat to inquire who they were. They asserted that they were Buckingham's men, who was near by with a large army, waiting for Richmond; and they urged him to land. But Richmond, suspecting fraud — the soldiers were in fact Richard's — sailed away to Normandy, whence he returned to Brittany. Here he learned that Buckingham had been beheaded and that Dorset and others were come to him. On Christmas Day in the church all took a solemn oath, Henry to marry Elizabeth, and the others to serve him as king. Then preparations began for a new attempt.

In England Richard had caught and put to death some of the conspirators, and had the others outlawed. Thomas Stanley, on account of his wife Margaret's acts came near being accounted one of the king's enemies, but the council absolved him, "as the woorking of a womans wit was thowght of smaule accounte", and ordered him to keep his wife at home under strict guard, removing all her servants from her.

Thus the conspiracy was crushed, but Richard was still in fear, "wherfor he had a myserable lyfe", and determined to end his trouble if possible. Messengers were despatched to the Duke of Brittany, promising him all the revenue from the lands of Richmond and those with him, if he would keep Richmond henceforth in prison. At this time the duke lay sick, and every thing was in the hands of Peter Landose, his treasurer. He, being in high disfavor with the nobility and thinking to win more power, not from any enmity to Richmond, whose life he had formerly saved, was ready to fulfil Richard's wishes. But Ely in Flanders got news of Richard's purpose, and warned Richmond, who contrived to escape into France, to the court of King Charles. — And now the earl of Oxford who had been imprisoned by King Edward in the castle of Hammes, came to Richmond, with his keeper, Sir James Blount.

Richard, disappointed in his attempt on Richmond's person, determined to attain his purpose in another way. So thinking whatever he might do but small matter in comparison with the horrible things he had done before, "ther cam therfor into his mynde matter the most wickyd to be spoken, and the fowlest to be commyttyd that ever was herd of". To prevent Henry's marriage with Elizabeth, he resolved to reconcile to himself the queen, that she might yield herself and her daughters into his hands, "and yf yt wer not possible to salve the sores immynent otherwyse, and that by hap it myght fortune his wyfe too dye, than he wold rather mary his nece himself than by thaffynytie aforesaid to danger the state". So he sent messengers to the queen promising "mountains" to her and her son Dorset. "The messengers being grave men, though at the first by reducyng [i. e. recalling] to memory the slawghter of hir soonnes they soomwhat wowndyd the quenes mynde, and that hir gryefe semyd scarse hable to be comfortid, yeat they assayed hir by so many meanes, and by so many fayre promisses, that withowt muche adoe they began to mollyfy hir (for so mutable is that sex), in so muche that the woman herd them willingly, and fynally sayd she wold yeald hir selfe unto the king; and so not very long after, forgetting injuryes, forgetting hir faith and promyse geaven to Margaret, Henryes mother, she first delyvered his dowghters into the handes of king Richerd; than aftir by secret messengers advysyd the marquyse her soon, who was at Parys, to forsake erle Henry, and with all spede convenyent to returne into England, wher he showld be sure to be caulyd of the king unto highe promotion. Whan the quene was thus qualyfyed, king Richerd receavyd all his brother's dawghters out of saintuary into the court" (p. 210).

All that remained was to "acquyte himself of marriage", but he was afraid, because he had of late counterfeited to be a good man. But his wicked intent won the mastery; he forbore to lie with his wife, and complained of her

10*

barrenness, especially to Rotherham, Archbishop of York, who, being wise in his generation, prophesied therefrom the queen's death. Richard now spread abroad a rumor that his wife was dead, either that Anne might on hearing it fall into a sickness, or to see how the people would take it if she should really die. When the queen heard of it, "supposing that hir days wer at an end", she demanded of her husband with tears why he had determined on her death. "Hereunto the king, least that he might seme hard hartyd (ferreus) yf he showld shew unto his wyfe no signe of loove, kissing hir, made answer loovingly, and comfortyng hir, bad hir be of good chere. But the quene, whether she wer dispatchyd with sorowfulness, or poyson, dyed within few days after". "Thys ys Anne that . . was soomtyme covenantyd ("desponsata", 1534 ed., "pacta", 1555 ed.) to prince Edward, soon to King Henry the sixt" (pp. 211—12).

Thus freed, Richard "began to cast an eye uppon Elyzabeth his nece, and to desyre hir in maryage; and because both the yowng lady hirself, and all others, did abhorre the wickednes so detestable", he determined to wait, especially as he was now troubled on every hand by the conspirators. Among them was William Stanley, whom Richard greatly distrusted; and when he applied for permission to go to his home, "for his pleasure as he sayd, but indede that he might be ready to receave erle Henry . . the king forbad him, and wold not suffer him to depart before he had left George lord Strange his soone as a pledge in the court" (p. 212).

News was now received that Oxford and Blunt had fled to Henry, and Richard sent to recover Hames castle which they had given over to the enemy. Then Richard heard that Henry was not succeeding in his attempt to gain aid at the French court; "which whan he belevyd to be so, as thowgh he had vanquisshed the whole warres, and had bene delyveryd from all feare, supposyd that ther was no cause why he showld take such care in a matter

of no danger" (p. 213). He therefore called home his
ships, but left men to guard the coasts, especially in Wales.
On the coast, to give notice of an enemy's approach, they
light lamps fastened upon great frames of timber, "and
with showtes through towne and fielde geave notice therof;
from thence others aftirward receave and utter unto ther
neighbors notice after the same sort. Thus ys the fame
therof caryed spedyly to all villages and townes, and both
country and towne arme themselves agaynst thenemy".
By such provision Richard was lulled into carelessness,
"for suche is the force of the divine justice, that as man
lesse seath, lesse provydeth, and lesse hede taketh when
he ys nighe the yealding of punishment" (pp. 213, 214).

Dorset, recalled by his mother, partly on this account
despairing of Richmond's success and partly suborned by
Richard's promises, fled from Richmond, but was overtaken
by Cheney and induced to return. Richmond now succeeded
in obtaining aid from King Charles, for which he left Dorset
and another as pledges, and at the mouth of the Seine
prepared his fleet. Here he heard of Richard's intention to
marry Elizabeth, which "pinchid Henry by the veray
stomak". He now determined to marry if possible the
sister of Walter Herbert, a man of great authority among
the Welsh, and so secure his aid, but the messengers
failed to reach him.

Receiving news that Richard Thomas and John Savage,
men of power in Wales, were ready to serve him, and
that Bray had money to pay soldiers, Henry set sail for
Wales with 2000 men on the 1st of August and came to
Milford Haven in Wales the seventh day after. [No speech].
Advancing through Darley he came to Haverford, where
he was well received, but learned that Thomas and Savage
were on King Richard's side. But the inhabitants of Pembroke sent to say "by Arnold Butler, a valyant man, de-
manding forgeavenes of ther former offences, that they
wer ready to serve Jaspar ther erle". Walter Herbert
was now said to be at hand with an army, and fear arose,

but the report was untrue. Now came over to Richmond a certain Griffin, and then John Morgan, and subsequently Richard Thomas, whom Henry had promised the perpetual lieutenancy of Wales. Henry now sent messages to Margaret his mother, to the Stanleys, to Talbot and others, and advanced to Shrewsbury.

Richard, who was at Nottingham, was informed that Henry had arrived, but that he "was utterly unfurnyshyd and feble in all things", while his own men were ready in all respects. So he thought the matter not much to be regarded, supposing that Henry would be captured by Herbert and Thomas. "But afterward, waynge with him self that a smaule matter in the warres made soome time great stirre, and that yt was a poynt of wysdom not to contemne the forces of hys enemye, though they were but smaule, he thowght best to provyde in time for the event to coom" (p. 219). So he sent at once for Northumberland, Brakenbury, Hungerford and others. Then it was reported to him that Henry had arrived at Shrewsbury; ,'with which message the king, much movyd, began with grief to be in a fervent rage, and cry vehemently out uppon the falshood of them who had broken promyse", and determined to go at once against his enemy. Henry advanced to Lichfield and thence to Tamworth, being met on his way by Hungerford and Burscher, who had fled from their leader Brakenbury by night. While on his way to Tamworth, Richmond, in great anxiety because he could get no word from Thomas Stanley, who did not appear openly on Richmond's side for fear of what Richard might do to his son, lingered on the road, lost all trace of his army, and wandered about till he came to a town three miles from his camp, where he spent the night in great fear of discovery. Next morning he returned to his army, who had been much alarmed for their leader, and said that he had been away of purpose to meet some secret friends. Afterwards he went secretly to Aderstone, and "here Henry dyd mete with Thomas and William

[Stanley], wher taking one an other by thand, and yealding mutuall salutation, eche man was glad for the good state of thothers, and all ther myndes wer movyd to great joy. After that they enteryd in cownsayle in what sort to darraigne battayl with king Rycherd" (p. 211).

In the meantime Richard had come with a huge number of men in arms to Bosworth, near Leicester. Here he refreshed his soldiers and "with many woords exhortyd them to the fyght to coome", the next day. "Yt ys reportyd that king Richerd had that night a terryble dreame; for he thowght in his slepe that he saw horryble ymages as yt wer of evell spyrytes haunting evydently abowt him, as yt wer before his eyes, and that they wold not let him rest; which visyon trewly dyd not so much stryke into his brest a suddane feare, as replenyshe the same with heavy cares: for furthwith after, being troublyd in mynde, his hart gave him theruppon that thevent of the battale folowing wold be grevous, and he dyd not buckle himself to the conflict with such lyvelyness of corage and countenance as before, which hevynes that yt showld not be sayd he shewyd as appallyd with feare of his enemyes, he reportyd his dreame to many in the morning. But (I beleve) yt was no dreame, but a conscyence guiltie of haynous offences, a conscyence (I say) so muche the more grevous as thoffences wer more great, which thowght [read: thowgh] at none other time, yeat in the last day of owr lyfe ys woont to represent to us the memory of our sinnes commyttyd, and withall to shew unto us the paynes immynent for the same, that, being uppon good cause penytent at that instant for our evell led lyfe, we may be compellyd to go hence in heavynes of hart" (p. 221—2).

The next day Richard arranged his forces for the battle. He drew out his vanward to a wonderful length, so full of footmen and horsemen that those who saw it were afraid; in the front were placed his archers under John duke of Norfolk. "After this long vanward folowyd the king himself, with a choyce force of soldiers" (p. 222).

Henry, who, "being departyd bak from the conference with his frinds began to take better hart", likewise arranged his forces and sent word to Thomas Stanley to come with his men. Stanley answered "that the earle showld set his owne folkes in order, whyle that he should coome to him with his army well apoyntyd. With which answer . . thowghe Henry wer no lyttle vexyd, and began to be soomwhat appallyd" he hastened to place his men in order. His vanward was small. In front of it he placed archers under the earl of Oxford; the right wing of the vanward was under Talbot, the left under Savage; he himself followed with one troop of horsemen and a few footmen. Henry's men numbered scarce 5000, besides the forces of the Stanleys, some 3000, while "the kings forces were twyse so many [and more, adds the translation. The original has "regiarum uerò copiarum bis alterum tantum fuit".] "Ther was a marishe betwixt both hostes, which Henry of purpose left on the right hand, that yt might serve his men instede of a fortresse, by the doing therof also he left the soon upon his bak; but whan the king saw thenemyes passyd the marishe, he commandyd his soldiers to geave charge uppon them". The battle was being hotly contested when Richard caught sight of Richmond; "wherfor, all inflawyd with ire, he strick his horse with the spurres, and runneth owt of thone syde withowt the vanwardes agaynst him". "King Richerd at the first brunt killyd certane, overthrew Henryes standerd, toygther [togyther] with William Brandon the standerd bearer", and threw the stout Cheney to the ground, "making way with weapon on every syde". Henry received Richard courageously and was holding him at bay better than his own soldiers would have expected, when William Stanley with his 3000 men came to the rescue. "Than trewly in a very moment the resydew all fled, and king Richerd alone was killyd fyghting manfully in the thickkest presse of his enemyes" (p. 224).

Among the men killed on Richard's side were John duke of Norfolk, Walter Lord Ferrers, Robert Brakenbury, and Richard Ratcliff. Catesby was executed at Leicester two days later. On Henry's side the chief loss was that of William Brandon. Among the captives was Henry, earl of Northumberland, who "as a frind in hart [uoluntarius amicus] was receavyd into favor" (p. 225).

"The report is that king Richerd might have sowght to save himself by flight; for they who wer abowt him, seing the soldiers even from the first stroke to lyft up ther weapons febly and fayntlye, and soome of them to depart the feild pryvyly, suspectyd treason, and exhortyd him to flye, yea and whan the matter began manyfestly to qwaile, they browght him swyft horses [read: "a swift horse"; orig. has "equum uelocem"]; but he, whe was not ignorant that the people hatyd him, owt of hope to have any better hap afterward, ys sayd to have awnsweryd, that that very day he wold make end ether of warre or lyfe, suche great fearcenesse and suche huge force of mynd he had: wherfor, knowinge certanely that that day wold ether yeald him a peaceable and quyet realme from thencefurth or els perpetually bereve him the same, he came to the fielde with the crowne uppon his head, that therby he might ether make a beginning or ende of his raigne. And so the myserable man had suddaynly suche end as wont ys to happen to them that have right and law both of God and man in lyke estimation, as will impyetie, and wickednes" (p. 225, 226).

Henry forthwith gave thanks to Almighty God, then from a hill near by commended his soldiers, commanded to cure the wounded and bury the slain, and thanked his nobles for their assistance. Thereupon Stanley set Richard's crown, found among the spoil, upon his head, "as thoughe he had bene already by commandment of the people [populi jussu] proclamyd king after the maner of his auncestors" (p. 226).

The body of Richard, nakyd of all clothing, and layd uppon an horse bake with the armes and legges hanginge downe on bothe sydes was browght to thabbay of monks

Franciscanes at Leycester, a myserable spectacle in good sooth, but not unwoorthy for the mans lyfe, and ther was buryed two days after without any pompe or solemne funerall" (p. 226).

Then follows a description of Richard. "He was lyttle of stature, deformyd of body, thone showlder being higher than thother (corpore deformi; altero humero eminentiore), a short and sowre cowntenance, which semyd to savor of mischief, and utter evydently (clamitare) craft and deceyt. The whyle he was thinking of any matter, he dyd contynually byte his nether lyppe, as thowgh that crewell nature of his did so rage agaynst yt self in that lyttle carkase. Also he was woont to be ever with his right hand pulling out of the sheath to the myddest, and putting in agane, the dagger which he did alway were. Trewly he had a sharp witt, provydent and subtyle, apt both to counterfayt and dissemble; his corage also hault and fearce, which faylyd him not in the very death, which whan his men forsooke him, he rather yealded to take with the sword, than by fowle flyght to prolong his lyfe, uncertane what death perchance soon after by sicknes or other vyolence to suffer (quam per turpem fugam, incertae ac fortasse pòst paulò morbo uel supplicio interiturae uitae parcere").

Speaking of Henry's restoration Vergil has a passage (p. 514 1st ed.) which does not appear in the translation because not in the 1556 edition. The last sentence of it (1556 ed. p. 531) appears in the translation, however, where Vergil shows avoidance of error would have brought good fortune to Henry and not Edward. I transcribe the passage as it is translated in Hall (p. 285), omitting a slight addition of Hall's own.

Thus Henry "after so many ouerthrowes beginnynge to reygne, lykely within short space to fall agayn, & to taste more of his accustomed captuitie & vsuall misery. This yll chance & misfortune, by many mēs opiniōs happened to him, because he was a man of no great wit [longe innocentissimus], whose study always was more to excell, other in Godly liuynge & vertuous example, then in worldly regiment, or temporall dominion, in so much, that in cōparison to the study & delectation that he had to vertue and godlines, he littel regarded, but in manner despised al worldly power & temporal authoritie, which syldome folow or seke after such persons, as frō them flye or disdayne to take them. But his enemies ascribed all th:s to hys coward stommack, afferming that he was a man apt to no purpose, nor mete for any enterprise, were it neuer so small: But who so euer dispiseth or dispraiseth, that which the cōmon people allow and marueyll at, is often taken of them for a mad & undiscrete person, but notwithstandyng the vulgare opiniō, he that folowyth, loueth and embraseth the contrary, doth proue bothe sad and wyse the wisedom of this world, is folishenes before God. Other there be that ascribe his infortunitie, onely to the stroke and punishment of God, afferning that the kyngdome, whiche Henry the .IIII. hys grandfather wrongfully gat, and vniustly possessed agaynst kyng Rychard the .II. and his heyres could not by very diuyne iustice, longe contynew in that iniurious stocke: And that therfore God by his diuine prouidence, punished the offence of the grandfather, in the sonnes sonne".

Next to More's biography, the history of Polydore Vergil is of greatest importance in the development of the Richard saga. More's work covered only the period from the death of Edward IV to the rebellion of Buckingham: Vergil's included the history of Richard from the reign of Henry VI to Richard's end at Bosworth. As More's work was included bodily in the succeeding chronicles, so was Vergil's history, bodily or as a basis, adopted for that part of Edward's and Richard's reigns not touched upon by More. As will be seen later, Grafton's continuation of Hardyng is Vergil's where it is not More's; Hall used Vergil in the same way, though with considerable additions; Grafton's chronicle copied Vergil's work as it appeared in Hall; Holinshed copied Hall and Grafton; Stow copied Hall. Thus the saga of Richard as it came to Shakespeare, so far as it is not More's is almost wholly Vergil's.

To Vergil is mostly due the definitive form of the accepted account of Richard's early life. By Vergil first is assigned to Richard a share in Prince Edward's death. Fabyan had reported that King Edward had questioned the captured prince and struck him with his gauntlet for an answer contrary to his pleasure; in Vergil question and answer are for the first time given. In Fabyan the prince is murdered by "the king's servants"; in Vergil the murderers are Clarence, Richard and Hastings. According to Vergil, Richard, as commonly reported, slew King Henry that Edward might have no more enemies to fear. No share in Clarence's death is ascribed to Richard by Vergil; and there is no suggestion in his account of Edward's reign that Richard at that time cherished any designs upon the crown. Throughout the account Richard appears, as he calls himself in Shakespeare's play, a pack-horse in Edward's great affairs, his devoted and faithful partisan. Thus it is that the later chronicles, following Vergil's account of Edward's reign, and then copying More's book, present two views of Richard, which if really less inconsistent with each other than has sometimes been asserted, have nevertheless a very different coloring. Shakespeare avoided all inconsistency, as Oechelhäuser pointed out, by adopting More's view of Richard's character from the beginning, while he used Vergil's account of the events in Richard's early life, as found in Hall and Holinshed.

Among the special contributions of Vergil's own to the history of this early period there is little that calls for special mention. To him however is due the anecdote dramatized by Shakespeare (R. III. 2, 1.) according to which Edward always called to mind, when ever any sued for a man's life, that none had sued for the life of his unfortunate brother Clarence. But if Vergil's own contributions are of no great importance, it is of great importance, considering the later acceptance of his account, to note what he included from the varying accounts of others. To him, for example, and not to Rous, was due the transmission of the famous prophecy about G. To him was due the accurate account of Warwick's mission to the Lady Bona of France, which More incorrectly reported as a mission to the king's daughter of Spain. To him and not to André is due the accepted account of the prophecy of Henry VI concerning the boy Richmond. To him it is due that the accepted picture of Warwick was that of a brave man, and not of a coward, as he was represented by the author of "The Arrival", by Warkworth and by de Comines. In the first two of these accounts Warwick dies an ignominious death, caught in his flight; in Vergil he is the bravest of the brave, slain as he fights alone in the very midst of the enemy — the Shakespearian Warwick.

Vergil's account of the events from Edward's death to Buckingham's rebellion presents some interesting points of comparison with that of More. It must not be forgotten, however, that it was unused by the later chroniclers, who all followed More.

In Vergil, as in André, Richard is represented as made protector by Edward — a provision in Edward's will, according to Vergil, and also of Edward's death-bed speech. The date set for the inception of Richard's purpose to reign is the death of Edward. He takes an oath of allegiance to Edward in York, as one of his hypocritical devices toward the attainment of his purpose. In the account of the Council meeting in the Tower it is notewortly that no mention is made of Shore's wife, and there is therefore no hint that Hastings in being connected with her was thus connected with her sorcery. Buckingham's speech at Guildhall presents a Richard entirely different from More's picture of the Richard whose movements were directed toward inducing the citizens to ask him to become king, while he himself protested against it. Accordingly there is no mention of any visit of the mayor and aldermen to Baynard castle. Vergil declares that there is no certain knowledge of the way in which the young princes were murdered — a noteworthy statement, considering that Vergil wrote long after the so-called confession of Tyrell, on which More depended, had been given to the world.

From this point on, Vergil's account — subsequently slightly increased by Hall, forms the definitive and accepted version of the closing events of Richard's reign. Thus he is responsible for the account of Richard's intrigues with Queen Elizabeth, his plot against his wife's life, his attempt to marry his niece, the conspiracy of Richmond, the short campaign that led to the battle of Bosworth, Richard's dream, and his brave death on the field of battle, refusing to fly on the swift horse provided for him. It is distinctive of the general sanity and impartiality of Vergil's account that he does not attempt to decide whether Anne's death was due to poison or to sickness. Richard's famous dream first mentioned by the Croyland continuator, is first described by Vergil.

Vergil's description of Richard's person is very similar to that of More. But there is no direct statement that he was hump-backed, the words "corpore deformi, altero humero eminentiore" leaving us somewhat in doubt as to that in which the deformity of body consisted. It is not impossible that the second phrase was meant as an explanation of the first, and that according to Vergil, Richard's deformity consisted only in having one shoulder higher than the other.

Richard's character as it appears in Vergil is practically the same as in More. His hypocrisy and craft are by no means so strongly emphasized, however; while on the other hand a real contribution is made in Vergil's picture of Richard's state of mind as his end approached.

The Richard whose conscience makes fearful forebodings of the battle's outcome, and who is yet determined to set his life upon the cast and stand the hazard of the die; who in the conflict enacts more wonders than a man, seeking for Richmond in the throat of death; who, abandoned even by those on whom he has most depended, fights on alone, with gigantic will crushing conscience, foreboding and fear, expending all his power in the unrelinquished pursuit of his purpose; the Richard, who, having ventured all for a kingdom, will die a king if he cannot live a king — this is Vergil's Richard.

In Vergil's handling of his story two things are especially noticeable. More had most vividly pictured the torment of conscience that followed upon Richard's murder of his nephews. This torment Vergil insists upon and emphasizes still further. It begins even before Hastings is put to death, produced by the consciousness of guilty intent; after this "the haynous guilt of wicked conscyence" so frets Richard at every moment that he lives in continual fear, and that he determines to rid himself of it by any means, even by the fresh crime of the princes' death — he is in "so far in blood, that sin will pluck on sin"; guilty of so many crimes that there is "no myschief, none adversytie" he does not fear; and last of all, conscience vitalizes its most terrible torments in the devils of that fearful dream which foretells Richard's end. With this insistence upon the power of conscience may be noticed the passage in which Richard, at the very moment when he has attained the end of his ambition, "the type of glory and promotion", and is accounted by all a happy man, perceives that he is beginning to slip from his height and that nought will avail to keep him there. This moment is the dramatic crisis of his career, and Vergil's Richard whose eyes are at this moment of success opened to see the end, is the Richard of Shakespeare whose first thought upon mounting his throne is

> Thus high . . . .
> . . . . is King Richard seated: —
> But shall we wear these honours for a day?
> Or shall they last, and we rejoice in them? (4 : 2.)

A more important contribution in Vergil's handling of the story is his favorite motive of the divine vengeance. This had been as we have seen to some extent employed by nearly every writer, most of all by André, who had shown in the cases both of Richard and of Edward the divine justice paying death for death. Vergil goes much farther than this. In his story Henry the sixth in all his calamities but pays the penalty for his grandfather's offence of usurpation; Margaret's disasters are the punishment for her complicity in the murder of Humphrey, the good duke of Gloucester; Henry's death is avenged by the destiny which leads the victorious members of the house of York to turn their hands upon each other; in the death of his children Edward pays the penalty for his perjury at York and for his murder of Clarence; Hastings perishes because he was of those that slew Prince Edward; Buckingham falls because he aided the wicked designs of Richard.

In such a view we are not far from that idea of destiny which, as Moulton and others have shown, rules Shakespeare's play of Richard III and forms its plot. There every bloody deed, every act of perjury and unfaithfulness in the whole long tragedy of the York-Lancastrian struggle is revenged of God; and each of the long row of murders becomes at the same time crime and punishment for crime. This conception, there can be little doubt, is due to the account of Polidore Vergil.

Shakespeare's application of the idea of Destiny to the character of Richard finds its germ also in Vergil. He too indicates that the hand of Destiny has been over Richard from the moment he conceives his wicked purpose. He cannot see that his intent means not his elevation, but the utter subvertion of his own house. Like every one who seeks to overthrow another, "his owne frawde, wicked and mischevous intent, his owne desperate boldenes" is really making him "frantyke and mad".

XIII. Rastell's "The Pastime of People or the Chronicles of Divers Realms".

John Rastell was born towards the end of the 15th century, and died in 1536. He married Elizabeth, the sister of Sir Thomas More. He was a printer by trade and published several legal works, including the first abbreviation of the English statutes, together with a Dialogue of Syr Thomas More and a number of other books. His best known book is "The Pastyme of People: the chronicles of dyuers Realmys and most specyally of the Realme of Englonde" published 1529.

This was, as the author declares upon the title page, "briefly compiled, and imprinted in Cheapside, by John Rastell". In the part covering the reigns of Edward IV, Edward V, and Richard III it is little more than an abridgement of Fabyan. He has, however, an extended account of current opinions coucerning the death of the princes and the disposal of their bodies, part of which seems to reappear in Hall and Grafton.

I quote from the 1811 edition of Dibdin.

"Of the maner of the dethe of this yonge kynge, and of his brother, there were dyuers opinyons; but the most cōmyn opinyon was, that they were smolderyd betwene two fetherbeddes, and that, in the doynge, the yonger brother escaped from vnder the fetherbeddes, and crept under the bedstede, and there lay naked a whyle, tyll that they had smolderyd the yonge kyng so that he was surely dede; and after y^t, one of them toke his brother from vnder the bedstede, and hylde his face downe to the grounde with his one hande, and with the other hande cut his throte bolle a sonder with a dagger. It is a meruayle that any man coude haue so harde a harte to do so cruell a dede, saue onely that necessyte compelled

Palaestra. X. 11

them, for they were so charged by the duke, the protectour, that if they shewed nat to hym the bodyes of bothe those chylderne dede, on the morowe after they were so cōmaunded, that than they them selfe shulde be put to dethe. Wherfore they that were so cōmaunded to do it, were compelled to fullfyll the protectours wyll.

And after that, the bodyes of these . II . chylderne, as the opinyon ranne, were bothe closed in a great heuy cheste, and, by the meanes of one that was secrete with the protectour, they were put in a shyppe goynge to Flaunders; and whan the shyppe was in the blacke depes, this man threwe bothe those dede bodyes, so closed in the cheste, ouer the hatches into the see; and yet none of the maryners, nor none in the shyppe, saue onely the sayd man, wyst what thynges it was that was there so inclosed. Whiche sayenge dyuers men coniectured to be trewe, because that the bones of the sayd chylderne coulde neuer be founde buryed, nother in the Towre nor in no nother place.

Another opinyon there is, that they whiche had the charge to put them to dethe, caused one to crye sodaynly, 'Treason, treason'. Wherwith the chylderne beynge a ferde, desyred to knowe what was best for them to do. And than they bad them hyde them selfe in a great cheste, that no man shulde fynde them, and if any body came into the chambre the wolde say they were nat there. And accordynge as they counselyd them, they crepte bothe into the cheste, whiche, anone after, they locked. And than anone they buryed that cheste in a great pytte vnder a steyre, which they before had made therfore, and anone cast erthe theron, and so buryed them quycke. Whiche cheste was after caste into the blacke depes, as is before sayde" (pp. 292—293).

XIV. The Continuation of Hardyng's Chronicle.

In 1543 Richard Grafton published from manuscripts in his possession two editions of the verse chronicle of John Hardyng. This ended with the beginning of Edward IV's reign, and Grafton added a prose continuation bringing the work down to the year of publication. In his preface "To the Reader" he stated:

"I haue here, to the vttermost of my poore wit, gathered and set foorth vnto you thesaid histories, not in metre, like as Iohn Hardyng hath dooen before, partely because would therby declare a dyfference betwene the former wrytyng of Iohn Hardyng and this my addicion, but specially that these excellent storyes should nether in sence nor wordes bee defaced of the eloquence and great grace that the autoures of thesame haue all readie geuen theim, and therfore haue I wrytten theim vnto you in prose and at length".

This continuation copied the work of More. What follows after is a translation of Polydore Vergil, somewhat mangled in places, often abridged, making omissions, many errors of translation and some slight additions; but in all essentials, nevertheless, a mere translation of Vergil. This fact, in spite of the clear statement in Grafton's preface that he sets forth what others have written, appears wholly to have escaped the attention of those who have previously noticed the continuation. Sidney Lee, in the Dic. Nat. Biog. sub Hardyng, says that Grafton "added a prose continuation by himself". Öchelhäuser, whose sole reference to Vergil is to say that he does not deserve mention as a writer of any importance on this period of history (p. 53), speaks always of the "Grafton'schen Fortführung von More's Arbeit" (p. 132) or of "dem späteren, nicht mehr von More herrührenden Theil der Chronik", without knowing that the continuation of the story in Hall, Grafton and Holinshed is based on Vergil's story. Morley (Eng. Writers, 7 : 270), mentions the continuation without assigning any authorship, and (8 : 359) calls it Grafton's first work as an original chronicler. Ellis, in the preface to his edition of the Hardyng Chronicle (1812), after speaking of More's work, says, "The remainder of the Continuation of Hardyng is indisputably Grafton's" (Introd.

XXI). The editor mentions two editions of Grafton's Hardyng both printed in January 1543 and differing in almost every page. One he prints, while the variant readings of the other are given in footnotes. Had he known that Grafton's continuation was a translation of Vergil he would doubtless have elected to print in the body of the work the other edition whose readings in more than three cases out of four are correct and faithful translation of the original while the others are not.

Most strangely of all, Dr. Lumby, who edited, in connection with his edition of More's Life, that portion of the Hardyng continuation which carries on the story from where More ceases to the end of Richard's life, seems never to have had a suspicion that he was dealing with a translation, a fact which led him to make some odd notes about incorrect and suspicious passages, about peculiar uses of language — really caused by literal translation of the original Latin — and on the wrong dating of the Battle of Bosworth, 1486 — which is Vergil's error — as evidence that the Hardyng continuation like More's work is rough and unrevised.

The account of the reign of Edward IV in the Hardyng continuation is in general a faithful translation of the work of Polydore Vergil. There are a very few slight additions and some slight omissions; in a few places the account of Vergil is abridged without doing any violence to the facts.

I note below the only important changes, quoting from Ellis's edition.

In the account of Edward's attempt in Warwick's house the edition used by Ellis follows Vergil (cf. p. 130); the other has "whether he wolde have violated the erles niece or another damosel in the erles house, all men knewe not" (p. 439).

The rumor that Warwick was angry because Edward proposed to marry his sister to the duke of Burgundy (cf. p. 130) is omitted.

In the edition used by Ellis, Vergil's account of Edward's escape from Middleton by bribery is follcwed; the other edition has: "But the kyng hym self spake fayre to the archebishop, and as the fame went, corrupted ether the bishop or his seruantes. So that one date he had licence to go a huntyng, and by the waie ther met with hym sir William A Parre, sir Thomas Abowrogh the lord Haward, and diuerse other of his seruantes, with suche a multitude, that the archebishop nor all his frendes durst not folowe the escape" (p. 443).

On the union of Prince Edward and Anne, the Hardyng continuation translates Vergil "Anne . . was maried and desponsed to prynce Edwarde" (p. 447).

In the mention of Edward's perjury at York as punished by the death of his children, the Hardyng continuation has, translating Vergil, "Of this thing I will speake more in Rychard the third". The account of Richard III. however, the continuation took not from Vergil but from More, and thus the passage referred to is wanting.

The description of Henry VI is omitted.

The account of Edward's proceedings in France is somewhat abridged.

Vergil's mention of Edward's reconciliation to God, and of his will, is omitted. Thus there is no statement in the Hardyng continuation that Edward appointed Richard protector.

More's work is adopted bodily by the Hardyng continuator: again without mention of the author.

The opening paragraphs of More are placed after the death-bed speech of Edward, and others a little later disarranged, so that the story here begins with More's account of Richard duke of York, preceded by a short introductory paragraph.

Of York's claim the continuation says in addition that the parliament where it was adjudged was "holden $\overset{e}{y}$ .xxx. yere of kyng Henry the .vi." (p. 468). The description of York as "a noble manne and a mightie" is omitted.

In the description of Richard's face, as "in states called warlye, in other menne otherwise" we have for the latter phrase "and amonge commen persons a crabbed face".

To the statement that Richard slew King Henry is added: "saiyng, 'Nowe is there no heyre male of kyng Edward the thyrde, but we of the house of Yorke'" (p. 469).

In speaking of Edward's last sickness there is added in parenthesis: "whiche continued longer then false & fantasticall tales haue vntruly & falsely surmised, as I my self that wrote this pamphlet truly knew".

To More's account of Richard's birth the Hardyng continuation adds that his mother "could not be deliuered of hym uncut". It states that Richard was in the north at the time of Edward's death, "for the good gouernance of the countrye" (p. 474).

The statement of Buckingham's message through Persall (the other edition has Persivall) appears in the Hardyng continuation at the very beginning of the story (p. 475) not, as in More, when the conspiracy of Buckingham against Richard is discussed. To the names of those arrested by Richard at Stony Stratford is added that of Sir Richard Hawte (p. 479).

To More's account of Richard's reverent bearing toward Edward, as his train entered the city, the Hardyng continuation adds: "saying to all men as he rode, 'Beholde youre prynce and souereygne lorde'" (p. 481).

The cardinal sent to induce the queen to give up her younger son is "my lorde cardinall archbishop of Cauntourbury" (p. 482) not of York, as in More.

In the account of the dedication of Westminster by St. Peter there is no mention of the angel or of St. Peter's cope.

The name of "the other lord" who accompanied the cardinal to the queen and took part in the discussion is given as "the Lord Haward" (p. 488).

The queen's mention of her taking refuge in the sanctuary when Edward was driven from the kingdom, and of the birth of her son there, is not in the Hardyng continuation. The passage, as Rastell indicates in a marginal note of his edition of More, "was not written by M. More in his history written by him in Englishe, but is translated oute of this history which he wrote in Laten". Several such passages from the Latin version occur, and none are in the Hardyng continuation, the author of which had evidently seen only the English version.

A second such passage omitted in the continuation is that in which More represents Richard as opening his purpose to Buckingham as soon as he had the children in his possession, and winning him to his side by means of "suttell folks" who showed him that he could not now go back, and by Richard's promise of the earldom of Hertford, with a quantity of treasure.

To the mention of Leicester as the seat of Hastings' power is added Northampton (p. 493). In the account of the Council Richard says "had bene a sleper", not "a slepe" as in More (cf. p. 91).

In the account of the meeting of the council where Hastings lost his head, the Hardyng continuation adds: "Then was the Archebyshop of Yorke and doctoure Morton byshoppe of Ely and the lorde Stanleye taken and dyuers other, whyche were bestowed in dyuers chambers" (p. 495). In the account of Hastings' warnings, the unnamed knight who came to escort Hastings to the Tower is named by the Hardyng continuation, which reads, "The same morning ere he were vp from his bed where Shores wife laye w^t hym all night, there came to hym sir Thomas Haward, soone to the lorde Hawarde (the whiche sturryng that mornyng very earlye) as it were of courtesye to accompaignie hym to the counsaill. but forasmuche as the lorde Hastynges was not readye he tarried awhile for hym and hasted hym awaye".

To the account of the beheading of Rivers and the others at Pomfret the Hardyng continuation adds: "Syr Thomas Vaughan, goyng to his deathe, saied, 'A wo woorth theim that toke the prophecie that .G. should destroy kyng Edwardes children, meaning that by the duke of Clarence lord George, which for that suspicion is nowe dead, but nowe remayneth Richard G. duke of Gloucetre, whiche nowe I see is hee that shall & wyll accomplishe the prophecye & destroye kyng Edwardes chyldren & all theyr alyes & frendes, as it appereth by vs this daye, whom I appele to the hygh tribunal of God for his wrongful murther and our true innocencye'. And then Ratclyffe saied, 'you haue well apeled, laye downe your hed'. 'Ye', quoth syr Thomas, 'I dye in ryght, beware you dye not in wrong'; and so that good knight was beheded and ẙ other .III. and buried naked in the monastery at Pomfret" (p. 501).

For More's "John Shaa" and "freer Penker" the Hardyng continuation has "Raffe Shaa" and "freer Pynkie" (p. 501).

In the review of the circumstances of Edward's marriage, where More mentions the sending of Warwick to claim the hand of "the kinges doughter of Spain", the Hardyng continuation, in accordance with its former account, substitutes "Bona syster to the Frenche kyng" (p. 502).

The anger of Warwick and his subsequent proceedings are omitted as having been mentioned before.

In the account of the appeal of the nobles and citizens to Richard at Baynard's castle, the Hardyng continuation makes Richard stand in the gallery, "w^t [with] a bishop on euery hand of him" (p. 513).

More's account of Richard's visit to Westminster, where he proclaimed himself king and pardoned Fogge is, together with the brief mention of the coronation, translated from the Latin history, and is therefore wanting in the Hardyng continuation. His account of the procession to Westminster is as follows.

"Rychard the thirde of that name, vsurped the croune of England, and opennly tooke vpon hym to be kyng the .XIX. daye of Iune, in the yere of our Lord a thousand foure hundreth and .LXXXIII. and in the .XXV. yere of Lewes the .XI. then beyng Frenche kynge, and the morow after, he was proclaymed kyng and with greate solempnitee rode to Westminster, and there sate in the seate royale, and called before hym the iudges of the realme, streyghtly commaundynge theim to execute the lawe without fauoure or delaye, with many good exhortacions (of the whiche he folowed not one) and then he departed towarde the abbaye, and at the churche doore he was met with procession, and by the abbot to hym was delyuered the sceptre of saint Edward, and so went and offred to saint Edwardes shrine, whyle ye monkes sange Te deum with a faynt courage, and from the churche he retourned to the palayce, where he lodged tyll the coronacion. And to bee sure of all enemyes (as he thought), he sent for five thousande menne of ye North against his coronacion whiche came vp euell apparelled and worsse harneyssed, in rustie harneys, neyther defensable nor scoured to the sale, whiche mustered in Fynesbury felde, to the great disdayne of all the lokers on" (p. 516).

On the fourth Richard visited the Tower with his wife; on the fifth he elevated certain of the nobles in rank, delivered Lord Stanley "out of warde for feare of his sonne the lorde Straunge, whiche was then in Lancasshyre gatheryng menne (as menne saied), and the saied lorde was made stuard of the kynges housholde, likewyse the archbyshoppe of Yorke was deliuered, but Morton bishop of Ely was deliuered to the duke of Buckingham to kepe in warde, whiche sent hym to his manoure of Brecknoke in Wales" (p. 516).

In the account of the murder of the princes, for More's statement that all attendants, "onely one called black Wil or William Slaughter except", were removed from the princes, the Hardyng continuation has: "one called blacke Wyll, and Wyllyam Slaughter onely excepte, whiche were sette to serue theim, and .IIII. other to see theim sure" (p. 520).

To More's statement that Tyrell devised that the princes should be murdered in their beds is added: "and no bloude shed" (p. 520). To the account of the disposal of the princes' bodies is added, "Some saie that kyng Rychard caused y̆ᵉ preest to take theim vp & close theim in lead put theim in a coffine full of holes hoked at y̆ᵉ endes with .II. bokes of yron, & so to caste them into a place called y̆ᵉ Blacke depes at the Thamis mouth, so y̆ᵗ thei shold neuer rise vp nor bee sene agayn" (p. 521). Here Rastell's account may have been the basis (cf. p. 162).

In the analysis of the Hardyng continuation's extension of More's story I concern myself with such changes and mistranslations only as are of importance from the form given to the facts of the story, or from later use by Hall and Legge.

Grafton welded Vergil's story to More's by passing directly from the last speech of Ely, as given by More (see p. 116), to Vergil's account of the duke's proposal to make Richmond king (see p. 144), by the short transitional statement that Ely's words induced Buckingham "to entre more plaine cōmunicacion with hym, so farre", that the bishop declared himself ready to help depose Richard (p. 525).

Almost at the very beginning of the continuation Grafton begins to mangle his original, by omitting Vergil's mention of the popular rumor that Buckingham helped Richard in order that the latter's crimes might eventually bring himself to the throne, and by stating that before the conversation between Buckingham and Ely, Buckingham — not Elizabeth, as Vergil has it — and Margaret had been in communication on the same matter before, and that moved by Buckingham she first approached Elizabeth through Lewis; and the whole passage is altered to suit this version. Carelessly enough, Grafton immediately after (p. 527) follows his original and represents Margaret as not learning "that the duke of Buckyngham had of him selfe afore entended the same matter" till after she had, in consequence of her understanding with Elizabeth, determined to send Urswick as a messenger to Richmond. The Hardyng continuation also gives us in effect a speech by Lewis to the queen which Hall afterwards elaborated and professes to quote verbatim as uttered by Lewis.

Richard's letters to Buckingham are not merely "most courteous (humanissimis)" but "enfarced and replenyshed with all humanytee, frendshippe, famylyaritee and swetnesse of woordes". The second letters are not merely "threatening (minaciter)" but "of a more roughe sorte, not wythoute manacynge and threatenynge". For Buckingham's cause of trust in Banister, "quem quia a puero bonum virum habuerat", Grafton writes: "because the same had bene and thē was his seruant". "Edwardus Ponyngus" becomes Edward Poyntz (and Lumby not finding anybody bearing both names confuses him with a certain Robert Pointz [see L.'s note, p. 182] instead of finding in him the Sir Edward Poynings who was a member of Henry's council and served him nobly as a general and administrator in Ireland and on the continent. Cf. Dict. Nat. Biog. sub Henry VII. and Hall, p. 424, 445, 452, 470, 478.)

The wind whereby Richmond sailed away from the trap set for him at Poole was, according to Grafton "euen appoynted hym of God to delyuer hym from that greate ieoperdy" (p. 531). Landose was hated by the lords of Brittany afterwards because he "tooke this matter in hande" — nor because, as Vergil says, the management of every thing was in his hands.

Grafton's account of Richard's attempt to win over Elizabeth is much abridged from his original; but as Hall has the full translation, we need not consider Grafton's account farther than to note a singular error of translation, of importance later.

Richard, he says, hoped to have "bothe her doughters oute of her handes into his owne". The orig. has "et se et filias". This might seem a slip in writing, for "both her daughters and herself", as Hall has "bothe of her and her daughters"; but later, for "primo filias in Ricardi potestatem tradit" we have again "deliuered both her doughters".

Later still, for "filias omnes fratris" we have a correct translation "al his brothers doughters".

In recounting Richard's dream, for the "visus est... videre circa se obuersari imagines quasi malorum demonum horrificas, & illas non sinere se quiescere", we have: "seming that he saw horrible deuilles appere vnto hym, & pulling and haling of hym that he could take no rest"; "which visyon fylled hym full of feare and also of heuy care", says Grafton, while Vergil says: "non tam subito pauore eius pectus perculit, quam anxiis impleuit curis". Richard rehearses his dream "vnto theim all" instead of the "many" of Vergil (p. 544).

In Richard's attack on Richmond, Grafton adds: "and like a lyon ranne at hym". The Hardyng continuation follows Vergil in giving the date of the battle of Bosworth as 1486. (So Hall). Grafton omits the fact that Richard came to the field with the crown on his head. The description of Richard "nimium elatum ac ferocem" is translated "a proude and cruell mynde", which gives a far different sense from the "corage hault and fearce", the correct rendering of the Polydore Vergil translation.

In the version of the Hardyng continuation there is little that calls for comment. Of the additions the only ones of importance are the story of the escape of Edward IV from Middleham Castle, which passed into Hall and Holinshed and so into Shakespeare; the statement that Richard appeared at Baynard's Castle between two bishops, which passed into Hall and so into Shakespeare: and the statement that the cardinal who went to the queen in sanctuary was the Archbishop of Canterbury. This too was adopted by Hall, and is supposed by the editors to have been adopted by Shakespeare, though that is, in spite of its unanimous acceptance by the editors, still a matter of doubt.

A certain tendency of the continuator to embellish his originals is seen in various places. Thus in the account of Richard's dream the devils are made to "pull and hale" him, and Richard's letters to Buckingham are described with additional adjectives destined to bring out more clearly Richard's hypocrisy. To hostility to Richard and his house are doubtless due the description of Richard's face as "crabbed", the speech put in Richard's mouth as he slays King Henry and the omission of More's praise of Richard's father.

XV. Hall's Chronicle.

Edward Hall was probably born in 1498 or 1499 and died in 1547. He was educated at Eton and King's College, Cambridge, and studied law at Gray's Inn. He entered politics and became a member of Parliament, where he showed himself a staunch supporter of Henry VIII, maintaining extreme theories of the royal supremacy.

His book appeared under the title of "The Union of the Noble and Illustre Famelies of Lancastre and York". It is said by bishop Tanner (Bibliotheca Britannica p. 372) to have been first printed by Berthelot in 1542, but there is no satisfactory evidence that this edition (still believed in by the author of the article on Hall in Dic. Nat. Biog. q. v.) ever existed. No copy exists with that date or with a dedication to Henry VIII, and the sole evidence in its favor is the existence of a copy in the Granville Library of the British Museum, and of another in the Public Library at Cambridge, containing leaves with initial blooming letters which differ in their form and rougher workmanship from those in the known perfect editions of 1548 and 1550. When we consider the many changes made in a single edition of many other important works of this period, this evidence affords no reason for disbelieving that the edition issued by Grafton in 1548 was the first. Additional evidence that the first edition of Hall followed the Hardyng continuation instead of preceding it is afforded by the way in which Hall expanded his translation of Polydore Vergil beyond that of the Hardyng continuation. Had Hall's fuller work, on the other hand, existed before the Hardyng continuation, the way in which the chroniclers of the time adopted whole the work of those who went before them makes it evident that the Hardyng continuator would have adopted Hall's work. We should have had, for example, Hall's extended speech of Lewis to the queen (not in Polydore Vergil, and only slightly sketched by the Hardyng continuation); we should have had the detailed conversation of Buckingham and Ely which Hall added to More's narrative, and the story of the flood that proved Buckingham's undoing.

That the one work was known to the author of the other is proven by various conicidences of language and statement for which the common original, Vergil, affords no basis.

Hall had before his death completed his chronicle to the twenty-fourth year of Henry's reign, 1532. By means of "diuers and many pamphletes and papers" which had belonged to Hall himself. Grafton brought down the account to the end of Henry VIII's reign. Another edition was issued in 1550 with a new preface (cf. Dic. Nat. Biog. sub Hall and Grafton).

Hall professed to have "compiled and gathered (and not made) out of diuerse writers, as well forayn as Englishe", his "simple treatise". His treatment of the reign of Edward IV is a translation of the work of Polidore Vergil, with large additions from de Comines on English affairs in France, a few details from Fabyan, and others the source of which it is impossible to determine. Many additions of his own also appear, as will be noted.

The following citations are made from Ellis's reprint, 1809.

The earliest mention of Richard in Hall is the statement (p. 253) that his mother after the death of her husband sent him with his brother George (Clarence) to Utrecht, "where they were of Philippe duke of Bourgoyne, well receyued and fested, and so there thei remayned, till their brother Edwarde had obteyned the Realme, and gotte*n* the regiment".

Hall adds to Vergil's account of the capture of Henry, the name of his captor, "one Cantlowe", from Fabyan.

In treating of Edward's marriage, Hall considers the statement of some that Warwick was sent to Spain to ask for his master the hand of Elizabeth sister of the king of Castile. He finds from the inscription on her tomb that the lady was at this time only six years of age, while Edward was over twenty-four; so that such a project was very unlikely. Certain it is, moreover, that application was made for the hand of Lady Bona. And therewith Hall comes back to Vergil's story, enlarging it in detail. His account of Edward's marriage is as follows: "The King being on huntyng in the forest of Wychwood besyde Stonnystratforde, came for his recreacion to the mannor of Grafton, where the duches of Bedford soiorned, then wyfe to syr Richard Woduile, Lord Ryuers, on whom then was altendyng a doughter of hers, called dame Elizabeth Greye, wydow of syr Ihon Grey knight, slayn at the last battell of saincte Albons, by the power of kyng Edward. This wydow hauyng a suit to y̆ kyng, either to be restored by hym to some thyng taken from her, or requyring hym of pitie, to haue some augmentacion to her liuyng, founde such grace in the kynges eyes, that he not onely fauored her suyte, but muche more phantasied her person, for she was a woma*n* more of formal countenaunce, then of excellent beautie, but yet of such beautie & fauor, that with her sober demeanure, louely lokyng, and femynyne smylyng (neither to wanton nor to humble) besyde her tounge so eloquent, and her wit so pregnant, she was able to rauishe the mynde of a meane person, whe*n* she allured and made subject to her, y̆ hart of so great a king. After that kyng Edward had well considered all the linyame*n*tes of her body, and the wise and womanly demeanure that he saw in her, he determined first to atte*m*pt, if he might prouoke her to be his souereigne lady, promisyng her many gyftes and fayre rewardes, affirming farther, $\tilde{y}$ if she would therunto condiscend, she might so fortune of his peramour and concubyne, to be chaunged to his wyfe & lawful bedfelow: which demaunde she so wisely, and with so couert speache aunswered and repugned, affirmynge that as she was for his honor farre vnable to be hys spouse and bedfelow: So for her awne poore honestie, she was to good to be either hys concubyne, or souereigne lady: that where he was a littell before heated with the darte of Cupido, he was nowe set all on a hote burnyng fyre, what for the confidence that he had in her perfyte constancy, and the trust that he had in her constant chastitie, & without any farther deliberacion, he determined with him selfe clerely to marye with her, after that askyng counsaill of them, whiche he knewe neither woulde nor once durst impugne his concluded purpose" (p. 264).

The causes of Edward's and Warwick's dissension are repeated as in Vergil. Speaking of the attempt of Edward on a lady in Warwick's house, Hall translates Vergil's "nec abhorret a ueritate" by "it erreth not far from truth", and adds that the lady was Warwick's daughter or niece. Treating of the conspiracy of Warwick with his brothers, Hall swells the speech put in Warwick's mouth by Vergil, and extends Vergi's account of Montacute's unwillingness.

"The lorde Marques [Montacute] could by no meanes bee reduced, to take any parte against kyng Edward till the erle had bothe promised hym great rewardes and high promocions, and also assured hym of the aide and power, of the greatest princes of the realme. Euē as the Marques vnwillingly, and in manner coacted gaue his consent, to this vnhappy coniuracion . . so with a fainte harte and lesse courage, he alwaies shewed hymself enemie to Kyng Edwarde, excepte in his laste daie: whiche lukewarme harte, and double dissimulacion, wer bothe the destruccion of him and his brethren" (p. 271).

Hall asserts that Clarence's opposition to his brother was caused by the grand marriages formed by Edward for his wife's relatives, "mariages", says Clarence at the conclusion of a speech to Warwick put into his mouth by Hall (who very often writes a speech where Vergil merely indicates one), "more meter for his twoo brethren and kynne, then for suche newe foundlynges as he hath bestowed theim on: But by swete saincte George I sweare, if my brother of Gloucester would ioyne with me, we woulde make hym knowe, that we were all three one mannes sonne, of one mother and one lignage discended, whiche shoulde be more preterred and promoted, then straungers of his wifes bloud" (p. 271).

Hall's account of King Edward's escape from Middleham varies from Vergil's and is very similar to that of the second Croyland continuation. "Kyng Edward beyng thus in captiuite, spake euer fayre to the Archebishop and to the other kepers (but whether he corrupted them with money or fayre promises) he had libertie diuers dayes to go on huntynge, and one day on a playne there met with hym syr William Stanley, syr Thomas of Borogh, and dyuers other of hys fren̄des, with such a great bend of men, that neither his kepers woulde, nor once curst moue him to retorne to prison agayn" (p. 275).

In describing Warwick's and Clarence's doings at Calais and in France, Hall copies the story of De Comines, including the message borne by the strange damsel to Clarence. Hall states that Edward was married to Anne, an evident mistranslation of Vergil's "despondetur".

At home Edward had succeeded in winning over Warwick's brother the Marquis Montacute, who "humbly yelded hymself, and vowed to bee euer true to the king (as he had doen before tyme) whom he with muche humanitie and faire woordes, did receiue and intertain".

Of the wretchedness and misery tasted by Edward in his flight, Hall says, "These soure sauces he tasted as a penaunce for his wanton liuyng, & negligent ouerseyng of thinges that he mighte well haue forsene & preuented, but his mynd was so geuen to pastyme, dalyaunce, & sensuall pleasure, that he forgat the olde adage, saynge, in tyme of peace prouyde for warre" (p. 284).

Of the proceedings about Edward in Burgundy Hall follows De Comines' account.

At Nottingham (not York, as in Shakespeare) there came to Edward "syr William Parre, syr Thomas a Borogh, syr Thomas Montgomerie, and diuers others of hys assured frends with theyr aydes, which caused hym at the fyrst co*m*ming to make Proclamacion in hys owne name, kyng Edward the .iiij. boldely sayng to hym, that they would serue no man but a kynge" (p. 292).

It was no marvel, says Hall, referring again to De Comines's story, that Clarence came over to Edward, "for as you haue hard before, thys marchandyse was labored, conduyted and concluded by a damsell, when the duke was in the French court, to the erles vtter confusion" (p. 293).

After following Vergil's description of the battle of Barnet, to which he adds the statement that Gloucester led the van, the King and Clarence the centre, and Hastings the rear, Hall adds further: "Some aucthors write, that this battail was fought so nere hande, that kyng Edward was constrained to fight his owne persone, & fought as sore as any man of his partie, and that the erle of Warwicke, whiche was wont euer to ride on horsebacke, from place to place, from ranke to ranke, comfortyng his men, was now aduised by the Marques his brother to relynquishe his horse, and trie the extremitie by hande strokes, whiche if he had been on his horsebacke, might fortune to haue escaped".

"This ende had Richard Neuell erle of Warwicke, whose stoute stomacke, and inuincible corage, after so many straunge fortunes, and perilous chaunces by him escaped, caused death before he came to any old age priuilie to stele on hym, and with his darte to take from hym all wordly and mundain affeccions: but death did one thyng, that life could not do, for by death, he had rest, peace, quietnes, and tranquillitie, whiche his life euer abhorred, and could not suffre nor abide" (p. 296).

Is Vergil's account of the battle of Tewkesbury Hall adds several important details. As at Barnet Gloucester led the van, with the king in the centre and Dorset and Hastings in charge of the rear. "The duke of Gloucester, which lacked no policye, valyantly with his battayle assauted the tre*n*che of the Quenes campe, whom the Duke of Somerset with no lesse courage defended, the duke of Gloucester for a very politique purpose, with all hys men reculed backe". Hereupon Somerset unwisely left his camp to pursue. "The duke of Gloucester takynge the auantage that he auentured for, turned agayn face to face to the duke of Somersets battayl, which (nothynge lesse thinkyng on, then of the returne) were within a smal season. shamefully discomfited". "The duke of Glocester entered the trenche, & after hym the kyng, where after no long conflict, the Quenes part went almost all to wrecke, for the most parte were slayne". "The Quene was fou*n*de in her chariot almost dead for sorowe, ỹ prince was apprehended and kepte close by syr Rychard Croftes. . . . After the felde ended, kyng Edward made a Proclamatio*n*, that who so euer could bring prince Edward to him alyue or dead, shoulde haue an annuitie of an .c. l. duryng his lyfe, and the Princes life to be saued. Syr Richard Croftes, a wyse and a valyant knyght, nothing mistrusting the kynges former promyse, brought furth his prisoner prince Edward, beynge a goodly femenine & a well feautered yonge gentelman, whome when kynge Edward had well aduised, he demaunded of him, how he durst so presumptuously enter in to his Realme with banner displayed. The prince, beyng bold of stomacke & of a good courage, answered sayinge, to recouer my fathers kyngdome & enheritage, from his father & grandfather to him, and from him, after him, to me lyneally diuoluted. At which wordes kyng Edward sayd nothyng, but with his hand thrust hym from hym (or as some say, stroke him with his gauntlet) whom incontinent, they that stode about whiche were George duke of Clarence, Rychard duke of Gloucester, Thomas Marques Dorset, and William lord Hastynges, sodaynly murthered, & pitiously manquelled. The bitternesse of which murder, some of the actors, after in their latter dayes tasted and assayed by the very rod of Justice and punishment of God" (pp. 300, 301).

Hall translates Vergil's account of the murder of king Henry and the description of his character. For Vergil's statement that Henry's body was brought without honor from the Tower, Hall has (evidently from Fabyan) "with billes and gleues pompeously (if you call that a funerall pompe)", and says that the conveyance to Chertsey was "without Prieste or Clarke, Torche or Taper, syngyng or saiyng" (p. 303).

There is no mention of the bleeding of Henry's wounds.

De Comines furnishes Hall with a full account of Edward's proceedings in France. Hall mentions Gloucester's dissatisfaction with the treaty of Picquigny. "But the duke of Gloucester and other to whom the French nation, was more odious than a tode, whose swordes thrusted for French blood, detested, abhorred, and cried out on this peace" (p. 314).

The account of Clarence's death is translated from Vergil without addition. Later Hall states that Edward was "set on by suche as enuied the estate of the duke of Clarence" (p. 337).

The war in Scotland is described at length, and Gloucester's activity and success emphasized. "Kyng Edward ...... muche commended bothe his valiaunt manhode, and also his prudent pollicie, in conueying hys busines, bothe to his owne purpose, and also to the profit of the Realme" (p. 336).

In treating of the death of King Edward, Hall departs from Vergil's account. He attempts to assign a cause for it. "Whether it was with the melencoly, and anger that he toke with the Frenche kyng for his vntruthe and vnkyndnes [in marrying the Dauphin to the lady Margaret of Austria, and not to his daughter Elizabeth. This was the cause assigned by de Comines.], or were it by any superfluous surfet (to the whiche he was much geuen) he sodainly fell sicke". As the end drew near he summoned his nobles "and thus in effect, to theim saied". There follows a long speech, entirely different from More's, which is given later. Thus Hall puts in Edward's mouth two wholly different speeches.

Edward first speaks of "the fraile and fadyng imbecilitie, of our humain nature, and the caduke fragilitie of the same". But so long as health flourisheth man thinks not of his end. This Edward speaks of himself, lamenting that he had not carried out "such pollitique diuises, and good and Godly ordinaunces" as he had determined to perform. He had meant "so to haue decorated this realme, with wholesome Lawes, statutes, and ordinaunces, so to haue educated" his children, that no foreign power would venture to attack them or the realm. All this he was now obliged to give over to those to whom he spoke, knowing "that neuer Prince bearyng scepter and croune, ouer realmes and regions, hath found or proued, more faithfuller counsailers, nor trewer subiectes". Such he confidently expected that they would be after his death to his children, "as the verie Images, and carnall portratures, of his stirpe, line and stemme".

Little peace had he had in life, but now he was summoned to eternal peace. "Therefore", continued he, "now for the perfecte, and vnmoueable confidence, that I haue euer had in you, and for the vnfained loue, that you haue euer shewed vnto me, I commende and deliuer into your gouernaunce, bothe this noble realme, and my naturall children, and your kynsmen. My children by your diligent ouersight, and pollitique prouision to bee taught, enformed, and instructed". Young as they were they could be trained to virtue or to vice, wherefore he implored them rather to "make theim riche in Godly knowledge, and vertueous qualities, then to take paine to glorifie theim, with abundance of worldely treasure, and mundain superfluitie".

"My kyngdom also, I leue in your gouernaunce, durying the minoritie of my children, chargyng you on your honors, othes, and fidelitie, made and sworne to me, so indifferently to ordre and gouerne, the subiectes of the same, bothe with iustice and mercie, that the willes of malefactors, haue not to large a scope, nor the hartes of the good people, by to muche extremitie, bee neither sorofully daunted, nor vnkyndly kept vnder: Oh I am so slepie, that I muste make an ende, and now before you all I commende my soule to almightie God, my sauior and redemer: my body to the wormes of the yearth, my kyngdom to the Prince my sonne, and to you my louyng frendes my harte, my trust, and my whole confidence. And euen with that, he fell on slepe" (pp. 339—341).

Having reached the end of Edward's reign, Hall now adopts the work of More bodily into his text, as the Hardyng continuation had done before him. In doing so he copied word for word the version of the Hardyng continuation. These two reprints of More are, according to Rastell, "very muche corrupte in many places, sometyme hauyng lesse, and sometime hauing more, and altered in wordes and whole sentences: muche varying fro the copie of his own hand. In Hall there are a very few slight verbal changes, from the Hardyng version and two important additions. These I note below. A few minute changes which are of importance only as showing the source used by later works are left till these are treated.

The opening paragraphs of More's work, dealing with the death of Edward IV and his character, Hall places after Edward's death-bed speech [by More].

Hall has Persival and not Persall as the name of the messenger sent by Buckingham to Richard.

Hall's account of the knight who accompanied Hastings

to the council varies a little from that of the Hardyng continuation, adding (as in More's original) that he was sent by the protector.

In the proclamation made by Richard against Hasting's, speaking of Shore's wife as being one of Hasting's counsel in the treason, Hall adds "with whom he laye nightly and namely the night passed next before his death" (p. 362).

Hall has the same accout as the Hardyng continuation of the negotiations for the lady Bona's hand, save that she is called sister to the French queen (not king).

In Buckingham's speech the case of Burdet, merely mentioned by More and the Hardyng continuator, is explained by Hall as follows:

"This Burdet was a marchau*n*t dwellyng in Chepesyd at y̆ signe of y̆ crounc ... This man merely [merrily] in y̆ rufflyng tyme of king Edwarde y̆ .iiij. his rage, saied to his awne some [sonne] that he would make hym inheritor of y̆ crounc, meanyng his awne house: but these wordes king Edward made to be mysconstrued, & interpreted that Burdet meant the crounc of the realme: wherfore within less space then .iiij. houres he was apprehended, judged, drawen and quartered in Chepesyde" (p. 369).

To the Hardyng continuation's account of the fifth of July Hall adds that Richard "created Eduard his onely begotten sonne, a childe of .x. yere olde, prince of Wales" (p. 375).

Then follows an extended account of the king's coronation, with the procession.

"After More's paragraph on the inward trouble that ensued to Richard after the murder of the princes, Hall branches off, returning for the moment to Vergil as his source. He copies Vergil's account of the people's sorrow and adds to it. "To murther a man", cried the people, "is much odious, to kyll a woman, is in manner vnnatural, but to slaie and destroye innocent babes, & young enfantes, the whole world abhorreth, and the bloud from the earth crieth, for vengaunce to all mightie God". Vergil's "Quid hic faciet aliis, cum suos crudeliter nullo eorum in se merito jugularit? pro certo habentes tyrannidem saeuissimam iam Rempublicam" (p. 540) is extended by Hall into: "a las what will he do to other that thus shamefully murdereth his awne bloud without cause or desert? Whom, wyll he saue when he slaith the poore lambes committed to him in trust? Now we se and behold y̆ the most cruel tyranny hath inuadyd the commonwealth, now we se that in him is neither hope of iustice nor trust of mercie but abundance of crueltie and thrust of innocente bloude" (p. 379).

Then follows Vergil's lament of the queen, with his reflection that the death of the princes was the penalty for Edward's broken oath at York and the death of his brother Clarence; the visit of Richard to York and the account of his procession there (extended from Vergil); Richard's return to London; the people's belief that "any blusteringe wynde perelous thunder or terrible tempest" was sent of God in penalty for Richard's crime; and Richard's determination to "tourn over the leffe" and show himself by his acts a good man.

Then Hall returns to More's story, as given in the Hardyng continuation, taking up the story of Buckingham's conspiracy, and follows to the end More's story, omitting, with the Hardyng continuation, Persival's message, as having been related before.

For the continuation of More's narrative, Hall, like the Hardyng continuator, makes use of Vergil's story; but unlike the Hardyng continuator, only as a basis, making himself large additions. He had besides the Hardyng continuation before him and makes use of its translation and changes in some places.

Vergil's story is not welded to More's by a hasty transitional paragraph but the speeches of Buckingham and Ely are continued at great length. Directly upon Ely's words "in the parsone of your grace", Hall goes on:

"The duke somewhat maruelynge at his sodaine pauses as though they were but parentheses, with a high coun-tenance saied" that Ely's manner made it plain to him that he had "some preiuie Imaginacion" which he feared to disclose. The duke assured him on his honor that he would "be as secrete in this case as the deffe and dumme person is to the singer, or the tree to the hunter". There-upon the bishop, perceiving the duke's desire "to be ex-alted and magnified" and his hatred and rancor toward Richard, spoke out boldly, "entendyng thereby to compasse how to destroye and vlterly confounde kynge Richarde, .. or els to sett the Duke so a fyer with the lesyer of ambicion that he hymselfe might .. escape". In reading ancient books the bishop had found it written that one owed a duty to one's parents, and one's kinsmen and friends, but one's native country "demaundeth as a debt by a natural bonde neither to be forgotten nor yet to be put in obliuion". This had caused him to reflect upon the present condition of the realm, which seemed likely to be exterminated. One hope he had for it, and that was in Buckingham him-self, as possessed of all qualities meet for a governor. "But on the other syde when I call to memorie the good qualites of the late protectour and nowe called kynge, so violated and subuerted by tyrannye, so chaunged & altered by vsurped aucthoritee, so clouded and shadowed by blynde and insaciable ambicion, ye and so sodainlye .. transformed from politike ciuilitie, to detestable tyrannie: I must nedes .. affirme, that he is neither mete to be a kynge of so noble a realme, nor so famous a realme mete to be gouerned by suche a tyraunte". Richard had slain many nobles, had accused his own mother of adultery, had declared his nephews bastards, had finally killed them. "The bloud of whiche sely and lyttel babes dayly crye to God, from the earthe for vengaunce. Alas my harte sobbeth, to remember this bloudy boucher and cruel monster". Wherefore he conjured Buckingham to take upon himself the crown and free his countrymen. For "yf any foren prynce . . ye the Turcke hym selfe woulde take vppon hym the regiment here and the crowne, the commons woulde rather admit and obey hym, then to lyue vnder suche a bloud supper and child kyller". If Buckingham refused the crown for himself, Ely implored him to "sett vp again the linage of Lancaster or auaunce the eldest doughter of kynge Edward to some highe and puyssaunte prince".

When Ely had finished "ẙ duke sighed and spake not of a great while", whereat the bishop was abashed; but Buckingham bade him not to be afraid, and promised to speak further on the morrow.

The next day Buckingham sent for the bishop. Taking off his bonnet he thanked God for His goodness that whereas the realm had been oppressed by great storms, a rule was about to be provided to His pleasure and the security of the realm. Then turning to Ely he said that for his frankness of yesterday he would make return by revealing all his thoughts. When Edward died, to whom he thought himself little or nothing beholden, he was naturally not inclined to favor Edward's children. Considering how the realm should be governed, an old adage sank into his head: "oft ruithe the realme, where chyldren rule, and women gouerne". He turned therefore against the young king, the queen and her kindred, who "toke more vpon them, and more exalted them selues by reason of the quene, then dyd the kynges brethrene, or any duke in his realme", and for his own "commoditie and emolumente" took part with Gloucester. "Whome I assure you I thoughte to be as cleane withoute dissimulacion, as tractable without iniurie, as mercifull withoute crueltie, as nowe I knowe hym perfectely to be a dissembler without veritie, a tyrante withoute pitie, yea and worse then the tyraunte phaleres . . . And so by my meanes, at the fyrste counsaill holden at London, when he was most suspected of that thynge that after happened . . . he was made Protectoure and defender, bothe of the kynge and of the realme, whiche aucthoritie once gotten, and the two chyldren partelie by policie broughte vnder his gouernaunce, he beynge moued with that gnawynge and couetous serpe*n*t, desyered to reigne". Richard proposed that he should be made protector till the king was twenty-four, and when he saw Buckingham "somewhat stycke at" this, because it was without precedent, and such a protector would not lightly give up his power, "he then brought in instrume*n*tes, autentike doctoures, proctoures, and notaries of the lawe, with deposicions of diuers wytnesses, testifieng kyng Edwards children to be bastardes". These Buckingham believed, "so agayn by my ayde and fauour, he of a protectour was made a kyng ... at whiche tyme he promysed me on his fidelitie, laiyng his hand in myne at Baynarde castel, that the .II. young princes should lyue, and that he would so prouide for them, and so mayntaine them in honorable estate. y^t I and all the realme ought and should be content. But when he was once crouned king ... he cast a way his old co*n*dicions as ye adder doeth her skynne. For when I myself sued to him for any part of the Earle of Hartfordes landes whiche .... Edwarde wrongefully .... withhelde from me, and also required to haue the office of the high constable shyppe of Englande .... in thys my fyrste suyte shewynge his good mynde towarde me, he dyd not onely fyrste delaye me, and afterwarde denay me, but gaue me such vnkynde woordes, with such tauntes and retauntes ye in maner checke and checke mate to the vttermost profe of my pacience". This feeling Buckingham concealed. "But when I was credibly enformed of the death of the .II. younge innocentes .. contrarie to his faith and promyse, to the whiche God be my iudge I neuer agreed nor condiscended. O Lord, how my veynes panted, how my body trembled, and my harte inwardelie grudged, in so muche that I so abhorred the sighte and much more the compaignie of hym, that I could no lenger abyde in his courte, except I shoulde be openly reuenged".

In this mood, having "fayned a cause to departe", Buckingham returned to Brecknock, meditating how to pull Richard from his throne. "I suddenly remembred that lord Edmond duke of Somersett my grandfather was with kynge Henrye the sixte in the .ɪɪ. and .ɪɪɪ. degrees from Ihon duke of Lancaster lawefully begotten: So that I thought sure my mother being eldest doughter to duke Edmonde, that I was nexte heyre to kynge Henry the sixte". But on his way home he met Margaret, countess of Richmond, the very daughter and sole heir to the duke of Somerset, Buckingham's grandfather's elder brother. She and her son Henry stood between him and the crown, a fact which he had clean forgotten. Yet Buckingham still thought of obtaining election as king, but meditating on the cares and troubles of that office, he decided against it. Margaret besought Buckingham that he would petition the king to allow her son to return to England, "and yf it were his pleasure so to do, she promised that the erle her sonne should mary one of kyng Edwardes daughters". This request Buckingham lightly passed over, but thinking upon it he came to a still bolder conclusion, namely to unite Richmond to Elizabeth, "by the whiche mariage bothe the houses of Yorke and Lancaster maye be obteyned and vnite in one, to the clere stablyshement of the title to the crowne of this noble realme".

At this devise the bishop was greatly rejoiced, and replied that it was necessary to consider whom to make privy of this "highe deuice and polliticke conclusion". He suggested therefore to make use of Reignold Bray, an old friend of the countess, who came to the duke, and returned with the news to his mistress.

Ely now meditated obtaining his own liberty, and suggested that if he were in his own isle of Ely he could make many friends for the enterprise. Buckingham was unwilling to let him go, as he relied strongly on Ely's wise advice; but the bishop, "beiynge wyttye as the duke was wylie", fled by night and came to Ely, whence he departed to Flanders (pp. 384—390).

Now begins again the use of Vergil. I indicate only the important additions and changes of Hall.

Hall, after his usual manner, has an extended speech by Lewis, the physician, to queen Elizabeth.

To the account of the abandonment of their leader by Buckingham's troops, Hall adds: "The duke with all his power mershed through the forest of deane entendyng to haue passed the riuer of Seuerne at Gloucester, and ther to haue ioyned in army with the Courtneys and other Westernmen of his confideracy and affinite, which if he had done no doubt but kyng Richard had bene in greate ieopardie either of priuacion of his realme or losse of his life or both. But so the chaunce, before he could attayne to Seuerne side, by force of continuall rayne and moysture, the ryuer rose so high that yt ouerflowed all the countrey adioyning, in somuch that men were drowned in their beddes, howses with the extreme violence were ouerturned, children were caried aboute the feldes, swimming in cradelles, beastes were drowned on hilles, whiche rage of water lasted continually .x. dayes, insomuch that in the countrey adioyning they call yt to this daie, the greate water, or the duke of Buckynghams greate water. By this inundacion the passages were so closed that neither the duke could come ouer Seuerne to his complices, nor they to hym, duryng the whiche tyme, the Welshemen lyngerynge ydely and without money, vitayle, or wages sodaynely scaled and departed: and for all the dukes fayre promyses, manaces and enforcementes, they woulde in no wise neither goo farther nor abide" (p. 394).

Of Banister Hall adds, "whom he [Buckingham] had tendrely broughte vp, & whome he aboue all men loued, fauored and trusted".

To the account of Buckingham's capture Hall adds that Banister betrayed him "to Ihon Mitton then shrief of shropshire, whyche sodaynely with a stronge power of men in harnes apprehended the duke in a litle groue adioyninge to the mansion of Homfrey Banaster, and in greate hast and euyll spede conueighed him appareled in a pilled blacke cloke to the cytie of Salsburie where kynge Richard then kepte his houshold".

"Whether this Banaster bewreyed the duke more for fear then couetous many men do doubt; but sure it is, that shortlie after . . . his sonne and heyre waxed mad and so dyed in a bores stye, his eldest daughter of excellent beautie was sodaynelie stryken with a foule leperye, his seconde sonne very meruelously deformed of his limmes and made decrepite, his younger sonne in a small puddel was stra*n*gled & drouned, & he beyng of extreme age arraigned & fou*n*d gyltie of a murther and by his clergye saued" (p. 395).

In speaking of Buckingham's suit to be admitted to Richard's presence Hall says: "whether it wer to sue for perdon and grace, or whether he being brought to his presence would haue sticked him with a dagger as men then judged" (p. 395).

Of the gale by which Henry was conveyed back in safety from his first attempt to land in England, Hall says, following the Hardyng continuation, that it was "sente them by God to delyuer him from that perell and ieopardie" (p. 396).

Vergil's statement that Richard put to death some of his own household is lengthened by Hall into: "Diverse of his houshold seruants whom either he suspected or doubted were by great crueltie put to shamefull death" (p. 397).

Vergil's simple statement that the order to keep Margaret Stanley close was fulfilled, becomes in Hall: "whiche commaundemente was a while put in execucion and accomplished according to his dreadfull commaundemente" (p. 398).

"Yet the wilde worme of vengaunce wauerynge in his hed could not be contented with the death of diuerse gentlemen suspected of treason, but also he muste extende his bloudy furye agaynste a poore gentleman called Collyngborne for making a small ryme of thre of his vnfortunate councilers, which wer the lord louell, sir Richarde Radclyffe his myscheuous mynion, and sir Wylliam Catesby his secrete seducer, whiche metre was.

> The Rat, the Catte and Louell our dogge
> Rule all Englande vnder the hogge.

Meanynge by the hogge, the dreadfull wilde bore whiche was the kynges cognisaunce, but because the fyrste lyne ended in dogge, the metrician coulde not obseruynge the regimentes of metre ende the seconde verse in Bore, but called the bore an hogge. This poeticall schoolemayster corrector of breues and longes, caused Collyngborne to be abbreuiate shorter by the hed, and too bee deuyded into foure quarters" (p. 398).

The truce with the Scots, merely mentioned by Vergil is given in full detail by Hall, together with an account of the negotiations. The truce was to last three years (p. 399). Hall adds that Richard, "to haue a double strynge to his bowe", "entreated a new aliaunce and mariage to be concluded betwene the prince of Rothsaye eldest sonne to the kyng of Scottes, and lady Anne de la poole daughter to Ihon duke of Suffolke and lady Anne suster to kyng Richarde, whiche suster he so muche fauoured that he studyenge all the weies by the which he might auaunce her offspringe and lignage, did not onely procure and seke meanes howe to make her daughter a pryncesse, and consequently a Quene, but also after the death of his sonne, he proclaymed Jhon erle of Lyncolne his nephew and her sonne, heyre apparaunt to $\overset{e}{y}$ crowne of England, dishencrityng kynge Edwardes daughters, whose brethren before you haue heard he shamefully killed & murthered" (p. 401).

To Vergil's statement that Landoise was ready to betray Richmond not because of any hatred toward him, Hall adds the reflection: "That cursed hungre of gold and execrable thirst of lucre, and inward feare of losse of aucthoritie, driueth the blynde myndes of couetous men and ambicious persones to euilles and mischifes innumerable, not remembring losse of name, obloquy of the people, nor in conclusion the punishment of God for their merites and desertes" (p. 403).

In the account of Richard's attempt to win over Queen Elizabeth, Hall makes several important changes. That the messengers first wounded the queen's mind by referring to the slaughter of her sons is omitted. For Vergil's "haud ita multo post oblita iniuriarum, immemor datae fidei Margaritae Henrici matri, primo filias in Ricardi potestatem tradit" (p. 550), we have: "And so she putting in oliuion the murther of her innocente children, the infamy and dishonoure spoken by [i. e. concerning] the kynge her husbande, the lyuynge in auoutrie leyed to her charge, the bastardyng of her daughters, forgettyng also y̌ feithfull promes & open othe made to the countesse of Richmond, ... blynded by auaricious affeccion and seduced by flatterynge wordes, first deliuered into kyng Richards handes her .v. daughters as Lambes once agayne committed to the custody of the rauenous wolfe". Ou Elizabeth's mutability Hall says: "Surely the inconstancie of this woman were muche to be meruelled at, yf all women had bene founde constante, but let men speake, yet wemen of the verie bonde of nature will folowe their awne kynde". For Vergil's "Ricardus ita placata Elisabeth regina, filias omnes fratris ex asylo in regiam recepit" (p. 550) we have: "After that kynge Rycharde had thus with glorious promyses and flatterynge woordes pleased and appeased the mutable mynde of quene Elyzabeth which knewe nothing lesse then that he moost entended, he caused all his brothers daughters to be conueighed into his paleys with solempne receauyng, as though with his newe familier and louyng entreteinement they should forget, and in their myndes obliterate the olde committed iniurie and late perpetrate tyrannye" (p. 407).

Of Richard's complaint to Rotheram of the barrenness of his wife, Hall adds that Richard thought "he would enucleate and open to her all these thinges, trustynge the sequell herof to take his effecte, that she herynge this grudge of her husband, and takyng therefore an inward thought, would not long lyue in this worlde" (p. 407). Of the supposition that Anne died by poison, Halls says it "is affirmed to be most likely" (p. 407). In the mention of Anne's relation to Prince Edward Hall translates Vergil's "desponsata" (1534 ed.) by "married", where the Harding continuation has "contracted".

On Richard's desire to marry his niece Hall translates "sed quia tantum nefas puella reclamante, omnes adhorrebant" (p. 550): — "But because all men, and the mayden her selfe moost of all detested and abhorred this vnlawfull and in maner vnnaturall copulacion" (p. 407).

When Henry sails from Brittany, for Vergil's "postquam Deum precatus est, ut felix faustumque esset" (p. 552) we have: "After that the erle had made his humble peticion, and devoute praier to allmightie God, besechynge him not only to sende him moost prosperous wynde and sure passage in his journey, but also effecteously desyrynge his goodnes of aide & comforte in his necessitie and victorie & supremitie· ouer his enemies —" (p. 410).

On Arnold Butler's message to Richmond we have: "For Arnold Buttler a valiaunt capitain, which first askynge perdon for his offences before tyme committed against the erle of Richmond, and that obteyned, declared to hym that the penbrochians were ready to serue & geue their attendaunce on their natural and immediate lord Jasper erle of Penbrooke" (p. 410). This involves a misconception of Vergil's statement, "Penbruchenses . . . per Arnoldum Bottelreium .. petita praeteritorum commissorum venia, se suo Gaspari comiti operam dare paratos esse significarunt" (p. 553). The offences were not Butler's only, but those of all the Pembrokians, in that they had accepted and served the earl of Pembroke created by

Edward IV since Jasper had been compelled to flee with Richmond to Brittany. Ellis's translation has rightly "ther former offences" and the Hardyng continuation "al former offences", giving the correct sense by a proper translation of the whole passage.

To Vergil's statement that Sir George Talbot came to Richmond's aid, Hall adds: "with the whole powre of the younge Earle of Shrewsburye then beynge in warde" (p. 411).

Of Richard's march to Bosworth, Hall says he sat "with a frownynge countenance and truculent aspect mounted on a great white courser" (p. 412).

Of the meeting of Richmond and Stanley, Hall says: "There the Earle came first to his fatherinlawe in a lytle close" (p. 413).

In the account of Richard's dream Hall follows Vergil closely but adopts from the Hardyng continuation the statement that the devils "pulled and haled hym". At the close of the paragraph Hall has a curious mistranslation of Vergil's "huic tristes migrare cogamur", which he renders "iocund to departe out of this miserable life".

To Richard's order of battle Hall adds that Norfolk's son, Thomas Earl of Surrey, was with him, and that Richard had "horsmen for wynges on both $\overset{e}{y}$ sides of his battail". Hall has long speeches of Richard and Richmond to their followers.

Richard's begins with praise of his "most faithfull & assured felowes, moste trusty & welbeloued cheuetains and elected captains, by whose wisdom & polecie" he had obtained the crown, "by whose puissaunce and valiauntness" he had enjoyed it in spite of the attempts of his enemies, and "by whose prudent & politike counsaill" he had so governed as to omit "nothing appertening to $\overset{e}{y}$ office of a juste prince". "So $\overset{t}{y}$ I may saie & truely affirme, that your approued fidelitie & tried constancye maketh me to beleue firmely & thinke, $\overset{t}{y}$ I am an vndoubted kyng & an indubitate prince. And although in $\overset{e}{y}$ adepcion & obteinyng of ẙ Garlande, I being seduced & prouoked by sinister counsail and diabolical temptacion did commyt a facynerous and detestable acte, yet I have with strayte penaunce and salte teryes (as I trust) expiated and clerely purged the same offence, which abhonimable crime I require you of frendship as clerely to forget, as I dayly do remember to deplore and lament the same". He calls their attention to the "case and perplexitie" before them, which demands proof of their allegiance, love, and duty. "I dought not but you know, howe the deuel .. hath entered into the harte of an unknown welshman .. excitynge him to aspire and couet oure realme .. ye se farther how a compaigne of traytors, thefes, outlawes and ronnegates of our awne nacion be ayders & partakers of his feate and enterprise ... : You se also, what a nomber of beggerly Britons & faynte harted Frenchmen be with hym arriued to distroy vs our wyfes and children". Like hares before the greyhound "astoned & amased with ẙ only sight" of the manly visages of Richard's soldiers they "will flee, ronne & skyr out of the felde". There are many signs of victory. "And to begyn with the earle of Richmonde Captaine of this rebellion, he is a Welsh mylke soppe, a man of small courage and of lesse experience in marcyall actes and feates of warre, brought vp by my brothers meanes and myne like a captiue in a close cage in the court of Fraunces duke of Britaine, and neuer saw armie, nor was exercised in marcial affaires", .. so for the Frenshmen & Brytons, there valiantnes ys suche, ẙᵗ our noble progenitors & your valiaunt parentes, haue them oftener vanquished & ouercome in one moneth, then they in ẙ beginnyng imagened possible to compasse & fynishe in a hole yere. Wherefore, ... like valiaunt champions auaunce furth your standards ... forward my captains, in whom lacketh neither pollicie wisdome nor puissaunce. . . . And as for me, I assure you, this day I wil triumphe by glorious victorie, or suffer death for immortal fame. For thei be maihmeed & out

of ẙ palice of fame disgraded, dieng w^tout renoune,
which do not as much preferre & exalte ẙ perpetuall honor
of their natiue countrey, as ther awne mortal & transitorie
life. Now sent George to borowe, let vs set forward, &
remember wel ẙ^t I am he which shall w^t high auaunce-
mentes rewarde & preferre ẙ valiaunt & hardy championes,
& punishe and turment the shameful cowardes & dreadful
dastardes" (pp. 414—416).

Richmond delivered his speech from a "lytell hyll so
that all his people myght se and beholde hym perfitly to
there great reioysyng: For he was a man of no great
stature, but so formed and decorated with all gyftes and
lyniamentes of nature that he semed more an angelical
creature then a terrestriall personage, his countenaunce
and aspect was cherefull and couragious, his heare yelow
lyke the burnished golde, his eyes gray shynynge and
quicke, prompte and ready in aunswerynge, but of suche
sobrietie that it coulde neuer be iudged whyther he were
more dull then quicke in speakynge (such was hys tem-
peraunce)" (p. 416).

Richmond began with an appeal to the justice of his
cause. "If euer **God** gave victorie to men fightynge in a
iust quarell? or yf he euer ayded such as made warre for
the welthe and tuicion of ther awne naturall and nutritiue
countrey? or if he euer succoured them whyche aduentured
there lyues for the relefe of innocentes, suppressynge of
malefactores and apparaunt offenders? No doubt my
felowes and frendes, but he of hys bountefull goodnes wyll
this daye sende vs triumphant victorye and a luckey
iourney ouer our prowde enemyes...: for yf you remember
... the very cause of our iust quarell, you shall appa--
antlye perceyue the same to be trewe, Godly, and vertuous.
... Our cause is so iuste that no enterprice can be of
more vertue, bothe by the lawes diuine and ciuile, for
what can be a more honest, goodly or Godly quarell then
to fight agaynste a Capitayne, beynge an homicide and
murderer of hys awne bloude and progenye? An extreme

destroyer of hys nobylytie, and to hys and oure countrey .. a deadly malle, a fyrye brande and a burden vntollerable". He and his followers "haue disheryted me and you and wrongefully deteyne and vsurpe ouer lawefull patrymonye and lyneall inherytaunce.... which persones for ther penaunce and punishment I doubte not but God of his goodnes will eyther deliuer into our handes as a great gayne and booty, or cause them beinge greued and compuncted with the pricke of ther corrupt consciences cowardely to flye ... : besyde this I assure you that there be yonder in that great battail, men brought thither for feare and not for loue, souldiours by force compelled and not w^t good will assembled: persons which desyer rather the destruccion then saluacion of ther master and captayn: And fynally a multitude: wherof the most part will be our frendes and the lest part our enemies. .... God appoynteth the good to confounde the yll .... If this be true ... who will spare younder tyraunt Richard ... vntrewely callyng hymself kyng ... the confusion of hys brother and murtherer of his nephewes ... bothe Tarquine and Nero: Yea a tyraunt mor then Nero, for he hath not only murdered his nephewe beyng his kyng and souereigne lord, bastarded his noble brethern and defamed the wombe of his verteous .. mother, but also compased all the meanes and waies .. how to stuprate and carnally know his awne nece .... Long we haue sought the furious bore ... let vs not feare to enter in to the toyle where we may suerly sley him ... Yf we wyn this battaill, ẙ hole riche realme of England .. shall be ours ... now is the time come to get abundaunce of riches and copie of profit ... Remember ẙ^{t} victorie is not gotten with the multitude of men, but with the courages of hartes and valiauntnes of myndes. The smaller that our nombre is, the more glorie is to vs yf we vanquishe, if we be ouercome, yet no laude is to be attributed, to the victors, consyderyng that .X. men fought agaynst one: and yf we dye so glorious a death in so good a quarell, nether fretyng tynne [tyme] nor cancarding obliuio*n* shal be able to obfuscate or race out of the boke of fame ether our names or our Godly attempt. And this one thyng I assure you, that in so iuste and good a cause, and so notable a quarell, you shall fynde me this daye, rather a dead carion vppon the coold grounde, then a fre prisoner on a carpet in a laydes chamber. . . . And now auau*n*ce forward trew men against traytors, pitifull persones against murtherers, trew inheritors against vsurpers, ẙ skorges of God against tirau*n*tes, display my banner with a good courage, marche furth like strong & robustious champions, & begyn ẙ battail like hardy conquerors, the battaill is at hande, & ẙ victorie approcheth, & yf we shamfully recule or cowardly flye, we and all our sequell be destroyd & dishonored for euer. This is ẙ daie of gayne, & this is ẙ time of losse, get this day victorie & be co*n*querers, & lese this daies battail & be villains & therfore in ẙ name of God & sai*n*ct George let euery ma*n* coragiously auau*n*ce forth his sta*n*dard" (pp. 416—418).

Hall follows Vergil's account of the battle, making several additions, only a few of which are important.

Vergil's statement that Henry had the sun at his back is enforced by the addition "and in the face of his enemies". The statement of the Hardyng continuation that Richard ran at Richmond "like a hungery lion" is adopted, and "with spere in rest" added. Concerning the slain duke of Norfolk Hall adds: "whiche was warned by dyuers to refrayne from the felde, in so much that the nyghte before he shoulde set forwarde towarde the kynge, one wrote on his gate.

    Jack of Norffolke be not to bolde
    For Dykon thy master is bought and solde.

Yet all this notwithstandynge he regarded more his othe his honour and promyse made to king Richard, lyke a gentleman and a faythefull subiecte to his prince absented not him selfe from hys mayster, but as he faythefully lyued vnder hym, so he manfully dyed with hym to hys greate fame and lawde" (p. 419).

Of the captured Earl of Northumberland Hall adds that he, "whither it was by the commaundement of kyng Richarde puttynge diffidence in him, or he dyd it for the loue & fauor that he bare vnto the Earle, stode still with a greate compaignie & intermitted not in the battaill" (p. 419).

Hall follow's Vergil's mistake in dating the battle a year too late, August 22, 1486.

To the statement that Henry gave thanks to God, Hall adds: "w^t deuoute & Godly orisons, besechyng his goodnes to send hym grace to auaunce & defende the catholike fayth & to mayntaine iustice & concorde amongest his subiectes & people, by God now to his gouernaunce committed & assigned" (p. 426).

The story of Lord Strange's rescue is likewise due to Hall. "I must put you here in remembraunce how that kynge Richarde puttynge some diffidence in the lord Stanley, which had w^t hym as an hostage, the lorde straunge his eldest sonne, which lord Stanley as you haue hearde before ioyned not at the first with his sonne in lawes armye, for feare that kynge Richarde woulde haue slayne the Lorde Straunge his heyre. When kynge Rycharde was come to Boswoorth, he sent a purseuaunt to the lord Stanley, commaundyng hym to auaunce forward with hys compaignie and to come to his presence, whiche thynge yf he refused to do, he sware by Christes passion that he woulde stryke of his sonnes hedde before he dined. The lorde Stanley aunswered the pursiuaunt that yf the kynge dyd so, he had more sonnes a lyue, and as to come to hym he was not then so determined: when kynge Richarde harde this aunswere he commaunded the lorde Straunge incontinent to be behedded, whiche was at that very same season when both the armyes had sight eche of other. The counsaillers of kyng Rychard pondering the time and the cause, knowynge also the Lorde Straunge to be innocent of his fathers offence, perswaded the kynge that it was now time to fight and not time to execucion, aduisynge him to kepe the Lorde Straunge as a prisoner till the battayll were ended, and then at Leyser his pleasure might be accomplished. So as God woulde kynge Rycharde enfryngyd hys holy othe, and the Lorde was deliuered to the kepers of the kynges tentes to be kept as a prisoner, whyche when the felde was done and their master slayne and proclamacion made to knowe were the childe was they submitted them selfes as prysoners to the Lord Straunge, and he gently receyued them and brought them to the newe proclamed king, where of him and of his Father he was receyued with greate ioye and gladnes" (pp. 420—21).

Of the bringing of Richard's body to Leicester, Hall adds that it "was trussed behynde a persiuaunt of armes called blaunche senglier or whyte bore, lyke a hogge or a calfe", "and all by spryncled with myre and bloude". Vergil's statement that Richard was buried "sine ullo funeris honore" is satirically paraphrased into "was with no lesse funeral pompe, and solempnitie enterred, then he woulde to be done at the beryng of his innocent nephiwes whome he caused cruellie to be murthered and vnnaturally to be quelled".

In the description of Richard, for Vergil's "of body deformed (corpore deformi)" Hall has "of body greatly deformed", for "little body (corpusculo)" he has "cruell body", and Vergil's "animum autem elatum ac ferocem" he translates not "courage high & fierce" but similarly to the Hardyng continuation "a proud mynde and an arroga*n*t stomacke" (p. 421).

The account is concluded by Hall with the words: "Thus ended this prince his mortall life with infamie and dishonor, whiche neuer preferred fame or honestie before ambicion tyranny and myschiefe. And yf he had continued still Protectoure and suffered his nephewes to haue lyued and reigned, no doubt but the realme had prospered and he muche praysed and beloued as he is nowe abhorred and vilipended, but to God whiche knewe his interior cogitacions at the hower of his deathe I remitte the punishment of his offences committed in his lyfe" (p. 421).

The work of More is a biography of Richard, and its feeling is throughout aroused by and directed toward the central figure of the story. Vergil's purpose was a far greater one, namely to write a history of England from the beginning down to his own time. Court historian as he was, in his account of the struggle of the Roses his sympathies were predominantly Lancastrian. Yet his account of this period is not written for itself alone, nor primarily devoted to proving justice of the Lancastrian contention. It always remains conditioned by the fact that is but a part of a far greater whole. The purpose of Hall was different from that either of More or of Vergil. It was, as the title of his book declares, to write the history of the contention between York and Lancaster, and the spirit in which he approached his task is seen in his introduction.

"What miserie, what murder, and what execrable plagues this famous region hath suffered by the deuision and discencion of the renoumed houses of Lancastre and Yorke, my witte cannot comprehende nor my toung declare nether yet my penne fully set furthe. . . . But the olde deuided controuersie betwene the forenamed families of Lancastre and Yorke, by the vnion of matrimony celebrate and consummate betwene the high and mighty Prince Kyng Henry the seuenth and the lady Elizabeth his moste worthy Quene, the one beeyng indubitate heire of the hous of Lancastre, and the other of Yorke was suspended and appalled in the person of their moste noble, puissant and mighty heire kyng Henry the eight, and by hym clerely buried and perpetually extinct. . . . What profite, what comfort, what ioy succeeded in the realme of Englande by the vnion of the fornamed two noble families, you shall apparantly perceiue by the sequele of this rude and vnlearned history. And because there can be no vnion or agrement but in respect of a diuision, it is consequent to reson that I manifest to you not onely the originall cause and fountain of the same, but also declare the calamities, trobles & miseries whiche happened and chaunced duryng the tyme of the said contencious discension" (pp. 1, 2).

To the picture of Gloucester's early career as transmitted by Vergil, Hall makes most important additions. It seems as if he must have been animated with a desire to show the real strength of Richard and the possibilities that lay in him, had not the desire of the throne warped his nature and brought on his downfall; and such a belief is made stronger by the words with which Hall closes his account of Richard's reign. Had Richard been content to remain Protector, "no doubt but the realme had prospered and he much praysed and beloued as he is nowe abhorred and vilipended". Thus to Hall more than to Vergil is due the apparent inconsistency between the two parts of the chronicles' accounts of Richard's career.

In Hall for the first time is Richard assigned an important part in the battles of Barnet and Tewkesbury. Here he appears as Edward's bravest and most skillful champion. We are not only told that in both battles he led the van; but his consummate strategy and unequalled courage at Tewkesbury are described in detail. In Hall's account it is Richard who leads and Edward follows; and to Richard does Edward owe his crown. Gloucester's warlike nature appears again in the account of the abortive campaign in France. Edward is glad to consent to a truce; Richard's sword thirsts for French blood, he detests, abhors, and cries out upon this peace. Again, Hall is the first to give Richard due credit for his campaign in Scotland. There is none of the condemnation of the Croyland continuator — who, it is worth remembering, is an eager excuser and supporter of the peace with France — and none of the lukewarm treatment of Vergil. In Hall's account appear Richard's "valiant manhood" and "prudent policy", and he wins the commendation not only of the king but of the whole realm.

But with the entrance upon More's work a new spirit appears. Nor is this More's spirit alone. Hall shows his own feeling by saying of Richard, "Lothe I am to remembre, but more I abhore to write the miserable tragedy of this infortunate prince, which by fraude entered, by tyranny proceded, and by sodayn death ended his infortunate life: But yf I should not declare the flagicious facies of the euyll princes, as well as I haue done the notable acts of verteous kinges, I shoulde neither animate, nor incourage rulers of royalmes, countreyes and seigniories to folowe the steppes of their profitable progenitors, for to attayne to the type of honour and worldly fame: neither yet aduertise princes being proane to vice and wickednes, to aduoyde and expell all synne and mischiefe, for dread of obloquy, and worldly shame: . . . Wherfore I will procede in his actes after my accustomed vsage" (p. 374).

This animus Hall reveals very clearly in his continuation, by the additions he makes to Vergil's account. His original is constantly embellished to bring out more strikingly the cruel nature and wickedness of Richard. Thus we have the account of Collingbourne's case, where Hall suppresses Collingbourne's real treason, and makes Richard put him to death for his scoffing rime alone. Where Vergil mentions the possibility that Richard poisoned his wife, Hall affirms that it is most likely. When Richard marches toward Bosworth it is "with a frowning countenance and truculent aspect". In Richard's speech to his soldiers, Hall, by a clever trick, makes him confess the crimes with which he is charged. The account of the taking of Richard to Leicester is embellished with further evidences of hostility. Richard is brought naked across the horse's back "like a hog or a calf" carried to market. His burial is attended, in Hall's mocking words, "with no less funeral pomp and solemnity than he would be done at the burying of his innocent nephews". In the description of Richard's person is seen the same desire to exaggerate. Vergil's statement that Richard was "of body deformed" becomes "of body greatly deformed"; and "little body" becomes "cruel body".

This is exaggeration of material supplied by Vergil; there is no new view of Richard's character in Hall save in a single point. Richard is represented as ready to perish, if need be, upon the field of battle, not as in Vergil, because recognizing the people's hate he is out of hope to have any better hap afterward; but in order that if he may not wear the crown in quiet he may by suffering a warrior's death win immortal fame. This devotion to fame, which does not appear in the Shakespearian Richard, was, as we shall see, in The True Tragedy made Richard's ruling passion.

To this exaggerated picture of Richard was of course to be expected an exaggerated contrast in Hall's picture of Richmond. Vergil had naturally declared him to have been sent of God, and in all respects treated him favorably; but there was no coarse flattery. Hall, moreover, outdoes Rous and embellishes André's picture of the "angelic" Richmond. His soldiers rejoice in the very sight of him, as he stands before them more like a creature of heaven than of earth, his hair yellow as burnished gold, his eyes and face shining, "formed and decorated with all gyftes and lyniamentes of nature".

In the general handling of Hall's story appears the same tendency to embellish and heighten the effect of the narratives that were his sources which has been noted in the descriptions of Richard and Richmond. This is especially seen in references to the murdered princes. No opportunity is lost to heighten the pathos of their end. They are constantly referred to as "innocent babes", "sely and little babes", "poor lambs" and the like; their blood cries to God for vengeance; Ely's heart sobs to think of them, Buckingham's veins pant and his body trembles. The whole impression of pathos and of horror approaches the description of the murder in Shakespeare's play, of which description it doubtless forms the germ. The same striving for effect is seen in the treatment of the Buckingham-Banister episode. In Hall, Buckingham is betrayed not merely by a retainer whom he had found honest from his youth; here Banister becomes one whom Buckingham had tenderly brought up and above all men loved, favored and trusted. In the same desire is doubtless to be found the reason why Hall adopts in the midst of More's story Vergil's lament of the queen for her murdered children.

The device of speeches, which had already been carried so far by André and More was a favorite rhetorical embellishment with Hall also. To those which he found in More and Vergil he added a second death-bed speech of Edward, a long continuation to More's speeches of Buckingham and Ely, a prayer of Richmond on sailing for England, speeches of Richard and Richmond to their soldiers, a prayer and speech of Richmond in thanksgiving for his success, and others. These speeches, troubled as they are by great prolixity, and by an abominable habit of doubling adjectives and nouns without adding anything to the sense — a fault in a slighter degree of More's work also — are nevertheless often very effective, and surpass all others in revealing the characters of those who utter them. It is this virtue which led to their frequent use in essence in Shakespeare's play.

Of material additions made to the saga by Hall the following are the most important: the account of the manner of Edward's escape from Middleham; the refusal of Montgomery and others at Nottingham to serve Edward unless he will claim the throne; the account of Prince Edward's capture and death at Tewkesbury, with the addition of Dorset's name as one of his murderers; the explanation of Burdet's case, mentioned in Buckingham's speech; Buckingham's statement of the taunts and re-taunts with which Richard met his request for the earldom of Hertford and his abhorrence toward the murder of the princes; the flood which leads to Buckingham's overthrow; the inscription found on Norfolk's gate; the account of Lord Strange's rescue.

All these passed into Shakespeare.

Hall's additions were largely adopted by the succeeding chroniclers, including Holinshed. But Holinshed, following Rastell's edition of More, and not Hall's version of it, and making use of other chronicles to increase and correct Hall's account of other events, does not have quite all of the material presented by Hall. Some of the omitted matter is found in Shakespeare's play, and thus we have the proof that Shakespeare used in its preparation not only Holinshed's chronicle, but Hall's as well. Oechelhäuser (Essay über König Richard III, p. 97 fn.) calls attention to one of these passages borrowed by Shakespeare from Hall, that, namely, where Richard appears in the gallery at Baynard's Castle "with a bishop on every hand of him". But Oechelhäuser adds that otherwise there is in the whole piece no indication that Shakespeare used any other source than Holinshed. That this is incorrect is shown by Wright in the preface of his Clarendon Press edition of Richard III, p. LXVII. Wright says, "Hall alone mentions Burdet's case, to which reference is made in III. 5. 76; ... and in Hall the scene of Buckingham's execution is the market-place at Salisbury, while in Holinshed it was at Shrewsbury". The former instance is correct; but in the latter Mr. Wright in turn has fallen into error. It is true that Holinshed says (3:418) that the captured Buckingham was brought to Richard at Shrewsbury, not Salisbury, as in Hall; but in Holinshed as in Hall, Buckingham is executed "at Salisburie, in the open market place". To the instances cited by Oechelhäuser and Wright may be added another. The reversal of Richard's fortunes in Richard III, Act IV, sc. III and IV (beginning) is evidently based on the passage from Polydore Vergil inserted by Hall in More's story: "And from thence forth [the murder of the princes] not onely all his counsailles, doynges and procedynges, sodainlye decayed and sorted to none effecte: But also fortune eganne to froune and turne her whele douneward from ᴊim" (p. 381).

A more striking instance, if all the editors be correct — which in spite of their unanimity is still open to some doubt — is the case of the messenger sent in Act III sc. I to the queen to ask for the young duke of York. Here the Qq. and folio have "Cardinal". In Act II sc. IV the Qp. have "Cardinal" and the folio "Archbishop" simply. In making the "Cardinal" of III 1 = Cardinal Bouchier of Canterbury, the editors must assume that Shakespeare followed Hall (p. 352) — preceded by Polydore Vergil and the Croyland continuator — and not Holinshed. The latter follows More, who has by a historical mistake not found in the Latin version, the Archbishop of York.

XVI. Grafton's Chronicle.

The date of Richard Grafton's birth is not known: he is supposed to have died in 1572. Though a member of the Grocer's Company, he is known almost wholly as printer and compiler of books. Coverdale's Bible (2nd ed.) was printed for him and Edward Whitchurch in Antwerp in 1537, Coverdale's corrected English translation of the New Testament at Paris in 1538 for the same persons. In 1539 Coverdale's Bible was printed for them in London. In 1539 "The Great Bible" was printed by Grafton and Whitchurch in London. Grafton was the printer of the first Book of Common Prayer, in 1549.

During Henry VIII's reign Grafton became printer to Prince Edward, was printer to the king during Edward's reign, and was printer to Lady Jane Grey, during her short assumption of power. He was imprisoned by queen Mary, but shortly released, and became a member of Parliament like Hall before him.

In the line of History Grafton first published Hardyng's Chronicle with the continuation already treated. In 1562 he issued "An Abridgement of the Chronicles of England", and this was reissued in 1563, 1564, 1570 and 1572.

In 1565 was issued "A Manuell of the Chronicles of England".

"A Chronicle at Large and Meere History of the affayres of Englande", known generally as "Grafton's Chronicle", appeared in 1568, in two volumes. In 1569 appeared a second edition, with a eulogy of Grafton by Thomas Norton (cf. Dict. Nat. Biog. sub Grafton).

The following citations are from the second volume of the two volume reprint by Ellis, 1809.

Hall had followed Vergil is his account of the reign of Edward the Fourth, making large additions, especially from De Comines.

Grafton adopted Hall's work bodily into his text, altering it only by a rare omission. He had at the same time Polydore Vergil and Fabian before him as an occasional brief addition shows.

All the additions noted in the summary of Hall are to be found in Grafton, save the speech of Warwick to his brothers, for which Grafton substitutes "the Erle of Warwick vttered a number of flattering and glosing wordes" and Hall's death-bed speech of Edward. Grafton evidently saw the absurdity of having two such speeches.

As Hall had done, Grafton adopted More's work, professing in the margin that the story was "now of late conferred & corrected by his [More's] awne copie". He does not mention that he likewise had Hall's chronicle or the Hardyng continuation before him and adopted many of his changes and additions without indicating that they are not in More.

Grafton has Hall's adoption from the Hardyng continuation that Richard entered the city "sayng to all men as he rode, beholde your Prince and souereigne Lorde" (p. 88) cf. p. 166.

The Cardinal who went to the Queen is called, as in More, the Archbishop of York (p. 89).

As in the Hardyng continuation and Hall the "other lord" is named "Lorde Haward" (p. 93).

All passages translated from More's Latin, and not in Hall, are in Grafton.

Grafton agrees with Hall and the Hardyng continuation in adding Northampton to Leicester as the seat of Hastings' power (p. 97; cf. sup. p. 167, Hall p. 359).

Richard, as in Hall (p. 359) and the Hardyng continuation (sup. p. 167) says "that he had bene a sleper" (p. 97). So, too, the addition on the fate of Stanley and others recurs; and the knight sent to accompany Hastings is named, Sir Thomas Howard (cf. sup. p. 167, Hall p. 361).

Hall's addition to the proclamation against Hastings, concerning Shore's wife "with whom he lay nightly etc." (cf. sup. p. 183) is adopted.

As in Hall the queen's kindred executed at Pomfret are named, including Hawte, and the speech of Vaughan (cf. sup. pp. 167—8) is given (p. 102, Hall p. 364).

Here too (p. 103) as in the Hardyng continuation (sup. p. 168) and in Hall (p. 365) Richard's preachers are named "Raufe Shaa" and "Fryer Pynkie".

As in Hall, for More's account of Warwick's embassy to Spain is adopted the statement of an embassy to ask for Lady Bona (p. 103), cf. p. 175.

Hall's addition to the account of the wooing of Elizabeth is admitted, cf. p. 175—6.

Hall's account of Burdet's case is copied, cf. p. 183.

The statement that Richard appeared in the gallery at Baynard's castle "with a Bishop on euery hand of him", which was first added to More's story by Grafton in the Hardyng continuation, and adopted by Hall, appears again in Grafton's Chronicle.

More's account of the procession to Westminster — translated from the Latin version — is followed exactly. Hall's paragraph on the proceedings of the fourth day of July is copied exactly, save that a slip in dating is corrected.

A list is given of the knights of the Bath created by Richard, and of the nobles who accompanied Richard in his procession to Westminster on the fifth of July. The coronation procession is described in detail.

From this point in the description of the coronation ceremonies till More is taken up again with the account of the murder of the princes, Hall is followed, with one or two slight changes and the omission of any mention of Richard's northern soldiers.

In the account of the murder of the princes Grafton has, as the Hardyng continuation (cf. sup. pp. 169, 170) and Hall (p. 378), the "IIII other" set to see the princes sure, Tyrell's device that there should be "no blood shed", and Hall's additional paragraph on the throwing of the princes' bodies into "the blacke depes" (p. 118).

Hall's paragraph from Vergil (extended) added after More's description of Richard's inward trouble (cf. p. 184) is adopted by Grafton.

Continuing to follow Hall, Grafton omits with him the statement of Buckingham's message to Richard through Persival (here called Persall, which is More's form of the name). He copies Hall's "Thys Duke as you haue heard before assoone as the Duke of Gloucester after the death of King Edwarde was come to Yorke, and there had solempne funerall seruice done for King Edward, sent to him a secret seruant of hys called Persall, with such messages as you haue heard before". Now Hall had transferred More's statement of this message to the very beginning of his account, but Grafton had failed to do so, having followed More exactly. Thus, omitted in this place also, the message nowhere appears in Grafton.

From the point where More's story ends, Grafton once more adopts Hall bodily into his text. There are some verbal changes, and a few omissions. I note the most important.

Buckingham is said to have been brought to Richard at Shrewsbury, not Salisbury, at in Hall. But the execution takes place at Salisbury (p. 135).

The treaty with the Scots is omitted, as well as the time of truce.

Henry's prayer to God before sailing on his second expedition (cf. p. 193) is omitted.

Hall's passage from Vergil, "whiche prycke of conscience allthough it strike not all waye, yet at the last daie, etc." is omitted.

Hall's speeches of Richard and Richmond before the battle are somewhat abridged, and Richmond's prayer to God after the battle is omitted.

The description of Richard, taken by Hall from Vergil, is omitted, doubtless as unnecessary after More's description.

XVII. Holinshed's Chronicle.

The date of Raphael Holinshed's birth is not known; he is supposed to have died in 1580. In the early part of Elizabeth's reign he obtained employment in London as a translator in the printing office of Reginald Wolfe. Wolfe had been engaged since 1548 on a universal history, working himself upon the English, Scotch, and Irish portions, with the aid of John Leland's collections, and in this task Holinshed assisted him. In 1573 Wolfe died, and his work passed into the possession of George Bishop, John Harrison, and Luke or Lucas Harrison, well-known publishers. They decided to limit the work to England, Scotland, and Ireland, and continued to employ Holinshed. William Harrison assisted in the work on the descriptions of England and Scotland, and Richard Stanihurst continued Holinshed's history of Ireland from 1509 to 1547.

The work was licensed for publication July 1, 1578, as "The Chronicles of England, Scotland, and Ireland", in two folio volumes. After Holinshed's death in 1580 (?) the publishers, with new associates, employed John Hooker as editor of a new edition. By him the work was continued, with the assistance of Francis Thynne, Abraham Fleming, and John Stow, to the year 1586. The new edition appeared in three folio volumes January 1, 1587 (1586 old Style), (cf. Dict. Nat. Biog. sub Holinshed). The following citations,

14*

are from the third volume of the London 1807—08 six volume reprint of the second edition of Holinshed.

Holinshed's account of the reign of Edward IV is based upon that of Hall. Sometimes Hall's account is adopted verbally; sometimes rewritten without essential change of fact; often abridged. Holinshed appears to have had a severe contempt for Hall's prolixity. Beside this the account of "The History of the Arrival of King Edward", is used, as communicated by Fleetwood, and adapted by Fleming (cf. p. 7). Further, there are excerpts from Stow (in turn sometimes from Warkworth and Fabian), from Fabian, an addition by Hooker, an item of Stow's from Euguerrant de Monstrelet, and one from John Rous. Most of these however refer to matters of interest in the city of London, and do not concern this summary. These additions belong to the second edition of 1586—7 Holinshed gives two accounts of the capture of Henry VI, Hall's and Stow's, which latter (as we have seen) was taken from Warkworth (cf. pp. 15, 224) and increased (by the statement that Warwick met the king and arrested him at Esildon, and that with Henry were "doctor Maning deane of Windsor, doctor Bedle, and young Ellerton") (p. 282).

Concerning Warwick's embassy to win a wife for Edward, Holinshed omits Hall's discussion as to whether Warwick went to Spain, and mentions only the embassy to France to ask for Lady Bona.

Hall's account of Edward's wooing of Elizabeth (cf. pp. 175, 176), is copied till towards the end. Holinshed's conclusion is: "with hir sober demeauoure, sweete looks, and comelie smiling (neether too wanton, nor too bashfull) besides hir pleasant toong and trim wit, she so alured and made subiect unto hir the heart of that great prince, that after she had denied him to be his paramour. with so good maner, and words so well set as better could not be deuised; he finallie resolued with himselfe to marrie hir, not asking counsell of anie man, till they might perceiue it was no bootie to aduise him to the contrarie of that his concluded purpose; sith he was so farre gonne that he was not reuocable, and therefore had fixed his heart vpon the last resolution: namelie, to applie an holesome, honest, and honourable remedie to his affections fiered with the flames of loue, and not to permit his heart to the thraldome of vnlawfull lust: which purpose was both princelie and profitable" (p. 284).

A comparison of Hall's and Holinshed's accounts with Shakespeare's scene (3 Hen. VI, III 2), shows that Shakespeare probably followed Hall. But cf. Hall's later account, p. 366, which Holinshed has.

Holinshed has Hall's speech of Warwick to his brothers, and the paragraph on the dissimulation of Marquis Montacute (cf. sup. p. 176); but Clarence's speech, together with his reasons for ill will toward his brother, is omitted. Here again, in 3 Hen. VI, IV 1, Shakespeare used Hall.

Hall's account of Edward's escape from Middleham is adopted by Holinshed, and the account from De Comines of Warwick's and Clarence's doings in France, the latter in somewhat abridged form. No essential fact is omitted, however. The story of the damsel sent by Edward to Clarence appears, and the statement that Prince Edward was "wedded" to Anne.

The reconciliation of Montacute to Edward (cf. sup. p. 177) is mentioned.

The story of Edward's flight is taken from Hall, but his addition on the "sour sauces" tasted by Edward in his flight (cf. sup. p. 177) is omitted. Edward's proceedings in Burgundy are related from Hall's account taken from De Comines.

Hall's passage from Vergil, on the misfortunes of Henry being caused by his grandfather's usurpation is omitted by Holinshed.

The story of Edward's landing in England and his further proceedings is taken from the "History of the

Arrival", which is followed in detail, with an occasional mention from Hall and some abridgement.

The passage on Henry of Derby, quoted on p. 7 is weakened into "where Henrie erle of Derbie, after called king Henrie the fourth landed, when he came to depriue king Richard the second of the crowne, and to usurpe it to himselfe" (p. 303).

Edward's proceedings are carefully detailed according to the "History of the Arrival", till he arrives at York. Here Holinshed includes Hall's account from Vergil of Edward's taking the oath to support Henry (cf. p. 133). "For this wilful perjurie (as hath beene thought) [a reference to Hall?] the issue of this king suffered for the father's offence the depriuation not onelie of lands and worldlie possessions but also of their naturall liues, by their cruel vncle Richard the third". To which Holinshed adds, "And it may well be. For it is not likelie that God, in whose hands is the bestowing of all souereigntie, will suffer such an indignatie to be doone to his sacred maiestie, and will suffer the same to passe with impunitie". With more to the effect that princes even more than private men are bound to keep their oaths (p. 305).

To the story of the men who met Edward at Nottingham and their demand that Edward should proclaim himself king, Holinshed adds from the earlier chronicler the name of Sir James Harrington.

As Holinshed proceeds with his account he is careful to temper the Yorkist tone of the chronicler's narrative. The offers made by Edward to Warwick which to the earlier writer seemed very fair considering the earl's "great and haynows offenses", Holinshed says "to manie seemed verie reasonable, considering their heinous offences". Warwick's demand, which the earlier writer says did not "in eny wyse stande with the Kyngs honowr and swretye", Holinshed says "was thought" in no wise so to stand. Yet in many places the original Yorkist wording is allowed to stand, and we find such expressions as "the pretensed authoritie of King Henrie" (p. 311).

Clarence's reasons for going over to his brother and the mediators between them, are stated as in "The Arrival" (cf. sup. p. 8) without mention of Hall's (De Comines') story of the damsel (p. 307).

Warwick's reception of Clarence's endeavors to reconcile him to Edward is given as in Hall (Vergil).

The story of the battle of Barnet is described from Hall, with additions from "The Arrival", and frcm Stow (Warkworth). From Hall, Holinshed adopts Vergil's statement that Warwick resolved to trust his brother Montacute, though suspicious of him; the arrangement of the troops; the speeches of Warwick and Edward to their men (abridged); the statement that Edward fought in person and that Warwick was forced to fight on foot; that Warwick fell in the midst of his enemies; that Montacute thought to succor his brother, but was overthrown and slain. From Warkworth through Stow come other and contradictory items: the story of Oxford's flight caused by the unfortunate mistake of badges; the statement that Montacute wore Edward's badge and was slain by one of Warwick's men for treason; and the story that Warwick was slain in flight. Edward's proceedings after the battle are related from Hall, but with the landing of Margaret Holinshed returns to "The History of the Arrival", admitting however from Hall (Vergil) an abridged account of Margaret's fear for her son, and her purpose to defer battle or send her son to sanctuary.

The story of the battle of Tewkesbury is again a compiled account, made up from "The Arrival" and Hall together. All that Hall has of Gloucester's conduct reappears, and where this conflicts with the account given by "The Arrival", in its praise of Edward, we find, "The king, or (as others haue) the duke of Glocester" etc.

The account of Prince Edward's death is given, however, not from "The Arrival", but from Hall, with only slight verbal changes. Queen Margaret's capture, on the other hand, is given not as in Hall, but as in "The Arrival", according to which Margaret was captured "in a poore house of religion", to which she had withdrawn on the morning of the battle. Herein Shakespeare in 3 Henry VI, V, IV & V, followed Hall.

The death of king Henry is described from Hall, to which account Holinshed adds that of "the Arrival", reworded. "Howbeit, some writers of that time, fauoring altogither the house of York, haue recorded, that after he vnderstood what losses had chanced vnto his freends, and how not onelie his sonne, but also all other his cheefe partakers were dead and dispatched, he tooke it so to hart, that of pure displeasure, indignation and melancholie, he died the three and twentith of Mai".

Hall's (Vergil's) account of Henry's character is copied by Holinshed, who, apropos of Henry's making account only of his sins, not of his losses, adds, "So then verie unlike it is, that he died of anie wrath, indignation, and displeasure bicause his business about the keeping of the crowne on his head tooke no better successe; except peraduenture ye will saie [returning in effect to Hall] that it greeued him, for that such slaughters and mischeeues as had chanced within this land, came to passe onelie through his follie and default in gouernment: or (that more is) for his fathers, his grandfathers, and his owne vniust vsurping and deteining of the crowne" (pp. 324—5).

Hall's account of Henry's burial is copied by Holinshed, but with the additions, that the corpse was conveyed to St. Paul's "on the Ascencion euen", a fact evidently obtained from Fabyan (cf. sup. p. 69); that at Paul's it was laid on the bier "or coffen bare faced, the same in presence of the beholders did bleed"; "From thense he was caried to the Black friers, and bled there likewise". The latter two items are from Stow, who got them from Warkworth.

From Stow (cf. inf. p. 225) is taken an account of the fate of Thomas Burdet of Warwickshire.

The story of Clarence's death is given as in Hall with all the different reasons assigned for it, but the order is changed, Clarence's complaint about his servant's death being given first, and the prophecy afterwards. Likewise is included later (p. 354) Hall's statement that Edward was set on by such as envied Clarence's estate. Cf. sup. p. 180.

From Hall is taken in abridged from the account of Gloucester's campaign in Scotland; but the paragraph in which the king praises him is omitted.

Hall is followed in the causes suggested for Edward's death; and Hall's death-bed speech of Edward is copied. It is preceded, however, by a statement meant to reconcile it with the effect of More's speech, quoted later.

"He began to make readie for his passage into another world, not forgetting (as after shall appeare) to exhort the nobles of his realme (aboue all things) to an vnitie among themselues. And hauing (as he tooke it) made an attonement betwixt the parties that were knowne to be scant freends, he commended vnto their graue wisedoms the gouernment of his sonne the prince, and of his brother the duke of Yorke, during the time of their tender yeares. But it shall not be amisse to adde in this place the words which he is said to haue spoken on his deathbed, which were in effect as followeth" —.

Like the Hardyng continuator, Hall, and Grafton before him, Holinshed introduced More's work into his own, and like Grafton he professed to print it "according to a copie of his owne hand, printed among his other works" (p. 360). Unlike Grafton, however, he very nearly does what he says. In general Holinshed followed More faithfully, with only the slightest of verbal changes, but he did have Hall and Grafton before him and admits the following alterations.

Concerning the "other lord" who accompanied the cardinal to the queen, Holinshed has in the margin: "The lord Howard, saith Edw. Hall" (p. 375).

To the account of Hastings' death Holinshed adds: "Thus began he to establish his kingdome in bloud, growing thereby in hatred of the nobles, and also abridging both the line of his life, and the time of his regiment: for God will not haue bloud thirstie tyrants daies prolonged, but will cut them off in their ruffe; according to Dauids words:
> Impio, fallaci, auidoque caedis
> Fila mors rumpet viridi in iuuenta" (p. 381).

Hall's addition to Richard's proclamation against Hastings that with Shore's wife "he laie nightlye and namelie the night last past next before his death" is admitted.

Hall's explanation of Burdet's case (cf. p. 183) is not admitted; and it may be supposed with Wright (Pref. to his Richard III, LXVII) that Holinshed believed this to refer to the case of the Warwickshire Burdet (cf. p. 217). Cf. Stow and what he says (inf. p. 228).

All the passages translated by Rastell from More's Latin are to be found in Holinshed. Concerning Richard's coronation he says, "But here to shew the manner of his coronation, as the same is inserted in this pamphet of Sir Thomas More, by Maister Eduard Hall and Richard Grafton (although not found in the same pamphlet) thus we find it by them reported". The report that follows combines Hall's and Grafton's accounts, but omits some of Grafton's details of the coronation.

To More's statement that after the murder of the princes Richard never had a quiet mind, Holinshed adds, "Than the which there can be no greater torment. For a giltie conscience inwardlie accusing and bearing witnesse against an offender, is such a plague and punishment, as hell itselfe (with all the feends therein) can not affoord one of greater horror & affliction" (p. 402)

Holinshed gives the name of Buckingham's messenger as Persall, following More, but in the margin stands "Persiuall, saith Ed. Hall" (p. 403).

Having finished More's story, Holinshed has a marginal note: "Here endeth sir Thomas Moore, & this that followeth is taken out of master Hall" (p. 403). But Holinshed had Grafton before him as well as Hall, as is abundantly shown by certain verbal deviations from Hall common to Grafton and Holinshed.

Holinshed agrees with Grafton in saying that Buckingham was brought to Richard at Shrewsbury; but like the latter agrees with Hall in saying that Buckingham was beheaded at Salisbury.

From Hooker is given the following anecdote. "King Richard came this yeare to the citie [of Exeter], but in verye secret maner, whome the maior & his brethren in the best maner they could did receiue, and then presented to him in a purse two hundred nobles; which he thinkefullie accepted. And during his abode here he went about the citie, & viewed the seat of the same, & at length he came to the castell: and when he vnderstood that it was called Rugemont, suddenlie he fell into a dumpe, and (as one astonied) said; Well, I see my daies be not long. He spake this of a prophesie told him, that when he came once to Richmond he should not long liue after; which fell out in the end to be true, not in respect of this castle, but in respect of Henrie earle of Richmond, who the next yeare following met him at Bosworth field where he was slaine" (p. 421).

From Hooker is given also a list of persons indicted for treason against Richard.

To Hall's and Grafton's statement that Collingbourne was beheaded for his rime solely, Holinshed adds the full indictment showing that the first charge was conspiracy to aid Richmond, and the second the writing and publication of certain rimes.

For the account of the Scotch treaty the reader is referred to the history of Scotland. But the statement that a truce was concluded for three years (which Grafton omitted) is included: as well as Hall's paragraph on the marriage of Anne de la Poole and the prince (duke, says Holinshed) of Rothsay.

From Stow is added by Fleming the history of the Earl of Oxford's career after the battle of Barnet (pp. 427—428).

To Hall's (Vergil's) account of Richard's winning over Elizabeth, Holinshed adds: "But it was no small allurement that king Richard used to ouercome hir (for we know by experience that women are of a proud disposition, and that the waie to win them is by promises of preferment) and therefore it is the lesse maruell that he by his wilie wit had made conquest of hir wauering will. Besides that, it is to be presumed that she stood in feare to impugne his demands by denials, least he in his malicious mood might take occasion to deale roughlie with hir, being a weake woman and of a timorous spirit" (p. 430).

Hall's prayer of Richmond on setting out from France is omitted by Holinshed (as by Grafton).

In Richard's speech to his army as reported by Holinshed (2^d ed.) occurs the well-known misprint by which Richard is made to say Richmond was brought up "by my moothers meanes" instead of "by my brothers means", as in Hall.

Hall's (Vergil's) mistake of 1486 as the date of the battle of Bosworth is corrected to 1485.

At the close of Hall's account, ending "to God . . . I remit the punishment of his offenses" Holinshed makes an addition: "whiche if the one be as manifold as the other, Gods iustice were not to be charged with crueltie. For by nature he is mercifull, slow to anger, and loth to smite: but yet eurie sinne (in respect of his righteousnesse) being deadlie (much more heinous and horrible) how can he but by iustice . . punish it seuerlie? And if he did it with ten thousand torments, who shall be so hardie as to expostulate and reason why he so dooth?"

Holinshed states that Henry VII had a tomb set up over Richard's grave, doing him the same honor that

Richard did to Henry VI, whose body he removed from Chertsey to Windsor.

"And now to conclude with this cruell tyrant king Richard, we may consider in what sort the ambitious desire to rule and gouerne in the house of Yorke, was punished by Gods iust prouidence.

For although that the right might seeme to remaine in the person of Richard duke of Yorke, slaine at Wakefield; yet maie there be a fault worthilie reputed in him so to seeke to preuent the time appointed him by authoritie of parlement to atteine to the crowne entailed to him and his issue; in whome also, and not onelie in himselfe, that offense (as maie bee thought) was dulie punished. For although his eldest sonne Edward the fourth, beeing a prince right prouident and circumspect for the suertie of his owne estate and his children, insomuch that not content to cut off all his armed and apparant enimies, he also of a gealous feare, made awaie his brother the duke of Clarence, and so thought to make all sure: yet Gods vengeance might not be disappointed, for (as ye haue partlie heard) he did but further thereby the destruction of his issue, in taking awaie him that onlie might haue staied the crueltie of his brother of Glocester, who inraged for desire of the kingdome, bereft his innocent nephues of their liues & estates.

And as it thus well appeared, that the house of Yorke shewed it selfe more bloudie in seeking to obteine the kingdome, than that of Lancaster in vsurping it: so it came to passe, that the Lords vengeance appeared more heauie towards the same than toward the other, not ceassing till the whole issue male of the said Richard duke of Yorke was extinguished. For such is Gods iustice, to leaue no vnrepentant wickednesse vnpunished, as especiallye in this caitife Richard the third, not deseruing so much as the name of a man, much lesse of a king, most manifestlie appeareth".

Here Fleming inserts from Guie, a comparison of Richard's act to that of Ludovico Sforza, duke of Milan.

"But to end with king Richard sometimes duke of Glocester, a title of dignitie ioined with misfortune and vnluckinesse (as is noted before)... As for King Richard, better had it beene for him to haue contented his heart with the protectorship, than to haue cast vp his snout, or lifted vp his hornes of ambition so high (and that with a setled intent) as to hacke and hew downe by violent blowes all likelie impediments betwixt him and home. Better (I say) had it beene for him to haue dwelt vpon his first honor, than to haue wandered in princelinesse; and better had it beene for him neuer to haue inioied the flattering prosperitie of a king, than afterwards to fall, and neuer to recouer losse or ruine, as is noted by the poet, saieng

T. Wat. in Am. Quer. 7.
Est melius nunquam felicia tempora nosse,
Quam post blanditias fortunae, fata maligna
Nec reparanda pati infortunia sortis iniquae.

Thus farre Richard the vsurper, vnnaturall vncle to Edward the fift and Richard duke of Yorke, brethren".

The account of Holinshed makes very little change in the form or content of Hall's. Richard's character remains as before, with its dark side made ever so slightly blacker by the omission of Hall's praise for his conduct in the Scottish war, and by an occasional additional phrase calculated to emphasize his cruelty and wicknedness. With this is emphasized by additions, especially in the long passage with which the account closes, the idea of the divine justice. The general attitude of Hall toward the House of York is preserved, in spite of the admission of portions from the Yorkist "History of the Arrival", for these do not stand alone, but side by side with the Lancastrian accounts, and are either so changed as to become Lancastrian in tone, or their accuracy is denied.

There is only one important addition of material. This is the anecdote of Richard's visit to Exeter, and the gloomy prophecy by which he connects Rougemont with Richmond.

Thus though Shakespeare may in writing Richard III have based his play almost wholly on the form of the saga which he found in Holinshed, yet in the formation of that saga Holinshed is of very slight importance. The proof that Shakespeare did use Holinshed in this play, Wright states as follows (Pref. to his R. III, VII): "To this source we owe the name of Friar Penker (III, 5, 104), which in Hall is Pynkie; the story of Richard's visit to Exeter (IV, 2, 107—111), and his alarm at the ominous resemblance of Rougemont to Richmond; and the statement in Richard's address to his army that Richmond had been maintained in Brittany 'at our mother's cost', an error which occurs in the second edition of Holinshed only". To this, however, more may be added. The reference in 1:2, 55, 6 to the reopening and bleeding of Henry's wounds rests upon Holinshed's account of Henry's burial (derived from Warkworth); there is no mention of the fact in Hall. Act III, sc. 1, 194—97,

> "And, look, when I am king, claim thou of me
> Th'earldom of Hereford, and the movables
> Whereof the king my brother stood possess'd".

rests upon a passage translated from More's Latin, and therefore not in Hall, but obtained by Shakespeare from Holinshed (More, Lumby's ed. p. 43).

XVIII. Stow's Annals.

John Stow was born 1528 and died 1605. Brought up to the trade of a tailor, he abandoned it to pursue historical investigations. In 1561 he published "A Summary of English Chronicles". This was often reprinted, ten times between 1561 and 1604. In 1580 he published his "Annales, or a Generale Chronicle of England from Brute until the present yeare of Christ 1580. (The titles of later edd. vary from this.) Other editions followed in 1592, 1601, 1605, with editions by Howes in 1615, 1631.

In 1598 was printed Stow's Survey of London (cf. Enc. Brit. sub Stow).

Stow's account of the reign of Edward IV is made up from many sources, among which were "The History of the Arrival", Warkworth, Fabyan, Hall, de Comines and others. In the following summary are noted only such points of his story as illustrate, correct or deviate strikingly from that of Hall, as before summarized.

In the first year of Edward's reign, "The 12. of March, Walter Walker a Grocer that dwelt in Cheape of London, for words spoken touching king Edward, was suddenly apprehended, condemned, and beheaded in Smithfield. This grocer is he, whom master Hall mistaketh to be Burdet" (p. 680).

Warwick's embassy is given simply as to Lady Bona, and Edward's marriage to Elizabeth Gray is merely mentioned without detail.

The account of Henry's capture is given as in Warkworth, save that "bysyde a howse of religione in Lancaschyre, by the mene of a blacke monke of Abyngtone" is omitted; and the addition that at Esyldon Henry was met and arrested by Warwick, "and forthwith his gilt spurs were taken from his feete, doctor Manning Deane of Windsore, doctor Bedle and young Ellerton being in his companie".

Clarence's separation from his brother is mentioned without the assignment of any reasons. Prince Edward is stated to have been married to [Anne] Warwick's daughter.

The story of Edward's return to England, of the reconciliation of Edward and Clarence, and of the battle of Barnet, are given as in Warkworth. Prince Edward's death is given as in Fabyan. "Edward . . . toke Queene Margaret prisoner with Prince Edward hir sonne, whom cruelly he smote on the face with his gantlet, and after his seruants slue him" (p. 695) [from the Liber Tewxburyiensis].

As in Warkworth King Henry is said to have been murdered, but no mention is made of Gloucester's presence at the Tower. Warkworth's account of Henry's burial, and the bleeding of his wounds is given, very slightly abridged in the wording only. Stow adds a long description of Henry's character, and incidents illustrating it.

Of Richmond no prophecy is mentioned. There is only the simple statement of his flight with the earl of Pembroke into Brittany (p. 699).

Edward's proceedings in France are related from de Comines (abridged). Gloucester's dislike for the truce is not mentioned.

The course of Edward's attempt to obtain Richmond is related in abridged form from Hall.

From Euguerrant (de Monstrelet) Stow relates the case of Burdet: —

"Thomas Burdet an esquire of Arrow in Warwickshire ... was beheaded for a word spoken in this sort (as was said). Edward in his progres hunted in Tho. Burdets park at Arrow, and slew many of his deere, amongst the which one was a white buck, whereof Tho. Burdet made great account, & therefore when he vnderstood thereof, he wished the buckes head in his bellie that moued the king to kil it. Which tale being told to the king, Burdet was apprehended and accused of treason, for wishing the buckes head horns and al in the kings belly. More he was accused of poisoning, sorcery & inchantment, whereupon he was condemned,.. and beheaded" (Stow p. 707).

In accounting for the death of Clarence Stow used only the indictment: —

"The 16 day of January began a parliament at Westminster, wherein George D. of Clarence . . was attainted of treason: In y̆ͤ which attaindor (which I haue read) is declared, that the said George . . against the king his soueraigne Lord, had caused diuers his seruants to informe the people, that Thomas Burdet his seruant (which was lawfully and truly attainted of treason) was wrongfully put to death. To his seruants of such disposition he gaue large summes of money, venison, &c. therewith to assemble the kings subiects, to feast them, and then to induce them

Palaestra. X. 15

to beleeue, that the said Burdet was wrongfully executed. He also by such his seruants, laboured to make the people beleeue that the king wrought by Negromancie, and vsed the craft to poison his subiects, such as him pleased, to the great disclander of the king, and incouraging his subiects against him. And ouer that, the said D. being in ful purpose to exalt himselfe and his heires to the regaltie and crowne of England, and cleerely in opinion to put aside from the same for euer, the king and his heires, vpon one of the falsest and most vnnaturall coloured pretence that man might imagine, falsely and vntruely published, that the king was a bastard, and not legitimate to raigne. And to continue this his most malicious and traiterous purpose after this seditious language among the people, he induced diuers of the kings naturall subiects to be sworne upon the blessed sacrament, to be true to him and his heires, none exception reserued of their allegiance: and after the same oth so made, he shewed to many, that the king had taken his liuelode from him, and his men were disherited, but he would indeuour to get them their inheritance, as he would do his owne: he shewed also, that the king inte$n$ded to consume him, in like sort as a candle consumeth in burning, whereof he would in briefe quite him. And ouer this, the said D. got an exemplification vnder the great seale of Henry the sixt late king, wherein was contained, that if the said H. and E. his son died without issue male, that $\overset{e}{y}$ said D. & his heires should be kings &c. Thus much for his attaindor.

And on the 11. of March, after he had offered his owne masse peny in the tower of London, he made his end in a vessel of malmesey".

The supposed causes of Edward's death are given as in Hall, but Hall's death-bed speech is omitted.

Stow copies de Comines' account of Edward's death and his comment on the deaths incurred in the struggle for the crown as caused by the wrath of God. Cf. p. 55, 56—7.

Like Holinshed, Grafton and Hall, Stow adopted bodily the work of Sir Thomas More. He is, however, the most faithful copyist of all, departing very seldom from More's text, and generally indicating the addition by a difference in print. After the entrance of Prince Edward into London, Stow adds, "The king was lodged in the bishops palace, where was kept a great counsell, and there was sworne to the king, the duke of Gloucester, the duke of Buckingham, and all the lords" (p. 726).

The passages from More's Latin are all included.

Like Grafton and Hall, Stow makes Richard say "that he had bene a sleper (More and Holinshed have "a slepe") that day".

Buckingham's reference to Burdet has against it in the margin: "T. Burdet esquire of Arrow in Warwickshire, looke Anno 1477" (p. 754).

More's account of the proceedings attending Richard's elevation to the crown is followed, but to it is added a reference to the 5000 men from the north, and the proceedings of the fourth, fifth and sixth of July, from Hall; but Richard is said to have been crowned on the seventh (p. 761).

Another additional paragraph recounts the taking and execution of certain rebels who had sent writings to Richmond, and who had purposed stealing Edward and his brother from the Tower, while their guards were extinguishing a fire set to draw them away (p. 762).

From the end of More's story, what "followeth is abridged out of Edward Hall" (p. 769).

There is little, therefore, to comment upon. Stow omits to say anything about Anne's death by poison, having only: "howsoeuer it fortuned" (p. 778).

Hall's long speeches of Richard and Richmond are omitted.

Richard the Third

up to Shakespeare.

Part II:

Richard in Poetry and the Drama.

I. The Song of Lady Bessy.

This curious ballad was published separately by Thomas Heywood in 1809, in Halliwell's Palatine Anthology 1850, and in the Percy Society's series. Two versions are known, one in a Ms. of the time of Charles II, and another, with some unimportant variations, is in the British Museum, Ms. Harl. 367. This, according to Halliwell, "appears to have been transcribed about the year 1600". Both versions are printed by Halliwell.

The author seems from internal evidence to have been Humphrey Brereton, as servant of Lord Thomas Stanley, afterwards Earl of Derby; and the date at which it was composed "must have been some time in the course of Henry VII's reign, or perhaps in the beginning of Henry VIII's" (Gairdner, Life of Richard III, p. 401).

The following synopsis contains all that is valuable to our purpose. For fuller knowledge the reader is referred to Gairdner's Life of Richard, and to the poem itself.

The "Lady Bessy" is the Princess Elizabeth, eldest daughter of Edward IV, who is here represented as the chief organizer of the conspiracy which brought Richmond to England, and ended in his defeat of Richard and marriage to Elizabeth.

Bessy comes to Lord Stanley and implores him, in return for the offices and possessions conferred upon him by her father, to bring Richmond home from Britanny and make him king. Stanley repulses her, but Bessy persists, reminding him of Richard's murdering the two princes, who should in right have reigned. Stanley again refuses, warning her that if Richard hears of her attempt she will be imprisoned or put to death. Bessy still continues, bringing forward a stronger argument. Once she saw her father weeping as he read a book, and as she came to him he revealed to her the cause of his sorrow.

> "For their shall never son of my body be gotten
> That shall be crowned after me;
> But you shall be queen and wear the crown:
> So doth expresse the prophecye!"

He gave the book to Elizabeth, and bade her show it to none save Stanley, and to rely upon him for aid. Him, therefore, she now petitions for soldiers and captains. Still denied by Stanley, she begs him for love of God to have pity on her. Only three days before Richard had sent to her

> "A batchelor and a bold baron,
> A Doctor of Divinitye",

to beg her to become his love, and he would poison his wife, and his son and heir as well. She would rather be burned than consent. Stanley still asserts his loyalty, and Bessy now brings forward her strongest argument. His loyalty will avail him nothing, for Richard has himself made known to her his purpose to hang or behead all the lineage of the Stanleys and the Talbots. Let him avert the danger by uniting with his brother, Sir John Savage, his sister's son, and Sir Gilbert Talbot, all of whom can bring great forces into the field. Stanley continues obdurate, sure that Richard cannot intend to betray him. Unsuccessful in all her appeals, Bessy falls in a swoon.

And now Stanley confesses to her, when she recovers, that he has but been trying her to see if she feigned. He has himself harbored thoughts of the same kind. They now take counsel together. Letters are written, with Bessy acting as scribe, to Lord Strange, Sir William Stanley, Sir John Savage, and Sir Gilbert Talbot, and these are despatched by Humphry Brereton, Stanley's esquire. All agree to meet Stanley in London. Brereton returns to Stanley, whom he finds walking in a garden with Richard.

On Stanley's complaint that he has not seen Brereton for a long while, the latter replies that he has been in the West country where he was born; and Stanley so commends the courage and loyalty of the West-country men that Richard is deceived and declares that half of England shall be Stanley's own.

On the third of May the conspirators meet Stanley and Bessy, and promise to make her queen. £19,000 of gold, with a love-letter and a ring from Bessy are despatched by Brereton to Richmond. He finds him at an abbey in Brittany, recognizing him from a description given by the porter.

> " 'A wart he hath', the porter said,
> 'A little alsoe above the chinn,
> His face is white, his wart is redd,
> No more than the head of a small pinn' ".

Richmond takes the letters and gold, and kisses the ring three times. After an unsuccessful petition to the King of France for men, money and ships, Richmond sends the messenger back with letters and the promise to Bessy that he will cross the sea for her.

On receipt of Richmond's messages, Bessy is sent into hiding at Leicester that she may not be burnt in a fire by Richard, and Stanley goes to the West. Lord Strange is sent to London to keep King Richard company. The conspirators call together their forces, and Richmond enters England. Hearing this news, the king calls together his lords, and summons Stanley to send him 20,000 men, or his son, Lord Strange, shall die. He likewise summons Sir William Stanley, who replies that on Bosworth field he will offer him such a breakfast "as never did knight to any king". Thereupon Richard determines that Strange shall die, and sends him to the Tower.

At Bosworth the forces of the conspirators meet. Richmond begs to lead the van, as he has come to claim his own right, and this is accorded him by Stanley. When Richard appears, and perceives that Stanley has ranged himself on Richmond's side he orders that Strange be executed at once. The intercession of Sir William Harrington, who begs that Strange be preserved till after the battle, when all the Stanleys will be in Richard's power, is of no avail. Strange's head is already upon the block, when Richard's ranks begin to break on every side, and the exigency of the situation enables Harrington to rescue Strange.

The battle rages and Richard's men begin to flee.

> "When King Richard that sight did see,
> In his heart hee was never soe woe: —
> 'I pray you, my merry men, be not away,
> For upon this field will I like a man dye;
> For I had rather dye this day
> Than with the Standley prisoner to be'".

Harrington urges the king to mount and save his life, but Richard answers,

> "'Give me my battle axe in my hand;
> I make a vow to myld Mary that is so bright,
> I will dye the king of merry England'".

And thus he falls among his enemies, the crown hewed from his head and his brains beaten out. In Leicester his corpse is viewed by the amiable Bessy who welcomes it with the remark,

> "'How like you the killing of my brethren dear
> Welcome, gentle uncle, home'".

She is then married to Richmond, and Sir William Stanley crowns them both.

The chief interest of this piece lies in the proof it affords that Richard's story appealed very early to the popular imagination and became subject to its shaping influence. Outside of the chronicles it appears first in the most popular form of literature, the ballad. Whether the song was originally composed by Brereton or not, that it was subjected to repeated changes by those who recited and copied it is clear as well from its contents, as from the variations in the two extant versions. A comparison with the chronicles is hardly necessary, the ground idea that the conspiracy owed its origin to Elizabeth being so palpably impossible as to make any other departure from history entirely natural. It is sufficient to note that the popular hate of Richard is shown in the unrelenting nature here ascribed to him, and in the taunt of the lady Bessy; while the popular favor for Richmond is shown by his appeal — contrary to the chronicle — to be allowed to lead the van. Both these traits recur in the most popular of the dramas, The True Tragedy of Richard III.

II. A Mirror for Magistrates.

The purpose of this epoch-marking work, the first edition of which appeared in 1559, and the reason for its title, are thus plainly set fort in the Introduction addressed "To all the Nobilitie, and All other in Office". Upon the magistrates of a realm depend its weal or woe. If the magistrates be good the people cannot be ill. They stand in God's place before their people, and should show the attributes of God, and notably justice. "What a foule shame were it for any nowe to take vpon them the name and office of God, and in their doings to shew themselues devils? God cannot of justice, but plague suche shameless presumption and hipocrisie, and that with shamful death, diseases, or infamye. How he hath plagued euil rulers from time to time, in other nations, you may see gathred in Bochas' [Boccaccio's] boke intituled: The fall of Princes, translated into English by Lydgate (a monke of the abbey of Bury in Suff.) How he hath delt with some of our countreymen, your auncestoure, for sundry vices not yet left, this boke named A Mirrour for Magistrates, shall in part plainlye set forth before your eyes.... For here, as in a mirror or loking glasse, you shal se if any vice be found, how the like hath ben punished in other heretofore, wherby admonished, I trust it will bee a good occasione to moue men to the soner amendment. This is the chief end why this booke is set forth, which God graunt it may talke according to the maner of the makers".

It was, then, a book of warning examples, set forth in the manner of Boccaccio's book, which furnished the suggestion for its publication. The legends are set in a framework of running comment, in which Baldwin, the editor, is represented as taking the place of Boccaccio, and the princes make their complaints to him. The different contributors gather about him, and opening "such bookes of chronicles" as they have "there present", proceed to select the various stories suitable to their purpose. What these chronicles were is indicated in the comment on the legend of Norfolk, where Hall, "whose chronicle in this worke", says the editor, "wee chiefly followed", and Fabyan are mentioned.

For the purpose of the work no period could offer better examples than that of the wars of the Roses, which had swept away so many of the nobles of England; and within that period no examples could he more striking than those furnished by the victims who met death at the hands of Richard III, and by the arch-tyrant Richard himself. All these had occupied stations of the highest rank, and had met death under circumstances of peculiar horror. Their falls had, moreover, in no case been the fall of the wholly innocent. In the lives of all had been great crimes, and to these their ends were traceable, either in the course of history itself, or in the belief in a just and avenging God. This belief appears with especial emphasis in the chief authority for this period, Hall's chronicle, whose main source, Polidore Vergil, had lost no opportunity to point out the crimes of his characters, and to declare with the greatest stress that in their downfall was to be seen the hand of a righteous and offended Deity. And Hall himself had contributed to make the same thought prominent, by his conception of the purpose of historical writing as a means of encouragement for the good and of warning for the bad, declaring that had not the lives of tyrants been put in remembrance, "young Princes and fraile gouernors might likewise haue fallen in a like pit, but by redyng their Vices and seyng their mischeueous ende, thei bee compelled to leaue their euill waies, and embrace the good qualities of notable princes and prudent gouernours: Thus, writyng is the keye to enduce vertue and represse vice" (Introd. to Hal.'s Chron., pp. V & VI).

It is not strange, then, that a very large proportion of the whole number of legends should belong to the period of Richard. In all, there were in the various editions, 96 poems, of which 50 belong to the period extending from the mythical coming of Brute to William the Conqueror. Of the 40 remaining, covering the period from William to 1540, 13 years before the first edition of the Mirror, 11, more than one-quarter, are connected with the story of Richard.

The Legends.

In the first edition, 1559, appeared:
    Henry VI, by Baldwin (?)
    George Plantagenet, Duke of Clarence, by Baldwin, according to Haslewood (cf. Introd. to his ed. p. XIX)
    Edward IV, by Skelton.

The second edition, 1563, added:
    Sir Anthony Wodvile, Lord Rivers, by Baldwin
    The Lord Hastings, by Dolman
    The Complaint of Henrie, Duke of Buckingham, by Thomas Sackville
    Collingborne, by Baldwin
    Richard Plantagenet, Duke of Glocester, by Segar
    Shore's Wife, by Thomas Churchyard.

This edition was reprinted in 1571, and again in 1574, this time entitled "The Last parte of the Mirour for Magistrates". Here 24 stanzas were added to the poem on Hastings. No new poems on this period were added in the various editions till 1610, when in Robert Niccols's edition appeared The Two Princes and Richard III (replacing Segar's poem). These, as post-Shakesperean, do not concern us.

These legends, with the single exception of Buckingham's Complaint, have no claim to be called poetry. Nor are they studies of character. They are nearly all mere biographies in verse, keeping generally close to their chronicle sources, but deviating sufficiently to indicate in places a decided advance in the Richard-saga, and in some of the episodes connected with Richard's story.

The citations in the following account are made from the edition of Haslewood, 1815.

1. How King Henry the sixte, a vertuous Prince, was after many other miseries, cruelly murdered in the Tower of London, the 22 of May, Anno 1471.

In this legend the only statement of importance to our purpose is contained in strophe 38.

> For there mine onely sonne not thirteene yeares of age,
> Was tane, and murdered straight by Edward in his rage:
> And shortly I my selfe, to stint all furder strife,
> Stabde with his brother's bloudy blade in prison lost my life".

Here the expression "to stint all furder strife" points to Hall as the source, who has (p. 303) "Poore kyng Henry ... was now in the Tower of London, spoyled of his life ... by Richard duke of Gloucester (as the constant fame ranne) which, to thintent that King Edward his brother, should be clere out of all secret suspicion of sodain inuasion, murthered the said kyng with a dagger". Fabyan (p. 662) has simply "was stykked with a dagger, by the handes of the duke of Gloucester". "Murdered straight by Edward in his rage" does not, perhaps, necessarily mean by Edward personally, a statement made by none of the chronicles.

2. How George Plantagenet, third sonne of the Duke of Yorke, was by his brother King Edward wrongfully imprisoned, and by his brother Richard miserably murdered the 11 of Jan. An. 1478.

Clarence begins his heavy plaint by declaring that he needs not to tell his name, for his wine bewrays him by the smell. He will set forth briefly his wealth, his woe, and causers of decay. After tracing his descent from Lionel, son of Edward III, and relating the death of his father, he passes to his brother Edward's successful attempt to gain the throne. Once king, Edward forgot his friends and despised his kin. Prepared by this unkindness, Clarence listened readily when Warwick tried to seduce him from his brother. "Witless, wanton, fond and young", he was conquered by love of Warwick's daughter, and fell. But at length he saw his error and returned to his brother, his desertion proving the death of Warwick. But Edward had two princelike sons, born to be punished for their parent's sin, and Edward's fear for these proved Clarence's downfall. For

26
"A prophesie was found, which sayd, a G
Of Edward's children should destruction bee.
27
Mee to bee G, because my name was George,
My brother thought, and therefore did mee hate".

But all such prophecies are falsest of the false, as Clarence shows at length, distinguishing them from the true prophecies, such as those of Merlin. This lore had been imparted to him by a faithful servant who set all his delight in study.

40
"He knew my brother Richard was the bore,
Whose tuskes shoulde teare my brother's boyes and me,
And gaue me warning therof long before".

He too prophesied the death of Clarence's wife, which came to pass. Then followed the project to marry the step-daughter of the Duke of Burgundy, to which the king would not agree. So

45
"face to face we fell at flat defiaunce
But were appeased by frends of our aliaunce".

But the marriage was dashed, whereat when Clarence's servant spoke his mind his enemies charged him falsely with an attempt to compass Edward's death by sorcery. The servant was condemned and put to death.

47
"This fierd my hart, as foulder doth the heath:
So that I could not but exclame and cry,
Agaynst so great and open iniury.

48
For this I was commaunded to the tower,
The king my brother was so cruel harted,
And when my brother Richard saw the hower
Was come, for which his hart so sore had smarted,
He thought it best take time before it parted:
    For he endeuoured to attayne the crowne,
    From which my life must nedes haue held him downe.

49
For though the king within a while had died,
As nedes he must, he surfayted so oft,
I must haue had his children in my guyde,
So Richard should besyde the crowne haue coft:
This made him ply the while the wax was soft,
    To finde a meane to bringe me to an ende,
    For realm-rape spareth neyther kin nor frend.

50
And whan hee sawe how reason can asswage
Through length of time my brother Edward's ire,
With forged tales hee set him newe in rage,
Till at the last they did my death conspire:
And though my truth sore troubled their desire,
    For all the world did knowe mine innocence,
    Yet they agreede to charge mee with offence".

A secret quest within the Tower followed the wishes of Clarence's brothers and condemned him to death.

52

"This feate atchiued, yet could they not for shame
Cause mee bee kild by any common way,
But like a wolfe the tyrant Richard came,
(My brother, nay my butcher I may say)
Unto the tower when all men were away,
   Saue such as were prouided for the feate:
   Who in this wise did straungely mee entreate.

53

His purpose was with a prepared string
To strangle mee: but I bestird mee so,
That by no force they could mee therto bring,
Which caused him that purpose to forgo:
Howbeit they bound mee, whether I would or no,
   And in a but of malmesy standing by,
   Newe christned mee, because I should not cry.

54

Thus drownde I was, yet for no due desert,
Except the zeale of iustice bee a crime:
False prophecies bewitcht king Edward's hart,
My brother Richard to the crowne would clime:
Note these three causes in thy rufull rime,
   And boldly say they did procure my fall,
   And death of deaths most straunge and hard of all".

This legend offers a most important addition to the saga. Till now there had been offered only a suggestion of Richard's connection with his brother's death. This was the cautious statement of More, copied into the Hardyng continuation and into Hall. "Somme wise menne also weene, that his drifte couertly conuayde, lacked not in helping furth his brother Clarence to his death: which hee resisted openly, howbeit somwhat (as menne demed) more faintly then he that were hartely minded to his welth. And they that thus deme think that he long time in king Edwardes life forethought to be king in case that the king his brother (whose life hee looked that euil dyete shoulde shorten) shoulde happen to decease (as in dede he did) while his children wer yonge. And thei deme, that for thys intente he was gladde of his brothers death the Duke of Clarence, whose life must needes haue hindered hym so entendynge, whither the same Duke of Clarence hadde kepte him true to his nephew the yonge king, or enterprised to be kyng himselfe. But of al this pointe is there no certaintie, and whoso diuineth vppon conjectures maye as wel shote farre as to short" (cf. p. 79).

This passage as found in Hall was evidently (cf. strophes 48 and 49) the primary source of the representation in the legend, but this goes far beyond More. Richard is here not merely the "helper furth" of Clarence's death, he is the actual causer of Clarence's condemnation, for Edward's waning wrath is fanned by him with "forged tales". A still farther advance makes Richard the actual murderer, attempting with his own hands to strangle his brother with a string, and failing, drowning him, with the assistance of his followers, in the butt of malmesey. Another crime has thus become firmly attached to Richard's name.

That this was, even before the Mirror for Magistrates, already the accepted view among the people, we have at least one sign. Hall copied More's statement from the Hardyng continuation without any other than merely verbal change, and the addition, "but this coniecture afterwarde toke place (as fewe dooe) as you shall perceiue hereafter" (p. 342), by which addition he apparently means to say that subsequent events made it apparent that Richard had even while his brother was alive desired the crown; and to indicate his belief that Richard did have something to do in helping his brother to his death. But in the Index of Hall's chronicle we find the following under "Richard". — "He put to death hys brother duke of Clarence, 380". Now the passage on p. 380 has nothing to say of Richard. It is the passage copied by Hall from Polidore Vergil (cf. p. 142) in which Vergil points out that the death of Edward's children was due to their father's crimes, first by his perjury at York. "And afterward by the death of the duke of Clarence his brother, he incurred (of likelyehod) the great displeasure toward

God". Under Edward's name, however, in the Index nothing is said of his connection with Clarence's death. Although the passage immediately preceding this upon p. 380 does refer to Richard, and there is a possibility that this fact led to a mistake on the part of a hasty index-maker; yet it seems very improbable that the mistake would have occurred had he not been possessed of the idea that Richard was Clarence's murderer.

But however the matter stood in the tradition of the people up to the publication of the legend in the Mirror for Magistrates in 1559, from this time on that Richard was his brother's murderer was the accepted view. Of this there is abundant evidence. Legge's Richardus Tertius (Shak. Lib. II, 1, p. 138) contains the statement "fratri suo mortem intulit Glocestrius", and The True Tragedy of Richard the Third (Shak. Lib. II, 1, p. 53) says of Clarence that he was "By Glosters Duke drowned in a but of wine". In Fletcher's Rising to the Crowne of Richard III, probably written before Shakespeare's play, Richard is likewise represented as his brother's "butcher". Shakespeare's representation of Richard's share in his brother's death had therefore a firmly established tradition behind it.

Strangely enough, this fact and its proofs have almost entirely escaped the notice of students of Shakespeare's play. With but a single exception, they regard Shakespeare's representation as his own extension of the suggestion in More. Thus, to quote but a few instances of many, Gairdner (Life of Rich. III, p. 41) says, "It is also made to appear [by Shakespeare] that it was Richard who got the order for his [Clarence's] death carried out, and that it was Richard who from the beginning had plotted his destruction by setting him and the king at enmity with each other. Of this view I must say that I find no warrant for it in any of the original sources of the history of Edward the Fourth's reign; and it seems to be derived entirely from a passage in More's Life of Richard III".

After quoting the passage, he continues, "The dramatist, of course, had not the means of saying, like the biographer, 'But of all this point there is no certainty'. So what in the first writer was a mere surmise was represented as a fact upon the stage to reflect the character intended.".

Tait (Dic. Nat. Biog. sub Clarence) says, "This surmise [of More] described by More himself as devoid of certainty, is the only positive foundation for Shakespeare's ascription of Clarence's death to Gloucester".

Courtenay (Comm. on the hist. plays of Sh. p. 64) says, "I do not find, even in Holinshed, the insinuation that Edward's jealousy of Clarence, and his consequent proceedings, were brought about or fomented by Gloucester. It is one of the instances which abound in the play; of that which may, indeed, be almost deemed its design, the blackening of the character of the king whom the grandfather of Queen Elizabeth had dethroned" (p. 71). "This is one of the cases in which Shakespeare has gone beyond his authorities in order to blacken Richard. Not a word is said by Holinshed or More of Richard's participation in the murder".

Lloyd (Crit. Essay on R. III) has: "The management of the death of Clarence by Gloster is mentioned [by More] as a suspicion which Shakespeare strengthened into a fact".

Skottowe (Life of Shak. p. 193) expresses himself to like effect. Other commentators tacitly refer the passage to More, by quoting his statement only in giving the sources of the play, or else have nothing to say about the source of the passage at all.

The single exception is Oechelhäuser, who in his Essay über König Richard III (Shakespereana, p. 67) after mentioning the passage in More, goes on to say: "Shakespeare war also nicht bloss nach seiner Quelle, sondern, wie sich bestimmt behaupten lässt, auch durch den damaligen allgemeinen Volksglauben berechtigt, Richard für den Anstifter dieses Mordes zu halten, fand überdies auch bei Holinshed die Andeutung über die von Richard beobachtete Tactik einer äusserlichen Parteinahme für Clarence, während er heimlich gegen ihn wirkte. Indirect beweist schon der Titel der ersten Quartausgabe: The Tragedy of King Richard the third. Containing his treacherous Plots against his brother Clarence u.s.w., dass der damalige Volksglaube Richard für den Mörder hielt; denn es ist undenkbar, dass Shakespeare, oder die Herausgeber, an so hervorragender Stelle einer geschichtlichen Thatsache erwähnt hätten, wenn diese nicht allgemein gekannt war und geglaubt wurde". He then points to the passage in The True Tragedy.

But even Oechelhäuser missed the strongest proof of his position, the legend in the Mirror for Magistrates, as well as the line in Legge's play and the indirect proof of Hall's Index.

That Shakespeare had not only the common tradition but the Mirror for Magistrates as well in his mind, is not improbable, thought it cannot be proved. The important effect assigned to the prophecy about G., which has been censured by Oechelhäuser and others, corresponds to the importance given it in the Mirror, and so does the method which Richard takes to accomplish his end. The lines (R. III 1, 1, 145—9)

"He cannot live, I hope: and must not die
Till George be pack'd with post-horse up to heaven.
I'll in, to urge his hatred more to Clarence,
With lies well steel'd with weighty arguments".

correspond very closely to

"And whan hee sawe how reason can asswage
Through length of time my brother Edward's ire,
With forged tales he set him newe in rage".

In both cases the drowning in the malmesy butt is treated as a final expedient when other means of murder prove inadequate.

The chronicle source of this legend was manifestly Hall, as shown throughout the poem.

3. Howe King Edward the fourth through his surfeting and vntemperate life, sodaynly dyed in the middest of his prosperity, the nynth of Aprill, Anno 1483.

This legend differs in character from the others, in that it is not a biography, but a lyric poem in seven strophes, devoted to the theme:

"What is it to trust to mutability?
Sith that in this world nothing may endure".

Edward points to his great prosperity, and marks its contrast to his sudden death, with the verse that forms the refrain of each strophe.

"Et ecce nunc in pulvere dormio".

The few events of Edward's life that are mentioned are confined to his fortifying and strengthening of various towns and castles, and are of no importance to this study. They do not appear to be drawn from the chronicles.

4. Howe Syr Anthony Woduile Lord Riuers and Scales, Gouernour of Prince Edward, was with his Nephue Lord Richard Gray and other causelesse imprisoned and cruelly murdered, Anno 1483.

After some introductory strophes, Rivers announces the usual theme, "How false and cumbrous worldly honors are", with the specific addition,

"How tyrauntes suffered and not queld in time,
Doe cut theyr throates that suffer them to clime".

The cause of his fall was "the abuse and scorning of God's ordinaunce" in that he and his kinsmen, raised to power by King Edward, had not married as God bade, but "wedded wiues for dignity and landes". He relates the anger of Clarence and Warwick, and the resulting death of his father and brother. When the realm became quiet and the queen was blest with children,

40
"I gouernd them, it was the king's desier:
This set theyr vncles furiously on fier,
That wee, the queene's bloud were assignde to gouerne
The prince, not they, the king's owne bloud and bretherne.

41
This causde the duke of **Clarence** so to chafe,
That with the king hee brainlesse fell at bate:
The counsaile warely for to kepe him safe
From raising tumults, as he did of late,
Imprisoned him: where through his brother's hate
He was condemnde, and murdered in such sort
As he him selfe hath truly made report".

Clarence had hated Rivers and his kinsmen, though they wished him well; but as Clarence maligned them, so Richard

47
"Maligned him, and beastly did him smother:
A deuelish deede, a most vnkindly part,
Yet iust reuenge for his vnnaturall hart".

Though Richard envied their state more than Clarence, yet he masked his feelings so successfully that he appeared their chiefest stay. Edward died, and Rivers started with his ward from Ludlow, dismissing at the request of council and queen — who had been urged thereto by Richard — the great train of men he had gathered for the prince's defence. Then

56
"The duke of **Glocester**, that incarnate deuill,
Confedred with the duke of **Buckingham**,
With eke lord **Hastings**, hasty both to euill,
To meete the king in mourning habit came,
(A cruell wolfe though clothed like a lambe)
And at **Northampton**, where as then I bayted,
They tooke theire inne, as they on mee had wayted".

Here lord Hastings is apparently represented as present at Northampton, but that this is not meant is shown in the further course of poem in which only the two dukes appear.

Events follow as narrated in the chronicle, the hypocritical friendliness, the securing of the inn-keys, the startled awakening of Rivers. An addition appears in River's dream:

68

"I saw a riuer stopt with stormes of winde,
Wheare through a swan, a bull, and bore did passe,
Fraunching the fysh and fry, with teath of brasse,
   The riuer dryde vp saue a litle streame,
   Which at the last did water all the reame.

69

Me thought this streame did drown the cruell bore
In litle space, it grew so deepe and brode:
But hee had kilde the bull and swan before:
Besides all this I sawe an ougly tode
Crall towarde mee, on which mee thought I trode:
   But what became of her, or what of mee.
   My sodayne waking woulde not let mee see".

Rivers is arrested, the conspirators hasten to Stony Stratford to the king, and there Gray, Vaughan and Hault meet the same fate as the earl. Returned to Northampton,

77

"There, loe! duke Richard made himselfe protector
Of king and realme, by open proclamation,
Though neyther king nor queene were his elector,
Thus hee presumde by lawles vsurpation".

Then follows the episode of the dish. Sent north to different castles the victims are finally united at Pomfret, where Ratcliffe puts them to death, with Vaughan crying out "This tyrant Glocester is the gracelesse G.".

83

"In part, I graunt, I well deserued this,
Because I causde not spedy execution
Bee done on Richard, for that murder of his,
When first hee wrought king Henrie's close confusion:
Not for his brother's hatefull persecution:
   These cruell murders painfull death deserued,
   Which had hee suffred, many had ben preserued".

The legend in general follows closely the chronicle account. It is noteworth here chiefly for its corroboration of the account of Clarence's death, in the foregoing legend, for the unfounded statement that Gloucester took upon himself at Northampton the usurped title of protector, and for the dream of Rivers, probably suggested by Hastings' dream in More's story. It is not impossible that it in turn furnished the suggestion of Clarence's dream in Richard III.

The chronicle source is Hall, as is shown by the whole course of the narrative, as well as by the discussion which ensues among the readers over the disagreeing accounts, of Fabian on the one side and More and Hall on the other, as to Dorset's relationship to the queen, and his whereabouts at the time of the prince's journey to London. The latter is here followed. "If by the way wee touch any thing concerning titles, wee follow therein Halle's chronicle. And where wee seeme to swarue from his reasons and causes of diuers doings, there wee gather vpon coniecture such thinges as seeme most probable, or at the lest most conuenient for the furderaunce of our purpose" (Haslewood's ed. II, 273). The latter reason may serve as general explanation for the Mirror's deviation from the chronicles.

That Hall was used, rather than More's biography as published by Rastell in 1557, is likewise conclusively shown by the mention of Hawte's name and by Vaughan's remark about the prophecy of G., neither of which occur in More.

In the introduction appears the statement, "You must imagine that he was accompanied with the lord Richard Gray, Hawt, and Clappam, whose infortunes hee bewaileth after this maner". No Clappam appears in the legend, and it is evident that his name is a mistake for Vaughan. None is mentioned either by the chronicles in this connection. A Clapham who was executed in 9th Edward IV for attempting to flee to Clarence and Warwick is mentioned by Fabyan, and it is perhaps this name retained in the reader's mind that has by a slip crept in here. If so, it shows that Fabyan was also consulted in the preparation of these legends, though his work appears to be responsible for nothing in them.

5. How the Lord Hastings was betrayed, by trusting too much to his euill counsaylour Catesby, and vilanously murdered in the Tower of London by Richard Duke of Glocester, the 13 of June, Anno 1483.

Hastings, determined to warn others from that which wroght his fall, is ready to yield up his fame as martyred saint, and reveal how

4
"Mens vniustice wreaked but God's iust ire,
And by wrong end, turned wreake to iustice hire:
O iudgements iust, by uniustice iustice dealt,
Who doubts of mee may learne, the truth who felt".

He was Edward's staff and joy, winning his favor by serving his lust with lovely women. Thus "God's sharpe wrath I purchast, my iust woe". Clinging to Edward always, he with him fought against Warwick, and when flight became necessary, fled with him to Holland, through all the dangers caused by the ships of the Easterlings. Returned to England, he fought for Edward in three bloody fields. At Tewkesbury

27
"My furious force, there forc'd perforce, to yeelde
The traytour foe".

And there when Prince Edward, produced by Crofts, had made bold answer to the king and been smitten by the gauntlet, him

29
"Clarence, Glocester, Dorcet and I Hastings slue:
The guylt whereof wee shortly all did rue.

30
Clarence, as Cyrus, drowned in bloud-like wyne,
Dorcet I furthered to his speedy pyne,
Of mee, my selfe am speeking president,
Nor easier fate the bristled boare is lent:
Our bloude have payd the vengeaunce of our guilt,
His fryed bones shall broyle for bloud he spilt".

With yet another murder did Hastings stain his hands, for after Edward's death he helped

36
"the boare, and bucke, to captiuate
Lord Riuers, Gray, sir Thomas Vaughan and Hawte".

39
"My selfe I slue, when them I damned to death,
At once my throate I riued, and reft them breath:
For that selfe day, afore or neare the howre.
. . . .
My head and body, in tower twynde like knyfe".

For there followed the double councils, the treachery of Catesby, in whom Hastings put all his trust, the scorned warnings of Stanley, the neglected omens as Hastings rode to the Tower, and finally the fateful meeting. Richard enters with courteous excuse, and commends Ely's strawberries; then

70
"Out goeth from vs the restlesse deuil againe:
Belike (I thinke) scarse yet perswaded ful,
To worke the mischiefe that did mad his scul:
    At last determind of his bloudy thought
    And force ordaynde to worke the wyle he sought.

71
Frowning he enters, with so chaunged cheare,
As for mylde May had chopped foule Januere:
And lowring on me with the goggle eye,
The whetted tuske, and furrowed forehead hye,
His crooked shoulder bristellike set vp.
With frothy iawes, whose foame he chawde and supd,
    With angry lookes that flamed as the fyer:
    Thus gan at last to grunt the grymest syre".

And so follows in detail the rest of that grim scene, ending in Hastings' death, and followed by the hypocritical attempt of Richard and Buckingham to deceive the citizens as to the real cause of the murder. Hastings finishes as he began, with the warning

"Marke God's iust iudgements, punishing sinne by sinn".

But the author ends the legend with words of praise for the man whom for his faithfulness

> "tyme and truth agree
> T'engraue by fame in strong eternity".

The legend follows closely the account of Hall, often, as in the council scene, being little more than a verse paraphrase embellished with reflections in extenso. In a few points the author varies from his authority. Thus, naturally perhaps, a more prominent part is assigned to Hastings in the battle of Tewkesbury than was his, and Hastings' part as assistant to Edward in his lust is emphasized, where the original merely suggests his companionship with Edward in his evil pursuits — "lord Hastynges, against whome the quene especially grudged for the fauoure that the king bare hym, and also she thoughte hym familier with the kynge in wanton compaignie" (Hall, p. 344). The author misses the reason for Richard's departure from the council, which was not, as here stated, that he was not yet fully persuaded to put Hastings to death, but that he might convey the impression that only during the interval had he learned of Hastings' "treason".

6. The Complaynt of Henry Duke of Buckingham.

Buckingham appears to warn those who trust too much to high honours, or seek to rule at court, and wisely weigh not how to wield the care. Born of noble ancestors, whose fate he relates, he was when Edward died a prince without a peer.

> 8
> "Ay me, then I began that hatefull yeere,
> To compasse that which I haue bought so deere:
> I bare the swinge, I and that wretched wight
> The duke of Glocester, that Richard hight".

For he joined with Richard to accomplish their secret plans.

> 9
> "What hee thought best, to mee so seemde the same,
> My selfe not bent so much for to aspyre,
> As to fulfill that greedy duke's desyre".

Eager to rule, Richard saw in the queen's kin his first hindrance, and Buckingham

12
"Unhappy wretch consented to their blood:
Yea kings and peeres that swim in worldly good,
In seeking bloud the end aduert you playne,
And see if bloud ey aske not bloud agayne".

Such was the fate of Cyrus, of Cambyses, Erutus and Bessus, of mightiest Alexander, when he had slain Clitus, his friend. Yet

25
". . . wee delighted in the state wee stoode,
Blinded so far in all our blinded trayne,
That blinde wee sawe not our destruction playne".

The queen's kin executed and Hastings murdered, all seemed smooth sailing. Richard was crowned and Buckingham became his chiefest peer. The princes were closely imprisoned, in hope that thus all strife might end. But rest fled from the conspirators.

35
"So wee, deepe wounded with the bloudy thought,
And gnawing worme that greu'd our conscience so,
Neuer tooke ease, . . .
. . . . of our deserued fall, the feares,
In euery place rang death within our eares".

For the wheel of fortune though it whirls up yet straight it whirleth down. The terror which Richard inspired could not prevent his subjects' hate. Such fear he felt thereof as Dionysius or fell Phereus did. And now Buckingham himself began to loathe Richard's cruelty, for he capped his crimes with the murder of his nephews.

50
"Ne could I brooke him once within my brest,
But with the thought my teeth would gnash withall:
For though I erst were by his sworne behest,
Yet when I saw mischiefe on mischiefe fall,
So deepe in bloud, to murder prince and all,
    Ay then, thought I, alas, and welaway,
    And to my selfe thus mourning would I say:

51

If neyther loue, kinred, ne knot of bloud,
His owne allegaunce to his prince of due,
Nor yet the state of trust, wherein hee stoode,
The world's defame, nor nought could forme him true,
Those gyltles babes, could they not make him rue?
    Nor could theyr youth, nor innocence withall
    Moue him from reauing them, theyr life, and all?"

But nought could move Richard; his heart was stone. Having accomplished all that he willed, and begun to realize the treason he had wrought,

53

"Then seemde hee first to doubt and drede vs all,
    And mee in chiefe, whose death all meanes he might,
    He sought to worke by malice and by might.

54

Such heapes of harme vpharbard in his brest,
With enuious hart my honour to deface,
And knowing hee, that I, which wotted best.
His wretched dryfts, and all his wretched case,
If euer sprang within mee sparke of grace,
    Must nedes abhorre him and his hatefull race:
    Now more and more can cast mee out of grace.

55

Which sodayne chaunge, when I, by secret chaunce
Had well percieude, by proofe of enuious frowne,
And saw the lot that did mee to aduaunce
Him to a king, that sought to cast mee downe,
To late it was to linger any stowne,
    Sith present choise lay cast before myne eye:
    To worke his death, or, I my selfe to dye.

57

Which heauy choyse so hastened mee to chose,
That I in part agrieude at his disdayne,
In part to wreake the dolefull death of those
Two tender babes, his sely nephewes twayne,
By him, alas, commaunded to be slayne,
    With paynted chere humbly before his face,
    Strayght tooke my leaue, and roade to Brecknocke place".

But fortune turned against Buckingham. The soldiers he had raised deserted him. Like Camillus, Scipio, Milciades [sic!] and Hannibal, he was abandoned by his country. Wandering and alone, he took refuge with Humphrey Banister, whom he had brought up, loved, and advanced. He too turned traitor and delivered his master to John Mitton, sheriff of Shropshire, and at Salisbury Buckingham lost his life.

Having told his tale thus far, the spirit of Buckingham falls in a swoon. From this he revives to utter in rage a curse upon Banister, calling upon Phoebe and Jove to bear witness to his words, and upon Alecto and Sibilla to aid him in his curse.

92
"Thou Banastaire, gainst thee I clepe and call
Vnto the gods, that they iust vengeaunce take
On thee, thy-bloud, thy stayned stocke and all".

94
"And thou caytyfe, that like a monster swarued
From kinde and kindnes, hast thy maister lorne,
Whom neyther trueth, nor trust wherein thou serued,
Ne his deserts could moue, nor thy fayth swonce,
How shall I curse, but wish that thou vnborne
    Had beene, or that the earth had rent in tway,
    And swallowed thee in cradle as thou laye.

95
To this did I, euen from thy tender youth,
Witsaue to bring thee vp? did I herefore
Beleue the oth of thy vndoubted troth?
Aduance thee vp, and trust thee euermore?
By trusting thee that I should dye therefore?
    O wretch, and worse then wretch, what shall I say?
    But clepe and curse gaynst thee and thine for aye.

96
Hated be thou, disdaynde of euery wight,
And poynted at where euer that thou goe".

98
"Deserue thou death, yea bee thou deemde to dye
A shamefull death, to end thy shamefull life".

And thus the curse runs on, invoking the death of Banister's eldest son in a boar's sty, the drowning of his second son in a puddle, and the striking of his daughter with leprosy, fates which according to Hall befel Buckingham's children.

"And after that, let shame and sorrowes griefe
Feede forth thy yeares continually in woe,
That thou maist lieue in death, and dye in life,
And in this sort forwaylde and weried so,
At last thy ghost to part thy body fro:
This pray I, Ioue, and with this later breath,
Vengaunce I aske vpon my cruell death".

Then with a final outcry against fortune Buckingham ceases, with the words that summarize his life,

"Who reckless rules, right soone, may hap to rue".

The view of Buckingham here given is in general that of More and Hall. An attempt is made, however, to make more definite than More had succeeded in doing the motive for Buckingham's revolt against Richard. An entirely new thought appears, namely, that the first impulse to dissension came from Richard's own guilty apprehension of the harm that might befall him if Buckingham with his full knowledge of his crimes should ever turn against him. The thought is worthy of Sackville, revealing his knowledge of human nature. The guilty soul, conscious of its own treachery, fears the like treachery in others, even its own accomplices. This apprehension leads to a determination to overthrow Buckingham so that harm may be out of his power, and the determination shows itself in words of disdain. Nothing is said of Buckingham's request for the Earl of Hereford's lands, which, in More, is represented as the cause of the "spitefull and minatory words" that fill Buckingham with hatred and mistrust.

To this the author adds a second motive, Buckingham's abhorrence of the murder of the princes.

"In part agrieude at his disdayne,
In part to wreake the dolefull death of those
Two tender babes"

Buckingham determines on rebellion. This second motive is adopted from the speech added by Hall to More's story — which gives no hint of such a motive — in which

Buckingham declares to Ely the reasons for his rebellion. Here after declaring that the taunts which followed his request for the Hereford lands tried his patience to its uttermost proof, Buckingham goes on to assert: "When I was credibly enformed of the death of the .ıı. younge innocentes, his awne natural nephewes contrarie to his faith and promyse, to the whiche God be my iudge I neuer agreed nor condiscended. O lord how my veynes panted, how my body trembled, and my harte inwardely grudged, in so muche that I so abhorred the sighte and much more the compaignie of hym, that I coulde no lenger abyde in his courte, excepte I shoulde he openly reuenged" (Hall, p. 387). This latter view of Buckingham's motives was, as will be seen later, adopted — probably independent of the Mirror for Magistrates — by Legge in his Richardus Tertius, where it leads to a further development, Buckingham's adhesion to Richard's plans for making himself king being there the result of his desire to save the lives of the princes. And the same passage from Hall is without doubt the source of the remarkable scene in Shakespeare's play, where Buckingham "grows circumspect" at Richard's proposal to murder the princes. With this is united the request for the Earl of Hereford's lands, and its contemptuous reception; but so united that as in the Mirror for Magistrates the contemptuous treatment springs from Richard's perception of the danger that may come to him from one who looks into him with considerate eyes, and from the immediately conceived resolve to put Buckingham out of the way, a resolve hinted at in Buckingham's parting words,

"O let me think on Hastings, and be gone
To Brecknock, while my fearful head is on'.

Sackville, Legge and Shakespeare probably arrived at their representations independently, but their work shows a development of Hall's view which leads far away from the uncertain one of More. The development begins with the Mirror for Magistrates, and from this moment the real cause of Buckingham's rebellion is found not in the reception of his request by Richard, nor in his pride and envy of Richard, urged on by the bishop of Ely, but in his horror at the tyrannical murder of the princes and his determination to avenge them. The reflex of the blackening of Richard that was shown in representing Richmond as an angel of light undergoes here a further extension in the person of Buckingham.

7. How Collingbourne was cruelly executed for making a foolish rhyme.

The legend has for its complaint that poetry has lost the freedom that it owned of yore. No tyrant suffers unavenged that his faults should be touched upon, and a tyrant was Richard, as Collingbourne found to his cost. His purpose was a good one, he had meant only to reform the wicked subjects of his rhyme.

35

"I neuer meant the king or counsayl harme,
Unles to wish them safty were offence:
Agaynst theyr powre I neuer lifted arme,
Nor pen, nor tongue, for any ill pretence:
The ryme I made, though rude, was sound in sence,
   For they therein, whom I so fondly named,
   So ruled all that they were foule defamed".

The legend needs to be noted here only because it adopts entirely the account of Hall, according to which Collingbourne was executed tyrannously for the rhyme alone. Fabyan had correctly stated that Collingbourne "was caste for sondry treasons: & for a ryme". Later Holinshed and Stow showed this in fuller detail (cf. p. 219). That Fabyan was used as well as Hall is shown by the account of the execution, which is not in Hall. The legend thus reveals the determination of the time to blacken Richard as much as possible, and admit nothing that could tell in his favor.

8. How Richarde Plantagenet Duke of Glocester murdered his brother's children, vsurping the crowne, and in the third yeare of his raigne was most worthely depriued of life and kingdome, in Bosworth plaine, by Henry Earle of Richmond after called king Henry the vij. the 22 of August 1485.

The kernel of the legend is the murder of the two princes, and with a rueful mention of this Richard begins his tale. Then, returning to the proper beginning of his story, he relates,

3
'The lords and commons all with one assent,
Protectour made me both of land and king,
But I therewith, alas, was not content:
. .   . .
    For I, desirous to rule and raigne alone,
    Sought crowne and kingdom, yet title had I none".

Again he turns to the gruesome deed and relates the pangs it cost him.

6
"Such terrours mee tormented, and my sprites fired
As vnto such a murder and shamefull deed required,
Such broyle dayly felt I breeding in my brest,
Whereby, more and more, increased mine vnrest".

Turning back again he mentions the death of Clarence.

8
"To cursed Cayn compare my carefull case,
Which did vniustly slay his brother iust Abel:
And did not I in rage make run that rufull race
My brother duke of Clarence? whose deth I shame to tel,
For that it was so straunge as it was horrible;
    For sure he drenched was, and yet no water neare,
    Which straunge is to bee tolde, to all that shall it heare".

Now at last Richard turns definitely to the princes. From this point the narrative follows Hall in detail. The murder is described not without some attempt at pathos.

15
"The wolues at hand were redy to deuoure
The seely lambes in bed, wheras they laye,
Abiding death, and looking for the howre,
For well they wist, they could not scape away".

17*

The deed brought hatred from nobles and people, and Buckingham raised his insurrection. And so the story advances to Richard's death at Bosworth, and ends like the other legends with an insistence upon the moral.

42
"Loe, heare you may behold the due and iust rewarde
Of tyranny and treason, which God doth most detest".

The legend is little more than a paraphrase of Hall's story, and has even less of the poetical afflatus than any of the others; a fact of which the editor takes notice by saying. "It was thought not vehement enough for so violent a man as king Richard had bene. The matter was well enough liked of some, but the meetre was misliked almost of all". The legend is noteworthy only in the repetition of the murder of Clarence by Richard, and in the correct statement that Richard was elected protector, as opposed to the statement of the Rivers legend that Richard usurped the protectorship. Of Richard's deformity nothing is said either here or elsewhere in the Mirror for Magistrates. Nor is anything said of the famous dream before the battle of Bosworth.

9. How Shore's Wife, King Edward the Fourth's Concubine was by King Richard despoyled of all her goods, and forced to doe open penaunce.

The legend of Shore's Wife begins with the wonted theme:

2
"In fortune's frekes, who trustes her when shee smiles,
Shall finde her false, and full of fickle toyes,
Her triumphe all, but fill our eares with noyse,
   Her flattring giftes, are pleasures mixt with payne,
   Yea, all her wordes are thunders threatning rayne".

This thought is extended through five strophes, and then Shore's wife avouches that of all this she is a proof, and proposes to rehearse her life as witness to its truth. Of noble birth she cannot boast, nor did fortune give her the gifts of gold; but beauty in the highest was hers. For that a king desired her, and who can withstand a king's desire?

20
"But cleare from blame my frends can not be founde,
Before my time my youth they did abuse:
In mariage a prentise was I bounde,
When that meere loue I knew not how to vse".

Willingly she yielded herself to Edward and ruled him by love, though he did reign a lord.

32
"I ioynde my talke, my iestures, and my grace,
In witty frames, that long might last and stand,
So that I brought the king in such a case,
That to his death I was his chiefest hand:
I gouernd him that ruled all this land:
   I bare the sword, though hee did weare the crowne,
   I strake the stroke that threw the mighty downe".

Yet the power thus won she never used to advance herself, but only to aid others.

34
"I tooke delight in doyng each man good,
Not scratting all myselfe as all were mine,
But lookt whose life in neede and danger stoode".

39
"I euer did vpholde the common weale,
I had delight to saue the guiltles blood:
Each suter's cause, when that I vnderstode,
I did prefer as it had bene mine owne,
And help them vp, that might haue bene orethrowne".

Yet all her bliss was turned to bale, for Edward died; and with his death all men who had sued to her and flattered her now turned their backs.

61
"As long as lyfe remaynde in Edward's brest,
Who was but I? who had such frends at call?
His body was no sooner put in chest,
But well was hee that could procure my fall:
His brother was myne enmye most of all,
   Protectour then, whose vice did still abound
   From yll to worse tyll death did him confound".

Richard feigned that she had tried to poison him, and for this feigned crime she paid open penance with taper in her hand. Shamefast she went, and pitied by the people.

65
"But what preuaylde the people's pitie there?
This raging wolfe would spare no giltless blood:
Oh wicked wombe that such ill fruit did beare,
Oh cursed earth, that yeeldeth forth such mud:
The hell consume all things that did thee good,
    The heauens shut their gates agaynst the spreete,
    The world tread downe thy glory vnder feete".

67
Woe worth the man that fathered such a childe,
Woe worth the howre wherein thou wast begate,
Woe worth the brests that haue the world begylde,
To norish thee, that all the worlde did hate:
Woe worth the gods that gaue thee such a fate,
    To lyue so long, that deserude so oft:
    Woe worth the chaunce that set thee vp aloft".

Had Richard punished her for justice' sake she could not have repined,

71
"But by yll will and powre I was opprest:
    Hee spoylde my goods, and left mee bare and pore,
    And caused mee to beg from dore to dore.

72
"What fall was this, to come from prince's fare,
To watch for crums among the blynde and lame?
When almes were delt I had an hungry share,
Because I knew not how to aske for shame,
Tyll force and neede had brought mee in such frame,
    That starue I must, or learne to beg an almes,
    With booke in hand, to say S. Dauid's psalmes".

Thus she wandered through the streets, clothed in beggar's garments.

75
"I had no house wherein to hyde my heade,
The open streete my lodging was perforce:
Full oft I went all hungry to my bed,
My flesh consumde, I looked lyke a corse:
Yet in that plight who had on mee remorse:
    O God, thou knowste my frends forsooke mee than,
    Not one holpe mee, that succred many a man.

76

They frownd on mee that fawnd on mee before,
And fled from mee, that followde mee full fast:
They hated mee, by whome I set much store,
They knew full well, my fortune did not last,
In euery place, I was condemnde and cast,
    To pleade my cause at bar it was no boote,
    For euery man did treade mee vnder foote.

77

Thus long I liu'd, all weary of my lyfe,
Tyll death approcht, and rid mee from that wo:
Example take by mee, both mayde and wyfe,
Beware, take heede, fall not to folly so:
A Mirour make by my greate ouerthro,
    Defy the world and all his wanton wayes,
    Beware by mee, that spent so yll her dayes".

The legend while otherwise based wholly on More's account of Jane Shore, as printed in Hall, makes an important change and extension in the matter of her beggary. All that the original has to say of this is, "I doubt not some man wyl thynke this woman to be to slight to be written of emong graue and weyghtie matters, whiche they shall specially thynke that happely sawe her in her age & aduersitie, but me semeth the chaunce so much more worthy to be remembred, in how much after wealth she fell to pouertie, and from riches to beggery vnfrended, out of acquaintance, after great substaunce after so great fauour with her prince, after as greate suite & sekyng to with all those which in those dayes had busynes to spede as many other men were in their tymes whiche be now famous onely by the infamy of their euill deedes, her doynges were not muche lesse, albeit they be muche lesse remembred, because they were not euyll, for men vse to write an euyll turne in marble stone, but a good turne they wryte in the dust, whiche is not worst proued by her, for after her wealth she went beggyng of many that had begged them selfes if she had not holpen them, such was her chaunce" (Hall, p. 364).

Here More is speaking of the later years of Jane Shore's life, when she fell into adversity and poverty and was forced to beg for help. And this is still more clearly evident because when More wrote, Shore's wife was still alive — she died in 1527 — and the passage in Hall was changed to fit the change in time. More's original reads: "in how much she is now in the more beggerly condicion, vnfrended and worne out of acquaintance, after good substance" etc., and "for at this day shee beggeth of many at this daye liuing that at this day had begged if she had not bene" (Lumby's ed. p. 55). After the death of Edward, Shore's wife was taken by Lord Hastings, and after his death and her condemnation by Richard she became the mistress of Dorset. Neither in More's passage nor in Hall's is there the slightest suggestion to connect her beggary with her condemnation by Richard, and the begging there mentioned is clearly not that of the professional beggar in the streets.

But the author of the legend in the Mirror for Magistrates makes her begging follow at once upon her condemnation by Richard, connecting it with Richard's spoiling her of her goods, and turning her into the common street beggar, with clapping-dish and staff and wallet; and her misery is pictured in such detail and extent that it becomes far more prominent in the legend than her penance in procession with taper in her hand. To this must be added that her connection with Lord Hastings and the interval of ease and good fortune which this afforded are not touched upon in the legend, and her wretchedness is made to follow at once upon Edward's death.

This picture of Shore's wife, and not that of the chronicle, became, as will be seen later, the basis of her representation in The True Tragedy of Richard the Third.

III. Legge's Richardus Tertius.

The first allusion to this work appears to be that of Sir John Harington, in his "Apologie of Poetry", 1591: "For tragedies, to omit other famous tragedies, that which was played at St. John's in Cambridge, of Richard III, would move, I think, Phalaris the tyrant, and terrefie all tyrannous minded men".

Thomas Nash, in his "Have with you to Saffron Walden", 1596, speaks of "his fellow codshead, that in the Latine tragedie of King Richard cries Ad urbs, ad urbs, ad urbs, when his whole part was no more than Urbs, urbs, ad arma, ad arma".

In Meres' Palladis Tamia, 1598, among "our best for Tragedy" is included "Doctor Leg, of Cambridge", in a list containing the names of Shakespeare, Marlowe, Peele, Kyd, and Johnson [sic].

Another paragraph declares, "As **Marcus Anneus Lucanus** writ two excellent tragedies; one called **Medea**, the other De incendio Trojae cum **Priami** calamitate: so Doctor Leg hath penned two famous tragedies; the one of Richard III, the other of The Destruction of Jerusalem".

Thomas Heywood, in his "Apology for Actors", 1612, quoted Harington's allusion.

Thomas Legge was born in Norwich in 1535. In 1552 he entered Corpus Christi College, Cambridge, whence he subsequently passed to Trinity College. There, after graduating B. A. in 1556—7, he became fellow. In 1560 he proceeded M. A., and in 1568 became fellow of Jesus College. In 1573 he was made master of Caius College. Some time between 1563 and 1574 he was regius professor of Civil Law, and in 1575 was given the degree of LL. D. In 1579 Legge was appointed commissary to the University, and in 1587 Vice-Chancellor. Again in 1593 Legge succeeded Dr. Still (the possible author of Gammer Gurton's Needle) in the Vice-Chancellorship, an office which he thus twice held. He became master in Chancery and doctor in the court of Arches. He died in 1607. Beside Richardus Tertius Legge wrote another tragedy, entitled The Destruction of Jerusalem. Of this Fuller says, "Having at last refined it to the purity of the Publique Standard, some Plageary filched it from him, just as it was to be acted". This play is generally considered Legge's last, but Fleay (Biog. Chron. Eng. Dram. 2 : 36) states that it was acted at Coventry in 1577. For this no authority is adduced. A play of this name appears according to Halliwell's Dictionary of Plays, p. 72, to have been acted at Coventry about the year 1577, but we have nothing to indicate that it was Legge's, and that a University play should have been acted in Coventry is on the face of it unlikely. (Cf. Morley, E. W. 10 : 369; Introd. to Shakespeare's Lib. Part 2, vol. 1; Fleay, Biog. Chron. sub nom.; Dict. Nat. Biog. sub nom.)

Information of the place, time, and circumstances of the production of Richardus Tertius is derived from the title of the Ms. in the Cambridge University Library. This reads:

Thomae Legge legum doctoris
Collegii Caio-goneviliensis in
Academia Cantabrigiensi
magistri ac Rectoris.
Richardus tertius Tragedia trivespa
habita Collegii Divi Johnis
Evangeliste
Comitii Bacchelaureorum
Anno Domini 1579
Tragedia in tres acciones devisa.

The Caius College, Cambridge Ms. (No. 125, 8⁰, 16/17 cent.) contains, together with the old plays Hymenaeus and Pedantius, "Thomae Legge legum Doctoris Collegij/ Goonevilli et Caij in Academia / Cantabrigensi, magistri ac / rectoris, Richardus / tertius tragoedia / trium vesperum/

Habita in Collegio Divi Johannis / Euangelistae Comitijs Bacchalaureorum / Anno 1573". This ascribed date of 1573, which no one who has written of the play appears to have noticed, I believe to be a mistake of the copyist. Legge was not made master of Caius until 1573, nor doctor of laws until 1575; and while of course he may have written the play before these titles came to him, it is far more likely that he wrote it after acquiring the prominent position of Master of Caius. Absolute evidence, however, is wanting and the possibility of so early a date is interesting.

Folios 42—62 of Ms. Tanner in the Bodleian Library at Oxford contain the first actio of Legge's play. The catalogue, however, did not recognize it as Legge's and none of the writers on the play seem to have been aware of its existence. Folio 42, beneath the list of characters, which is the same as that of the Cambridge University Library Ms., has: "Acted in St. Johns Hall before the Earle of Essex 17 March. 1582". Considering that the list of actors is the same as that for 1579, this date also, in spite of the circumstantial statement of the presence of the Earl of Essex may be considered open to some doubt.

Fleay, followed by others, conjectures that the play was also prepared with epilogue and prayer for performance before the Queen in 1592. He relies on the following evidence. Dec. 2, 1592, the Vice-Chamberlain, Lord Burghley, wrote to Cambridge and to Oxford, asking that the students should prepare English comedies to be acted at Christmas before the Queen, who could not at this time be entertained by the London actors, on account of the plague. Dr. Still, Vice-Chancellor of Cambridge, replied Dec. 4, alleging want of practice in English plays, and the unwillingness of the principal actors to play in English. This appears to have given offence to the Queen. Legge, who had succeeded Still as Vice-Chancellor, wrote to Burghley in January, 1593, referring to this offence, and stating that men had been sent to Oxford to witness the

Queen's entertainment there, that they might be better prepared to obey her directions. Now on Sep. 24 and 26, 1592, the Queen had graciously received at Oxford the Latin plays, Bellum Grammaticale and W. Gager's Rivales. The latter had been previously performed in June 1583 in Christ Church Hall. "If Gager's Latin revamped was graciously received, why not Legge's?" is Mr. Fleay's question (cf. Fleay, Chron. Hist. Eng. Stage, p. 79 and Collier, Hist. Dram. Poetry 1 : 296).

In all this, I cannot find any conclusive evidence that Legge's play had been rearranged for a performance at this time before the Queen, although it may have been so. Fleay finds it unlikely that Still, who had already written a successful English play [Still's authorship of Gammer Gurton's Needle is, however, by no means certain], would have objected to the use of English, if a Latin play had not been already prepared; and the point may be well taken. But there is nothing to show that this play was Legge's, whose letter was written, just as Still's had been, in his official capacity as Vice-Chancellor, and gives no indication of any further personal interest in the matter. The epilogue does not place it beyond doubt that the play was ever acted or intended to be acted before the Queen; and if such was the case, it may have been on the occasion of its first performance, a supposition of Fuller, accepted by Legge's editor, Field, for which, however, there likewise seems to be no evidence (cf. Cooper, Athen. Cant., p. 457).

The most satisfactory argument for a presentation before the Queen is the character of the piece itself. Few plays could naturally have been so attractive to Elizabeth. Its champion and victor was her own grandfather, and its result the foundation of her own royal house. Her father had been the direct offspring of that union of the houses of Lancaster and York in which the great struggle ended, and she had been taught to feel herself the most glorious fruit which that union had produced, the perfect fulfilment of its promise. No play could more fully have satisfied her pride. Its character and the great reputation which it enjoyed make it almost inconceivable that Elizabeth, if she had not seen the play on the occasion of its first presentation, should have been offended when it was proposed to produce it before her; and it is still less conceivable that if such had been the intention, Still and Legge should have failed to notify Burghley and the Queen of the fact. It is, therefore, most unlikely that a production before the Queen was intended for Christmas 1592. Elizabeth may well have seen Richardus Tertius at its first presentation, but evidence of that fact is meagre and far from conclusive.

Some seven manuscripts of Richardus Tertius are known to be in existence. Three are at Cambridge, in Emmanuel College, Caius College, and the University Library, two are in the British Museum, one (of the first actio) is in the Bodleian, and according to Mr. Field there is "at least one in private hands". The play was edited by Barron Field for the Old Shakespeare Society in 1844 from the Emmanuel Ms., with blanks supplied by the Ms. in the University Library. It was again printed by Hazlitt, in his edition of Shakespeare's Library, Part 2, vol. 1. As it stands here, as Mr. Fleay remarks, "it sadly wants editing", for it contains "nearly a thousand errors". All references in the following account are to this edition. In the quotations I have followed the text, only occasionally supplying the correct reading in brackets. The sense is almost always clear, if one will bear in mind that the punctuation is utterly untrustworthy. Periods, especially, are constantly wrongly inserted or omitted.

The position of Richardus Tertius in the development of the drama in England is of the highest interest and importance. With our present meagre lists of the University plays and our almost utter ignorance of their contents it is impossible to say much of them with certainty; but according to our present knowledge Richardus Tertius appears to have been the first real history-play, or "Chronicle History" written in England. Bale's Kyng Johan had been acted in 1561, and was the first play to introduce an English monarch upon the stage; but it has no title to be called a history, following as it does the lines of the old moralities. Gorboduc, or Ferrex and Porrex, the first tragedy, 1562, takes its story from the chronicles, but this belongs to mythical and not actual English history. The University plays, as well in English as in Latin, appear to have been down to 1590 and later confined almost wholly to Biblical or classical material. Nowhere in the list appears a play that deals with English history, save Legge's, and a transcript of his play by Henry Lacey in 1586.

To Legge, therefore, was due the turning of the drama in England in an entirely new direction. It was he who first perceived that English history as related by the chroniclers possessed as great a store of dramatic material as the classical saga, or Biblical story, the chief objects of the academic study of the time. It was he who while the national consciousness and pride were swelling under the great events of Elizabeth's reign, first gave them a new object and incitement in the history of England's past, presented in living form upon the stage.

That the play had a large influence there can be no doubt. It is true that we seek in vain in the lists of University plays for another play beside Lacey's transcript that deals with English history. Purely academic taste continued to find its favorite motives elsewhere. But its influence is not to be sought here. That the play won a great reputation as preeminent among the University tragedies is shown by the allusions of Harington and Meres. Fuller (Worthies, Norwich, p. 277) says that the piece was presented with great applause, and indicates its effect upon the student actors by the anecdote that Palmer, afterwards Dean of Peterborough, who acted King Richard, "had his head so possest with a Princelike humor, that ever after, he did what then he acted, in his Prodigal expences, so that (the Cost of a sovereign ill befiting the Purse of a Subject), he died Poor in Prison". The number of extant Mss. and the fact that it was copied by Lacey are other proofs of its popularity. This reputation cannot have been without great effect upon the band of University men composed of Marlowe, Lodge, Peele and Green, who were well acquainted with the body of University plays, and sometimes assisted in their presentation, who reveal their influence in their own works, and who were the first to bring out the national historical drama, begun by Legge, upon a popular stage and in a popular form.

Marlowe was a student in Cambridge, at Benet, now Corpus Christi, College as early as Mar. 17. 1581, and must have heard much of the play as well as read it. If, as the Bodleian Ms. declares, it was acted in 1582 also at St. John's, Marlowe undoubtedly saw the play. Green, who took his B. A. degree at St. John's College in 1578, just before Legge's play was produced there, took his M. A. degree in 1583 at Clare Hall in the same University. He was therefore probably present when the play was given; was at any rate residing in Cambridge at the time. Nash, who belongs to the same group, though he wrote no English history-play, resided at St. John's for almost seven years, from 1581, took part in a Latin play there, and shows his acquaintance with Legge's play by the previously quoted allusion to the amusing mistake of a flurried actor. Lodge was a student at Oxford, where he took his B. A. in 1597. Peele, the most important in the list next to Marlowe, was also a student at Oxford for nine years before 1581, and in June 1583 assisted Dr. Gager in producing his Latin plays of Dido and Rivales.

Considering these facts, and the evidences of University training in the anonymous history-plays of King John and Henry V, which were among the earliest, it is not unreasonable to suppose that Legge's play was not only the first of its line, but that it largely furnished the direct incitement to that dramatizing from the chronicles of the careers of English monarchs which established a national historical drama in popular form upon the popular stage. The inspiration which led Legge alone among the writers of University tragedies to treat English material is not far to seek. Could we be certain that the play was, as is supposed by Fuller, originally prepared for production before Elizabeth, we should feel sure that the material presented itself to Legge as most apt for a compliment to the Queen; and such a belief is by no means to be rejected, even if the play was not given before her. Compliments to the Queen, on a large as well as on a small scale, were not confined to performances before her. Further, the play itself leaves no doubt that Legge recognized in the Richard of the chronicles, not only in the purpose and result of his whole career, but in a multitude of its details as well, a wonderful resemblance to some of the characters of that Senecan drama which was the ideal and model upon which the University tragedies were formed. That aspect of Richard which had in some measure attracted the notice of Rous and especially of André was for Legge the chief thing: Richard as a Senecan tyrant was the object of his presentation.

Thus it happens that the Richard of Legge's play is in no sense, as is the case with Shakespeare's Richard, the creation of the playwright. There is indeed in the whole play exceedingly little for which Legge himself is responsible, and which is not to be found in the chronicles or in Seneca. The author found a most slavish following of the chronicles consistent with his purpose, for the Senecan traits of Legge's Richard are largely in the Richard of the chronicles. The work of the Latin dramatist was almost wholly employed not to add, but to emphasize ideas and situations recognized as peculiarly his own. What the resultant was of this combination of Chronicle and Seneca is revealed by the analysis of the play. Before turning to this, however, it is necessary to indicate more exactly the sources from which Legge drew his historical materials.

The Historical Sources of Richardus Tertius.

Richardus Tertius derives its historical material from More's biography of Richard, with its continuation by Hall, whose material in turn was obtained from the history of Polidore Vergil, increased by sundry bits from the continuation of the Hardyng chronicle, and additions of his own. This does not necessarily mean that Legge made use of More and Hall directly. More's work, as shown in Part I, first appeared in the continuation of Hardyng, 1543, in mutilated and inaccurate form, with a few additions. In this shape it was copied by Hall's chronicle in the editions of 1548 and 1550. It then appeared in Rastell's folio editions of More's works, 1557, printed "fro the copie of his own hand". In this form it was copied into Grafton's chronicle, 1568, where, however, some bits were retained from the Hardyng continuation, and at least one important addition, the description of Richard's coronation, was made. In form still more closely like the Rastell edition it appeared in Holinshed, 1578. More's story, which broke off abruptly in the midst of a conversation between Buckingham and Ely, was continued in the Hardyng continuation by a translation, somewhat abridged and changed, of Polidore Vergil. The continuation in Hall's chronicle was likewise based on Polidore Vergil, but had many more additions. This was adopted almost unchanged into Grafton's chronicle, and into Holinshed, where some bits of Grafton's wording are also found. Further additions were made in the second edition of Holinshed, 1587, which appearing eight years later than Legge's play does not here come into consideration. It remains to be determined, therefore, in what book or books Legge made use of More's story and its continuation.

1. That he did not make use of More in the Rastell edition is shown by the appearance in the play of various additions from the Hardyng continuation and from Hall, as appears in detail in the analysis of the play.

That Polidore Vergil was not used in the original is likewise shown by the presence in the play of additions made by Hall, as well as by evident translation of Hall's version of Vergil.

Thus we are reduced to a consideration of the Hardyng continuation, Hall, Grafton and Holinshed.

2. That Legge made use of the Hardyng continuation appears to be proved by the following.

P. 207, col. 2, the Queen, sollicited by Lovell in Richard's behalf, sends her daughters to the court, where Richard receives them with the words

Geminas vides sorores: ô faustum diem.

In the passage in which Hall treats of this matter (pp. 406, 7) we find, "He clerely determined to reconcile .. his brothers wife quene Elizabeth .. beleuynge .. that she would not sticke to commite .. to him the rule and gouernaunce both of her and her daughters" (a translation of Vergil's *et se et filias*); "first deliuered into kyng Richard's hands her .v. daughters" (for Vergil's *primo filias in Ricardi potestatem tradit*); and again, "he caused all his brothers daughters to be conueighed into his paleys" (a translation of Vergil's *filias omnes fratris*). Grafton and Holinshed follow Hall. But for these three statements we have in the Hardyng continuation, "he doubted not but shortely to finde the meanes to haue both her daughters out of her handes into his owne"; "and first she deliuered both her daughters into the handes of kyng Richard"; and (this time in correct translation) "after he had recyued al his brothers daughters from the sanctuary into his palayce". The conclusion appears inevitable that in writing this scene Legge used the Hardyng continuation; and this in spite of the fact that in the dramatis personae of this Actio appear five daughters of Edward (four mute). They must all have appeared in the scene between Lovell and the queen, where they do not speak, but are addressed, without their number being indicated. But only two — geminas sorores — are received by Richard, and for this the Hardyng Continuation must have been responsible.

There does not elsewhere appear in the play a passage found only in the Hardyng continuation. On the other hand much that is found in Legge's play, in Hall's continuation of More, and hence copied (mostly) into Grafton and Holinshed, the Hardyng Continuation fails to give. Thus there do not appear in it:

p. 194 "Buck." to the end of the conference with Ely;
198 Bray's speech;
200 Guilford's large army (frequens caterva);
200 The basis of Richard's lament over the death of his son;
201 Buckingham's sickness (stomachi dolore);
201 Buckingham's disaster by flood;
202 The delivery of Buckingham to Mitton, sheriff of Shropshire;
203 Richmond's first attempt to land (shown by "Dorcestrium", which is not in the H. C.);
204 The marriage of Richard's niece, and the truce with the Scots;
206 The Queen's relation of her injuries;
216 The inscription on Norfolk's gate;
216, 17 The Orations of Richard and Henry;
216 Answer of Stanley and postponement of the execution of Strange;
219 Speech and prayer of Henry after the battle;
219 The return of Strange.

This shows that though used on occasion the Hardyng continuation gave but slight help in the composition of the play.

3. Grafton's Chronicle was also used. This is seen in "The Shewe of the Coronation" (p. 184) the order of which is detailed as follows:

    Trumpetts
    Choristers
    Singing-men
    Praebendaries
    Bishopps
    Cardinall
    Heralds
    Aldermen of London
    Esquires, Knights, Noblemen
    Gilt spurs borne by the Earle of Huntingdon
    St Edward's stafe. Earle of Bedford
    The point of $\overset{e}{y}$ sword naked. E. of Northumberland
    The great mace. Lord Stanly
    Two naked swordes, E. of Kent, L. Lovell
    The grete scepter. Duke of Suffolke
    The ball wth the crosse. E. of Lincolne
    The sword of estate. E. of Surrey
    Three togather. The Kinge of heralds
    The Maior of London with a mace on the right hand the
        gentleman usher on the left hand,
    The King's crowne. Duke of Norfolke
    The Kinge under a canopy betwixt two Bishopps
    The Duke of Buckingham wth a white staffe caringe up
        the King's traine
    Noblemen
    The Queen's scepter
    The white dove wth a white rod
    The Queene's crowne
    The Queene wth a circlet on her head under a Canopie
    The Lady Margaret bearinge up the Queene's traine
    A Troupe of Ladies
    Knights and Esquires
    Northren Souldiers well armed.

While the procession is advancing it is commented upon and explained by a "Civis" to a stranger "Hospes", who is visiting the city.

    A description of the coronation procession first appeared in the Hardyng continuation, and was copied by Hall

(p. 375). Grafton gave a more extended description, which from a nearly contemporary account, published in Excerpta Historica (p. 379—384) appears to be nearly correct. Holinshed's description is not as a whole so extended as Grafton's, and differs from it in some other respects. Where it happens to be fuller it appears from the Exc. Hist. account to be correct. A comparison of Legge's procession reveals the following:

1) "The Queene wth a circlet on her head under a canopie" is surely from Grafton, who has "Anne... and hauing a canapy ouer her head, and on euery corner of the same was a Bell of Golde and on her head was a circlet of Golde, set with many precious stones". Hall has "Anne... betwene two bishoppes, and a canabie ouer her hed, borne by the Barones of the portes. On her hed a riche coronall sette with stones and pearle". Holinshed agrees with Hall, save that he has "coronet". The word "circlet" in Legge shows the use of Grafton, as well as the omission of the bishops and barons. Legge would hardly have omitted the bishops had they been in his text, for he has them with Richard, as does Grafton.
2) "Knights and Esquires" must likewise be from Grafton, who has "ladies... and after them a great number of knights and Esquires". These are not mentioned in Hall or Holinshed.
3) A negative proof of the use of Grafton is found in the comments of the spectators on the significance of the dove (p. 183).

Hosp.
Quid alba Reginae columba denotat?
Hosp. [Read: Civis]
Notat avis innocentiam nihil nocens.

Grafton has "rod with the doffe which signifieth innocencie". Holinshed here omits the significance, and Hall has no such explanations whatever. The significance might, of course, have easily been added by Legge himself, but as it appears otherwise in Grafton alone, its presence may be regarded as cumulative proof of the use of Grafton.

4) "Choristers", "singing-men" and "Praebendaries" probably came from Grafton. In none of the chronicles do they appear in the description of the coronation. But Grafton's "and forthwith there came up before the King & the Queene bothe priests and clarkes, that song most delectable and excellent musick" seems a more likely ground for the insertion than Hall's statement that after the king and queen had taken their seats in the abbey "diuerse songes" were "solemply songe".

That Grafton was, however, not the only authority used for the Shewe of the Procession is proved by the inclusion of the "Northren Souldiers well armed", who are mentioned in Hall and Holinshed, but not in Grafton or More.

4. This case, with others mentioned below, proves that in addition to the Hardyng continuation and Grafton, Legge used Hall or Holinshed or both of them. Which of the two he used, or whether he did use both it seems impossible to determine, for aside from the cases mentioned in 2 and 3 there appears to be nothing in the play for which there are not at least two authorities. In Hall and Holinshed, and not in Grafton, are

p. 184 "Northren Souldiers well armed";
216 Richard's oration, many lines of which are direct translations of lines in Hall and Holinshed, but not in Grafton, who abridged the speech as he found it in Hall;
217 Henry's speech, of which the same thing, in less degree, is true;
218 Henry's prayer.

Thus there is sufficient proof that Legge drew from one of these two or both.

The sole argument going to show that on a given occasion Hall and not Holinshed or Grafton was used is that in the arrests made by Gloucester at Stony Stratford (p. 143) Hawte is mentioned — "proditorem patriae perfide voco Haute simul". In the corresponding passages of the four chronicles Hawte is mentioned by Hall alone. More and Holinshed do not speak of Hawte at all; but unfortunately for our purpose Grafton mentions his name later when speaking of the execution of those arrested on this occasion. Hence the proof is not absolute for the use of Hall, for Legge may have transferred the name from that passage. When however Legge's customary faithfulness to the immediately related passage is considered, it remains very probable that the mention here of Hawte is an indication of the use of Hall.

For other passages which have no basis in Holinshed Grafton always stands beside Hall. Thus either Hall or Grafton may have been authority for

- p. 140 Buckingham's message to Richard (mentioned in a later passage by More and Holinshed);
- 149 Gloucester's words "Eduardus en rex etc.";
- 153 The Queen's speech (as shown by the parenthesis in it, which corresponds to the arrangement of Hall and Grafton, not that of More and Holinshed);
- 160 The mention of Northampton;
- 162 Gloucester's speech — arrest of Stanley, York and Ely;
- 169 Postponement of coronation to Nov. 2.
- 174 "Burdetti — cui quod jocatus est" (the word jocatus points to the explanation in Hall and Grafton only);
- 177 The presence of the bishops with Richard (from the Hardyng Con.);
- 190 The speech of Brakenbury from "jugulare civem" (from Pol. Vergil);
- 200 Richard's lament for his son.

For the exclusive use of Holinshed in any given passage there is no proof. Where Hall fails, Grafton always has the same passage. Thus to either Holinshed or Grafton may be due

 p. 1–3 Buckingham's order "pracite etc." (which here appears before the greeting to the king, as in Holinshed, Grafton and More, not after it, as in Hall);

 145 "Packs and coffers" in stage direction;

 151 et seq. The scene with the Queen (probably; as the word "recidiva" in the speech of the queen 151, 2, appears to correspond rather with the "recidiuation" of More, Holinshed and Grafton than the "resiluacion" of Hall and the Hardyng Con.);

 153 The birth of the prince in prison (from More's Latin, first appearing in Rastell's ed. 1557 and so not in Hall);

 156—158 The temptation of Buckingham and his agreement with Richard (from More's Latin);

 180 Richard's speech in court of King's Bench (from More's Latin).

If either Hall or Holinshed was not used that one is probably Holinshed, which appeared in the latter half of the year before Legge's play was produced, if 1579 be the earliest date. The composition of this may well have begun at an earlier period.

The foregoing section will have made clear that in the analysis of the play the reference of passages to More or Polidore Vergil is a reference to the original and not the immediate source, and the same may be the case with references to Hall.

Analysis of the Play.

Citations from Seneca are made from the edition of Leo, Berlin, 1879.

The argument of the first actio covers the period from the death of Edward IV to the condemnation of Shore's wife. It corresponds in all respects to an outline of the story in Hall, save that here, as in the Dramatis Personae, the young king is said to be fifteen years old. More calls him "a thirtene yeare of age", and this was followed by Hall and all who copied More. Rous and others varied from this, but I have been unable to find anywhere an authority for fifteen. In fact, the prince was twelve and a half years old. It is possible that Legge's statement was conditioned by the apparent age of the student actor, but a greater difficulty must have existed in the case of the young duke of York, whose age is correctly given as eleven. The argument states that Richard, homo nimia ambitione elatus, perceived in the tender age of the prince an easy path for himself to the throne.

The opening scene of the play discloses the queen lamenting to the Cardinal Archbishop of Canterbury the death of her husband, and expressing her fears for the safety of her son, who is coming up from Wales to be crowned. The tone of her words is entirely Senecan, a lament over the cares that attend a throne. The note is struck in the opening words of the scene, which sound at the same time the ground-note of Richard's whole tragedy:

> Quicumque laetis credulus rebus nimis
> confidit, et magna potens aula cupit
> regnare, blandum quaerit is malum.

The words are an imitation of Troades 1—3:

> Quicumque regno fidit et magna potens
> dominatur aula nec leves metuit deos
> animumque rebus credulum laetis dedit
> me videat et te Troia.

with a reminiscence of Oedipus 6, 7:

> Quisquamne regno gaudet? O fallax bonum,
> Quantum malorum fronte quam blanda tegis!

cf. also Agamemnon 57 et seq.

The queen hastily reviews her marriage to Edward, and the joy she won thereby, dashed too soon by the nobles' scorn of her birth, and the death of her father and brother, brought about by Clarence. The establishment of her kindred about the prince caused yet more dissension, and again the fates brought disaster in the death of her husband.

> Nec tristis haec contenta peste sors fuit
> prius malum majoris est gradus mali
> Exhalat aegrotum maritus spiritum,
> et fata rumpunt regis impia manu
> saevae sorores, invident virum mihi
> mortale fatis luditur genus. sibi
> spondere quiquam non potest tam stabile
> fortuna quod non versit anceps. sordida
> manet domus tantum beata, dum timet
> virtus ruinas magna.

cf. Her. Fur. 208—9:

> finis alternis mali
> gradus est futuri.

Her. Fur. 181:

> durae peragunt pensa sorores.

Oct. 925—6:

> Regitur fatis mortale genus
> nec sibi quisquam spondere potest
> firmum et stabile.

Her. Fur. 199—200:

> humilique loco sed certa sedet
> sordida parvae fortuna domus:
> alte virtus animosa cadit.

Now the young prince is on his way to London to be crowned, a new cause for fear, for even if no dauger threatens from without, from the house of Lancaster, there may yet be danger within.

The cardinal seeks to comfort her, but she rejects his consolation. She has good cause to fear, for, following the advice of many — an advice given at Gloucester's instigation, according to the argument — she has deprived the prince of a large train, in order not to renew the ancient enmity healed at Edward's bedside. Thus she may have left him naked to his enemies. "A mighty hatred presses hard our house, ambition rages. Gloucester brought his own brother death; will his ambition spare his nephew?"

While the cardinal is still endeavoring to diminish her fears, a messenger enters. The prince, he announces, has reached Northampton in safety. In accordance with the queen's letters, Rivers has dismissed all soldiery from about the prince, and is accompanying him alone with Gray. So far the news is encouraging, but to the queen's anxious question whether Gloucester has met the king, the messenger replies that both he and Buckingham have sent most friendly letters and promised to join the king shortly. The queen is thrown back into her former fear.

> Postquam favor flatu secundo vexerit
> ratem procul: reliquit idem languidus
> alto mari, multisque jactat fluctibus.
> Res prosperae si quando laetari jubent,
> rursus revolvor in metus, nec desinit
> animus pavere laeta quamvis cerneret.

The first three lines are an imitation of Octavia 877 et seq.:

> O funestus multis populi
> dirusque favor, qui cum flatu
> vela secundo ratis implevit
> vexitque procul, languidus idem
> deserit alto saevoque mari.

The cardinal again interposes, urging that her fear is giving easy credence to sinister prophecies; while the queen insists that experience has taught her that fear is wisdom, an interchange of epigrams in Senecan stichomythia ensues, with an occasional line actually imitated from Seneca. E. g.:

> Hoc facile credunt qui nimis miseri timent,

an imitation of Hercules Furens, 314, 15:

> Quod nimis miseri volunt
> hoc facile credunt.

The scene ends with another insistence upon the theme with which it opened.

> Timere didicit quisquis excelsus stetit,
> rebusque magnis alta clauditur quies.
> Auro venenum bibitur ignotum casae
> humili malum, ventisque cunctis cognita
> superba summo tecto nutant culmine.

This is from Thyestes 447 et seq.:

> dum excelsus steti
> nunquam pavere destiti atque ipsum mei
> ferrum timere lateris . . . .
> . . . . scelera non intrant casas,
> . . . .
> venenum in auro bibitur —

and Octavia 890 et seq.:

> bene paupertas
> humili tecto contenta latet
> quatiunt altas saepe procellas
> aut evertit Fortuna domos.

As for the facts of the scene, they correspond almost exactly to the chronicle. There is, however, no statement there that Rivers dismissed all Edward's soldiers. More and his copyists state that the prince was being brought up "with a sober company", and there was in fact a train of two thousand soldiers. The scene itself is not in the chronicle, where the archbishop of Canterbury first comes to the queen to obtain the duke of York.

The view of Richard is not quite clear. He is ambitious and he hates the queen. It is directly stated, too, as in the Mirror for Magistrates that he was the cause of Clarence's death. But it does not appear whether this was in pursuance of a purpose to obtain the throne. The statement of the argument, while not necessarily inconsistent with this view, would seem to indicate that Richard's purpose was first definitely conceived after the death of Edward. But at all events, Richard appears as a man whose hatred for the queen's kin and whose ambition she has long known and feared. He has not hesitated to bring his own brother to death, and the queen, before there has been the slightest overt act of hostility on Richard's part, is full of a lively dread that he will not spare his nephew. Of other events in Richard's previous career, good or bad, there is no mention: Legge contents himself with the one murder as an indication of Richard's ruthless character. Yet he has contrived, largely by the employment of Seneca, to give to the opening scene an intense feeling of anxious suspense. A tyrant and his tyranny are at hand. At their approach the royal victim feels the vanity of earthly glory, the certainty that what is high must fall. In expressing that feeling of herself she unconsciously prophesies and asserts the punishment of the author of her downfall. Richard is climbing high, but after all only to reach a point from which fall is sure. It is the same thought which in Shakespeare's play Richard urges upon Dorset, and accepts with unconscious fatalism when turned upon himself.

    Marg. They that stand high have many blasts to shake them:
            And if they fall, they dash themselves to pieces.
    Glou. Good counsel, marry: learn it, learn it, marquess.
    Dor. It toucheth you, mylord, as much as me.
    Glou. Yea, and much more.   R. III. 1:3:259 et seq.

The scene now changes to Northampton, where Gloucester has arrived and greets Rivers with words expressing the "frendly chere" of the chronicle. Rivers replies courteously, and subsequently excuses himself to go to sleep. Then ensues a council between Gloucester, Buckingham, and Hastings, who, contrary to the chronicle, is also represented as present. Richard addresses Buckingham in the words which the chronicler represents him as having sent to those whom he knew to be at variance with the queen, "some by mouthe, some by writynge and secrete messengers". Legge makes Richard's complaint more personal than in the original, "I" being often substituted for "we", and makes more direct Richard's charge that the queen was responsible for Clarence's death, and that he himself escaped the like fate only by his own sagacity. Buckingham agrees in Richard's view of the danger, and mentions — following the chronicle's anecdote of the message through Persival — that he has already sent Richard word to the same effect. Richard proposes the arrest and removal of Rivers, at which Buckingham and Hastings — whose presence in this scene is doubtless due to the statement of the chronicle that Richard with the words above mentioned set on fire especially Buckingham and Hastings — express fear of a popular uprising. Their fears are set at rest, and they swear — in Senecan terms — fidelity to Richard, who has throughout the scene declared his own fidelity to the young prince. Rivers, the keys of whose inn have meanwhile been taken into the conspirators' possession, and the ways beset by their guards, now appears, expressing his anxiety as to what this sudden change may mean, and approaches the dukes to learn the cause. He is met with the charges mentioned in More, and is not allowed to defend himself, but is hastily arrested and dragged off the stage, crying out upon the treachery of Fortune. Thus the scene extends through a whole night, following very closely, with constant translation of the original, the account of More.

Thereupon follows the meeting of Gloucester and Buckingham with the king, and the arrest of Gray and Hawte exactly as narrated in Hall. Gloucester greets the king with "Rex vivat aeternum Britanus inclytus", Buckingham with, "Tibi beatum firmet imperium deus". Beside this, Gloucester makes strong profession — again in Senecan terms — of his fidelity. There is but one change from the account of the chronicle. There the king weeps because his servants are changed; Legge improves by making him weep at the arrest of his brother, Gray.

The story of Richard's sending a dish from his own table to Rivers, and bidding him be of good cheer is related by a scene between a servant of the king and one of Richard's, in which the king's servant laments the downfall of his master, which, he clearly sees, Gloucester's ambition is destined to bring about.

The action again shifts to London, where the queen receives the news of the disaster to her kinsmen, and holds conference with the Archbishop of York. The scene is a good example of Legge's dramatic method. So far as the facts are concerned the scene follows closely the paragraph of More which is its basis, and as usual little is omitted, even of the minor details. Where More puts words into the mouths of the characters, Legge translates them into his Latin. But the form and manner of the scene are wholly Senecan. In the anguish and unrest of the queen the author saw a close resemblance to the condition of unhappy Phaedra, after the rejection of her suit to Hippolytus. Accordingly, the scene is modelled upon that of Seneca, so far as the differing circumstances allow. The moment chosen for presentation is that of the arrival of the Archbishop at the sanctuary. He is met by an ancilla, corresponding to the nutrix of Phaedra, who bewails the evils that have fallen upon the house of York.

> Quis est malorum finis? heu! heu! quam diu
> Regina victa luctibus diris gravat?
> Quae possidet ferox Erinnis Regiam.
> Tortos vel angues Megara crudelis vibrans
> Luctumque majorem prior luctus vocat
> Et vix malis Regina tantus sufficit.

The ancilla then relates to the Archbishop, as the nutrix does to the chorus of Phaedra, the state of the unfortunate queen.

> Splendens honore antistes Eboracensium
> Diros tibi renovare me casus jubre
> Postquam Luna fessis suaserat,
> et caeca nox horreret, amisso die
> Increbuit aula, vinculis Riverium
> duris premi et Graium nepotem: tum locus
> quis principem capiat, tenere neminem.
> Postquam paterent tanta reginae mala,
> animus tremore concitus subito stupet,
> Solvuntur (heu) labante membra spiritu

> Postquam trementes misera vires colligit,
> en, talibus mox astra pulsat vocibus
> O dura fata parcite . . . .
> . . . .
> Non sustinet labante mox collo caput
> Largo madescunt imbre profusae genae
> cor triste magnis aestuat doloribus,
> cultum decorum regiae vestis procul
> removet, et eximii rubores muricis
> Quieta nunquam constat, huc, illuc, fugit,
> tolli jubet iterumque poni corpora.
> Et semper impatiens sui status, cito
> mutatur, et coelum quaerelis verberat.

Compare with this the nutrix's description of Phaedra. Phaed. 360 et seq.:

> Spes nulla tantum posse leniri malum,
> finisque flammis nullus insanis erit.
> . . . .
> erumpit oculis ignis et lassae genae
> lucem recusant, nil idem dubiae placet
> artusque varie iactat incertus dolor,
> nunc ut soluto labitur moriens gradu
> et vix labante sustinet collo caput,
> nunc se quieti reddit, et somni immemor,
> noctem querelis ducit; attolli iubet
> iterumque poni corpus et solvi comas
> rursusque fingi: semper impatiens siu
> mutatur habitus . . . .
> . . . .
> lacrimae cadunt per ora et assiduo genae
> rore irrigantur, qualiter Tauri iugis
> tepido madescunt imbre percussae nives.
>   Sed en, patescunt regiae fastigia.
> reclinis ipsa sedis auratae toro
> solitos amictus mente non sana abnuit.

Phaedra. Removete, famulae, purpura atque auro inlitas
> vestes, procul sit muricis Tyrii rubor.

As the abode of Phaedra opens to reveal her and her servants hurrying to remove their mistress's purple and gold-embroidered garments, so in Legge's scene a curtain is drawn, revealing the queen in sanctuary with her daughters, while her servants are bringing her possessions in haste and heaping them up about her.

From here to the close of the conversation between the archbishop and the queen the scene follows closely the narration of the source, Senecan influence manifesting itself only in invocations to the "rector potens Olympi", and in the curse which the queen utters against Hastings:

> Ille, ille nostri durus hostis sanguinis
> Hastingus, ille principi exitium parat:
> En, vindices mater deos supplex precor
> Dirum caput flammis nefandis abruant.

Compare Oct. 227, 28:

> utinam nefandi principis dirum caput
> obruere flammis caelitum rector paret.

The besetting of the Thames and all ways to the sanctuary by Gloucester's servants, the tumultuous meetings of nobles and citizens, the meeting of the lords, with the advice of Hastings to defer any action until Gloucester and Buckingham arrive, which follow in More's story, are drawn together by Legge into one scene. Here occurs the line referred to by Nashe, the summons to the citizens, "Urbs, urbs, Cives, ad arma, ad arma". The diverse divining upon this dealing appears in expressions of hostility to the queen, "Dii feminae tam triste vindicent nefas", and prayer for the prince, "At te deus, pusille princeps, muniat". The Archbishop of York declares the common fear that Gloucester's actions are due to his desire for the crown — "furens repetit Ambitio thronum? et poscit in praedam sibi?" — and Hastings calms the agitation with the words ascribed to him by the chronicle.

Escorted by the mayor and Gloucester, the young king now enters London. He greets the city in the style of the Senecan Agamemnon and Thyestes returning to their homes, and declares his joy to be greater than that of the Greeks beholding their native land after the Trojan war, greater even than the joy of shipwrecked Ulysses.

> Ubi barbaras sedes mutavimus ferae
> gentis, revertor sospes ad patrios lares.
> Urbis superbae clarus hic pollet nitor,

> Regnique splendet majus inclyti decus.
> Urbs chara, salve tanta: nunquam gaudia
> post tot ruinas Asiae Argivis nunquam
> optata patriae regna et Argolicas opes
> cum bella post tam longa primi viserent.
> Vix hospiti tot lustra tam laetum tibi
> redditum licet tantis miser naufragiis
> ereptus esses dux Cephalenius parant
> Quam crescit amissae voluptas patriae
> hospes diu postquam carebas, et suos
> negant aspectus longum iter mihi.

Cf. Agam. 782—5:

> Tandem revertor sospes ad patrios lares
> o cara salve terra tibi tot barbarae
> dedere gentes spolia, tibi felix diu
> potentis Asiae Troia summisit manus.

and Thy. 404—409:

> Optata patriae tecta et Argolicas opes
> miserisque summum ac maximum exulibus bonum,
> tractum soli natalis et patrios deos
> (si sunt tamen di) cerno, Cyclopum saevas
> turres, labore maius humano decus,
> celebratra iuveni stadia.

Gloucester shows his devotion to the prince, with words corresponding to those put in his mouth by Hall, — "saying to all men as he rode behold your prince and souereigne Lord".

> Eduardus en rex vester, o cives mei,
> honore fulgens regio en potens puer
> chare Britannis principem vides tuum
> virtute praestantem fidelis abdite.

A soliloquy by Hastings follows, to impart the result of the first meeting of the council, the election of Gloucester to the protectorship and the taking of the great seal from the Archbishop of York, as recorded by More. Hastings exults that his enemies lie in prison at Pontefract, and prays that their death be near at hand.

The rest of the fourth Actus is devoted to a reproduction of More's account of the meeting of the council in which Richard proposes that the duke of York be brought from sanctuary, and of the efforts of the cardinal Archbishop of York to induce the queen to deliver him up. All the speeches of the original are given in extended detail. As noted elsewhere, it is here the archbishop of York, as in More and Holinshed, and not, as in Hall's historically correcter account, Canterbury, who goes to the queen. He is accompanied by Buckingham and Howard, who represent the "divers other lords" of More. Howard's presence is indicated by Hall and Holinshed, who ascribe to him a certain speech assigned in More's original simply to "another lord". This again is another instance of Legge's minute faithfulness to his source; — an interesting contrast to the manner of Shakespeare, who makes Hastings accompany the cardinal, and at the latter's invitation, no regard being paid to More's suggestion that Richard sent others to make the matter more sure.

The farewell of the queen to her son affords the dramatist a fine opportunity for rhetoric. Nothing could be more touching than More's simple words: "And there withall she said unto the child: Farewel, my own swete sonne, God send you good keping, let me kis you ones yet ere you goe, for God knoweth when we shal kis togither agayne. And therewith she kissed him, and blessed him, turned her back and wept and went her way, leauing the childe weping as fast" (p. 40). But with this Legge could not be content. The queen's words are extended by him over forty lines. His dramatic model furnished him with the scene of Andromache yielding up her young Astyanax to be sacrificed by her victorious foes, and Andromache's words of sorrowful parting are therefore made the example of Elizabeth's:

      O dulce pignus, alterum regni decus,
      spes vana matris, cui patris laudes ego
      demens precabar frustra, avi longas dies
      tibi patronus adsit tot pro cellis arbiter
      mundi deus, tutoque portu collocet

> impulsa vela, maestaeque matris accipe
> infixa labris oscula infoelix tuis.

cf. Troades 766—70:

> O dulce pignus, o decus lapsae domus
> summumque Troiae funus, o Danaum timor,
> genetricis o spes vana, cui demens ego
> laudes parentis bellicas, annos avi
> medios precabar, vota destituit deus.

The "avi longas dies", which in Andromache's mouth have meaning, referring to the aged Priam, in Elizabeth's become absurd. She can hardly be supposed to refer to Richard duke of York, who was only forty-eight years old, when he perished at Wakefield, four years before Elizabeth became acquainted with his son; and Elizabeth's own father was dead.

Nor is the speech as a whole well applied to the young prince, of whose safety the queen has at least some hope. It is a rare slip for Legge, who in general fits his borrowings well to his own necessities.

The queen's long wail continues, with an appeal to her son to suffer her tears, even if his noble soul prevent any of his own. She has been trained to weep by the death of Edward her lord, but when he died another Edward remained to take his place, and her kinsmen were by her side in power. Now they are overthrown, her brother lies in prison, and the king himself is in the custody of the dreaded Richard. In the loss of her second son the queen's last hope is gone.

> In hoc fuit una spes lapsae domus.

The whole passage contains many similarities to the passage in the Troades. Thus

> an quicquid potest
> flebilius esse regis Eduardi nece

is a reminiscence of. Tro. 784—5

> flebilius aliquid Hectoris magni nece
> muri videbunt;

Tum turma suffulsit meorum nobilis

has caught up a phrase from Tro. 779:
puer citatas nobilis turmas ages.

Petam mater simul
viventis oculos ad [ut] mea claudam manu

is from Tro. 788—9:
concede paucas, ut mea condam manu
viventis oculos.

at suos planctus tamen
concede matri

is probably an imitation of Tro. 801—2:
pauca maternae tamen
perfer querelae verba

and the immediately following lines
En, sume fletus matris, e misero patris
quicquid relictum funere

are from Tro. 807—8:
et sume lacrimas, quidquid e misero viri
funere relictum est.

The lament concludes with a simile from the Troades doubtless entirely in accord with the taste of the academic audience for which Legge wrote, but to a modern mind destructive of that sympathy with the mother's feeling which the rest of Legge's rhetoric has not yet rendered entirely impossible.

Qualis remota matre crudelis leo
praedam minorem morsibus vastis premens
raptavit ore; talis sinu meo
crudelis avulsit nepotem patruus.

cf. Tro. 794—99:
fremitu leonis qualis audito tener
timidum iuvencus applicat matri latus
at ille saevus matre summota leo
praedam minorem morsibus vastis tenens
frangit vehitque: talis e nostro sinu
te rapiet hostis.

It is doubtless likewise his dependence on Seneca that leads Legge most strangely to put into Howard's mouth a description of the queen's manner as she takes leave of her son.

> en candidas profusa lachrymis genas
> variis tenellos filii artus implicet,
> amplexibus suprema spargens oscula,
> nec plura singultus sinit anhelans loqui.
> Haesitque medio rapta gutture egredi
> vox jussa, nec reperit viam infoelix amor.
> Quid matris adeo chara vexas pectora?
> post terga discedens relinquit filium.

All this, of course, took place before the audience, and was to be seen and heard by them. Why it should be related by Howard is a mystery. But his words are the extended reproduction of the last sentence quoted above from More.

In the opening scene of the fifth Act is dramatized the passage from More's Latin which in Rastell's edition of More's English history of Richard, and thus in Grafton and Holinshed, but not in the Harding continuation or in Hall, follows directly upon the obtaining of the duke of York; that, namely, which recounts Richard's craft in securing the support of Buckingham, who, according to More, "had repented the way that he had entered" (cf. p. 90). The "suttell folks" that broke the matter to Buckingham are in the drama represented by Catesby. In a soliloquy preceding the entrance of Buckingham he indicates the present situation. The protector is drawing rapidly toward the accomplishment of his purpose. His prey is within his grasp, the crown is almost ready to his hand. All who oppose him he is ready to make way with, save Buckingham, whom he expects to win to his side. The situation of Richard reminds the dramatist of that of Atreus in Seneca's play, as he sees the hated Thyestes and his two young sons fallen into his power. Hence the soliloquy of Catesby characterizing Richard's position is based upon that of Atreus characterizing his own (cf. Thyestes 491—503). The likeness in the characters of Atreus and Richard, and in the fact that each murders his two young nephews, is striking, and as will be seen Legge returns to it again and again.

Buckingham is characterized in this interview both by Catesby's words, "animo tumet superbus", and his own,

> At si quis excelsa potens aula, levis
> Immunis imperio deae suae potest
> jactare foelicem statum haud fragili loco.
> Excelsus id Buckinghamus heros potest.

This view appears to rest on a later passage in More's story, where in recounting the reasons for Buckingham's conspiracy he says, "Very trouth it is, the duke was an high minded man, and euyll could beare the glory of an other" (cf. p. 114). In the conversation Catesby repeats the declarations given in More's paragraph, that the young king will revenge on Buckingham the imprisonment and death of his relatives; that repentance and an attempt to repair his offence will only ensure his destruction at the protector's hands; and that the sole way out of the dilemma is to put vengeance out of the young king's power by raising the protector to the throne.

The scene is skillfully managed. Catesby reveals in solemn and impressive words the anger of the young king and his purpose to have vengeance. Buckingham at first treats the matter lightly: a boy's brief anger, he replies, is soon extinguished.

A boy's wrath it is, replies the tempter, but the rasher because it is a boy's.

Time will diminish it. Nay, for his mother will urge it on.

But Gloucester shared the crime. True, yet vengeance will be satisfied with the punishment of one.

Gloucester's authority will restrain the boy's wrath. Yes, so long as he is a boy.

But he will always fear his uncle. Nay, a king fears no one.

Buckingham begins to waver. What plan will save him? Catesby's reply opens up new horrors. That plan

only, he answers, which will forbid the prince your death.
What, cries Buckingham, will the queen's wrath urge on
her son so far? To Buckingham's fearful question Catesby
replies with the crafty suggestion, Her dead son can
work no injury. The duke stands aghast. Is then the
sole remedy the death of the prince? At once Catesby
brings his strongest batteries to bear.

> Vinci nisi scelere novo scelus nequit
> Quoddam scelus honestum necessitas facit
> Plagis tenetur capta dispositis fera
> Quasi vinculis uterque servatur nepos
> levi peribunt Claudii nutu ducis
> periere jam jam, si tibi nunc consulas.

With the first line cf. **Agam.** 115:

> per scelera semper sceleribus est iter.

and **Phaed.** 721:

> scelere velandum est scelus.

Lines 3 and 4 have their source in the passage mentioned
above from the **Thyestes**.

For Buckingham too there is danger.

> Glocestrium munit satelles clam ducere
> mores notat secretos excubitor tuos
> qualem tuorum minime falsam putes,
> adversus illum forte si quicquam pares
> Nihil timendum si vides, time tamen
> incerta multorum fides: constans nihil:
> Inimica crede cuncta: turbatus solet
> simulare multa vultus, et finget dolos
> Fratri Thyestes liberos credens suos
> mistum suorum sanguinem genitor bibit.

The statement concerning the spies is from More, the
manner of the warning Senecan. The last line is **Thy.** 917.

Buckingham is on the point of yielding. To repent
of his share in bringing about the fate of the queen's
kinsmen would be cowardly. On the one side is the certain
danger from the queen mother and the king; on the other
the protection offered by the supreme power of Gloucester.
Catesby clinches his case with an argument Buckingham

cannot ganisay. If a hastened fate deprives the king of life — the threat is apparent — Gloucester will surely be king. With Buckingham's aid he can win the crown without such a sacrifice. By supporting Richard he will not really be bringing on the catastrophe, for that is unavoidable; and he will save the lives of both the princes. The conquest is complete. The duke promises his aid, satisfying himself with the thought that after all the prince's loss is slight, if he thus preserves his life. For if he were king yet his mother would rule, not he.

It is evident from this scene that Legge adopted that view of Buckingham which the latter gives of himself in his conversation with the Bishop of Ely, as far as the duke's disposition toward the prince is concerned. The passage in point is: "So agayn by my ayde and fauour, he of a protectour was made a kyng .... at which tyme he promysed me on his fidelitie, laying his hand in myne at Baynarde Castel, that the II young princes should lyue" (Hall, p. 387). The view is the same as Shakespeare's, whose "high-reaching Buckingham grows circumspect" at the thought of the princes' death. On the other hand, of the alternative views suggested by More, "that this duke was priuy to al the protectours counsel, euen from the beginning", and that only after the persuasions of certain subtle folk "to thys wicked enterprise, which he beleued coulde not bee voided, hee bent himselfe and went through", Shakespeare selects the first and Legge the latter.

The motive suggested by Catesby, that Buckingham by assenting to Richard's plans will save the king, is not due to Legge. It stands already in the passage from More, "There was no way left to redeme his offence by benefites; but he should soner distroy himself than saue the king, who with his brother and his kinsefolkes he saw in such places imprisoned, as the protectour might with a beck distroy them al". What is peculiar to Legge is the emphasis he gives to the motive. It is led up to in the construction of the scene: it is the first really effective move of Catesby in his play upon Buckingham, and the last, with which he completes his conquest; it forms the real ground of Buckingham's decision. Thus the duke's character stands in Legge's play on a higher plane than in any of the histories or in Shakespeare.

In the conversation between Buckingham and Catesby is, perhaps, best seen the real value of the Senecan stichomythia, so often adopted by Legge. It forms an excellent medium for the expression of a contest of minds in which one character urges and the other resists. Such is its constant and regular use in Seneca. It is used in the same way by Shakespeare in his play of Richard III. Here it lacks much of the philosophical and apothegmatic character common to it in Seneca, but it gains thereby in point and real effectiveness.

In the next scene, which continues the dramatization of the passage from More's Latin, the two dukes come to an agreement. Buckingham complains of the danger from the young king, and demands that he be imprisoned. Richard professes horror, and agrees that the king's terrible plans must be averted. Though his life be spared, he must be restrained in prison.

> Tremulos per artus horror excurrit vagus
> Juvenile novi regis ingenium ferox
> indocile, flecti non potest? frangi potest.
> si patiamur, exitium parat nobis grave.
> redimere vitam vinculis regis licet.

In the first line will be recognized a formula that appears with many variations in Seneca. It is as constantly used by Legge. Line 3 is Thy. 200.

Richard proceeds hypocritically to declare his sorrow at taking away his brother's realm. Everywhere the partisans of Lancaster will laugh at the fallen house of its rival. Yet their lives must be guarded from danger and the state from woes; and he therefore demands his brother's sceptre, his by right of blood. To Buckingham he promises the earldom of Hereford, and that his son shall marry Buckingham's daughter.

The two now consult with Catesby as to their further steps. It is decided to remove the princes to the tower and to institute divided meetings of the council. The nobles are to be summoned to the coronation and all is to proceed as if in order. Under cover of the preparations Richard may attain his purpose. The people are to be won by money or by fear. To ascertain the feelings of the nobles is more difficult, but Richard believes himself equal to the task.

> Quasi publicis de rebus annus nimis
> quos suspicor solicitus usquam consulam
> dum multa proponam dubius et volvimus
> secreta regni, mens patebit abdita.

This bit of craft, as well as the suggested means for winning the people are Legge's own. The use of money is doubtless adopted from the lattier passage of More, in which Richard is said by large gifts to have himself unsteadfast friendship; while constraint of the people through fear is the wonted proceeding of the Senecan tyrant. The other facts are from the passage from More's Latin.

On Hastings alone Richard does not need to exercise his arts. Hastings is open in his faithfulness to the young king. Yet he may possibly be won, and to Catesby is assigned the task of trying him. Now in More's story it is left in doubt whether Catesby ever did try him or not. "Catesby, whither he assayed him or assaied him not, reported vnto them, that he founde him so fast, and hard him speke so terrible woordes that he durst no further breke". As in the case of Buckingham's agreement to Richard's plans, Shakespeare adopted the one alternative, and Legge the other. In Shakespeare's play Hastings is really approached and declares his fidelity. In Legge's Catesby seizes the chance to ensure his master's downfall. Left alone by the dukes, he begins to soliloquize,

> Quid nunc agis Catesbeie? quin tibi consulas:
> nunc avoca actus animi, nunc fraudes, dolos.
> Totum Catesbeium. . . . .
> . . . .
> praeesse solus tu potes Lecestriae
> successor Hastingi: duces credent magis:
> bene est: pereat, ut nostra crescat gloria
> Infausta dirus rumpat ensis viscera.
> Studere fingam Regulis durum nimis,
> flecti nec ulla pertinax posset prece.

Here Catesby becomes in a certain degree the representative of the Senecan Ulysses. cf. St. 613—14:

> nunc advoca actus, anime, nunc fraudes, dolos,
> nunc totum Vlixen.

Why Legge preferred to represent Catesby as not going to Hastings is evident from Catesby's speech: he found it more consistent with More's statement that Catesby, "fering lest their motions might with the lord Hastinges minishe his credence, wherunto onely al the matter lenid, procured the protectour hastely to ridde him. And much the rather, for that he trusted by his deth to obtaine much of the rule that the lorde Hastinges bare in his countrey; the only desire whereof, was the allectiue that induced him to be partener and one specyall contriuer of al this horrible treson". None of this comes to expression in Shakespeare, where the character of Catesby appears only in outline. He is the devoted follower and assistant of Richard, but of the purposes and motives that govern him nothing is said.

In the following scene Stanley makes known to Hastings his fears as to the meaning of the separate councils. Hastings endeavors to calm his anxiety by telling him that his faithful friend Catesby is always at the other council. Stanley fears he may prove untrue, but Hastings declares his complete confidence in him. Again Stanley urges that they fly before it is too late. "Serum est cavendi tempus in mediis malis" (Thy. 487). But Hastings is confident that he stands in the highest favor with Richard and Buckingham. Besides, to fly were to argue themselves guilty of some crime, and if brought back they would surely be destroyed. Hastings would rather fall through the guilt of another than by his own cowardice.

> Trans ista (crede) nulla quam demens times.
> Rude prius in coelum chaos mutabitur,
> prius astra terris haereant, flamine salum,
> quam fallat astrinctam fidem Catsbeius.

cf. Octavia 222—25:

> Iungentur ante saeva sideribus freta
> et ignis undae, Tartaro tristi polus,
> lux alma tenebris, roscidae nocti dies,
> quam —

The scene is a faithful transcript of the passage in which More recounts the conversation of Stanley and Hastings anent the separate councils (cf. p. 90—91). But Hastings' scornful refusal to fly is from the later passage where he answers the messenger whom Stanley sends to relate his warning dream. Shakespeare likewise combines the two passage in the answer Hastings gives to Stanley's messenger in his play.

There follows now a scene of a nature like that of several others in the play, a scene in which Richard and his helpers consult and agree upon events that are brought to pass in later scenes. In one point only is this scene not superfluous to the action, in that here Catesby makes report of his fictitious trial of Hastings. But for Richard's character it is very important. In Shakespeare's play Richard pursues his course toward the goal without a single faltering step. He knows at what he aims, and how to hit it. Of his success he is not one moment in doubt, and until he is successful there never comes upon him a moment when he is oppressed by the fearful magnitude of his undertaking. Satellites and helpers he must have, but of the services they render he is always the inspirer. If for a moment they seem to suggest and guide, they offer only what he has before instilled into them, and he is still the leader where he seems to follow. They may hesitate, but he never does. So long as Buckingham leads in the right path, Richard like a child will go by his direction. But when at last Buckingham checks at Hastings' fate, inquiring, "What shall we do?" it is Richard whose answer comes like a flash. "Chop off his head, man; — somewhat we will do".

To all this the Richard of Legge's scene presents a striking contrast. To his helpers Catesby and Howard he reveals a deep anxiety over the success of his plots; fear and hope are shaking his very soul; his ambition is master of him, not he of it.

>   Spes concutit mentem metusque turbidam,
>   trepidumque gemino pectus eventu labat.
>   Imago regni semper errat ante oculos mihi,
>   et usque dubium impellit ambitio gravis
>   turbatque pectus: flamma regni concita
>   nescit quiescere: sceptra nunc tantum placent.
>   Non desinam dum summam votorum attigi.
>   Multum exagitat incerta nobilium fides
>   cui nostra certus consilia credam haud scio:
>   Nec sunt loco tuto sitae fraudes meae.

Howard essays to encourage his anxious master.

>   Quid pectus anxium tumultu verberas?
>   nescit timere quisquis audet magna; jam
>   regnum petis; fortuna fortes adjuvat,
>   ars prima regni poste te cives metu
>   retinere: qui cives timet rebelles excitat.
>   Audebit omnia quisquis imperio regit
>   et dura tractat sceptra regali manu.

The thoughts are those with which an Atreus, a Nero, an Etrocles, a Lycus feeds himself. cf. Thyestes 205—7, Oct. 443, Phoen. 654—59, and Her. Fur. 353. In Richard's heart the words of Howard fall on good soil. He answers,

>   Pectus nihil perturbat ignavus metus
>   Excede pietas mente si nostra lates.
>   Tuetur ensis quicquid invitum tenes.
>   Aperire nunc ferro decet fraudi viam,
>   mactetur hostis, quisquis obstabat mihi.

The speech is an echo of that of Lycus, Her. Fur. 344—5

> quod civibus tenere te invitis scias
> strictis tuetur ensis

and of that of Nero, Oct. 469

> tollantur hostes ense suspecti mihi.

Howard now urges that the prisoners at Pontefract be immediately put to death, but Gloucester is reserving them that all his foes may fall together. Turning to Catesby he asks his news from Hastings, and Catesby replies that Hastings' thoughts are wholly directed against Richard's head. He has refused to further the protector's plans.

> Prius profundat arctus Ithicum
> fretum et rapax consistet aqua Siculi maris.
> Noxque atra terris ante splendorem dabit.

The words are borrowed from Thy. 476—482. Richard bursts out in anger. Hastings' blood alone can atone for his words. But how?

> at qua via mactabo vesanum caput?

It is the question that Atreus addresses to his satellite, when meditating revenge upon Thyestes. Cf. Thy. 244

> profare, dirum qua caput mactem via?

It is Catesby who is ready with the plan to accuse Hastings' mistress, Jane Shore, of plotting Richard's death. Hastings is sure to defend her and this will lay him open to a charge of treason. Gloucester adopts the plan. A council meeting in the Tower is ordered, and Howard is instructed to see that Hastings is present. Imprisonment is determined on for Ely, York, and Stanley.

On the following morning, accompanied by Howard, Hastings approaches the Tower. He wonders that his horse stumbles so often, and prays that the omen may be averted. Then his thoughts turn to Stanley's dream of the boar, and he derides his friend's fears. He meets the priest and the pursuivant, and converses with them as in More's story, rejoicing that this day they are beheaded who on the occasion of his former meeting with the pursuivant were triumphing in his fall. Then he rides on, urged forward by Howard, who pities in his heart the man who is hastening so unconsciously to his fate. More's account is followed throughout, except that the name of Hastings' companion was obtained from Hall, who first added it, or from Grafton, who copied Hall.

The next scene is that of the famous council. Buckingham greets the assembled nobles in behalf of the still absent Richard and assures them of the protector's anxiety for the speedy crowning of the young king, toward whom he cherishes all faithful loyalty. Then Richard enters with an apology for his late appearance. From this point on More's narrative is followed in minute and complete detail. Hastings, arrested, bursts out into lamentations.

> Quis nostra digne conqueri potest mala?
> heu, quas miser voces dabo? quae lachrimis
> nostris Aëdon exhibet luctus graves?
> o machinator fraudis et diri artifex
> sceleris; mearum prodidit fallax amor
> blandaque tectum fronte secretum malum,
> cur invident severa fata vitam: in mea
> quid morte tam potens erit versutia? etc.

It is the same Senecan cry against Fortune that Rivers utters upon his arrest. The speech is made up of a considerable number of Senecan reminiscences. cf. Oct. 914—16. Tro. 750, Oct. 376—79, Oed. 6, 7, Oct. 904—5

> invidet etiam
> cur in patria mihi saeva mori?

In response to Hastings' words Gloucester urges on his hesitating soldiers, and again Hastings bursts out with a despairing cry against Fate.

And he goes on to recall Stanley's dream and the other warnings he had received. cf. Oed. 980—6.

Then he is hurried away to his death, bidding earth farewell.

At once Gloucester calls the citizens together to account to them for Hastings' death. His story to them, supported by his and Buckingham's rusty armor. the promise of the citizens to spread his report, while among themselves they declare their entire lack of faith in it, the proclamation of Richard's herald, with the jokes of the bystanders when it becomes evident that the proclamation was composed long before the time named by Richard as that when he had his first intimaticn of the conspiracy, are all detailed in close conformity to the story of More. Only to increase the pathos of Hastings' fall a nuntius is introduced to relate to the citizens the manner of his death.

> Postquam ad locum durus satelles traxerit,
> ad astra tollit heros lumina:
> ex ore casto concipit Deo preces
> Quaecumque nostra contumax superbia,
> supplitia meruit (inquit) ô numen sacrum,
> utinam meo jam jam luatur sanguine
> Vix ultimas moratur carnifex preces
> quin solvit illico ense corporis obicem.

There is no authority for the passage, further than that the last two lines may have been suggested by More's statement, "heuely he toke a priest at aduerture, and made a short shrift, for a longer would not be suffered, the protectour made so much hast to dyner". This, however, occurred before Hastings was taken to the place of execution, and his prayer is not a shrift. The rest may have been suggested by the death of Hercules, Herc. Oct. 1691 et seq.

To the character of Hastings as he appears in More's story Legge's play adds nothing, a greater share in the action is assigned him by making him, contrary to history, take part with Richard and Buckingham at Northampton in bringing Rivers and his companions to their fate (a situation inconsistent with the later scene in which the lords receive advice from Hastings in London, before Gloucester and the king have arrived); but even here his part is chiefly confined to an expression of anxiety lest Richard's measures prove dangerous. A part is also assigned him in the deliberations that lead to the removal of the duke of York from his mother, where he agrees that the boy must be obtained by force if necessary. But these slight additions merely make more conspicuous his historical hostility to the queen and her circle. For the rest, he is as in More and Shakespeare, "very faithful, and trusty ynough, trusting to much". In the treatment of no character do Legge and Shakespeare approach so nearly as in that of Hastings, chiefly because in the plays of both the chronicle is most closely adhered to, and because both found of dramatic value nearly all that the history related of Hastings. From this point of view a comparison of the final scene in Hastings' life as it appears in Shakespeare's play and as it appears in Legge's is of great interest. In both Hastings makes a farewell speech, which in both, to avoid monotony, is broken by the words, in Legge of Gloucester, in Shakespeare of Lovell, hastening him to his death. In both speeches the tone is the same. The earl laments his folly that would not take the warnings plainly offered, repents the pride that has led him to triumph over his enemies, and bewails the momentary fleeting grace of mortal men. But in Shakespeare appears another thought: Hastings recognizes in his downfall the fulfilment of Margaret's curse. His fall is indeed Richard's crime, but it is none the less punishment for the perjury he committed when he swore faithful friendship to his foes at Edward's bedside, and for his share in Prince Edward's death. Legge gives no look into Hastings' past and his view is the partial one of More; Shakespeare, influenced by Polidore Vergil, takes the whole man as his soul stands naked before its Creator, and shows in his fate the hand of a divine Nemesis.

ludunt genus
mortale caeca fata: praemonstrant malum
vitare quod vetant tamen,

cries Hastings in Legge. But in Legge Hastings' fate is blind and undeserved; in Shakespeare it is the fate he has woven for himself. It is not the neglected warning of Stanley's dream or of his stumbling horse that has prevented escape; it is his blindness to the fact that the deeds which won him the momentary grace of men have forfeited the grace of God. Legge's view is Senecan; Shakespeare's Christian.

The actio ends with a solemn procession, in which Shore's wife does open penance as a harlot. The train consists, as indicated by a marginal note in English, of "A Tipstaffe, Shore's Wife in her petticote, haveinge a taper burninge in her hand, The Verger, Singinge men, Praebendaries, The Bishope of London, Citizens". As the procession advances there is sung a prayer against adultery.

1. Fidem tuere conjugum
   Lectum probo libera
   Defende privatos thoros
   Furtiva ne laedat Venus.

2. Quemcunque facti penitet
   Purga solutum crimine
   Exempla sanet posteros
   Furtiva ne foedet Venus.

"Furtiva Venus" is the Senecan phrase for adultery (cf. Agam. 275). The song may be said to correspond in a general way to the Senecan chorus, and its theme is the same as that of several in the Octavia and the Agamemnon.

As the procession winds along, the watching citizens are captivated by the beauty of the culprit.

En Shora tremulum cereum gerens manu
Induta poenas linteo infames luit,
Regum inclyta meretrix tyranno dat duci
poenas, pater descende Jupiter, et thoro
tam grata pignora nunc tuo rape: nam tuam
Laedam vel Europam, puta deserere polum,
Oh misera, me miseret tui piget, pudet:
(Licet impudica mulier, et minus proba)
Privare vita dum nequit Dux Claudius
spoliare fova quaerit iratus tibi.

The comments of the citizens are based on More's statement that Shore's wife "went so fair and louely, namelye while the wondering of the people caste a comly rud in her chekes... that her great shame wan her much praise. And many good folke also, that hated her liuing, and glad wer to se sin corrected, yet pitied thei more her penance, then rejoyced therein, when thei considred that the protector procured it, more of a corrupt intent then ani vertuous affecion". The lat two lines are based on the statement, "Now then by and bi, as it wer for anger, not for couetise, the protector sent into the house of Shores wife.. and spoiled her of al that euer she had, aboue the value of II. or III. M. marks". Legge puts the admiration of the people into Senecan form, making the good citizens of London play the same part, and utter the same classical comparisons, as the Chorus which in the Octavia praises the beauty of Poppaea. cf. Oct. 762—72. This is one of the most striking of a hundred examples of the fundamental absurdity of Legge's method. But in respect of such speeches, it may be remarked, the popular drama long continued to be nearly as faulty as Legge's play. In the former, it is true, London citizens do not make direct appeals to the classical gods; but down to the master work of Shakespeare classical allusions are common enough in the mouths of even the lowest characters. The absurdity is more prominent in Legge largely because the two influences in his play, the classical and the Christian are more than once in striking contrast to each other.

A short Epilogue, summing up the criminal steps that Richard has thus far taken in his bloody progress to the throne, forms the final word of the actio.

Actio Secunda.

The second actio, like the first, is preceded by an Argument containing an outline of the events in this part of the play.

The first scene is another of those preparatory scenes with which the play is "padded" (cf. p. 301). Gloucester, Buckingham, and Lovell deliberate as to the measures to be taken to obtain the crown. Hastings is dead, Ely and Stanley in prison; what is the next step? This time the scene itself, as well as its facts, is based on the story of More, who indicates that Richard held such a council. "Then thought the protectour, that while men mused what the mater ment, while the lordes of the realme wer about him out of their owne strenghtis [that is, gathered in London for the coronation, and so far from their homes, where their power lay], while no man wist what to thinke nor whome to trust, ere euer they should haue space to dispute and disgest the mater and make parties, it wer best hastly to pursue his purpose, and put himself in possession of the crowne, ere men could haue time to deuise ani wais to resist. But now was al the study, by what meane thys matter being of it self so heinouse, might be first broken to the people, in such wise that it might be wel taken. To this counsel they toke diverse etc." In accordance with More, it is in this scene that Richard proposes to have declared the bastardy of Edward's children as well as the bastardy of Edward himself. In Gloucester's manner as he makes the infamous suggestion of his mother's crime there is none of the skilful treatment by which Shakespeare indicates an apparent reluctance on Richard's part. More says "he would that point should be lesse, and more fauorably handled, not euen fully plain and directly, but that the matter should be touched aslope craftely, as though men spared in that point to speke al the truth for fere of his displeasure". Here all Richard's hypocrisy is reserved for the people; he shows no pretence of shame to Buckingham, but reveals to his confederate by the crafty suggestion the uttermost depths of his character. Shakespeare, however, makes Richard an abler and wiser man than this. He knows better than to reveal himself farther than is necessary, even to his helper. The suggestion is apparently forced from him by the exigency of the case; and the crime is to be but slightly touched on, not for the sake of effect upon the people, but out of regard for his mother.

> Nay, for a need, thus far come near my person,
> . . . .
> Yet touch this sparingly, as't were far off;
> Because, my lord, you know my mother lives.
> R. III, 3:6.

In Legge's Richard, however, there is none of this. He makes this proposal as bluntly and with as little sign of shame as the other; and it is not till he gives instructions to Dr. Shaw for his sermon that he suggests that the matter be "touched aslope".

The part played by Buckingham in the scene is almost entirely passive. It is he who expresses the necessary fears and anxieties, and utters the conventional; "what, pray, is to be done?" and "How shall this be accomplished?" His sole helpful suggestion is that of the name of Dr. Shaw, after Lovell has shown the necessity of calling on a preacher. Richard, who seems wholly free from the fears he has formerly shown, beside the suggestion of Edward's and his mother's adultery — which could naturally come from no one but him — suggests the name of the Mayor as the proper tool to use upon the citizens, and that Buckingham shall address them in Guildhall. But it is Lovell who is the really fertile manager and determiner of the course to be taken. To him Legge assigns the proposal of measures described by More as coming from Richard himself — the taking advantage of the fact that the nobles are in London far from their strength and in utter darkness as to what is going on or the best course to pursue. It is Lovell who suggests the proclamation postponing the coronation to the second of November (a fact added by the Hardyng continuator to More's story, and copied by Hall and Grafton, not by Holinshed; cf. p. 279). It is Lovell, too, who shows the necessity of bringing to their assistance some man of great influence among the citizens; who devises the scheme of making religion a cloak for Richard's plans and through the sermon of an able and respected minister giving his claims the additional weight of apparently divine authority; and it is he, finally, who devises the master-stroke by which Richard is to appear at the proper point in Shaw's sermon, that his appearance, coinciding with Shaw's words, may make them believe him "specially chosen by God and in maner by miracle".

The effect of assigning Lovell so important a place is inevitably a weakening of Richard's role. Here again it is evident that Legge had no such conception of Richard's character as that which in Shakespeare's play makes him not only dominant in every scene where he appears, but the one driving force throughout the whole play till after he has obtained the throne. Further, Legge was not great enough as a dramatist even to perceive the full value of the material furnished him by More. In this scene is a second notable proof of the inferiority of Legge's Richard to More's.

That more active roles as counsellors are assigned by Legge to Lovell, Catesby, and Ratcliffe than are theirs in the chronicle appears again to be largely due to the influence of Seneca. Their relation to Richard naturally recalled the position of the confidants in the Senecan plays, though it is not wholly like. The confidants who oppose their masters' passions are naturally out of the question; though traces of opposition are not wanting in Richard's confidants. But there are other confidants in Seneca whose opposition is not strong enough to withstand the urging of their masters, whose counsellors and assistants they become. They advise the means of bringing their masters' passions to satisfaction, and act as their agents in carrying out the plans determined upon. To these Lovell, Catesby, and Ratcliffe bear a distinct resemblance, and their words, while mostly determined by the chronicle story are not without Senecan imitation. For the council scenes themselves, which are rarely even suggested by the chronicle, the frequent similar scenes in Seneca are without doubt largely responsible.

The mayor of London and Dr. Shaw are summoned before Richard and he explains to them his wishes and plans, to which they give ready assent.

The sermon of Dr. Shaw is not delivered upon the stage, but related by one citizen to another. The first citizen enters soliloquizing upon the dangerous condition of affairs.

>Qnousque scinditur Britannia litibus
>Luctusque cumulat luctibus fatum grave?
>dirum premit recens malum? pene modum
>severa fata nesciunt. Numquam domus
>Irata plena caedibus pacabitur?
>haeresve nullus sceptra impune geret?

A terrible danger is threatening the state.

>Glocestrium ducem
>ambire regnum murmurat secreta plebs
>Patrui nefas crudele, tetrum, parvuli
>latent in obscuro nepotes carcere,
>in Commitiis de certo ascriptus dies.
>Glocestrii tantum ducis frequens Cliens
>attrita pulsat limina: illic emicat
>illustris aulae splendor, istuc confluunt
>mitiora quisquis supplici implorat prece.
>Quicunque Regis nuda calcat limina
>et principis servus fidelis veseret
>illum minus edocta vulnerat cohors.

These lines make it clear that the scene is founded upon the passage in which More relates the misgivings of the people while the divided council meetings were taking place, before the fateful meeting at which Hastings lost his life. There "began there, here and there about, some maner of muttering amonge the people, as though al should not long be wel, though they neither wist what thei feared nor wherfore; were it that before such great thinges mens hartes of a secret instinct of nature misgiueth them, as the sea without wind swelleth of himself somtime before a tempest, or were it that some one man, happely somwhat perceiuing, filled mani men with suspicion, though he shewed few men what he knew. Hobeit somwhat the dealing self made men to muse on the mater, though the counsell were close. For litle and little all folke withdrew from the Tower, and drew to Crosbies place in Bishops gates strete wher the protectour kept his household. The protectour had the resort, the king in maner dessolate". Upon this same passage is likewise founded a scene in both the True Tragedy and Shakespeare's play. Curiously enough, in both these the scene is pushed backward in time and is made to follow immediately upon king Edward's death; while Legge pushes it forward to a time just before Richard's accession.

To the first citizen enters now a second, who relates to him the sermon of Dr. Shaw with Gloucester's late appearance, the failure to move the people, and the withdrawal of the wretched Shaw to his home. In all More's story is faithfully and completely followed, save that the text "Spuria vitulamina non agent radices altas" [Book of Wisdom IV] becomes for the metre's sake

   Semen beatum thorus adulter denegat
   Proles nec altas spuria radices dabit.

The text reads in Hall "spuria vitulamina non dabunt radices altos", and Legge's use of dabit may possibly be rightly regarded as an aditional proof of his use of Hall.

The scene closes with a summons into the Guildhall, before which, apparently, the citizens are conversing, to listen to an address from Buckingham. Here again More's account of the assembly together with the speeches is reproduced complete.

The scene at Baynard Caste follows, again a complete transcription of More's account down to the comments of the citizens on their way home "that these matters bee Kynges games, as it were stage playes". Richard appears in the gallery between two bishops, according to the addition made to More's story by the Hardyng continuator and copied by Hall and Grafton but not by Holinshed (cf. p. 279).

At the close of Shaw's sermon, says More, "the preacher gate him home and neuer after durst looke out for shame, but kepe him out of sight lyke an owle. And when he once asked one that had bene his olde frend, what the people talked of him, al wer it that his own conscience wel shewed him that thei talked no good, yet when the tother answered him that there was in euery man's mouth spoken of him much shame, it so strake him to the heart, that within fewe daies after he wishered and consumed away". This conversation is now made by Legge the occasion of a special scene. Shaw enters with tottering step and wretched countenance, to be greeted by his friend, who reproaches him for his continued absence from the public view, and begs to know the gloomy thoughts over which he is brooding. Then Shaw reveals the terrible woe which the consciousness of crime has brought him.

> Heu mihi animus semet scelere plenus fugit,
> vetat quae scire pectus oneratum malis,
> mentisque consciae pavor, dolor aestuat,
> animus non potest venenum expellere.
> . . . .
> Noctu diem voco, repeto noctem die,
> semper memet fugio, non possum scelus.

In vain does his friend seek to convince him that he can heal the evil and atone for his crime. Shaw insists that death alone can expiate so gross a fault. All the arguments of his friend (advanced and answered in Senecan stichomythia) are of no avail; after as before, his feeling is

> necat quisquis jubet
> vivere: quisquis mori jubet vitam dedit.
> tantum potest placere quidquid displicet.

Then comes the fateful question mentioned by More.

> De me viri quid loquuntur futiles?

The answer is

> Te sceleris arguunt nefandi conscium.

In the composition of this scene was present a remembrance of the famous scene in the Phoenissae, in which Oedipus, bowed down by his woes and resolved on death is dissuaded by Antigone. Of verbal likenesses there are not many but they are sufficient to prove the connection. Cf. with the first lines above, Phoen. 217—17:

> me fugio, fugio conscium scelerum omnium
> pectus, manumque hanc fugio, et hoc caelum et deos.

> quisquis mori jubet vitam dedit

appears to be modelled on Phoen. 212:

> quidquid potest
> auferre cuiquam mors, tibi hoc vita abstulit

and Phoen. 304:

> ideoque leti quaero maturam viam
> morique propero —

> Sceleris novi mater prius natu[m] scelus,

which occurs in the conversation, is evidently modelled on Phoen. 269:

> scelerisque pretum maius accepi scelus.

The close correspondence of thought in the two scenes is equally good proof of the connection.

After the answer of his friend, Shaw perceives a throng of people approaching; it is the new king, Richard, on his way to Westminster Hall, where in the court of King's Bench he intends to take upon himself the crown, and adress the lawyers. Shaw flees from the sight of the citizens, while his friend enters to hear the words of Richard that he may report them to Shaw.

Richard's speech begins with a Senecan turn of More's words "declared to the audience, that he woulde take vpon him the crowne in that place there, wher the king himself sitteth and ministreth the law; because he considred that it was the chiefest duety of a kyng to minister the lawes".

> Juvabat Astreae locatum sedibus
> et hoc tribunali tremendo Minois

auro caput sepire primum fulgido,
Justaque cives leges regere patriae
Rex providere debet id potissimum.

The "as pleasant an oration as he could", which according to More the king proceeded to delives, resolves itself into a speech of praise and promise of honor to the lawyers, and a declaration that now at last the state has reached a condition of peace which it shall be his care to foster. He promises to put aside all enmities and sends for his old enemy Fogge from sanctuary and takes him by the hand. As usual More is closely followed throughout, the few additional words, as indicated above, being used to fill out the oration.

An epic scene follows. A citizen and his guest, a stranger, are awaiting the coronation procession of Richard. They have been talking of the evil condition of the state, and occupy the time with discussing, in Senecan fashion, the position of the king. The citizen, while at heart opposed to Richard's proceedings defends them from the point of view that all things are to be pardoned in a king; while the stranger represents the Senecan morality.

. . . .
Hosp. Tibi reguli duo? nefas regere patruum
hi dum supersint
Civis.   Hoc facit regni sitis:
in arce regni carceris caeci luem
patiuntur.
Hosp.   O scelus
Civis.   sed principis tamen
Hosp. Magis hoc nefandum
Civis.   Propter imperium simul.
Hosp. Pietas decet regem, nec impio licet
parare regnum pretio.
Civis.   Semper tamen
imperia constant pretio bene quolibet.
. . . .
Jam parce dictis: tempori decet obsequi
nuper nimis blande salutat obvios:
abjicere se cogit mens mali conscia,
regemque vultus pene servilis docet.

The theme and its treatment are wholly in accord with those of the discussion between Seneca and Nero in the Octavia 440 et seq., and of the discussion between Jocasta and Eteocles in the Phoenissae 651 et seq. The complete passages should be compared. There are especial verbal resemblances to Phoen. 664, Tr. 258, Med 55, Oct. 455, 6, and Oed. 703—4. What is true of this is true of the scene in general, that the thought is wholly Senecan, while close verbal resemblances, with few exceptions, are slight.

The last three lines of the citation are based on More's description of Richard's return from the scene at Westminster Hall. "In his returne homewarde, whom so euer he met he saluted. For a minde that knoweth it self giltye, is in a maner dejected to a seruile flattery".

The citizen now relates to his friend those acts of the day preceding the coronation for the account of which we are indebted to the Harding continuator, copied by Hall, Grafton, and Holinshed. York has been delivered from prison and likewise Stanley, for fear of his son in Lancashire, while Ely has been given into Buckingham's charge. The procession now approaches, and the rest of the scene is occupied with the explanations by the citizen of the meaning of the royal insignia. This, as well as the order of the procession, which is given at length in English under the head of "The Shewe of the Coronation" is taken from Grafton. Cf. p. 276).

The actio concludes with the direction, "During the solemnity of the Coronation lett this songe followinge be songe wth instruments.

>Festum diem colamus assensu pari
>quo principis caput corona cingitur.
>>Decora Regni possidet
>>Regis propago nobilis
>>Illustre principis caput
>>fulva corona cingitur.
>>Nunc voce laeti consona
>>cantum canamus principem.
>>Regnum premebat dedicus
>>Libido Regio polluit.

The words, "During the solemnity of the coronation" in the direction, as well as the statement of Hall that after they had entered the Abbey and were seated in their seats of estate divers songs were solemnly sung, seem to indicate that not only the procession but the coronation ceremonies as well were given in dumb shew on the stage. But I do not regard this as by any means certain.

An epilogue to this actio is wanting.

Actio Tertia.

The argument of the third actio bears a new character. Instead of being a mere synopsis of the events to follow, it takes the form of an impassioned speech to the participants in the action, addressed to them by Furor, an evident imitation of the Furia in the Thyestes. There the fury sets the action in motion by forcing the shade of Tantalus to spread madness in his own home, detailing to him the long series of fearful crimes he is to cause. Here the fury urges Richard on to the deeds that are to prove his destruction.

> Quorsum furor secreta volvis pectora
> minasque spiras intimas, nec expedis
> faces tuas? scelus expleas Glocestrium:
> Glocestrios invise[a] rex olim tuos
> et sceptra jactes, praetium sane necis,
> dubiosque regni volve fraterni metus.
> Decora spetant ora Eboracum stupens
> miretur excelsum decus vulgus leve.
> Quorsum moras trahis lenes totus miser
> fias, magisque saeviat nefas breve.
> Aude scelus mens quicquid atrox cogitat,
> Regnumque verset ultimum Regio scelus.
> Nondum madebant caede cognata manu:
> nondum nepotes suffocantur Regii
> et frustra poscas neptis incestos thoros:
> imple scelere domum patris tui.

Then comes an incitement to Buckingham, and finally to the avenging Richmond.

>   illico
> discat furor saevire Buckinghamius:
> macta tyrannum, deme sceptra si potes:
> sed non potes: paenasque dignas perferes
> tanti tumultus. En venit Richmondius,
> exul venit, promissa regna vendicat,
> regnique juratos prius thoros: age,
> stringantur enses, odia misce, funera
> diramque stragem: impone finem litibus.
> En regnet exul, rex nec auxilium impetret,
> tuaque cadat (Henrice) Richardus manu.
> Actum est satis: parcam furor Britanniae
> post hac, novasque jam mihi quaeram sedes.

As in the speech of the fury in Thyestes events are ordered which precede those that are presented in the play itself, so here are mentioned the visit of Richard to Gloucester and his second coronation in York (related by Hall from Vergil), which do not appear in the play.

Of verbal imitation of the passage in the Thyestes there is not much. Line 6 is perhaps a reminiscence of Thy. 32—34:

> superbis fratribus regna excidant
> repetantque profugos; dubia violentae domus
> fortuna reges inter incertos labet

Line 16 is from Thy. 53:

> imple Tantalo totam domum,

and the concluding lines, in which the fury, having accomplished her work, promises a final farewell to Britain, are a reminiscence of those in which Tantalus, having accomplished his work, is bidden to depart. Thy. 105—7:

> actum est abunde, gradere ad infernos specus
> amnemque notum.

The opening scene discloses Brakenbury, Constable of the Tower, revolving with himself in horror the fearful command he has received from Richard, through John Green, to put to death the young princes in his charge. Richard's terrible ambition is never free from fear so long as the princes live; in the midst of his triumph he is ever

conscious of the unrighteousness of his position, and
fearful therefore of its loss.

> Horrere nunquam cessat imperii sitis
> curis nec unquam solvitur aegra ambitio
> famam occupans
> incerta sortis cogitans ludibria
> quamque facili injusta ruit impetu potentia,
> regnique ludibrium nimis statum tremens,
> dum spiritu vescatur aetherio nepos.

The "sitis imperii", "aegra ambitio", "incerta sortis ludibria"
are Senecan commonplaces often repeated in varying
phrase. And cf. Phoen. 660 and Thy. 215—17.

Before the question of obedience to Richard's command
Brakenbury wavers. The debate with his own fears is
terrible. Richard's character he knows only too well;
punishment for disobedience is certain; he must obey. And
yet in spite of his fear he cannot. Shame flees from the
halls of kings: from his poor home it will not out.

> solumne regnum non timet
> maculam? quid aula pertinax fugis pudor
> humilemque casam quaeris? aulam deserat
> quisquis pie vivet.

It is another variation of the favorite Senecan comparison
between the palace and the hut.

At last Buckingham has reached his resolve: he will
not obey. If his fate awaits him he will meet it gladly.

To him enters now Tyrell, charged by the king to
receive the keys and execute the murder. As he comes
he too is debating with his hesitating heart, convincing it
that the deed must be done, the king obeyed. By the
time he accosts Brakenbury he has succeeded in putting
himself in the king's place: his conversation with Brakenbury is that of a tyrant urging and supporting his crimes
against the reasoning of a philosopher. The argument is,
in fact, that of Nero and Seneca in the Octavia. Here
the tyrant urges that the commands of a king must be
obeyed; his opponent, that it is the part of a king to

command only what is right. Thus such lines of the Octavia as e. g.

    Oct. 459 Nero.   Jussisque nostris pareant.
           Seneca.   Justa impera:
      451 Nero.   Fortuna nostra cuncta permittit mihi
      454 Seneca. Id facere laus est quod decet, non quod licet

are reflected in Legge's

        Tirell.   An non decet mandata Regis exequi?
        Braken. Nunquam decet jubere regem pessima.

Verbal resemblances to Seneca are, however, mostly to the speech of Eteocles in the Phoenissae. Legge's line

      regnare non vult esse qui inivsus timet,

is Phoen. 654; and

      ars prima sceptri posse te invidiam pati

is another expression of the same thought, changed in a single word, from the speech of Lycus, Her. Fur. 353:

      ars prima regni est posse invidiam pati.

      Invis a nunquam imperia retinentur diu

is Phoen. 660.

More's answer of Brakenbury "that he would neuer putte them to death to dye therefore" is Senecanized into

      Sequar lubens, quocunque me fata vocant

in imitation of Oed. 296:

      Sed quo vocat me patria, quo Phoebus, sequar.

The conclusion of the argument is Tyrell's demand for the keys.

As regards the facts of the scene, More's story is followed, as always. But the entrance of Tyrell is not preceded by any statement explanatory of his presence. The story of his selection by Richard to execute the murder, which both in Shakespeare's play and the True Tragedy forms the occasion of a special scene, is characteristically preserved by Legge to be afterwards, in Senecan fashion, related.

The murder of the princes follows. While Tyrell is within, arranging the murder with Forrest and Dighton, Brakenbury stands without, waiting for the news of the terrible deed which he has no power to avert. The moment forms the climax of the play and affords the most tempting occasion for the display of Senecan rhetoric. The beginning of Brakenbury's soliloquy expresses the horror of the moment.

> O caeco regnandi libido, ô scelus
> Regis furentis triste nimis, ô patrui
> Nefanda sceptra, quae suorum sanguine
> madent. Propinquae vos manus heu destruunt,
> ô nobiles pueri, pupillos oppermunt.
>
> Heu quis Caucasus
> lachrymis potest, aut decus Indus parcere?

It is the Senecan cry of horror at the deeds of an Atreus,

Thy. 734—5   o saevum scelus
. . . .
. . . . . . an ultra manis aut atrocius
natura recipit?

Thy. 1047—50   tale quis vidit nefas?
quis inhospitalis Caucasi rupem asperam
Heniochus habitans quis ve Cecropiis metus
terris Procrustes?

a cry repeated in many forms in the bloody dramas which Legge imitated. The soliloquy is not all a Senecan wail, however. A touch of something like pathos is given it when Brakenbury calls to mind — the incident is from More's narrative — the prince's reception of the news that his uncle had usurpt the crown.

> Amissa postquam regna cognovit puer,
> et possidere rapta sceptra patruum:
> Sic fatur infoelix lachrymis genas rigans
> at imo pectore trahens suspiria,
> Regnum nihil moror: precor vitam mihi
> hanc patruus ne demat

> Imago semper errat aute occulos mihi
> tristis gementis principis, nec desinit
> pulsare moestum animum quaerela Reguli.

Now Tyrell returns. He has left Forrest and Dighton within, ready to begin their deadly task; in a moment the announcement will be made that it has been performed. And here Legge shows how fatal to all dramatic common sense a too great devotion to Senecan art could be. While they are waiting for the terrible news, while every thought of Legge's audience, and still more every thought of the participants, should be fixed upon the tragedy, Brakenbury takes occasion to ask how the king received his refusal to execute the princes, and Tyrell relates the whole long story of Richard's anger, the page's suggestion of Tyrell and his subsequent selection. The whole passage in More is faithfully copied. Further than this, More's simple statement that at Brakenbury's refusal Richard took great "displeasure and thought" is expanded into a twenty-one line picture of an anger that amounts almost to madness, with a classical comparison of Richard to Orestes.

> Ut ista primum novit, ingenti statim
> stupore torpet, sanguis ora deserit,
> totusque cineri similis expallet simul
> suspiria imis efflat e percordiis,
> saevaque cordi proximum feriens latus,
> regale subito deserit solium, furens
> graditur citatis passibus, quassans caput,
> tacitoque secum dirus immungit sinu,
> ubi sanguis e fornace veluti denuo
> proruit adustus, fervidis torrat genas
> rubetque totus, puncio velut mari
> immersus, aut minio fuisset perlitus.
> Oculi scintillant flammei obtuitu truci
> velutique setis horret erectis coma.
> His tanquam Orestes accensus facibus fuit
> Nam de suorum caede convellunt pares
> utrumque furiae: discrepapt uno tamen.
> Agitatur umbra matris ille mortuae:
> gravi nepotum ast ille vivorum metu.
> Et gravitur in te exarsit ira turbida,
> responsa rex qua nocte percepit tuae.

The source of this description I have been unable to find. It appears not to be from Seneca; but nearly as surely it is not Legge's own. It is barely possible that it was suggested by the description of Oedipus, Oed. 915 et seq.

In the account of the page's suggestion Legge appears to have had a slight perception of the absurdity of making Tyrell himself relate to Brakenbury how the page declared him a man ready to do anything to win the king's favor; but a modern reader will hardly agree that all is made right by the parenthetical "audacter istud audio [audeo] nunc dicere" which the author puts in Tyrell's mouth.

The long narration is at last finished, and Dighton appears with the words, "Uterque suffocatur exanguis puer". True to his role Brakenbury greets the news with "Hei mihi, per artus horror excurrit vagus", while Tyrell merely inquires the manner of their death. This is a simple account of their suffocation, keeping close to More, and with no attempt at any such pathetic embellishment as that which in Shakespeare's play characterizes Tyrell's account of the murder. As in the chronicle account the bodies of the dead princes are now revealed. Brakenbury bursts out into Senecan lamentation.

> Videone corpora Regulorum livida?
> funestus heu jam caede puerili thorus
> Quis lachrymas durus malis vultus negat.
> Hei mihi, perempti fraude patrui jacent.
> Quis Colchus haec? quae Caspium tangens mare
> gens audet? etc.

The passage is an imitation of Tro. 1104—09, the wail of Andromache over her son's shattered body.

Tyrell — who has no word of human regret — orders the burial of the bodies, and returns the keys to Brakenbury, who is left alone to utter another long lament.

> O saeva nostri temporis credulitas
> ô regis animus dirus! ô mens barbara,
> secura turbans jura naturae ferox!
> Tune innocentes principes, pueros pios

monstrum Procustes, tune mactasti tuos?
ô terra, coelum, moestumque regnum Tartari,
scelus videtis triste? etc.

The long passage is compounded in imitation of various bits from Seneca; of which Thyestes' lament over the bodies of his two sons slain by their uncle, and Hippolytus's cry of horror when Phaedra's criminal design is made plain to him, are the most important; cf. Thy. 1006—16 and Phaed. 671—81. The close of Brakenbury's speech is taken from the passage which Hall inserted into More's narrative from Polidore Vergil, and corresponds to the words, "To murther a man is much odious, to kyll a woman, is in manner vnnatural, but to slaie and destroye innocent babes, & young enfantes, the whole world abhorreth, and the bloud from the earth crieth, for vengaunce to all mightie God ... a las what will he do to other that thus shamefully murdereth his awne bloud without cause or desert? Whom wyll he saue when he slaith the poore lambes committed to him in trust? now we se and behold $\overset{t}{y}$ the most cruel tyranny hath inuadyd the commonwealth, now we se that in him is neither hope of iustice nor trust of mercie but abundance of crueltie and thrust of innocente bloude" (Hall, p. 379).

With this exception of Brakenbury's part the scene is a faithful transcript of More. Brakenbury's presence in the scene has no foundation in the chronicle. In Shakespeare's play he does not appear at all in this connection, and in the True Tragedy he takes himself out of the way after delivering up the keys. But this scene is the climax of Legge's play, and its proper handling required — in Legge's mind — an abundance of Senecan rhetoric. This could not well be assigned to the murderers, and Brakenbury was introduced to supply the need. Legge's treatment of the scene is highly significant of the entire artificiality of the Senecan method. Shakespeare, who likewise allows the murder to be related, felt as well as Legge the desirability of heightening the effectiveness of the scene. He did so by following the natural course which, as has been shown, the chronicles had successively pursued: he heightened the pathos of the narration by adding a rhetorical embellishment that was calculated to bring out the innocent youth and beauty of the tender victims; and added a human touch of his own in putting this into the mouths of the remorseful murderers themselves. The Senecan method acted differently. Here the sole embellishment is declamation. The murder is drily and hastily related, and its natural pathos is lost in the classic wail which runs the gamut from Procrustes to Nero. Add to this the absurdity of Tyrell's long narration, destroying all suspense on the part of the waiting listeners, and Legge's climactic scene becomes his most conspicuons failure.

To the same strain of declamatory woe the passage in which Hall, copying Vergil (cf. p. 142), relates the sorrow of the queen on receiving the news of her sons' murder, lent itself readily. In Legge's scene Elizabeth appears troubled with forebodings that have been increased by frightful dreams.

> Eheu recenti corda palpitant metu
> gelidus per artus vadit exangues tremor,
> Nocturna sic me visa miseram territant,
> Et dira turbant inquietam somnia
> . . . .
> Jam cuncta passim blanda straverat quies,
> somnusque fessis facilis obrepsit genis
> vidi minantem concito cursu heu aprum
> natosque frendens dente laniavit truce
> utrosque saevus mactat. Aetheriae potens
> dominator aulae, fata si quid filiis
> dirum minantur, in hoc caput crescat furor,
> matremque prius jam fulmen irati petat.

This preparatory situation is imitated from that of Andromache in the Troades, to whom appears in sleep the form of Hector warning her to save their son. Cf. Tro. 435—443, 452, 3.

The second scene of the Octavia also had an influence upon this. The ancilla of Legge's scene corresponds to the nutrix to whom Poppea relates her vision, Oct. 712 et seq., and the frightful character of her dream corresponds more closely than Andromache's to that of the queen's. In the latter, however, the boar, tearing the children with savage tusks, is undoubtedly drawn from the dream of Stanley, related by More. The following lines of the Octavia are especially to be compared, 712—18:

> Confusa tristi proximae noctis metu
> visuque, nutrix, mente turbata feror,
> defecta sensu. laeta nam postquam dies
> sideribus atris cessit et nocti polus
> . . . .
> somno resolvor; nec diu placida friu
> quiete licuit.

Cf. also with the complete passage Phaed. 959—63, 623—4, Oct. 55—6, 738, Phoen. 443—4.

The rest of the scene follows the chronicle exactly in facts, including the queen's swoon. This, however, offers opportunity for imitating the passage in the Troades in which the swoon of Hecuba is described. Thus Legge's

> Labefacta mens succumbit: assurge: hei mihi,
> rursus cadentem misera spiritum leva
> spirat, revixit, tarda mors miseros fugit,

corresponds to Tr. 949—954

> at misera luctu mater audito stupet;
> labefacta mens succubuit, assurge, alleva
> animum et cadentem, misera, firma spiritum.
> . . . .
> . . . .
> spirat, revixit, prima mors misera fugit.

There is also the inevitable change of the avenging Christian God into Jupiter with the avenging thunderbolts. Legge's

> Te, te, precor supplex mater genibus minor,
> qui vindicans flammas vibras tonans pater,

> et hunc vibrentur tela perjurum tua,
> spolies Olimpum irate fulminibus tuis,
> et impium coeli ruina vindicet

contains reminiscences of Ag. 528, Thy. 1085 et seq., Oct. 229, and other passages.

The ancilla consoles the queen as the nutrix does Medea. Cf.:

> Quin placida cogites, animumque mitiga,
> Mentemque sana turbidam curis leva.

with Medea 425, 6:

> Recipe turbatum malis
> era, pectus, animum mitiga.

The queen's lament follows the chronicle closely, with the addition of a reference to Procrustes and the savage Colchian.

There is no announcement made in the play to Richard himself that the children have been put to death, and no indication that the fact has any effect upon his nature. Thus the murder forms the climax of the play only in the sense that it marks the height of Richard's success and that thereupon begin to appear the adverse influences which will bring about his fall. More's hint that "after this abhominable deede done, he neuer hadde quiet in his minde. hee neuer thought himself sure" remained without effect upon the playwright that otherwise follows him so faithfully. On his next appearance Richard is, to be sure, in deep trouble, but the trouble is caused by his external losses and dangers, not by "stormy remembrances of his abhominable dede". In Legge's refusal to make use of this part of the material furnished him by More is without doubt again to be seen the influence of Seneca.

The Senecan hero is, as Rudolf Fischer says (Zur Kunstentwicklung d. engl. Trag., p. 18), "in nature and will always one, possessed by one passion, and looking toward one goal". So completely is this true that an Atreus, an Eteocles, a Lycus, a Nero, appear in Seneca rather as personifications of certain passions than as individuals possessed of and governed by them. These passions are poured out in repeated monologue and dialogue. To their expression is added the expression of joy at the prospect or attainment of their satisfaction, of fear and anger at the prospect or arrival of failure. For as these passions strive toward satisfaction they meet with opposition. A faithful servant remonstrates against the purpose of Atreus, Jocasta endeavors to restrain Eteocles, the plans of Lycus are checked by Megara. Seneca strives to restore Nero to reason and virtue. Thus the dramas are throughout dramas of emotion rather than action, dramas of which, to quote Fischer again, problems of feeling and processes of the soul form the real kernel. Yet, though the soul of the Senecan tyrant is affected by joy, and by fear and anger, its ruling passion is never in the slightest altered by them; and though opposed it is never swerved from its direction. In other words, while the soul is always in conflict it is never in conflict with itself. Conscience is unknown in Seneca. Hence, there is no "poetic justice" in Seneca. The wicked passion is usually satisfied; and if not satisfied its punishment is wholly external. The outraged Universal is never shown to be unbroken.

Now the historical picture of Richard, both as colored by Polidore Vergil and as colored by More, presented Legge a Richard with a conscience and punished by his conscience. That Richard became the Richard of the True Tragedy, a Faust, whose conscience drives him toward a repentance to which he cannot attain; and it became the Richard of Shakespeare, on whom the universal Nemesis wreaks complete revenge through the coward conscience that so afflicts him. But it is not the Richard of Legge. Prominent as is the part of conscience in his historical model, it is put wholly aside. Richard's one passion is his from first to last, accompanied by joy, fear and anger, opposed by the passions and aims of others, but unchanging and unswerved. It knows no pity and no remorse. And punished as it is, it is punished only externally, that is, in truth not punished at all. Legge's Richard is not only Senecan in conduct, but Senecan in essence.

From the announcement to the queen the play passes at once to the conversation at Brecknock between Buckingham and Ely. There has been no indication of a break between Richard and Buckingham, and the latter's last appearance was in the procession at Richard's coronation. The whole long conversation between the bishop and the duke is given, as found in More and in Hall's continuation, and there follow the summoning of Bray, the employment of Lewis, the physician, the flight of Ely, and the conference of Lewis with Queen Elizabeth, all in close dependance on the chronicle.

Only the beginning of Buckingham's conversation with Ely requires comment. Here Legge's skill has again failed a little. More's story relates that "parceiuing by the processe of their communicacions the dukes pride now and then balke oute a lytte breide [exclamation] of enuy toward the glory of the king, and therby feling him ethe to fal out yf the matter were well handled: he [Ely] craftelye sought the waies to pricke him forwarde taking alwaies thoccasion of his comming. . . . . For when the duke first began to praise and bost the king, and shewe how much profit the realm shold take by his reign; my lord Morton aunswered" etc. Legge, however, instead of skilfully confining Buckingham's expressions to a little exclamation of envy here and there, commits the mistake of making him utter at the very beginning the strongest condemnation of Richard.

> Quot caedibus cruentat insanas manus?
> Quot destinavit ad necem mentis furor?
> dicere nequeo, nec verba sufficiunt mihi:
> dolor tacere jussit. O nullo scelus
> credibile in aevo, quodque posteritas negat.
> Patruus nepotes patris heu regno expulit.
> Tantum exuit regno? necem miseris dedit
> Fraenos dolor vix patitur, ulcisci cupit.

Thus when subsequently Buckingham does praise the king,

> Cujus tamen regno scio prudens caput
> consulere, pax florebit aequa civibus
> Laudandus ergo, cura quem regni tenet,
> et cui suorum civium chara est salus,

the words seem wholly out of place, and Ely's comment,

> superbus eructat animus, nec continet
> sese, secretam miscet iram laudibus,

it not only does not fit the speech of Buckingham that immediately precedes it, but it is rendered absurd by what has gone before. Buckingham's wrath is certainly not secret. This treatment is caused by Legge's individual view of the duke's character. As already stated (cf. p. 297) Legge adopts that view of Buckingham which he gives of himself in the speech in which Hall makes him reveal himself to Ely. According to this, Buckingham falls away from Richard because he murders his nephews. This view Legge tries to unite with the account of More, making such changes as appear necessary. Hence it is not signs of envy, but of wrath, secretam iram, which Ely recognizes in Buckingham's words. But the changes are insufficient to prevent a misfit.

The scene between Lewis and the queen affords opportunity for imitating the scene in the Hercules Furens in which Amphitryon comforts Megara with the hope of an approaching end to her woes. Lewis's address,

> Regina servans conjugis casta fide
> lectum jugalem, siste misera lachrimas,
> adesse spera jam malis finem tuis,

corresponds to that of Amphitryon, Her. Fur. 309—13:

> o socia nostri sanguinis, casta fide
> servans torum natosque magnanimi Herculis,
> meliora mente concipe atque animum excita,
> aderit profecto, qualis ex omni solet
> labore, maior.

The queen's reply,

> Quod pepulit aures nuntium laetum meas?
> quid audio? num misera mens est credula?
> haec facile credunt, quod nimis miseri volunt.
> sed quod volunt, fortuna contumax vetat.
> Prona est timori[s] semper in pejus fides,

corresponds to that of Megara with the succeeding words of Amphitryon, 313—16:

> Meg. Quod nimis miseri volunt
> hoc facile credunt. Amph. Immo quod metuunt nimis
> nunquam moveri posse nec tolli putant:
> prona est timoris semper in peius fides.

Buckingham next appears, with a speech to his soldiers, used by the author as a means of imparting the facts given in the chronicle concerning Richard's unsuccessful letters urging Buckingham to repair to the court; and concerning the other rebels who intend to join the duke in his enterprise. The beginning of the speech, with its expressions of indignant anger at the tyrant, is modelled on Senecan examples. Cf. Her. Fur. 920—4 and Tr. 258—9.

For the first time since his coronation Richard now appears once more upon the stage. He was then at the pinnacle of his success; he was king of England and in a young prince of Wales saw the establishment of a dynasty. Now his downward course has begun. His son is dead; Buckingham is arrayed in arms against him; there is a greater danger preparing by Richmond over seas. The basis of the scene is that Senecan view of Polidore Vergil which Hall imported into More's story (cf. p. 206). "And from thenceforth not onely all his counsailles, doynges and procedynges, sodainely decayed and sorted to none effecte: But also fortune beganne to froune and turn her whele douneward from him, in so much that he lost his only begotten sonne called Edwarde in the .iij moneth after he had created hym prince of Wales" (Hall, p. 381).

It cannot be too strongly insisted that to Polidore Vergil through Hall, rather than to More, is due the introduction of this dramatic reversal of fortune, not only in Legge but in all the literary treatments of Richard's story, including Shakespeare's. It is true that immediately following Richard's coronation More indicates a turn in the tide. "Now fell ther mischiefes thick. And as the thing euill gotten is neuer well kept, through all the time of his reygne, neuer ceased there cruel death and slaughter, till his own destruction ended it". Here, however, the mischiefs are the deaths and bloodshed following Richard's coronation, not the misfortunes that befall Richard himself. First among the mischiefs mentioned is the murder of the princes. There is here no idea of an evil fate that dogs Richard's footsteps till he for an instant tastes the cup of success, then snatches it from his lips. Another reversal, following upon the murder of the princes, is emphasized by More, but it is a reversal in Richard's inner nature. Now for the first time does conscience begin to speak; he never has quiet in his mind, never thinks himself sure. This is the reversal on which, as will be seen, the True Tragedy lays the chief stress. To his moving picture of Richard's inward anguish More adds, "Now hadde he outward no long time in rest. For hereupon sone after began the conspiracy, or rather good confederation" of Buckingham. But here again, though the quick beginning of trouble is indicated, it is treated merely as a fact following in the natural course of the narration, not as the swift penalty of Fate.

But the conception of Polidore Vergil, as has been shown (cf. p. 160), introduces a Nemesis throughout the whole story of the York-Lancaster struggle. Each of the chief participants pays the penalty of his crimes, and yet, as in Seneca, "dum punitur scelus, crescit". For many Richard is the instrument of Fate. In the murder of Clarence (in Shakespeare, not Vergil), of the queen's kinsmen, of Hastings, even of the innocent princes, he punishes a former crime. Until this moment Richard's course is upward, and he has no suspicion that the hand of Fate is likewise against himself. Now without warning fortune reverses her wheel. Here lies the dramatic kernel of Shakespeare's whole play. The first part of it, down to Hastings' death (spoken of in anticipation), he found in the Vergilean version, adopted into all the chronicles, of the course of the struggle down to the death of Edward III. Then in the midst of More's story, Vergil's application of the same principle of Nemesis to Richard himself was preserved in the passage inserted by Hall, but not copied by Holinshed. It is to this conception, and doubtless largely to this passage, that we owe the words of Richard, when in Shakespeare's play at the moment of his coronation he forebodes a change.

> Thus high, by thy advice
> And thy assistance, is King Richard seated:
> But shall we wear these honors for a day?
> Or shall they last, and we rejoice in them?

To this conception, and still more clearly to this passage is due the arrangement of scenes 3 & 4 of Act IV. In scene 3 the murder of the princes is announced to Richard. His last great deed is accomplished. That the scene may be more truly climactic, the death of Anne is put forward in time and mentioned here. Every project that Richard cherishes, has been, or bids fair to be, successfully carried out.

> The son of Clarence have I pent up close;
> His daughter meanly have I match'd in marriage,
> The sons of Edward sleep in Abraham's bosom,
> And Anne my wife hath bid this world good night.
> Now, for I know the Breton Richmond aims
> At young Elizabeth, my brother's daughter,
> And by that knot looks proudly o'er the crown,
> To her I go, a jolly thriving wooer.

Thriving! It is the last time that he can say the word. There enters Catesby, with

> Bad news, my lord; Ely is fled to Richmond,
> And Buckingham, back'd with the hardy Welshman,
> Is in the field, and still his power increaseth.

At the moment of success, when all seems sure, trouble comes. Richard must take the field to defend what he has won. There follows the comment of Fate, from the lips of the figure in whom Shakespeare personified his Nemesis:

> So, now prosperity begins to mellow
> And drop into the rotten mouth of death.

It is the Vergilean conception and not More's. Not till later in the play appears the mental anguish on which More lays all his stress. And even then, when Shakespeare reveals that the completion and perfection of the work of Nemesis lies not in Richard's external losses, but in Richard's own tortured soul, he adopts a view which is Vergil's as well as More's, and one which Vergil insists upon most strongly in connection with that very dream wherein, in Shakespeare, Richard recognizes the affliction of his coward conscience.

Thus while on More, as every one has noticed, depends almost the whole material fabric of Shakespeare's play; as nobody seems to have noticed, the ideal fabric depends on Polidore Vergil.

It is this Vergilean conception that imparts to Richard III much of the Senecan character that has often been remarked in it. To the student of Shakespeare much of the interest of Legge's play consists in its revelation of the Senecan side of Richard's story. Nowhere is this more apparent than in this scene, where "fortuna fallax" has her greatest triumph. Here the same Vergilean conception is the basis; and Legge's Senecan imitations show how Senecan that basis is.

Richard appears, bewailing his troubles.

> O saeva fata semper, ô sortem asperam
> cum saevit et cum parcit ex aequo malam
> Fortuna fallax rebus humanis nimis
> insultat, agili cuncta pervertens rota.
> Quos modò locavit parte suprema, modò
> ad ima eosdem trudit et calcat pede.

> Subitio labantis ecce fortunae impetu
> quis non potentem cernit eversam domum?
> Heu gnatus, heu primò unicus periit mens
> (ô dura fata, et lugubrem sortem nimis)
> qui clara patris regna sperat mortui.
> Ut ille magnt parvus armenti comes,
> primisque vixdum cornibus frontem gerens
> cervice subíto celsus, et capite arduus
> gregem paternum ducit, et pecori imperat.
> O suave pignus, ô decus domus
> Regalis, ô Britanniae fumus [funus] tuae,
> O patris heu spes vana, cui demens ego
> laudes Achillis bellicas, et Nestoris
> annos precabar, luce privavit deus.
> Nunquam potenti sceptra gestabis manu
> felix, Britanno jura nec populo dabis,
> Victasque gentes sub tuum mittes jugum.
> Non Franca subiges terga, non Scotos trahes
> in tua rebelles imperia sine gloria
> jacebis alto clausus in tumulo miser.

The first two lines are from Med. 431—2:

> O dura fata semper et sortem asperam,
> cum saevit et cum parcit ex aequo malam!

cf. also Tr. 1056:

> O dura fata, saeva miseranda horrida!

With the lines on Fortune cf. Ag. 56—64, 71—2:

> o regnorum magnis fallax
> Fortuna bonis, in praecipiti
> dubioque locas nimis excelsos;
> nunquam placidam sceptra quietem
> certumve sui tenuere diem;
> alia ex aliis cura fatigat
> vexatque animos nova tempestas.
> non sic Libycis syrtibus aequor
> furit alternos volvere fluctus
> . , ...
> ut praecipites regum casus
> Fortuna rotat.

cf. also Her. Fur. 524, Tr. 259 et seq., Oed. 11, et al., Thy. 597 et seq. The idea is the most prominent one in all Seneca. The reversal of Fortune's wheel is in the passage from Vergil.

Richard's lament for his son is, like the lament of Queen Elizabeth, a close imitation of Andromache's lament for her son, together with a simile taken from Ulysses' description of the boy. For the latter. cf. Tr. 537—540:

> sic ille magni parvus armenti comes
> primisque nondum cornibus findens cutem
> cervice subito celsus et fronte arduus
> gregem paternum ducit ac pecori imperat.

For Tr. 766—770 see the passage on p. 291—292; and cf. in add. Tr. 771—774:

> Iliaca non tu sceptra regali potens
> gestabis aula, iura nec populis dabis
> victasque gentes sub tuum mittes iugum,
> non Graia caedes terga, non Pyrrhum trahes.

From his dead son Richard passes to the conspiracy of Buckingham and that of Richmond, and relates his unsuccessful attempt to induce Buckingham to return to court. Hesitating and doubting what to do, he resolves by new and useful laws, by liberality to the citizens, by the erection of a college for priests, and by general uprightness, to regain the favor of the people, which he has lost by the murder of the princes. All this, except the account of his dealings with Buckingham, which is from More, is from the passage copied by Hall from Polidore Vergil, which thus passes practically entire into Legge's play.

From the middle of the conversation of Buckingham and Ely (cf. p. 116) More's story ceases to be the basis of the play, and Hall's continuation — copied also by Grafton and Holinshed — takes its place.

The abandonment and flight of Buckingham follows, related to Richard by a messenger. The circumstantial account follows Hall in detail. Richard gives orders for the ports to be guarded, and for a fleet to ward off Richmond, and makes proclamation of a reward for the capture of Buckingham. All the details are from Hall's account.

A messenger now appears with the news of Buckingham's capture through the treachery of Banister. Richard greets the news with savage joy.

> Si non fides me sacra regno continent,
> tentabo mea stabilire sceptra sanguine,
> et regna duro saevus imperio regam.
> Nunc ergo dux poenas gravissimas luat.
> Obrumpat ensis noxium tristis caput,
> nullamque pene carnifex reddat moram.
> Regnare nescit, odia qui timet nimis.

With the last line cf. Phoen. 654:

> Regnare non vult esse qui invisus timet,

and other passages cited on p. 302. The other lines are probably based on the following, from the passage inserted by Hall from Vergil. "But afterwarde euidentlie to all persones it appeared, that onely feare (whiche is not a maister long in office and in continual aucthoritie) and not justice, caused kynge Rycharde at that verie tyme to waxe better and amende his synneful life, for shortelie the goodnes of the man whiche was but payncted and fraudulent, sodainlie wexed coulde and vanished awaie (Hall p. 381)".

Richard now turns his attention to the case of Margaret, formerly Countess of Richmond and now Lord Stanley's wife, who has been sending letters to her son. Stanley is to guard his wife closely at home, keeping all servants away from her, that she may have no opportunity to send further letters. As a pledge of his own fidelity he shall leave with Richard his son Lord Strange as hostage. As Stanley's name does not appear in the scene-heading and as he makes no reply, it cannot be determined whether he is supposed to be present and addressed by Richard, or whether Richard is revealing in soliloquy the directions he intends to give Stanley. The former may be the case, as mutes do not appear in the scene-headings (cf. e. g. the priest met by Hastings); but if so it is still strange that Stanley does not reply. The passage follows a paragraph in Hall, p. 398, but the detention of Lord Strange is from a later passage, Hall p. 408, in which Stanley, intending to prepare for Richmond's arrival, applies for leave to go home.

Buckingham, apparently on his way to execution, now appears with a soliloquy embodying the usual declamatory Senecan lament against deceitful fortune, on which Legge has already rung so many changes. It offers an interesting comparison to the similar scene in Shakespeare.

> O blandientis lubricum sortis decus!
> ô tristis horrendi nimis belli casus!
> heu, heu fatis mortale luditur genus.
> Quisquam ne sibi spondere tam firmum potes͏̈
> quod non statim metuenda convellat dies!
> Cujus refulsit nomen Anglis inclytum
> modò, pallidos nunc ad lacus trudor miser.
> Quid (heu) juvat jactare magnos spiritus?
> Fallacis aulae fulgor (heu) quos perdidit?
> Heu blanda nimium dona fortunae! mare
> non sic aquis refluentibus turget, aut undis
> turbatus ab imis pontus Euxinus tumet,
> ut caeca casus heu fortuna magnatum vocat.
> Funestus heu dirusque Richardi favor
> quid illa deplorem miser tempora, quibus
> fretus meo consilio aper frendens, sibi
> regnum cruento dente raptum comparat?
> En, hujus ictu nunc atroci corruo.
> Natale solum, illustre decus ô Angliae,
> horrenda quae te fata nunc manent? ferox
> postquam jugo tyrannus oppresum tenet
> heu, heu, miser Stygeas ad undas deprimor,
> Crudelis et collo securis imminet.

With this cf. Oct. 924—28, 34, 35, Agam. 64, 72.

It will be noticed that here, as in Shakespeare, Buckingham recognizes that his death is a just return for the aid he has rendered Richard. In Shakespeare this recognition is rendered more impressive by Buckingham's broken oath of service to Edward's children and his wife's allies, and by his remembrance of Margaret's curse, through which he is included in the effect of the universal Nemesis. Both scenes rest on the passage copied by Hall from Polidore Vergil (p. 395). "This death (as a reward) the duke of Buckyngham receaued at the handes of kyng Richard, whom he before in his affaires, purposes and enterprises had holden susteyned and set forwarde aboue all Godes forbode. By thys all men maye easelye perceaue that he not onley loseth bothe his labour, traueyle, and industrie, and ferther steynethe and spoteth his ligne with a perpetuall ignomony and reproche, whiche in euyll and mis[c]hiefe assisteth and aydeth an euyll disposed person, considerynge for the mooste parte that he for his frendely fauoure should receaue some greate displeasure or infortunate chaunce. Beside that God of his iustice in conclusion appoyncteth to him a condigne peyne and affliction for his merites and desertes".

The following scene is another of the several preparatory scenes in which are determined by Richard and his counsellors the measures to be subsequently pursued. As in the other scenes, Richard appears weak, vacillating, and fearful. His counsellors must support and encourage him, and it is they who propose the further steps he is to take.

Richard's opening words reveal him in the lowest depths of despair, not only fearful, but certain that his fate is at hand.

> Quid me potens fortuna fallaci nimis
> blandita vultu gravius ut ruerem, edita
> de rupe tollis! finis alterius mali
> gradus est futuri: dira conspirat manus
> in me rebellis, torqueor metu miser.
> disrumpor aestuante curarum salo.
> Richmondiensis ille perfidus comes
> in transmarinis ambit (heu) regnum locis:
> In cujus arma jurat turba civium
> inimica: mox hujus mali tanti metu
> famulos cruenta morte mulctavi meos.
> at fama vexat turgidum pectus magis:

> thalamos jugales filiae Richmondio
> comiti studet regina mater jungere.
> O triste facinus, hostis in nostra potens
> regnabit aula, meque fatis destinat.

With this compare Oct. 377—280:
> Quid me, potens Fortuna, fallaci mihi
> blandita vultu, sorte contentum mea
> alte extulisti, gravius ut ruerem edita
> receptus arce totque prospicerem metus?

Agam. 101—2:
> quidquid in altum Fortuna tulit
> ruitura levat.

and Her. Fur. 208—9:
> finis alterius mali
> gradus est futuri.

A messenger enters with the news that Richmond is on the seas. He is represented as one of the soldiers who have been guarding the coast, and relates the unsuccessful attemps of Richmond to land on the coast of Dorset, and his escape from the snare set for him by the soldiers (Hall 396). Again Richard breaks out into a wail against Fortune.

> Cur ludis inconstans nimis misera dea?
> nuper locatum me levas summa rota,
> auraque molli prosperos affers dies:
> illico supinum lubrico affligis solo.
> Quam varia, quam maligna, quam levis dea?

cf. Oct. 452:
> levis est dea [Fortuna]

and Med. 219—220:
> rapida fortuna ac levis
> praecepsque regno eripuit.

To Lovell falls the duty of encouraging the despairing king.
> Cur vexat animum cura vesanum gravius?
> ubi prisca virtus? pellat ignavos metus
> excelsus animus: fortis haud novit metum.

cf. Phoen. 77—78:
> sed flecte mentem, pectus antiquum advoca
> victasque magno robore aerumnas doma.

cf. also the passage in the Oedipus where Jocasta strives to teach Oedipus the duty of a king.

Oed. 82—88
     Quid iuvat, coniunx, mala
 gravare questu? regium hoc ipsum reor:
 adversa capere, quoque sit dubius magis
 status et cadentis imperi moles labet,
 hoc stare certo pressius fortem gradu:
 haud est virile terga Fortunae dare.
 Oed. Abest pavoris crimen ac probrum procul,
 virtusque nostra nescit ignavos metus.

There is nothing to fear, continues Lovell, from the dead Buckingham, the other rebels are buried in the ground, while the Scots are held in loyalty by the promised marriage and the truce recently concluded. (Hall p. 393, and 401, cf. p. 191. The "rebelles" are Browne, Clyfforde, Sentleger, Rame and others executed by Richard. Hall p. 397). Richard's ambassadors are in Britanny and their promises will doubtless avail to induce the Breton duke to restrain Richmond (Hall p. 403).

Catesby is ready with another proposal. If the mission to Britanny fails, then let Richard break up the marriage between Richmond and the princess Elizabeth. Richard eagerly seizes the suggestion. Elizabeth shall be put to the sword.

 Rapietur illico, finietque nuptias
 districtus ensis, Tartaro nubet prius.

But this Richard's counsellors believe to be going too far. It will give the lie to the new course of humane and liberal action by which he has been winning the people to himself.

 At est asyli grande violati nefas:
 meliora cogita. . . . . . .
 et nuper allectus tibi populus fuit
 quem plurimis dudum modis colere studes
 statim scelere perculsus inani, oderit.

The opposition reminds one of that of the satelles to his master Atreus,

Thy. 204, 5   Fama te populi nihil
            adversa terret?

as well as of Seneca to Nero, Oct. 440 et seq.
But Richard is bound that it shall be so.

> Taedasne demens patiar invisas mihi
> meoque sceptro contrahi? nunquam accidet.
> Scelesta nostrum firmat impietas thronum
> audebo quodvis: scelere vincendum scelus:
> violare jura facile regnanti licet.
> In rebus aliis usque pietatem colas.
> Stringatur ensis: Regna tutatur cruor.

It is the speech of a Nero, determined to rid himself of his enemies. Cf. Oct. 462, 3, 469:

> An patiar ultra sanguinem nostrum peti,
> inultus et contemptus ut subito opprimar?
> tollantur hostes ense suspecti mihi

Oct. 451 Fortuna nostra cuncta permittit mihi
     456 Ferrum tuetur principem.

Also Phaed. 721:

> scelere velandum est scelus.

Lovell, however, suggests that the queen may possibly be induced to allow her daughters to come to court, and Catesby is ready with a more infamous proposal. If it should happen that Richard's wife should die, he might marry his niece. Again the suggestion is eagerly seized by Richard, who is ready to go to any length.

> Placet, quod inquis! potius quam regnum ruat,
> tentanda cuncta: triste consilium tamen
> dum vivit uxor: hanc decet laetho dari.

From Lovell again comes the suggestion of the best means of bringing about the queen's death; the spreading abroad of the rumor that she is already dead, the abstinence from her bed, and the conveying to her of the information that her husband cannot endure her sterility. All is welcome to Richard.

> Mactabo potius, ense laethali, prius
> tollam veneno, quam mea pestis throni
> cladesque fuerit.

Lovell and Catesby are despatched to persuade the queen-mother, and Richard is left alone to meditate upon the situation. Throughout the scene he has appeared intensely fearful of the dangers pressing upon him, unready in devices to ward them off, but entirely ready to undertake any crime that will ensure his throne. Such he reveals himself in his soliloquy.

> Animum tumultus volvit attonitus, rupit
> regni metus, quiescere nec usquam potest,
> sanare nunc malum queo solum, face
> neptem jugali si maritus jungerem
> Uxor sed obstat: scelera novimus prius
> quid conjugem cessas veneno tollere?
> aude anime, num peccata formidas tuam?
> sero pudet: peracta pars sceleris mei
> olim fuit maxima: pium esse quid juvat?
> post tanta miserum facinora, nihil facis.
> Parat animus nefanda, parva nec placent.
> Regnum tuemur: omnis in ferro salus.

This is the tyrant pure and simple, without any great qualities, another Lycus, whose words Legge puts into Richard's mouth, cf. Her. Fur. 341:

> omnis in ferro salus.

That Richard should speak the words of Lycus is especially fitting, for the two tyrants stand in the same position. Each holds a sceptre gained by crime, each is hated by his people, each hopes by a criminal marriage to make his place sure.

The facts of the scene are all taken from Hall's account.

In the following scene Lovell approaches the queen. In accordance with Hall's account he first "excuses and purges" Richard "of all things before against her attempted or procured". The excuse is Senecan, taken from the scene between Lycus and Megara in Hercules Furens.

> Dum vincere cupis, arma delectant magis
> nescit modum sibi strictus ensis ponere:
> at placida victori magis pax expedit.

cf. Herc. Fur. 403—405, 408—10:

>arma non servant modum;
>nec temperari facili nec reprimi potest
>stricti ensis ira, bella delectat cruor.
>   sed nunc pereat omnis memoria:
>cum victor arma posuit, et victum decet
>deponere odia.

Richard, so Lovell asserts, is sincerely repentant and would show this by placing her daughters brilliantly in marriage — a promise not in Hall nor in the other chronicles, but a historical fact, cf. Gairdner, Life of Richard III — and by all kinds of honors to her son Dorset, if he will return from Richmond. Having done his best, Lovell awaits the queen's answer, which is not at once given.

>Quid moesta terram conticescis intuens?
>errore quid pectus vago versas tuum?

At last the queen speaks. She indignantly enumerates the injuries mentioned by Hall, "the murther of her innocente children, the infamy and dishonoure spoken by [i. e. of] the kynge her husbande, the lyunge in auoutrie layed to her charge, the bastardying of her daughters".

>Ergo filiorum sanguine madentes manus?
>non liberos crudelis occidit fratris?
>nostrosque conspersit thoros falsa labe?
>an non potest matri scelestus parcere,
>infame generi vulnus inflixit suo
>saevire ferrum cessat, ubi regnat furor?

Though based on Hall there is a distinct reminiscence of the scene in the Hercules Furens, where Lycus, endeavoring to win over Megara, is met by her with the reproach of his crimes. Cf. Her. Fur. 370—3:

>Lycus.   Quid truci vultu siles?
>Megara. Egone ut parentis sanguine asperam manum
>   fratrumque gemina caede contingam?

But after a long discussion, part of it, naturally, in Senecan stichomythia, the queen, though still fearful, is overcome by desire for the welfare and honor of her children.

> O filiae charissimae, heu, heu, filiae,
> dotare vos thalamis beatis rex parat,
> abite, vos fortuna quò miseras jubet.

A messenger is at once despatched by the queen to her son Dorset, urging him to return. The facts of the interview are in all the chronicles, from Hall on. Vergil and the Hardyng continuator have not the enumeration which the queen's speech seems to follow.

Richard welcomes his two nieces with concealed eagerness, expresses his pity for their ill-fortune, and promises them noble marriages. Of his own designs upon Elizabeth no hint is given as yet. His wife still lives. The scene seems to be based on Vergil's account as it appears in the Hardyng continuation, not as in Hall. (See p. 274—275).

While Richard is speaking, Anne approaches, "with lamentable countenance and sorrowful cheer". The Archbishop of York has conveyed to her the news that Richard scorns her as barren, and the rumor spread abroad among the people that she is already dead has likewise come to her ears. Her woeful complaint to her husband gives the content of the corresponding passage in Hall, and Richard's answer, denying any purpose to procure her death, and encouraging her with a promise to manifest his love as soon as he shall have composed the rebellion, corresponds to the "fair words", "dissimuling blandiments" and "flattering lesyngs" (*i. e.* lies) mentioned by Hall.

There enters a messenger to announce that Richmond has escaped from the plots laid for him by Richard. At the king's request he relates the story of Richmond's escape from Landoise as recounted by Hall. To this is added the news that Oxford has escaped from the castle of Hammes where he has been so long confined, and has joined Richmond. The tidings are met with the usual Senecan lament.

> O nuntium infestum! ô nitida pallatia,
> passura graviorem exitum Oedipodae domo'
> O luce splendens principis falsa decus!
> O sors acerba! ô fata Regnis invida!
> Sed parce diis demens scelere quos irritas.
> Opaca regna Ditis, et caecum Chaos,
> exangue vulgus, numen abstruxi Jovis,
> et quicquid arcet, huc novos spargite dolos.
> Vestras manus Richmondium vocat nefas,
> ut spiritus illico scelestos expuat,
> nisi graviores expetat poenas dolor.

This is another variation of the well-known refrain; and the comparison with the house of Oedipus is another manifestation of the fact that Richard is regarded as a Senecan hero. For the Senecan commonplaces "opaca regna Ditis" and "caecum Chaos" cf. Her. Fur. 95, Med. 637, Agam. 752, Oct. 556, Phoen. 234, et al. For "exsangue vulgus" cf. Oed. 597. Of special infence on the passage was Med. 740—1:

> comprecor vulgus silentum vosque ferales deos
> et Chaos caecum atque opacam Ditis umbrosi domum.

The lament is scarcely finished when another messenger enters with the news that Anne is dead — a message likewise greeted with a lament, though it is this time hypocritical.

> O dira fata! saeva nimis ô numina!
> res possident mortalium certi nihil;
> consors unica vitae, et chara conjux, vale.

For the second line see Agam. 61.

That Anne died by poison is clearly indicated by the manner of her death as described by the nuntius

> Postquam lugubris sedisset moesta diu,
> suspiria gravibus mista cum singultibus
> heu saepe fundit: saepe falsis lachrymis
> diris querelis conjugem ingratum premit.
> Tandem inquietam capit attonitus furor,
> nuncque huc et illuc currit erranti gradu,
> tanquam tumultum patiens in se turbidum:
> statimque quaerit (voces infractae sono)

> Quae cor revellit dextera crudelis meum?
> An non est maritus, inquit? heu fidele cor
> valde est ineptum munus ingrato viro.
> Postea pupillae prorsus occultae latent,
> et solum aperta pallidè albugo micat:
> vomitiones inde crebras extulit,
> animaeque in altum saepe deliquium cadit:
> Artus per omnes frigidus sudor meat
> orisque subitò nitidus evanuit color:
> frons flava marcet, livida ardent tempora
> et palpebrarum omnes defluunt pili
> Caerulia turpi labia liquescunt situ,
> et lingua (visu horribile) specie lurida
> prominet hiante ex ore solito grandior,
> unguesque nunc haud amplius clari nitent
> sed quasi veneno perliti pereunt: cadit
> tandem misera luctata fatis foemina.

The source of this remarkable description I have not been able to find. There is no corresponding passage in Seneca. Yet it is entirely comparable to such passages as those in which the Senecan nuntius describes the murder and sacrifice of the sons of Thyestes, or the execution of Astyanas and Polyxena, and is intended to produce the same effect of horror. It proves that Legge did not refrain from the opportunity offered by the death of the princes because of any artistic dislike for Seneca's sensationalism. Whatever its immediate source, the motive of the passage is wholly Senecan.

Richard is unmoved by the terrible description. His thoughts turn at once to his niece, who at this very moment opportunely appears.

> Sed neptis huc dubio venit gradu mea
> tentare procus hujus instituam thoros.

The words remind one of Shakespeare's Richard III, 4, 3, 39—44:

> Anne my wife hath bid the world good night.
> Now for I know the Breton Richmond aims
> At young Elizabeth my brother's daughter,
> . . . .
> To her I go, a jolly thriving wooer.

But in Shakespeare's play there is no wooing-scene between Richard and Elizabeth; and for such a scene there is no warrant in the chronicles, where the only reference is: "The king thus (accordyng to his long desire) losed out of the bondes of matrimony, beganne to cast a foolyshe phantasie to Lady Elisabeth his nece, making much suite to haue her ioyned with him in lawfull matrimony. But because all men, and the mayden herselfe moost of all, detested and abhorred this vnlawfull and in maner vnnaturall copulacion, he determined to prolonge and deferre the matter till he were in a more quietnes" (Hall p. 407, from P. Vergil). Here there is nothing said of a personal meeting between Richard and the princess. How Legge came to introduce such a meeting is easily discovered from the scene itself. A Senecan tyrant, in a situation similar to Richard's, likewise endeavors to strengthen his position upon the throne by a marriage which he fails to accomplish. This is Lycus, who in the scene from the Hercules Furens already referred to, woos Megara and is rejected with scorn. Still another unsuccessful wooing is made the theme of a whole play of Seneca, viz. Phaedra's suit to Hippolytus. It was these that induced Legge to introduce Richard's personal wooing, and upon them his own scene is formed. It is interesting to note in this connection that for Shakespeare's likewise historically unfounded scene of the wooing of Lady Anne by Richard, Theodor Vatke in the Jahrbuch der deutsch. Shak.-Gesellschaft, 4:67 (referred to by Cunliffe, Infl. of Seneca on Eliz. Tragedy, p. 78) suggested a comparison to the wooing of Megara by Lycus. Here we have a wooing by Richard that is certainly founded on that of Lycus. In all these cases the wooed is repelled by the wooer's crimes, and against their influence he has to contend. In both Shakespeare and Legge the criminal declares his repentance and offers to expiate his crimes with death. In Shakespeare alone is the suitor successful. A comparison of the two scenes is of the highest interest, and I quote that of Legge entire.

Rex.
O regia de stirpe derivans genus,
et digna sceptris virgo: postquam (proh dolor)
rapuere fata conjugem tam tristia:
quae sit magis mihi juncta Regali face,
quàm genere quae regis superbo nascitur?
Sociemus animos, et thori sponde fidem,
accipe maritum. Quid truci vultu siles?

Filia.
Egone, ô nefandum scelus, expiandum rogis
nullis! egone manus misera conjux meas
rubente mortuorum sanguine imbuam?
Olimpus uxori deerit ante suae,
Luanque [Lunaque] gubernabit diem, noctemque sol:
Prius Aetna gelidas emittet ardens aquas,
Nilusque vagus ignitas laminas vomet.
Egone silebo parvulos misera invidos
tibi nepotes, at mihi charos fratres
crudelitèr tua peremptos dextera?
Sceleste patrue? prius ab extremo sinu
Hespera Tethys lucidum attollet diem:
Lepus fugabit invidum priùs canem.
Punit nefandum quamvis abditum scelus
Jupiter, et astutos sinit nunquam dolos.
Humeros premebant saxa Sisiphi lubrica
saevus Procustes asperam poena[m] luit,
quoniam suos vim necarunt hospites.
Non hospites tu, sed nepotes (heu) tuos
nuper relictis fasciis miser necas.

Rich.
Agedum effrenatas virgo voces amove,
ne ob unum scelus corpora pereant duo.
Cruore solium fateor acquiri meum
et innocentium morte: sic fatis placet.
Cecidere fratres? doleo; facti poenitet
sunt mortui? factum prius nequit infci
num flebo mortuos? lachrymae nil valent.
Quid vis facerem? an fratrum geminam necem
hac dextera effuso rependam sanguine?
faciam? paratis ensibus pectus dabo:
et si placet magis, moriar ulnis tuis
ignes, aquas, terram, aut minacem Caucasum
petam, petam Tartara, vel umbrosum nemus

atrae Stygis; nullum laborem desero
si gratus essem tibi, virago regia.
Filia.
Sit amor, sit odium, sit ira, vel sit fides;
non curo: placet odisse, quicquid cogitas.
Tuus priùs penetrabit ensis pectora,
libido quàm cognata corpus polluat.
O Jupiter saevo peritus fulmine.
Cur non trisulca mundus ignescit face?
Cur non hiulca terra devorat illico?
Immane portentum ferocis principis,
terrore superans Gorgoneum genus.
Rich.
Pessima, tace: solum silet in armis fides,
nihil ne valet amor? nihil thorus movet
regius? acerbae neque lachrymae valent?
est imperandi principi duplex via,
amor et metus: utrumque regibus utile.
Cogere.
Filia.
si cogas mori sequor lubens.
Rich.
Moriere.
Filia.
Grata mors erit magis mihi
et praestat aerumnis mori oppressam statim
quam luce curis obsitam frui diu.
Rich.
Moriere demens.
Filia.
Nil minaris amplius?
mallem mori virgo, tyranno quam viro
incesta vivere, diis, hominibusque invida.
Rich.
Hem quid agis infoelix? thoros spernet tuos.
Regina vivas, sis mea, miseros sile
fratres.
Filia.
Miser non est quisquis mori seiet.
Rich.
Anne lubens? en nullus est ferro metus,
strictusque nescit ensis unquam parcere.

                    Filia.
Neronis umbrae, atque furiae Cleopatrae
truces resurgite, similem finem date
his nuptiis, qualem tulit Oedipodae domus.
Nec sufficit fratres necasses tuos principes?
Et nobili foedare caede dexteram?
quin et integram stuprare quaeras virginem
maritus? ô mores, nefanda ô tempora!
at saeva priùs evadat ales viscera:
in me feras priùs tuas atrox nemus
emitte, vel quod triste monstrum nutrias,
quam casta thalamos virgo sequor adulteros.
                    Rich.
Discessit, et nostros fugit demens thoros
negligit amores stulta virgo regios.
Nunc ista differam; minae forsan cadent
rabidae puellae, patriae dum consulo.

Cf. this with the scene Her Fur. 332—523. I select the most important lines.

    Lyc.   alieno in loco
haut stabile regnum est; una sed nostras potest
fundare vires iuncta regali face
thalamisque Megara.
                      non equidem reor
fore ut recuset ac meos spernat toros:
temptemus igitur, fors dedit nobis locum,
namque ipsa
           iuxta praesides astat deos
              o clarum trahens
a stirpe nomen regia, facilis mea
parumper aure verba patienti excipe,
pacem reduci velle victori expedit,
victo necesse est — particeps regno veni;
sociemur animis, pignus hoc fidei cape:
contige dextram. quid truci vultu siles?

    Meg. Egone ut parentis sanguine aspersam manum
fratrumque gemina caede contingam? prius
extinguet ortus, referet occasus diem,
pax ante fida nivibus et flammis erit
et Scylla Siculum iunget Ausonio latus,
priusque multo vicibus alternis fugax
Euripus unda stabit Euboica piger,

Lyc.
: patrem abstulisti, regna, germanos, larem
patrium — quid ultra est?
sequitur superbos ultor a tergo deus.
Thebana novi regna: quid matres loquar
passas et ausas scelera? quid geminum nefas
mixtumque nomen coniugis nati patris?
quid bina fratrum castra? quid totidem rogos?
riget superba Tantalis luctu parens
maestusque Phrygio manat in Lipylo lapis.
Haec te manent exempla.

Lyc.   Agedum efferatas rabida voces amore
                cruento cecidit in bello pater?
cecidere fratres? arma non servant modum;
nec temperari facile nec reprimi potest
stristi ensis ira.

Meg.   non vincet fidem
vis ulla nostram; moriar, Alcide tua.

Lyc. Cogere. Meg. cogi qui potest nescit mori.

Lyc. Moriere demens.

Most of the breaks not supplied by the historical foundation will be found in the following. Herc. Fur. 494—500:

Megara. Vmbrae Creontis et penates Labdaci
et nuptiales impii Oedipodae faces,
nunc solita nostro fata coniugio date.
nunc, nunc, cruentae regis Aegypti nurus,
adest multo sanguine infectae manus.
dest una numero Danais: explebo nefas.

Phaed. 613—616:

Phaedra. non me per altas ire si iubeas nives,
pigeat gelatis ingredi Pindi iugis
non, si per ignes ire et infesta agmina,
cuncter paratis ensibus pectus dare.

Phaed. 567—574:

Hipp. Sit ratio, sit natura, sit dirus furor:
odisse placuit, ignibus iunges aquas
et amica ratibus ante promittet vada
incerta Syrtis, ante ab extremo sinu
Hesperia Tethys lucidum attollet diem
et ora damnis blanda praebebunt lupi
quam victus animum feminae mitem geram.

Phaed. 680—1:
>cur dextra, divum rector atque hominum, vacat
>tua nec trisulca mundus ardescit face?

cf. also Tr. 576—7:
>Andr. Si vis, Ulixe, cogere Andromacham metu,
>vitam minare; nam mori votum est mihi.

Richard's chagrin at his defeat in his purpose to marry Elizabeth is now swallowed up in the joyful news received by messenger from Brittany, who declares that Richmond has found it impossible to obtain aid and has given up his expedition. This gives the author an opportunity to vary Richard's Senecan laments with an expression of joy.

>Festum diem celebrare jam laetos decet,
>ô mihi dies albo lapillo nobilis!
>Jam sors beatis mitior rebus fluit.
>Quot modò procellas concitat frustra Comes
>et quàm graves nuper minatur exitus?
>Quin in suum redibit authorem scelus. etc.

In Richard's words is to be traced the influence of Med. 985, Agam. 402—3, Tr. 870 and Thy. 435. The scene is based upon the chronicle account (Hall p. 408), in which Richard receives the news reported above. Whereupon he "eyther beynge to light of credence, or seduced and deluded by hys craftie taletellers, greatly reioysed as though he had obteyned the ouerhand of his enemyes with triumph and victorie, and thought hymselfe neuer so surely delyuered of all feare and dreadfull ymaginacions, so that he needed nowe no more once for that cause eyther to wake or breake his golden slepe". Hence, as in Legge's speech, he summons home his ships, but that he may not be entrapped gives orders for a strict watch on the coast and on the frontiers of Wales.

From Richard's fancied security the play passes, with dramatic contrast, to the actual invasion of Richmond, to which the last act is given up. In the first scene the arrival of Richmond on the coast of Wales is announced by a nuntius, who alarms the inhabitants.

> Quis me per auras turbo raptat concitus?
> fuge, fuge, civis, haeret à tergo Comes:
> minatur horrendum furor Richmondius:
> portum pedite Milfordium immani premit.
> totamque calcat proditam sibi Walliam:
> furens comes toti minatur Angliae.

At the news men rush away in fear, while wives cling to them imploring not to be abandoned, and an aged mother beseeches her son not to leave her.

> Matris tuae solamen ô fili mane.
> Sin hostibus domum relinques perfuga,
> scrutetur ensis nota quondam filio
> ubera; tuo mater peribo vulnere.

The speech of the nuntius contains a reminiscence of that with which the nuntius announce the crime of Thyestes. Thy. 623—5:

> Quis me per auras turbo praecipitem vehet
> atraque nube involvet, ut tantum nefas
> eripiat oculis?

while that of the old woman may perhaps have been influenced by the speech of the nutrix to Deianira in Hercules Oetaeus 925, 6:

> Per has aniles ecce te supplex comas
> atque ubera ista paene materna obsecro.

The scene is inconsistent with the chronicle, which states that Richmond "was applauded and receauved of the people with greate ioye" (Hall p. 410); and it lacks dramatic purpose, unless Legge had some notion of showing thereby the reputation of his hero, for in the following scene Richmond is welcomed by Rhesus Thomae (— Thomas ap Rice), the leader of these very people, as

> heros Britanniae gentis auxilium unicum
> optatus Anglis civibus . . . tuis.

Legge's whole purpose demands the representation that Richmond comes, not as an enemy or an object of fear, but as a welcome deliverer. Of course Seneca is responsible for the "furor Richmondius" and the "furens comes". The scene is based upon the passage in which Hall (from Vergil), apropos of Richard's order strictly to guard the coast, explains the way in which the arrival of an enemy is reported. "For the custome of the countreys adioynyng nere to ỹ see is (especially in the tyme of war) on euery hill or high place to erect a bekon w̃ a greate lanterne in the toppe, which maie be sene and discerned a great space of. And when the noyse is once bruted that the enemies approche nere ỹ land, they sodeinly put fyer in the lanthornes and make showtes & outrages from toune to toune and from village to village. Some ronne in post from place to place admonishyng the people to be ready to resist the ieopardy, and defende the perell. And by this pollecy ỹ fame is sone blowen to euery citee & toune, in somuche that aswell the cytezens as the rural people be in short space assembled and armed to refell and put back the newe arryued enemies (Hall p. 409)".

Richmond signalises his arrival in Britain by a speech in which the justice of his cause and his position as God's avenger are asserted. None of the chronicles, from the Hardyng continuation on, mention a speech of Henry upon his arrival in England, although Bernard André puts such a speech into his mouth, an "Ad Angliam salutatio ad suosque secunda justaque oratio (cf. p. 62)", and Fabian mentions that he "knelyd downe vpon the erth and with meke countenaunce and pure deuocion began this psalme 'Judica me Deus et decerne causam meam' (cf. p. 73)". All the plays however, have such a speech — in the True Tragedy and Shakespeare after Richmond has marched some ways from the coast, but as it is his first appearance the situation is the same; and it is probably based not only upon dramatic requirement but upon general historic tradition.

In Legge the speech is naturally colored by reminiscences of Seneca.

> optata tandem tecta cerno patriae,
> miserisque nosco maximum exulibus bonum.
> ô chare salve terra, sed salve diu,
> frendentis apri dente lacerata impio.
> Da (patria) veniam, bella si geram pia,
> da quaeso veniam: causa commovit tua;
> dirumque principis nefas bellum vocat.
> Rex est peremptus: occupat regnum Nero:
> cum rege fratre parvulus periit puer.
> Solum tuentur templa reginam sacra.
> Regum cruoris ultor adveni pius:
> poenas dabit Richardus Henrico: dedit,
> si nostra clemens vota concedat Deus.

Richmond's greeting to his native land is based on the passages from the Agamemnon and the Thyestes already imitated in the speech of the young king on his return to London (cf. p. 289—290). The rest is undoubtedly made up from Richmond's speech to his soldiers (Hall, p. 417), in which a like comparison of Richard to Nero occurs. With the whole speech cf. also the speech of Octavia, Oct. 222—251, especially 248—251.

> utinam suorum facinorum poenas luat
> Nero insitivus, Domitis genitus patre,
> Orbis tyrannus qui premit turpi iugo
> morumque vitiis nomen Augustum inquinat.

Richmond is welcomed by Thomas ap Rice, who assures the doubting earl (as usual, in Senecan terms) of his fidelity, and is promised the government of Wales in return. The facts are all from the chronicles (Hall p. 411).

In the next scene are comprised the various events which, according to the chronicle account, occurred during Richmond's march from Lichfield to Tamworth. Here, it is related, Sir Walter Hungerford, Sir Thomas Burchier and diverse others, having abandoned their leader Brakenbury, "by nocturnall wandryng, and in maner by vnknowen pathes and vncertain waies searchyng, at the last came to the earle Henry" (Hall, p. 413). In this same march occurred the mischance by which Richmond lost his army in the darkness, while he lingered behind it "disconsolate, musyng, and ymagenynge what was best to be done" because he could get no tidings from his step-father, Lord Thomas Stanley. Legge in his scene introduces the two parties wandering in the night. Ou one side of the stage Hungerford and Burchier converse, praying in Senecan terms that day may linger till they have reached their destination.

> At ô quieta noctis almae tempora,
> tuque miseris praebens opem Phoebi soror,
> adhuc tuere: differas Titan diem,
> donec tyranni tuti ab armis, inclyti
> tentoria Henrici comitis attingimus.

A soldier appears, crying

> Foelix tuas fugio per umbras caeca nox
> mactetur ense quisquis obstabit mihi.

while, according to the marginal direction, "heare allso divers mutes, armed souldiers, run over the stage one after another to ẙ Earle of Richmond".

On the other side of the stage Richmond is "wandering"

> Quis his locus, quae regio quae regni plaga?
> ubi sum? ruit nox: heu ubi satellites
> Inimica cuncta: fraude quis vacat locus
> quem quod rogabo? tuta sit fides, vide,
> nativus artus liquit internos calor,
> rigore frigent membra: vix loquor metu:
> tremesco solus, cura mentem concoquit. etc.

The speech is noteworthy because it shows in Richmond's case, as we have before seen in Richard's, of what influence Legge's Senecan model was in altering the conception of the chronicle. Of Richmond's feelings in the present situation the chronicle says that he was disconsolate, musing, melancholy and pensive. He is "not a lytle afeard" because he cannot be assured of Stanley, but this fear has nothing in it of cowardice. It is the fear not of danger but of failure. Having lost his army, he is represented as "takynge greate thought and muche fearyng least he should be espied, and so trapped by kynge Richardes skoute watche". Even this is the natural anxiety of a man playing a great game, which a false move threatens to make him lose. But Legge's model demanded that the expression of feeling should be declamatory, that anxiety should be made terror, fear horror. Thus the anxious Richmond is reduced to the position of a coward; his limbs grow stiff with terror, he can scarce speak for fear. At the same time it must be said, as something of an offset to this, that such expressions were doubtless taken by neither author nor audience at their full value. They must have possessed to a certain degree a stamp of conventionality that prevented the ascription to Richmond of quite so deep a fear as the words themselves denote.

Legge's immediate model is indicated by the opening lines of the speech, which are an imitation of Herc. Furens 1138—9

> Quis hic locus, quae regio, quae mundi plaga?
> ubi sum?

Immediately following the speech of Richmond is a speech by Oxford, who welcomes the returning leader; and makes known the anxiety his soldiers have felt concerning their absent leader. According to the chronicle Richmond spent the night at "a very lytle village beynge aboute .III. myles from his armye", and "the next morenynge early in the dawnynge of the daye he retourned". Thus between the twe speeches a whole night has elapsed and the scene has been entirely changed, a fact sufficiently indicated by the speeches themselves. This treatment is distinctive of Legge's thoroughgoing disregard of the unities of time and place, a disregard which, of course, was almost wholly forced upon him by the extent of his material. It is of especial interest to observe the Elizabethan movement away from these, at least supposedly, Senecan canons not merely beginning, but carried to an extreme, within the University circle itself, and in a play whose whole method, so far as it is not determined by the material, is Senecan.

In reply to Oxford Richmond gives as excuse, "Solum juvat secreta saepe volvere". Here is a variance from the chronicle, where Richmond excuses himself "not to haue gone oute of hys waye by ignoraunce, but for a pollecie deuysed for the nones he went from his campe to receaue some glad message from certeyne of his preuy frendes and secret alies" (Hall p. 413). In the chronicle no mention is made of Oxford, whose speech represents the statement, "As he [Richmond] was not merye beynge absent from hys compaignie, lykewyse his armie much marueled and no lesse mourned for hys sodeyne and intempestious absence" (Hall, p. 413). The scene ends with the reception of Burchier and Hungerford, who assure the earl that Richard's troops are following him only through fear.

In the next scene Henry meets his step-father, Stanley. For purposes of comparison with Shakespeare and the **True Tragedy** I quote the scene entire.

Henri.
Nisi vota fallunt, vitricus venit meus,
domus suae Stanleius eximium decus.
verumne video corpus? an fallor tua
deceptus umbra? spiritus vires capit:
exultat animus, et vacat pectus metu.

Stanl.
Et nostra dulce membra recreat gaudium:
generum juvat videre: complexus mihi
redde expetitos. Sospitem qui te dedit,
det tua vicissim coepta perficiat deus;

Henri.
Dabit, tuo si liceat auxilio frui.

Stanl.
utinam liceret quae velim.

Henri.
Quidni potes?
quid non licebit.

Stanl.
saepe quod cupio tamen
non absque magno perfici potest damno.

Henr.
Quidnam times, dum patriam juvis tuam?
Stanl.
Quod vita chara filii fuit mei.
Henr.
Serat Richardus obsidem fidei tuae.
Stanl.
Ne te juvarem, pignori datum tenet.
Henr.
O suodolum scelus, ô tyrannum barbarum!
amore quos fidos parum credit sibi,
horum fidem crudelis exprimit metus.
Stanl.
Iram coerce, pectus et nobile doma
palam juvare si nequeo, furtim tamen
subsidia nunquam nostra deerunt tibi.
Henr.
Discescit: heu, me lenta vitrici fides
perturbat: hujus quanta spes fulsit mihi?
Frustra at quaerelis pectus uritur anxium,
vanisque juvat implere coelum quaestibus:
quin triste praecipitare consilium decet.

The chronicle account of this meeting is as follows. Richmond "prevely departed agayn from his host to the toune of Aderstone, where the lord Stanley and sir William his brother with their bandes were abidynge. There the Earle came first to his father inlawe in a lytle close, where he saluted hym and Sir William his brother, and after diuerse congratulacions and many frendely embracynges, eache reioysed of the state of other, and sodeinly were surprised with great ioye, comfort and hope of fortunate successe in all their affaires and doynges. Afterward they consulted together howe to geue battaile to kynge Richarde if he woulde abide, whome they knewe not to be farre of with an houge army" (Hall, p. 413, from Vergil). The first words of Henry in this scene are not to be taken as indicating that Legge intends to vary from the chronicle, and make Stanley come to Richmond — as in Shakespeare's play — instead of the reverse. "Vitricus venit meus" is entirely consistent with a meeting to which, as in the chronicle, both parties come from some distance and approach each other. "Came first to his father-in-law", in the chronicle account, means "met his father-in-law for the first time since the landing". Richmond's words of apparent surprise are no indication of an unexpected visit from Stanley, for they are only another case of Senecan imitation. Cf. the passage in the Hercules Furens where Amphitryon welcomes Hercules,

Herc. Fur. 618—625 Vtrumne visus vota decipiunt meos,
   an ille domitor orbis et Graium decus
   tristi silentem nubilo liquit domum?
   estne ille natus? membra laetitia stupent etc.

and cf. Oed. 203—4:
   adestne clarus sanguine ac factis Creo
   an aeger animus falsa pro veris videt?

Legge does, however, vary from the chronicle in the content of the conversation. In the chronicle account there is nothing said of Lord Strange or of the impossibility of Stanley's rendering open aid. The conversation is entirely joyful, and all have "great ioye, comfort and hope of fortunate successe". That the conference was at all unsatisfactory to Richmond is also contradicted by the surprise with which Richmond on the morning of the battle receives a refusal from Stanley, for whose troops he has sent. The entirely altered complexion of Legge's scene appears to be caused by the inclusion here of other passages in the chronicle. Thus the reference to Lord Strange comes from the passage describing the state of Richmond's mind as he loitered behind his troops: "he was not a lytle afeard because he in no wise could be assured of his father inlawe Thomas Lorde Stanley, whiche for feare of the distruction of the Lorde straunge his sonne (as you haue heard) as yet enclyned to neyther partie". Stanley's answer, with Richmond's depression, but determination nevertheless to push on his plans, appears to be adopted from the passage relating to the morning of the battle, when Richmond "sent to ẙ lord Stanley (which was now come wᵗ his bande in a place indifferently betwene both yͤ armies) requiryng him wᵗ his men to approche nere to his army & to help to set yͤ souldiours in array, he answered yᵗ therle should set his awne men in a good order of battaile while he would array his compaigny, & comme to him in time conuenient. Which answere made other wise then therle thought or would haue iudged, considering yͤ oportunite of the time & the waite of yͤ busines, & although he was there wᵗall, a litle vexed, began somewhat to hang yͤ hedde, yet he wᵗout any time delaiyng compelled by necessite, after this maner instructed & ordred his men" (Hall p. 414).

That the scene depends on these passages is made more certain by the fact that in Richmond's speech as he wanders in the night no mention is made of Stanley's fear for his son, and this would have to be mentioned somewhere; while the message to Stanley before the battle does not appear in the play. It is very unlikely that Legge with his scrupulous inclusion of nearly everything in the chronicle would have omitted this had it not been already included in effect.

From this scene we pass to the morning of the battle. Richard's troops are already under arms, and Norfolk stands awaiting his leader. Richard approaches, pale and disturbed. In response to a question from Norfolk he relates his dream.

>   Norfolciae charum caput, dux nobilis,
>   cujus fuit mihi semper illustris fides;
>   falso celabo nihil fronte perfidus.
>   Horrenda noctis visa terrent proximae.
>   Postquam sepulta nox quietem suaserat,
>   altusque teneris somnus obrepsit genis:
>   subito premebant dira furiarum cohors,
>   saevoque laceravit impetu corpus tremens,
>   et foeda rabidis praeda sum daemonibus:
>   somnosque tandem magnus excussit tremor,
>   et pulsat artus horridus nostros metus.
>   Heu! quid truces minantur umbrae Tartari?

The facts of the dream are in the chronicles (from Vergil, "improved" by the Hardyng continuator. cf. p. 172). For the introduction are used the same Senecan passages as for the queen's dream. The "terrible devils" of the chronicle are Senecanized into "diva Furiarum cohors", from Thy. 250. The conclusion is from Oct. 734—738:

> tandem quietem magnus excussit timor;
> quatit ossa et artus horridus nostros tremor
> pulsatque pectus; . . . .
> . . . .
> heu quid minantur inferum manes mihi.

Norfolk scoffs at dreams and urges Richard to arms.

> Jam strictus ensis optimum augurium canit.

Richard is at once himself.

> Nil pectus ullus verberat tremulum metus,
> ignava nec quassat tumultus corpora
> audere didicimus priùs: telis locos
> hostes vicinos jam premunt, bellum vocant:
> acies in armis nostra ex adversis stabit.

That Richard should relate his dream is in accordance with the chronicles, but there is no mention of cheer and encouragement from his friends. Norfolk plays the part of the Senecan confidant, as for example the nutrix who encourages Poppaea after her fearful dream. So too in Shakespeare's play Richard confesses to Ratcliffe that he has had a fearful dream — though he does not, cannot, relate it; confesses for the first time that he fears. As here from Norfolk he receives the answer

> Quid somnia tremis? noctes et vanas minas?
> quid falsa terrent mentis et ludibria?

so in Shakespeare he hears Ratcliffe say,

> Nay, good my lord, be not afraid of shadows.

What distinguishes the conception of Shakespeare's scene wholly from that of Legge's is the character of those shadows and of Richard's fear.

> Rich. By the apostle Paul, shadows to-night
> Have struck more terror to the soul of Richard
> Than can the substance of ten thousand soldiers,
> Armed in proof and led by shallow Richmond.

It is his own conscience, not Richmond, that the Shakesperean Richard fears. But Legge takes no account of the "punccion and pricke of his synfull conscience" which the chronicle saw in Richard's dream. Legge's Richard requires encouragement against his fear of defeat at the hands of Richmond.

Richard, restored to his courage, now leaves Norfolk to his reflections. These make it evident that he is not so sure of success as has appeared before the king.

> Quid agimus? hem quid caeca fata cogitant?
> quidnam parat suspecta civium fides?
> inventa nuper scripta me talia monent:
> NORFOLCIENSIS INCLYTE
> NIL COEPERIS AUDACIUS:
> NAM VENDITUS REX PRETIO
> RICHARDUS HEROS PERDITUR.
> At nulla nostram macula damnabit fidem:
> Richardi nunquam signa deseram.

This represents the passage added by Hall to Vergil's story. "Ihon Duke of Norfolke .. was warned by dyuers to refrayne from the felde, in so much that the nighte before he shoulde set forwarde towarde the kynge, one wrote on his gate.

> Iack of Norffolke be not to bolde
> For Dykon thy maister is boughte and solde.

Yet all this notwithstandynge he regarded more his othe honour and promyse made to king Richard, lyke a gentleman and a faythefull subiecte to his prince absented not him selfe from hys mayster, but as he faythefully lyued vnder hym, so he manfully dyed with hym to hys greate fame and lawde" (Hall p. 419).

Richard's oration to his troops is little more than an abridged translation of the speech in Hall. It is, for rhetorical purpose, made to end with

> Aut moriar hodie, aut parabo gloriam.

As Richard ends his speech a Nuntius enters making known the reply of Stanley that if Richard slays George Stanley he has more sons to take his place. With difficulty does Norfolk induce Richard to postpone the death of the young lord till after the battle. The facts of this scene are all from the account first added by Hall to Vergil's story (cf. p. 199—200).

Richmond's speech to his soldiers, like Richard's, follows in the main in condensed form the original in the chronicle. For the purpose of a parallel to Richard's speech Henry's is made to end with the words:

Aut perdat, aut peribit, hoc certum est mihi.

"Heare $\overset{e}{y}$ battell is joyned", says the marginal direction. The battle takes place off the stage, and its course is indicated by directions in English. Thus after Richmond's speech we read, "Uppon his retourne [i. e. his departure from the stage to the battlefield without], lett gunns goe of, and trumpetts sound, wth all stir of Souldiers wth out $\overset{e}{y}$ hall, untill such time as $\overset{e}{y}$ lord Stanly be one $\overset{e}{y}$ stage ready to speake". This corresponds to the chronicle's "When kynge Richard saw the earles compaignie was passed the marresse, he commaunded with al hast to sett vpon them, then the trompettes blew & the souldiours showted and the kyngs archers couragiously let fly there arrowes" (Hall p. 418).

Next Stanley appears, hurrying on his soldiers to the assistance of Richmond. This is based on the chronicle's statement: "The terrible shot ons passed, the armies ioyned, & came to hande strokes ... at whiche encounter the lord Stanley ioyned with therle" (Hall p. 418).

"Let heare bee the like noyse made as before, as soone as $\overset{e}{y}$ Lord Stanley hath spoken, who followeth the rest to the feild. After a little space, let the L. Northumberland come with his band from $\overset{e}{y}$ feild, att whose speach let the noyse cease". Northumberland's speech is as follows.

> Northumbriorum illustre nil damnes genus,
> nostramve lunam (miles) ignavam putes,
> quod tella fugiens hostium terga dedi
> Immane regis execror tandem scelus:
> horreo suorum sanguine ma(n)dentes manus.
> Suasit vetustas fatidica regi fore
> victoriam, manus prius si conferat
> Mutata quàm sit luna. Luna nos sumus:
> Mox ergo lunam (milites) mutavimus,
> tyrannus ut dignas scelere poenas luat.

For this the only basis in the chronicle is the statement that among those who submitted themselves to Richmond after the battle "was Henry the IIII. erle of Northumberlande, whiche wither it was by the commaundement of kyng Rycharde puttynge diffidence in him, or he dyd it for the loue & fauor that he bare vnto the Earle, stode still with a greate compaignie & intermitted not in the battail" (Hall p. 419). Northumberland's reference to himself as the moon is explained by the fact that the badge of the Percies is "a crescent argent, within the horns per pale, sanguine and gules charged with a double manacle fesser ways or". For the prophecy of the king's victory if he engaged in battle before the moon changed, a victory which the Northumbrian moon prevents by changing at once, I have not been able to find any source Even the statement of Northumberland's refusal to take part in the battle did not enter the historical account till Hall, who added it to Vergil's simple statement that the earl submitted and was received into favor (cf. p. 199).

Upon this speech follows, "Let hear be the like noyse as before, and after a while let a captain run after a souldier or two wth a sword drawne driveinge them againe to the feild, and say as followeth.

> Centurio
> Ignave miles, quo fugis? nisi redis meo
> peribis ense.

After the like noise againe, let souldiers run from ye feild, over the stage one after the another, flinginge of their harnesse, and att length let some come haltinge and wounded. After this let Henerye, Earle of Richmond come tryumphing, haveinge y̆ body of K. Richard dead on a horse: Catesby and Ratcliffe and others bound".

Now appears a Nuntius who with the introductory words

> Sedata lis est, Juditium Mavors tulit
> Jacet Richardus, at Duci similis jacet,

recounts the manner of Richard's death. All corresponds to the chronicle account down to the closing words

> O laude bellica inclytum verè ducem,
> Si saeva Gallus arma sensisset tua,
> vel perfidus fallens datam Scotus fidem.
> Sed sceleris ultor coelitum potens pater
> est sero vitam, sed satis ultus tuam.

These are Legge's equivalent for the passage with which Hall closes his account of Richard's life. "Yf he had continued still Protectoure and suffered his nephewes to haue lyued and reigned, no doubt but the realme had prospered and he muche praysed and beloued as he is nowe abhorred and vilipended. but to God whiche knewe his interior cogitacions at the hower of his deathe I remitte the punishment of his offences committed in his lyfe". Thus Hall opens up a view of future punishment for Richard in the next world: with Legge Richard's death is penalty enough, sero sed satis.

Upon the announcement of the Nuntius follows the prayer and speech of Henry, a curious compound of the Christian feeling of the chronicle, and the classical feeling of Seneca.

> Rector potens Oympi, et astrorum decus,
> terrestrium qui pastor et fidelium,
> et principum cujus est potestas cordium:
> tu laeta Regibus trophaea collocas:
> Nitida caput cingis corona regium,
> Solus deorum falsa vincis numina,
> hostesque generi affligis invidos suo:
> Ingens honor debetur et gratia tibi,

> qui splendidum triumphum indulseras.
> Cedit tuis armata jussibus cohors.
> Si straga quis saeviret Astyages ferox
> Phrygiove Pelops rege natus Tantalo.
> Expectet ille Cyrum, et ultorem tremat.
> Henricus audebat Richardum pellere.
> At tu nitentis ô gubernator poli
> Quem terra colit et vasta mundi fabrica,
> dum corpus aura vescitur, nec ultimum
> diem claudunt fati sorores invidae,
> teneros levis dum nutrit artus spiritus,
> te laude perpetua canemus, debitas
> tibi afferemus gratias, potens deus:
> Tu belluam meis domandam viribus
> mitis dabis, heu civibus pestem suis.
> At vos graves passi dolores milites,
> curate mox inflicta membris vulnera,
> crudele ne quo serpat ulcus longius.
> Reliqui sepulcra mortuis mites date.
> Et inferis debetur excellens honor.

Here not much corresponds to the original, which reads, "He kneled doune and rendred to almightie God his harty thankes w̐ deuoute & Godly orisons, besechyng his goodnes to sende hym grace to auaunce & defende the catholike fayth & to mayntaine iustice & concorde amongest his subiectes & people, by God now to his gouernaunce committed & assigned: Which praier finyshed, he replenyshed w̐ incomperable gladnes, ascended vp to the top of a littell mountaine, where he not only praysed & lawded his valiaunt souldiours, but also gaue vnto theim his harty thankes, w̐ promyse of condigne recompence for their fidelite & valiaunt factes, willing & commaundyng al the hurt & wounded persones to be cured, and the dead carcases to be deliuered to ẙ sepulture" (Hall, p. 420).

The Senecan influence is apparent throughout the speech, though no close imitation of any given passage is to be distinguished. "Rector potens Olympi, et astrorum decus, nitentis gubernator poli" are paralleled by Her. Fur. 205, 459, Med. 531 et al., while on the other hand the lines:

> terrestrium qui pastor es fidelium,
> et principis cujus est potestas cordium.

are entirely Christian. The punishment of Pelops is, of course, a favorite Senecan theme, but Astyages and Cyrus do not occur in the plays.

As Henry's speech ends, there appears Lord Strange, who has escaped as by a miracle from death at Richard's hands. With him he brings as prisoners certain men whom he delivers to Henry, only to have them returned to himself. Who these men are appears not from the scene but from the chronicle. "The Lorde was deliuered to the kepers of the kynges tentes to be kept as a prisoner, whyche when the felde was done and their master slayne and proclamacion made to knowe w(h)ere the childe was, they submitted them selfes as prysoners to the Lord Straunge, and he gently receyued them and brought them to the newe proclamed king, where of him and of his Father he was receyued with greate ioye and gladnes" (Hall, p. 420). The scene bears a strongly lyrical character through a speech of congratulation put in the mouth of Strange, and the play ends with the words of Henry,

> Regno mihique gratulor: regno, gravi
> quòd sit tyranno liberum: porro mihi,
> quod sceptra regni tracto regalia mei.
> Quare supremo regna qui dedit deo
> laudes canamus ore supplices pio.

A stage direction follows. "Let a noble man putt on $\overset{e}{y}$ Crowne upon kinge Henries head att the end of his oration (in accordance with the chronicle account in which Stanley crowns Richmond with Richard's crown, found on the field), and $\overset{e}{y}$ Song sunge wch is in $\overset{e}{y}$ end of the booke. After an Epilogue is to bee made, wherein lett bee declared the happy uniteinge of both houses, of whome the Queenes majestie came, and is undoubted heyre, wishing her a prosperous raigne". Which, after briefly recounting the events of the act, the following Epilogue does, tracing the descent of this union of York and Lancaster down to

> Elizabetham, patre dignam filiam
> canosque vencentem seniles virginem.
> Quae regna tot Phoebi phractis cursibus
> commissa rexit pace foelix Anglia,
> quam dextra supremi tonantis protegat
> illus et vitam tegendo protrahet.

Other Senecan Imitations.

Under this head I include such imitations as are not closely interwoven with the fabric of the play, and hence have not found a place in the foregoing analysis. They are chiefly dramatic formulae and conventionalities, but not without interest and meaning when compared with those used by the makers of Elizabethan English plays. Many examples of these have already been quoted. The numbers prefixed to quotations from the play refer to the pages and columns of Hazlitt's edition (Shak. Lib. II,1).

For the sake of completeness I have added a few further imitations that have not been included elsewhere. But in general I have refrained from entering upon the almost interminable task of noting those Senecan imitations which consist merely of short phrases, such as "caecum chaos, Venus furtiva, sitis regnandi etc.", a sufficient number of which have already been quoted to serve as examples. Legge's work is sown with these: classical and especially Senecan phraseology is adopted wherever possible. It would be of no value to note all possible examples, when once their character and extent has been recognized. Considerations of space compel me to confine these further comparisons usually to a single example of the classes in which they may be divided.

1. Indication of approaching persons.

    a) of major characters, e. g. of Richard:

    > 163,2 Sed ecce retrodux venit dubio gradu
    > quassans caput torvo supercilio furit.

Further 215,2. Cf. Oct. 436:

> Sed ecce gressu fertur attonito Nero
> trucique vultu.

and Tr. 999—1000

> Sed en citato Pyrrhus accurit gradu
> vultuque torvo

b) of minor characters, nuntius, servant, etc.

> 144,1 Quis huc minister advolat celeri pede
> Quo nunc adeo generose praecipitas gradu?
> 166,1 Sed hic gradum confert ad arma serviens
> Quid civibus clamare quaerit publice?

cf. Agam. 408

> Sed ecce, vasto concitus miles gradu
> manifesta properat signa laetitiae ferens.

and Phaed. 991

> Sed quid citato nuntius properat gradu
> rigatque maestis lugubrem vultum genis.

2. Addresses

a) to major characters, e. g. to Queen:

> 198,2 Regina servans conjugis casta fide
> lectum jugalem
> 205,2 o socia thalami regis olim, foemina
> illustris

cf. Her. Furens 309

> o socia nostri sanguinis, casta fide
> servans torum.

Such addresses are carried much farther in Ricardus Tertius than in Seneca. Naturally, there is often slight or no verbal resemblance; but the source of their manner is made sufficiently evident by the passages quoted above.

b) To Nuntius and other bearers of news.

> 156,2 ut gesta res est, quaeso paucis expedi.
> 202,1 hostis quibus captus dolis sit, explica.
> 203,2   Gesta quae sunt, explica.
> 208,2 Effare, carcerem cur evasit tetrum?

cf. Thy. 633
> effare et istud pande, quodcumque est malum

Also Herc. Oet. 1607, Tr. 1065—7, Thy. 639—40, and Herc. Oet. 748. Similar passages are Phaed. 996, Agam. 413, Oed. 212, 914, Thy. 626.

3. Expressions of horror and presentiment of evil.

> 142,1 nescio quid animus triste presagat malum
> horrent timore membra: cor pavet metu.

cf. Her. Fur. 1147—8

> paveo: nescio quod mihi
> nescio quod animus grande presagit malum.

Of this there are very many examples.

4. Encouragement to put away anxiety.

> 146,2 metus remitte, pone curas anxias
> . . . .
> Quicquamne gravis animos levat miseros dolor?

cf. Agam. 916

> pone iam trepidos metus.

Also Thy. 921, Phaed. 404, Her. Fur. 311, and Phaed. 435, 438.

5. Time indications — morning and night.

> 139,2 at ubi suum mundo diem reparat coma
> Radiante Tytan, et leves umbras fugat.

cf. Oct. 1—4

> Jam vaga caelo sidera fulgens
> Aurora fugat, surgit Titan
> radiante coma mundoque diem
> reddit clarum.

Also Phaed. 677—8

> tuque, sidereum caput,
> radiate Titan.

6. Sleep.

> 140,1 Jam laxat artus languidos gratus sopor
> Lectoque fessa membra componi juvat
> placidam quietem noctis opto proximae.

cf. Phaed. 100—1
>   non me quies nocturna, non altus sopor
>   solvere curis.

and Oct. 116—17
>   membra cum solvit quies
>   et fessa lumina oppressit sopor.

cf. also Her. Fur. 1065 et seq.

7. Oaths.

142,1
>   Polus tristi prius
>   jungetur orco, sydera natabunt aquis
>   amicus ignis fluctibus saevus erit
>   vincet diem nox: quam meam damnes fidem.

cf. Oct. 223—6
>   iungentur ante saeva sideribus freta
>   et ignis undae, Tartaro tristi polus
>   lux alma tenebris, roscidae nocti dies
>   quam —

8. Tyrannical and barbarous crime.

149,1 Nec ullus Isther audet Alanis feris
praebens fugam violare, nec rigens nive
tellus perenni hircana, vel sparsus Scytha.

cf. Thy. 627—32
>   Quaenam ista regio est? Argos et Sparte, pios
>   sortita fratres, et maris gemini premens
>   fauces Corinthi, an feris Hister fugam
>   praebens Alanis, an sub aeterna nive
>   Hyrcana Tellus an vagi passim Scythae?
>   Quis hic nefandi est conscius monstri locus?

9. Invocation of the Deity.

146,1 Rector potens Olympi, et altitonans pater
198,2 Te, te potens mundi arbiter supplex precor

cf. Herc. Fur. 205
>   O magnae Olympi rector et mundi arbiter
>   quisquis gubernas . .

Agam. 581—2
>   pater
>   altisona quatiens regna

Also Her. Oet. 530, Phaed. 1134, and Thy. 1077—8.

10. Miscellaneous Imitations.
>140,2 inani voce pulsantes Jovem
>200,1 stulte nimis votisque pulsando Jovem

cf. Herc. Oet. 1671
>superosque et ipsum vocibus pulsans Jovem.
>142,2 Quo me trahitis? Quam jubet poenam potens
>fortuna? Quae nunc me manent miserium malum?
>. . . . .
>Nam quae salutis spes reliquitur mihi?

cf. Oct. 899
>Quo me trahitis?

Oct. 893—5
>nunc ad poenam
>letumque trahi flentem miseram
>cernere possunt.

Oct. 906
>Sed iam spes est nulla salutis.

Of this class the name is legion.

The following illustrates Legge's desire to classicize wherever possible. For the general statement of Hall, p. 358, "The brother hath been the brother's bane" we have

>154,1 Romana fraterno madebant sanguine
>moenia.

The Character of Richard in Richardus Tertius.

Having followed Richard's course through the play, let us here sum up what that study has revealed concerning his nature. What has been the influence of Seneca upon the character of More's Richard? And how closely does the Richard that results from that influence resemble the Richard of Shakespeare?

The external events in dealing with which Legge's Richard reveals his character remain almost exactly the same as in the story of More and Vergil. His personal wooing of Elizabeth and the extended scenes with his counsellors are the only important variations which the desire to imitate Seneca was strong enough to introduce. The same situations and the same problems are met here as in More and Shakespeare. Any variation in Richard's character is therefore due to the author's conception, and not to variation in what Richard is called upon to face.

The ruling passion of More's Richard is also that of Legge's — ambition, the caeca libido regnandi. For here the historical and the Senecan models agree. Ambition is the main spring of all his action, the centre of his whole character. Accordingly, of all the deeds in Richard's former life which More and Vergil mention, and which in Henry VI play so important a part in revealing the fundamental traits in the youthful Richard from which the later Richard sprang, Legge thought it necessary to retain but one. Here, under the influence of a tradition later than More, he goes beyond his chronicle sources; Gloucester is not merely the secret urger of Clarence's death, he is Clarence's murderer. This one former deed is the mark and sign of Gloucester's ambition, the prophecy of all the bloody deeds to come. As in the Senecan tyrant, Richard's ambition for the crown is not merely his chief passion, but his only one. It is neither tempered nor intensified by any other characteristic. There is in him none of that "daemonic energy of will" which in Shakespeare's Richard must have an outlet, and finds it in ruling others of less intellect and power. There is not even in Legge's Richard any hatred of mankind caused by, or by him connected with, the misshapen form that marks him out from other men; for, curiously enough, in Legge's play there is not one word of Richard's deformity. His is the lust to rule, pure and simple, like that of Lycus and Eteocles, not born of hate of other man, nor born of conscious strength of mind.

For Legge's Richard is not a strong man. More's Richard is strong: strong in fertility of resource, strong in craft, strong in courage. In Shakespeare these qualities are raised almost to the sublime. Richard is not only the resourceful, he is the guide and director of every action; till his day comes, the absolute master of events. But Legge's Richard is conspicuously lacking in resource; he is dependent on his counsellors. He consults with them as the Senecan tyrant with his confidants, and is guided by their advice. They direct his moves and he follows. They suggest again and again what in More's story is Richard's own device. His one resource is the one resource of the Senecan tyrant — the sword; his cry is always "tollantur hostes ense". He knows of but one way to prevent the marriage of Richmond and Elizabeth, "finiet nuptias districtus ensis", "Regna tutatur cruor". If a crafty way is proposed by which Anna may be induced to die of sorrow, Richard's way is readier, "mactabo potius ense laethali". If Elizabeth refuses him he flies to his one argument, "Strictus nescit ensis unquam parcere". To Legge's Richard as to Seneca's Lycus, there is but one way of safety — "omnis in ferro salus".

The craft of More's Richard he does to a certain extent retain. The loud professions of loyalty that cover purposed treachery, the open friendliness that covers secret enmity, and to a slight degree the devising of pitfalls for his foes are to be found in Legge also. Yet this dissimulation is after all somewhat commonplace. More's description of Richard's deceit has a greater effect upon the reader than the instances of its practice. For when these are narrated the problem for deceit is stated only when it has been solved, problem and solution appear together. In the drama the problem appears before its solution, there is between the two the element of suspense, and there is the feeling of surprise and pleasure when the right solution is proposed. Further, narrated deceit lacks the personal element. But in the drama we have not merely craft facing a problem, we have a deceiver facing men. He see the influence of one man upon another, see the problem in process of solution in the conflict of two minds, perceive all the shades of feeling, all the touches of thought and phrase, by which the end is reached. And when the end is reached we admire not merely the ingenuity that solves the problem but the power also which conquers a man.

But Legge wholly fails to avail himself of the opportunity afforded by his dramatic art. It forces him to omit More's description of Richard's dissimulation, but he does not supply its loss. Many of the crafty schemes of More's Richard are by Legge ascribed to his helpers. Much of his deceit is narrated, and that which appears in dialogue lacks dramatic power because closely translated from More's narrative. In the only conflict of wits upon which Richard enters — the wooing scene — he is defeated. There is otherwise no pitting of mind against mind, no conflict in which Richard is victor. Of that devilish ingenuity with which in Shakespeare Richard molds every occasion to his purpose, of that masterly certainty with which every stroke of his superb mind always hits its mark, of that exquisite diplomacy through which his helpers are made to feel themselves the guides and masters of his fortune while he but follows, there is no trace in Legge. Legge's Richard has no sign of intellectual influence over those about him. He wins them because their plans and aims coincide with a part of his, or are served by his; he does not hold them by force or craft of mind.

Nor is Legge's Richard courageous. More's Richard and Shakespeare's knows no fear but that of conscience. Next to his superb intellect that which makes Shakespeare's Richard admirable in spite of his crimes is his unfaltering courage. But Legge's Richard throughout the play is terribly beset by fear. Before he attains the throne he is devoured with fear lest he shall not attain it, and requires the commonplace encouragement of his satellites "fortuna fortes adjuvat". Having obtained the throne he is devoured by fear lest he shall lose it.

> "torqueor metu miser
> disrumpor aestuante curarum salo",

is now his continual cry. Only on the field of Bosworth is Richard courageous, and here the author follows the universally known and accepted story.

The tide of emotions which Richard feels, he does not lock up in his own breast, but pours out for all to hear. Every change of situation, every loss or success brings a fervid declamation from his lips. This is the most striking contribution of Seneca to the character of Legge's Richard. All his torturing fears lest he may not win the crown, his sorrow at the death of his son, his rage at the rebellion of Buckingham, his dread of Richmond, his joy if fortune favors him by throwing Buckingham into his power or by checking for a moment Richmond's plans, his absolute despair when Richmond's star seems to be in the ascendant, all are revealed in a flow of Senecan declamation.

The man who is given to the loud and constant expression of feeling is not often the man of action. So it is with Legge's Richard. From the moment of his coronation to his appearance on the field of battle Richard makes not one step of his own motion to aid himself. Once or twice he gives directions to his helpers; Anna he murders and Elizabeth he woos, but in Legge both times acting upon the suggestion of others. Otherwise till the final scene he appears only as the man who sees his fate moving upon him and can find nothing better to do than stand and pour out his terror and despair. Shakespeare's Richard has no feelings to lay bare to the world, either of joy or of sorrow. When Buckingham revolts he lets fall no word to show that he is disturbed.

> "Come, I have learn'd that fearful commenting
> Is leaden servitor to dull delay.
> Delay leads impotent and snail pac'd beggary,
> Then fiery expedition be my wing".

When Legge's Richard hears the news he gives no sign of action: all his deeds are "fearful commenting". When

Richmond is repelled from the coast by a storm, there falls no word of emotion from the lips of Shakespeare's Richard; only

"March on, march on, since we are up in arms:
If not to fight with foreign enemies,
Yet to beat down these rebels here at home".

Legge's Richard thinks only of Richmond's escape from the hands of his soldiers, and responds with a wail at the fickleness of Fortune. Fortune rules him; he has no thought of the energy with which Shakespeare's Richard is determined to rule Fortune.

Not that Shakespeare's Richard does not feel. The news of Richmond's approach has power to more him so that he forgets the directions he would give, loses self-command, changes his mind. But the revelation that his nerve is shaken comes through the betrayal of his mind, not that of his will. He utters not a word of fear. That word one thing alone has the power to extort from him — his conscience. When this asserts dominion over him he cries at last, "I fear, I fear". But Legge's Richard, like the Senecan tyrant upon whom he is modelled, knows no conscience. And therewith he is raised out of the plane of the human and the real, into a sphere where he becomes merely the embodiment of an abstract passion — like the Lycus and the Eteocles who in becoming the heroes of the Senecan drama cease to be men.

Thus in Legge's play, as in Seneca, the ethical foundation on which every work of true art must be built does not exist. Richard receives no punishment adequate to his crimes. He has been king and dies like a king, fighting bravely, in the midst of his enemies. It is an end such as the real Richard might have wished for himself, had he been in truth the ruler of his fate. We know that there must be something more.

Part of that "something more" one may be inclined to find in the "boiling sea of cares" with which Legge's Richard is from the first beset. He has wished to reign and in attaining his wish has found his punishment. It is a great theme, and might have been furnished with a Senecan text, the prophecy of Jocasta over Eteocles (Phoen. 5,6):

" poenas et quidem solvet graves
regnabit: est haec poena".

But if Legge meant to read this lesson he gives no sign of it. Expressly he declares that Richard's punishment is in his death. By the corpse of Richard the nuntius who makes known the manner of his end declares

"Sceleris ultor coelitum potens pater
Est sero vitam sed satis ultus tuam".

Formal Imitation of Seneca.

Hitherto our comparison of Richardus Tertius with the plays of Seneca has been confined almost wholly to similarities of language. These, it has been shown, are mostly connected with similarities in the situations and in the thoughts furnished by the chronicle material. Only occasionally are the thoughts at bottom other than those of the chronicle, though so often clothed in Senecan garb. The chronicle material was accepted as a whole, and the Senecan imitation is in general rigidly confined to the limits allowed by it.

But this raw material was to be presented in the form of a drama, had to be shaped in an artistic mold; and here the play wright was in a wider sense the author of his product. How far did he adopt the Senecan mold? How much of the form, as well as the language, of the play is due to Seneca?

In answering this question I make use of the results of the study of Seneca's plays in Rudolf Fischer's "Zur Kunstentwicklung der englischen Tragödie".

Material — Theme — "Fable".

Since the raw material of the chronicle is adopted in practical entirety into the drama, remains unworked by the poet, a comparison under this head is really a comparison of the chronicle story with Seneca, and the content of material and "fable" in the play fall together. Legge's material was the history of the life and death of an English king — in place of Greek saga English history which had also — unknown to Legge — to a considerable degree become saga. In place of the mythic characters of a long-past heroic age Legge had characters who had lived less than a century before his play was produced.

His theme is the struggle of a tyrant to win a throne, and his unsuccessful defence of that throne once gained. The theme of the large majority of the Senecan plays is in essence "marriage, with its different complications and consequences". Thus the two themes seem to stand entirely apart. But in the development of the Senecan theme through various plays appears the figure of the tyrant. In the Octavia the chief figure is the Roman tyrant Nero, who drives from him his innocent wife that he may complete a criminal union, and who to fulfil his purpose is ready to undertake any crime against his nearest relatives and against his people. In the Thyestes appears the tyrant Atreus, who, in avenging himself upon his adulterous brother, slays his two young and innocent nephews. In the Hercules Furens the tyrant Lycus, who has by murder made his way to the throne, to establish himself there in security woos one whose relatives he has murdered. In the Phoenissae the tyrant Eteocles is eager to win the throne at any cost to those bound to him by the closest ties. All these situations are reproduced in the life of Richard as given in the chronicles. In Seneca the tyranny with its ambition to rule, its cares and fears, its successes and falls, is not indeed the main theme; but it is there, powerful and strong, occupying a large portion of the action. Thus the theme of Richardus Tertius corresponds to a subordinate theme of four Senecan plays — the career of a tyrant.

For the "fable" of the drama itself, Seneca adopts

only the last phase of the "material-fable"; each play begins shortly before the final moment of the total action, or is confined to an action which is short and simple. Legge's play, on the contrary, is a chronicle-history, and covers the whole career of the tyrant from the inception of his purpose, to its expiation by death. Herein he abandons the classical unities, and presents a play which springing from the desire of classical imitation, and clothed in classical dress, is nevertheless in essence romantic.

In the character of the scenes, therefore, a wide difference from Seneca is to be expected. As in Seneca the drama is limited in general to one short period of time and to one place, precedent events and events happening elsewhere must appear in epic form. Again, in Seneca the want of action entails that many of the scenes instead of producing events, either external or within the souls of the characters, must be given up to the expression of feeling caused by what has preceded or by what is expected to follow; and as this feeling is fixed and unchanged these scenes must be wholly lyrical. In Legge's play, however, with its enomous extent, we should expect a far larger proportion of dramatic scenes. But there is a further consideration. The very extent of Legge's material forced him to reproduce most of it in epic form, and hence the presence of a large proportion of epic scenes is no proof of a special Senecan influence. That can be established only of the content and manner of these scenes. The lyrical element, on the other hand, being unnecessary to the action was almost wholly within the power of the playwright. If a large proportion of such scenes is found Senecan influence in this may be concluded.

A comparison between Legge and Seneca in regard to the proportions of these scenes is, however, a matter of much difficulty. In the first place, the establishment of the scenic divisions in Legge's play is not wholly easy.

The scenes are not numbered, but are generally indicated by printing the names of the characters engaged in each in capitals at the head. Often not all the names appear, but the divisions are usually trustworthy. Some changes, however, are necessary. Thus on p. 180 Actio 2, Actus 4, a new scene (2) must be assigned to Gloucester. On p. 203, the same must be done for Buckingham's speech, 3 : 3 : 4. On p. 205, though we have **Richardus Rex Solus** in capitals at the head, the speech as clearly belongs to the preceding, with which I include it, as does Norfolk's speech on p. 216, where Dux Norf. is not capitalized. On p. 205 we have as scene-heading **Lovell: Regina Elizab. Rex Richardus**. But Richard does not appear in the conversation between Lovell and the queen, which takes place in the sanctuary. On p. 207 he welcomes his two nieces into his palace, to which they have been sent. It seems on the whole best to indicate a new scene, 3 : 4 : 3. On p. 218 I have assigned separate scenes to the Centurio, 3 : 5 : 11, and to the Nuntius and Henry. The scenic divisions in general, while not so limited as those of Seneca, are often more limited than those of a Shakesperian play.

Further, a difficulty arises from the fact that Legge's scenes are often of a more mixed nature than those of Seneca. For example, in Seneca the relating of news by a nuntius is regularly assigned a scene by itself, whereas in Legge such a message is more than once followed by an expression of sorrow or joy, in extent equal to or greater than the message itself. Or the news may be followed by a dramatic half-scene. Such scenes I have had therefore to count twice in the following tables. Nor is it quite always possible to determine to one's own satisfaction whether a scene is chiefly epic or lyric. Absolute exactness in separating the different elements by scenes is therefore not practicable; but it is general proportions that we are seeking, and to this extent the tables given below are trustwortly.

Epic Scenes.

In a total of 58 scenes there are 25 cases distributed in 21 scenes where, with one exception, a large part, and usually the predominating part of each scene is taken up by the giving of news. Of the scenes 2 are chiefly lyric, 2 chiefly dramatic, 1 is half dramatic, and 2 half lyric. In 11 cases the news-giver appears as "nuntius"; in 15, the news-givers have parts in the play. Of these, 4 have entirely minor parts — civis (2), servus (1), Ancilla (1); 10 major parts — Richard (2), Q. Eliz., Buck., Arch. Ebor., Hastings, Catesby, Ludovic, Dighton, Tirell, 1 each. Of the 15, Ancilla, Civis (1), Catesby, and Tirell may be said to correspond to the confidants in Seneca.

The Senecan proportions are: cases 19; nuntius 7 + 2 (nuntius named) = 9; confidants 8; other major figures 2. The Senecan plays cover (not considering the fragmentary Phoenissae) a little over 11,000 lines; Legge's play circa 4650. Thus the number of cases is proportionally to the number of lines far greater than that in Seneca, but for this Legge's material is responsible. Within the number of cases we have the following proportions.

	Legge	Seneca
Nuntius	11 : 25	9 : 19
Confidants	4 : 25	8 : 19
Other major figures	10 : 25	2 : 19

Thus Legge makes use of the nuntius nearly as often proportionately as Seneca, but on the other hand assigns proportionately nearly four times as often the role of newsgiver to his chief characters.

In the 25 cases all but one deal with events that happen during the course of the play. Hence, as in Seneca, it is natural that the majority should be found in the last actio. The cases are thus distributed: Actio I, 7; Actio II, 2; Actio III, 16.

The handling of these scenes shows a great constrast to Seneca. In Seneca they are generally monologues addressed directly to the public or the chorus. In Legge the news is regularly delivered to one of the characters of the play, by the nuntius usually to Richard. Only 6 times is news delivered in a soliloquy (including the news of Richard's death, and of the proposed treatment of Stanley and his wife, a case which I have here considered as epic, though it may be dramatic).

In nature of content and in manner the scenes approach more closely those of Seneca. As in Seneca they give news of events which it is impossible to present dramatically upon the stage, or they describe events which the author's feeling prevents him from wishing to put upon the stage. To the latter class belong the descriptions of the way in which characters lose their lives, a class of which Seneca's plays offer so many examples. To their influence is to be assigned Legge's refusal to produce on the stage the deaths of Hastings, of the princes, of Anna and of Richard himself; and equally to their influence are to be assigned the descriptions of the deaths of Hastings and Anne, for which there is no suggestion in the chronicles.

In this connection it may be noted that in these epical scenes of Legge there is, with the exception of the first scene, in which the queen gives information of events precedent to the play, nothing which Shakespeare chose to put upon the stage, save the scene between Richard and Stanley, which may, as has been seen, be dramatic in Legge also. Much of Legge's minor information is omitted entirely by Shakespeare, as unnecessary; while the deaths of the princes, of Anna, and of Richard, he likewise relates. On the other hand, bits of news which in Legge are too insignificant even to give an epic nature to the scenes in which they appear are sometimes produced dramatically by Shakespeare, notably and distinctively in the case of Richard's dream. So too the long conferences over the proposed procuring of the Duke of York, and the speech of Buckingham to the citizens, dramatic in Legge, appear epically in Shakespeare, while the cardinal's conference with the queen, and Buckingham's with Ely fall away entirely.

In manner Legge's epic scenes are Senecan so far as the nature of the news they give will allow, and naturally most completely so when their content was not furnished by the chronicle, as in the description of Hastings' and of Anna's death. Like the Senecan messages they are sustained and declamatory, rarely interrupted but often introduced by a short question or urgent direction (cf. p. 372). As in Seneca, the case is a rare exception in which there is a dialogue of interchanging question and answer, as in the first scene of the play.

They are Senecan further in that they seldom become the impulse to action. In 4 cases only of the 25 do they lead to a decision; in Seneca in 2 out of 19. Their regular consequence is, as in Seneca, not action but the expression of feeling, usually sorrow, rarely joy.

A chief difference from the Senecan messages consists in the fact that Legge's rarely exceed 25 lines and are generally under this. In Seneca they are short (up to 20 lines) in but three cases; of medium length (up to 100 lines) in 9; and long (up to 200 lines) in 7. Here again the chronicle is responsible. In the epic as in the dramatic portions of his work Legge generally confines himself to his authority, rarely extending or embellishing what it furnished. Thus while in Seneca one fifth of the total length of the nine plays exclusive of the Chorus is occupied by epic scenes, of Legge's play only about one ninth is epic.

Lyrical Scenes.

Under this head are to be placed, as in Fischer's study of Seneca, all scenes which, in spite of their often naturally epic or dramatic introduction or conclusion, have for their chief object the expression of feeling, whether for the purpose of characterizing the speaker, or for the purpose of moving the listener.

In the 58 scenes of the play there are 17 scenes or important parts of scenes in which the expression of feeling is the sole or most important content. As emotion follows naturally upon news received, or is caused by presentiment of news to be received it is natural that in 8 cases the scenes, according to the often non-Senecan scenic division of the play, should have also been noted as epic. In two cases the preceding part of the scene is dramatic. The scenes are thus distributed: — Actio I, 5; Actio II, 1; Actio III, 11.

This distribution corresponds in general to that of the Senecan plays, where beginning and end are much more strongly lyric than the middle parts, "an indication of especially emotional opening and close of the plays". In total amount the lyrical portions cover about one-fifth of the play, far less than Seneca's one-third. Yet though the proportion is smaller, when we consider that for comparatively few of these scenes is there warrant or suggestion in the chronicle, and that they show constant verbal imitation of the Senecan plays, with but one or two exceptions more extended by far than that in the epic and dramatic scenes, the conclusion is unavoidable, that the lyric scenes of the play are generally due to Senecan influence.

Dramatic Scenes.

In the total of 58 scenes there remain 34 which can be characterized as predominantly or largely dramatic, a little more than half. In total amount, however, the dramatic passages cover a little more than two-thirds, very considerably more than Seneca's less than one-half. This corresponds with what was to be expected from the nature of Legge's material. To this amount the long conferences and speechs transferred in their full length from chronicle to play materially contributed.

Of the scenes 8 are monologues, including 5 adresses to soldiers,
    8 are dialogues,
   10 are conferences of 3 persons,
   8 „   „   „ more than 3 persons.

Proportions.

	Seneca			Legge		
Mon.	8 : 46 =	circa	1 : 6	8 : 34 =	circa	1 : 4
Dial.	28 : 46 =	„	3 : 5	10 : 34 =	„	3 : 10
3 Pers.	10 : 46 =	„	1 : 5	8 : 34 =	„	1 : 4

Thus the dramatic monologue is one and one-half times as frequent as in Seneca, for which excess the addresses to soldiers are responsible; the dialogue is half as frequent; scenes with three speakers a little more frequent. Scenes with more than three speakers the Senecan drama like the Greek did not of course allow. Here Legge's arrangement was largely conditioned by his material. Too many persons by far play a part in the story as given by the chronicles for Legge to avoid the occasional use of such scenes. They had either to be related by a nuntius or placed on the stage.

The arrangement of the dramatic scenes in the play is as follows.

```
Actio I    Act. 1—0 dramatic scenes
                2—2
                3—2
                4—2
                5—5

Actio II   Act. 1—2
                2—1
                3—2
                4—1
                5—0

Actio III  Act. 1—0
                2—3
                3—0
                4—4
                5—10
```

In Actios I and II the beginning is undramatic, the close strongly dramatic, which corresponds generally to the Senecan arrangement, in which the beginning is almost wholly undramatic, the close usually dramatic, though sometimes quiet. This, when the character of the opening scenes is considered (cf. the analysis of the play), is certainly to be ascribed to Senecan influence.

Otherwise in the division of the dramatic scenes no special Senecan influence can be established.

Such influence in the dramatic scenes is, however, apparent in the frequent use of stichomythia, of which there are six cases in the play. Like Seneca Legge does not confine himself to balancing single lines, but balances half-lines as well.

The Chorus.

The Chorus, as such, is lacking in Legge. Yet we find a chorus at the end of Actio I singing in the processions before Shore's wife a song in reprobation of lust, which reminds one of the chorus in Phaedra 958—88; a song occurs in the "Show of the Procession" following Actio 2; and at the close of Actio 3 "ye song" is "sunge wch is in ye end of the booke". The position of these songs corresponds to that of the Senecan chorus which intervened between the acts, and in the Hercules Oetaeus and the Octavia brought the play to its conclusion. The didactic element of the Senecan chorus appears often in the body of the play.

Construction.
Organization of the Material.

The play is unique in that it is divided not only into Acts and Scenes, but into three Actios or parts. These, as indicated by the title of the University Ms., were presented on three several evenings. They may be compared to the three parts of Henry VI, but the comparison is only external. In the latter case each of the parts forms a play by itself, with the complete organization of a play; the parts of Richardus Tertius are in no sense plays by themselves, and are independent only in so far as the conclusion of each marks an important step in Richard's career; 1, the removal of Hastings (and even here it is the entirely subordinate punishment of Shore's wife that fills the eye at the very last); 2, the attainment of the throne; and 3, the death of Richard. This division into Actios is therefore wholly accidental, adopted to fit external circumstances. As the actios have no play organization their division into Acts and scenes is also largely external and inorganic; and they afford no basis of comparison with Seneca. Such a comparison can only be a very general one. Legge's arrangement is, with the changes I have before indicated.

Actio I, Act. 1 — 1 sc.
        „ 2 — 3 „
        „ 3 — 3 „
        „ 4 — 3 „
        „ 5 — 7 „
        17 scenes.

Actio II, Act. 1 — 2 sc.
        „ 2 — 2 „
        „ 3 — 2 „
        „ 4 — 2 „
        „ 5 — 1 „
        9 scenes.

Actio III, Act. 1 — 3 sc.
        „ 2 — 5 „
        „ 3 — 4 „
        „ 4 — 7 „
        „ 5 —13 „
        32 scenes.

Thus a rather lively beginning is followed by a comparatively quiet middle actio, and an extremely lively conclusion. In each of the first and last actios the movement increases in force, so far as number of scenes is concerned, till the end, and this agrees with the character of the scenes, the dramatic scenes, as has been shown, increasing likewise toward the end. In Seneca Acts 1 and 4 are quiet, 2 and 3 moderately lively, 5 sometimes quiet and sometimes lively. There is therefore little similarity in Act and Scene organization between Seneca and Legge, a fact in large measure caused by the course of the latter's material.

In arrangement of scenes according to the number of speakers Seneca's plays show

    Monologues $40:104 =$ ca. $4:10$
    Dialogues $51:104 =$ „ $5:10$
    Three speakers $13:104 =$ „ $1:10$

Legge's play has

Monologues	13:58 =	a little more than	1:5	
Dialogues	21:58 =		3:8	
Three speakers	14:58 =	„ „ „	1:4	= 5:12
More than 3 speakers	10:58 =	„ „ „	1:6	

Thus in Legge the monologue is little more than half as frequent as in Seneca, the dialogues three-fourths as frequent, the scenes with three speakers or more four times as frequent. This again corresponds with what was to be expected from the more dramatic nature of Legge's material. The comparison is an imperfect one, owing to the fact that Legge's scenes are often more complicated than those of Seneca, and would not infrequently, if arranged in Senecan fashion, be divided once or even twice. A strictly Senecan division would increase the number of monologue scenes by at least three.

Here a formal comparison of Richardus Tertius with Seneca must end. In the construction of the play the arrangement of the figures, their distribution through the play, is conditioned by the material. Such too, on the side of composition, is the case in the arrangement of the action. How far Senecan imitation is to be seen in the characters has been considered in the analysis of the play.

If now we summarize our answer to the question How much of the form of Legge's play is due to Seneca? we have the following result.

The main character of the play upon its formal side is not Senecan. It makes the widest departure from the unities of place and time, adopts a fable covering a long period and full of dramatic action — is essentially non-classical. Accordingly, the dramatic scenes of the play occupy two-thirds of its content, where Seneca's dramatic scenes cover but one-half. The epic and lyric scenes are correspondingly limited. So also scenes with more than two speakers are far more frequent than in Seneca, monologues and scenes with two speakers less frequent.

Certain minor particulars of the form are, however, due to Seneca: in the epic scenes, relation of deaths in place of their dramatic presentation, the presence of two of these relations, in general the manner of the epic scenes, the frequent appearance of the "nuntius"; generally, the presence of the lyric scenes, and their manner; the lack of dramatic scenes at the beginning of the play and of Actio III; quite possibly the presence of the songs at the end of each act. To this may be added the fact that the metre is, naturally, the same as Seneca's — the iambic tetrameter.

Other similarities, like the notable resemblance of Legge's theme to a subordinate but prominent theme of Seneca, are not due to imitation.

Legge's imitation of Seneca is therefore predominantly verbal, not formal.

The Relation of Legge's Richardus Tertius to Shakespeare's Richard III.

It is not easy to see how Shakespeare should have been acquainted with the work of Legge, and comparison of the two plays affords no evidence for the supposition. Common variations from the common source are very few, and in nearly all cases of too slight a nature to give rise to the suspicion that Shakespeare borrowed from Legge. An example of this kind is the fact that in both plays it is Norfolk who interferes to procure the postponing of Strange's execution till after the battle. Norfolk's "After the battle let George Stanley die" sounds very like Norfolk's "Post bella gnatus patris expiet scelus". But the verbal resemblances of the scene are sufficiently accounted for by the passage in the chronicle, and the substitution of Norfolk's name for "the counsaillers of kyng Richard" of the chronicle, may, in the absence of other similar instances, be set down to chance.

The case is different with the scene in which Richmond meets his step-father, Stanley. Here occurs a common variation from the chronicle in Stanley's statement that he cannot help Richmond as he would, in the mention of Lord Strange's predicament, and in the troubled thought's of Richmond caused by his father's words. But Legge's scene is much more closely imitated by The True Tragedy, and it is likely that the latter, rather than Legge immediately, is responsible for the passage in Shakespeare. The same is true of Richmond's speech on entering England — if any other source than a sense of dramatic fitness is necessary to account for such a speech. There is a certain resemblance between Legge's

> "o chara salve terra, sed salve diu
> frendentis apri dente lacerata impio"

and Shakespeare's

> "The wretched, bloody, and usurping boar,
> That spoil'd your summer fields and fruitful vines",

for which The True Tragedy passage, where "the boar" is not mentioned, will not account. On this, however, one cannot build much.

Perhaps the strongest resemblance not accounted for by the chronicle is that between the wooing scenes with Anne and with Queen Elizabeth in Shakespeare, and the scene with the princess Elizabeth in Legge. For the Shakespeare scene with Anne there is not, it is well known, the slightest chronicle foundation. Quite as remarkable as the conception of this scene is the tone of the scene between Richard and Elizabeth. Many lines are, as has often been pointed out, strongly Senecan in character. Notably alike in both plays is the plea with which Richard answers the charge of murdering his nephews; in Legge, "sic fatis placet", in Shakespeare. "All unavoided is the doom of destiny". Notable too is is the frequent use of Senecan stichomythia.

Yet here again, with so little to corroborate, there is not enough to warrant the assertion of Legge's influence. One can only venture the suggestion that if, as many critics think, Shakespeare's play is a revision of an anterior play, especially if, as Mr. Fleay feels sure, this anterior play was Marlowe's, it may have been subject to Legge's influence, and so account for the presence in Shakespeare's play of some of the resemblances here noted. It is difficult to compare the wooing scenes and not cherish a suspicion that such was the case.

IV. Lacey's Richardus Tertius.

The existence among the Mss. in the British Museum of another play bearing the same title as Legge's has long been known. Nobody seemed, however, to have given the piece more than the hastiest examination, and it was designated by Farmer "a childish imitation" of Legge's play. It was mentioned in Field's introduction to Legge's Richardus Tertius (Shak. Soc. Pub. 1844) on the authority of Halliwell as "a poor imitation", and it appeared under the same designation in Halliwell's Dictionary of Plays, 1860. It is, in fact, nothing less than a transcript of Legge's play, made, as appears from Ms. Harl. 6926, by Henry Lacey in 1856, for presentation at Trinity College, Cambridge. A second Ms. is Harl. 2412. The establishment of this fact was due to the authors of the Athenae Cantabrigienses, 1861. cf. vol 2, p. 41.

V. The "Tragical Report of King Richard the Third".

August 15, 1586 was entered in the Stationer's Register "A tragical Report of King Richard the Third, a Ballad. This is not extant, and nothing further is known of it. Streevens seems to have thought that it may have been a play, as he says, "It may be necessary to remark that the words, song, ballad, enterlude and play were synonymously used" (quoted in Boswell's Malone, vol. 21, p. 19);

but there is absolutely no ground for the assumption. Mr. Fleay once thought that the ballad was called forth by the production of The True Tragedy, but this opinion he abandoned later.

VI. The True Tragedy of Richard the Third.

Attention appears first to have been called to this play when Steevens in his notes to Shakespeare's Richard III quoted the following entry from the Stationers' Register under date of June 19, 1594, for Thomas Creede: "An enterlude, intitled the tragedie of Richard the Third, wherein is shown the deathe of Edward the Fourthe, with the smotheringe of the two princes in the Tower, with the lamentable ende of Shore's wife, and the contention oft he two houses of Lancaster and Yorke". That the play here mentioned was in existence was unknown to the general public until Boswell in his edition of Malone's Shakespeare, 1821, printed a large portion of it from a copy wanting the commencement. Commenting upon it, he stated that he thought it "unnecessary to point out the particular passages in which a resemblance can be traced" between the True Tragedy and Shakespeare's play, but thought that the reader "would be satisfied that Shakspeare must have seen it when he sat down to the composition of his own play". Elsewhere he says "it appears evidently to have been read and used by Shakspeare". The authorship Boswell was inclined to ascribe to the author of Locrine, on the strength of the resemblance of Richard's soliloquy on revenge to two passages in that play.

Augustine Skottowe, in his Life of Shakespeare, 1824, I, 266—7, found some resemblances between this play and Shakespeare's. The passages are noted later. From these he concluded that Shakespeare "grafted on his own view of the subject such hints as he conceived conducive to its improvement".

Collier, in his edition of Skakespeare, 1844—1853, 5, 342 and foll., commented upon the play at some length, transcribing from a perfect copy in the possession of the Duke of Devonshire, the following title-page, and calling attention to its correspondence with the entry in the Stationers' Register: "The True Tragedie of Richard the Third: Wherein is showne the death of Edward the fourth, with, the smothering of the two yoong Princes in the Tower: With a lamentable ende of Shores wife, an example for all wicked women. And lastly the coniunction and ioyning of the two noble Houses, Lancaster and Yorke. As it was playd by the Queenes Maiesties Players. London Printed by Thomas Creede, and are to be solde by William Barley, at his shop in Newgate Market, neare Christ doore. 1594. 4°".

Collier then considered the peculiarities of the play, calling particular notice to the Induction and conclusion, as well as the style in which it is composed. As he found no allusion to the Spanish Armada in the Epilogue, while other public events of less prominence are touched upon, he thought that "we may perhaps infer that the drama was written before the year 1588". Elsewhere he says, "It is perhaps the most ancient printed specimen of composition for a public theatre, of which the subject was derived from English history".

Boswell's belief that Shakespeare had used the play was rejected by Collier, who declared that "we cannot trace any resemblances, but such as were probably purely accidental, and are merely trivial". He found the nearest approach of the two plays to each other to be "just before the murder of the princes, where Richard strangely takes a page into his confidence respecting the fittest agent for the purpose".

In 1844 the play was edited by Barron Field for the old Shakespeare Society. In his introduction he agreed with Boswell that Shakespeare must have seen "this humble work of his predecessor". Besides pointing out

in his notes "several parallel ideas", he considered that the line
"King. A horse, a horse, a fresh horse",
was sufficient proof that Shakespeare considered Nature as his property and that he had a right to seize it wherever he found it. The page episode, which Collier had found strange, and the nearest approach of the two plays, can hardly be called strange, remarked Field, as it is found in More's story.

The True Tragedy was reprinted with Field's introduction by Hazlitt in Part II vol. 1 of his edition of Shakespeare's Library, 1875. All references in the following study are to this edition.

Historical position, nature, and style of the play.

Scarcely less interest attaches to the position of The True Tragedy in the development of the English historical drama than to that of Legge's Richardus Tertius. We can no longer hold of it with Collier that we have in it "perhaps the most ancient printed specimen" of an English history-play, nor with Fleay in his earliest opinion, that it was "the first chronicle history in its full sense". It will be shown later that it was clearly preceded by several others, including the three parts of Henry VI. But as Legge's play was of a mixed type, a presentation of the form and material of a chronicle-history in the artistic garb of the Senecan play, so The True Tragedy is of a mixed type, unique in the union which it presents of the English chronicle-history and the tragedy of revenge.

As a history-play The True Tragedy is undoubtedly the first in which the interest is fixed upon one central and dominating figure. It is not the first to abandon the loose and unorganized method of writing chronicle-histories which spread out the events of a period in their historical succession without attempt at unity; for in the Edward II of Marlowe these plays had already advanced to a point where the historical events are not detailed purely for their own sake, but are unified by their relation to a central figure, and where the history-play becomes in a high degree a study of character. But the figure of Edward, though central, is not dominating, and secondary figures like those of Isabel and Mortimer attract a good share of the interest to themselves. The Richard of The True Tragedy is not only central but dominating, not merely attracts the chief interest but absorbs practically all of it. The play is not the chronicle-history of a reign, it is purely the history of a character.

This was the result of two influences. The chronicle story, the historical source of the play, offered many inducements to such a treatment. Richard as he there appears is always the central figure, and his personal career, mental as well as external, is the main theme of the work. But this could not alone suffice to produce a character-play like The True Tragedy. The effect of a faithful following of More's story, without discrimination and without selection, is shown in Legge's play. There Richard's story is treated in the first manner of the chronicle-histories, and in the multitude of events related at length the influence and dominating position of the central character is largely lost. But The True Tragedy shows such a selection of scenes and such a subordination of details that the figure of Richard is always before the actual or the mental eye. Everything — excepting the secondary story of Shore's wife — is subservient to the purpose of portraying this one character.

This treatment could only be the result of such a conception of Richard as led to the desire to make the story, not of his acts and fate, but of his inner nature, the chief interest of the play; and for this conception More's work did not furnish the sole suggestion. Since the appearance of Tamburlaine and Faustus Marlowe had been the master of the stage and the teacher of playwrights. The success of these plays was due to the genius with which he had riveted attention and interest upon one figure, the gigantic force of whose character, or the terrible struggle of whose soul, formed the single object of the play. Imitation of Tamburlaine was the more natural to the author of The True Tragedy because of the many traits in which the historic Richard resembled Tamburlaine, and because Marlowe's play, though mostly imaginary, was also a history-play. Imitation of Faustus was the more natural because of More's and Vergil's description of the struggle in Richard's soul. What the effect of this imitation of Tamburlaine and Faustus was upon the figure of Richard I show elsewhere; here it is sufficient to say that the influence is great enough to show that to it is largely due the shaping of The True Tragedy as a study of character.

That the author stood in the full current of all that was popular upon the stage is shown by the fact that The True Tragedy is not only a history-play, but a play of revenge. How many such plays, and what, had preceded, it is impossible to determine, but the genus had certainly for some time been well established. The Misfortunes of Arthur, The Spanish Tragedy and Locrine at least had gone before; and The Battle of Alcazar and James IV, if they did not precede it, must have appeared at about the same time.

The revenge tragedy in England derived its origin, as plays like The Misfortunes of Arthur show, from those plays of Seneca which have for their subject the terrible history of the house of Pelops — the Thyestes and the Agamemnon. Here from father to son passes the spirit of revenge, the crime that punishes crime ever meeting punishment in turn. As inspiring agents in this horrid course of sin appear the ghosts of the dead, Tantalus in the Thyestes, Thyestes in the Agamemnon. When the Senecan theme of revenge entered the Elizabethan drama the Senecan machinery entered with it: the ghost is inseparable from the revenge-play. With this went, too, the Senecan descriptions of the torments suffered by the victims, the wheel of Ixion, the stone of Sisyphus, the flames of Tartarus, all the pangs of the classical Hades.

But with all this adoption of theme and machinery, the tragedy of revenge underwent in England a certain simplification and gained in directness. In the Senecan plays the ghosts of the dead inspire madness in their descendants; Tantalus is forced by the fury to stir up crime in his grandchildren, Thyestes seeks revenge not upon his brother but upon his brother's son, Agamemnon. In the English play the ghost regularly calls for revenge upon the one who has committed the crime against him, and that revenge as regularly follows. The cry for revenge has become adapted to the natural English thought that he who commits the crime is the one who deserves to suffer punishment: his children are innocent of their father's sin. Not that the punishment of the father in his offspring does not appear at all in the English plays. It appears, for example, in one of the first, if not the first, The Misfortunes of Arthur, which stands most directly under Senecan influence; and it appears in Shakespeare's York-Lancaster tetralogy, where the princes suffer for the crime of their father Edward. Yet here the thought that the father is punished through his children, not that the children are punished in his stead, is uppermost. In general, the Greek doctrine of a Nemesis that endures from generation to generation has been supplanted by the English doctrine of righteous retribution upon the really guilty.

Another characteristic of the English revenge-play is that the ghosts have a more important part than in the Senecan play. Often they appear at the end of the play to exult over the attainment of their revenge, as does the ghost of Gorlois in The Misfortunes of Arthur. Sometimes they watch the course of the play, as the ghost of Corineus in Locrine, or of Andrea in The Spanish Tragedy, who converses with Revenge between the acts and thus serves "for Chorus in this Tragedy". Sometimes the ghost is of one murdered before the play begins, sometimes of one murdered in the course of the play. Sometimes the ghost appears to the guilty one, oftener to the agent of revenge. In all these variations the general rule holds true that the ghost of the English revenge-play has a far more important part than in the Senecan play, and its appearance during the course of the action is nearly always frequent.

Such are the most striking characteristics of the revenge plays which exercised an influence upon The True Tragedy. How do they there appear?

That the motive of revenge should have been introduced in a chronicle-history play need excite no surprise. It had already been used in two history-plays, The Misfortunes of Arthur and Locrine, whose subjects were taken from the mythical history of England, found together with the actual in the chronicles. Thence to its application in a play taken from actual English history was but a short step. Yet there seems always to have been a feeling that the machinery of ghosts belonged naturally to a world remote in time or space from the immediate English world, and was best employed therefore in plays whose action was laid in a far-past romantic time, or in a foreign land. The True Tragedy and Shakespeare's Richard III remained the only chronicle-history plays from actual English history that employed any of the motives of the revenge plays. And here, it will be seen, these motives were subjected to a special treatment calculated to render them better adapted to the nature of the play in which they were employed.

At the beginning of The True Tragedy appears in regulation fashion the ghost of Clarence, murdered before the play begins, by his brother Richard. He appears with the regulation cry of Vindicta, and prays that Revenge may come quickly, then leaves the stage not to appear again. The tone of the play as a play of revenge has been set at the start. But it has no enforcement whatever, until the end of the play is nearly reached. Then it appears again in the ghost soliloquy of Richard.

But here the usual course of the revenge tragedy is changed. The ghosts of the murdered, crying revenge, do not actually appear. They are represented as the creatures of Richard's imagination, diseased in consequence of his guilty conscience. The ghosts have ceased to be mere external machinery, used to awaken the spectator's sense of horror; they have become a means of revealing the torments of a guilty soul. And thus the spirits of the murdered do in truth obtain revenge.

That The True Tragedy is the first play to show this union of the revenge-play ghost and the torments of conscience cannot be asserted, for a like conception appears in Greene and Lodge's A Looking Glass for London and England, and in Greene's James IV, both of uncertain date. They are certainly not far removed in time from The True Tragedy.

In the ghost soliloquy occurs a passage that represents all nature, as well as the 'ghosts of the murdered, as calling out for revenge.

This conception is found in the earlier play of Locrine. But there the thought is uttered by the ghost himself. Here we have the same advance, for the cry of inanimate nature is likewise heard in The True Tragedy only by the imagination distorted by conscience.

In literary form The True Tragedy reveals some striking pecularities. It is written partly in verse, partly in prose, which interchange without any apparent reason. In the verse, the old heavy blank-verse, bearing close resemblance to that of the old King John, has the chief place; but with it appear ballad metre (as also in King John), septenaries, in rimed couplets and unrimed, and unrimed lines of every possible length. These are often combined in fantastic fashion. Thus in a single

26*

speech (of Rivers, p. 75—6) we have $\underbrace{4 \times 3a}$ $\underbrace{4 \times 3a}$ $\underbrace{5b}$ $\underbrace{4 \times 3b}$ $5 \times 3x$ $\underbrace{5c}$ $\underbrace{5 \times 3c}$ $\underbrace{4 \times 3d}$ $\underbrace{4 \times 3d}$. The greatest freedom occurs near the beginning, but there is much license throughout.

As it stands, the play is wretchedly corrupt and abominably printed. Not only is prose printed as verse and verse as prose, but there are many passages from which it is impossible to extract any sense at all. For some of the corruption no ignorance of the printer will account, and we must believe that the copy which lay before him was in many respects far from the original. Dorset appears in the early part always as "Lord Marcus" while later he is correctly called "Lord Marquesse Dorset". Catesby appears first as "Casbie", but always after as "Catesby" and "Catsby". The Sir Richard Hawte of the chronicle appears always as "Hapce" or "Hape", an inexplicable change. Scene-headings and directions are often palpably wrong. The play does indeed require careful editing, as Mr. Fleay suggests, but even the carefulest could not bring entire consistency out of the confusion.

Some of the inconsistencies, which have an importance in the interpretation of the play, will be touched on in the analysis, and others under the question of authorship; most, however, are unimportant and may be left unnoticed.

The Historical Sources of The True Tragedy.

As with Legge's play and all other works which treat of Richard's story, the ultimate source of The True Tragedy is More's biography, with the additions made by Hall. An investigation of the play to determine in what works the author made use of More's and Hall's story shows the following as immediate sources.

1. The True Tragedy used Hall's Chronicle or the Harding continuation. This is apparent from the following passages.

    a) p. 66. "And horsemen ayders vnto him [Buckingham], is my Lord Chamberlaine, and my Lord Hastings".

Hastings was himself lord Chamberlain. The author
— here as elsewhere exceedingly careless in the use of
his authorities — evidently used Hall or the Hardyng con.,
which have "Henry duke of Buckyngham, and Willyam
lord Hastynges, and lord Chamberlain" (Hall, p. 348).
More (p. 14) has "Edwarde Duke of Buckingham, and
Richarde Lorde Hastinges and chaumberlayn". Holinshed
(p. 366) has "William lord Hastings then chamberlain".
Grafton has "Richard the Lorde Hastings a noble man,
then Lord Chamberleyn".

> b) p. 77. "Buc. Gentlemen on afore keep your
> roomes, how now Lord Gray doo you iustle in
> the presence of the King? This is more then
> needs".

The passage occurs after greetings have been exchanged
with the king. This agrees with the order of Hall, who
with the Hardyng con. has (p. 349) after the exchange
of greetings, "The duke of Buckyngham said aloude, on
afore gentlemen, and yomen kepe your roumes, and therewith in $\check{y}$ kynges presence they picked a quarel to the
lord Richard Grey". In More, and in Grafton and
Holinshed following him, the command of Buckingham is
given as the company approaches the king. "To whome
the Duke of Buckingham saide, goe afore, Gentlemenne
and yomen, kepe youre rowmes. And thus in a goodly
arraye thei came to the kinge, and on theire knees in
very humble wise salued his grace" (p. 17). Then follows
the quarrel.

> c) p. 95. "The Kings pleasure is this, that he wil
> haue no blood shead in the deed doing".

cf. Hall (p. 378), "that they shoulde be murtherd in their
beddes and no bloud shed". The Hardyng con. and
Grafton have this latter clause, but it is wanting in More
and Holinshed.

Corroborative, if less conclusive are the following.

d) p. 52.
"Richard Plantagenet of the House of Yorke,
. . . .
Had as the chronicles make manifest,
In the two and twentith yeare of Henry the sixth,
By act of Parliament intailed to him
The Crowne and titles to that dignitie".

Hall and the Hardyng con. alone in the corresponding passage mention a date for the Parliament — which is, to be sure, not the "two and twentith" but the thirtieth year. [This again is an error. It was really the thirty-ninth year, as given correctly by Hall, p. 249]. This passage was doubtless the cause why The True Tragedy has a date here, though the usual careless treatment of authorities appears. Twenty-two is a favorite number of the author, who sets it elsewhere also inaccurately. It was perhaps borrowed from the twenty-two years of Edward's reign, mentioned on the next page, 53.

e) p. 64. "Enters **Page** and **Perciuall**", with the ensuing scene in which Percivall delivers the message from Buckingham to Richard.

The message is mentioned in this place by Hall, and the Hardyng con.; in More and Holinshed the passage occurs at the beginning of the account of Buckingham's conspiracy, though it refers to this time. Grafton has not the message at all (cf. p. 210), though he mentions it, and gives the name of the messenger. The name of the messenger occours as Persivall in Hall and in one edition of the Hardyng con. In More, one edition of the Hardyng con., Grafton and Holinshed the name is Persall, but in the margin of Holinshed stands, "Percival saith Ed. Hall". Thus the passage and the name may have been obtained from Holinshed, though it is less natural to suppose so.

f) pp. 67—8. "The Duke of Buckingham is vp in the Marches of Wales with a band of men".

This follows immediately upon the scene with Percival. In Hall (p. 347) occurs "The duke sente backe the messanger with greate thankes and diuerse priuey instruccions by mouthe, whiche Persiuall did somuche by his trauaill that he came to the duke of Buckyngham his master into the marches of Wales, and eftsones with newe instruccions met with the duke of Gloucester at Notyngham". So also the Hardyng con. More (p. 86) has "The messenger sent back with thanks, and some secret instruccion of the protectors mind, yet met him again with farther message from the duke his master, within few dayes after at Nottingham". Thus the "Marches of Wales", while not an impossible addition of the author of the play, is in all probability from Hall or the Hardyng continuation.

g) p. 69. "Sir Hapce", pp. 76 and 77, "Sir Richard Hape", in the train of the young prince and arrested by Gloucester, is the Sir Richard Hawte mentioned by Hall and the Hardyng con. He is mentioned by Grafton also, but not here, only in the later passage, where the execution is described. More and Holinshed do not mention Hawte at all. Thus his inclusion here, while possibly from Grafton is probably from Hall or the Hardyng con.

2. Another chronicle authority beside Hall or the Hardyng continuation was also used.

a) p. 82. The Cardinal Archbishop of York asks the Duke of York from his mother.
Hall and the Hardyng con. have the Archbishop of Canterbury. More, Grafton and Holinshed have the Archbishop of York.

b) pp. 127—8. The Epilogue from the death of Henry VIII cannot be founded on Hall or the Hardyng con., which end with Henry's death.

3. If Hall was not used then Holinshed was used. At the close of Edward's death-bed speech we have:
> "For I am so sleepie, that I must now make an ende,
> And here before you all, I commit my soul to al mighty God,
> My sauiour, and sweet redeemer, my bodie to the earth,
> My Scepter and Crowne to the yoong Prince my sonne".

This is nearly word for word from the first death-bed speech of Edward, written by Hall and copied by Holinshed only. (Cf. pp. 182, 217.)

4. "The Earl of Westmorland and Northumberland, are secretly fled".

I suggest elsewhere (see p. 409) that this reference may have been taken from Holinshed. It offers the single direct argument for the use of Holinshed, and is, of course, inconclusive.

This is all that can be absolutely proved with regard to the chronicle authorities for the play. An attempt at a closer limitation must deal with the question of probabilities.

A decision between Hall and the Hardyng continuation is assisted by the following consideration. For everything in the play that is based on the chronicles, with the exception of 2, a) and b), and 4, Hall will account. This is not the case with the Hardyng continuation, which has nothing to say of the truce with the Scots and the marriage of Richard's neice (T. T. p. 108), the proclamation of the Earl of Lincoln as heir apparent (p. 92), the offence of Arnold Butler (p. 112), Lord Stanley's refusal to come to Richard and the postponed murder of George Stanley (p. 119), and the safe return of George Stanley (p. 126). The greater extent of Hall's authority makes it therefore highly probable that Hall was used, and this probability is strengthened by the fact that Hall's Chronicle was extremely popular and constantly used by the dramatists of the day; while the Hardyng continuation had been succeeded in popular favor not only by Hall but by Grafton and Holinshed, all of which contained much more material.

As between More, Grafton, and Holinshed, there seems, in the first place, little reason to suppose that More was used. In all known instances his story was used through the medium of one of the chronicles. Further, it will not account for any of the passages under 1, above, and ends at the beginning of Buckingham's conspiracy. As the chronicles were certainly used it is unlikely that the author should have cared to consult as well More's less complete original.

Between Grafton and Holinshed a decision is more difficult. Grafton fails to account for several of the passages mentioned under 1, and has no statement of the duration of the truce between the Scotch and English, given by Hall and Holinshed as three years, and changed by The True Tragedy to six (p. 91). Holinshed on the other hand fails totally for all the passages under 1. But the "Westmorland" passage seems to point to the use of Holinshed, and for the Epilogue from the beginning of Elizabeth's reign Holinshed alone will account, if it be assumed that here, as is clearly the case in the rest of the epilogue, a chronicle account is the basis. This, however, cannot be shown with certainty. But the author reveals on every page that his study of his authorities was exceedingly hasty and inaccurate. This renders it more probable that he used the well-known and popular Holinshed rather than the less well-known and older Grafton, the use of which has not, I believe, been proved for any of the productions of the Elizabethan popular stage. The same argument is a still stronger reason for believing that the Hardyng continuation and More's biography in Rastell's edition were not used in preference to Hall. With a dramatist like Legge there would be no such presumption.

We may conclude, therefore, with practical certainty that the author of The True Tragedy used Hall, and regard it as most probable that he used Holinshed rather than Grafton in addition.

5. The True Tragedy made use of The Mirror for Magistrates for the story of Shore's Wife. This is shown,

a) By the whole conception of Shore's wife's punishment. The open penance in procession receives the barest mention, being limited to "Goe from me to the Bishop of London, and see that she recieue her open penance". This is absolutely all, and is followed in the same sentence by the direction, "let her be turned out of prison, but as bare as a wretch that worthily hath deserved that plague", and orders that no one shall relieve or pity her. Her appearance from this time on is confined to her unsuccessful begging of those whom she has assisted; while her previous appearance has been in the nature of preparation for this, since there she obtains the promise of help from those whom she has aided, in case of misfortune to her, which promise in the later scenes they fail to keep. This corresponds entirely to the legend in the **Mirror for Magistrates**, where as here her poverty in caused by Richard's spoiling her of her goods, and where as here, comfortless and hungry, she begs in the streets, of those who have before benefited by her kindness. This is wholly contrary to the representation of More and Hall, in whose work Jane Shore's beggary has nothing to do with Richard's confiscation of her goods, occurring only late in her life; where there is no suggestion that she begged in the streets; and where her beggary receives only slight mention, while her penance in procession is described at length. Cf. the analysis of the legend, and the comments on its relation to its source (pp. 260—4).

b) Shore's wife first appears in the play with an apostrophe to Fortune. So in the poem she introduces her story with a tirade against Fortune, carried out through five stanzas. The thought in both places is the same: Fortune flatters, suddenly to deceive; lifts high, only to let fall.

c) In the play, Shore's wife after receiving the news of Edward's death is next told that Gloucester has been made protector. Whereat she exclaims:

> "Ah me, then comes my ruine and decaie,
> For he could neuer abide me to the death,
> No he alwaies hated me whom his brother loued so well".

There is no chronicle or historical authority for the statement that Richard especially hated Shore's wife. She received no notice from him till she became a convenient means of working Hastings' death; and her condemnation to punishment was, as represented by More, the result of a pretended morality on Richard's part, and the confiscation of her goods the result of covetousness and not of his anger. Both condemnation and confiscation were the consequences of the situation produced by the plot against Hastings, united, doubtless, with a desire to throw odium on the dead Edward. The passage has its source in these lines in the Mirror for Magistrates legend.

> "His [Edward's] body was no sooner put in chest,
> But well was hee that could procure my fall:
> His brother was myne enemye most of all,
> Protectour then, whos vice did still abound".

The last line does not necessarily, and, as the further course of the poem shows, passing at once to Richard's charge that Shore's wife attempted to poison him, probably does not, mean to say that Richard was Protector at once after Edward's death; but it is easy so to understand it, and that the author of The True Tragedy did so understand it, and from it derived the appointment of Richard by the king, seems to be shown by the lines preceding the three quoted above.

> "Shor. But say Lodwicke, who hath the King made Protector,
>   During the innormitie [minority] of the young Prince.
> Lod. He hath made his brother Duke of Glosier Protector.
> Shor. Ah me, then comes my ruine, etc."

The connection of the announcement of Richard's protectorship with what follows renders it more than probable that this too is drawn from the same passage in the Mirror for Magistrates. That it is not drawn from the chronicles I show elsewhere (cf. p. 264).

d) Certain verbal resemblances point to the same origin.
1. cf. "For tho he was king, yet Shore's wife swayd the swoord" (p. 90) with the poem's

> "I gouernd him that ruled all this land:
> I bare the sword, though he did weare the crowne".

Here the resemblance is absolute proof of imitation. In More there is nothing of the kind.

2. "But my friends should have preferd discipline before affection, for they know of my folly, yea my own husband etc." This appears to mean that her friends should have restrained her, instead of, out of love for her, letting her go her own way; but there can be no doubt that the lines are reminiscences of the Mirror for Magistrates,

> "But cleare from blame my frends can not be founde,
> Before my time my youth they did abuse:
> In mariage a prentise was I bound".

The passage in Hall (More) will not account for the resemblance. "This woman was borne in London, well frended, honestly brought vp, and very well maryed, sauyng somewhat to sone, her husbande an honest and a young citezen, godly and of good substaunce, but forasmuche as they were coupled or she were well rype, she not very feruently loued for whom she neuer longed".

3. "Now shall Shore's wife be a mirrour and looking glasse to all her enemies" (p. 60). Cf. in the concluding lines of the poem "A Mirour make by my great ouerthro", and the whole purpose of the Mirror for Magistrates. The intention of the play, as evidenced by its title, was the same as that of the Mirror, to make of Shore's wife "an example for all wicked women".

e) "I will shun her company and get me to my chamber, and there set down in heroical verse, the shamefull end of a Kings Concubin". This seems clearly to be a reference to the poem in the Mirror for Magistrates. For a further discussion of the passage see pp. 439—431.

Analysis of The True Tragedy.

In analysing Legge's Richardus Tertius it was possible, while describing the nature and content of the play, to give at the same time nearly completely its relations to its historical and literary sources, for these were limited to two, the chronicles' history of Richard and Seneca's plays. The case is very different with The True Tragedy. It is not the first of its species, but was preceded by many, historical plays, plays of revenge, and others, which exercised influence upon it: and at the same time it stands in close relation to at least one play that follows it, Shakespeare's Richard III. It has seemed best, therefore, owing to their importance, to assign to separate sections such questions as the relation of the play to Legge, to Marlowe, to Henry VI and to Richard III. and to confine the analysis to showing the nature of the play, with its relation to its historical sources, and to such works other than these of Legge and Marlowe as reveal resemblances to it.

The introduction to the play is formed by a scene between Truth and Poetrie, to whom enters the ghost of Clarence, crying

> "Cresce, cruor: sanguis satietur sanguine: cresce,
> Quod spero citò. O citò, citò, vendicta".

These, the first words of the play, indicate upon one side the character it is to bear — that of a revenge tragedy, in which the problem of the play is the attainment of revenge by one murdered previously to the action. Thus, for example, in The Spanish Tragedy the ghost of Andrea, in The Misfortunes of Arthur (1588) the ghost of Gorlois, set the play in motion and indicate that its end is to revenge the wrongs they have suffered. In other of the revenge plays, as e. g. Locrine (probably written before 1587) and The Battle of Alcazar (1591 or earlier) the ghosts appear during the course of the play itself. In nearly all these revenge-plays appears the cue-word, vindicta. Thus in The Spanish Tragedy, Hieronyma, mourning his son, appears reading

>"Vindicta mihi —
>Ay, heaven will be revenged of every ill",

and with this Biblical quotation (Deut. 32 : 35, 41 : 43; Ps. 94 : 1; Rom. 12 : 19; Heb. 10 : 30), it is likely, the word first enters the Revenge Tragedy. Then it became a favorite cry of the ghosts. In The Battle of Alcazar "Enter three ghosts crying Vindicta", and in Locrine the ghost of Albanact cries out to Humber "Vindicta, Vindicta". The True Tragedy shows itself at the beginning, then, fully in the current of the revenge plays; and its connection with them is shown in several other passages.

When Clarence's ghost has disappeared, Poetry turns to Truth, and there ensues the following dialogue.

> "Poetrie. Truth well met.
> Truth. Thankes Poetrie, what makes thou vpon a stage?
> Poet. Shadowes.
> Truth. Then will I adde bodies to the shadowes,
> Therefore depart and giue Truth leaue
> To shew her pageant.
> Poet. Why will Truth be a Player?
> Truth. No, but Tragedia like for to present
> A Tragedie in England done but late,
> That will reuiue the hearts of drooping mindes.
> Poet. Whereof?
> Truth. Marry thus."

Thereupon Truth sets forth the circumstances attendant upon the steps of Richard Plantagenet's attempt to win the crown, the death of Richard, of Henry and of Clarence,

>"By Gloster's Duke drowned in a but of wine".

Poetry inquires what shield it was that the ghost of Clarence let fall.

> "Truth. A sheild conteining this, in full effect,
>   Blood sprinkled, springs: blood spilt, craues due revenge:
>   Whereupon he writes, Cresce cruor etc." —

Truth then describes Richard:

> "A man ill shaped, crooked backed, lame armed, withall,
>   Valiantly minded, but tyrannous in authoritie.
>   So during the minoritie of the yoong Prince
>   He is made Lord Protector ouer the Realme".

Turning now directly to the audience, Truth makes known the immediate situation.

> "Gentiles suppose that Edward now hath raigned
>   Full two and twentie yeares, and now like to die,
>   Hath summond all his Nobles to the court,
>   To swear alleageance with the Duke his brother,
>   For truth vnto his soune the tender Prince".

Then Truth and Poetry leave the stage, and the play proper begins.

The source of Truth's explanation is evidently More's introduction to his story of Richard, which is on the whole closely followed. This does not, however, account for the statement of Clarence's death at Richard's hands, nor for the appointment of Richard as protector. For an explanation of these see pp. 241 ff. and 411. That the mention of a date for the Parliament in which Richard Plantagenet made known his claims points to the use of Hall or of the Hardyng continuation, I have shown p. 406.

The allegorical figures of Truth and Poetry in connection with the ghost of Clarence convey an indistinct reminiscence of the introduction to The Spanish Tragedy, where the likewise allegorical figure of Revenge appears with the ghost of Andrea, and before the fourth act explains the dumb show, as Truth here explains the action of the ghost of Clarence.

[Scene 1.] The opening scene is the reconciliation scene at Edward's bedside, described by More. Those present are Edward, Lord Hastings, Lord Marcus [— Lord Marquis Dorset], and Elizabeth. "To them **Richard**" follows in the scene-heading, but he does not appear. That he was meant to do so, and that we have here a corruption or alteration of the original, I show elsewhere. Edward's speech to his lords follows, in abridged form, at the beginning almost word for word, the speech put in his mouth by More. He calls their attention to the plight in which he lies, and begs them at his death to cease from their quarrels and forgive each other. To Dorset and Hastings — following More's account — he addresses himself especially. They are at first unwilling to yield, and the king despairs, but finally at the entreaty of Elizabeth and of Edward they join hands and unite in an oath of friendship. Edward then again addresses them, committing the young prince to the government of Gloucester as Protector, and bidding Elizabeth be loyal to her brother. Then, the sleep of death approaching, he commends his soul to the Redeemer and dies.

The final words of Edward show the use of the death-bed speech written by Hall, cf. p. 407—8. The reluctance of Dorset and Hastings to agree is not from the chronicles. I have suggested a probable source for it on p. 493.

During the course of the scene Elizabeth refers to Edward as "the aged King my father". But Edward died when only 41. The representation of Edward as aged corresponds to that of Brutus in Locrine. Here, likewise in the first scene, Brutus dying, addresses his lords and his children, with whom is Guendolen, his niece, — which may possibly account for the presence here of Elizabeth, who is not mentioned by the chronicles. Locrine is bidden to imitate his "aged father's steps", Guendolen will not contradict her "aged father's [Corineus'] will", Albanact is bidden, later, like Locrine, to imitate his "aged father's steps". The expression occurs repeatedly. This is the first indication of resemblances to the old plays of this group, many of which appear later.

Cf. the king's "But what saith Lord Marcus and Lord Hastings What, not one word?" with the old Henry V

(Shak. Lib. II, 1, 343): "Pardon, good father, not a word: ah he will not speak one word". With the final words and death of Edward, cf. those of Henry in the old Henry V, p. 347.

[Scene 2.] Shore's wife enters with an apostrophe to Fortune.

"O Fortune, wherefore wert thou called Fortune?
But that thou art fortunate?
Those, whom thou fauourest be famous,
Meriting mere mercie,
And fraught with mirrors of magnanimitie,
And Fortune I would thou hadst neuer fauoured me".

Hursly, her maid, remonstrates that she should not exclaim against Fortune, who has caused her advancement, but Shore's wife reveals the fact that she fears the death of the King. If he goes she will be left unprovided for, and her foes will triumph. There enters now Lodwicke, a messenger from Lord Hastings, with the request that she will come to his master. Of him she inquires news of the King's health, and after some ambiguous replies from which she takes courage, he informs her that the king is dead. She bursts out into lament.

"Ah sweete Edward, farwell my gracious Lord and souereigne,
For now shall Shore's wife be a mirrour and looking glasse,
To all her enemies".

She prophesies that all her friends will fall from her. Her fear is increased by the news that Richard has been made Protector, "for he could neuer abide me to the death". Lodowicke comforts her with the words that his lord, Hastings, will always help her, and promises her the land she has begged for him, should she ever be in want.

Now "Enter a **Citizen** and **Morton** a seruing man". The citizen welcomes Morton, and begs for the return of money he has lent. Morton cannot give it, for he is uncertain of his own; the King is dead. The citizen is forced to content himself, for he too is conscious of coming danger, and has heard rumors that the young king will never reign — "The King looseth his right they say". They now perceive Mistress Shore, and greet her. Both are much beholding to her, Morton for his place, the citizen for the life of his son, and both thank her heartily. She warns them that she fares not as well as once, and may some day be driven to try her friends. She then departs with Lodowicke and Morton to betake herself to Hastings, and the citizen is left to comment on the situation. For Shore's wife, though the King is dead, there is yet Lord Hastings; for himself, if all customers serve him as Morton has done, he is likely to keep a bad household of it.

As I have shown, pp. 410—3, the part of Shore's wife is drawn from the legend in the Mirror for Magistrates. The scene is wholly a prophecy and foreboding of what is to befall her. One great loss she has suffered, though she still has friends, but what will happen if Hastings should fail her?

The passage between the citizen and Morton is doubtless from the passage in More where he speaks of the citizens foreboding danger, their hearts misgiving them by a secret instinct of nature, as the sea without wind swells before a storm. Cf. the fuller discussion of this passage, pp. 126—7. The passage is, like that with Shore's wife, one of foreboding, but it is the foreboding of a danger not to one person only, but to the state. Crudely written as it is, if well acted it could not have failed of effect.

[Scene 3.] "Enters **Richard, Sir William Casbie** (= Catesby) Page of his chamber, and his traine". Richard bids his followers farewell, directing them to look to their charges, and they depart, Catesby uttering as he leaves the wish,

"Cas. Renowned and right worthie Protector,
 Whose excelency far deserues the name of king then protector,
 Sir William Casbie wisheth my Lord,
 That your grace may so gouerne the yoong Prince,
 That the Crowne of England may flourish in all happinesse".

Richard is left alone. The parting words of Catesby have roused him, and he pours out a soliloquy that reveals all his ambition, the crimes his ambition has caused in the past, and that which it will cause in the future.

"Rich. Ah yoong Prince, and why not I?
Or who shall inherit Plantagines but his sonne?
And who the King deceased, but the brother?
Shall law bridle nature, or authoritie hinder inheriance?
No, I say no: Principalitie brooks no equalitie,
Much less superioritie,
And the title of a King is next vnder the degree of a God,
For if he be worthie to be called valiant,
That in his life winnes honour, and by his sword winnes riches,
Why now I with renowne of a souldier, which is neuer sold but
By waight, nor changed but by losse of life,
I reapt not the game but the glorie, and since it becommeth
A sonne to maintain the honour of his deceased father,
Why should I not hazard his dignitie by my brothers sonnes?
To be baser than a King I disdaine,
And to be more then Protector, the law deny,
Why my father got the Crowne, my brother won the Crowne,
And I will wear the Crowne,
Or ile make them hop without their crownes that denies me;
Haue I remoued such logs out of my sight as my brother Clarence
And king Henry the sixt, to suffer a child to shadow me,
Nay more, my nephew to disinherit me,
Yet most of all, to be released from the yoke of my brother
As I terme it, to become subiect to his sonne,
No death nor hell shall not withhold me, but as I rule I will raign.
And so raign that the proudest enemy shall not abide
The sharpest shoure. Why what are the babes but a puffe of
Gun-pouder? A marke for the soldiers, food for fishes,
Or lining for beds, deuices enough to make them away,
Wherein I am resolute, and determining, needs no counsell.
Ho, whose within?"

Not at the moment of Edward's death did this Richard conceive his purpose to reign. It has been with him ever since he began to take part in his brother's wars, and has guided his every act. Henry and Clarence have been removed as logs from his path, and now at last he has been freed from the yoke of his brother's reign, under which he has chafed. Shall he now after all this submit to the rule of a boy? Though he never for a moment

27*

fails to see that all law is against him, arguments are not wanting to feed himself with. He is his father's son, imbued with his father's spirit. Upon him descends the duty of upholding his father's crown. Has he not fought for it, for father and for brother, giving all the power that was in him for them, and what has he reaped? The glory of a soldier, to be sure, but the gain of all his valiancy has gone to another. And now, conscious of all his long service in the winning of that crown, he must stand and see it fall to a child, who knows nothing of the past, and has made no sacrifices for that which is put in his hands by fortune. Even now the child cannot rule. Richard must rule, but for another. The child will reign. Shall he not make one last easy blow at fate, at this cruel chance which is depriving him of that which he feels he should rightly inherit, of that which he himself has won? Death and hell shall not withhold him from it.

Such appears to be the meaning of Richard's soliloquy. That it reveals the same Richard as the Richard of 3 Henry VI I shall try to show elsewhere (cf. p. 487 et seq.).

In addition to the passage there (p. 493) quoted from 2 Henry VI compare with Richard's "Ile make them hop without their crownes", from James IV (before 1592):

"On pain of death, proud bishop, get you gone,
Unless you headless mean to hop away".

While Richard has been speaking he has heard someone stirring within, and in response to his call appear the page and Percival.

"Per. May it please your Maiestie.
Rich. Ha villaine, Maiestie.
Per. I speake but vpon that which shall be my good Lord.
Rich. But whats he with thee?
Page. A Messenger with a letter from the right honourable The
[Duke of Buckingham".

[For Per. in the first and third lines, read Page. Richard's question and the page's answer make evident the reason for the change.] At the greeting Richard turns aside to soliloquize.

"A how this title of Maiestie, animates me to my purpose,
Rise man, regard no fall, haply this letter brings good lucke,
May it be, or is it possible,
Doth Fortune so much fauour my happinesse
That I no sooner deuise, but she sets abroach?
Or doth she but to trie me, that raising me aloft,
My fall may by the greater, well laugh on sweete change,
Be as be may, I will neuer feare colours nor regard ruth,
Valour brings fame, and fame conquers death".

The words are significant in two ways. At the moment of entrance upon the actions that are to accomplish his purpose, while all promises fair, Richard has a moment's foreboding of the end. It is the same foreboding that Shakespeare's Richard feels, when having mounted his throne he asks.

"But shall we wear these glories for a day?
Or shall they last, and we rejoice in them?"

This fore-indication of what is to follow is a favorite device of the author of The True Tragedy.

The last line of Richard's speech throws especial light upon the character. Looking forward to the end, he shows that his ambition reaches beyond death. Not power, but fame, is his object, and "fame conquers death". Death will be no adequate punishment for this Richard's crimes, as Legge thought it for his Richard. On the "majesty" passage cf. p. 493. On Richard's reference to Fortune see p. 479.

Richard now turns to Percival. The letter he has brought contains the offer of Buckingham to join with Richard, and Richard gladly accepts, though Buckingham has long been his foe. Buckingham proposes to remove the Prince from the Queen's friends, and Richard eagerly agrees, as "it is the only way" to his purpose. At the coronation both the dukes shall be present, and there, says Richard,

"by the helpe of thy Lord, I will so plaie my part
That Ile be more than I am, and not much lesse than I looke for".

Percival conveys by word of mouth the message of his master that he has a brave company of men in readiness, and that Hastings will join him. That news is a surprise to Richard. "Sounes, dares he trust the Lord Hastings?" Assured that Hastings is secret, Richard promises to meet Buckingham the next day. This day he cannot, he "must first set a screene before the fire for feare of suspition", and urge on the controversy between the kinsmen of the King and those of the Queen. Then opening himself to Percival, whose trust to Buckingham he considers sufficient warrant, he says, "I climbe Perciuall, I regard more the glorie then the gaine, for the very name of a King redouble[s] a mans life with fame, when death hath done his worst". And the same thought breaks out again in his soliloquy after Percival is gone.

> "Why so, now Fortune make me a King. Fortune give me a kingdome, let the world report the Duke of Gloster was a King, therefore Fortune make me a King, if I be but King for a yeare, naye but halfe a yeare, nay a moneth, a weeke, three dayes, one daye, or halfe a day, nay an houre, swounes half an houre, nay sweete Fortune, clap but the Crowne on my head, that the vassals may but once say, God saue King Richards life, it is inough".

Absurdly crude as this is, the thought is clear enough, and its expression the more vigorous for its crudeness. It is the title of King that Richard seeks; that once attained even death cannot deprive him of fame and glory.

The message of Percival is of course taken from the account of More (cf. p. 406). The are however some differences. The proposal to remove the Prince from the Queen's kindred is made here, as in Shakespeare's play, to come from Buckingham; and Buckingham is represented as having brought Hastings into the conspiracy, whereas in More's account they were both brought in by Richard. Buckingham himself is represented as an old foe of Richard. This is probably caused by the statement of More that Buckingham and Hastings, "not bearing eche to other so muche loue, as hatred both vnto the Quenes parte" accorded with Gloster. The author deals with the chronicles throughout in the most arbitrary fashion. Richard's presence in London is, of course, contrary to the chronicle, agreeing in this with Shakespeare's play. The presence of the page, and the prominent part he has throughout, is also contrary to More's story, in which he appears only in connection with the procurement of Tyrell. The Moor's Boy in The Battle of Alcazar may here have had influence. Cf. especially the battle-scenes in the two plays.

I have elsewhere offered proof that Hall or the Hardyng continuation was used for this scene. Cf. p. 406.

The page now enters and Richard inquires what he has heard about the Court.

"Page. Ioy my Lord for your Protectorship for the most part.
Some murmure, but my Lord they be of the baser sort.
Rich. A mightie arme wil sway the baser sort, authority doth
[terrifie".

The thought is Senecan. The page conveys the further news that the king is coming up to his coronation with Rivers, Gray and the rest. It is rumored, too, that Buckingham is up in the Marches of Wales with a band of men, and aiming at the crown. Richard laughs at the idea, but sees the necessity of immediate action. "In trust is treason, time slippth, it is ill iesting with edge tooles, or dallying with Princes matters, Ile strike while the yron is hote, and Ile trust neuer a Duke of Buckingham, no neuer a Duke in the world, further than I see him". He goes out and the page is left to comment.

"Page. I see my Lord is fully resolued to climbe, but how hee climbes ile leaue that to your iudgements, but what his fall will be thats hard to say: But I maruell that the Duke of Buckingham and he are now become such great friends, who had wont to love one another so well as the spider doth the flie: but this I haue noted, since he hath had the charge of Protector, how many noble men hath fled the realme, first the Lord Marcus sonne to the Queene, the

Earl of Westmorland and Northumberland, are secretly fled: how this geare will cotten I know not. But what do I medling in such matters, that should medle with the vntying of my Lordes points, faith do euen as a great many do beside, medle with Princes matters so long, til they proue themselues beggars in the end. Therefore I for feare I should be taken napping with any words, Ile set a locke on my lips, for feare my tongue grow too wide for my mouth".

Richard's words are indicative of a directness and swiftness of action not unlike that of Shakespeare's Richard, and reveal at the same time an unreadiness to trust another which — with the exception of the Percival episode — is characteristic of him throughout. He will rely as far as possible on himself, and make use of others only when it is unavoidable.

The words of the page contain almost the only hint of the comic in the whole play. In this respect it corresponds to the old King John and is notably different from the old Henry V. In the statement of the page as to the noble men who have fled we have one of the many remarkable examples in the play of a complete "muddling" of the historical events. No one fled, of course, till after the capture of the Queen's kinsmen. Then Dorset fled with the Queen to sanctuary. His flight from the country did not follow till after the failure of the rebellion started by Buckingham. The earl of Northumberland remained on Richard's side and abandoned him only at the battle of Bosworth. There is no earl of Westmoreland in the story. I venture to suggest, as explanation of the statement, that the author may have caught it up from Holinshed's account of the rebellion of the earls of Westmoreland and Northumberland in 1569. In the margin of vol. 3, p. 235 stands "The earle of Northumberland and Westmerland rebelled", and later (p. 336) comes the statement "the two earles of Northumberland and Westmerland were fled" — first to Durham and then to Scotland.

[Scene 4.] "Enter the yoong **Prince,** his brother, **Duke of Yorke, Earle Rivers, Lord Gray, Sir Hapce, Sir Thomas Vaughan**".

In this heading the Duke of York appears by mistake, as he is subsequently shown to be in London. "Sir Hapce" is a remarkable mutilation of Sir [Richard] Hawte.

The Prince is on his way toward London, and has nearly reached Northampton when he receives letters from his mother, bidding him dismiss his train lest Northampton should prove too small to receive them, and lest Gloucester should think they came of malice against him and his blood. A discussion ensues, in which Rivers urges that the train should not be dismissed, because the two factions may easily fall apart once more, and because Buckingham is up in the Marches of Wales and the Protector is joined with him for some reason unknown. Buckingham is thought to be a friend to the king, but Richard is misdoubted as a foe. At Gray's suggestion Rivers is left at Northampton to confer with the two dukes and discover their purpose; while in accordance with the Queen's letters and the young King's desire the train is dismissed. Rivers consents, and takes his leave, while the young King in distress promises, if he lives, to root out this malice and envy, and make them weary who first began the mischief. Gray and Vaughan applaud the speech as evidence of kinglike resolution and a toward nature. The party then proceeds.

The scene is in general drawn from More's account, but there are differences. Rivers urges the greenness of the league of amity as a reason for retaining the train, contrary to More, where the same fact is urged upon the Queen by Gloucester's emissaries as a reason for dismissing the train. Rivers is left behind to discover the purpose of the dukes, while in More his presence in Northampton is left unaccounted for; and, chief difference of all, Richard's authority is recognized, — "We have the Prince, but they the authoritie", while More's effort had been to conceal or deny the fact that Richard had any authority.

The fear lest Northampton might be too small for the train is derived from More's statement that Buckingham and Richard found the King preparing to leave Stony Stratford free for them "because it was to streighte for bothe companies" (Lumby's ed. p. 17).

[Scene 5.] "Enters an old Inne-keeper and **Richard's Page**".

The scene is the Inn at Northampton where Rivers is lodged. The page is giving orders for the entertainment of Richard and his followers, and with especial emphasis that Richard's lodging is to be prepared as near to Rivers' as possible, and that after all are gone to bed he shall bring to Richard the keys of all the rooms. These orders awaken the strongest reluctance on the part of the host. To lock in his guests like prisoners seems to him little better than treason.

> "Page. Treason villaine, how darest thou haue a thought of treason against my Lord? Therefore you were best be brief, and tell me whether you will do it or no?
> Oste. Alasse what shall I do? who were I best to offend? shall I betrai that good olde Earle that hath laine at my house this fortie yeares? Why and I doe hee will hang me: nay then on the other side, if I should not do as my Lord Protector commands, he will chop off my head, but is there no remedie?"

He at last consents, but greatly against his will.

The situation is of course derived from More, as well as the taking of the keys. Otherwise the scene is the author's. We have in it further evidence of the close relations between The True Tragedy and the other plays of its group. Rivers was about the age of King Edward, having been born about 1542, not at all an old man. But the expression "good old man" is very common in the old plays, and in the old King John occurs a passage especially apropos to the present one.

King John, p. 262
> "O strangle not the good olde man,
> My hostesse oldest guest".

cf. also Edw. III, IV, 4, 149—50
> "Ah good olde man, a thousand thousand armors,
> These words of thine have buckled on my backe".

Selimus, l. 1549
> "I smile to see how that the good old man" etc.

So too of the Mayor of York, 3 Hen. VI 4, 7.
> "The good old man were fain that all were well".

The representation of Rivers like that of Edward as aged is therefore the adoption of a device common in the popular plays of the time to increase pathos.

Following this scene comes the stage-direction "Enters the mother **Queene**, and her daughter, and her sonne, to sanctuary".

The direction appears wholly out of place. The arrest of the Queen's kinsmen, which in reality caused her to fly to sanctuary, has not yet occurred, nor has she received any disturbing news. But that the direction was meant to be here, and has not been misplaced by the printer or copyist is shown by the fact that when the Queen next appears she is in sanctuary and it is there that she receives the news of her kinsmen's arrest.

[Scene 6.] In the next scene Rivers is heard calling from his chamber. He perceives that his key is gone, and that he has been betrayed; yet as Gloucester and Buckingham enter he turns to salute them gently. This is in accord with More's "he determined vppon the suretie of his own conscience, to goe boldelye to them, and inquire what thys matter myghte meane". Gloucester turns on him at once.

> "Thou wretched Earle, whose aged head imagines nought but
>   [treacherie,
> Like Iudas thou admitted wast to sup with vs last night
> But heauens preuented thee our ils, and left thee in this plight.
> Greeu'st thou that I the Gloster Duke, shuld as Protector sway?
> And were you he was left behind, to make vs both away?"

This follows More's, "whome as soone as they sawe, they beganne to quarell with hym, and saye that hee intended to sette distaunce betwene the Kynge and them, and to brynge them to confusion, but it should not lye in his power". "And when hee beganne (as hee was a very well spoken manne) in goodly wise to excuse himself, they taryed not the ende of his aunswere, but shortely tooke him and putte him in warde". The play differs in allowing Rivers to defend himseld boldly and at length, Buckingham commenting on his words with

"A brauly spoken good old Earle, who tho his lims be num
He hath his tongue as much at vse, as tho his yeares were yong"

Rivers boldly defies Richard to his face,

"The Chronicles I record [take to witness], talk of my fidelitie, &
[of my progeny,
Wher, as in a glas y^u maist behold, thy ancestors & their trechery.
The wars in France, Irish conflicts, & Scotland knowes my trust,
When thou hast kept thy skin vnscard, and let thine armor rust.
. . . .
Was this the oath, which at our princes death.
With vs thou didst combine?
But time permits not now, to tell thee all my minde:
For well tis known that but for feare, you neuer wold have clind".

What this last line is intended to mean I do not know. The first lines are pure invention, as contrary to history and to the chronicles as they are absurd. At the age of nineteen Richard distinguished himself as his brother's chief champion, at Barnet and Tewkesbury, 1471; accompanied his brother on his invasion of France, 1475, where the chronicles represent him, "whose swordes thrusted for French bloude" (Hall, p. 314), as the only one dissatisfied with the purchased peace; and in 1482 waged war in Scotland with success, and receivede therefor the thanks of King and Parliament. As for Rivers' record, he is mentioned in the chronicles as successful in tournament at Smithfield against the Bastard of Burgundy, and as accompanying Edward to France, where with the rest he acquiesced in the truce. There is no mention of him as present at Barnet or Tewkesbury or as taking part in the Scotch wars. Of Irish conflicts there appear to have been none in Edward's reign. It is probable that the speech is a free extension of More's statement, "To the governaunce and ordering of this yong prince .. was there appointed .. Lord Rivers .. a right honorable man, as valiaunte of hande as politike in counsayle".

Finally Rivers is despatched to Pomfret, and leaves with a blessing upon the "yoong and tender babes" at whose life he perceives Richard is aiming. According to More the departure of Rivers took place after the arrest of the others, and the return of the whole party to Northampton. It is ordered that the ways be guarded — following More — and Richard departs for Stony Stratford, where, says he, "happily ile say grace to the Princes dinner, that I will make the devoutest of them forget what meat they eat".

[Scene 7.] The scene is now transferred to Stony Stratford, where the Prince, Gray, Vaughan and Hapce are awaiting Rivers. Gray is anxious because of his charge, and because no word has been received from Rivers, which makes him think that Rivers and the Protector have quarrelled. The King essays to comfort him.

> "Why good vnkle comfort your selfe, no doubt my vnkle Earle Riuers is well, & is comming no doubt with my vnkle of Gloster to meet us, else we should haue heard to the contrarie. If any haue cause to feare, it is my selfe, therefore good vnkle comfort your selfe and be not sad".

Gray listens gratefully, and promises to conceal his feelings and entertain Buckingham and Richard properly when they come. At this moment they enter.

Thus far the scene is wholly the author's invention. On the character of the young Prince see pp. 441—3. Cf. also with the passages there quoted, this from The Battle of Alcazar (p. 434, col. 1):

> "Brave boy, how plain this princely mind in thee
> Argues the height and honour of thy birth!
> And well have I observ'd thy forwardness: —

> Which being tender'd by your majesty,
> No doubt the quarrel open'd by the mouth
> Of this young prince impartially to us,
> May animate and hearten all the host
> To fight against the devil for Lord Mahamet".

This scene, again, has for purpose the fore-indication of disasters to come.

"Enters **Richard, Duke of Buckingham,** and their traine". Richard greets his royal nephew with all show of courtesy, as does Buckingham, but as soon as the united trains start on, Buckingham picks a quarrel with Gray, who has accidentally brushed against him. Richard at once chimes in, with the charge that the justling is the sign and result of Gray's inward hate. The attempt of the King to calm the opponents is unsuccessful, and Gray, Vaughan and Hapce are arrested. Buckingham charges that Gray has conveyed money out of the Tower to relieve their enemies the Scots, and Richard charges him with governing the Prince without the Protector's authority. Gray replies that they have authority from the mother Queen, and that the delivery of the money to the Scots was made by a general consent of them all, and he has their hands to show for his discharge. All is of no avail. The King is in despair. His authority is set at naught, his crown is so beset with sorrows that grief will kill him ere he can enjoy his kingdom. As his authority is useless he descends to entreaty, and begs to be allowed to bail all the prisoners, or at least Lord Gray. He knows that his uncle conceals no treason or dangerous secrets. Richard replies that he conceals "secrets that are too subtil for babes". They are using him like a child, and Richard proposes to defend him. There is nothing to fear. His authority is only under the King, and he intends to win the just recompense of a true subject, but having received the Protectorship from the dead Edward, he proposes to use it as he sees fit. The King is forced to content himself, unhappy as he is; Gray is removed, and they start for London, Richard promising to appoint by the way trusty officers for the King. The scene closes with

> "Buc. Sound trumpet in this parley, God saue the King.
> Rich. Richard".

"There is character", comments Field, "in still making Gloucester try the sound of his greatness".

The scene follows in general the account of More, as reported by Hall and the Hardyng continuation, but as usual there are considerable changes. Richard's Protectorship is again recognized, by his opponents, who assert against him the authority of the Queen. Gray, instead of Dorset, is the one here represented as taking treasure from the Tower, and its application is given, as to the Scots, not as in More, to send men to the sea, i. e. fit out a fleet and supply it with soldiers. Gray's statement that this was done by general consent agrees with More's "by the whole counsaile at London". More's statement, however, is false. Under any circumstances, Gray (Dorset) could not have had Buckingham's or Richard's signature or consent thereto, as both were absent from London at the time. Richard had himself just settled all conflicts in Scotland, and was therefore the last man to know that the delivery of money to the Scots was a good and necessary purpose. It is significant that More and the chroniclers who follow him do not venture to suggest what the purposes were for which the men at sea were to be used; and the play makes the confusion worse. The King's lament over his empty authority, as well as Richard's answer to his remonstrance, is not from More. Cf. pp. 483, 506. The "trusty officers" whom Richard appoints are the "newe seruantes" whom More says they set about the King.

On Richard's substitution of his name in the cry "God save the king" cf. p. 506—7. With, "Yes, secrets that are too subtil for babes. Alasse my Lord you are a child, and they use you as a child", cf. from the old King John.

"Ah boy, thy yeares I see are farre too greene
To looke into the bottome of these cares".

[Scene 8.] The scene now changes to Westminster, where the Queen, with the young duke of York and her daughter Elizabeth, appears in sorrow. They implore her to reveal the cause of her heaviness, and urge her to forget her grief for their dead father, in beholding his image in his children. But she is mourning not for the dead husband but for the Duke and the King, who, she fears, is coming up to an untimely coronation. Her nightly dreams are dreadful. "Me thinks as I lie in my bed, I see the league broken which was sworne at the deathe of your kingly father, tis this my children, and many other causes of like importance, that makes your aged mother to lament as she doth". Elizabeth though only forty-five or forty-six years old is represented as aged like her husband and Rivers, to increase the pathos, and the scene is again one of foreboding. It may be taken for granted that the author makes Elizabeth take sanctuary so early because of her dreams and a general fear. This feeling corresponds to that manifested by the Queen in Legge's first scene, but not to More, where the Queen and her friends are represented as "nothynge earthelye mystrustynge (Lumby's ed. p. 14).

For a possible source of the dreams cf. p. 478.

Now enters a messenger with "ghastly looks" and makes known the heavy news that the Queen's kinsmen have been arrested and sent to Pomfret. The Prince is already in London, at the bishop's palace in the Protector's hands. The Queen inquires if the messenger be not servant to the Archbishop of York, and as she receives an affirmative answer the Archbishop himself appears, with letters from the Council. The Queen, who looks upon her kinsmen as sure to be murdered, forebodes still heavier news. The Cardinal greets the Queen from Gloucester, and makes known the determination of the Council that the Duke shall come to the King. The Queen declares she will not send him to be butchered.

> "Car. Your grace misdoubts the worst, they send for him only to haue him bedfellow to the King, and there to staie & keep him company. And if your sonne miscary, then let his blood be laid vnto my charge. I know their drifts and what they do pretend, for they shall both this night sleepe in the Tower and to morrow they shall both come forth to his happie coronation. Vpon my honour this is the full effect, for see the ambusht nobles are at hand to take the Prince away from you by force, if you will not by faire meanes let him go".

The Queen declares she will lose her life before he shall get her boy away from her, and asks if he will break sanctuary. The Cardinal, expressing surprise that she should have thought it necessary to take sanctuary at all, advises her to let the boy go, and she with no further sign of reluctance gives him up.

The scene from the entrance of the messenger follows More only generally. The first meeting between the Queen and the Archbishop is wholly omitted, and the second meeting is joined immediately to the scene with the messenger, by the palpable device of making him the servant of the Archbishop. The conversation is very much condensed from More's account. The Archbishop's speech is from More, except the statement that the King is to be crowned on the morrow. His words regarding the Queen's flight to sanctuary, "A heauie case when Princes flie for aide, where cut-throates, rebels and bankerouts should be", are from Buckingham's speech in the Council as reported by More. In the condensation all the pathos of More's description of the parting of the Duke and his mother is lost, and with entire lack of art the Queen is made to pass from a determination to give up her life rather than her son, to a consent to resign him, without any argument or conflict between. That the scene was not drawn from More in Hall or the Hardyng continuation I have shown on p. 407. On the greeting with which the

Palaestra. X.   28

messenger is received, and his answer, see pp. 496 and 508.

[Scene 9.] The play now turns once more to Richard. There enter "foure watchmen" and with them Richard's page, who proceeds to inform the audience in soliloquy of the present situation.

> "Page. Why thus by keeping company, am I become like vnto those with whom I keepe company. As my Lorde hopes to weare the Crown, so I hope by that means to haue preferment, but instead of the Crown, the blood of the headles light vpon his head: he hath made but a wrong match, for blood is a threatner and will haue reuenge. He makes hauocke of all to bring his purpose to passe: all those of the Queens kinred that were committed to Pomphret Castle, hee hath caused them to be secretly put to death without iudgement: the like was neuer seen in England. He spares none whom he but mistrusteth to be a hinderer to his proceedings, he is straight chopt vp in prison. The valiant Earle of Oxford being but mistrusted, is kept close prisoner in Hames Castle. Againe, how well Doctor Shaw hath pleased my Lord, that preached at Paules Crosse yesterday, that proued the two Princes to be bastards, whereupon in the after noone came down my Lord Mayor and the Aldermen to Baynards Castle, and offered my Lord the whole estate vpon him, and offered to make him King, which he refused so faintly, that if it had bene offered once more, I know he would haue taken it, the Duke of Buckingham is gone about it and is now in the Guild Hall making his Oration. But here comes my Lord".

Here the historical statements of the chronicles are again terribly "muddled". The Queen's kindred were, according to More (incorrectly), executed on the same day as Hastings; Oxford was imprisoned in Hames Castle by Edward IV not long after he recovered his throne; Shaw's Sunday sermon was followed on Tuesday by Buckingham's speech, and that on the next day by the visit of the Mayor and citizens to Baynard's Castle, where Richard did finally accept the offer to make him King. All this, of course, followed the death of Hastings. The confusion is so great as to render the play's description of Richard's course to the crown absurd.

While the page is speaking enter Richard and Catesby. Richard has determined to cut off Lord Hastings, for, he says, "he hath bene all this while partaker to our secrets, and if he should by some mislike vtter it, then were we all cast away". Catesby consents with the words, "Nay my Lord, do as you will, yet I have spoken what I can in my friend's cause". Richard turns to the page to ask him if he has the men in readiness as he directed, and bids Catesby have his weapons ready, as he is about to enter the Court. He has "been a long sleeper" but means to be awake anon to some of their costs. After Richard and Catesby have gone out, the page explains that there is to be a meeting of the Council which will cost Hastings and Stanley their best caps. He has half a dozen ruffians ready — evidently the "foure watchmen" — and when Richard knocks on the table they will rush in crying "treason" and lay hands on Stanley.

The representation of Catesby as pleading for his friend Hastings is another remarkable variation from the chronicle account. The reason urged by Richard for doing away with Hastings is another. Not the secrets he might reveal, but the opposition he offered to Richard's further plans — "lest his life should have quailed their purpose" — formed the cause of his destruction according to More. The reason here urged is the same as that assigned by the Mirror for Magistrates for Richard's turning against Buckingham. Cf. p. 254. Otherwise the facts of the passage are from More's account. On the page's "Blood is a threatner and will haue revenge" cf. p. 414, and also from The Battle of Alcazar (Dyce, Green and Peele, p. 437) "Blood will haue blood, foul murder scape no scourge".

Only the close of the famous Council scene appears on the stage. Richard, Catesby and others enter pulling Lord Hastings.

"Rich. Come bring him away, let this suffice, thou and that accursed sorceresse the Mother Queen hath bewitched me, with assistance of that famous strumpet of my brothers, Shores wife: my withered arme is a sufficient testimony, deny it if thou canst: laie not Shores wife with thee last night?

Hast. That she was in my house my Lord I cannot deny, but not for any such matter. If.

Rich. If villain, feedest thou mee with Ifs & ands, go fetch me a Priest, make a short shrift, and dispatch him quickly. For by the blessed Saint Paule I sweare, I will not dine tell I see the traytors head, away Sir Thomas, suffer him not to speak, see him executed straight & let his copartner the Lord Standly be carried to prison also, tis not his broke head I haue giuen him, shall excues him.

Exit with Hastings".

Here, though when Hastings appears he has already been arrested, the author introduces the charges made by Richard in the Council, following strictly More's account.

Catesby is ordered to have a Herald proclaim in the city the indictment of Hastings — which Catesby informs him is already finished — and promises him the place of his friend Hastings, if Buckingham, who all this while has been laboring with the citizens to make Richard king, succeeds in his purpose. Catesby goes on his mission and Richard turns to the page. "Now sirrha to thee, there is one thing more vndone, which grieues me more then all the rest, and to say the truth it is of more importance than all the rest". The page urges him to reveal it, but Richard hesitates; the matter is too weighty for so mean a man. Not until the page presses him repeatedly does he at last bring it out. "I would haue my two Nephewes the yoong Prince and his brother secretly murthered. Sownes villaine tis out, wilt thou do it? or wilt thou betray me?" The page is forward to assist, mentions the name of Terrell, a poor gentleman hoping for preferment, and promises to bring him to Richard. The Protector bids him be circumspect and liberal, and promises reward. He then entrusts the page with a further mission.

"Now that Shores wifes goods be confiscate, goe from me to the Bishop of London, and see that she receiue her open penance, let her be turned out of prison, but so bare as a wretch that worthily hath deserued that plague: and let there be straight proclamation made by my Lord the Mayor, that none shall releeue her nor pittie her, and priuie spies set in euerie corner of the Citie, that they may take notice of them that releeues her: for as her beginning was most famous aboue all, so will I haue her end most infamous aboue all. Haue care now my boy and win thy maisters heart for euer".

The proclamation by the herald is from More's story, as likewise the offer of the page to procure a murderer in Tyrell. Richard's hesitation to make known his wish is an artistic touch added by the author. According to More's story he went to Tyrell, who lay in a chamber outside his own. That Buckingham should be at the Guildhall, urging the citizens to make Richard king, while the latter is engaged in making way with Hastings is an absurdity connected with the absurd arrangement of events in the page's speech. The confiscation, and the open penance of Shore's wife are from More, but the turning of her out of prison to beg in the streets, is, as I have shown, from the legend in the Mirror for Magistrates, cf. p. 410. The proclamation by the mayor that none shall relieve her, and the setting of spies to see that nobody does so, are again an addition by the author. But cf p. 440—1.

[Scene 10.] "Enter **Shore's** Wife".

She appears lamenting the dishonor and folly of her former life, and the cruelty of the Protector that constrains her to beg in the streets. Lodowicke now enters, bewailing the deaths of many peers and the imprisonment of the young King "by the outrage of the Protector, who hath proclaimed himselfe King, by the name of Richard the third". The circumstances which have led to this do not appear. In Lodowicke Shore's wife recognizes one for whom she had procured the restoring of his lost lands, and approaches to beg a trifle. Lodowicke — absurdly enough — fails to recognize her until she makes known her name and begs a return for her former kindness to him. The answer she receives has been prophesied in the earlier scene.

> "Lod. A gods what is this world, and how uncertaine are riches? Is this she that was in such credit with the King? Nay more that could command a King indeed? I cannot deny but my lands she restored me, but shall I by releeuing of her hurt myselfe, no: for straight proclamation is made that none shall succour her, therefore for feare I should be seene talke with her, I will shun her company and get me to my chamber, and there set downe in heroicall verse, the shamefull end of a Kings Concubin, which is no doubt as wonderfull as the desolation of a kingdome".

Shore's wife laments the evident falling away of all those whom she aided when Edward was king and she "swayd the sword". She sees the citizen approaching, the life of whose son she saved, and determines to try him. As the citizen enters he is commenting on the improvement in affairs under Richard's rule. The ruffians on the Thames have been put down, the frays in the streets suppressed, and a truce concluded with Scotland for six years. The petition of Shore's wife he refuses in still coarser fashion than Lodowicke's.

Another lament by Shore's wife follows. Morton, the serving man, now enters. Him too she will try, though he is least able to help her. Morton like the others has a piece of information to offer. Richard has proclaimed John, Earl of Lincoln, heir to the crown — of Richard's son, here as in Shakespeare's play, nothing is said —, the young princes are reported to have been murdered, and strangest of all Buckingham has turned from Richard and gone down to Brecknock, where he means to raise a power to pull down the usurper. Shore's wife applies to Morton for relief and makes known her name, only to be greeted with the answer, "A foole, and euer thy owne enemy". Yet the servant is not so hard-hearted as the others. He is about to part with her his small means, when Richard's page enters. Seeing himself watched, Morton too denies her, and departs. The page approaches to twit Shore's wife with her misery. He suggests that if she need maintenance she may fall to her old trade. But she is truly repentant, and leaves the stage for good with the words,

> "Therefore sweet God forgiue all my foul offence,
> And though I haue done wickedly in this world,
> Into hell fire, let not my soule be hurld".

In this scene only the information conveyed by Lodowicke, the Citizen, and Morton is from More. The mention of a truce with Scotland for six years indicates the use of More through Hall, cf. p. 408. The rest is a dramatization of the legend in the Mirror for Magistrates.

On Lodowicke's proposal to set down in heroical verse the shameful end of a King's concubine, Mr. Fleay (Biog. Chron. 2 : 242) says, "Lodowick, sc. 10, who in this passage is certainly the Lodowick of Edward 3, is going to write the Shore story in 'heroical verse', as 'the shameful end of a King's Concubine, which is no doubt as wonderful as the desolation of a kingdom'. Shore's Wife was written in verse by A. Chute, S. R. 16th June 1593, and in Drayton's Heroical Epistles, which were certainly written years before their publication in 1599. See Spenser's allusion to him as Aetion in Colin Clout's come home again, 1595, where this "Heroical" work is distinctly indicated. As other of these Epistles relate to the story of Edward the Black Prince and the Countess of Salisbury, which story is also connected with Lodowick in Edward 3 . . ., I have no doubt that Drayton is meant in both plays".

Mr. Fleay is surely wrong. Apart from the unlikelihood that Drayton's Epistle was in existence previous to The True Tragedy — a question which I shall consider later, — the following is amply determinative. Drayton's Heroical Epistles contain two letters, one written by Edward to Shore's wife, pleading for her favor, the other Shore's wife's answer, denying him at first, but at the end allowing him to see that he has won her love.

There is certainly here no "shameful end of a Kings Concubin", and the epistles do not therefore fulfil the absolute requirement of the reference. But that requirement is fulfilled by the poem in the Mirror for Magistrates, from which, I have shown, the whole part of Shore's wife in the play was drawn. That poem is written in the metre — the iambic pentameter rimed — known then, as often now, by the name of heroical or heroic verse. Puttenham e. g. in his The Arte of English Poesie 1589 (Arber's Reprint, pp. 75, 76), says of Chaucer, "His meetre Heroicall of Troilus and Cresseid is very graue and stately, keeping the staffe of seuen, and the verse of ten". This is a far more natural meaning for the "heroicall verse" of Lodowicke's remark, than a reference to the "heroicall epistles" of Drayton, so called because, following Ovid, he conceived his characters to be in a sense heroical. Further, if this were a reference to Drayton's work we should undoubtedly have some reminiscence of it in the play. But there is absolutely none.

There is just one thing which in the slightest upholds Mr. Fleay's theory, and that he does not appear to have noticed. In the "Note of the Chronicle Historie" appended by Drayton to the epistle of Shore's wife (Spenser Soc. ed. 2 : 75) occurs the following. "Richard the third causing her to do open penance in Paules Church-yard, commaunding that no man should relieue her", etc. In the latter clause is a certain resemblance to The True Tragedy which is not found in More or the chronicles, aed one much more difficult of explanation than that mentioned by Mr. Fleay. If it could be made a probability that Drayton's epistle with its note was in existence in 1589 or 1590, it might be thought that the author of the play took this command from Drayton's note, where it applies to Shore's wife's penance in procession, and applied it to her begging, which he took from the Mirror for Magistrates. There is not the slightest proof, however, that the poem was in existence so early, and it is rather unlikely that the Notes were made till the poems were published in 1599. The most probable explanation is that the statement in both play and Note has a common source which we have been unable to find; or that Drayton took the statement from The True Tragedy, which is more likely than the reverse. The possibilities are too many, in the absence of any other indication of connection between The True Tragedy and Drayton's work, to warrant one in asserting that the author of the play was acquainted with the Heroical Epistles.

[Scene 11.] The next scene is laid at the Tower. Tyrell has brought a letter to Brokenbury from the King, in which the latter is commanded to deliver up the keys to Tyrell for one night. This he does, at the same time giving Tyrell to understand that he knows for what purpose he is there. "For the king oftentimes hath sent to me to haue them both dispatcht, but because I was a seruant to their father being Edward the fourth, my heart would neuer giue me to do the deed". Tyrell bids him not bother about the matter, which is between the King and himself; and "good Sir Robert" leaves in tears. Tyrell then calls up Miles Forest, who reports that he has procured two pitiless villains. "One of their names is Will Sluter [later called Slawter] yet the most part calles him blacke Will, the other is Jack Denten [Douton]". They are summoned, and Tyrell assures himself that they are pitiless. Tyrell informs them that the King "will haue no blood shead in the deed doing", and aske their advice on the best way to proceed. Forest proposes to shoot the princes with pistols as they sit at supper, Will to take them by their heels and beat their trains out against the walls, Denten to cut their throats — admirable proposals to prevent bloodshed! Tyrell decides that while the Princes are asleep Forest shall call up the murderers and they shall smother them between two feather beds. At this point the two princes enter. York is lovingly solicitous for his brother, who is grieving, not, as he explains, for himself, but because their uncle the Protector has fallen so far from love and duty as to keep them prisoners. York tries to comfort his brother with an assurance that their uncle will soon let them go, and begs Forest, who approaches, to tell his kingly brother some merry story, for he is melancholy. The King will have no stories, but inquires who it was that he has seen walking with Forest in the garden.

> "For. My Lord, it was one that was appointed by the King to be an ayde to Sir Thomas Brokenbury.
> King. Did the King, why Myles Forest am not I King?
> For. I would have said my Lord your vnckle the Protector.
> King. Nay my kingly vnckle I know he is now, but let him enioye both Crowne and kingdome, so my brother and I may but enjoy our liues and libertie".

The King now perceives Slawter and Denten, and cries out, "Who are they whose gastly lookes doth present a dying feare to my liuing bodie?" On hearing their names he starts. "Slawter, I pray God he come not to slaughter my brother and me, for from murther and slaughter, good Lord deliver vs". The two Princes then retire to rest, accompanied by Forest, who bids the murderers wait till he calls them up. Meanwhile Denten is stricken with remorse, and requires the threats of his companion to summon him back to his resolution. Forest now appears.

> "For. But ho sirs, come softly, for now they are at rest.
> Will. Come we are readie, by the masse they are a sleepe indeed.
> For. I heare they sleepe and sleepe sweet Princes, neuer wake no more, for you haue seene the last light in this world.
> Jack. Come presse them downe, it bootes not to cry againe, Jack vpon them so lustily. But maister Forest now they are dead what shall we do with them?
> For. Why goe and bury them at the heape of stones at the staire foote, while I goe and tell maister Terrell that the deed is done.
> Will. Well we will, farewell maister Forest".

Tyrell enters, inquiring if the deed has been despatched. Forest informs him that it has, and that the children are buried at the stair foot. "Anon ile carry them where they shall be no more founde againe, nor all the chronicles shall nere make mention what shall become of them". Tyrell departs to inform the King.

The basis of the scene is More's account, as given in Hall and the Hardyng continuation.

Variations and additions appear in the following. The King sends "oftentimes", instead of once, to Brakenbury to put the children to death. Brakenbury's reason for not doing so is an addition, as well as his conversation with Tyrell. The conversation between Tyrell and the murderers is an addition. On its origin cf. p. 484. The conference on the means of the murder was perhaps suggested by More's, "Sir James .. ceuysing before and preparing the meanes". The scene with the Princes is mostly invention. The King's melancholy is drawn from More's, "The prince .. with that young babe hys brother, lingered in thought and heauiness til this tratorous death deliuered them". The author not unskilfully distinguishes the two brothers in feeling, and makes an approach toward giving them real characters, a faint suggestion of the treatment they receive in Shakespeare's play. On the slip by which the King learns that Richard has assumed the crown, see p. 508—9. The introduction of the murderers to the Princes is, of course, invention. On the remorse of Denten cf. p. 510. It should be noted that the murder takes place on the stage in full view of the audience — contrary to Legge and to Shakespeare. This is wholly in keeping with the general tone of the play, which has much of the character of the bloodier and more horrible revenge plays. Forest's promise to bury the Princes where they shall never be found again is taken from More's statement that a priest of Brakenbury's buried them in another place, which could not be known by reason of his death. In More's account it is Tyrell who directs the burial at the stair foot.

Of the two murderers Mr. Fleay says (Biog. Chron. 2:315), "One of the actors in it, Sc. 11, is called Will Slaughter, 'yet the most part calls him Black Will', i. e. the Black Will of Arden of Faversham, q. v., which had no doubt been acted by the same man. Another actor is called Jack Douton (Dutton) or Denten, an accomodation of the Dighton of history to the actor's real name". Accordingly, in Mr. Fleay's list of the Queen's men (Chron. Hist. of Stage, p. 34) may be found "William Slaughter. See the old play on Richard 3". Of Arden of Feversham Mr. Fleay says (Biog. Chron. 2:28), "The tragedy of Arden of Feversham was acted publicly. In it a principal murderer has for name Black Will. This name is historic, being taken from the chronicle account of the murder in 1551. But an allusion to this Black Will in the old Richard 3 shows that Arden was previously on the stage, acted by the Queen's men, and that the part of Black Will was taken by an actor called William Slaughter or Slater; possibly the father of the Martin Slaughter, actor, who sold old plays (Query plays that had belonged to the Queen's men) to Henslow, and has therefore been elevated by Collier and his follower Halliwell to the dignity of authorship. The passage runs thus: — 'Forest. "One of their names is Will Sluter, yet the most part calls him Black Will; the other is Jack Denten". Now, Forest and Deighton were the names of the 'murderers', according to the chronicles. No William Slaughter is found in them. He is introduced here as a bit of 'gag' addressed to the groundlings for the sake of the wretched pun. For the same reason Deighton is changed to Denten, which was a variant spelling of Dounton, known as an actor". Acting upon the belief he at that time entertained that The True Tragedy was acted in 1585 or 1586, Mr. Fleay therefore dated Arden 1585'.

By the Revels accounts (cf. Cunningham, Extracts from the Acc'ts of the Revels at Court, Introd. p. XXXII), and otherwise, we know that there was in the Queen's compagny a John Dutton, and Mr. Fleay's conjecture that the variations in the name of the second murderer were caused by accomodation to the actor's name may be correct; but he has fallen into a sad mistake with regard to the other murderer. A little closer reading of More's story would have shown him the statement, "forthwith was the prince and his brother bothe shet vp, and all other remoued from them, onely one called black Wil or William Slaughter except, set to serue them" (Lumby's ed. p. 83). And this statement is in all the chronicles. The author of the play simply made him one of the murderers, assigning to Forest a general superintendence of the affair, instead of making Forest and Dighton the two murderers, according to More. Thus both the name William Slaughter and the nickname Black Will are in the chronicle source, as is the case with the Black Will of Arden of Feversham. All the conclusions of Mr. Fleay are therefore worthless.

[Scene 12.] The play now turns to Buckingham, who enters with dagger drawn. Banister, who has betrayed him, is in his power and forced to plead for life. He pleads that the proclamation was death to him that harbored Buckingham, and that he must obey his Prince. Buckingham declares that the thousand crowns offered as reward were the real inducement and is about to slay Banister when a Herald enters and arrests him as a traitor. Buckingham bursts out into a wild tirade against Richard.

> "Ah Richard, did I in Guild Hall pleade the Orator for thee, and held thee in all thy slie and wicked practices, and for my reward doest thou alot me death? Ah Buckingham, thou plaidst thy part and made him King, and put the lawfull heires besides: why then is Buckingham guiltie now of his death? Yet had not the Bishop of Ely fled I had escaped".

At this point "enters six others to rescue the **Duke**". Buckingham entreats them to lay their weapons by. He tells them that Richmond is about to land at Milford Haven, and bids them go to his aid. On his knees he prays that Richmond may succeed and marry Elizabeth, as he has promised. He had hoped to raise up a lawful king, but it was too late, the Princes were smothered in the Tower. "Sweet Edward and thy brother, I nere slept quiet thinking of their deaths. But vaunt Buckingham, thou was altogither innocent of their death". Then turning to Banister he curses him.

> "But thou vilain, whom of a child I nurst thee vp, and hast so vniustly betraid thy Lorde? Let the curse of Buckingham nere depart from thee. Let vengeance, mischiefes, tortures, light on thee and thine. And after death thou maist more torture feele, then when Exeon turnes the restlesse wheele. And baune thy soule were ere thou seeme to rest. But come my friends, let me away.
>
> Her. My Lord, we are sorie. But come laie handes on Banister".

Why Banister should be arrested does not appear. It may be the author's extension of the hint contained in Hall's "As for his thousand pound kyng Richard gaue him not one farthing, saiyng that he which would be vntrew to so good a Master would be false to al other" (p. 395). Buckingham's passage with Banister, and the intervention of the six would-be rescuers, are the author's invention. The Herald represents Mitton, Sheriff of Shropshire. The proclamation is given from the chronicles, save that the reward is stated as 1000 crowns instead of £ 1000. The contents of Buckingham's two speeches are from the chronicles, down to his mention of the Princes. Here The True Tragedy, which represents Buckingham as revolting from Richard before the murder, is nearer the historical fact than the chronicles, which, following Hall, represent Buckingham as revolting partly, at least, on account of the murder. Apparently (cf. "it was too late") Buckingham is represented as at first intending to restore the Prince to his throne, an invention of the author's. I have suggested the Buckingham legend in the Mirror for Magistrates (cf. p. 225) as the source of the curse against Banister. The language of the curse shows close resemblance to the other plays of the group, especially the revenge plays. Cf. The Spanish Tragedy (Haz. Dods. 4:58).

> "O God! confusion, mischief, torment, death and hell".

Arden of Feversham I: 337.

> "Hell-fyre and wrathful vengeance light on me".

The wheel of Ixion is a favorite allusion, introduced like much of the machinery of the revenge plays, from Seneca. Cf. especially Spanish Tragedy, p. 9:

> "And poor Ixion turns an endless wheel",

and in The Battle of Alcazar, Act IV, end, the curse of Abdelmelec on the opposing army and king:

> "Then let the earth discover to his ghost
> Such tortures as usurpers feel below;
> Rack'd let him be in proud Ixion's wheel,
> Pin'd let him be with Tantalus' endless thirst,
> Prey let him be to Tityus' greedy bird,
> Wearied with Sisyphus' immortal toil:
> And lastly for revenge, for deep revenge,
> Whereof thou goddess and deviser art,
> Damn'd let him be, damn'd, and condemn'd to bear
> All torments, tortures, plagues, and pains of hell".

[Scene 13.] Richard now appears for the first time since his coronation. Much has happened since that time, the Princes have been murdered, and Buckingham has revolted and been captured. All this Richard has not been able to bear unmoved.

> "King. The goale is got, and golden Crowne is wonne,
> And well deseruest thou to weare the same,
> That ventured hast thy bodie and thy soule,
> But what bootes Richard, now the Diademe,
> Or kingdome got, by murther of his friends,
> My fearefull shadow that still followes me,

>   Hath summond me before the seuere iudge,
>   My conscience witnesse of the blood I spilt,
>   Accuseth me as guiltie of the fact,
>   The fact a damned iudgement craues,
>   Whereas impartiall iustice hath condemned.
>   Meethinkes the Crowne which I before did weare,
>   Inchast with Pearle and costly Diamonds,
>   It turned now into a fatall wreathe,
>   Of fiery flames, and euer burning starres,
>   And raging fiends hath past ther vgly shapes,
>   In Stygian lakes, adrest to tend on me,
>   If it be thus, what wilt thou do in this extremitie?
>   Nay what canst thou do to purge thee of thy guilt?
>   Euen repent, craue mercie for thy damned fact,
>   Appeale for mercy to thy righteous God,
>   Ha repent, not I, craue mercy they that list,
>   My God, is none of mine. Then Richard be thus resolu'd,
>   To place thy soule, in ballance with their blood,
>   Soule for soule, and bodie for bodie, yea mary Richard,
>   That's good, Catesbie.
> Cat.   You cald my Lorde, I thinke?
> King.   It may be so".

While Richard has been pouring out his anguish Catesby has entered, and Richard eagerly grasps at the relief of his presence. But he is not yet restored to self-control. As he converses with Catesby about his troubles he repeatedly misunderstands the remarks of his faithful subordinate to be aimed at him, and bursts out into rage that has to be calmed by Catesby. He is overwhelmed with trouble. Buckingham is in rebellion; but Catesby is able to relieve him here with the news of the duke's execution. Of Richmond Catesby knows little, but Richard has only too full information. Margaret is conspiring to bring home her son, and has arranged a marriage between him and the Princess Elizabeth. This news, indeed, Catesby has heard of.

> "King.   Why then there it goes,
>   The great duiell of hell go with all.
>   A marriage begun in mischiefe, shall end in blood:
>   I thinke that accursed sorceresse the mother Queene,

> Doth nothing but bewitch me, and hatcheth conspiracies,
> And brings out perillous birds to wound,
>> Their Countries weale,
>> The Earle is vp in Armes,
>> And with him many of the Nobiltie,
>> He hath ayde in France,
>> He is rescued in Brittaine,
> And meaneth shortly to arriue in England:
> But all this spites me not so much,
> As his escape from Landoyse the Dukes Treasuror,
> Who if he had bene prickt foorth for reuenge,
> He had ended all by apprehending of our foe,
> But now he is in disgrace with the Duke,
> And we farther off our purpose then to fore,
> But the Earle hath not so many byting dogs abroad,
> As we haue sleeping curres at home here,
> Readie for rescue".

The facts mentioned in the passage with Catesby are from the chronicle. Richard's soliloquy shows the same conception of his punishment as Shakespeare's. It is not merely his external losses, as in Legge, that drive him to despair, it is the guilty conscience, witness of the blood he has spilt. The constant determination, the savage and cruel will, are not proof against assaults from within. Nor is it merely in his hours of sleep that Richard's will grows feeble and conscience asserts her power. He is always pursued by the fearful shadow. Yet further, this Richard has his moments when he thinks on repentance, of appealing to God for mercy, and all his strength of will is required to turn him back. Here the influence of Marlowe's Faustus is plainly to be seen (cf. p. 481—2), an influence revealed even more clearly in other plays of the group to which The True Tragedy shows close relation. Compare from A Looking Glass for London and England (Dyce's Green p. 142):

> "Methinks I hear a voice amidst mine ears.
> That bids me stay, and tells me that the Lord
> Is merciful to those that do repent.
> May I repent? O thou, my doubtful soul,

> Thou mayst repent, the judge is merciful!
> Hence tools of wrath, stales of temptation!
> For I will pray and sigh unto the Lord".

and from Friar Bacon and Friar Bungay, 176 col. 1,

> "Yet, Bacon, cheer thee, drown not in despair;
> Sins have their salves, repentance can do much:
> Think mercy sits where Justice holds her seat,
> And from those wounds those bloody Jews did pierce,
> Which by thy magic oft did bleed afresh,
> From thence for thee the dew of mercy drops,
> To wash the wrath of high Jehovah's ire,
> And make thee as a new-born babe from sin. —
> Bungay, I'll spend the remnant of my life
> In pure devotion praying to my God".

What distinguishes The True Tragedy from other imitations and keeps it closer to the original, is that Richard, moved by his conscience to think of repentance forces himself by his own will to turn away from it. He has his moments of weakness when feeling is uppermost, but his will is still indomitable. And here is the essential characteristic of the Shakespearean Richard also.

With the "raging fiends" in "Stygian lakes" cf. Locrine 5:4,

> "The snarling curs of darken'd Tartarus
> Sent from Avernus' ponds by Rhadamanth".

Much closer connection with this and other plays of the group is shown in Richard's next soliloquy.

As Richard confers with Catesby there enter Lord Stanley and his son George. Richard at once asks the former for news of his stepson Richmond, which Stanley professes to be unable to give. The King expresses distrust in rough fashion, and declares his belief that Stanley's request to be allowed to depart to his home is made merely that he may help Richmond. Stanley protests, and is finally permitted to go, on promise that he will use his forces against Richmond and leaving his son George as a pledge. The facts of the scene are from the chronicle account, with some slight changes and misunderstanding.

Now enters Lovell, whom Richard has sent to the Queen concerning his suit to her daughter Elizabeth.

"King. How now Louell, what newes?
   What saith the mother Queene to my sute?
Lou. My Lord very strange she was at the first,
   But when I had told her the cause, she gaue concent:
   Desiring your maiestie to make the nobiltie priuie to it.
King. God haue mercy Louell, but what saith Lady Elizabeth?
Lou. Why my Lord, straunge, as women will be at the first.
   But through intreatie of her mother, she quickly gaue
   consent. And the Queene wild me to tel your grace, that
   she meanes to leaue Sanctuary, and to come to the court
   with al her daughters".

Here is an important variation from the chronicle account. According to this, "men bothe of wit and grauitie" — here, as in Legge, represented by Lovell, see p. 344 — are sent to persuade the Queen to come to court with her daughters. Nothing is said of Richard's suit for her daughter, for Anne is not yet dead; and the chronicles have expressly "queene Elyzabeth which knewe nothing lesse then that he moost entended" (Hall, p. 407). The princess's consent is still further away from the chronicles, according to which "the mayden her selfe moost of all detested and abhorred this vnlawfull and in manner vnnaturall copulacion" (Hall, p. 407). The reality of the Queen's consent is rendered doubtful by the fact that in the next scene she sends messages of welcome to Richmond, and we have in consequence the same uncertainty here as attaches to her consent in Shakespeare.

That, however, Richard should make suit to the Queen for her daughter's hand is not contrary to the chronicles, as we have "making much suite to haue her ioyned with him in lawfull matrimony" (Hall, p. 407). What is contrary is that this suit should be joined to the request that the Queen leave sanctuary and bring her daughters to Court.

Richard is inquiring about "the Scottish Nobles that met at Nottingham" when there enters a messenger.

29*

"King. Gogs wounds who is that? search the villaine, had he any dags about him?
Mess. No my Lord I haue none.
King. From whence comes thou?"

He comes from Nottingham, and Lovell, Catesby and the page press about him with the eager question, "Is the marriage concluded betweene the Scottish Earle and the Lady Rosa?" Richard is angered by their officiousness.

"King. Nay will you giue me leaue to tell you that? Why you villianes will you know the secrets of my letter by interrupting messengers that are sent to me? Away I say, begone, it is time to looke about: away I say, what here yet villaines?"

In his disturbance of spirit Richard is so hasty that he has no thought of the messenger, who has news to deliver, and does not therefore obey Richard's bidding. He informs Richard that the marriage of his niece has been concluded, and brings the further news that Captain Blunt has revolted and fled to Richmond with his prisoner, the Earl of Oxford. Richard bursts out again in a passion.

"O villaines, rebels, fugetives, theeues, how are we betrayd, when our owne swoordes shall beate vs, and our owne subiect seekes the subuertion of the state, the fall of their Prince, and sack of their Country, of his, nay neither must nor shall, for I will Army with my friends, and cut off my enemies & beard them to their face that dares me, and but one, I one, beyond the seas that troubles me: wel his power is weake, & we are strong, therefore I wil meet him with such melodie, that the singing of a bullet shal send him merily to his logest home".

The historical content of the scene is peculiar. Nothing is advanced to show why such importance is given to the marriage of Richard's niece, and it is not further mentioned in the play. The name of Richard's niece was Anne de la Poole, and "the faire Lady Rosa" is only to be explained as a corruption of her husband's name, the prince of Rothsay. The agreement for this marriage was made at the same time as the truce mentioned much earlier in the play.

Richard's greeting of the messenger is a dramatization of More's "Where he went abrode, his eyen whirled about, his body priuily fenced, his hand euer on his dager, his countenance and maner like one alway ready to strike againe". On the passage in which Richard bids all depart, see p. 512.

"It is time to look about" is a favorite expression of the old plays. Cf. Mucedorus (Delius' ed. p. 11):

>"When heaps of arms do hover overhead,
>'Tis time as then (some say) to look about'.

and the old King John, p. 179,

>"Arthur, away, tis time to look about".

With "send him to his longest home" cf. Locrine (Doubtful Plays of Sh., Tauchnitz, p. 193),

>"Never shall these blood-sucking mastiff curs
>Bring wretched Sabren to her latest home".

Arden of Feversham, IV, 1

>"Theyle be your ferry men to long home"

Titus Andronicus, I, 83,

>"Those that I bring unto their latest home".

[Scene 14.] Richmond now makes his first appearance, accompanied by the Earl of Oxford. P. Landoys and Captain Blunt. He welcomes them to England, which he claims as his right and inheritance.

>"Richard but usurps in my authortie,
>For in his tyrannie he slaughtered those
>That would not succour him in his attempts,
>Whose guiltlesse blood craues daily at Gods hands,
>Reuenge for outrage done to their harmlesse liues.
>Then courage countrymen, and neuer be dismay'd,
>Our quarels good, and God will helpe the right,
>For we may know by dangers we haue past,
>That God no doubt will giue vs victorie".

Oxford and Blunt plight their faith to follow Richmond till he conquers. Landoys unites with them, ready to follow his leader to death, but hoping, if the Queen keep her word, to see the union of the houses of York and Lancaster. Richmond thanks them, and promises if he be made king,

> "I will so deale in gouerning the state.
> Which now lies like sauage shultred groue,
> Where brambles, briars, and thornes, ouergrow those sprigs,
> . . . .
> And neuer leaue to follow my resolue,
> Till I haue mowed those brambles, briars and thornes
> That hinder those that long to do us good".

Oxford adds that they have escaped the greatest danger, Richard's garrison at Milford Haven, and need not feel dismayed because Buckingham is taken.

The speech of Richmond is not based on any of the chronicles. It may perhaps be imitated from Legge's speech of Richmond at his landing. Cf. the remarks on that passage, p. 356, and see also p. 479. For a comparison with Shakespeare's speech and scene see p. 513. Oxford and Blunt accompanied Richmond to England, but that Landoyse should be made one of his followers is an absurdity for which there is not the slightest foundation.

In his first speech Richmond manifests as in Shakespeare, though not so clearly, his claim to be God's agent in punishing the tyrant. With his words compare old Henry V (Sh. Lib. II 1, p. 363),

"Hen. V My Lords and louing Countreymen
> Though we be fewer, and they many,
> Feare not, your quarrel is good, and God wil defend you.
> Plucke vp your hearts, for this day we shall either haue
> A valiant victorie, or an honourable death".

The latter passage follows the chronicle (Hall, p. 67) quite closely, and the speech in The True Tragedy is probably based on Richmond's speech before the battle of Bosworth (Hall, p. 467). Influence of the Henry V speech is not impossible, however, as Richmond's arrangement of battle at the close of this scene appears to be influenced by the Henry V battle arrangement which is part of the speech from which the above is taken.

When Oxford has finished there enters a messenger with letters from the mother Queen and from Lady Stanley, Richmond's mother. He mentions the names of several who are coming to Richmond's aid, "the Lord Fitz Harbart the earle of Pembrokes sonne and heire", "Sir Prise vp Thomas", "sir Thomas vp Richard", "Sir Owen Williams", "sir Thomas Denis", and "Arnoll Butler". At the latter name Richmond grows angry. "Doth Arnoll Butler come, I can hardly brooke his trecherie, for hee it was that wrought my disgrace with the King" [i. e. Edward]. He is soon appeased and turns to the arrangement of his battle.

> "Because I will be foremost in this fight,
> To incounter with that bloodie murtherer,
> Myselfe wil lead the vaward of our troope,
> My Lord of Oxford, you as our second selfe,
> Shall haue the happie leading of the reare,
> A place I know which you will well deserue,
> And Captaine Blunt, Peter Landoye and you,
> Shall by in quarters as our battels scoutes,
> Prouided, thus your bow-men Captaine Blunt,
> Must scatter here and there to gaull their horse,
> As also when that our promised friends do come,
> Then must you hold hard skirmish with our foes,
> Till I by cast of a counter march,
> Haue ioynd our power with those that come to vs,
> Then casting close, as wings on either side,
> We will giue a new prauado on the foe,
> Therefore let vs toward Aderstoe amaine,
> Where we this night God-willing will incampe,
> From thence towards Lichfield, we will march next day,
> And neerer London, bid King Richard play".

There is no mention in the chronicles of Richmond's receiving messages from the Queen. He sent messengers to his mother, the Stanley and others, and they "retourned to hym the same daye that he entered into Shrewsburie, and made relacioun to hym that his frendes were ready in all poyntes to doo all things for him which either they ought or might do" (Hall, p. 411). The names of Richmond's helpers are chiefly from the chronicles. But they have received the usual careless treatment. "Lord Talbut, the Earle of Shreuesbury's sonne and heire", is in the chronicle "Sir George Talbott with the whole poure of the young Earle of Shreusbury then beynge in warde"; "Lord Fitz Harbart" was really Sir Walter Herbert, second son of the first Herbert Earl of Pembroke, and not his heir, who was named William like his father. This William was transferred from the earldom of Pembroke to that of Huntingdon in 1479. "Prise up Thomas" = Rice ap Thomas. The curious and wholly unfounded reference to Butler is the author's invention, based on Hall's "Arnold Butler a valiaunt captain, which first askynge perdon for his offences before tyme committed against the erle of Richmond and that obteynd". This I have shown elsewhere (cf. p. 193) is a mistranslation of Polidore Vergil. The offences were those of all the Pembrokians, and consisted evidently in serving the Earl of Pembroke set up for them by Edward, after their former lord, Jasper, who now returned with Richmond, had been driven out. "Owen Williams" and "Sir John Denis" are not mentioned in the chronicles, but, curiously, in the sketch of the persons occupied in one act of a play on Richard found in the papers of the Actor Alleyn (cf. p. 531) the same name occurs. "3 sce. Ansell, Dang^r. Denys, Hen. Oxf. Courtney, Bouchier and Grace. To them Rice ap Tho. and his Souldiers". The other names would seem to indicate that here also Denis was one of those who came to Henry.

Richmond's battle arrangement differs notably from that of the Chronicles, which have, "In $\overset{e}{y}$ Frount he placed the archers, of whome he made captain John erle of Oxford: to the right wing of $\overset{e}{y}$ bataill he appoynted, sir Gylbert Talbott to be $\overset{e}{y}$ leder: to $\overset{e}{y}$ left wing he assigned sir John Sauage, & he w^t $\overset{e}{y}$ aide of $\overset{e}{y}$ lord Stanley accompaignid with therle of Pembroke hauyng a good compaignie of horsmen and a small nomber of footmen" (Hall p. 414). But compare old Henry V p. 363.

> "Now my Lords I wil that my vncle the Duke of Yorke,
> Haue the auantgard in the battell.
> The Earle of Darby, the Earle of Oxford,
> The Earle of Kent, the Earle of Nottingham,
> The Earle of Huntington, I wil haue beside the army,
> That they may came fresh vpon them.
> And I myselfe with the Duke of Bedford,
> The Duke of Clarence and the Duke of Gloster,
> Wil be in the midst of the battell.
> Futhermore, I wil that my Lord of Willowby.
> And the Earle of Northumberland,
> With their troupes of horsemen, be continually running like Wings on both sides of the Army:
> My Lord of Northumberland, on the left wing.
> Then I wil that euery archer prouide him a stake of
> A tree, and sharpe it at both endes,
> And at the first encounter of the horsemen,
> To pitch their stakes down into the ground before them,
> That they may gore themselues vpon them,
> And then to recoyle backe, and shoote wholly altogither,
> And so discomfit them".

The latter may have been imitated in the True Tragedy passage. Richmond's order of march was, according to the chronicle (Hall 411—13) Shrewsbury, Newporte, Stafforde, Lichefelde, Tomwoorth. He did not encamp in Aderstone, but visited Lord Stanley "in a little close" near that place.

[Scene 15.] The page enters.

> "Page. Where shall I find a place to sigh my fill,
> And waile the griefe of our sore troubled King?
> For now he hath obtaind the Diademe,
> But with such great discomfort to his minde,
> That he had better liued a priuate man, his lookes are gastly,
> Hidious to behold, and from the priuie sentire of his heart,
> There comes such deepe fetcht sighes and fearefull cries,
> That being with him in his chamber oft,
> He mooues me weepe and sigh for company,
> For if he heare one stirre he riseth vp,
> And claps his hand vpon his dagger straight,
> Readie to stab him what so ere he be.
> But he must thinke this is the iust reuenge,

> The heauens haue poured vpon him for his sinnes,
> Those Peeres which he vnkindly murthered,
> Doth crie for iustice at the hands of God,
> And he in iustice sends continuall feare,
> For to afright him both at bed and boord,
> But staie, what noyse is this, who haue we here?"

This is evidently based on the passage on More from which was drawn the motive for the greeting of the messenger in scene 13. "Where he went abrode, his eyen whirled about, his body priuily fenced, his hand euen on his danger, his countenance and maner like one always ready to strike againe, he toke ill rest a nightes, lay long wakyng and musing, sore weried with care and watch, rather slumbred than slept, troubled wyth feareful dreames, sodainely sommetyme sterte vp, leape out of his bed and runne about the chamber, so was his restles herte continually tossed and tumbled with the tedious impression and stormy remembrance of his abominable dede".

While the page is speaking there enter soldiers, who explain that they have revolted from Richard and are on their way to Richmond. The page, foreboding the overthrow of his master, goes in to tell him.

That many soldiers revolted to Richmond is related in the chronicle. That we have a scene here showing this is perhaps due to the influence of Legge's play. See p. 366—7.

[Scene 16.] Richmond now enters, on his way by night to meet his stepfather Stanley. Oxford, who begs to accompany him, remonstrates against his night expeditions, and relates the fear of the soldiers caused by his last night's absence, Richmond turns him away, saying that he has promised his father that none shall come but himself. In the meeting that ensues between Stanley and Richmond the former relates the precarious position of his son George, and declares he cannot render open aid. At this Richmond is in despair, a despair increased by the knowledge that Richard's forces number 20,000 while his own are but 5000. Yet conscious of the justice of his cause he determines not to lose hope.

On this scene and its relation to those of Legge and Shakespeare see pp. 360 ff., 475 f., and 515.

According to the chronicles Richmond had 5000 beside 3000 under the Stanleys; "the kynges nomber was doble as muche & more" (Hall, p. 414). 20,000 appears to have been a favorite number in similar passages of the old plays. Cf. e. g. True Tr., p. 116

"Rich. What number do you thinke the king's power to be?
Stan. Mary some twentie thousand".

with Jack Straw (Haz.-Dods. 5 : 385)

"Treas. My friend, what power have they assembled in the field?
Mess. My lord, a twenty thousand men or thereabout".

[Scene 17.] Before the next scene, as motto to its contents, appears "Quisquam[ne] regno gaudes [?] ô fallax bonum". Cf. p. 475.

"Enters the King and the Lord Louell.

King. The hell of life that hangs vpon the Crowne,
　The daily cares, the nightly dreames,
　The wretched crewes, the treason of the foe,
　And horror of my bloodie practise past,
　Strikes such a terror to my wounded conscience,
　That sleep I, wake I, or whatsoeuer I do,
　Meethinkes their ghoasts comes gaping for reuenge,
　Whom I haue slaine in reaching for a Crowne.
　Clarence complaines, and crieth for reuenge.
　My Nephues bloods, Reuenge, reuenge doth crie.
　The headlesse Peeres come preasing for reuenge.
　And euery one cries, let the tyrant die.
　The Sunne by day shines hotely for reuenge.
　The Moone by night eclipseth for reuenge.
　The Stars are turned to Comets for reuenge.
　The Planets chaunge their coures for reuenge.
　The birds sing not, but sorrow for reuenge.
　The silly lambes sits bleating for reuenge
　The screeking Rauen sits croking for reuenge.
　Whole heads of beasts comes bellowing for reuenge.
　And all, yea all the world I thinke,

>   Cries for reuenge, and nothing but reuenge.
>   But to conclude, I haue deserued reuenge.
>   In company I dare not trust my friend,
>   Being alone, I dread the secret foe:
>   I doubt my foode least poyson lurke therein.
>   My bed is vncoth, rest refraines my head.
>   Then such a life I count far worse to be,
>   Then thousand deaths vnto a damned death:
>   How wast death I said? who dare attempt my death?
>   Nay who dare so much as once to thynke my death?
>   Though enemies there be that would my body kill,
>   Yet shall they leaue a neuer dying minde.
>   But yow villaines, rebels, traitors as you are
>   How came the foe in, preasing so neare?
>   Where, where, slept the garrison that should a beat them back?
>   Where was our friends to intercept the foe?
>   All gone, quite fled, his loyaltie quite laid a bed?
>   Then vengeance, mischiefe, horror, with mischance,
>   Wild fire, with whirlewinds, light vpon your heads,
>   That thus betrayd your Prince by your vntruth.
> King. Frantike man, what meanst thou by this mood?
>   Now he is come more need to beate him backe".

The conversation that follows with Lovell is corrupt, but Richard's speech is evidently delivered in soliloquy, for Lovell, inquiring the cause of Richard's trouble, is repulsed with the words, "The cause Buzard, what cause shoulde I participate to thee? My friends are gone away, and fled from me, keep silence villaine, least I by poste do send thy soule to hell, not one word more, if thou doest loue thy life".

Richard's soliloquy, the best-known passage in the play, was without question suggested by the chronicle account of his dream. In the horrors that come to him Richard recognizes the effect of his wounded conscience, and this too has its basis in the interpretation put by the chroniclers (following Polidore Vergil) upon his dream. But this is the extent of the chronicle influence. The terrible devils pulling and haling him have here become the ghosts of those whom he has murdered, and the whole conception of the passage is borrowed from the revenge-plays, the influence of which has been nearly wanting since the introduction of Clarence's ghost. With this soliloquy should be especially compared

Locrine, Act 5, sc. 4

> "The boisterous Boreas thund'reth forth revenge:
> The stony rocks cry out on sharp revenge:
> The thorny bush pronounceth dire revenge.
> Now Corineus, stay and see revenge,
> And feed thy soul with Locrine's overthrow".

James IV (Dyce's Green p. 217, col. 2)

> "Methinks I hear my Dorothea's ghost
> Howling revenge for my accursèd hate:
> The ghosts of those my subjects that are slain
> Pursue me, crying out, "Woe, woe to lust!"

A Looking Glass for London (Dyce's Green p. 142)

> "Groaning in conscience, burden'd with my crimes,
> The hell of sorrow haunts me up and down,
> Tread where I list, methinks the bleeding ghosts
> Of those whom my corruption brought to naughts
> Do serve for stumbling-blocks before my steps;
> The fatherless and widow wrong'd by me,
> The poor oppressèd by my usury;
> Methinks I see their hands rear'd up to heaven,
> To cry for vengeance of my covetousness".

The first quoted passage, which Boswell thought a proof that The True Tragedy and Locrine had the same author, is of course no proof of that fact, but the resemblance is far too close to deny a connection between the two. That cannot be set aside by the statement that such repetitions as this of the word revenge "is one of the commonest artifices of rhetoric" (Field's introd. p. 50). The same cannot be so strongly asserted of the other passage cited by Boswell,

Locrine 5:2

> "Behold the heavens do wail for Guendolen;
> The shinning sun doth blush for Guendolen;
> The liquid air doth weep for Guendolen;
> The very ground doth groan for Guendolen".

Of these plays, Locrine, assigned by Fleay to so early a date as 1586, though not published till 1595, and Looking Glass must have preceded The True Tragedy, and the others may have done so. The passage here is clearly dependent upon the influence of the revenge-plays, and it is to them through The True Tragedy that we owe the ghost scene in Shakespeare. See pp. 515—8.

With the first lines of Richard's speech compare also Old King John, p. 224

> "Yet John your lord . . . .
> Will (as he may) sustaine the heauie yoke
> Of pressing cares, that hang vpon a Crowne".

The thought is expressed often in the old plays, doubtless originally from Seneca.

The habit of ending soliloquies with "but to conclude" is likewise common in the old plays. Cf. eg. King Henry's speech in 3 Henry VI, 2:5; 2 Henry VI, 4:1; Sp. Tragedy (Haz. Dodsley 4:124).

It is to be noted that we have here no single dream, and that Richard does not, as in the chronicle, make known to others the cause of his trouble. On the King's final words to Lovell cf. p. 524, c.

As Richard repels Lovell, Catesby enters with the news that Stanley refuses to come, and that when threatened with the death of his son he has replied that he has another son left to make Lord Stanley. Richard, with a wild outcry, wishes to send at once for George Stanley and behead him. Catesby and Lovell endeavor to dissuade him, but he is not to be moved. As they hesitate to follow out his bidding he turns upon them with the question, "Why sirs why fear you thus", and implores their help.

> "Both. We will my Lord.
> King. We will my Lord, a Catesbie, thou lookest like a dog, and thou Louell too, but you will runne away with them that be gone, and the diuel go with you all, God I hope, God, what talke I of God, that haue serued the diuell all this while. No, fortune and courage for mee, and ioyne

> England against mee with England, Ioyne Europe with Europe, come Christendome, and with Christendome the whole world, and yet I will neuer yeeld but by death onely. By death, no die, part not childishly from thy Crowne, but come the diuell to claime it, strike him down, & tho that Fortune hath decreed, to set reuenge with triumphs on my wretched head, yet death, sweete death, my latest friend, hath sworne to make a bargaine for my lasting fame, and his, I this verie day, I hope with this lame hand of mine, to rake out that hatefull heart of Richmond, and when I haue it to eate it panting hote with salt, and drinke his blood luke warme, tho I be sure twil poyson me. Sirs you that be resolute follow me, the rest go hang your selues".

And Richard goes out to his final battle. There is no change in his heart as he faces the decisive hour. A moment he thinks of God and repentance, then resolutely turns away. Death if death come, cannot refuse him the one thing that has been his highest purpose, lasting fame. Crown, power, life may go, but he has been a king and like a king will die. All the chronicles unite to speak of Richard's brave death, and Legge had followed them. What especially distinguishes The True Tragedy Richard from Legge's is that this courage is his characteristic throughout. It can only be attacked from within by his conscience, and that is not strong enough to overcome his will.

The crude and savage expression of the revenge plays clings to this speech. With the last gruesome words of Richard, cf. Arden of Feversham, II; 2 : 105, 6,

> "From hence nere will I wash this bloody staine,
> Til Ardens hart be panting in my hand".

and I, 159—60,

> "Ile send from London such a taunting letter
> As she shall eat the hart he sent with salt".

Selimus, 1302 et seq.:

> "He should have done as I do mean to do;
> . . . .
> Then teare the old man peece meal with my teath
> And colour my strong hands with his gore-blood".

1385, 6:
> "I would rip up his breast and rend his heart
> Into his bowels thrust my angry hands".

Locrine (p. 191):

> "Find me young Sabren, Locrine's only joy,
> That I may glut my mind with lukewarm blood,
> Swiftly distilling from the bastard's breast".

[Scene 18.] "The battell enters, **Richard** wounded with his Page".

> "King. A horse, a horse a fresh horse.
> Page. A flie my Lord, and saue your life.
> King. Flie villain, looke I as tho I would flie ⊢"

First shall earth receive his dead body. He looks up to the gloomy heavens, where the sun refuses to shine, and thinks, "down is thy sun, Richard, never to shine again". Yet the old spirit returns. Faint he will not, for even yet Fortune may yield him a quiet crown — if not he can at least die a king. Then "enters **Richmond** to battell againe, and kils **Richard**".

For a closer examination of the above-quoted passage and comparison with Shakespeare, see pp. 518—20.

[Scene 19.] "Enters **Report** and the **Page**". Of the page Report requests "the certain true report of this victorious battle", and the page relates to him that Richard has been slain and Richmond is conqueror. Slain too are the Duke of Norfolk, sir Robert Brokenby (Brakenbury), and Lovell. Catesby is this day beheaded at Leicester for taking part with Richard. Then the page turns to describe his master's courage in the battle". "Richard came to fielde mounted on horsback, with as high resolve as fierce Achillis mongst the sturdie Greekes". To meet him came Richmond and the battle joined. "But in the skirmish which continued long, my lord gan faint", and Richmond preceiving this sounded a fresh alarm. "But worthie Richard that did neuer flie, but followed honour to the gates of death, straight spurd his horse to encounter with the Earle, in which encountry Richmond did preuaile, & taking Richard at aduantage, then he threw his horse and him both to the ground, and there was woorthie Richard wounded, so that after that he nere recouered strength. But to be briefe, my maister would not yeeld, but with his losse of life he lost the field".

This account of the page is not wholly true to the chronicle. The deaths of Norfolk and of Brakenbury are in the chronicle account. Catesby is there said to have been beheaded "II daies after". Here his death takes place on the same day, immediately after the battle, another of the numerous historical absurdities in the play. Lovell was not killed, but escaped, as the chronicles state, to the sanctuary of St. John's at Colchester (Hall has Gloucester by mistake), and lived to take part in a rebellion against Henry, dying 1487. The account of Richard's death is also much changed, and not to his advantage. In the chronicle account (cf. p. 152) there is no fainting on Richard's part, nor does Richmond prevail in his encounter with Richard and overthrow him, but "with stode his violence and kept him at the swerdes poincte without aduantage longer then his compaignons other thought or iudged", when William Stanley suddenly came upon the scene with his 3000 men, and, forsaken by his followers, Richard was beaten down amid the throng of his enemies.

The figure of Report, allegorical like the figures of Truth and Poetrie in the introduction to the play, finds something of a parallel in the figure of Rumour in Sir Clyomon and Sir Clamydes, and in the Rumour who speaks the Induction of Shakespeare's 2 Henry IV. There, however, Rumour fulfils his nature and delivers news; here, curiously, Report is the recipient of news. His part would be somewhat justified if a hint were given that he receives news only to spread it; but there is no such hint.

With "With as high resolue as fierce Achillis mongst the sturdie Greekes", cf. old King John, p. 245

Palaestra. X.   30

"With which I shall surprise his liuing foes,
As Hector's statue did the fainting Greekes".

With "but followed honour to the gates of death" cf. Battle of Alcazar, Act 1, 1, 122

"But follow to the gates of death and hell".

and Arden of Feversham II, 5, 166

"I, to the gates of death to follow thee".

[Scene 20.] Now "Enter **Earle Richmond, Earle Oxford, L. Standley,** and their traine, with the crowne". Richmond, turning to his followers, proposes since God has given them the fortune of the day that they first give thanks unto his Deity. He then returns his thanks to those who have helped him, expresses sorrow for those who have fallen and promises pay to the remaining. To his stepfather he gives special thanks for his unlooked for aid. Stanley praises his son's resolution, and Oxford vows eternal love, doubting not to see him as honored among his countrymen "as Hector was among the Lords of Troy or Tulley mongst the Roman senators".

There now appears the mother Queen with Elizabeth. The Queen is greeted kindly by Richmond, and inquires for her son Dorset. Her fears are set at rest by the information that he has been left in France as pledge for men and munition, which Richmond, driven by force of tempest to that shore, was forced to ask for. Richmond promises that he shall now return home, and begs for the hand of Elizabeth. Stanley crowns his son by election of the peers, and he is hailed Henry the Seventh.

Richmond then turns to Elizabeth herself and asks for her hand, and she, dutifully committing herself to her mother's disposal, "for when our aged father left his life, he willed vs honour still our mothers age", is by the latter bestowed on Richmond. All would now be joy were it not that George Stanley is missing. Of his safety there seems no hope. But just at this moment George appears, with two messengers, and relates how these two, sent by Richard to murder him, had, knowing how innocent he was, shifted him away when the battle joined.

"Rich. Now seeing that each thing turnes to our content,
 I will it be proclaimed presently, that traytrous Richard
 Be by our command, drawne through the streets of Lester,
 Starke naked on a Colliers horse let him be laide,
 For as of others paines he had no regard,
 So let him haue a traytors due reward.
 Now for our marriage and our nuptiall rytes,
 Our pleasure is they be solemnized
 In our Abby of Westminster, according to the ancient
             [custom due,
 The two and twentith day of August next,
 Set forwards then my Lords towards London straight,
 There to take further order for the state".

The messengers now turn to the audience, and the first, with the words,

 "Thus Gentles may you heere behold,
 The ioyning of these Houses both in one,
 By this braue Prince Henry the seauenth"

relates in brief the history of his reign. The second messenger follows and relates the reigns of Henry VIII and Edward VI, the princess Elizabeth does the same for Mary — the summary here is only a statement of her marriage, length of reign, and death — and the Queen concludes with Elizabeth.

 "Worthie Elizabeth, a mirrour in her age,
 By whose wise life and ciuill gouernment,
 Her country was defended from the crueltie
 Of famine, fire and swoord, warres fearfull messengers.
 This is that Queene as writers truly say,
 That God had marked downe to liue for age.
 Then happie England mongst thy neighbors Iles,
 For peace and plentie still attends on thee:
 And all the fauourable Planets smiles
 To see thee liue in such prosperitie.
 She is that lampe that keepes faire Englands light,
 And through her faith her country liues in peace:
 And she hath put proud Antichrist to flight,

And bene the meanes that ciuill wars did cease:
Then England kneele upon thy hairy knee,
And thanke that God that still prouides for thee.
The Turke admires to heare her gouernment,
And babies in Iury sound her princely name,
All Christian Princes to that Prince hath sent.
After her rule was rumord foorth by fame.
The Turke hath sworne neuer to lift his hand,
To wrong the Princesse of this blessed land.
Twere vaine to tell the care this Queene hath had,
In helping those that were opprest by warre:
And how her Maiestie hath stil bene glad,
When she hath heard of peace proclaim'd from far.
Ieneua, France and Flanders hath set downe,
The good she hath done, since she came to the Crowne.
For which, if ere her life be tane away,
God grant her soule may liue in heauen for aye.
For if her Graces dayes be brought to end,
Your hope is gone, on whom did peace depend".

There are as usual several variations from the chronicle account in this final scene. Henry's thanks to God and to his soldiers follow the chronicle, as well as his crowning by Stanley with Richard's crown, found among the spoil on the field. But Richmond's election by the peers is of course a chronological impossibility. The chronicles have "as though he had byne elected king by the voyce of the people" (Hall, p. 420). The presence of the Queen and the Princess Elizabeth on the field is of course unwarranted. Dorset's absence in France as a pledge is from the chronicles, but the reference to the tempest was evidently taken from the account of Richmond's first attempt to invade England. He was at that time aided by Charles of France and Francis of Brittany, but it was not till after this that Dorset came to him, fled, and was brought back, and then first was given to Charles as pledge. The account of Strange's escape with the two murderers varies from the chronicle, in that they are represented as sent to murder him by Richard, who declines to postpone the execution. According to the chronicle Richard did consent to postpone it, and delivered him "to the kepers of the kynges tentes to be kept as a prisoner" (Hall, p. 420), and these yielded themselves to him after the battle. The account is not quite consistent, either, with the previous scene, in that though Richard refuses to spare Stanley, nothing is said of sending two murderers, and no time intervenes to allow of it. The marriage of Henry and Elizabeth took place Jan. 18, 1486 "The two and twentith day of August next" would have been exactly one year from the battle, which took place Aug. 22, 1485. From this date the author with his customary lack of care evidently caught up his line.

On the source of the Epilogue see p. 409. The references in the passage devoted to Elizabeth's reign are not always clear. "And she hath put proud Antichrist to flight" probably refers to the defeat of the Armada, but may refer to the restoration of the Protestant religion. The help given to France may refer to 1560—62, when there was great strife between Condé and Guise, whom Elizabeth tried to reconcile, sending "aide to Monsieur Vidame, Captaine of Newhaven against such as sought to subuert both Religion and the estate" (Speed, p. 1159); but it is more probable that it refers to 1589— July 25, 1593, when the Queen sent money, munitions, ships, and soldiers to the aid of Henry of Navarre. Help was sent to the Netherlands 1585—1587. The reference to Geneva is probably an allusion to the return from that city of many able Protestants who had there taken refuge during the reign of Mary.

The Character of Richard in The True Tragedy.

Crude and inartistic as The True Tragedy is in dramatic organization and in expression, it presents in the character of its hero a conception that is strong, definite, and interesting. Legge's Richard, subjected to the influence of Senecan models, is decidedly weaker than the Richard of More and the chroniclers. The influences which since Legge's play had been at work in the popular drama, and to which The True Tragedy was subject, were, on the other hand, calculated to strengthen the portrait of Richard when he next appeared on the stage. Since Legge's play the genius of Marlowe had produced a Tamburlaine, and till long after Shakespeare had become the real master of the stage, the figure of Tamburlaine exercised a determinative influence in the conception of the popular dramatic hero. From the moment he appeared, no play built upon a single character could present its hero as weak, hesitating, emotional or directed by others. Ruthless and regardless he might be, cruel in action and savage in expression, but always self-centered, and always master.

In Dr. Faustus Marlowe had presented yet another distinct type, and one which had hardly less influence than Tamburlaine. Tamburlaine was the unwavering of soul, fixed in purpose from beginning to end, and his drama had been that of conflict with the external world and with Fate; the drama of Faustus was the conflict within his own soul, the conflict with his own conscience.

The Richard of The True Tragedy is a combination of these two types. That he should be such was not only a natural consequence of the popularity of Tamburlaine and Faustus, but a natural result also of the chronicle picture of Richard which was the historical basis of the play. Like Tamburlaine, the chronicle Richard was the ruthless and determined follower of an ambition to be king; and like Faustus, he was pictured as suffering fearful conflict with his conscience. Legge, with the Senecan tyrant always in mind, had found no place for conscience in his Richard; in the Faustus-Richard it could play a mighty part.

But there was, as we have seen, still a third influence at work upon The True Tragedy, that of the revenge plays; and for this too there was opportunity in the story of Richard. Murderer of his brother and nephews, of Hastings and other peers, he gave abundant occasion in the play for the appearance — in fact or in imagination — of their spirits to cry revenge. And thus a second punishment was provided for him in addition to the anguish of a wounded conscience.

The Richard of The True Tragedy is then the outcome of these three influences grafted upon the material furnished by the story of More and Vergil as repeated in the chronicles, and conditioned without doubt by the Richard of 3 Henry VI or its original. What is in sum the result as we have traced it through the play?

At his first appearance Richard shows himself possessed of one thought and passion; to him, as to Tamburlaine, "the title of a King is next vnder the degree of a God". There is but one thing for a man possessed of this idea to strive for, and from the beginning Richard has been making his way toward the crown. Henry and Clarence have been removed as logs from his path, from the yoke of his brother he has been released, and from the one remaining step the fear of death and hell shall not withhold him — as they cannot withhold Tamburlaine. Yet Richard is not above seeking to give himself grounds for his action. He is Plantagenet's son, and should be heir of his crown as he is of his spirit; he is the winner of the crown though he has not worn it.

Yet from the first, unlike Tamburlaine, Richard recognizes that he is in the hands of Fortune. He does not superbly assume success and mastery of Fate. Fortune may raise him only that his fall may be the greater. Here is for a moment the thought of Legge's Richard. But it is only for a moment. In general this Richard's thoughts are widely removed from those of Legge's. Legge's Richard seeks the place and power of king; if Fortune removes him from his place by death he is punished. But this Richard cannot be punished by death, for it is not the power of the throne at which he aims, it is the fame and glory of the name of king. The title of king once attained, Death itself cannot deprive him of what he has sought.

If the vassals but once cry 'God save king Richard' it is enough. This is the characteristic which separates the Richard of The True Tragedy from that of Legge on the one side and from that of Shakespeare on the other.

The characteristics revealed in pursuit of his purpose are in full accord with the nature thus made known at the start. The method of this Richard is direct and forceful. He has little use for hypocrisy. Of the Proteus-nature of Shakespeare's Richard, as of the superb intelligence that directs his craft, there is here almost no trace. There is but one scene in the whole play where Richard himself appears as deceiver — that with the young King —, and here the deception is that of the downright lie. This is almost the only remnant of the dissimulation asserted so strongly by More, and even here the direct and forceful nature of Richard appears in his words to the prince to whom he professes loyalty, "during the minoritie of your grace, I will use my authoritie as I see good". This Richard has little more need of craft than has Tamburlaine.

Like the nature so is its expression, forceful and savage. Richard can rave over trouble, but he cannot sorrow or whine over it. Where the Spakesperean Richard keeps his tongue and lets no word escape him, revealing his trouble only by nervous and inconsiderate action, The True Tragedy Richard breaks out into wildest anger, in words charged with all the horror of the crudest revenge plays. The crudity is repulsive, often absurd, but it is forceful and strong. It is the expression of the cruel and pitiless Tamburlaine, freed from bombast, but lacking all the poetry of Tamburlaine, and with the bombast replaced by the gruesome.

When in the first speech of Richard he argues with himself the reasons for his action, he shows that he is not free from the influence of conscience. Something within him requires to be satisfied, and he strives to satisfy it. If then death offers no real punishment, conscience may

Here the story of More and Vergil shows its chief influence. As Richard goes on in his frightful course, conscience asserts its power. It tears his soul with anguish, as in the story of More, and we have the page's moving description of his master's fear, taken directly from that source. But Richard's conscience drives him farther, drives him like Faustus to the thought of repentance. He thinks of purging himself of guilt, of craving mercy from a righteous God. Yet, as with Faust, it is but for a moment, the old imperious will re-asserts itself, and the thought is put aside.

It is noteworthy that with this Richard conscience asserts its power not, as in Shakespeare, only when sleep has placed the will in abeyance. Sleeping or waking he hears its cry. If in this respect this Richard's will is weaker than Shakespeare's Richard's, the fact that it can overcome the more violent attack reveals at the same time its strength.

Noteworthy, too, is the manner in which his wounded conscience reacts upon him. Not only does it reveal itself as in More's story in his sleepless nights, his dreadful dreams, the fear of every new-comer that keeps his hand always upon his dagger; waking he sees terrible visions that strike despair to his heart. And these visions are not merely those of the dream that Vergil relates, — for from this dream, doubtless, are drawn the "raging fiends" which Richard sees in Stygian lakes prepared to come to him; but, as in the tragedies of revenge, he sees the spirits of those whom he has murdered, all crying 'let the tyrant die'. To his distorted imagination all things in nature have joined in the cry: he has not only become the enemy of men; from the whole world, even the inanimate and unhuman, he is an outcast.

It marks a great advance over the old revenge plays that the ghosts — with the exception of Clarence's, at the beginning — do not appear, but are represented as the product of Richard's diseased mind. Thus they are made to fulfil a purpose which is not theirs in the older plays; they lead the thought back to their cause in the guilty, tortured conscience of the criminal, and so reveal the punishment that even now is his.

So when Richard dies upon the field of battle, dies possessed of that for which he had longed, the glory and the fame of kingship, and with it the fame of a courage undaunted and a will unrelenting to the last, we feel that he has yet not escaped his punishment. He has paid and will yet pay for all he has won.

Thus The True Tragedy makes a long step forward in the literary treatment of the figure of Richard as it had been developed through the century of chronicles and in the play of Legge. He has not yet the characteristics of diabolical craft, of over-mastering intelligence, of power to rule, he has not yet become the subject of true art. But strength and energy and an all-conquering will are his, and with these the ethical germ which alone justifies the portrait drawn by the true artist — the Richard of Shakespeare.

The Influence of Legge's Richardus Tertius upon The True Tragedy.

That the author of The True Tragedy should have been acquainted with Legge's play is, a priori, not improbable. The authors of the early plays from the beginning of Elizabeth's reign down to Shakespeare were nearly all University men. If such was the case with our author, he can hardly have escaped some knowledge of Richardus Tertius. The True Tragedy belongs to the same group as the old King John, and The Famous Victories of Henry V, which like it were written for the Queen's company; and commentators have not been slow to associate with these the names of University men like Peele, Lodge and even Marlowe. In the play itself, it must be confessed, evidences of a thorough-going University education are wanting: but this is the case with the other plays also. There are however some traces of a certain amount of classical training, as the Latin speech of Clarence's ghost, the Latin quotation preceding Richard's ghost soliloquy, and the references to Ixion's wheel, Stygian lakes, etc., though the latter count for very little, being common property among the playwrights of the day. The quotation Quisquam regno gaudet, ô fallax bonum, the printer's corruption of Quisquamne regno gaudet? o fallax bonum. Oed. 6, tends to show an acquaintance with Seneca's plays, and its application to Richard reveals that the author was alive to the Senecan aspect of Richard's story, and renders it more probable that the author may have read Legge's play.

All this is however highly unsatisfactory. Anything approaching a real proof that the author made use of Legge's play must appear in the general construction of the play, and in the use of situations peculiar to Legge and not in the chronicle sources.

In this too appears a considerable difficulty. For Legge, as has been shown, in the construction of his play followed the chronicle story with nearly complete faithfulness, and such deviations as he made were mostly suggested by Seneca. Aside from the story of Shore's wife, and the introduction up to the meeting of Richard and Buckingham with Rivers, the scenes of The True Tragedy are mainly only the chief scenes of the chronicle story, in which an agreement with Legge can be set down to the common source. Points of profitable comparison are therefore few. These few, however, while they do not perhaps amount to an absolute proof of the use of Legge, and while in general deviations in The True Tragedy from the chronicle story are to be ascribed to the influence of other plays upon the popular stage, leave little doubt that the author was acquainted with Richardus Tertius, and made occasional use of it.

1. The most striking instance is the scene of Richmond's meeting with Stanley. This scene in Legge deviates

widely from the chronicle (cf. p. 360 et seq). There the meeting is represented as one of joy and hope. The participants "suddenly were surprised with great joy, comfort, and hope of fortunate success in all their doings", and there is nothing in the meeting to disturb this feeling. In Legge's scene, on the contrary, Richmond is overwhelmed with vexation, doubt and despair. Stanley has refused the expected aid, and assigns as cause the danger to his son, George Stanley, who in the chronicle account of the meeting is not so much as mentioned. With Legge's scene, and not with the chronicle, The True Tragedy wholly agrees. As in Legge, Stanley explains the situation of his son, and to Richmond's request for help in the battle replies he cannot give it. Richmond declares that the news goes to his heart and is in utter despair of victory. In both cases Stanley comforts his downcast step-son, and promises secret aid. Cf.

> Stan. Why sonne, see how contrarie you are, for I assure you, the chiefest in his company are liker to flie to thee, then to fight against thee: and for me, thinke me not so simple but that I can at my pleasure flie to thee, or being with them, fight so faintly, that the battell shall be wonne on thy part with small encountring".

with Legge's

> Stanl. Iram coerce, pectus et nobile doma
> Palam juvare si nequeo, furtim tamen
> subsidia nunquam nostra deerunt tibi.

In both cases the scene closes with Richmond encouraging himself against his own despair, and turning forward to the battle. The correspondence throughout the scene is, when the wide variance from the chronicle is considered, too close to leave much doubt that Legge's scene was the basis of the other.

2. In The True Tragedy, p. 215, Oxford remonstrates with Richmond for his absences by night. "Good my Lord haue a care of your self, I like not these night

walkes and scouting abroad in the evenings so disguised, for you must not now that you are in the vsurpers dominions, and you are the onely marke he aimes at, and your last nightes absence bred such amazement in our soldiers, that they like men wanting the power to follow Armes, were on a sodaine more liker to flie then to fight". For this the chronicle has only, "As he was not merye beynge absent from his compaignie, lykewyse his armie muche marueled and no lesse mourned for hys sodeyne and intempestious absence" (Hall, p. 413). Here there is no mention of Oxford, and no remonstrance, and the expression of the soldiers' feeling is mild in comparison with that of the play. In the corresponding scene in Legge, however, we have likewise Oxford remonstrating with Richmond, and the tone of his words is much closer than that of the chronicle to that of The True Tragedy.

Com. Oxon. Ingens premebat cura sollicitos (comes
    illustris) animos horror excussit gravis,
    dux milites quòd absens deseris,
    dum nocte caeca summa montium juga
    vincunt, nec ullus jussa privatus facit.
    mox triste pectus moeror invasit gravis:
    nunc voce miles frustra compellat ducem.

3. Just previous to this scene between Oxford and Richmond is a scene in which soldiers flee across the stage to Richmond, and are accosted by the page, to whom they declare their purpose to abandon Richard. The flight of soldiers is mentioned in the chronicle, and just previous to the night absence of Richmond and his meeting with Lord Stanley. When, however, the general loose and arbitrary arrangement of scenes in The True Tragedy is considered, it is corroborative proof of Legge's influence to find in it the same arrangement as that of Richardus Tertius — the flight of Richard's soldiers, then Richmond's night absence and Oxford's speech, then the meeting of Richmond and Stanley.

4. On p. 81 of The True Tragedy, the queen, while awaiting the arrival of the young king from Wales, says

to her son and daughter, "A sweet children, when I am a rest my nightly dreams are dreadful. Me thinks as I lie in my bed, I see the league broken which was sworne at the death of your kingly father, tis this my children . . that makes your aged mother to lament as she doth". It seems not unlikely that the queen's dreams, which are not mentioned by the chronicle, were suggested by the scene in Legge where the queen has a dream portending danger to her two boys in the Tower. This she relates to her maid with the introductory words,

> Nocturna sic me visa miseram territant.
> Et dira turbant inquietam somnia.

The dream is Legge's invention, a doublet, so to speak, of Hastings' dream, with imitation of Seneca (cf. p. 326—7). Prophetic dreams, while not very uncommon in Elizabethan poetry, are not to be found in many of the plays which are at all likely to have had influence upon The True Tragedy. The nearest resemblance is in Soliman and Persida (Haz. Dodsley, 5, 360), where Persida when it is announced to her that her lover Erastus has been condemned and executed, exclaims

> "My nightly dreams foretold me this,
> Which, foolish woman, fondly I neglected".

Here the verbal resemblance is not close enough to suggest connection, and there is no resemblance in the situations. The same is true of Selimus, where Solyma relates a foreboding dream to her husband, and of Arden of Feversham, where Arden has a dream presaging his death. Legge's scene is far more likely to have been the source of that in The True Tragedy than any of these.

The scene should also be compared with Legge's first scene, where as here the queen is represented as burning with anxiety for her son, who is on his way from Wales. Of such anxiety on the part of the queen, as well as, naturally, any scene in which such anxiety is expressed, there is no suggestion in the chronicles.

5. In The True Tragedy Richard sends Lord Lovell to the queen in sanctuary. The chronicles have only, "the messengers being men both of wit and grauitie". But in Legge Richard likewise sends Lord Lovell. Here is another correspondence like that in the case of Oxford.

6. On p. 65 of The True Tragedy Richard asks himself in soliloquy,

> "Doth Fortune so much favour my happinesse
> That I no sooner deuise, but she sets abroach?
> Or doth she but to trie me, that raising me aloft,
> My fall may be the greater"?

The latter lines seem almost a translation of the following, also spoken by Richard in soliloquy, in Legges play (p. 203).

> Quid me potens fallaci nimis
> blandita vultu, gravius ut ruerem, edita
> de rupe tollis!

The lines of The True Tragedy may perhaps quite as well be an imitation of Octavia, 377—380, which Legge imitated. In that case they would at least bear testimony to the author's acquaintance with Seneca, and thus to the University education necessary to an acquaintance with Richardus Tertius.

7. The fact that Richmond has a speech upon his appearance in England may also be due to the influence of Legge's play. But cf. p. 356.

These are all the passages for which it seems plausible to suggest Legge's influence. Though few, their character seems to justify the statement previously made, that while they do not furnish an absolutely satisfactory proof that Legge's play was occasionally used in the composition of The True Tragedy, they yet leave little doubt that such was the fact.

The Influence of Marlowe upon The True Tragedy.

That Shakespeare's Richard III was modelled under the powerful influence of Marlowe has long been recognized. As each of Marlowe's plays is built upon one character who embodies a single passion, the development and exercise of which forms the play, so Shakespeare's play is built upon the one character of Richard, who is likewise animated by one great passion, the story of whose exercise is the story of his whole career. Richard has the same gigantic intensity of purpose, the same Titanic energy and power that characterize Marlowe's Tamburlaine. Now the same thing is true of the Richard of The True Tragedy. The figure lacks all the art of Shakespeare's, but that very fact throws into more striking prominence the elemental force by which he is driven; and the very crudity of its expression makes clearer the resemblance to Marlowe's Tamburlaine. There is the same savagery, the same wild, unrestrained expression of a determined will, without any of the artful cunning of Shakespeare's Richard; and most of all there is the same animating purpose. Shakespeare's Richard is animated by a thirst for power, because he feels his ability to rule; it is, in reality, the power itself for which he longs. The Richard of The True Tragedy, like Tamburlaine, thirsts not so much for power as for the glory and the fame of power. It is the title of king that allures him, the report of the world that Gloster was a king. This gigantic elemental force of character, this direct and downright expression of will, this thirst for glory and fame, are not characteristics of More's Richard; and they are still more evidently wanting in that portrait of Richard which Legge drew from More and Seneca. With Marlowe they first became characteristics of a dramatic hero.

For a full realization of the dependence of The True Tragedy upon the Marlowe ideal it is necessary to have the whole play in mind, to follow Richard's part from beginning to end. Here I must confine myself to the consideration of some passages in which the dependence upon Tamburlaine and also upon Faustus is clearest. To this I add certain passages in which further imitation is possible.

1. On Richard's first appearance (p. 63) he delivers a long soliloquy in which his purpose and the spirit which animates him are revealed. Here we read:

> "Principalitie brooks no equalitie,
> Much less superioritie,
> And the title of a King, is next vnder the degree of a God".

Later, in the scene with Percival (p. 66) we have, "I climbe Perciuall, I regard more the glorie then the gaine, for the very name of a King redouble[s] a mans life with fame, when death hath done his worst". The influence of Tamburlaine is evident, especially of Act 2 scene 5.

> "Tamb. Is it not passing brave to be a king,
> And ride in triumph through Persepolis?
> Tech. O, my lord, it is sweet and full of pomp!
> Usum. To be a king is half to be a god.
> Ther. A god is not so glorious as a king:
> I think the pleasure they enjoy in heaven,
> Cannot compare with kingly joys in earth".

With Tamburlaine first the comparison of a king to a god enters English dramatic literature.

2. On Richard's first appearance after the coronation and the murder of the princes, he is represented conformably to the chronicle story as oppressed by his guilty conscience.

> "My fearefull shadow that still followes me,
> Hath summond me before the seuere judge,
> My conscience witnesse of the blood I spilt,
> Accuseth me as guiltie of the fact,
> The fact a damned judgement craues,
> Whereas impartiall iustice hath condemned'.

Thus far agreement with More. But More's account stops with the mention of Richard's anguish and unrest. The True Tragedy goes farther. It represents Richard as conceiving the idea of repentance, of an appeal to God for mercy. Then his old spirit revives and he turns away.

"Meethinkes the Crowne which I before did weare,
Inchast with Pearle and costly Diamonds,
Is turned now into a fatall wreathe,
Of fiery flames, and euer burning starres,
And raging fiends hath past ther vgly shapes,
In Stygian lakes, adrest to tend on me,
If it be thus, what wilt thou do in this extremitie?
Nay what canst thou do to purge thee of thy guilt?
Euen repent, craue mercie for thy damned fact,
Appeale for mercy to thy righteous God,
Ha repent, not I, craue mercy they that list.
My God, is none of mine".

So too the same feeling is apparent in the final despairing conference between Richard, Lovell, and Catesby (p. 120).

"King. . . . A Catesbie, thou lookest like a dog, and thou Louell too, but you will runne away with them that be gone, and the diuel go with you all, God I hope, God, what talke I of God, that haue serued the diuell all this while. No, fortune and courage for mee".

Here is plainly to be seen the influence of Marlowe's Faustus. With that play first appears the character who, having turned away from God in pursuance of a gigantic ambition, is attacked by remorse, meditates and debates with himself repentance, but returns to his former purpose. In the plays that followed Marlowe's the character and the situation often recur: before Marlowe they never appear.

Not impossibly the "raging fiends" of the passage in The True Tragedy are likewise drawn from Faustus, where Lucifer, Belzebub and Mephistophilis threaten the wavering Faustus, and where in the final scene the devils enter to carry him away. But cf. pp. 172, 194.

3. Another point of contact between these two plays has been suggested by Professor A. Brandl, in the introduction to his edition of the Schlegel-Tieck Richard III. This is in the final scenes in the lives of Faustus and Richard. As Faustus' hour draws nigh the heavens become overcast with laboring clouds and mists, in which Faustus recognizes the menace of an angry God. So in

The True Tragedy Richard recognizes in the watery heavens and darksome clouds a prophecy of his own destruction. Of this gloomy sky on the day of the battle of Bosworth the chronicles say nothing, stating in fact the exact contrary. Cf. p. 198.

4. In The True Tragedy, p. 79, the young king is represented as enraged at his inability to save his kinsmen Rivers and Gray, whom Gloucester and Buckingham have arrested.

"King. A Gods, and is it iustice without my consent? Am I a King and beare no authoritie? My louing kindred committed to prison as traytors in my presence, and I stand to giue aime at them. A Edward, would thou laist by thy fathers side or else he had liued till thou hadst bin better able to rule. If my neere kindred be committed to prison, what remains for me, a crowne? A but how? so beset with sorrows, that the care & grief wil kil me ere I shall enioy my kingdome. Well since I cannot command, I wil intreat".

In the chronicle story there is no hint of such reflection on the part of the young king.

With this passage and the whole scene cf. the scene in Marlowe's Edward the Second (Dyce's ed. p. 288), in which Edward's nobles arrest against his will Gaveston and Kent. Edward remonstrates in vain.

"K. Edw. Nay, then, lay violent hands upon your king:
Here, Mortimer, sit thou in Edward's throne;
Warwick and Lancaster, wear you my crown.
Was ever king thus over-ruled as I?
Can. Learn, then, to rule us better, and the realm".

Edward's remonstrances having no effect, he perceives that he must entreat.

"K. Edw. It boots me not to threat; I must speak fair".

But even entreaties are without avail; he is obliged to submit.

This passage is the likeliest source of that in The True Tragedy.

31*

5. It is likely that the scene (p. 94) in which Tyrell instructs the two murderers is imitated from the like scene in Marlowe's Edward the Second, in which Mortimer instructs the murderer Lightborn. Cf. the following. True Tr. p. 94.

"Ter.   Myles Forest, haue you got those men I spoke of, they must be resolute and pittilesse.
For.   I warrant you sir, they are such pittilesse villaines, that all London cannot match them for their villainie".

The murderers are called in and Tyrell addresses them.

"Ter.   Come hither sirs, to make a long discourse were but a folly, you seeme to be resolute in this cause that Myles Forest hath deliuered to you, therefore you must cast away pitie, & not so much as thinke upon fauour, for the more stearne that you are, the more shall you please the King.
Will.   Zownes sir, nere talke to vs of fauour, tis not the first that Iack and I haue gone about".

From Edward II (Dyce p. 217):

"Mort.   Lightborn, come forth! Art thou as resolute as [thou wast?
Light.   What else, my lord? and far more resolute.
. . . .
Mort.   But at his looks, Lightborn, thou wilt relent.
Light.   Relent! Ha, ha! I use much to relent.
Mort.   Well do it bravely, and be secret.
Light.   You shall not need to give instructions; 'Tis not the first time I have killed a man'".

Henry VI and The True Tragedy.

The generally prevailing view of the date of The True Tragedy, which, depending largely on the results of Collier's hasty and imperfect examination assigns it to a time previous to 1588, has led to viewing the play as existing independently of others, and to a failure to connect it in any way with Henry VI or plays on which this was based, for it is improbable that these existed before 1588. Mr. Fleay, however, whose latest opinion assigns the play to a much later date, regards it as "evidently meant as a continuation of the series 1 Henry 6 and The Contention of York and Lancaster", all three plays having belonged to the Queen's men, while The True Tragedy of Richard Duke of York, the original, or a shortened acting copy of 3 Henry VI, according to varying opinions, was "a rival continuation of Pembroke's men" (Biog. Chron. 2, 315). Mr. Fleay evidently means not that The True Tragedy is an immediate continuation of The Contention, but that, Pembroke's men having produced the T. Tr. of Richard Duke of York, the Queen's men continued the story with the T. Tr. of Richard III, hearing a similar title. Compare Fleay's Chron. Hist. of the Stage p. 406, where he says "Richard 3, True Tragedy of . . . evidently a sequel to Richard Duke of York, True Tragedy of".

With this view I agree. For leaving aside the vexed and apparently insoluble problem of the relation of 1 Hen. VI, The Contention, and Richard Duke of York to each other and to the perfected Henry VI, it seems clear that the play before us is dependent upon 3 Henry VI, or its original, for its conception. In the first place, knowing that the Queen's company had 1 Hen. VI and The Contention (2 Hen. VI) as well as The True Tragedy, it is more natural to suppose that The True Tragedy grew out of these than that it preceded them, though the latter is of course possible. The probabilities that The True Tragedy followed are increased by two other considerations. The three parts of Henry VI bear all the marks of that early group of history-plays whose main idea seems to have been to present all the material which the chronicle offered for a certain period, without any serious attempt at giving it unity or a single dramatic purpose: and this is still more evidently the case with The Contention and The True Tragedy of Richard Duke of York, in which one may see earlier stages of 2 and 3 Henry VI. Such too was the case with Legge's play, with the old plays of King John and Henry V, and to a large degree with Edward II. The True Tragedy of Richard III marks a distinct advance upon this stage. Even allowing for the secondary story of Shore's wife, and for the fact that in the chronicles the story of Richard's reign is largely unified by the character of Richard, there remains in this respect a clear margin of progress in the badly mangled and at best inartistic drama. Again the fact that The True Tragedy begins practically where 3 Henry VI ends is, while not determinative, at least corroborative evidence that it was meant to follow it.

But upon these external probabilities we are not compelled to rely. The play itself offers internal evidence that it followed Henry VI.

1. The introduction, based upon More's introduction to his story, and in general following this closely, has a few changes, one of which appears to have a bearing upon this question: — More's statement (as it appears in Hall), that Richard Plantagenet, duke of York, "began not by warre, but by lawe to calenge the crowne of Englande, puttyng his claims in the parliament etc." This becomes, in the introduction to the play,

> "Richard Plantagenet of the House of Yorke,
> Claiming the Crowne by warres, not by dissent [descent]
> Had as the Chronicles make manifest,
> . . . .
> By act of Parliament intailed to him
> The Crowne".

Is it unreasonable to suppose that this change with its direct contradiction of More's statement was produced by the author's knowledge that in the play of the Queen's Company which handled the period previous to the decision of Parliament, the Duke of York had indeed been engaged in warring for his claim, and that the end of that play was formed by the battle and York's victory at St. Albans? Too much stress it not to be laid on this, but it appears to offer the first indication of a connection with previous plays which the further course of the play reveals much more clearly.

2. The introduction is an introduction to the events which begin the play, but not to the motives which condition these events. Richard's murders of King Henry and of Clarence are mentioned, but the reason for them does not appear. Richard is described and his choice as Protector stated, but his feelings and motives, which have caused the situation with which the play opens, and which are to govern what follows, are not made known. These appear first in the soliloquy with which Richard makes his entrance.

> "My father got the Crowne, my brother won the Crowne,
> And I will uear the crowne,
> Or ile make them hop without their crowne that denies me:
> Haue I remoued such logs out of my sight as my brother [Clarence
> And king Henry the sixt, to suffer a child to shadow me,
> Nay more, my nephew to disinherit me,
> Yet most of all, to be released from the yoke of my brother
> As I terme it, to become subiect to his sonne".

Now More had suggested as a possibility that Richard had a hand in helping Clarence to his death, in order to further his own ambition, and this, it has been shown, became the accepted view, appearing in the Mirror for Magistrates and in Legge's play. But neither More nor anybody after him, chronicler or poet, suggested that Richard's murder of Henry was caused by his purpose to put out of the way all who stood between him and the crown. This murder was regarded by all the chroniclers as the result of a purpose to prevent the possibility of further danger from the House of Lancaster, and such is the view of the Mirror for Magistrates — "to stint all furder strife". First in 3 Henry VI (T. T. of R. D. of York) is the murder of Henry made a part of Richard's attempt to win the crown. Here his purpose is indicated as far back as the time when Edward first woos Elizabeth Gray.

"Glo. Would he were wasted, marrow, bones, and all,
That from his loins no hopeful branch may spring,
To cross me from the golden time I look for!
And yet, between my soul's desire and me —
The lustful Edward's title buried —
Is Clarence, Henry, and his son young Edward,
And all th' unlook'd for issue of their bodies,
To take their rooms, ere I can place myself".

From this moment he makes known his purpose to hew his way out of these difficulties with a bloody axe. Prince Edward is murdered, Henry follows, and the play closes with Richard's promise to "sort a pitchy day" for Clarence. In The True Tragedy soliloquy, Richard's mention of having removed King Henry as a log from his path is so meagre as to be convincing that Henry's murder as the result of Richard's purpose must have been well known to the audience that heard this play. Had this not been the case, the author could hardly have failed to speak of the matter more at length, and naturally in the Introduction, where the cause of Henry's murder is not suggested. Such previous knowledge must have been obtained from 3 Henry VI (T. T. of R. D. of York). Clarence's death, which does not appear in 3 Henry VI, it was easily possible for The True Tragedy to omit. It was prepared for in 3 Henry VI, and the appearance of Clarence's ghost at the beginning of The True Tragedy with its cry for vengeance, and Truth's comment upon it, were sufficient to leave the audience in full knowledge of the relation of his death to Richard's story.

It must be said that Oechelhäuser takes a different view from that here given of More's words, in regard to Richard's purpose in the murder of Henry. In these, according to Oechelhäuser, "wird Eduard's IV. Auftrag oder Mitwissenschaft an diesem Mord ausdrücklich in Abrede gestellt und derselbe bereits mit Richard's Absichten auf die Krone in Verbindung gebracht". He thinks therefore that Shakespeare did not go beyond his source. The passage requires careful examination. It reads (Lumby's ed. p. 6) "Frende and foo was muche what indifferent, where his aduantage grew, he spared no mans deathe, whose life withstoode his purpose. He slew with his owne handes king Henry the sixt, being prisoner in the Tower, as menne constantly saye, and that without commanndement or knoweledge of the king, which woulde vndoubtedly, yf he had intended that thinge, haue appointed that boocherly office, to some other then his owne borne brother. Some wise menne also weene" that he helped Clarence to his death etc. Here is a distinct suggestion, it must be admitted, that Henry's death was necessary to a purpose of Richard's. The question is, what purpose? That More does not mean the purpose to obtain the crown, he shows by what follows. After giving the supposition of the "wise men", that Richard helped Clarence to his death, he goes on to say, "And they that thus deme, think that he long time in king Edwardes life [the Latin has "jam olim viuente adhuc Edwardo"] forethought to be king in case that the king his brother (whose life hee looked that euil dyete shoulde shorten) 'shoulde happen to decease (as in dede he did) while his children wer yonge. And thei deme, that for thys intent he was gladde of his brothers death". From this it is clear enough that in speaking of Henry's murder More had no intent to suggest that Richard's purpose to seek the crown had then been conceived. The suggestion is made in the most cautious form that some people suppose that Richard had a hand in Clarence's death, and supposing this, they suppose also that while Edward was still alive he had this intent. If More had meant that Richard had this intent in Henry's murder it would not first be brought forward in connection with Clarence's. And if More is so cautious in this matter, going on to say that in all this there is no certainty, that it is pure conjecture, how much less likely that he meant to put forward the conjecture in connection with Henry's death.

What More did mean is shown by the treatment the statement received in the chronicles that copied it. The first copier, the Hardyng continuator, showed what he understood by adding a clause to the passage, making it read: "He slewe in the towre kynge Henry the sixte, saying, 'Nowe is there no heyre male of kyng Edward the thyrde, but we of the house of Yorke" (p. 469). In other words, Richard's purpose was to establish his own house in security by removing all other claimants to the throne. The same passage appears in Hall, in whose pages the process of blackening Richard reaches its height, and in Grafton. Holinshed, who copied More's work from the Rastell edition, has not the added clause. Here is, therefore, no contradiction, as Oechelhäuser seems to think, to the purpose as stated in the account of Henry's death given under the tenth year of Edward's reign, "that king Edward his brother, shoulde be clere out of all secret suspicion of sodain inuasion" (Hall, p. 303) or, as Holinshed has it, "to the intent that his brother King Edward might reigne in more suretie" (p. 690). The chronicles, it must be further remembered, and not More's original, were the direct sources of Shakespeare's plays, as of The True Tragedy.

Another proof that More's words do not have the meaning that Oechelhäuser ascribes to them is that none of the later works down to Henry VI makes the suggestion that Richard's murder of Henry was part of his efforts toward the crown, though as we have seen, Richard's murder of Clarence had already in the Mirror for Magistrates become a fact. Yet in The True Tragedy this view is treated as already well known. How is it likelier to have become known than through that play which adopts a view of Richard's purpose that sets it back even before the death of Prince Edward, the play whose treatment of the historical sources is conditioned by a purpose to show Richard's character as wholly villanous from the start?

3. There is another indication in Richard's opening soliloquy of a preceding play. Urging to himself his claim upon the crown, he says:

"For if he be worthie to called valiant,
That in his life winnes honour, and by his sword winnes
[riches,
Why now I with renowne of a souldier, which is neuer
[sold but
By waight, nor changed but by losse of life,
I reapt not the gaine but the glorie, and since it becommeth
A sonne to maintaine the honour of his deceased father,
Why should I not hazard his dignitie by my brothers sonnes?"

The passage is evidently more or less corrupt (at least the two buts of lines 4 and 5 are unjustifiable) but the sense is clearly that Richard is basing his claim partly upon the renown he has won as a valiant soldier in battles the glory of which he reaped but not the gain. Here a knowledge on the part of the audience of Richard's renown as a soldier seems to be taken for granted. The battles in which Richard showed his valiancy must have been shown before the eyes of the same audience. Not only is the soldier Richard made prominent in 2 Henry VI, where Richard so fights for his father that he wins from him the commendation, "Richard hath best deserved of all my sons" (3 Hen. VI 1,1) — a service and a prowess wholly unhistorical — but he plays the same part as constant valiant champion of his brother. But the harvest is not his. That 3 Henry VI (T. T. of R. D. of York) was in the author's mind is clearer still from the fact that this thought which marks Richard's first appearance in The True Tragedy was his last in 3 Henry VI. In the closing scene of that play Edward reviews the war that has made him securely king.

"K. Edw. Once more we sit in England's royal throne,
Re-purchased with the blood of enemies.
What valiant foemen, like to autumn's corn,
Have we mow'd down in top of all their pride!
. . . .
Young Ned, for thee, thine uncles and myself
Have in our armours watch'd the winter's night;
Went all-afoot in summer's scalding heat,
That thou mightst repossess the crown in peace.
And of our labours thou shalt reap the gain.

> Glo. [aside] I'll blast his harvest, if your head were laid;
> For yet I am not look'd on in the world.
> This shoulder was ordained so thick to heave;
> And heave it shall some weight, or break my back: —
> Work thou the way, — and thou shalt execute".

The likeness in the thought is unmistakeable, and the verbal resemblance in "thou shalt reap the gain" renders the connection of the two passages still more probable.

4. Further in the soliloquy Richard seems to feel himself the representative of his dead father. "Who shall inherit Plantagines but his sonne?" "Since it becommeth a sonne to maintaine the honour of his deceased father, why should I not hazard his dignitie by my brothers sonnes?" The hint, though slight, is, when taken in connection with the other and stronger proofs that 3 Henry VI was here used, sufficient to warrant one in believing that here again was in mind the portrait of Richard as he appears in that play. There he is the true inheritor of his father's spirit, and feels himself such. Edward inherits his father's title, Richard his father's nature. The fact and Richard's consciousness of the fact appear repeatedly (cf. Kuno Fischer, S. Char. R. III, p. 79 et seq). The words of Richard in The True Tragedy soliloquy sound like a far-off echo of his words in 3 Henry VI 2, 1.

> "Rich. Richard, I bear thy name; I'll venge thy death,
> Or die renowned by attempting it.
> Edw. His name that valiant duke hath left with thee;
> His dukedom and his chair with me is left.
> Rich. Nay, if thou be that princely eagle's bird,
> Show thy descent by gazing 'gainst the sun:
> For chair and dukedom, throne and kingdom say;
> Either that is thine, or else thou wert not his".

I turn now to certain other passages not bound up like the preceding with the foundation motives of the play, which likewise point to influence from Henry VI.

5. With "Ile make them hop without their crownes that denies me", and the whole passage cf. from the 1619 quarto of The Contention:

"I'll come after you, for I cannot go before,
As long as Gloster bears this base and humble mind:
Were I a man, and Protector, as he is,
I'd reach to th' crown, or make some hop headless:
. . . .
Who is within there?"

This in 2 Henry VI I, 2 reads

"Follow I must: I cannot go before,
While Gloster bears this base and humble mind.
Were I a man, a duke, and next of blood,
I would remove these tedious stumbling-blocks
And smooth my way upon their headless necks.
Where are you there, Sir John?" . . .

Thereupon enters Hume.

"Hume. Jesus preserve your royal majesty!
Duch. What say'st thou? majesty! I am but grace.
Hume. But, by the grace of God, and Hume's advice,
Your grace's title shall be multiplied.
[Your grace's state shall be advanced ere long]"
1 Part of Cont.

In like manner, as Richard is uttering the soliloquy in The True Tragedy, he hears some one stirring and calls "Ho, whose within?" In response appear the Page and Percival, and the following ensues.

"Per. May it please your Maiestie.
Rich. Ha villaine, Maiestie.
Per. I speake but vpon that which shall be my good Lord".

There is a pun on the word grace in The True Tragedy p. 81 which may be an imitation of that in the passage from 2 Henry VI:

"Yorke. May it please your grace.
Queen. A my son, no more grace, for I am so sore disgraced.
that without Gods grace, I fall into dispaire with myself".

6. The reconciliation-scene by Edward's deathbed has a peculiar nature, in that Dorset and Hastings when urged to reconciliation refuse, quarrel in the presence of the despairing king, and only at length through the entreaties

of the king and of the princess Elizabeth are induced to become friends. In the chronicle account there is nothing of this. After the king's speech all are moved to weeping, and answer "as they thoughte shoulde stande with his pleasure. And there in his presence (as by their woordes appeared) eche forgaue other and ioyned their handes together, when as it after appeared by their dedes their hartes were far asunder" (Hall, p. 345). There is here no hesitancy on the part of the opponents, no quarrelling and no entreaty. Now in I Henry VI 3, 2 there is a reconciliation-scene where Henry implores Gloucester and Winchester to make friends. Here appear the quarrelling in the king's presence, entreaties, the king's despair, and the final truce. How close the parallel is may be seen from the following comparison — which is meant not as a substitute for the full scenes, which should be compared, but to bring out the chief points of resemblance.

The True Tragedy.	I. Henry VI.
Appeal of King.	Appeal of King.
Tacit refusal.	Tacit refusal.
King. "These words strike a second dying to my soule". Cf. also earlier in scene, "It is folly to speake to them .. [I] must die being thus tormented in minde".	King. "O, how this discord doth afflict my soul".
Intercession of Elizabeth.	Intercession of Warwick.
"Ah yeeld Lord Hastings, And submit your selues to each other: And you Lord Marcus, submit your selfe".	"My lord protector yield; yield, Winchester".
Continued opposition of lords.	Continued opposition of lords.
Hast. "No, I am resolute, except thou submit".	Win. "He shall submit or I will never yield".
Hastings submits through regard for dying king.	Gloc. "Compassion on the king commands me stoop".
Lord Marquess is urged to follow his example. He finally yields.	Winchester urged to his example. He finally yields.

In the case of the Henry VI passage there is in the chronicles an actual contention between the parties, though on paper mostly. Charges are brought forward on either side, the case is adjudicated by council, and through Bedford (in the play, Warwick), Gloster and Winchester are directed to declare friendship to each other and join hands, and this is done (cf. Hall, pp. 130—136). The play dramatises this, makes it an actual verbal scene, but in general all corresponds to the fact. Charges are made on each side, by word of mouth, a reconciliation is brought about by Warwick, each gives the other his hand. In other words, the scene is the chronicle relation dramatised.

In both cases, of course, the chronicles were used. They account for most of Shakespeare's scene, for less of the True Tragedy's. The resemblance of the rest seems too close to be accidental. The quarrel by word of mouth, and the necessary ensuing hesitation of the principals to make up, together with the mediation which is actually in the chronicle, make it most likely that Shakespeare's scene in Henry VI had the chronicle alone as its basis. It follows that The True Tragedy came after Henry VI.

7. On p. 70 of The True Tragedy we have a brave speech of the young king apropos of the dissension between the two parties in his kingdom.

"King. Ah gods, if I do live my fathers yeares as God forbid but I may, I will so roote out this malice & enuie sowne among the nobilitie, that I will make them weary that were the first beginners of these mischiefes.
Gray. Worthily well spoken of your princely Maiestie
Which no doubt sheweth a king-like resolution.
Vaugh. A toward young Prince, and no doubt forward to all vertue, whose raigne God long prosper among us".

On p. 77 the king comforts the arrested Gray, who says, "The sweet joyce of such a grape would comfort a man where he halfe dead, and the sweete words of such a Prince would make men careless of mishaps, how dangerous soeuer".

Of all this there is nothing in the chronicles, where there is no indication of the king's early ripeness. But compare 3 Henry VI 5, 4, where the young prince Edward, son of Henry VI, makes a brave speech whereupon Oxford cries,

> "Women and children of so high a courage
> And warriors faint! Why 't were perpetual shame.
> O brave young prince! thy famous grandfather
> Doth live again in thee: long mayst thou live
> To bear his image and renew his glories".

and 3 Henry VI 2, 2, where the same prince makes another knightly speech and Clifford says,

> "Why that is spoken like a toward prince".

The representation of the one Edward as toward and brave may well have been drawn from that of the other.

Minor resemblaces are the following.

8. On p. 81 of The True Tragedy a messenger entering is greeted by York with the words, "What art thou that with thy ghastly lookes preaseth into sanctuary, to affright our Mother Queene". So in 3 Henry VI, 2, 1, a messenger is greeted by Richard with the words,

> "But what art thou, whose heavy looks foretell
> Some dreadful story hanging on thy tongue?"

9. Cf. True Tragedy p. 118,

> "Where, where slept the garrison that should a beat them back?"

with 3 Henry VI 5, 1,

> "Where slept our scouts, or how are they seduc'd,
> That we could get no news of his repair?"

10. Cf. True Tragedy, p. 66

> "And where by the helpe of thy Lord, I will so plaie my part,
> That ile be more than I am, and not much lesse than
> [I looke for",

with 3 Henry VI 3, 1, 56.

> "King Hen. More than I seem, and less than I was born to".

The True Tragedy and Shakespeare's Richard III.

The opinions of some of the more important critics on the question whether Shakespeare, in preparing Richard III, made use of The True Tragedy, have already been cited in the introduction to this play. They show that opinion has been by no means unanimous, but that in later times the current has set most strongly toward the belief first expressed by Collier, that Shakespeare's play was composed wholly independently. The present state of general opinion appears to agree with Oechelhäuser (Essay über R. III in Shakespeareana, p. 134), who says, "Ob Shakespeare dies Drama überhaupt gekannt hat, ist sehr zu bezweifeln und keinenfalls zu erweisen", and with Kuno Fischer (Sh. Charakterentwicklung R. III, p. 32), who says, "Ob nun Shakespeare die letzteren [Legge and the T. T.] gekannt hat oder nicht, abhängig von ihnen ist er in keiner Weise".

Among the few who have ranged themselves upon Boswell's side in addition to Skottowe with his four parallels, and Barron Field, who, besides what he has to say in his introduction, points out some resemblances in his notes, the most important name is that of Lloyd, author of the Critical Essays which appeared with Singer's edition of Shakespeare in 1856, and were afterward issued separately in 1858 as Essays on the Life and Plays of Shakespeare. Lloyd believed "that Shakespeare knew this play there can be little doubt, partly from agreement in general course, though that was aided by common dependence on another source, and still more from correspondence of terms and of tone in particular passages".

Three of these he instanced, and they will be mentioned later.

Verplanck in like manner refers to the ghost scene and the call for the horse.

By these commentators was especially emphasized the resemblance between the line of The True Tragedy,

"A horse, a horse, a fresh horse" and Shakespeare's, "A horse, a horse, my kingdom for a horse"; and this resemblance led Halliwell, the most conservative of critics, to put himself so far upon their side as to say in the Introduction to his edition of Richard III, "with the possible exception of one line, where the king calls for 'a horse, a fresh horse' there does not appear to be grounds for supposing that he derived a single hint from his predecessor". Against the assumption that even this line was adopted by Shakespeare from The True Tragedy appeared Oechelhäuser, who (Shakespeareana, p. 134) called attention to the line in The Battle of Alcazar, "A horse, a horse, villain, a horse!" "Somit", says he, "zerfällt jeder Beweis, dass Shakespeare das alte Drama gekannt oder benutzt habe". With regard to further resemblances he says, "Vereinzelte Anklänge in Inhalt oder Form ergaben sich von selbst aus der Benutzung gleicher Geschichtsquellen".

In spite, however, of the strong belief that Shakespeare did not use the play, it does not appear that any of those who held it made a careful and thorough examination of the passages cited by Skottowe and Field, or critically compared the plays throughout, with reference to their sources. Does not appear, I say, for though such examination may have been made, none of these writers has published any such examination of the passages of Skottowe and Field, or done much more than content himself with a sweeping denial of their thesis.

I propose here to indicate and examine all resemblances between the two plays for which their common sources are not clearly reponsible, and to draw therefrom, if possible, some more definite and authorized conclusion than has yet been arrived at, as to the probability of Shakespeare's use of The True Tragedy. It must be premised that if, as Halliwell, James Russell Lowell, Fleay and others think, Shakespeare's play was founded upon still another old play (cf. p. 532—3), and if, what is not impossible, this play had made use of The True Tragedy, the straining and sifting process undergone in the two plays would naturally leave the hints adopted from The True Tragedy fewer and harder to recognize. It is no satisfactory settlement of the question in advance to call attention to the fact that resemblances here are few, whereas in Shakespeare's Henry IV and King John the parts adopted from the old plays are many and extensive. The question remains whether the few resemblances are, as Collier declares, "merely trivial", and whether it is natural to suppose them "purely accidental".

1. In the Introduction of The True Tragedy, p. 53, Truth, explaining to Poetry the nature of Richard, and following therein in general the description of More, says,
>"So during the minoritie of the yoong Prince
>He is made Lord Protector ouer the Realme",

and goes on to relate how Edward on his death-bed
>"Hath summond all his Nobles to the Court,
>To sweare alleageaunce with the Duke his brother,
>For truth vnto his sonne the tender Prince,
>Whose fathers soule is now neare flight to God,
>Leauing behind two sonnes of tender age,
>Fiue daughters to comfort the haplesse Queene,
>All vnder the protection of the Duke of Gloster".

And on his death-bed, p. 57, Edward commits the government of the young Prince "to my brother the Protector".

In Shakespeare's play, 1:3, we have:
>"Q. Eliz. Oh, he [the Prince] is young, and his minority
>Is put unto the trust of Richard Gloucester,
>A man that loves not me, nor none of you.
>Riv. Is it concluded he shall be protector?
>Q. Eliz. It is determined, not concluded yet:
>But so it must be, if the king miscarry'.

Here the meaning is not wholly clear. Wright (Clar. Press R. III, p. 137) explains, "It is resolved upon, though no formal record of the fact has been made". Oechelhäuser finds in Elizabeth's words a reference to More, according to whom Richard's protectorship was "erst nach seiner Ankunft in London in Rath förmlich beschlossen". However this may be, Shakespeare's conception is clearly that Edward appoints Richard protector — as Oechelhäuser agrees, cf. p. 88, "Edward stirbt, Richard, nun Protector etc." — and in accordance with this, Richard is spoken of as protector immediately upon his arrival with the Prince, 3:1:141, before there has been time for a meeting of the council. Further, of a ratification by the council of Richard's appointment there is no word in Shakespeare's play.

That it was the desire and intention of Edward that Gloucester should be protector there can be little doubt; and his appointment as such by Edward in his will is distinctly stated by André and by Polidore Vergil. Edward's first will, made years before, does not mention Richard, but the final will is not on record. But though this appointment may be fact, it is not stated by any of the chronicles — More, Fabyan, Hall, Grafton or Holinshed — which Shakespeare can have used. Legge does not call Richard protector till after his appointment by the council. In the Mirror for Magistrates, in the legend of Rivers, Richard proclaims himself protector at Northampton, "Though neyther king nor queene were his elector"; while in the legend of Richard we have:

"The lords and commons all with one assent,
Protectour made me both of land and king".

The statement of More, which is not quite correctly referred to by Oechelhäuser, in fact represents Richard's selection by the council not as a ratification, but as an appointment. "The Duke of Gloucester bare him in open sighte so reuerentelye to the Prince, with all semblaunce of lowlinesse, that from the great obloquy in which hee was soo late before, hee was sodainelye fallen in soo greate truste, that at the counsayle next assembled, hee was made the onely manne chose and thoughte most mete, to bee protectoure of the king and hys realme, so that (were it destenye or were it foly) the lamb was betaken to the wolfe to kepe" (Lumby's ed. pp. 22—23). It was part of More's purpose to conceal the fact that Richard was possessed of any authority when he came to Northampton and Stony Stratford. According to him, Richard's conduct was out and out usurpation. So we have no explanation from More why Rivers remained behind the king at Northampton, whither he had, as a matter of fact, gone to explain to Gloucester, whose claim to authority he recognized, the measures he had taken for the king; and so, according to More, Richard's appointment as protector was due to his hypocritical show of loyalty. More's story was followed by all the chroniclers, and so faithfully, that Hall in that portion of his story for which Polidore Vergil was chief authority deliberately omitted Vergil's statement that Edward in his will made his two sons his heirs and committed them to the tuition [i. e. protectorship] of Richard. Cf. p. 138.

That Shakespeare's conception was far away from More's is shown not only by the omission of any council appointment, but by the mention of his protectorship before Edward dies, and by the fact that this mention is made by the queen to Rivers himself.

For the source of this view in The True Tragedy an explanation has already been offered. It appears to have been drawn from the legend of Shore's wife in the Mirror for Magistrates. Even if not from that source the representation is entirely in keeping with the author's exceedingly careless treatment of his authorities. Such is not the treatment of Shakespeare, who would never, with More before him, have made Richard protector at this time, merely through reading the passage in the Mirror for Magistrates, and for whose deviations from his historical sources a dramatic purpose is usually clearly evident. Here no such purpose is apparent. We seem confined to the conclusion that Shakespeare, or his original, if one existed, borrowed the view from The True Tragedy.

2. For the first scene of The True Tragedy, the reconciliation scene by Edward's bedside, we have the following heading. "Enter **Edward the Fourth, Lord Hastings, Lord Marcus** and **Elizabeth. To them, Richard**".

The heading shows that Richard is supposed to be present at this reconciliation, entering during the course of the scene. As a matter of fact Richard does not show his presence by speech. That it is not the heading that is at fault is shown in the first place by the heading itself. A simple mention of "Richard" might be a mistake, but "To them, Richard" is too definite a suggestion to have easily crept in through carelessness on the part of copyist or printer. But there is conclusive proof that Richard was intended to be present. The Introduction states just before, p. 53, that Edward has summoned his nobles

"To sweare alleageaunce with the Duke his brother",

and in the later scene between Richard and Rivers (p. 74) the latter asks,

"Was this the oath which at our princes death,
With vs thou didst combine?"

Rivers himself was not present at the death-bed scene, but appears to be speaking as the representative of his faction. But there is no point in the scene where anything seems to have dropped out, and no reference to Richard that implies his presence.

Where corruption of this kind exists, conjecture only is possible. The two other passages make it tolerably certain that in this scene, in its original state, Richard was present, and united in the oath of amity and allegiance to the young Prince. Such presence is not justified by the chronicles. Richard was in the North, at York, when Edward died, and from there rode to Northampton, where he met Buckingham and Rivers. That he joined in the oath of amity at all is nowhere suggested. Thus Shakespeare's predecessor had already led the way in a deviation from the authorities, calculated to make Richard's guilt all the greater. Whether Richard was meant to be present in the scene or not, he joined at all events in the oath of amity, and in breaking it added another crime of perjury to the rest. If the indications are correct, he did it, as in Shakespeare, at Edward's bedside, with the rest of the quarrelling nobles.

3. The scene between Morton and the citizen, p. 61, though doubtless based on the passage in More's story in which he speaks of the "mutteringe amonge the people, as though al should not long be well" (cf. p. 90), as Shakespeare's scene certainly is, shares with that scene a certain deviation from the original. More speaks of this mistrust as occasioned by the double council meetings. The author of The True Tragedy precedes Shakespeare in making — much less skillfully — a scene of this, and in placing it directly after the death of King Edward. Uncertainty and mistrust follow, the moment he is gone, and that the Duke of Gloucester is full of danger is suggested by the citizen's, "The King looseth his right they say".

4. Richard in the scene with Percival, Buckingham's messenger, says,

> "I do accept of his grace, and will be as readie to put in practise
> To the vttermost of my power, what ere he shalbe to deuise;
> But whereas he hath writ that the remouing of the yoong
> Prince from the Queenes friends might do well,
> Tell him thus, it is the only way to our purpose".

Shakespeare likewise makes this suggestion come from Buckingham. The scene in The True Tragedy is from More (cf. p. 422), and Shakespeare's passage was, it may be, suggested by the same, though in his case the message becomes "the story we late talked of". But in More, Buckingham sends the message that he will take whatever part Richard wishes. There is no suggestion from Buckingham as to what that part shall be. In The True Tragedy, before Shakespeare, it is Buckingham who in this point directs, and Richard who accepts his suggestion.

5. On p. 69 of The True Tragedy we have a discussion between Rivers, the young King, and the members of his train, over the letters of the Queen, bidding them dismiss their over-large company. The reasons urged in the discussion are from More's statement of Gloucester's persuasions conveyed to the Queen. "And the lordes about the kyng, should assemble in the kynges names muche people, thei should geue ẙ lordes betwixt whom & them ther had bene some tyme debate, an occasion to feare and suspecte least they should gather this people, not for the kynges saue guard, whom no man impugned, but for their destruction, hauyng more regarde to their old variaunce then to their new attonement, for the whiche cause they on the other parte might assemble men also for their defence, . . . and thus should all the realme fal in a roare, . . . & then all the world would put her & her kynred in the blame, saiyng that they had vnwysely and vntruely broken the amytie and peace whiche the kynge her husband had so prudently made betwene her kynred and his, whiche amyte his kynne had alwaies obserued" (Hall).

In The True Tragedy we have for this:

"King. Right louing vnckles, and the rest of this company, my mother hath written, and thinks it conuenient that we dismisse our traine, for feare the towne of Northampton is not able to receiue vs: and againe my vnckle of Gloster may rather think we come of malice against him and his blood: therefore my Lords, let me here your opinions . .

Riu. Then thus may it please your grace, I will shewe my opinion. First note the two houses of Lancaster and Yorke [an absurd mis-statement of the opposing parties!], the league of friendship is yet but greene betwixt them, and little cause of variance may cause it breake, and thereby I think it not requisite to discharge the company because of this".

Compare now the two with Shakespeare's scene 2:2.

"Buck. Me seemeth good, that with some little train,
Forthwith from Ludlow the young prince be fetch'd
Hither to London, to be crown'd our king.

Riv. Why with some little train, my Lord of Buckingham.

Buck. Marry, my lord, lest, by a multitude,
The new-heal'd wound of malice should break out;
Which would be so much the more dangerous,
By how much the estate is green and yet ungovern'd.
. . . .
Glou. I hope the king made peace with all of us
And the compact is firm and true in me.
Riv. And so in me; and so, I think, in all:
Yet, since it is but green, it should be put
To no apparent likelihood of breach,
Which haply by much company might be urged:
Therefore I say with noble Buckingham,
That it is meet so few should fetch the prince".

The agreement between the two passages and especially the agreement between the two speeches of Rivers, is far closer than the agreement of either scene with the chronicle. That there is any discussion at all is an invention shared by both scenes, and that in both plays pure chance should lead the two authors to assign precisely to Rivers such similar speeches is hardly to be thought of. There are, besides, other verbal resemblances which strengthen the belief in a connection between the two scenes.

It may be noted that the Shakespearean passage with the exception of Buckingham's first speech appears first in the folio. The apparent connection with The True Tragedy is additional proof that it belonged to the original complete form of the play.

6. The young King in this discussion gives evidence of a maturity for which the chronicle offers no hint. It has already been suggested (p. 496), that this may find its source in 3 Henry VI. The same ripeness is still more extensively shown by the Prince in Shakespeare's play. That The True Tragedy may have been partly responsible for this is suggested not only by its precedence in the conception but by the likeness in the following passages.

From The True Tragedy:

"King. Ah gods, if I do live my fathers yeares as God forbid but I may, I will so roote out this malice & enuie sowne among the nobilitie, that I will make them weary that were the first beginners of these mischiefes.

Gray. Worthily well spoken of your princely Maiestie,
Which no doubt sheweth a king-like resolution.
Vaughan. A toward yoong Prince, and no doubt forward to all vertue".

Cf. Sh. Rich. III, 3 : 1:
"Prince. An if I live until I be a man,
I'll win our ancient rights in France again
Or die a soldier as I lived a king.
Glou. Short summers lightly have a forward spring".

7. After the arrest of his kindred (p. 79) the young king remonstrates with the words, "I know my vnkle will conceale no treason or dangerous secresie from vs". Richard replies, "Yes, secrets that are too subtil for babes. Alasse my Lord you are a child, and they vse you as a child: but they consult and conclude of such matters, as were we not carefull, would proue preiudicial to your Maiesties person".

For this the chronicle has only "Yee my lieage quod the duke of Buckyngham, they have kept the dealyng of these matters farre from the knowledge of your good grace" (Hall, p. 349).

In Shakespeare's play, 3 : 1, occurs a similar passage. The King declares, "I want more uncles here to welcome me", and as in The True Tragedy Gloucester, not Buckingham, replies,

"Sweet prince, the untainted virtue of your years
Hath not yet dived into the world's deceit:
No more can you distinguish of a man
Than of his outward show; which, God he knows,
Seldom or never jumpeth with the heart.
Those uncles which you want were dangerous;
Your grace attended to their sugar'd words,
But look'd not on the poison of their hearts:
God keep you from them, and from such false friends!"

8. At the close of the discussion scene (p. 80) we have:
"Buc. Sound trumpet in this parley, God saue the King.
Rich. Richard".

Compare Richard III 1:3, where Margaret's curse is turned upon her by Gloucester. The long curse ends with

"Thou rag of honour! thou detested —
Glou. Margaret".

The situation is entirely different, but the trick is in a sense the same. In the older play Buckingham utters a blessing, so to speak, which Richard by the insertion of his name causes to his own satisfaction to fall upon himself. In the other case, by substituting Margaret's name he causes a curse meant for him to fall on her, likewise to his own satisfaction.

9. On p. 80 we have a scene in which the Queen appears in sorrow after the death of Edward, and is comforted by her children, Elizabeth and the Duke of York.

"Yorke. May it please your grace to shew to your children the cause of your heavines, that we knowing it, may be copartners of your sorrowes.
Queen. Ay me poore husbandles queene, and you poor fatherlesse princes.
Eliz. Good mother expect the liuing, and forget the dead. What tho our Father be dead, yet behold his children, the image of him selfe.
Queen. Ay poore Princes, my mourning is for you and for your brother, who is gone vp to an vntimely crownation".

This should be carefully compared with Shakespeare's Act 2, sc. 2, between the Duchess of York and Clarence's son and daughter. In both scenes the children implore the sorrowing mother to reveal the cause of her grief. In each case the reply is that she is not sorrowing for the death of the children's father, but for another cause. Especial resemblance exists between The True Tragedy's "What tho our Father be dead, yet behold his children, the image of him selfe", and the words of the Duchess of York in Shakespeare's scene,

"I have bewept a worthy husband's death,
And liv'd by looking on his images"

and between The True Tragedy's, "Good mother, expect the liuing and forget the dead", and the words of Rivers to the Queen in Shakespeare:
> "Drown desperate sorrow in dead Edward's grave,
> And plant your joys in living Edward's throne".

It is scarcely necessary to say that for neither scene is there any chronicle authority.

10. Cf. the reception by the Queen of the news of her kinsmen's arrest:
> "Yorke. What art thou that with thy gastly lookes preaseth into sanctuary to affright our mother Queene?
> Mess. A sweete Princes, doth my countenance bewray me. My news is doubtfull and heauie"

with the reception of the same news in Shakespeare 2 : 4.
> "Enter a Messenger.
> Arch. Here comes a messenger. What news?
> Mess. Such news, my lord as grieves me to unfold".

11. Cf. Richard's words (p. 85), "They say I haue bin a long sleeper to-day" with Shakespeare 3 : 4. 24, "I have been long a sleeper". For this More has, "bene a slepe that day". Grafton, Hall and Holinshed have "been a sleeper".

12. Field compares the council scene (p. 86) in The True Tragedy with Shakespeare's. For myself I see no resemblances for which the common source will not account.

13. On p. 96 of The True Tragedy we have:
> "King. What was he that walked with thee in the Gardeine, me thought he had the keyes?
> For. My Lord, it was one that was appointed by the King to be an ayde to sir Thomas Brokenbury.
> King. Did the King, why Myles Forest, am not I King?
> For. I would haue said my Lord your vnckle the Protector.
> King. Nay my kingly vnckle I know he is now, but let him enjoye both Crowne and kingdome, so my brother and I may but enjoy our liues and libertie".

Cf. Shakespeare's Act 4, sc. 1.
> "Brak. The king hath straitly charged the contrary.
> Q. Eliz. The king! who's that?
> Brak. I mean the lord protector".

Skottowe was the first to call attention to this coincidence, and Field did the same after him. It is a coincidence that cannot be explained away as "purely accidental"; nor is there any direct chronicle foundation for it. Hall (p. 378) has, from More, "The Prince assone as the Protectour toke vpon him to be kynge, and left the name of protectoure, was thereof advertised and shewed that he should not reigne, but his vncle should haue the crowne. At which word the prince sore abashed beganne to sighe and sayd: Alas I would myne vncle would let me haue my life although I lese my kyngedome". In The True Tragedy the Prince learns of his uncle's intentions only by a slip on the part of Forest — an artistic as well as artful improvement upon the chronicle. But it is still in connection with the chronicle passage. Shakespeare, however, makes use of the stroke before Richard has become king, and the blow falls as a warning upon the Queen; it does not fall upon the Prince. The author of The True Tragedy was therefore clearly the inventor, and Shakespeare adopted the clever invention.

14. The passage in The True Tragedy in which the murderers receive their instructions from Tyrell was, probably, as has been shown (cf. p. 484) imitated from Marlowe; and the same is probably true of the scene in Shakespeare's play in which Gloucester instructs the murderers of Clarence and that in which they murder him. There are indications, however, that go to show that Shakespeare had also in mind the scene in The True Tragedy. Cf. with the two passages on p. 484, the following from Richard III, 1:3:

"Glou. How now, my hardy, stout resolved mates!
Are you now going to dispatch this deed?
. . . .
But sirs, be sudden in the execution,
Withal obdurate, do not hear him plead;
For Clarence is well-spoken, and perhaps
May move your hearts to pity, if you mark him.

First Murd. Tush!
>Fear not, my lord, we will not stand to prate;
>Talkers are no good doers: be assured
>We come to use our hands and not our tongues".

Gloucester's speech bears considerable resemblance to the last speech of Tyrell. More conclusive is the fact that in both the murder scenes the murderers, in the T. T. one, in Shakespeare both, in turn, have a fit of repentance. The unrepentant murderer in both scenes upbraids the repentant one. Cf. The True Tragedy's, "Why, you base slaue, are you faint hearted" with Shakespeare's, "Why, fool" — "What art thou afraid?"; and the proposal in The True Tragedy, when Denten recovers from his repentance, "but come, lets too it", with Shakespeare's "Sec. Murd. come, shall we fall to work?" (other eds. "shall we to this gear?"). Here there was no common model, for in the Marlowe murderers there is no hint of repentance. Lloyd also called attention to this resemblance, saying, "The germ of much of dialogue of the murderers of Clarence seems among other parallels to be found here".

15. Cf., p. 98 of The True Tragedy,
>"Ter. How now, Myles Forest, is this deed dispatcht?
>For. I sir, a bloodie deed we haue performed".

with Shakespeare 1:4:267,

"Sec. Mur. A bloody deed and desperately dispatch'd" (Qq. "performid").

16. True Tragedy pp. 101, 102. Prof. Brandl (Introd. to his ed. of Schlegel-Tieck trans. of R. III) calls attention to the fact that both here and in Shakespeare, Richard, at his first appearance after obtaining the crown, is represented as already troubled by fear that his kingdom shall not last.

17. True Tragedy, pp. 102—3. The purpose of the scene between Richard and Catesby is to show how Richard is unnerved by Richmond's conspiracy and by his conscience. He does not know whether he has called Catesby or not,

misunderstands Catesby's hope that his troubles will be overcome as a hope that he himself will be overcome, and flies into a passion when Catesby praises Richmond. The same purpose is apparent in Shakespeare's scene, 4:4, between Richard, Catesby, and Ratcliffe.

18. Upon this scene, in both plays follows the scene between Richard and Lord Stanley. The scenes are too long to copy here entire, but the following parallel brings out the chief resemblances. In both plays the scene opens with Richard asking for news.

The True Tragedy.	Sh. Richard III.
"Now Lord Standley, what newes".	"Stanley, what news with you?"

In both cases Stanley answers ambiguously and is upbraided therefor by Richard.

| "Oh good wordes Lord Standley, but giue me leaue to gleane out of your golden field of eloquence how braue you plead ignorance". | "Heyday, a riddle! neither good nor bad! Why dost thou run so many mile about. When thou mayst tell thy tale a nearer way?" |

In both cases Stanley disclaims intimate knowledge of Richmond's plans and any sympathy with them. Richard disbelieves him and declares his belief that Stanley intends to aid Richmond.

Stanley asks leave to depart to his home in the north. Richard distrusts his purpose:

| "Ay sir, that you might be in Cheshire and Lancashire, then should your Postes passe inuisible into Brittaine, and you to depart the realme at your pleasure, or else I to suffer an intollerable foe vnder me, which I will not". | "Ay, ay, thou wouldst be gone to join with Richmond: I will not trust you, sir". |

Richard than changes his mind and allows him to go, provided he leaves his son as pledge.

[T. T. con.]
"Thou shalt goe, leauing me here thy sonne and heire George Standley for a pledge, that hee may perish for thy fact if need should be".

"Thou art set free for our defence . . . to preuent his purpose with thy power".

[Sh. R. III con.]
"Well,
Go muster men; but, hear you, leave behind
Your son, George Stanley: look your faith be firm,
Or else his head's assurance is but frail".

In answer to Richard's question, "Where is thy power then to beat him back?" Stanley has previously promised to muster men.

The chronicle basis of this is as follows. Richard gave credence "least of all to the Lord Stanley, because he was ioyned in matrimony with the lady Margarete mother to the erle of Richmond, as afterward apparauntly ye maie perceaue. For when the sayde lorde Stanley woulde haue departed into his countrey to visite his familie, and to recreate and refreshe his spirites (as he openly sayde) but the truth was to thentent to be in a perfight readines to receaue the erle of Richmond at his first arriuall in England: the king in no wise would suffre hym to departe before that he had left as a hostage in the courte George Stanley lorde Straung his first begotten sonne and heire". The common source will not by any means account for all the resemblances in the wording, conception, and course of the scene. This passage is one of the four which Skottowe mentions as proof that Shakespeare used The True Tragedy, and Field also refers to the resemblance.

19. On p. 108 of The True Tragedy Richard receives a letter by the hand of a messenger, and while he reads it his followers press questions on the messenger. Richard is angered by this and orders them all away, forgetting that he has not listened to what the messenger has verbally to deliver

"King. Away, I say, begone, it is time to looke aboute: away I say, what here yet villaines?

Mess. My Lord, I haue some what to say besides.
King. Then speake it, what hast thou to say?"

Here is betrayed the same lack of self-control that appears in Shakespeare's scene, 4:4, where Richard on the receipt of bad news sends Catesby to Norfolk, forgets to give him a message to take, then storms when he sees him waiting.

"Dull, unmindful villain,
Why stay'st thou here, and go'st not to the duke?"

20. Richmond appears for the first time (p. 109) accompanied by "Earle Oxford, P. Landoys, & Captain Blunt". The presence of Landoys is hard to account for, and of course absurd. But while it is perhaps natural that Oxford and Blunt should be Richmond's companions, it is worth noting that Shakespeare has a like scene, 5:2, with Richmond, Oxford, Blunt, and Herbert, who balances Landoys of The True Tragedy. In both cases Richmond opens the scene with an address of encouragement to his companions, introduced in the older play by, "Welcome deare friends and louing countrymen", in Shakespeare by, "Fellows in arms and my most loving friends". He urges them on against Richard, who "but usurps in my authoritie" (T. T.), "the wretched, bloody, and usurping boar" (Sh.), and closes with inspiring words.

T. T. "Then courage countrymen, and neuer be dismayed,
Our quarels good, and God will helpe the right,
For we may know by dangers we haue past,
That God no doubt will giue us victor_e".

Sh. "In God's name, cheerly on, courageous friends,
To reap the harvest of perpetual peace
By this one bloody trial of sharp war".

Then follow in both cases speeches from Richmond's companions, which, it must be admitted, do not bear any resemblance to each other except in the general effect of hope and purpose to undergo the struggle with constancy. In both cases Richmond's speech is delivered not at landing as in Legge, but after he has proceeded some way into England.

Palaestra. X.

21. Page 111 of The True Tragedy enters a messenger from the "mother queene" with a letter from Richmond's mother, Margaret. Richmond's first words are, "Welcome my friend, how fares our mother & the rest?" Is it mere chance that makes Richmond's greeting in Shakespeare's play to his father Stanley,

> "All comfort that the dark night can afford
> Be to thy person, noble father-in-law!
> Tell me how fares our loving mother?"

There is in the chronicle story nothing to hint at this solicitude on Richmond's part for his mother. It may be noted that in both plays we have a list of names of those who come to Richmond's help.

22. Page 115 of The True Tragedy Richmond meets Stanley. Between this scene and that of Shakespeare there are several striking resemblances. In both, Stanley hurries over his answer to Richmond's question — in The T. T. as to his father's health, in Shakespeare as to his mother's — with the words that he must be brief. In both is the reference to George Stanley — not in the chronicle account of the meeting — in both the statement that Stanley is unable to assist Richmond openly, but will aid him as best he may, in such fashion as will not endanger George Stanley's life — no mention of which diplomacy is made in the chronicle report. In both scenes Stanley warns Richmond to prepare for battle on the next day — not in the chronicle. In both the meeting takes place at night — contrary to the chronicle. Richmond's trouble in The True Tragedy because Stanley will not render open aid seems reflected in his statement in Shakespeare,

> "Ill strive with troubled thoughts, to take a nap".

23. (Page 116.) At their meeting Richmond asks of Stanley, "What number do you thinke the kings power to be?

Stan. Mary some twentie thousand . . .
Rich. And we hardly fiue thousand, being beset with many enemies, hoping vpon a few friends, yet dispair not Richmond".

In Shakespeare (5 : 3 : 9) Richard asks a like question of Norfolk.

"Who hath descried the number of the traitors?
Norf. Six or seven thousand is their utmost power.
Rich. Why our battalia trebles that account;
Besides, the king's name is a tower of strength,
Which they upon the adverse faction want".

The chronicles mention the numbers on both sides, when detailing the order of battle, but without statement of the effect of numbers on the leaders' spirits. The passages may well be entirely independent of each other, yet it is not without some significance that both authors have given dramatic value to the bald statement of their source, by making it reveal the natures of the leaders. As Shakespeare gives the passage to Richard its artistic value is heightened by the "dramatic irony" by which he is represented as thinking his name a name to conjure with.

24. That the soliloquy of Richard (p. 117) in which he cries out in torment that the ghosts of all whom he has slain come crying for revenge, is a distinct advance upon the chronicle, in which Richard dreams of horrible devils pulling and haling him, has been shown pp. 460—2, together with some parallels from other plays.

That the scene in Shakespeare where the ghosts appear to Richard in his dream is merely an extension of the scene in The True Tragedy seems by far the most probable explanation. This has been asserted by Skottowe, Field, Lloyd and Verplanck, and those who have opposed the view that Shakespeare gathered hints from The True Tragedy have never troubled themselves to answer their argument. Neither the older or the later play derived the idea directly from the chronicles, whose view, taken from Polidore Vergil and the additions of the Hardyng continuation, is that the devils were a vivid representation to

Richard of his future punishment, a representation summoned up by "his conscience pricked with the sharp sting of his mischeuous offences". Cf. the full passage, p. 151. The ghosts of the murdered clamoring for revenge is a totally different conception. Neither is it the conception of any of the works that deal with Richard down to these two plays. It is not likely that the two hit upon the idea independently. The True Tragedy had been on the stage and certainly attracted considerable attention some time before Shakespeare's play was written. The idea was clearly derived from the revenge tragedies. Now The True Tragedy, as has been shown, is partly a tragedy of revenge, and shows repeatedly its dependence upon the plays of this genus. The ghost of Clarence with its cry of Vindicta sounds the note of revenge at the very start, and the words of Richard in this scene "The Sunne by day shines hotely for revenge" etc., likewise show connection with other revenge plays. In short, the substitution of the ghosts of the murdered for the devils of the chronicle is entirely in accord with the nature of The True Tragedy as a whole. Shakespeare's play on the other hand, while it is in a high sense a revenge play, has very little in common with the revenge plays of the time. It is a Nemesis play, like those of the Atridae. Its kernel is the Nemesis of Richard's own nature, the Nemesis of the conscience he has tried to suppress. Entirely in accord with this idea is the tone of the words which the ghosts address to Richard, and of the words he utters to himself as he wakes. There is no cry for revenge, and the word itself does not occur in the speeches of the ghosts. They appear in Shakespeare not, as in the revenge plays, to satisfy themselves; they come to press home on Richard the fact of his guilt. He has refused to face his guilt before; now he must face it. And so they become indeed pricks of conscience, and throng to the bar of his soul, "crying all 'Guilty! guilty!'" The fact that they are made to address Richmond as well as Richard is a further indication that we have here a development of the simpler idea natural to the revenge tragedies.

The comparison of the two plays makes it evident that the appearance of the ghosts was a natural invention of the author of The True Tragedy, sprung from the conception of his play: it seems equally clear that the appearance of the ghosts in Shakespeare's play was not adopted directly from the revenge plays. He found them naturally substituted for the devils in Richard's dream, found them united with the terrors of a wounded conscience, upon which his thought laid all the stress in picturing Richard's anguish, and made use of them because he saw their adaptability to his own purpose.

There are not wanting indications of connection in the wording as well as the conception of the two passages. Cf. from The True Tragedy

> "Meethinkes their ghosts comes gaping for revenge,
> Whom I haue slaine in reaching for a Crowne
> . . . .
> And every one cries let the tyrant die"

with Shakespeare's

> "Methought the souls of all that I had murther'd
> Came to my tent, and every one did threat
> To-morrow's vengeance on the head of Richard"

and with the final words of each of the ghosts, "Despair and die".

Cf. also (with Lloyd), from The True Tragedy

> "The hell of life that hangs upon the crown,
> The daily cares, the nightly dreams
> . . . .
> And horror of my bloody practise past,
> Strikes such a terror to my wounded conscience"

with the words of Richard to Ratcliffe in Shakespeare's play,

> "Shadows to-night
> Have struck more terror to the soul of Richard
> Than can the substance of ten thousand soldiers".

In connection with the ghosts, Shakespeare's 3 : 1 : 143—5,

"York. I shall not sleep in quiet at the Tower.
Gloster. Why what should you fear?
York. Marry, my uncle Clarence' angry ghost".

is not impossibly a reminiscence of the appearance of Clarence's ghost in The True Tragedy.

The likeness in the two passages does not end here. There is in The True Tragedy passage something of the same delirium in Richard's words as in Shakespeare; and there appears the same spirit and the same recovery from despair that characterize Shakespeare's Richard.

"Then such a life I count far worse to be
Then thousand deaths vnto a damned death:
How wast death I said? who dare attempt my death?
Nay who dare so much as once to thinke my death?
Though enemies there be that would my body kill,
Yet shall the leaue a neuer dying minde".

In both plays follows upon the passage Richard's fear that his friends will prove untrue.

25. In the scene (p. 120) where Richard resolves on the death of Lord Strange we have:

"King. His trecherous father hath neglect his word and done imparshall wast by dint of sword, therefore sirrah go fetch him. Zownes draw you cuts who shall go, I bid you go Catesby".

Field compares Shakespeare's Act 4 sc. 4, the passage in which the unnerved Richard bids Catesby go before he has his message (cf. p. 512—3). There is no resemblance in the situation, and I cannot think that Shakespeare could have obtained a hint for his scene from this passage of The True Tragedy.

26. On p. 121 of The True Tragedy we have

"The battell enters, **Richard** wounded, with his **Page**.
King. A horse, a horse, a fresh horse.
Page. A flie my Lord and saue your life.
King. Flie, villaine, looke I as tho I would flie, no first shall this dull and senceless ball of earth receiue my body cold and void of sense".

Cf. Shakespeare's play, 5:4
"King Richard. A horse! A horse! my kingdom for a horse!
　　Catesby. Withdraw, my lord; I'll help you to a horse.
King Richard. Slave! I have set my life upon a cast.
　　　　And I will stand the hazard of the die".

 This is the famous passage which has been urged as proof by all supporters of the theory that Shakespeare borrowed from The True Tragedy. The chronicles have only, "They began to suspect fraude and to smell treason, and not only exhorted but determinately aduysed hym to saue hym selfe by flyght; and when the loss of the battayle was imminent and apparante, they brought to hym a swyfte and a light horse to conuey hym away. He ... answered (as men saye) that on that daye he would make an end of all battailes or els ther finish his lyfe" (Hall, p. 420). Oechelhäuser thought to find a source for Shakespeare's line equally as likely as The True Tragedy in the line of The Battle of Alcazar, "A horse, a horse, villain, a horse!" and declared that thus every offered proof that Shakespeare used the older play fell to the ground.

 But Oechelhäuser's rebuttal is not satisfactory, as a little examination will show. The scene in The Battle of Alcazar from which the line is drawn runs thus (5:1:71 et seq.):

　　　　"Enters the Moor and his Boy, flying.
The Moor. Villain, a horse!
　Boy. O, my lord, if you return, you die!
The Moor. Villain, I say, give me a horse to flie,
　　　　To swim the river, villain, and to fly.
　　. . . . .
　Boy. O my lord,
　　　　These ruthless Moors pursue you at the heels,
　　　　And come amain to put you to the sword!
The Moor. A horse, a horse, villain, a horse!
　　　　That I may take the river straight and fly.
　Boy. Here is a horse, my lord,
　　　　As swiftly pac'd as Pegasus:
　　　　Mount thee thereon and save thyself by flight".

In this passage the Moor's cry is for a horse to fly with. In The True Tragedy and in Shakespeare

Richard's cry is for a fresh horse to go once more against his foes. It is not at all certain that The Battle of Alcazar may not have followed The True Tragedy, as the earliest date for its production is, so far as known, 1591. If it preceded, it is entirely possible that the passage in The True Tragedy imitated The Battle of Alcazar, with which, as shown elsewhere, it has much in common. The page here corresponds exactly to the Boy of The Battle of Alcazar. Those who prefer with Oechelhäuser to think that Shakespeare too borrowed from The Battle of Alcazar are forced to face the fact that Shakespeare's play shows no other trace of connection with this play, and to believe in the likelihood that he, entirely independent of a play that had appeared some time before his own, and which like the Contention and The True Tragedy of R. Duke of York, which he certainly continued in his Richard III, would naturally have attracted his attention, not only likewise thought of a line in The Battle of Alcazar, but changed the passage of his chronicle authority to a conception not that of The Battle of Alcazar but exactly the same as that of The True Tragedy, and wrote lines that closely correspond. The likelihood is all the other way, if we consider these two passages alone. But they do not stand alone.

27. Immediately following upon the words quoted above from The True Tragedy, Richard continues, "you watry heauens rowle on my gloomy day, and darksome cloudes close up my cheerfull sownde, downe is thy sunne Richard, neuer to shine again, the birdes whose feathers should adorne my head, houers aloft & dares not come in sight, yet faint not man, for this day if Fortune will, shall make thee King possest with quiet crown". Richard looks up to the dark and gloomy clouds, the watery heavens above him, where no sun is to be seen, and draws therefrom an ill-boding prophecy of his own fate. Down is his sun too, and never to rise again. Yet once more he brings his will to bear, encourages himself and fights on.

Cf. with this Shakespeare's Act 5, sc. 3, where Richard inquires "who saw the sun to-day?" and perceiving that "he disdains to shine" draws the gloomy prophecy therefrom,

"A black day will it be to somebody.
Ratcliff, ...
. . . the sun will not be seen to-day;
The sky doth frown and lower upon our army.
I would these dewy tears were from the ground".

Then comes the reaction.

"Not shine to-day! Why, what is that to me
More than to Richmond? for the selfsame heaven
That frowns on me looks sadly upon him'.

That Shakespeare drew his passage from The True Tragedy there can be little doubt, when it is observed that the chronicle account gives an entirely different description of the day. According to it the sun was shining! "Betwene both armies ther was a great marryse which therle of Richemond left on his right hand, for this entent that it should be on that syde a defence for his part, and in so doyng he had the sonne at his backe and in the faces of his enemies" (Hall, p. 418).

28. The heading of the last scene in Shakespeare's play reads in both quartos and folio, "Alarum. Enter Richard and Richmond; they fight. Richard is slain. Retreat and flowrish. Re-enter Richmond, Derby bearing the crown, with divers other Lords". This is generally changed in modern editions to "Enter Richard and Richmond, fighting; and exeunt fighting", "else Stanley could not afterwards enter with the latter . . . bearing the crown, and say, 'So, here, this long-usurped royalty . . have I pluck'd off'".

In The True Tragedy, after Richard's call for his horse etc., comes the stage-direction, "Enters Richmond to battell againe, and kils Richard". Then "Enters Report and the Page", who relates to the other the course and result of the battle. Then "Enter Earle Richmond, Earle Oxford, L. Standley, and their traine, with the Crowne".

The fact that in both plays "with the crown" is made a part of the stage-direction is indicative of connection between the two. If this is the fact, the direction of The True Tragedy would support the original direction of Shakespeare's play, which makes Richmond kill Richard upon the stage. Then the direction "Re-enter Richmond" might naturally follow, the scene between Report and the Page having been omitted. As has often been remarked, especially by Lowell (cf. Rolfe's ed. of Richard III, p. 33), the close of the play bears signs of hasty treatment. Thus Stanley tells Richmond that George Stanley is living and safe in Leicester town, though he has had no time to learn any such fact. Precisely of the same character is the statement of the Page in The True Tragedy immediately following the death of Richard and before the re-entrance of Richmond, that Catesby "is this day beheaded on a stage at Lester, because he took part with my Lord the King".

In the page's account we have,

> "But worthie Richard that did neuer flie, but followed honour to the gates of death, straight spurd his horse to encounter with the Earle".

Cf. Catesby's words, Richard III 5:4:4,5,

> "His horse is slain, and all on foot he fights,
> Seeking for Richmond in the throat of death".

Cf. also Stanley's response to Richmond's words in The True Tragedy,

> "Well spoken sonne, and like a man of worth, whose resolution in this battle past, hath made thee famous 'mongst thy enemies",

with Shakespeare's scene, where Richmond likewise speaks first, and Stanley replies, "Courageous Richmond, well hast thou acquit thee".

29. Cf. in the Epilogue of The True Tragedy,

> "Then happie England mongst thy neighbor Iles,
> For peace and plentie still attends on thee:
> And all the fauourable Planets smiles
> To see theee liue in such prosperitie"

with the Epilogue in Shakespeare's play

"And let their heirs — God, if thy will be so —
Enrich the time to come with smooth-faced peace,
With smiling plenty, and fair prosperous days".

30. I append a few resemblances of a purely verbal nature.

a) P. 77 "But in good time they come" (as Richard and others enter), p. 107 "But see in good time here he is" (as Lovell enters). This introduction is a noteworthy peculiarity of Shakespeare's play. Thus 2 : 1 : 45

"And in good time, here comes the noble duke"
3 : 1 : 24 "And in good time, here comes the sweating lord"
3 : 1 : 95 "Now, in good time, here comes the Duke of York"
3 : 4 : 21 "In happy time, here comes the duke himself"
4 : 1 : 12 "And in good time here the lieutenant comes".

This formula so specially favored in Richard III is not common. "Good time" in this sense occurs only twice elsewhere in all Shakespeare and "happy time" twice, but never in this formula "And in good (happy) time here comes" etc. — The formula does not occur in the known plays of Peele, Green, or Marlowe (in The Jew of Malta Abigail replies to demand to open the door, "In good time, father"), not in I, II, III Henry VI (1 : 3 "You're come to Sandal in a happy hour"), and not in the old play of Henry V. It occurs once in the old King John, "And in good time, welcome my lord Chattilion", in Arden of Feversham once (I 1, 291) "In good time see where my husband comes", and in Mucedorus once.

b) A favorite phrase of The True Tragedy is "no doubt" in such expressions as (p. 70) "Which no doubt sheweth a king-like resolution", "A toward young prince and no doubt forward to all vertue", etc. Cf. Richard III 1 : 2 : 45, "Young, valiant, wise, and, no doubt, right royal". This use of "no doubt" — "undoubtedly" occurs 10 times in The True Tragedy, and 15 times in Richard III. Elsewhere in Shakespeare it occurs: in 1 play (Hen. V) 3 times; in 2 (Temp. and Hen. VIII) twice; in 6 plays once each (including 3 Henry VI). In I and II Henry VI it does not occur at all.

c) Cf. p. 119 of The T. Trag. "King. Keep silence villaine, leaste I by poste do send thy soule to hell", with Richard III, I : 1 : 146, "Till George be pack'd with post-horse up to heaven".

d) Cf. p. 87, "I am acquainted with one James Terrell .. with him my Lord will I so worke, that soone at night you shall speake with him", with Richard III, 4 : 3 : 31, 32

> "Come to me, Tyrell, soon at after supper,
> When thou shalt tell the process of their death".

In concluding this section, I wish to emphasize that I by no means assert that in all the instances here brought together Shakespeare borrowed from The True Tragedy. I have endeavored to include every case in which a careful examination discovered a resemblance that cannot be accounted for by the common chronicle source of the two plays. Even where resemblances may be accidental the probability of accident decreases with increasing numbers, and it was therefore necessary to omit none, in order that the total extent of resemblance might be seen. But I believe a conservative judgment, re-examining the instances I have brought forward, will agree that in this number are some resemblances too important to be called trivial and too close to be accidental, and conclude that Shakespeare certainly did make use of The True Tragedy.

The Date of The True Tragedy.

Having examined the relations of the play to such other works as show resemblances to it, we are now in a position to consider the question of the date at which it was written.

In this, as in the question of the relationship of the play to Shakespeare's, the opinion of Collier has generally been accepted by those who have not cared to examine the question for themselves. This was that "as in this sort of Epilogue no allusion is made to the Spanish Armada, though other public events of less prominence are touched upon, we may perhaps infer that the drama was written before the year 1588". Of late years the attempt to establish a closer date has been taken up by Mr. Fleay, and his opinion, after some rather remarkable wavering and contradictions, has been expressed in favor of a date considerably later than that suggested by Collier as the later limit.

On page 64 of his Chronicle Hist. of the Stage, Mr. Fleay says, "Richard III, as played by the Queen's men c. 1587, was the first play of that kind", viz. "the first chronicle history in its full sense". On page 67 of the same book he says of The Famous Victories of Henry V, "This play . . cannot be later than 1588 and was probably anterior to all other 'histories', being far inferior to the early plays on John, Richard III" etc. "I believe it to have been acted c. 1585—6". In his later book, A Biograph. Chr. of the Eng. Drama, 2, 28, Mr. Fleay says, "This Richard 3 was almost certainly acted early in 1586 or late in 1585, before the theatres were closed for the plague. The ballad founded on it was entered S. R. Aug. 15". This was A tragical Report of King Richard the Third, a ballad. Entered S. R. Aug. 15, 1586, cf. p. 395. But on page 315 of the same volume we find, apparently as the result of a later and closer examination, the following remarkable change. "It was played at Court (see prayer at the end), and therefore cannot date later than 1591; but as it was evidently meant as a continuation of the series 1 Henry 6 and The Contention of York and Lancaster it cannot be much earlier".

With this latter opinion the results of the foregoing study practically agree. The extreme under limit for the date is furnished by the entry in the Stationers' Register, June 19, 1594. The play was published "As it was playd by the Queenes Maiesties Players", and a knowledge of the history of their company, as traced by Mr. Fleay, enables us to push back the date considerably farther.

From 1583 to December 26, 1591 the Queen's men acted at The Theater. That they then suffered at least partial disruption seems to be proved by the fact that that they presented no plays at court during the holidays. In the previous year they had presented "enterludes" on New Year's Day, Sunday after New Year (Jan. 3), Twelfth Day (Jan. 6), and Shrove Sunday (Feb. 14). After this time they did not appear at Court. In 1593 a company under the same name, "probably the mere débris of the old one" was acting down to May 3. April 1 to April 8, 1594 the Queen's men, as we learn from Henslow's Diary, were acting with Sussex's men at The Rose. After this they disappear from the stage. Further knowledge of their history is obtained from the history of the plague, which forced the closing of the theatres from July to December, 1592, and from May to Christmas 1593 (cf. Fleay, Chron. Hist. of Stage, Cunningham, Revels at Court, Introd. p. XXXII).

Thus we have 1592 Jan. to July, 1592, Dec. to May, 1593, in which the play may possibly have been produced. It was not produced while the Queen's men were acting with Sussex's men, Apr. 1—8, 1593; and it is extremely improbable that it was newly written for the remnant of the Queen's company which acted after 1591. There are traces of many of the old Queen's men's plays passing over to Strange's and Sussex's companies, and early in 1594 several other plays of the Queen's men beside The True Tragedy, including The Contention and the old Henry V, came into the hands of the printer Creede. The plays played by the Queen's men and Sussex's in 1594 were old plays. Every thing points to the fact that from 1592 on the remnant of the old company made use of a previously acquired stock of plays.

December 1591 is therefore the latest date which can with probability be assigned as the under limit for the play. This is the same as that set by Mr. Fleay on the ground of the prayer for the Queen at the end, but Mr. Fleay would have considerable difficulty in showing that the presence of such a prayer is proof that the play was acted at Court.

Let us now turn to the question of the upper limit. Here Mr. Collier's remark that the Armada is not mentioned in the Epilogue is of absolutely no weight. The line "And she hath put proud Antichrist to flight" may so well be a reference to the defeat of the Armada, that, even though it may be a reference to the overthrow of the Catholic religion prevailing under Mary, it certainly cannot be used as a satisfactory basis of argument.

Far more satisfactory is an examination of the influence of other plays upon The True Tragedy. Here I believe I have sufficiently shown in the foregoing study that Marlowe's Tamburlaine and Faustus, and very likely Edward II, were imitated. Little argument can be drawn from the other old plays with which The True Tragedy shows connection, for in most cases the dates of these are not established; but many show even more strongly the influence of Tamburlaine and Faustus, and their resemblances to The True Tragedy are additional proof that it stands under the same influence. Faustus was very certainly produced in 1588, and some time must have elapsed before imitations appeared.

The so-called "archaic" form of The True Tragedy cannot be allowed weight in opposition to this. We have ballad-metre in the old King John, which appeared after Tamburlaine, and both the old King John and Henry V show similar absurdities of expression. Crude as the form certainly often is, in face of the clear influence of Marlowe it must be regarded as a survival, the work of an inferior artist, not as an indication of very early date.

Further, it has, I believe, been satisfactorily shown that The True Tragedy implies the pre-existence of 3 Henry VI, or The True Tragedy of Richard Duke of York, if that he regarded as an original of 3 Henry VI — an opinion with which I do not agree and which finds less and less support, but which it has seemed unwise to consider here. This, it is generally agreed, cannot be dated much earlier than 1590.

We may conclude, therefore, that The True Tragedy was very certainly written between 1589—1591, and probably somewhere between July 1590 and December 1591.

The Authorship of The True Tragedy.

This question is of so dark a nature that the most careful investigation yields no satisfactory result. The views of Boswell (Malone's Shakespeare), Lloyd (Essay on R. III) and Fleay (Biog. Chron. 2, 315) are merely groundless suppositions which need no refutation. The sole conclusion is that there are no data upon which one can found even a reasonable conjecture.

VII. Chute's Shore's Wife.

"Beawtie dishonoured written vnder the title of Shores wife", by Anthony Chute or Chewt, was entered on the Stationers' Register, June 16, 1593, and published in the same year, "imprinted by John Wolfe".

It consists of 167 six-line stanzas, relating the career of Jane Shore. The narration, as in Churchyard's legend in the Mirror for Magistrates, is supposed to be made by "her wronged ghost". Only two copies are known to be in existence and as both are in private hands, and the poem has never been reprinted, the general public must content itself with the description in Corser's Collectanea Anglo-poetica, Part IV pp. 390—6.

Corser quotes several stanzas, but as his object is to illustrate Chute's style, absolutely no idea of the material contents of the poem is to be obtained from them.

That it was written some time before publication is suggested by the author's calling it in the dedication "the first invention of my beginning Muse", and "myne infant labours"; and by Harvey's mention of it in the introductory letter to his Pierces Supererogation, 1593.

VIII. Fletcher's The Rising to the Crowne of Richard the thirde. Written by him Selfe.

This was written by Giles Fletcher, the elder, and published in 1593 in a volume whose full title is "Licia or Poemes of Love, in Honour of the admirable and singular vertues of his Lady, to the imitation of the best Latin Poets and others. Whereunto is added the Rising to the Crowne of Richard the third". This was reprinted by Grosart, Misc. Full. Worthies, 1876. The dedication is dated September 4, 1593.

The poem follows the manner of the legends in the Mirror for Magistrates, which was revived at this time by such poems as Chute's Shores Wife, 1593, Churchyard's reprint in 1593 of his legend of Shore's wife in the Mirror for Magistrates, and Daniel's Complaint of Rosamond, 1592. Cf. Morley, Eng. Writers, X. 214.

To these poems and to the legend of Elstred (in the Mirror for Magistrates, 1574?) reference is made at the beginning of Fletcher's work.

Richard, relating his story in person, mentions these three unfortunates and declares their fate but a trifle compared with his own.

> "Nor weepe I nowe, as children that have lost,
> But smyle to see the Poets of this age,
> Like silly boats in shallowe rivers tost,
> Loosing their paynes and lacking still their wage.
> To write of women, and of womens falles,
> Who are too light for to be fortunes balles".

He cannot think that his honor was stained so long as that which he sought and gained was a kingdom. The story is confined to Richard's upward course, ending where his sorrows began. Richard's nature, derived from his father, his murder of Henry VI and of Clarence, the downfall of the queen's kinsmen, the queen's sorrow and flight to sanctuary, her conference with the Archbishop of York, the removal of the duke of York from sanctuary by one who, as in Shakespeare, is called simply "Cardnall", the murder of the Princes — merely mentioned, not pictured — Hastings' downfall and the securing of Buckingham to Richard's side, the sermon of Dr. Shaw, and the final attainment of the crown, form the leading points of the poem.

In general the story of More is the basis. It is noteworthy, however, that Clarence is represented as himself plotting to be king, that Richard is made his brother's "butcher", that the murder of Henry is made a part of Richard's plots to gain the crown, and that Richard is called Lord Protector at the same time when he brings about the fall of Rivers and Gray. Thus the poem furnishes additional evidence that these were all matters of accepted tradition when Shakespeare wrote.

That Fletcher used Holinshed is shown by the allusion to the winning of Buckingham:

"To match our children I did him persuade,
And Earle of Hereford he himself be made".

This is from one of the passages translated from More's Latin, which Hall does not have but which is in Holinshed. Cf. p. 223.

Poetically the work has no value. The queen's parting from her son is the only situation in which the writer strives at all for effect; and Richard's character is barely outlined. His real spirit appears only in the assertion that even now he does not repent:

"For meaner things men wittes and lives have spent"

and he scorns all such as blame his fortune. More's simile of the sea swelling before a storm is used by Fletcher as by Shakespeare (R. III II, 3, 44). Cf. p. 126—7.

IX. Henslowe's Play on Richard III.

Among the papers of Edward Alleyn, the actor, and son-in-law and partner of Philip Henslowe, the theatrical manager, is preserved at Dulwich College, on the back of a note from one Robert Shaa to Henslowe, the following memorandum.

"1 sce. W^m· Wor. and Ansill, and to them the plowghmen.
2 sce. Richard and Q. Eliza. Catesbie, Lovell, Rice ap. Tho., Blunt, Banester.
3 sce. Ansell. Daug^r· Denys, Hen. Oxf. Courtney, Bouchier and Grace. To them Rice ap. Tho. and his Souldiers.
4 sce. Milton, Ban. his wyfe and children.
5 sce. K. Rich. Catesb, Lovell, Norf. Northumb. Percye".

This evidently refers to a play upon the subject of Richard III, projected for Henslowe's company, the Admiral's men. It was probably, Collier suggests, "the scheme of an entire act, drawn up by concert, and as a guide, between two or more dramatists engaged on the same play". The date of the play, or whether, in fact, the play was ever written, is wholly unknown. As however, it is not probable that Henslowe's company was without a play on so popular a subject during the nineties, it is quite possible that the above is a bit from a play used during this period and replaced by Jonson's Richard Crookback in 1602. Not impossibly it preceded Shakespeare's. The character of Banister, omitted by Shakespeare, is here retained. "Denys" may be the "sir Thomas Denis" mentioned in the True Tragedy (see p. 455). Cf. on the memorandum, Collier, Memoirs of Edward Alleyn, pp. 121—2.

X. A Possible Original Play of Shakespeare's Richard III.

It is an opinion strongly held by many critics that Shakespeare's Richard III is a revision of an older play. As no such play is extant and there is nothing but con-

34*

jecture upon which to conclude that it ever existed, the subject is beyond the province of this work. For the sake of completeness it may be allowed to indicate briefly some of the reasons offered for this opinion.

The second quarto, 1602, professed to be "newly augmented", and the same profession was made by all the succeeding quartos. Yet all merely copied the first quarto, 1597, and offered no additions. There are those who do not see in this a publisher's device to sell more copies, but believe that the play was, as averred, an augmentation.

The evidence for this is of course almost wholly internal. Especial attention is called to metrical licenses like those of the anterior period, "the prolonged stichomythia conducted and relieved with art and feeling that remind of the Greek tragedians" (Lloyd, Critical Essay on R. III), and the conception of Margaret, which Fleay (Chron. Hist. of Shak., p. 276) thinks plainly due to Marlowe. Certain passages are felt to be too weak to be the product of the same hand that wrote others. James Russell Lowell (cf. Introd. to Rolfe's R. III, p. 33) says, "It appears to me that an examination of Richard III. plainly indicates that it is a play which Shakespeare adapted to the stage, making additions, sometimes longer and sometimes shorter; and toward the end he either grew weary of his work or was pressed for time, and left the older author, whoever he was, pretty much to himself". With this opinion harmonizes, as Rolfe remarks, the statement of Fleay (in Ingleby's Shakespeare: The Man and the Book, Part 2, p. 139) that the folio text up to a point in act V, sc. 3 was printed from a prompter's copy, but was from this point supplemented by the quarto of 1602, the prompter's copy being probably deficient toward the conclusion. Elsewhere (Chron. Hist. of Shak., p. 276) Mr. Fleay thus states his idea of the origin of the play. "There can be little doubt that in this, as in John, Shakespeare derived his plot and part of his text from an anterior play, the difference in the two cases being that in Richard III. he adopted much more of his predecessor's text. I believe that the anterior play was Marlowe's, partly written for Lord Strange's company in 1593, but left unfinished at Marlowe's death, and completed and altered by Shakespeare in 1594".

Halliwell believed that "some of its weakness and excessively turbulent character" is without doubt due to the use of an anterior play, and mentions the rising of the ghosts as indicative of such use, and offers also the only bit of external evidence. "No copy of this older play is known to exist, but one brief speech and the two following lines have been accidentally preserved:
>"My liege, the Duke of Buckingham is ta'en,
>And Banister is come for his reward" —

from which it is clear that the new dramatist did not hesitate to adopt an occasional line from his predecessor [the first line — R. III IV, 4, 529, "My liege, the Duke of Buckingham is taken], although he entirely omitted the character of Banister. Both plays must have been successful, for, notwithstanding the great popularity of Shakespeare's, the more ancient one substained its ground on the English stage until the reign of Charles I." (Outlines of the Life of Shakespeare, 4th ed., p. 124). The lines above quoted are taken from "a little volume of excessive rarity entitled, A New Booke of Mistakes, or Bulls with Tales and Buls without Tales, but no lyes by any meanes, 1637, — In the play of Richard the Third, the Duke of Buckingham, being betraid by his servant Banister, a messenger, comming hastily into the presence of the King to bring him word of the Duke's surprizall, Richard asking him, what newes?, he replyed, — My leige, the Duke of Banister is tane = And Buckingham is come for his reward'. The high probability of Shakespeare's drama having been founded on an anterior one encourages the belief that the first of the lines just given belonged, in its genuine form, to the older play" (Halliwell's Outlines, notes to 5th ed. p. 512).

It must be noted that the possibility is not excluded, that the play here mentioned was later than that of Shakespeare.

In concluding this brief notice, it may be said that the majority of those who believe in the existence of an earlier play agree with Halliwell, rather than Fleay, that Richard III is nevertheless essentially Shakespeare's.

XI. Drayton's Heroical Epistles.

On page 439 I have mentioned the argument of Fleay that the words of Lodowicke, in Scene 10 of The True Tragedy contain a reference to Drayton's Heroical Epistles. I there postponed to this place the question of the date of these poems.

Their existence before 1595, though not published till 1599, is assumed by Mr. Fleay from the well-known reference in Spenser's Colin Clout, 1595.

> "And there though last not least is Aetion,
> A gentler shepheard may no where be found:
> Whose muse full of high thoughts inuention,
> Doth like himself Heroically sound".

In finding here a reference to Drayton's Epistles Mr. Fleay is supported by the pretty commonly accepted view of the many who believe that Aetion is meant for Drayton. That, however, it must be remarked at the outset, still remains, and probably always will remain, a matter of conjecture.

But even if this is accepted, it does not necessarily follow that the last line refers to the Heroical Epistles. The "like himself" is commonly interpreted, by Mr. Fleay also, as referring to Drayton's pseudonym of Rowland, under which he appears in Idea: The Shepherds Garland, 1593, wherein he praises Spenser's Faerie Queene. If now we assume that the Heroical Epistles preceded The True Tragedy we must make the further assumption that Drayton was already known to Spenser under the pseudonym of Rowland at least three years before the appearance of Idea. But again, the identification of Drayton with Aetion rests upon the assumption that Aetion stands here for Idea, both being used to mean "first-cause" in Greek, and so, as synonyms, interchangeable. Idea of course was not a pseudonym of Drayton, and it is a little difficult to see why its synonym should be used as a name for the poet. At all events, everything in the argument points to a reference arising from the 1593 volume Idea. And admitting that the "doth Heroically sound" may well refer to the Heroical Epistles, it is in view of all the circumstances equally natural to believe that it is simply a compliment on the "high thought's invention" in the poem Idea coupled by the word "heroically" to the name of the poet, Rowland.

Whatever support Mr. Fleay derived for his theory from the reference in The True Tragedy I believe I have removed, and I may here say, without entering upon a detailed proof of the statement, that the assumption of a reference to Drayton in the Lodowick of Edward III appears to be equally unfounded. The play is far away from the story which Drayton gives in his Epistles, and upon the correctness of which he in his notes insists.

Lastly, it is on the face of it unlikely that these poems, if composed before 1591, should not considering Drayton's activity in publishing between 1591 and 1597, have been published till 1599. The style of the Epistles is far superior to that of his earlier published work, and furnishes thus an internal proof of its later composition.

These considerations show how impossible it is with any great show of reason to assign the Epistles to a date earlier than The True Tragedy, and the case is little better for a date earlier than Shakespeare's Richard III. Some of the epistles must have been later, as in the epistle of Surrey to Geraldine, Nash's Jack Wilton, completed June 27, 1593, published 1594, was used (cf. Morley, Eng. Writers X: 321); and in the epistles of Margaret and

Suffolk, Shakespeare's Henry VI was used, as shown by the fact that Margaret and Suffolk appear as lovers, by the prophecy of the witch of Eye that Suffolk would die by water, and the fact that Suffolk's ship is attacked by pirates, for none of which representations is there authority in the chronicles. Compare also the reference to Richard, quoted below. To this add that Drayton's words, "Two or three poems written by sundry men have magnified this womans (Shore's wife's) beautie" must include a reference to Chute's poem 1593, as this caused Churchyard to issue his Challenge, containing a reprint of the legend in the Mirror for Magistrates, whose authorship he claims as his own. The circumstances imply that no poem — certainly none of importance — had been written on Shore's wife save his own and Chute's, for between the former and the latter nothing had been written that aroused interest enough in the subject to induce Churchyard to put forth a public claim to the earlier poem.

It is not probable therefore that the epistles of Edward to Shore's wife and of Shore's wife to Edward were written before Shakespeare's play, but in the absence of a certain date I give below a brief synopsis of these epistles, with the reference to Richard contained in the epistle of Margaret to Suffolk.

1. Que<u>e</u>ne Margaret to William de-la-Poole Duke of Suffolke.

> "And now I heare his [Yorke's] hate full duchesse chats,
> And rips vp their descent vnto her brats,
> And blesseth them as Englands lawfull heires,
> And tels them that our diadem is theirs.
> And if such hap her goddesse Fortune bring,
> If three sonnes faile, sheele make the fourth a King
> He that's so like his Damme, her yongest Dicke,
> That foule, ill-fauored, crookebacke stigmatike,
> That like a carcas stolne out of a tombe;
> Came the wrong way out of hir [his] mother's wombe;
> With teeth in's head, his passage to haue torne,
> As though begot an age e're he was borne".

cf. 3 Henry VI 135—138

"Q. Marg. But thou art neither like thy sire nor dam;
But like a foul mis-shapen stigmatic,
Mark'd by the destinies to be avoided
As venom toads, or lizards' dreadful stings".

2. Edward the fourth to Shores wife.

In this epistle Edward bewails that Fortune has been kinder to the City than to the Court, in giving so beauteous a woman to Shore. When the report of her beauty was brought to him he could not believe it, but when he saw her he thought report too poor, and urges that she will show fairer at Court, as jewels show fairest in richest setting. He relates how he came disguised to the city to see her. Shore called him into his shop to show and sell him jewels. Edward wanted his fairest jewel, which he would not sell. Then follows extravagant praise of her beauty. Her cheeks with their roses and lilies surpass the gardens of the Italians, her lips and teeth the rubies and pearls of India, the transparence of her skin the crystal of Pole and Dane. Her garments, whatever they may be, surpass the French, her locks make her husband's gold seem but dross. Her touch turns all to gold, she is sweeter than all perfumes, her hand is whiter than lawn. All ache to see her and having seen her scorn to look at anything else. Such a powerful effect hath beauty. The merchant, the cynic, soldier, lawyer, tradesman, and sweating clown, all alike are fond of fair women. Learning and Art have a place only to note and describe her beauty. Such perfection belongs not in a city shop, but in a Prince's sumptuous gallery. Edward urges her to prove the difference

"Betwixt a vulgar and a kingly love"

and in conclusion declares that delays breed doubts, and while time tarries Love grows sickly and Hope daily starves.

3. The Epistle of Shore's wife to king Edward the fourth.

She begins to write quaking, as a child playing on the lute a new lesson before his master. She wishes she had been a humble shepherd's wife

> "Nor seene the golden Cheape, nor glittering Change,
> To stand a Comet gaz'd at in the skies".

Her beauty has been praised before, but never so much admired as by Edward. That he should stoop from the beauties of his court to a poor citizeness seems unbelievable; London is so full of beautiful women. She praises England's beauties above those of other nations. She ends this vein, for she feels she is drawing on her own indignity.

> "And what though married when I was but yong,
> Before I knew what did to loue belong,
> Yet he which now's possessed of the roome,
> Cropt beauties flower when it was in the bloome".

Her husband trusts her, she cannot deceive him. She has repulsed others, she must repulse the King.

> "Yet rather let me die the vildest death,
> Then liue to draw that sinne-polluted breath".

And yet Edward knows that women are least angry often when most they chide. Men know too well how to woo women, how to flatter.

> "Who would have thoght, a King that cares to raigne,
> Inforcde by loue, so Poet-like should faine".

Edward has overpraised her beauty, yet she knows, and he too, that women secretly like best those who admire them most. Churlish husbands enjoy their wives' favors, but keep them at home and allow them no pleasures: what wonder that they will stray when tempted? And when the temptation comes from a king?

> "When Kings once come, they conquer as they list.
> . . . .
> And thus by strength thou art become my fate,
> And mak'st me loue euen in the midst of hate".

To this epistle Drayton adds an interesting note. "Her stature was meane, her haire of a dark yellow, her face round & ful, her eie gray, delicate harmony being betwixt each parts proportion, & each proportions colour, her body fat, white, and smooth, her countenance cheerefull, and like to her condition. That picture which I haue seen of hers, was such as she rose out of her bed in the morning, hauing nothing on but a rich mantle cast vnder one arme ouer hir shoulder, and sitting on a chaire on which her naked arme did lie".

XII. Index Table of Some of the Sources of Shakespeare's Richard III.

The following table is intended to serve in a certain degree as index to some of the results of the foregoing study in their relation to Shakespeare's play. It is not meant to be self-explanatory, and for the full importance and bearing of each item the reader is referred to the body of the work. Nor is there any attempt to repeat the work of Oechelhäuser's essay, and indicate at large the relations of Shakespeare's play to its sources. It is meant solely to call attention to some sources and influences of which Oechelhäuser and others do not take sufficient or any account, to indicate more fully than has elsewhere been done what Shakespeare drew from Hall alone and what from Holinshed alone, and at the same time to indicate the development in the chronicles of the more important events and facts mentioned by Shakespeare — the history of which is given in full in Part I of this work.

"Holin.-Hall" means that either authority may have been the immediate source. A series of authorities is arranged in order from the last to the first. The Hardyng continuation is generally not mentioned because it almost always agrees with Hall, and Hall's own contributions to the story are regularly indicated. Grafton is omitted as a mere copier of Hall so far as the facts here mentioned are concerned.

Richard III.

1:1 Richard's deformity. Extended from Holin.-Hall (Hard. con.), from More and Vergil (the latter's description blackened by Hall). Deformity first in Rous.
Richard's monstrous birth. Holin.-Hall (Hard. Con.) from More. First in Rous.
Richard's plots vs. Clarence. Cf. M. for M. "Clarence" str. 50. More?
The G. prophecy. Holin.-Hall, from Vergil. Mentioned first by Rous.

1:2 Richard woos Anne. Cf. Richardus Tertius, Richard and Elizabeth.
Richard's murder of Henry. Holin.-Hall, from Vergil and More. Earlier in Fabyan, André, Rous et al.
Richard's share in murder of Prince Edward. Holin.-Hall, from Vergil.
The bleeding of Henry's wounds. Holin. alone, from Warkworth.

1:3 Richard determined on as Protector. From The T. Trag. (?) influenced by M. for M. Earlier in Vergil and André.
Rivers, Dorset and Hastings standers-by at Prince Edward's murder. Hastings shares in murder in Holin.-Hall, from Vergil.
Dorset shares in murder, Holin.-Hall (first).
Rivers, Shakespeare's addition.
Margaret's curse averted. Cf. The T. Trag. (p. 507).
Richard's murder of Clarence. From T. Trag. or tradition as evidenced by T. Trag., Legge, M. for M., Hall's Index.

1:4 Clarence condemned for perjury by Warwick's Ghost. Suggested by Holin.-Hall, from Vergil.
Clarence's death a punishment for perjury and murder of Prince Edward. Holin.-Hall, from Vergil.
Murder scene. Cf. T. Trag. and Ed. II.

2:1 Reconciliation scene. Holin.-Hall, from More.
Richard's presence in this scene. Cf. T. Trag.
Edward declares that none have appealed for Clarence. Holin.-Hall, from Vergil.

God's justice on Ed. for Clarence's death. Holin.-Hall, from Vergil.

2:2 Lamentation scene. Suggestions from T. Trag.?
Discussion on number of train and Rivers words. From T. Trag.?
Buckingham's suggestion that Prince be removed from Queen's kinsmen. Cf. T. Trag.

2:3 Foreboding of citizens. Holin.-Hall, from More. Cf. its position here with that in T. Trag.
Message concerning arrest at Stony Stratford Hawte omitted shows use of Holin. alone? From More.

3:1 "Sweet prince, the untainted virtue of your years" etc. From T. Trag.?
Archbishop of Canterbury sent to Queen. Hall alone (Hard. con.).
Early ripeness of Prince and his words "An if I live" etc. Influence of T. Trag.?
Promise of the earldom of Hereford and movables. Holin. alone, from More's Latin.

3:3 Omission of Vaughan's reference to G prophecy show use of Holin. alone? From More.
Gray and Rivers die for standing by when Prince Edward is murdered. Names added by Shakespeare; their punishment suggested by Holin-Hall, from Vergil.

3:4 "I have been long a sleeper". Holin.-Hall, but cf. T. Trag.
Hastings' punishment for murder of Pr. Edward. Holin.-Hall, from Vergil.

3:5 Friar Penker. Holin. alone, from More.
Burdet's case explained. Hall alone.

3:7 Enter Gloster between two Bishops. Hall alone, Hardyng con. Later in Grafton also.

4:1 "The king!" .. "I mean the lord protector". From T. Trag.

4:2 Buckingham's reluctance to countenance death of princes. Holin.-Hall. First in Hall's speech of Buckingham.
The earldom of Hereford and the movables. Cf. 3:1. Holin. alone, from More's Latin.
Henry VI's prophecy concerning Richmond. Holin.-Hall, from Vergil. Earlier in André.
Richard's visit to Rougemont. Holin.-alone.

4:3 Richard's murder of Anne. Holin.-Hall ("most likely") from Vergil (an alternative possibility). First in Rous (as a fact).
4:4 Richard's reversal of Fortune. Hall alone, from Vergil.
"Edward for Edward pays a dying debt". Holin.-Hall, from Vergil.
Richard and Elizabeth. Cf. Legge.
Richard unnerved in scene with Catesby. Cf. T. Trag.
Richard and Stanley. From T. Tragedy. Holin.-Hall, from Vergil.
5:1 Buckingham's death a righteous punishment. Holin.-Hall, from Vergil.
5:2 Richmond's speech and words of his followers. Cf. T. Trag.
5:3 Meeting of Stanley and Richmond. From T. Trag. (?), from Legge.
The ghosts. Suggested by T. Trag.
Richard's soliloquy. Cf. T. Trag.
The gloomy, foreboding day. From T. Trag.
Norfolk's scroll. Holin.-Hall (first).
Richmond's and Richard's speeches to their troops. Holin.-Hall (first).
"At our mother's cost". Holin. alone.
Rescue of Lord Strange. Holin.-Hall (first).
5:4 "A horse, a horse". From T. Trag.
5:[5] Scene heading. Cf. T. Trag.
Final speech of Richmond. Cf. T. Trag.

Addendum.

To p. 267, l. 3 et seq. This passage was written before the appearance of the Jahrbuch der deutschen Shakespeare Gesellschaft for 1898, where, in our catalogue of the Latin university plays, p. 258, Dr. Keller gives the date 1573 assigned to Legge's play by the Caius College Ms., as he was the first to discover. It should be said that both Keller and Brandl (ibid. p. 222) accept the date as correct. In a private letter Dr. Keller writes, "Was das Datum des Ms. Caius Coll. betrifft, so mag darauf hingewiesen werden, dass die beiden anderen Cambridger Mss. 1579 als Aufführungsdatum angeben: das eine direkt, das andere durch die Spielerliste. Unter den drei Stücken des Caius Ms. ist ein zweites, für das eine Aufführung i. J. 1579 durch die Spielerliste eines anderen Ms. bezeugt scheint: Hymenaeus. Das ist aber wohl so ziemlich der einzige Punkt der gegen das Datum 1573 spricht".

Corrigenda.

Page
- 3. l. 3 he read be
- 20. l. 2 plain read plain.
- l. 21 came read same.
- 22. l. 10 meagrest read meagerest
- 23. l. 8 idigne read indigne
- l. 16 numeribus read muneribus
- 24. l. 27 Rudlow read Ludlow
- 25. l. 13 Burgurdiones read Burgundiones
- 31. l. 17 he read be
- l. 35 Edingburgh read Edinburgh
- 53. l. 31 dele could get there
- 58. l. 28 is read of
- 62. l. 26 adress read address
- 68. l. 35 nor read not
- 70. l. 29 dynerse read dyuerse
- 77. l. 18 tbe read the
- 78. l. 9 little, read little.
- 80. l. 35 After soueraintye supply ;
- 85. l. 8 semblaunee read semblaunce
- l. 21 the read he
- 86. l. 22 Jurther read Further
- 87. l. 27 to read so
- 88. l. 12 bath read hath
- 89. l. 27 euer read euen
- 90. l. 16 grantes read granted
- 91. l. 28 sutteties read suttelties
- 92. l. 14 when had read when he had
- 93. l. 4 stewed read shewed
- l. 6 enery read euery
- 99. ll. 5 and 9 Peuker read Penker
- 101. l. 18 vitulamnia read vitulamina
- l. 30 surety read surely
- 104. l. 19 no read not

Page
- 110. l. 11 thinket read thinketh
- 111. l. 2 sleping read sleeping
- 112. l. 18 light read light"
- 116. l. 31 expiravit read expiravit"
- 119. l. 4 of historical read of English historical
- 128. l. 10 Henry I read Henry VII
- 132. l. 26 he read be
- 144. l. 10 began read begun
- 161. l. 20 coucerning read concerning
- 163. l. 7 because would read because I would
- 166. ll. 11—13 Dele to It
- l. 13 It read The Continuation
- 168. l. 31 His read Its
- 170. l. 19 so farre", dele comma
- 171. l. 24 nor read not
- 174. l. 19 dele period
- 175. l. 19 altending read attending
- 176. l. 24 Vergi's read Vergil's
- 179. l. 5 Is read To
- 182. l. 27 hand. read hand".
- 182. l. 28 changes, read changes
- 183. l. 4 Hasting's read Hastings
- l. 5 Hasting's read Hastings'
- l. 8 accout read account
- l. 30 "After read After
- 185. l. 11 vlterly read vtterly
- 187. l. 21 any read my
- 188. l. 26 devise read device
- 192. l. 22 On read Of
- 194. l. 20 huic read hinc
- 195. l. 5 abhonimable read abhominable
- 201. l. 12 justice read the justice

Page				Page			
204.	l.	19	moreover read however	359.	l.	26	twe read two
207.	l.	13	has read has,	376.	l.	32	man read men
212.	l.	13	Euguerrant read Enguerrant	380.	l.	13	more read move
				384.	l.	36	trustwortly read trustworthy
217.	l.	9	from read form				
218.	l.	18	(inf. p. 228) read (inf. p. 227)	388.	l.	33	adresses read addresses
				395.	l.	20	1856 read 1586
225.	l.	11	Euguerrant read Enguerrant		l.	29	Streevens read Steevens
231.	l.	11	as read a	396.	l.	13	oft be read of the
235.	l.	13	fort read forth	406.	l.	27	occours read occurs
	l.	28	auncestoure read auncestours	408.	l.	20	neice read niece
				411.	l.	31	Glosier read Gloster
236.	l.	19	he read be	413.	l.	3	431 read 441
242.	l.	5	farre read to farre	421.	l.	15	dele period
247.	l.	38	poem read the poem	422.	l.	29	The are read There are
254.	l.	18	dele period				
255.	l.	19	swome read sworne	428.	l.	7	himseld read himself
	l.	35	Buckingham's read Banister's		l.	16	death. dele period
					l.	29	receivede read received
262.	l.	18	that read that death				
264.	l.	32	he read be	435.	l.	29	revenge read reuenge
266.	l.	35	Cantabrigensi read Cantabrigiensi	436.	l.	20	and promises read and Richard promises
282.	l.	30	dauger read danger		l.	36	he read be
299.	l.	18	lattier read later	440.	l.	29	aed read and
305.	l.	30	nothing, a read nothing. A	441.	l.	28	aske read asks
					l.	31	trains read brains
308.	l.	9	lat read last	446.	l.	17	baune read banne
313.	l.	33	Caste read Castle	452.	l.	1	had read has
314.	l.	12	wishered read withered	455.	l.	36	Stanley read Stanleys
				458.	l.	7	on (second) read of
315.	l.	19	pretum read pretium		l.	31	absence, read absence.
	l.	26	adress read address	463.	l.	9	his read this
326.	l.	14	conspicuons read conspicuous	467.	l.	32	age read aye
				472.	l.	23	Spakesperean read Shakespearean
341.	l.	19	attemps read attempts				
347.	l.	18	inflence read influence	487.	l.	14	uear read wear
				491.	l.	9	4 and 5 read 3 and 4
355.	l.	17	announce read announces	510.	l.	19	of dialogue read of the dialogue
358.	l.	4	Ou read On				

Palaestra. X.   35

Bibliographical Index

of Works Referred to in the Foregoing Study.

André, Bernard, Historia Regis Henrici Septimi. Ed. Gairdner. (In Rerum Britannicarum Medii Aevi Scriptores.) London, 1858.
Buck, George, History of the Life and Reigne of Richard the Third. London, 1646.
A Chronicle of London, from 1089 to 1483. London, 1827.
The Chronicles of the White Rose of York. London, 1845.
Collier, J. P., History of English Dramatic Poetry. London, 1831.
Commynes, Philippe de, Memoires. Ed. Dupont. Paris, 1840.
Cooper, C. H. and T., Athenae Cantabrigienses. Cambridge, 1861.
Corser, Thos., Collectanea Anglo-Poetica. 1860.
Courtenay, Thos. P., Commentaries on the Historical Plays of Shakespeare. London, 1840.
Historiae Croylandensis Continuatio. In Rerum Anglicarum Scriptorum Veterum Tom. I. Ed. Fell. Oxford, 1684.
Cunliffe, J. W., The Influence of Seneca on Elizabethan Tragedy. London, 1893.
Cunningham, Peter, Extracts from the Accounts of the Revels at Court in the Reigne of Queen Elizabeth and King James I. London, 1842.
Draiton, Michael, Works. (Spenser Soc. Publ. 45, 46.) Manchester, 1888.
Excerpta Historica, or Illustrations of English History. London, 1833.
Fabyan, Robert, The New Chronicles of England and France. Ed. Ellis. London, 1811.
Fischer, Kuno, Shakespeare's Characterentwicklung Richard's III. Zweite Ausgabe. Heidelberg, 1889.
Fischer, Rudolf, Zur Kunstentwicklung der englischen Tragödie von ihren ersten Anfängen bis zu Shakespeare. Strassburg, 1893.
Fleay, F. G., A Biographical Chronicle of the English Drama, 1559—1642. London, 1891.

Fleay, F. G., A Chronicle History of the London Stage, 1559—1642. London, 1890.
— A Chronicle History of the Life and Work of William Shakespeare. London, 1886.
Fuller, Thos., The History of the Worthies of England. London, 1662.
Gairdner, James, History of the Life and Reign of Richard the Third. London, 1878.
Grafton, Richard, Chronicle or History of England. London, 1809.
Greene, Robert, Life and Complete Works. Ed. Grosart. Huth Library, 1881—3.
Greene, Robert, and George Peele (q. v.), Dramatic and Poetical Works. Ed. Dyce. London, 1874.
Hall, Edward, Chronicle containing the History of England, Henry IV—Henry VIII. London, 1809.
Halliwell [-Philipps], J. O., A Dictionary of Old English Plays. London, 1860.
— Outlines of the Life of Shakespeare, 4th ed. London, 1884. 5th ed. London, 1885.
Hardyng, John, Chronicle, containing an Account of Public Transactions from the Earliest Period of English History to the Beginning of the Reign of King Edward the Fourth. Together with the Continuation, by Richard Grafton, to the Thirty Fourth year of King Henry the Eighth. Ed. Ellis. London, 1812.
Hazlitt, W. Carew, A Select Collection of Old English Plays. Originally published by Robert Dodsley in the year 1744. Fourth Edition. London, 1874.
History of the Arrivall of Edward IV in England and the Final Recouerye of His Kingdomes from Henry VI. Ed. Bruce. London, 1838.
Holinshed, Raphael, Chronicles of England, Scotland, and Ireland. London, 1808.
Ingelby, C. M., Shakespeare: the Man and the Book. London, 1887.
Leland, John, De Rebus Britannicis Collectanea. Ed. Thos. Hearne. Oxford, 1715.
Lloyd, W. W., Essays on the Life and Plays of Shakespeare. London, 1858.
Marlowe, Christopher, Works. Revised Edition. Ed. Dyce. London.
A Mirror for Magistrates. Ed. Haslewood. London, 1815.
More, Thomas, Opera Omnia. Frankfurt and Leipsic, 1689.
— History of King Richard III. Ed. Lumby. Cambridge, 1883.
Morley, Henry, English Writers. London, 1887—1895.
Oechelhäuser, W., Shakespeareana. Berlin, 1894.

Palatine Anthology; A Collection of Ancient Poems and Ballads. Ed. Halliwell. London, 1850.
Pauli, Reinhold, in Lappenberg-Pauli, Geschichte von England. Hamburg, 1834—1858.
Peele, George, Works. Ed. Bullen. London, 1888. [See Greene.]
Puttenham, George, The Arte of English Poesie. Arber's English Reprints, 15. London, 1860.
Rastell, John, The Pastyme of People. Ed. Dibdin. London, 1811.
Rous, John, Historia Regum Angliae. Ed. Hearne. Second Edition. Oxford, 1745.
Seneca, L. Annaeus, Tragoediae. Ed. Leo. Berlin, 1879.
Shakespeare, William, Works. Ed. Collier. London, 1844—1853.
— Plays and Poems. Ed. Malone [and Boswell]. London, 1821.
— King Richard the Third. Ed Rolfe. New York, 1896.
— Dramatische Werke, übersetzt von v. Schlegel und Tieck. Ed. Brandl. Leipzig und Wien, 1897—1899.
— King Richard the Third. Ed. Wright. Oxford, 1893.
— Works. Ed. Verplanck. New York, 1847.
Shakespeare's Library. Second Edition. Ed. Hazlitt. London, 1875.
Skottowe, Augustine, The Life of Shakespeare. London, 1824.
Speed, John, The History of Great Britaine under the Conquests of ye Romans, Saxons, Danes and Normans. London 1611.
Stow, John, The Annales of England. London, 1592.
Tanner, Thos., Bibliotheca Britannico-Hibernica. London, 1748.
Turner, Sharon, History of England during the Middle Ages. London, 1814.
Vergil, Polydore, Anglicae Historiae Libri XXVI. Basel, 1534.
Three.Books of Polydore Vergil's English History. From an Early translation. Ed. Ellis. London, 1844.
Warkworth, John, A Chronicle of the first Thirteen Years of the Reign of King Edward the Fourth. Ed. Halliwell. London, 1839.
Warner, B. E., English History in Shakespeare's Plays. New York, 1894.

DATE DUE			
MAY 1 9 ~~'79~~		APR 2 5 2000	
APR 1 8 ~~1989~~		APR 0 7 2002	
DEC 9 1982		JUN 1 6 2006	
DEC 3 1987			
FEB 1 4 1995			
ILL: 7994198 7-24-02			
JUL 1 0 2006			

HIGHSMITH 45-220